Corruption,
Global Security,
and World Order

CORRUPTION, GLOBAL SECURITY, AND WORLD ORDER

ROBERT I. ROTBERG

Editor

WORLD PEACE FOUNDATION
Cambridge, Massachusetts

HARVARD KENNEDY SCHOOL PROGRAM
ON INTRASTATE CONFLICT
Cambridge, Massachusetts

AMERICAN ACADEMY OF ARTS & SCIENCES
Cambridge, Massachusetts

BROOKINGS INSTITUTION PRESS
Washington, D.C.

Copyright © 2009
World Peace Foundation and American Academy of Arts & Sciences

WORLD PEACE FOUNDATION
P.O. Box 382144
Cambridge, Massachusetts 02238-2144

AMERICAN ACADEMY OF ARTS & SCIENCES
136 Irving Street
Cambridge, Massachusetts 02138

Corruption, Global Security, and World Order may be ordered from:
Brookings Institution Press, c/o HFS, P.O. Box 50370, Baltimore, MD 21211-4370
Tel.: 800/537-5487 410/516-6956 Fax: 410/516-6998 Internet: www.brookings.edu

Library of Congress Cataloging-in-Publication data

Corruption, global security, and world order / Robert I. Rotberg, editor.
     p.   cm.
   Includes bibliographical references and index.
   Summary: "Discusses global ramifications of deeply embedded corruption by criminals and criminalized states. Explores trafficking issues—how nuclear/WMD smugglers coexist with other traffickers. Examines how corruption deprives citizens of fundamental human rights, assesses the connection between corruption and the spread of terror, and proposes remedies to reduce and contain corruption"—Provided by publisher.
     ISBN 978-0-8157-0329-7 (pbk. : alk. paper)
   1. Political corruption. 2. Transnational crime. 3. Security, International. 4. Nuclear nonproliferation. I. Rotberg, Robert I. II. Title.
   JF1081.C6733 2009
     364.1'323—dc22   20090208

9 8 7 6 5 4 3 2 1

Printed on acid-free paper

Typeset in Minion

Composition by Cynthia Stock
Silver Spring, Maryland

Printed by R. R. Donnelley
Harrisonburg, Virginia

Contents

Preface   vii

1   How Corruption Compromises World Peace
and Stability   1
Robert I. Rotberg

2   Defining Corruption: Implications for Action   27
Laura S. Underkuffler

3   Defining and Measuring Corruption:
Where Have We Come From, Where Are We Now,
and What Matters for the Future?   47
Nathaniel Heller

4   Corruption in the Wake of Domestic
National Conflict   66
Susan Rose-Ackerman

5   Kleptocratic Interdependence: Trafficking,
Corruption, and the Marriage of Politics
and Illicit Profits   96
Kelly M. Greenhill

6   Corruption and Nuclear Proliferation   124
Matthew Bunn

7   To Bribe or to Bomb: Do Corruption
and Terrorism Go Together?   167
Jessica C. Teets and Erica Chenoweth

8   Corruption, the Criminalized State,
    and Post-Soviet Transitions   194
    Robert Legvold

9   Combating Corruption in Traditional Societies:
    Papua New Guinea   239
    Sarah Dix and Emmanuel Pok

10 The Travails of Nigeria's Anti-Corruption Crusade   260
    Rotimi T. Suberu

11 The Paradoxes of Popular Participation in Corruption
    in Nigeria   283
    Daniel Jordan Smith

12 Corruption and Human Rights:
    Exploring the Connection   310
    Lucy Koechlin and Magdalena Sepúlveda Carmona

13 Leadership Alters Corrupt Behavior   341
    Robert I. Rotberg

14 The Role of the Multi-National Corporation
    in the Long War against Corruption   359
    Ben W. Heineman, Jr.

15 The Organization of Anti-Corruption:
    Getting Incentives Right   389
    Johann Graf Lambsdorff

16 A Coalition to Combat Corruption: TI, EITI,
    and Civil Society   416
    Peter Eigen

17 Reducing Corruption in the Health and Education Sectors 430
    Charles C. Griffin

18 Good Governance, Anti-Corruption,
    and Economic Development   457
    Jomo Kwame Sundaram

Contributors   469

Index   477

Preface

Global security and world order are threatened as never before by myriad sources of instability. Foremost is the collapse of macroeconomic stability and fiscal certainty. Next, possibly, is the lack of concord among the powers of the world, with Russian, Chinese, and American competition and mutual suspicion preventing the confident resolution of a number of outstanding and intractable subsidiary issues. Some of those concern the spread of nuclear weapon capacity and the resilience of terror and terroristic movements. Additionally, tyranny continues to stalk the globe, especially in Africa and Central Asia and parts of Southeast Asia and Latin America. As the chapters in this book show, corruption is at the very center of all of these contentious global anxieties, fueling their fury and magnifying their intensity. This book, in novel and path-breaking ways, explores the enabling ties between corrupt practice and security, corrupt practice and human rights and development, and corrupt practice and the maintenance of tyranny. It also provides abundant studies of key egregious national examples.

This book emerged out of rich conversations at the American Academy of Arts and Sciences stimulated, originally, by Robert Legvold's deep knowledge of Russia and the Russian near abroad. The Academy and its Committee on International Security Studies, the Program on Intrastate Conflict at the Kennedy School of Government, and the World Peace Foundation subsequently organized a series of heuristic meetings in 2007 and 2008 to discuss modern ramifications and implications of deeply embedded corruption, especially as it posed novel (or at least hitherto largely unexplored) threats to world order. This book is the result.

This resulting volume builds on essays originally prepared for discussion at one or more of the joint meetings. Each has been revised multiple times; I am grateful to my fellow contributors for the painstaking care with which each contributor approached the tasks of writing and revision, and—with equal fervor—to Emily Wood for her assiduous attention to the daunting details of copy-editing, fact-checking, and marshalling so many authors and subjects. The result is a tribute to the contributors and to her.

The authors and I are also grateful to Alice Noble and Elizabeth Huttner at the Academy for hosting us so well (and for Martin Malin's guidance earlier), and for Katie Naeve and Vanessa Tucker, of the Program, for keeping us focused and well-organized during the long months from inception to completion. Charles Norchi participated in our discussions and made lasting contributions to this book's architecture.

The sponsorship at the Academy of the Committee on International Security Studies, chaired so ably by Carl Kaysen and John Steinbruner, enabled this project and book to become a reality. I appreciate the committee's confidence and backing throughout the process of testing initial ideas and maturing them into a completed product. The committee wisely encouraged us to embrace corruption in all of its security facets.

The World Peace Foundation, led by Philip Khoury, its chair, and other trustees also strengthened the conceptual foundations of the project and eventual book. I am appreciative, too, for the continued backing for this and other projects of Graham Allison, director of the Belfer Center for Science and International Affairs at the Kennedy School of Government, and his and my other colleagues within the always intellectually engaged and lively Center.

Robert I. Rotberg
March 1, 2009

Corruption, Global Security, and World Order

ROBERT I. ROTBERG

1

How Corruption Compromises
World Peace and Stability

Corruption is a human condition and an ancient phenomenon. From Mesopotamian times, if not before, public notables have abused their offices for personal gain; both well-born and common citizens have sought advantage by corrupting those holding power or controlling access to perquisites. The exercise of discretion, especially forms of discretion that facilitate or bar entry to opportunity, is a magnetic impulse that invariably attracts potential abusers. Moreover, since nearly all tangible opportunities are potentially zero-sum in their impact on individuals or classes of individuals, it is almost inevitable that claimants will seek favors from authorities and that authorities, in turn, appreciating the strength of their positions, will welcome inducements.

Until avarice and ambition cease to be human traits, corruption will continue to flourish. Self-interest dictates the using and granting of favors. Merit will determine outcomes and advancement only in a minority of nations, and the riptide of corruption—even in the most abstemious nations and societies—always exists as an undertow to be resisted. Indeed, in many nations, obtaining even rightful entitlements in a timely fashion, or at all, is characteristically subject to inducement. Almost everywhere, and from time immemorial, there is a presumption that most desirable outcomes are secured through illicitly pressed influence or hard-bought gains.

United States Senate seats are, in one case, almost exchanged for cash. Nigerian governmentally awarded construction contracts are procured for no less than a hefty percentage of the total project value. The outcomes of Thai elections are determined almost entirely by the purchase of votes and voters. So too were U. S. elections in the early days of the republic; Americans, who readily understood the importance of influence and access from their founding days, always feared the power of corrupt politicians. French politicians and political parties have long depended on corruptly illegal flows of funds from wealthy corporations or individuals, or foreign polities, a continuing scandal that was investigated and exposed in the 1990s.[1]

Dickens and Eliot were as fully aware in the British nineteenth century of the power of corrupt practice as were much earlier authors and commentators. Eliot's *Felix Holt, The Radical,* for example, bemoans parliamentarians being unashamed "to make public questions which concern the welfare of millions a mere screen for their own petty private ends." She also writes that "corruption is not felt to be a damming disgrace," using the word itself explicitly. Felix Holt's and Eliot's own remedies for corrupt practice seem to be the force of an aroused public opinion, certainly a form of accountability.[2]

This book takes as givens that corruption is common everywhere in the early twenty-first century, that almost no nations and no collections of leadership are immune to the temptations of corruption, that we know more than ever before about the mechanisms and impacts of corruption, that corrupt practices are more egregious and more obscenely excessive in the world's newer nations, and that what is truly novel in this century is that corruption is much more a threat to world order than ever in the past.

Corruption is no longer largely confined to the political sphere, where wily politicians and their officials siphon money from the state, fiddle bids, or demand emoluments for giving citizens what is rightfully theirs. There is a new critical security dimension to corruption, compromising world peace and stability. Now areas of the globe are positively at risk because of corrupt practices within states and the impact of such practices across transnational borders.

This volume shows how the peace of the world is systematically compromised by corruption that facilitates the possible proliferation of weapons of mass destruction; that assists the spread of terror and terroristic practices; and that strengthens the malefactors who traffic illicitly in humans, guns, and drugs, and who launder money. Corrupt practices undercut noble international efforts to improve the health, educational attainments, welfare, prosperity, and human rights of the inhabitants of the troubled planet. No arena of human endeavor is now immune from the destructive result of corruption. Indeed, as Robert Legvold's chapter demonstrates forcibly, numerous areas of the globe, especially within the post-Soviet sphere, are now controlled by criminals and criminalized states whose entire focus is the promotion of corruption. In Africa there are such states, too, Zimbabwe and Equatorial Guinea offering the foremost examples.

This book hence argues that hoary forms of corruption persist alongside and facilitate the spread of the newer, more potentially destructive modes of corruption. It also indicates that as great as are the wages of sin within national borders and national governments—and almost nothing has diminished those rewards—they are just as large if not much greater across borders. There has been a quantum leap in all forms of trafficking, particularly the trafficking of humans (mostly women and children, and some male slaves) and in drugs, with new beachheads for South American–derived cocaine and marijuana in Africa and Afghan heroin in Asia and the ex-Soviet hinterland. Light weapons and small arms are smuggled along some of the same routes, and nuclear and other WMD smugglers often co-exist with human and drug traffickers—all varieties encouraged by open or corrupt borders and officials at all levels. Some of the criminalized states specialize in such activities. Other nation-states, such as North Korea, depend on the open sores of corruption to accrue foreign exchange. Kelly Greenhill's chapter explores many of these trafficking issues, Legvold deals with the post-Soviet space, and Matthew Bunn's chapter follows the devious, pernicious, WMD trails.

Because the newer forms of corruption depend on the old and, indeed, could not exist without the old methods and practices, this book explores the theory and practice of traditional corruption (Laura Underkuffler); it shows how extreme forms of traditional corruption persist and operate (Rotimi Suberu, and Sarah Dix and Emmanuel Pok), or flourish following internal wars (Susan Rose-Ackerman); estimates levels of corruption (Nathaniel Heller); and explores its rationale (Jomo K. S.).

Lucy Koechlin and Magdalena Sepúlveda Carmona's chapter examines the various ways in which corruption deprives citizens of fundamental human rights, employing experiences in Malawi as an instructive case. Jessica Teets and Erica Chenoweth assess the plausibly tight connection between corruption and the spread of terror. Daniel Jordan Smith's chapter on Nigerians' participation in corruption shows how the mass of citizens, in one large, corrupted country, react to and collaborate intimately with the corrupt endeavors of their leaders.

The remaining chapters in the volume are about ongoing efforts and strategies to reduce and contain, hardly ever to eliminate, corruption. They are optimistic, but not conclusive, essays. Peter Eigen, the founder of Transparency International (TI), writes about TI's current work and newer endeavors such as the Extractive Industries Transparency Initiative. Johann Graf Lambsdorff, the originator of the Corruption Perceptions Index, evaluates a number of accountability mechanisms and urges attention to bottom-up reforms. I write about the importance of leadership action in dampening the enthusiasm for and the continued practice of corruption. Ben W.

Heineman, Jr. provides a blueprint for good corporate practice so as to prevent, or at least limit, corporate conniving with corrupt practices within nations. Charles Griffin shows how the leakage and wastage of official funds in the crucial health and educational sectors, especially in the developing world, can be reduced.

All of the contributors to this volume define corruption according to the standard formulae employed either by the World Bank, TI, or Global Integrity. Those formulae are variants of "the abuse of public office for private gain" theme, and many cite the well-accepted, more elaborate, and refined definition offered decades ago by Nye.[3] Because there are no meaningful taxonomic differences between the various theoretical definitions, whether simple or complex, there has been no attempt in this volume to impose a single form of words to describe the acts and behaviors that collectively are labeled as corruption. More controversially, there is a consensus among the contributors that persons who are not officials, per se, can still act corruptly if they take advantage of their quasi-governmental roles to defraud a public and enrich themselves. Many of the individual cases in Bunn's chapter, for example, behaved corruptly despite their want in many cases of elected or appointed national office.

Somewhat less controversially, in terms of theory, the contributors to this book largely reject any moral distinction between venal corruption—the large-scale stealing of state revenues or resources, often through contract and construction fraud—and lubricating or petty corruption. Scott once suggested that lubricating corruption, especially "speed money," gave political influence to ethnic and interest groups that were effectively disfranchised or otherwise marginalized, and therefore served as an important political safety valve.[4] Certainly, petty corruption of certain kinds can be said to be more annoying than developmentally destructive; underpaid policemen and functionaries are by this measure arguably extracting "taxes" from citizens who are otherwise not contributing significantly to the national tax base. Each consumer may pay relatively minor amounts to obtain permits, licenses, and passports that should by right be procured freely. But the overall cost to society as a whole in cash and in time may still be significant and damaging to GDP growth. Moreover, the moral fabric of any society is rent as much, if not more, by the perpetuation of lubricating than by venal corruption. The sheer scale of the collective extraction is immense. Where there have been country and household studies, the toll taken by bribes on household incomes can be severe, as in Kenya.[5] Leaders cannot uplift their nations and ensure stability and prosperity without eliminating both varieties of corruption. The

Singapore example makes that case, as does the analogical case of the battle against petty crime in cities like New York.[6]

Corruption Calibrated

Underkuffler dissects the older and the new definitional paradigms of corruption. Corrupt practices are illegal. Ostensibly, corruption involves violations of law. But not all violations are equally corrupt, and petty bribes are not on par with charging massive rents on resources or construction contracts. Nor are certain kinds of corrupt acts—nepotism and various forms of patronage—necessarily illegal. More salient, corruption involves breaches of duty, "owed to the public of an intentional and serious nature," that result in private gain.[7] Someone who embezzles public funds obviously breaches his or her duty and also acts illegally. But what about a public official who merely exaggerates the extent of a disability? For Underkuffler, calling corruption a breach, even a betrayal, of duty does not fully capture the "loathsomeness" that corruption entails.[8] Making such actions treacherous or stealthy may help, but it is the act, not how it is performed, that is corrupt.

A more promising definition of corruption begins with the notion of the subverted public interest. Or perhaps corruption is merely an indication of market failure and the failure of appropriate allocative mechanisms? Thus, rent-seeking and corruption are harmful and inefficient on rational, not moral, grounds. But are they always? Sometimes corrupt acts improve efficiency.

Underkuffler critiques all of the available definitions. She prefers a moral definition that explicitly condemns corruption as evil, citing theorists from ancient and early modern times, as well as contemporaries. For her, corruption's moral core needs to be recognized. In popular terms, she writes, it is "the transgression of some deeply held and asserted universal norm."[9] Moreover, it shows an individual's disregard for shared societal bonds. Where and when amorality (corruption) prevails, society and individuals suffer. Thus combating corruption becomes a moral obligation. The fabric of society is irreparably sundered so long as corruption is condoned, or permitted to prevail.

How much of the world is corrupt? Or in how many countries do corrupt practices prevail? Given that we can find corruption in almost every nation, and that TI's Corruption Perceptions Index annually ranks 180 countries according to their perceived levels of corruption, both of those questions may be unhelpful. Indeed, of the 180 countries ranked, a good 120 exhibit worrying levels of corruption. But hard numbers—actual numbers of corrupt payoffs within a given country, actual numbers of corrupt "incidents," however defined, and so on—are impossible to quantify. The World Bank estimates that globally $1 trillion is paid each year in bribes, but that is a ballpark figure.[10] The numbers of corrupt persons brought to trial is not particularly helpful, except possibly in Singapore. We know that various venal developing-world leaders have salted away billions in Swiss and other secret bank accounts. We know that obscene heads of state have constructed many mansions in their own countries or purchased properties abroad, in Europe, Hong Kong, and Malaysia. But, aside from local "bribe paying" surveys in a few countries, we cannot know the full financial cost, nationally or globally, of corruption. Nor can we begin realistically to estimate such huge numbers, or their regional or national quantities. All anyone can report is that in some particularly wide-open nation-states the amounts skimmed from the public by politicians and their ilk are very large, dwarfing in some cases legitimate sources of GDP. Unfortunately, too, in Africa, if not in Asia, much of the capital that is purloined leaves Africa and therefore has little multiplier effect. In Suharto's Indonesia, at least, some illicit gains were deployed internally, and were "productive" at home.

Because good answers and good numbers are scarce, and the directions and contours of corruption are unspecified, Nathaniel Heller's chapter attempts to indicate what is now known, and how existing knowledge can be extended and deepened. Part of the problem of aggregating corruption is that the most sophisticated, existing measurement tools depend on indirect calibrations—on third-party surveys that are subject to selection bias. Moreover, as refined as TI's Corruption Perceptions Index has become, it is impossible to be certain that each survey retains the same definition of corruption, or that those persons being surveyed are reacting to complementary definitions.

Second-generation methods of estimating corruption are also indirect, for they measure anti-corruption effectiveness, accountability mechanisms, budget transparency, and so on. Sometimes experts give opinions, with varying degrees of authority. Household surveys have often been employed, too. But few of these second-generation efforts have covered as many countries as the well-established first-generation proxies.

Locally generated assessments of corruption might be helpful, as Heller suggests, but they would inevitably be subject to claims of bias and intimidation. He also asserts that qualitative descriptions may be as useful as quantitative measurements even though the comparability across countries of national qualitative studies would be questionable. He urges more attention to leadership and political will as integral components of the to-be-developed third-generation methods of assessing corruption's impact.

Rose-Ackerman, among others, has refused to accept the heuristic utility of the Scott distinction between types of corruption and their societal consequences. In her books and essays, especially her chapter on corruption in post-conflict societies in this volume, she suggests that "corruption is a symptom that state and society relations are dysfunctional."[11] In developing countries, especially those emerging from civil warfare, all of the conditions that are typically conducive to the proliferation of corruption in developing and other countries are magnified by parlous and porous controls, weakened accountability mechanisms, and heightened greed. Emergency and developmental assistance provide incentives for public officials, local or international contractors, or technically astute outsiders to profit from their positions or their knowledge. Organized crime (as in Guatemala) also thrives in post-conflict situations, especially where arms and other trafficking has become customary. Indeed, depending on how peaceful outcomes are achieved, criminals may well capture and plunder the new states.

Rose-Ackerman's chapter compares the post-conflict cases of Angola, Burundi, Guatemala, Kosovo, and Mozambique. Corruption propensities varied in those cases, according to the kinds of governments that were in power during war-time and whether they were truly representative or not, the character of the peace bargain (who were the victors?), underlying economic (whether there were resource rents) and social situations—including income inequalities, the extent of war-related physical destruction and population displacement, and the impact on each country of outsiders—neighboring nations, international lending institutions, criminals, and so on. Rose-Ackerman suggests that it matters if international organizations in such cases are or are not interested in creating democratic and accountable public institutions; in several past situations they preferred stability over integrity, and permitted corruption to thrive.

Her conclusion is that successful, sustainable anti-corruption efforts depend on addressing the underlying conditions that create corrupt incentives. Neither the empty rhetoric of moralizing nor witch hunts against opponents will accomplish lasting reform. New states should not permit corruption to fester, and must avoid allowing narrow elites to monopolize economic and political opportunities. Otherwise these groups may use their power to monopolize rent-seeking opportunities and undermine growth. A free market, operating within legal boundaries, can limit corrupt opportunities, but in a post-conflict situation, with a weak state, "an open-ended free market solution . . . can lead to widespread competitive corruption" as individuals and firms operate outside the law.[12]

Rose-Ackerman recommends that post-conflict peace agreements explicitly incorporate anti-corruption accountability measures. She thinks that during any period when they might be in charge, international peacekeepers might be able to institute effective anti-corruption reforms, if their presence is acceptable to the local population, and if international donors can manage reconstruction trust funds to facilitate peace-building and prevent local officials from appropriating or channeling them illicitly. The imposition of effective international controls on money laundering and on the export of corrupt rents is also valuable.

Crime, Nuclear Weapons, and Terrorism

Corrupt practices facilitate all kinds of illicit transactions, especially—as Rose-Ackerman explains—in the post-conflict space. Greenhill strengthens and extends that analysis by exploring, in her chapter, the intimate connection between corruption and corrupt political actors and all forms of transnational trafficking—humans, drugs, guns, organs, and so on. Global criminals and global criminality flourish in the twenty-first century at levels and across continents to a degree that is dramatic in their reach and power. None of this furtive industry is possible without corrupt assistance, at borders and deep within nation-states that are both strong and weak. Greenhill calls this symbiotic relationship "kleptocratic interdependence." Little of this activity is new, but what is new, along with its size and growth trajectory, is the global security threat that criminalized kleptocractic interdependence poses for world order.

Transnational criminal organizations are violent, control markets, and infiltrate the legitimate economy. They smuggle humans, especially immigrants, women, and children; they run guns; traffic drugs and organs; launder large profits; and evade taxes. In order to exist efficiently, they routinely pay off enabling politicians and officials, including the most lowly border guard. "Corruption," writes Greenhill, "offers criminal groups the means to penetrate markets with relatively low transaction costs and then to exploit those markets largely unregulated. . . ."[13]

Corrupted officials look the other way, facilitate illicit activities of all kinds, forestall prosecutions or dismiss offences, prevent legislation and regulation, and prevent competition. Moreover, in some nation-states, officials have participated intimately in criminalized export operations, such as cocaine and heroin movements, and have altered regulatory environments to ease such trafficking. Corruption, in this dimension, shapes state policies. In some countries, such kleptocratic interdependence amounts to state capture, or what Legvold terms criminal and criminalized states. The examples of this licit and illicit fusion multiply in the post-Soviet space, in Asia, Africa, and Latin America.

Greenhill epitomizes kleptocratic interdependence as the division of state responsibilities between non-state actors and officials, the privileging of private gain over public good, rampant greed at all levels inside and outside government, the privatization of national coffers, and the total absence of accountability. Politicians and their bureaucratic allies are purchased openly by non-state actors, warlords, and criminal entrepreneurs. Elections and other democratic mechanisms are financed and "owned" by the syndicates. In these contexts, Greenhill quotes a Mexican politician as remarking that "'a politician who is poor, is a poor politician.'"[14] Yet, controlling power may also shift in some instances from the criminals to the criminalized politicians—the Milosevics, Fujimoris, and Mugabes of different eras. Overall, however, symbiosis—effective partnership—works best for both parties, as in post–World War II Japan and Taiwan. Lee Kuan Yew understood the need to break decisively with criminals to create an effective, stable Singapore.

Contrary to what one might infer, these transnational criminal organizations prefer to base themselves in well-functioning countries, mostly in democracies. They may profit from control of weak states, but they tend to headquarter themselves, like most successful international corporations, in nations that rank relatively non-corrupt on TI's Corruption Perceptions Index, Nigeria excepted.

The durable ties between corrupt regimes and transnational crime and transnational trafficking pose major global security problems because of the ability of criminal organizations to subvert stability and growth in poor countries, by their skill at sapping such impoverished places of revenue and legitimate modernization, by their undermining of the moral fabric of weak and fragile societies, and by their negative reinforcement of the least favorable kinds of leadership in developing countries. But these unholy partnerships also exacerbate already high levels of crime and predation, through human and drug trafficking and money laundering; seriously contribute to the perpetuation of regime venality; and by facilitating the spread of small arms and light weapons make civil wars possible and lethal. Additionally, the networks that are controlled by criminals and facilitated by corrupt politicians can enable the spread of weapons of mass destruction (as Bunn's chapter shows) and fund and supply terroristic actors and insurgent movements. Only with the diminution of corruption can the reach of the tentacles of criminal enterprise be rebuffed and reduced.

Bunn makes an even stronger point, relevant to every effort that will be made in the Obama period, to contain the spread of nuclear weapons and fissile material: Corruption was a central enabling factor in every case of nuclear proliferation, and will be directly relevant now and into the future. Nuclear theft can hardly exist without corrupt partners, corrupt officials and border guards, and corrupt trafficking routes. Bunn discusses the known cases of pilfering and smuggling, and their links to other kinds of transnational crime. Essential to his examination of such issues is a conscious extension of the usual definition of corruption that applies to non-public office-holders as well as to office-holders who abuse their positions for private gain. Many of the offenders whom he discusses used their privileged access to key information or materiel to supply state secrets or proprietary and unlicensed technology to rogue nation-states for personal benefit.

Pakistan was the center of one of the central networks of corruption and proliferation, as Bunn describes. It became a premier export enterprise, supplying centrifuge and other key forms of technology to Iran, Iraq, Libya, and North Korea, at least. More than twenty countries were involved, with abundant illicit transfers of cash, payoffs at many levels, and different kinds and levels of corruption. Designs and equipment, and maraging steel, found their way illicitly to those who had nuclear aspirations. The result of this web of intrigue, chicanery, and money laundering was nuclear weaponization and its spread, fueled by various degrees of corrupt practice and payment.

At another level, terrorist groups may not have sought highly enriched uranium, suitable for a bomb, but they have sought and may in future seek highly enriched uranium or plutonium sufficient to construct a crude nuclear device. They could only obtain such supplies corruptly, or through direct theft. Al Qaeda apparently has made repeated efforts to purchase stolen nuclear material and ex-Russian warheads. Guards at nuclear sites are particularly open to corrupt inducements. Jobs in such establishments are sometimes for sale. And smugglers, whether inside or outside criminal syndicates, will smuggle anything for profit.

Bunn's chapter advocates a series of reforms that are capable of capping or at least reducing the kinds of corrupt practices that facilitate the spread of WMD. He wants governments to retrain and educate individuals who have access to nuclear materials and facilities, compel corporations to promote tough security cultures within their own domains, improve controls in and at sensitive installations, and adhere to the spirit and letter of UN Security Council Resolution 1540, which obligates member states to establish domestic controls to prevent proliferation of weapons and their means of delivery. Additionally, Bunn calls for the codification of international standards to defeat criminals and terrorists and to safeguard stockpiles and other places where nuclear supplies are stored. He suggests upgrading detection methods and technical systems. Rigorous accounting systems will be necessary to ensure the rapid detection of theft. Tighter border security will also be essential. So will improved legislation and universal jurisdiction, with stiffer penalties.

Like Bunn, Teets and Chenoweth show how corruption and corrupt actors facilitate the spread of critical new global insecurities. The authors evaluate two hypotheses regarding the relationship between corruption and terrorism. First, that terrorists may be motivated directly by the presence of corrupt regimes; they can mobilize followers to take up arms to extirpate corrupt and thus illegitimate governments. Second, in states where rule of law is weak and criminalization flourishes, terrorists can accumulate funds, weapons, forged documents, and so on. Terrorist organizations can take advantage of existing criminal organizations to traffic in guns, drugs, and humans (as Greenhill describes), or can create their own networks of criminality to move cocaine, opium, heroin, or marijuana; purchase and trade in small arms and light weapons; or transport women and children across borders. Teets and Chenoweth posit that terrorist attacks will come from inside highly corrupt nation-states but will not necessarily target those same states.

They tested those conclusions quantitatively, using models to investigate the true relationship between corruption rankings, drug trafficking, arms imports, money laundering, and terrorist incidents. The results indicate that higher levels of corruption in a country increase the number of terroristic attacks that originate in that county. Moreover, nation-states that facilitate illicit trafficking of all kinds produce heightened numbers of terrorist attacks. Major arms-importing countries that are corrupt also produce terrorist attacks. Yet, whereas money laundering is associated with increased numbers of terrorist organizations, drug trafficking is linked to reduced numbers of terrorist groupings. This latter finding means that drug trafficking and terrorism do not go together, despite contrary evidence from the Taliban in Afghanistan and the FARC in Colombia (a case which they investigate).

Corruption enables terrorists (in Colombia and Afghanistan, for example) to purchase arms and materiel, but also to transport illicit goods both in and out of their homelands to, say, Russia, and receive large numbers of weapons in return. Corrupted Russian military officials and corrupted customs inspectors at both ends of the connection, and in Jordan—as a refueling stop—were critical to the FARC's success. Indeed, the FARC could not have prospered in Colombia without a concatenation of corrupt connections internally. Likewise, the Taliban in Afghanistan and Pakistan cannot mobilize and gain weapons and territory without the connivance of corrupt Afghan and Pakistani army officers and personnel.[15] There is a reasonable suspicion that corrupt militaries in Sri Lanka and Uganda—two more examples—permitted the insurgencies in both countries to grow stronger than they otherwise might have. The case of the FARC demonstrates that corruption facilitates, more than it motivates, terrorism. It also makes evident that terrorism cannot flourish without a global supply chain; effective action against terrorism can be focused on corrupt facilitators as well as the terrorist organizations themselves. To attack terrorism, world order should combat corruption, especially among customs and other border officials.

Russia and the Near Abroad

The intertwining of criminality and corruption is readily seen in the post-Soviet space in Eastern Europe and Central Asia, as well as in Mother Russia itself. As Legvold's chapter reminds us, eight of twelve post-Soviet states cluster toward the bottom of TI's Corruption Perceptions Index. But this condition is of concern not only for the welfare of citizens in Russia and its former dependent states. Legvold asserts that the levels of massive corruption that envelope Russia and its periphery directly threaten international welfare and international security in profound ways. Corruption in Russia and its near beyond is implicated in regional conflict, global terrorism, and the potential proliferation of WMD. It threatens health outcomes beyond the Russian sphere and fuels illicit trafficking of humans, arms, and all things criminal.

Among the post-Soviet nations are several places that are criminal states, i.e. where the core activity of the state is criminal and the state itself depends "overwhelmingly on the returns from illicit trade" to exist and pay its way.[16] Abkhazia, South Ossetia, Transdniestr, and Nagorno-Karabakh are prominent examples.

Others are criminalized states, places where corruption is extensive—where the highest levels of the state and the entire apparatus of the state are "suffused" with corrupt practice. Legvold suggests that the distinction between criminal and criminalized is that in the latter the nation-state's core may not be corrupt, but the "process" by which the state acts is indeed corrupt. These states are also "captured," as Greenhill and Legvold explain, and as indicated earlier, the business of the state is "privatized." Russia, Ukraine, Uzbekistan, Kyrgyzstan, Moldova, Armenia, and Azerbaijan are criminalized examples.

The remaining post-Soviet places are corrupt, even Georgia and Mongolia, excepting the Baltic nations.

In the criminal and criminalized states, there is systemic corruption (as in the Soviet Union itself), usually with the apex of the state at the controlling center of a widespread network of corruption. Decentralized examples also exist, but the prevailing pattern in Russia, its near abroad, and in Africa and Asia is centralized systemic corruption that captures and controls the state for the benefit of a relatively few principal agents. Legvold's chapter offers rich empirical detail on who got and gets what, who controlled which industry, who embezzled how much from state coffers, and on and on. Legislation, entrance to university, evasion of the military draft, securing land titles, arranging medical treatment, and the overall cost of "doing business" each had its defined price in Russia and beyond. In the first four years of this century, the average bribe increased from the equivalent of $10,000 to $136,000.[17]

In Russia, as in the globe's systemically corrupt states, local officials routinely collaborate with predatory business interests, are "indifferent to the law and property rights," and are ready, even determined, to share illicit spoils. Extortion is normal compensation for sanctioning someone else's corporate endeavor. So is theft by functionaries. The main preoccupation of bureaucrats is rent-seeking, particularly through the interpretation of regulations. Moreover, there is no accountability or transparency. The courts are weak and the press is often brave but outgunned.

In Russia and its neighbors, as almost everywhere, these corrupt practices and lack of accountability limit economic growth and reform, lead to market distortions and inefficiencies, and diminish political stability by discrediting government and breaking the social contract between ruler and ruled. Sometimes, as in the color revolutions earlier in this century, citizens actually took to the barricades and brought down ex-Soviet regimes primarily because they were perceived as being corrupt.

Corruption in these criminalized states, especially where they harbor spent nuclear fuel or missiles and the components of missiles, threatens world order directly. Both Bunn and Legvold report instances of smuggled weapons-grade fuel and other analogous cases. Russia has also harbored perpetrators and itself has directly engaged in weapons smuggling, thus helping to fuel civil wars in many parts of Africa and Latin America. So has Ukraine. Its Transdniestr neighbor indeed specializes in this kind of trade. Russia (and China) also traffic in counterfeit manufactured goods and pharmaceuticals, in copyrighted items and other contraband, and in humans. About 1 million women may have been spirited out of Russia to the West between 1995 and 2005, a proportionally greater number from Ukraine in a comparable time period, and fully 10 percent of Moldova during the 1990s. Russia also smuggles wildlife and animal parts supplied by poachers and corrupt security officials and has decimated the sturgeon population in the Caspian Sea. Afghan heroin also moves across and into Russia and the Ukraine, harming those countries and Europe. Nothing moves without corrupt gains at every transit point. In some of the smaller post-Soviet states those rents help to sustain the highest reaches of the nation.

Legvold's sober chapter is inherently pessimistic. As far as reforms, he concludes that "little will change" until new leaders come to power who attempt to end the criminalized or the criminal states.[18] Change must come from within despite the palpable rewards of business as usual through rampant systemic corruption.

Nigeria and Other Corrupted Countries

The other case studies contained in this volume are equally brutal in their surveys of political and largely internal corruption in Papua New Guinea and Nigeria and in the six other country cases discussed by Rose-Ackerman and Koechlin and Sepúlveda Carmona. Papua New Guinea (PNG) is unlike Russia and largely devoid of transnational implications and trafficking, but Nigeria is implicated in a raft of transnational activity and is heavily involved in almost every form of cross-border and transcontinental illicit action, even the smuggling of children as slave labor.

There are few nation-states as corrupt and corrupted as Papua New Guinea. Dix and Pok suggest that corruption there is rampant and unchecked, with the state having been captured by criminalized forces. They also indicate that PNG is more infected than other places with systematic nepotism, costing millions of dollars in its separate provinces alone. Curiously, they report that in this unusual example of state corruption, petty (lubricating) corruption appears less widespread than national-level venal (administrative) corruption. It is also opportunistic rather than systemic, possibly because most PNG citizens are subsistence farmers with limited involvement in their government or with its officials.

All of these standard forms of corruption flourish in PNG despite accountability institutions such as an ombudsman, a fraud squad, a financial intelligence unit, a formal code of conduct for parliamentarians, an audit act and an auditor general, a proceeds of crime act, and a national anti-corruption alliance that coordinates inter-agency investigations and prosecutions. Dix and Pok discuss the weaknesses of each of these anti-corruption approaches within the PNG context, as well as the cavalier quality of the courts. Another reason for the inability of such well-meant mechanisms to stem corrupt practice in PNG, they write, is the pervasiveness of an indigenous culture of tolerance for corruption.

The people of PNG, like the people of so many other new nation-states, are accustomed to receiving cash in exchange for their votes, to paying off the police, to offering bribes to obtain telephone lines, and so on. But the six million people of PNG also appreciate that linguistic and ethnic kin need to work together in a network of reciprocity that is held together by corrupt practice, including the block buying of votes and large-scale nepotism.

Even so, the authors argue, Papua New Guineans are not always indifferent to the stain of corruption despite the overhang of social network obligations, especially if the offenders are from a different ethnic or linguistic group. The ombudsman does at least receive abundant complaints.

Western institutions lack legitimacy in PNG, especially when they are opposed by an elaborate system of exchange that has its roots in the culturally sustained practices of more than 800 distinct ethno-linguistic entities and innumerable cross-cutting kinship networks. These traditional practices have become a system by which politicians and officials view public office as opportunities to accumulate wealth and status for themselves and also for their networks—their *wantoks*. The spoils of office are expected to be shared, specifically through patronage.

Dix and Pok suggest that the spread of educational opportunity in PNG, a semi-literate country, may help break down the traditional support for cronyism and other incentives for corruption. So will a better educated population allow civil society, including church groups, to grow and become more active in opposing or at least questioning the ripeness of corruption in PNG.

The authors despair that Westernized institutional instruments may not be able to cope, no matter how strengthened, with corrupt demands that are enshrined in practice and now incorporated into the expectations of the "big men"—the political persons at the apex of PNG village, provincial, and national authority. However, it is to these "big men" that Dix and Pok look for possible ameliorations of corrupt practice. They think that a diminution of corruption in PNG will come only when "not so bad" leaders attempt to alter how their countrymen view the conjunction of tradition and corruption. When leaders begin to say that it is customary to be transparent and not underhanded, then the people of PNG may reduce their acceptance of prevailing approaches to corruption.

Nigeria also has its big men, its ethnic and kin networks, and its traditions of gift exchange, but Nigeria, compared to most other nation-states in Africa and to PNG, is well-educated and sophisticated. Corruption is common and expected in virtually all circumstances. As Smith's chapter makes perfectly clear, Nigerians use corrupt methods to cope with the vicissitudes of daily life, assume that the web of corruption cannot easily be evaded, and still resent its exactions and rail regularly about how corrupt acts impose heavy costs on their everyday existence. Unlike the atmosphere in PNG, Nigerians have never condoned corruption or the heavy toll that it exacts on their lives.

Nigerians, reports Smith, "participate in forms of corruption that perpetuate their victimization."[19] They want to employ social networks of patronage, as in PNG, but ordinary Nigerians believe that elites have hijacked the patronage system to serve their own interests. Accountability mechanisms have also been perverted. The post-colonial state is the problem, because the dominant class plays by its own rules, not by society's rules. It has captured the state and should share its resources more broadly than it does. Ordinary Nigerians bemoan what corruption does to them, but they still seek to participate in it to gain access to schooling, health care, and jobs. "Who gets to . . . a position of power and then refuses to help his people?"[20] Big men must enrich themselves; they must fulfill the expectations of family and community.

At the same time as Nigerians understand the cultural underpinning of corrupt practice, they are aware that its level has far exceeded what can be explained by kinship, obligations of patronage, and responsibilities to home communities. They are disturbed by the crookedness of their fellow Nigerians—by scams and attempted scams. But they feel powerless to reduce corruption levels even as they seek to benefit from particular personal flows of clientelism.

Nigeria does not lack for official accountability organizations, several of which have worked effectively in the local battle against corruption. Nevertheless, on TI's Corruption Perceptions Index for 2008, Nigeria ranked two-thirds of the way down, at 121 of 180. It also was among the bottom ten of forty-eight African countries in the 2008 Index of African Governance, to some extent because of its poor ratings on corruption, rule of law, security, and other critical categories of governmental performance.[21]

Suberu explains why and how Nigeria's "unprecedented" official campaign against corruption since 1999 has essentially failed, its potential success being undermined time and again by acts of political commission or omission. Human Rights Watch, quoted by Suberu, suggests that much of the corruption and accompanying violence that permeates Nigeria is indeed criminal.[22]

The country's principal perpetrators of corrupt practice are elite politicians at local, state, and national levels.

Although Suberu agrees with Smith that ordinary Nigerians are "active participants" in the social reproduction of corruption, the onus is on the ruling class. Indeed, Suberu says that the petty corruption that has long been endemic to Nigeria is "conspicuously trivial" compared to the "monumental" scale of corruption that is and has been for decades orchestrated by the nation's rulers.[23] According to the chairman of Nigeria's Independent Corrupt Practices and Other Related Offenses Commission (ICPC), two-thirds of Nigeria's earnings from oil, about $500 billion, have been stolen by Nigerians from the nation's treasury.[24] Gift-giving, favoritism, nepotism, and most of the forms of corruption that are common everywhere, as in PNG, occur throughout Nigeria and constitute a culture of corruption. But corruption's chief fuel in Nigeria's modern times has been the massive wealth and abundant rents that flowed from petroleum and its export. Key members of the executive, legislators, state governors, judges, policemen, and even (or especially) military officers have all stolen outrageously. Between 1999 and 2007, thirty-one governors (Nigeria has thirty-six states) were indicted by anti-corruption agencies for embezzlement, money laundering, false declaration of assets, and illegal purchasing of properties outside of and inside Nigeria.

The country's several anti-corruption agencies, and its penal code, have never been equal to the task of curbing corrupt practices. The provisions of the code have rarely been enforced and the agencies, no matter how active, have been unable to prevent the perversion of public office for private ends. Nor have public education campaigns and well-meant efforts led by military rulers in the 1980s. Instead, successive rulers of Nigeria have manipulated anti-corruption efforts and statutory agencies, removed key personnel who dared to close in upon miscreants who were high-level politicians at the national and state levels, starved the agencies of funding, and in many additional ways compromised even the boldest institutional efforts to curb corruption. Impunity also persists for executives and for Nigerians who were the big thieves in pre-1999 governments. The absence of clean elections further undercuts the credibility of national anti-corruption institutions and compromises their autonomy and their integrity.

Human Rights

Koechlin and Sepúlveda Carmona also dissect a national case—Malawi—but the primary argument of their chapter is that the prevalence of untrammeled corruption in the nation-states of the developing world seriously threatens human rights, as well as fairness and social justice, rule of law performance, and so on. Because the protection and empowerment of the globe's most vulnerable and disadvantaged are core values of human rights norms, and because corruption helps directly and indirectly to immiserate the world's already-poor and citizens of all income levels everywhere, the persistence of corrupt practices, as in the post-Soviet and other cases cited earlier, diminishes human rights. Furthermore, write Koechlin and Sepúlveda Carmona, major international conventions specify those specific human rights and impose obligations on nation-states. When human rights are undermined or attacked by corruption, those who are deprived of their rights are able to protest, or at least to draw attention to such often-ignored impacts of corruption. Linking corruption and human rights also should encourage increased public and official support for anti-corruption initiatives.

The claim that Koechlin and Sepúlveda Carmona make is often overlooked in the anti-corruption literature and in anti-corruption initiatives to boost accountability, such as the UN Convention against Corruption (UNCAC) and TI's National Integrity System (NIS). But the salience and potential power of an emphasis on human rights in battling corruption is strong, amplifying other efforts at enhancing accountability. Adding an awareness that corruption harms human rights could assist in the transformation of a culture of corruption into a culture of accountability—the goals of both the UNCAC and NIS. Koechlin and Sepúlveda Carmona urge anti-corruption reformers to understand and take advantage for the first time of the instrumental potential of a human rights–based approach in the battle against corruption.

In Malawi, Koechlin and Sepúlveda Carmona show that the nation-state has assumed a welter of human rights obligations by ratifying a number of international and regional covenants and conventions. Its constitution also enshrines human rights, creates a commission on human rights, installs an official ombudsman, and offers other bodies with broad mandates to protect and promote human rights. Malawi has also ratified the UNCAC, has enacted potent legislation against corruption, and has a strong Anti-Corruption Bureau, now bolstered by the report in 2009 of a forward-looking Anti-Corruption Commission authorized by the president and parliament and chaired by a well-respected former senior government official turned corporate leader.

Despite adherence to human rights and anti-corruption protocols, Malawi is ranked as a country that has hardly eliminated the taint of corrupt practice. In 2008, TI ranked Malawi 115 of 180 countries. That means that most citizens are still marginally enfranchised and subject to corrupt abuse that undercuts their economic and social rights. Where citizens fail to realize their full rights to life, to education, to health, and so on, and where that failure is in some measure attributable to corruption, Malawi is not fulfilling its treaty and constitutional obligations.

The authors' argument is that in Malawi, as elsewhere, endemic corruption—the misappropriation of public funds and the misuse of positions of power—and a culture of executive and other impunity that perpetuates social, economic, and political inequalities together constitute human rights abuses. But this connection between corruption and human rights may be underappreciated locally. With recognition of the intimate linkages between the two, and an awareness of how Malawi's progressive rules and intentions are being undercut by persistent corruption, it is at least plausible that the local anti-corruption crusade could be strengthened. Instead of treating human rights and corruption as parallel concerns, a common strategy in Malawi and elsewhere that combines the two would help. So would the employment of core economic, social, and cultural rights as a frame of reference to add a new dimension to and thus assist the struggle against corruption. Viewing corruption as a violation of human rights would emphasize its baleful impact on vulnerable citizens. Such a view would add a valuable normative dimension.

Battling Corruption

The last third of this volume sets out a strategy, admittedly mixed and mostly untested, capable of combating corruption. It combines best practices in the anti-corruption effort with novel and recently introduced initiatives. Every chapter in this section, indeed in the entire book, has something to say about how accountability overall and within particular jurisdictions can be strengthened. Accountability and transparency, after all, are the key antidotes to the perpetuation of corruption, but they can be achieved in myriad ways, some more plausibly effective than others. Together with strengthened measures of accountability, several of the chapters' authors advocate swift and certain punishment for corrupt offenders. Zero tolerance for offenders is also proposed by some. But everyone involved in the great battle against corruption nationally and internationally knows how hard it is in most nation-states to target corrupters and corruptees, much less to punish them decisively. The struggle against corruption will be won, most of our authors agree, in the courts of public opinion and by giving backbone to national political wills. This last point was confirmed in 2009 by a public opinion survey in Kenya's major cities: Three-quarters of respondents believed that the Kenyan government overwhelmingly lacked the political will to fight corruption. "Most of the institutions of governance," said TI's leader in Kenya, "had been captured by corrupt, narrow vested interests"—even the judiciary and the official anti-corruption commission.[25]

Corruption flourishes because rulers and ruling classes condone and, often, actively participate in its nefarious pursuits. My chapter in this volume argues that pro-active leadership by heads of state and heads of government can do more to reduce corrupt practices than almost anything else. This approach complements Heineman's chapter on corporate responsibility. In both the political and the corporate spheres, we argue, leadership action is decisive. My chapter cannot conclusively demonstrate empirically that politicians, bureaucrats, and lower-level operatives solicit bribes and demand percentages of contracts because leaders (and their immediate superiors) turn the other way or seem (despite rhetoric to the contrary) to condone such actions by subordinates down the line. There is no certain way to prove that a culture of corruption, once unleashed, is responsible for examples of greed at the top or at the bottom of official lists. But we can argue from the few successful anti-corruption examples that committed leadership is essential if a polity seeks definitively to cleanse itself of corruption. A small number of political and corporate leaders with vision have done just that, not for moral but for profoundly instrumental reasons. In both arenas, prosperity, better living standards, and good earnings followed successful anti-corruption initiatives that were enunciated and then pursued systematically for decades until a reformed political culture (or corporate culture) had been achieved.

My chapter examines the very few successful anti-corruption cases in the developing world to show the critical inputs of leadership. But, once again, the successes are suggestive, rather than conclusive. No one has tested side-by-side two nation-states following different leadership trajectories. Correlations and circumstantial evidence support my contention, however, that human condition defaults toward corruption; only decisive and committed leadership action can intercede. Moreover, piety and moral appeals are meaningless. Heads must roll. Pronouncements must be followed by exemplary punishments, the higher the better. Moreover, the heads of state or of government must themselves be blameless, with no hints of embellishment or unfair perquisites. If not, their legitimacy will obviously be tainted and lower-ranking officials will take their cue from rumor or physical evidence of special advantage. The policeman on the beat watches what his captain does, and copies him or her. Ordinary police seek bribes if those to whom they report do so, and likewise on up the line. Cabinet ministers skim contracts because they can get away with it, but also because everyone else is doing it. Why should anyone miss out on the advantages of office, of position, of authority? In this manner corruption becomes a way of life in much of the developing world and in large swathes of the developed world, such as Russia and China. Only decisive political will—visionary leadership—can stanch corruption.

Heineman offers a prescription for the creation of effective internal corporate anti-corruption cultures that are infused with high integrity and high performance. He wants governments to mandate sustainable anti-corruption behavior by their corporate citizens. Since external corrupting pressures inevitably tempt multi-national corporate managers who must meet arbitrary financial goals, Heineman advocates clear and well-articulated rules that apply to all employees at all levels in all situations and countries under all circumstances. Not only should obvious infractions be sanctioned, such as bribe-giving and extortion-paying, but every manner of additional compromising payment, however clandestine, must also be outlawed. So must special arrangements with spouses or associates (or straws) of powerful recipient country leaders and for political contributions of all kinds. As Heineman writes, "a strong anti-corruption program requires a robust integrity culture," together with unambiguous guidelines.[26] But, as in the political sphere, corporate leaders must act decisively against miscreants and malefactors who cross the company integrity line. The leaders themselves must operate with integrity.

The best corporations, like the best polities, will educate and train their employees to avoid wittingly or unwittingly involvement in corrupt behavior. Heineman provides abundant examples of good practices, and shows how those practices can be applied across multi-national corporations. He emphasizes that "what is right" always trumps "what is legal." Bribe-taking and -giving are not only corrupt and demoralize the internal culture of a corporation, but they also lead to actions such as the falsification of the books and dishonesty that eat away at the core of a modern multi-national enterprise.

Accountability in an anti-corrupt business is enhanced—as it is in the political realm—by giving employees "voice," by empowering whistle-blowing (Lambsdorff is an advocate also), and by creating ombudsmen-like avenues for reporting potential infractions of the rules. Heineman further recommends compensating corporate leaders for performance with integrity, not just for performance. That rule has an obvious analogy for nation-states.

If multi-national corporations refuse to bribe, pay percentages of a construction contract to an influential minister, or give attractive gifts to the president's wife or mistress, it may be possible for them to assist anti-corruption initiatives in selected developing countries and, also, to remove incessant temptation among officials accustomed to competing for emoluments with their envious colleagues. If, in line with Heineman's idealistic prescription, multi-national corporations behave with a new integrity, at least one major corrupting influence will be removed and reform, strengthened. But Heineman makes clear that a strong affirmative corporate culture depends, in important part, on robust enforcement of national laws against multi-nationals as required under the OECD Convention on Combating Bribery of Foreign Public Officials. He also shows that the record of signatory nations to the convention has been, on balance, disappointing.

Lambsdorff offers a number of anti-corruption strategies for both governments and private firms. Investigating such measures statistically, he stresses the need for bottom-up endeavors, not only repressive punishments (which do not always deter) from the top. Likewise "zero-tolerance" sometimes produces perverse results. His research also shows that solid rules-based approaches alone do not raise a country's ratings in the TI Corruption Perceptions Index. Even limits on individual office-holder discretion and overly restrictive procurement guidelines—even debarment—have their costs as well as their likely benefits.

Corruption sometimes flows from adverse incentives. This is the known consequence of artificial price or quantity restrictions, import quotas, and limited import and other licenses. A reverse policy, offering monetary and other inducements for non-corrupt behavior, is difficult to administer and produces perverse moral hazards. Moreover, as Lambsdorff reminds us, "honesty" incentives are unlikely to outbid the rewards that are provided by corrupters. Establishing an effective value system, as Heineman and others advocate, is obviously better, but is only capable of being developed if the actions of leaders and all of their followers strengthen their legitimacy. Mere compliance systems are insufficient. However, leniency for self-reporting that leads to effective prosecution does have its benefits. Such a policy provides incentives for corrupt parties to report each other. Indeed, Lambsdorff wants corrupt actors to be "seduced to betray each other so as to destabilize corrupt transactions."[27]

Grassroots initiatives by civil society are what Lambsdorff calls a core contributor to anti-corruption efforts. Press freedom is another bottom-up contribution to the effort; countries with high levels of press freedom have lower levels of perceived corruption. Leniency and self-reporting are also bottom-up strategies. Overall, bottom-up efforts need to "highlight the economic returns from acting with integrity." Relying on morality will not do.[28]

When Eigen created TI in 1993, he little knew how successful his efforts would be in energizing the battle against corruption. As a World Bank official with extensive experience in Africa, he understood well how the rot of corruption had undermined the bank's well-intended efforts to contribute to

Africa's economic growth and development. That was among his motives in establishing a new NGO that would build coalitions in many developing countries (now more than 100) to combat the spread of corruption. (His chapter devotes a few modest paragraphs to the founding of TI.) As a by-product came the now well-regarded and carefully researched survey of surveys—TI's Corruption Perceptions Index (developed by Lambsdorff)—and the more recent Bribe Payer's Index. Later, Eigen and TI invented Integrity Pacts for governments and all bidders for public contracts. These instruments constituted pledges not to solicit or pay bribes, with accompanying monitoring systems.

Eigen almost singlehandedly brought corruption out of the closet and compelled the bank, other donors, and governments everywhere to acknowledge the existence and the corrosive scale of corruption. Corruption, Eigen and TI emphasized, was a systematic and recognized way to undertake business by most European multi-national corporations. It was also tax deductible, legal, and condoned. (The U.S. Foreign Corrupt Practices Act of 1977 had uniquely prohibited the bribing of foreign officials.)[29] The modern concern with and assault on corruption begins with Eigen and the founding of TI. The 1999 OECD Convention on Combating Bribery of Foreign Public Officials and the 2003 UN Convention against Corruption (UNCAC) are direct outcomes of Eigen's efforts. (There were 140 ratifications by nation-states of UNCAC through 2008, although what such ratifications actually imply about implementation is problematic.)

Now, as Eigen's chapter in our book indicates, he is active in bolstering the capacity of civil society to battle corruption. He also believes that anti-corruption efforts may be strengthened by the Extractive Industries Transparency Initiative (EITI). Originated by a coalition of NGOs calling themselves Publish What You Pay, EITI encourages its corporate and governmental signatories to declare their payments openly, i.e., to declare how much Exxon-Mobil is paying Cameroon in annual petroleum royalties, for example.

EITI monitors data on financial flows to see that extractive industries are reporting what is paid to governments and that governments are allowing companies to do so. Thirty-seven oil, gas, and mining companies have endorsed EITI. Resource-rich countries first become candidate countries (twenty-three in 2009). After independent validations, they can become compliant countries. EITI intends to become the gold standard for revenue transparency for extractive industries. It may also expand soon into the timber exporting sector.

In another sectoral diagnosis, Griffin offers a set of prescriptions capable of reducing corruption in the health and educational arenas of developing countries. On average, in such nation-states, health and education budgets account for more than half of central government expenditures. Foreign assistance is often concentrated on the enlargement of health capacities and on educational improvements in low- and middle-income countries, but to what effect? Since many of these countries are perceived as thoroughly corrupt, according to TI, and since accountability and fiduciary controls are often lamentably weak, many of the funds supposedly devoted to strengthening health and education in the developing world are wasted.

Griffin goes beyond standard definitions of corruption to include blatant absenteeism or the failure to deliver appropriate (and expected) services under the usual rubric of abusing public office for private gain. He also discusses ghost workers, the abuse of shady procurement systems, collusion among bidders, inadequate tracking mechanisms that facilitate peculation, falsified claims, and a host of other scams that either adulterate or jeopardize health outcomes and reduce educational opportunity in needy countries.

One method of combating these common deficiencies is to design new educational and health programs that empower citizens, not bureaucracies, and shift performance risks from government to private suppliers. Griffin wants to make teachers in schools responsible to students, hospital administrators and physicians to their patients. In El Salvador (and in Bangladesh and New Zealand), school management is decentralized, with parent-teacher associations in charge of overseeing central government disbursements and instructional outcomes. The health market is much more difficult to strengthen in analogous ways, but subsidized insurance that follows individual patients (as in China, Ghana, Kenya, and many other countries) helps. Principals, in other words, should be in charge of agents, not the other way around. By such means can greater accountability and transparency be achieved, and corruption reduced markedly.

Jomo urges those who battle corruption to avoid laundry lists of governance reforms. It is impossible, he writes, to address all kinds of corruption simultaneously. He suggests that anti-corruption efforts should focus on those types of corruption that are most damaging to development. In many circumstances, economic growth is a necessary condition for effectively addressing corruption. He argues that ostensible governance-enhancing reforms such as decentralization may unintentionally create new opportunities for rent-seeking. Even privatization, which is seemingly intended as a policy intervention to reduce public sector corruption, unwittingly creates new opportunities. Condemning all rent-seeking also obscures the many ways in which rent-seeking in the developing world may be regulated appropriately and channeled for development. Furthermore, encouraging profit maximization and the seeking of competitive advantage is to be encouraged, not always deprecated.

Together, the contributors to this expanded approach to the age-old problems of corruption agree—even without being able to quantify their accord—that corruption in the twenty-first century infects much more of human activity than ever before. Globalization in all of its ramifications has made it much easier than in previous centuries to propagate corrupt pursuits, and for corrupt officials to facilitate all manner of transnational and transcontinental forms of crime. Indeed, absent corrupt channels, the world would be more secure, less anxious about the spread of WMD and terror, and less affected by illicit trafficking of myriad kinds.

The authors each propose remedies: enhanced transparency and heightened awareness by media investigators and civil society; an aroused public opinion; tougher and more certain punishment; decisive anti-corrupt leaders who set a positive example personally and politically; adherence to internationally set standards and new initiatives like EITI and the OECD convention; and new, enforceable sanctions against money laundering, trafficking, and innumerable kinds of shady activities. No singular attack on corruption will reduce its spread and pernicious importance. But a combination might, especially if all of the remedies and responses offered throughout this book are deployed strategically to overwhelm the global practice and threat of corruption.

Notes

1. Ari Adut, *On Scandal: Moral Disturbances in Society, Politics, and Art* (New York, 2008), 129–174.

2. George Eliot, *Felix Holt, The Radical* (New York, Crowell edition, nd, but circa 1870; orig. pub. London, 1866); Charles Dickens, *Little Dorrit* (London, 1855). This novel, by Dickens, was first published as a serial novel between 1855 and 1857. Although decried by many nineteenth-century critics, it is now praised as a tale that disparages modern social and political corruption.

3. Joseph S. Nye, "Corruption and Political Development: A Cost-Benefit Analysis," *American Political Science Review,* LXI (1967), 417–427. For additional definitions and ways of understanding the different definitions, see Peter John Perry, *Political Corruption and Political Geography* (Brookfield, VT, 1997), 12–18.

4. James C. Scott, *Comparative Political Corruption* (Englewood Cliffs, 1972), 67.

5. Transparency International-Kenya, "Kenya Bribery Index 2008" (Nairobi, 2008), available at www.tikenya.org/documents/KenyaBriberyIndex08.pdf (accessed 18 February 2009).

6. For Singapore, see Robert I. Rotberg, "Leadership Alters Behavior," chapter 13 in this volume. Susan Rose-Ackerman says in her chapter that "strong leadership and good morals are not sufficient." See Susan Rose-Ackerman, "Corruption in the Wake of Domestic National Conflict," 86.

7. Laura Underkuffler, "Defining Corruption: Implications for Africa," 30.

8. Ibid., 31.

9. Ibid., 38.

10. World Bank Institute, "Worldwide Governance Indicators: 1996–2006" (Washington, D.C., 2007), available at www.govindicators.org (accessed 18 February 2009).

11. Rose-Ackerman, "Corruption in the Wake," 86.

12. Ibid.

13. Kelly Greenhill, "Kleptocratic Interdependence: Trafficking, Corruption, and the Marriage of Politics and Illicit Profits," 99.

14. Ibid., 103.

15. Richard A. Oppel, Jr., "Corruption Undercuts U. S. Hopes for Improving the Afghan Police," *New York Times* (9 April 2009).

16. Robert Legvold, "Corruption, the Criminalized State, and Post-Soviet Transitions," 196.

17. Ibid., 201.

18. Ibid., 229.

19. Daniel Jordan Smith, "The Paradoxes of Popular Participation in Corruption in Nigeria," 286.

20. Ibid., 297.

21. Transparency International, "Corruption Perceptions Index" (2008), available at www.transparency.org/policy_research/surveys_indices/cpi/2008 (accessed 18 February 2009); Robert I. Rotberg and Rachel M. Gisselquist, *Strengthening African Governance: Ibrahim Index of Governance, Results and Rankings 2008* (Cambridge, MA, 2008), available at http://belfercenter.ksg.harvard.edu/project/52/intrastate_conflict_program.html?page_id=224 (accessed 18 February 2009).

22. Rotimi Suberu, "The Travails of Nigeria's Anti-Corruption Crusade," 260.

23. Ibid., 261.

24. Ibid., 264.

25. Derek Kilner, "Watchdog Says Graft Could Cause More Election Violence in Kenya," *Voice of America Online* (9 March 2009), available at www.voanews.com (accessed 14 April 2009). Job Ogonda is the TI leader quoted.

26. Ben W. Heineman, Jr., "The Role of the Multi-National Corporation in the Long War against Corruption," 362.

27. Johann Graf Lambsdorff, "The Organization of Anti-Corruption: Getting Incentives Right," 409.

28. Ibid., 410.

29. Lambsdorff's chapter is critical of the full effectiveness of this act.

LAURA S. UNDERKUFFLER

2

Defining Corruption: Implications for Action

The problems that result from public officials' participation in corruption, and allegations of such problems, plague emerging and established governments. It is easy to deplore the existence of corruption; it is far more difficult to determine what corruption truly is and why we deplore it as a social and political evil.

For those who are actively involved in fighting corruption, an in-depth examination of what appears to be a definitional question might seem to be a misplaced effort. Obviously, the definition of corruption is important in the shaping of legal prohibitions and controls. In addition, there are issues of cultural relativity in one's understanding of corruption—for instance, one man's bribe may be another man's gift.[1] However, as those on the front lines of corruption-fighting efforts rightly point out, there are many acts that are universally condemned as corrupt. For instance, as Noonan famously observes, "Not a country in the world . . . does not treat bribery [somehow defined] as criminal on its law books."[2] If there is overwhelming agreement that bribery, the illegal skimming of profits, and bid-rigging are corrupt acts, what more—in a general sense—can be gained from an examination of this definitional issue?

This chapter examines the conceptions of corruption that are usually found in the academic and operational literature and explores the issues that these findings raise. I argue that these conceptions, although useful, fail to capture significant and substantial aspects of prevailing beliefs about what corruption is. Furthermore, I argue that what is missing from these theories—in particular, the conviction that corruption is a moral evil—has distinct implications for the identification and control of this governmentally and societally destructive phenomenon.

Understanding Corruption: Mainstream Theories

Corruption, as an idea in politics and government, has been the subject of extensive academic analysis and commentary. For many years, political scientists, sociologists, and legal academicians have generally assumed a particular understanding of corruption and proceeded to study its causes, effects, and methods of prevention. Corruption, for instance, has been assumed to be bribery and like acts, with little attention given to the precise contours of this idea or what the use of this idea added to the simple list of prohibited acts.

In the 1970s and 1980s, this approach changed and more sophisticated analyses began to appear. This change was fueled by developments that were internal and external to the academic field. Political scientists such as Robert Klitgaard and economists such as Bruce Benson and John Baden began to focus on the nature of corruption as critical to how we envision corruption and whether it operates as a positive or destructive social force. Legal academicians, prodded by a general movement toward the merger of law with other disciplines, were no longer satisfied with the curt simplicity of statutory or other legal definitions. In addition, because of the importance of corruption and allegations of corruption in national and international politics and governance, additional attention to the core concept was inevitable.

A uniform understanding of corruption has not emerged from these academic efforts. Although there is a popular understanding of corruption that is shared by politicians, journalists, and "the man on the street," academic theorists have advanced a multiplicity of meanings, with more or less scrutiny or explicit understanding of the underlying idea. There are, however, several approaches that are dominant in theorists' work and that can be readily identified. In the following discussion I consider these theories and their ability to capture what, in "corruption," we believe to be at stake.

Corruption as the Violation of Law

As Scott's classic work begins, "Corruption, we would all agree, involves a deviation from certain standards of behavior. The first question which arises is: what criteria shall we use to establish these standards?"[3] If public corruption is the concern, perhaps the most obvious place to start is this: corruption involves a violation of law.

This understanding is based upon a common-sense observation. When one thinks about corruption by government actors, one tends to think of crimes such as bribery, fraud, extortion, embezzlement, kickbacks on public contracts, and so on. There seems to be a strong correlation between what one believes to be *illegal* acts and what one believes to be corrupt. Indeed, some observers would go further: if an official's act is prohibited by law, as established by government, it is corrupt; if it is not so prohibited, it is not corrupt, even if it is otherwise undesirable.[4]

The association of corruption with illegality has a tremendous advantage: it imports all of the safeguards that we associate with legal procedures and legal rules into our treatment of this phenomenon. How useful, however, is this theory in identifying the essence of corrupt behavior? When one examines corruption-as-illegality, one finds serious problems. Consider, for instance, the following statements:

— "A" has broken the law.

and

— "A" is corrupt.

The meaning of these statements is different. Burglars, bank robbers, perpetrators of assault, or even many white collar criminals (for instance, those who have engaged in simple theft or tax evasion) are not considered "corrupt." Although "corrupt" acts may be a subset of "illegal" acts, the meaning of these two ideas is clearly not the same.

Indeed, the lack of congruence between "illegality" and "corruption" is evident even when consideration is limited to illegal acts that are generally assumed to be within an imagined core of corrupt conduct. Consider, for instance, payments made to induce an abuse of power for the achievement of private ends. As Scott observes, this would include "acts as diverse as a peasant's minute payment to a public hospital orderly to ensure his seeing a doctor and a large tax firm's generous bribe to a politician in return for his fiddling with tax laws to its advantage."[5] Although both acts might be equally illegal, and within our general understanding of the kinds of acts that corruption involves, we would hesitate to call them equally corrupt—if, indeed, the first is corrupt at all.

Notions of illegality are far broader than notions of corruption. In addition, and at the other end of the spectrum, what is illegal may fail to capture what one (nevertheless) firmly believes to be corrupt conduct. For instance, the products of machine politics—such as pork-barrel legislation, nepotism, and legal patronage—are commonly regarded as corrupt, even if they are not illegal. Indeed, since corruption can capture the machinery of government, and can bend the products of government (the law) to its will, it is apparent that the "legal" or "illegal" nature of conduct cannot be depended upon to identify corrupt or non-corrupt acts. Corrupt actors, who control the levers of legislative and executive power, cannot be expected to condemn themselves. If corruption can infect the law, then "corruption" and "legal status" cannot be the same.

There is no guarantee that the law will condemn all corrupt conduct. Nor is there a guarantee that the law will, as a fundamental matter, implement the values in which the common condemnation of corruption lies. Although one generally assumes that the law implements broader ethical or moral notions, there is no necessary connection between legality and what those ethical or moral notions prescribe—a connection that "corruption" seems to demand.

In other words, although a judgment of illegality may be placed on corrupt conduct, it is not the *illegality* that makes the conduct corrupt. Rather, there are other pre-existing reasons for believing that particular conduct is corrupt; pre-existing reasons that illegality does not capture.

Corruption as the Breach of Duty

The breach-of-duty conception of corruption is common in the legal academic and political science literature.[6] According to this theory, public corruption is the breach of a duty owed to the public of an intentional and serious nature, which involves, as the result of that breach, anticipated private gain.[7]

When one considers bribery, extortion, embezzlement, and other forms of public corruption, there is no doubt that intentional, serious breaches of duties by public officials, motivated by private gain, are involved. However, are these elements sufficient to capture corruption's meaning?

There are serious problems with this approach. Public officials' intentional, serious breaches of duties may range from the acceptance of a $20 bribe by a police officer to the exaggeration by a city treasurer of his medical condition to remain on city-paid disability leave. Both seem to fall within the ambit of the breach-of-duty theory, which includes the violation of legal, social, and organizational norms. Although the first is clearly corrupt, the corrupt nature of the second is far less certain. Whatever its wrongfulness, the latter act does not involve the kind of loathsome wrongfulness that is ordinarily associated with corrupt acts.

Indeed, the wrongfulness that the breach-of-duty theory involves may not—in its extreme form—involve ethical or moral wrongs at all. A breach of a "public duty" is a breach of established laws, regulations, or other rules of conduct established by those who wield the powers of government. Although one might wish to anchor these duties in broader notions of "right" or moral conduct, the idea of corruption as breach-of-duty does not require this linkage. As many writers have noted, such "moralistic" notions are an additional gloss that the breach-of-duty model does not, of itself, involve.[8] In some cases, the norms or duties that are transgressed might be, from an ethical or moral point of view, more worthy of condemnation than their breach.

The idea of corruption as the intentional and serious breach of duty by a public servant seems to describe what many corrupt acts involve, but this idea alone is not enough. The idea of breach of public duty is both more and less than the core concept. It is more in that it includes behavior that is not corrupt. It is less in that it fails to capture the societal opprobrium or loathsomeness that corruption involves.

Corruption as Betrayal and Secrecy

In an effort to capture the particular, opprobrious nature of corruption, some breach-of-duty theorists have added elements to their understandings of corruption. Under one approach, theorists have added the *betrayal* of those whom the official serves.[9] It is not enough that a public official (intentionally) acts in a way that is contrary to his sworn duty; this breach must be of a type that excites particular social condemnation. The public official must not simply disappoint the public; he must *betray* it.

The idea of betrayal of trust by public officials does tap into the emotional reservoir that corruption evokes. However, corruption-as-betrayal suffers, as a general matter, from the same inadequacies as does the breach-of-duty theory on which it is based. For instance, betrayal of trust, like breach of duty, is something that one ordinarily assumes to be morally condemnatory, but this is not necessarily so. Strictly speaking, one who betrays a trust is simply one who acts differently from the way that others had reason to expect. The "order" that the public duties and the inculcation of trust were to uphold may be congruent with broader moral values, or it may not. For betrayal of trust to always be (by definition) of an opprobrious nature, the idea of the honoring of trust *itself* must be elevated to a morally iconic status—something that (in view of the fallibility of government) betrayal-of-trust theorists are generally loath to do. Corruption is, in short, a *particular kind* of breach of duty; it is a *particular kind* of betrayal of trust.

In an effort to capture this further, elusive characteristic of corruption, some corruption-as-betrayal theorists have added *treachery or secrecy* as an integral part of the corrupt transaction. For instance, Brasz defines corruption as "the stealthy exercise of derived power" to the detriment of the public, "under the pretence of a legitimate exercise of [that] power."[10] This element of secrecy does figure prominently in images of corrupt acts. As one commentator observes, the practical difference between campaign contributions and bribes may be that in the former, "parties openly espouse the ends which

... contributors hope to achieve as a result of their largesse."[11] However, on deeper reflection, it is obvious that secrecy cannot be what distinguishes corrupt from non-corrupt acts. An otherwise innocent transaction is not transformed into a "corrupt" act solely because it is done in secrecy. Conversely, an official who takes bribes openly should not be exempt from prosecution.[12] A breach of duty or betrayal of trust, done in secret, is (perhaps) quite likely to be corrupt. Although this setting might increase the odds that the transaction is corrupt, it is not in the act's secrecy that we locate its wrongfulness.

Corruption as Inequality

A more sophisticated approach to the role of secrecy in public corruption is presented by theorists who view secrecy (and corruption generally) in democratic-governance terms. According to this approach, it is not secrecy *qua* secrecy that is the problem with corrupt acts; it is that secrecy is incompatible with the way in which the public expects democratic government to be conducted. In this view, "[t]ransactions between citizens and politicians [for example] can be judged corrupt when they subvert or circumvent a democratic process and its associated values of openness, equality, equity, and accountability."[13] Secrecy, by this understanding, is important as an instrumental matter: it is important because it allows the subversion of the ideals of democratic governance, particularly, the equal treatment of all citizens.[14]

The observation that corruption involves a denial of equality seems to be a true one. Corruption—whether bribery, extortion, kickbacks on public contracts, or nepotism—quintessentially involves the denial of equality. Does this, however, successfully identify corruption's central core?

Upon closer analysis, a fundamental question haunts this theory: equality of what? The idea of simple equality—or equal treatment of similarly situated persons—is inadequate to distinguish corrupt from non-corrupt decisions or acts. In the political sphere, for instance, similarly situated persons are often not treated equally for reasons that we accept. Despite the ideal of political equality, legislators, mayors, or other officials are not expected to spend equal time listening (in person) to each citizen or considering equally each citizen's written request. It is accepted that for many reasons, citizens will have differing abilities to influence government policy, ranging from their personal stakes in the matter, to the intelligence of their views, to the number of citizens who share their positions. Although equality might be an operative concept in strictly bureaucratic corruption (for instance, the mechanical processing of import or export duties), equality is not of much help in more sophisticated contexts. All unequal opportunities to make one's case are not condemned, nor are all unequal benefits that result from official policies. Although inequality is often the result of much of what we believe to be corrupt conduct, it is not inequality itself that identifies the corrupt core.

Public Interest Theories

The problems with the preceding theories—particularly that they do not adequately grapple with the deeper normative ideas that associate betrayal, secrecy, or inequality with corruption—have led some theorists to advance an understanding of corruption that is more distinctly normative in nature than these previous theories. This approach "explicit[ly] and simply assert[s] that corruption involves the subversion of the public interest."[15] The core notion of this theory is that there is a "public" or "citizenry" that has distinct interests, and that these interests are damaged by private-regarding (corrupt) conduct. Self-seeking behavior, in this approach, may have personal or factional goals, but what is important is that public interest is sacrificed in favor of the corrupt actor's personal interests or of the interests of others whom she chooses.[16]

An obvious issue that public interest theories present is this: *what is* the public interest? More particularly, "*whose evaluation* of the public interest is to be operationalized?"[17] There is no guarantee that members of a governing elite, let alone all government actors or all citizens, will share a particular view of the public interest in any given situation. Indeed, substantial arguments can be (and have been) made that the public interest may sometimes require practices that are generally believed to be corrupt. For instance, bribes and other payoffs might be a justified means to assimilate new groups into the existing political system or the way to circumvent bureaucracy in the service of economic entrepreneurs.[18]

Public-interest corruption theories suffer from the same problem as do legally based theories, trust-based theories, and the like: such theories capture more than corrupt conduct in some cases, and less than corrupt conduct in others. As Scott observes, "we can imagine many acts [that] we would commonly call corruption—e.g., placing destitute immigrants illegally on the city payroll—that could be considered in the public interest, just as we can imagine acts against the public interest—e.g., the legislative creation of tax loopholes for the rich—which, however much they smack of favoritism, are not commonly seen as corrupt."[19] Although violation of the public interest is involved in corruption, once again, it is not enough, alone, to identify corruption's core.

Economic Theories

In recent years, certain commentators have turned to the use of economic theories as a way to understand corruption. Economic theories are generally: 1) those that see corruption as the rectification of market failure, or as the reallocation of undesirable power arrangements; or 2) those that use economic analysis to provide a normative baseline to identify corrupt acts.

Under the first approach, "corrupt acts" are identified in explicitly value-neutral and market-oriented terms. Under this theory, public and private (including "corrupt") interests are simply conflicting claims that are mediated through legal and non-legal market mechanisms. When legal schemes fail to reflect market pressures and realities, non-legal ("corrupt") transactions serve to reestablish the appropriate market equilibrium.[20] Corruption is a kind of "underground" or "black" market that arises "when the institutional structure precludes private owners from allocating their resources in a competitive [way]."[21] As Tilman observes, modern bureaucracies often implement what is, in effect, a mandatory pricing model of market economics. When there is a serious disequilibrium between the supply (of bureaucratic goods) and demand, the centralized allocative mechanism, which is the ideal of modern bureaucracy, may break down. This breakdown is corruption.[22]

The idea of corruption-as-illegality is crucial here: the acts that are deemed to be "corrupt" under this model are those that are not permitted by the governing legal order.[23] However, illegality is given no operational or normative significance beyond this simple guideline. There is nothing that makes the legally sanctioned system of rights superior, in any moral or other sense, to any other system. Indeed, it is because of the undesirability of the legally sanctioned system—i.e., its inefficiency—that a system of underground "rights modification" (corruption) arises.[24]

The fundamental theoretical contribution of this theory—that corruption can, in fact, have positive economic, social, or political outcomes—was a revolutionary insight in its time, even if controversial and now largely discredited.[25] From the point of understanding the *idea* of corruption, however, this theory adds little. Corruption as expressed in this theory is a restatement of the idea of corruption-as-illegality or corruption-as-breach-of-duty, theories whose deficiencies were exposed above. Therefore, the usefulness of this theory lies not in its unique definition of corruption, but in its distinct understanding of the consequences of the corrupt act. However, the explicitly value-neutral nature of corruption that underlies this theory is less congruent with common understandings of corruption than are the other theories that have been explored.

Within the second approach, economic ideas are used to develop a distinctly normative understanding of corruption. Corruption is defined as personal rent-seeking by government officials in derogation of the duties that they have to their principals (higher officials, the public) as established by law.[26] Such an approach acknowledges that rent-seeking might be a positive or useful phenomenon in this context, as it may allow for productive activities that existing laws or other public duties do not permit.[27] However, these theories carry a distinctly normative imprint. From an economic point of view, rent-seeking or corruption inevitably "introduce[s] costs and distortions, encourages excessive public infrastructure investment," and "discourages legitimate business investment."[28] In addition, these theorists subscribe to the idea that the rule of law is of great societal value, and that the delegitimization of government rules by corruption carries its own overwhelming costs.[29]

To the extent that these theories rely upon illegality as corruption, they add little that is new. The idea that the efficiency of actions determines their corrupt or non-corrupt nature is different, and deserves closer examination.

The idea that the efficiency of corrupt acts should be considered in policymaking is an obviously useful one. We should be reluctant—for whatever reason—to ignore economic costs. However, is the efficiency or inefficiency of particular acts truly useful in the identification of their corrupt or non-corrupt nature? After even cursory reflection, it is apparent that this idea falls short. Certainly all inefficient actions are not corrupt, as "corruption" is generally understood. Actions by government actors can be incompetent, wasteful, market-thwarting, or otherwise inefficient, and not necessarily be corrupt. By the same token, corrupt actions are not necessarily inefficient. An official could grant a special favor to his brother, and in fact achieve greater "efficiency" for other, specified government ends. Although financial distortions and inefficiency may characterize many corrupt acts, and although they may be reasons to condemn corrupt acts, the root of corruption cannot be captured in purely economic terms. For those economic theories that retain the "corrupt" act as a meaningful notion, which identifies particularly opprobrious conduct, more is needed beyond economic tests.

Combination Theories

Thus far, we have found that none of the mainstream understandings of corruption, alone, adequately captures the meaning of corruption. However, there is another possibility that needs to be considered. Perhaps these theories could successfully capture the idea of corruption if they were considered in combination, rather than separately. For instance, Philp offers what might be called a "combination theory." He states: "We can recognise political corruption when:

1) a public official ('A'),

2) in violation of the *trust* placed in him by the public ('B'),

3) and in a manner which harms the *public interest,*

4) knowingly engages in conduct which *exploits* the office for clear *personal and private gain* in a way which runs contrary to the *accepted rules and standards* for the conduct of public office within the political culture,

5) so as to benefit a third party 'C,' by providing 'C' with access to a good or service 'C' would not otherwise obtain."[30]

This theory combines ideas of betrayal of trust, secrecy, subordination of the public interest, illegality, and breach of duty. All of these must be present before an act is "corrupt." Do these elements, in combination, successfully capture the idea's core?

When one considers the over-inclusivity of mainstream theories, the layering of requirements in this way is helpful. Under this approach, corruption is not the violation of any law, or the breach of any duty, or the subversion of any public interest; corruption is only those violations, breaches, or subversions that involve (for instance) secrecy, betrayal, and self-dealing. Since all of these characteristics are associated with corrupt conduct, requiring their simultaneous fulfillment does narrow the scope of acts within that category.

However, combination theories such as this one do not eliminate the problems identified previously. Although, presumably, the number of acts that are identified by these overlapping requirements are reduced, a way to distinguish corrupt from non-corrupt conduct is still lacking. For instance (to use Philp's theory) there are certainly fewer acts that violate the law or other public "rules and standards," harm the public interest, and involve a breach of trust, for personal gain, than that simply have one of these characteristics alone. Yet, all acts that share these characteristics are not corrupt. For instance, a healthy government employee could call in sick or feign disability, and thereby violate applicable rules and standards, harm the public interest, and breach the public trust, all for personal gain, but this action would not, in the absence of other conduct, be considered "corrupt." Other elements could be added to this combination theory to make it more robust; for instance, it could be additionally required that the act involve secrecy or inequality. However, for all of those cases where these elements will help to narrow the field, they will create problems of under-inclusiveness in other cases, by excluding acts (such as overt bribes, or "equal" bribing opportunities) that are nonetheless corrupt.

Combination theories can be seen, in a sense, as kaleidoscopic presentations of mainstream theories: the elements of separate theories can be combined and recombined in complex combinations that are richer or more exacting than those elements alone. The fundamental problem, however, remains. Corruption is more than illegality, breach of duty, betrayal, secrecy, inequality, the subversion of the public interest, and inefficiency, whether those elements are considered alone or together. In other words, although all of these theories identify elements that are often important characteristics of corrupt acts, these elements are not the *essence* of corruption—they are not, alone or in combination, all that compose the corrupt core.

Corruption: A Deeper Understanding

This chapter has demonstrated that mainstream formulations of corruption—although useful as far as they go—fail to capture what composes the core of corruption.

What is missing? It is that corruption is an explicitly moral notion; corruption describes, in general parlance, a powerful, all-consuming evil. This idea, although often unarticulated, permeates both popular and technical discussions of the subject. Furthermore, because of the power of this idea, any approach to corruption that fails to reckon with its moral aspect will be both descriptively and programmatically inadequate.

The idea that political or public corruption is a deeply moral concept can be found in classical accounts, as well as in contemporary political theory. Both Platonic and Aristotelian notions of democratic governance, its maintenance, and its decline warned of the morally eviscerating nature of political corruption.[31] Scholars of the medieval and early modern eras have found that ideas of corruption and evil were fused throughout the writings of these periods in Britain and France.[32] For instance, in his famous dictionary penned in the eighteenth century, Johnson defines corruption as "[w]ickedness; perversion of principles."[33] In this view, "[t]o say that corruption is wrong is rather like saying that murder is wrong. Both statements express what is, in effect, a conceptual truth or a grammatical necessity."[34]

This equation of corruption with moral evil has survived and thrived in contemporary accounts of the phenomenon. Contemporary accounts strongly associate political corruption with moral decadence, degeneracy, and decay.[35] Corruption, in these accounts, is more than evidence of bad (or illegal) conduct; it is evidence of a moral "virus" or "cancer," an "infestation" of "evil," all of which often seems to have religious roots.[36] Such associations can be found in virtually any major city newspaper's account of a recent corruption scandal. For instance, a recent article reported that the vice mayor of Beijing, Wang Baosen, committed suicide in 1996 after having been presented with evidence implicating him and his staff in "systemic corruption." "Wang was guilty of squandering public funds, acquiring expensive real estate, and booking hotel suites for 'pleasure-seeking,' according to officials. 'He was morally degenerate and lived a rotten life,' the Xinhua news agency said."[37] In an article about rampant corruption in India, a former attorney general of the country was quoted as saying that "'[i]t's spread like a cancer.'" "'It's reached a terminal state. There is a complete breakdown in [moral] values.'" The question, the story continued, is "whether the country's very soul has been irredeemably warped."[38] Discussing the fall-out from the indictment on corruption charges of American super-lobbyist Jack Abramoff, a columnist wrote that "the scandal literally had Republicans, led by President Bush, turning money Abramoff gave them [as campaign contributions] over to charity, as if casting away their sins."[39] As Smith observes in his contribution to this volume, "[t]he social morality of [corrupt] behavior figures much more prominently in popular assessments of corruption than any technical definition."[40]

Indeed, the idea of corruption as a moral concept is so powerful that it seeps into the work of many contemporary theorists, even as they take pains to exclude moral content from their definitions of the word. For instance, although Klitgaard describes his theory of corruption as a breach-of-duty model, he acknowledges that "'corrupt' invokes a range of images of evil. . . . There is a moral tone to the word."[41] Leys, who criticizes what he calls a "moralising approach" to corruption, nonetheless describes corruption in terms of the "strength of the rules of private morality" and assaults "on moral rules."[42]

Looking for the essence of corruption in the violation of law, breach of duty, betrayal of trust, poor economic outcomes, and the like will be viscerally unsatisfactory if, at the same time, corruption's explicitly moral core is not recognized. Corruption, in its popular conception, is not simply the breach of some neutral or politically chosen standard; it expresses the transgression of some deeply held and asserted universal norm.

Furthermore, corruption—under this understanding—carries more than the threat of an individual transgression; it presents a vital threat to the larger societal fabric of which it is a part. The popular visualization of corruption as a "cancer" or "virus" is not incidental; it is a critical part of what this idea of corruption attempts to convey. Corruption, in this view, is not simply an official's poor choice or bad act; it is a threatening exhibition of the actor's self-involvement, self-indulgence, and disregard for the restraint of societal bonds. Corruption in this sense threatens more deeply—it is a "cancer" or a "virus" precisely because it challenges the existing order more deeply. It substitutes personal self-seeking, family or clan loyalties, or other parochial goals and loyalties for larger societal identification and societal goals.[43] As such, corruption is not simply an aberrant act committed by a reprobate actor; it is a repudiation of the idea that a fabric of shared values is necessary to undergird societies and governments.

As a result of this characteristic, public corruption is intuitively assigned a far greater and more powerful role than it is, for example, in the simple monetary loss or other individual consequences of the corrupt individual's action. When a corrupt individual holds public office, his corrupt character indicates the danger of *systemic damage.* The corrupt politician, police officer, or judge does not simply threaten harm to particular individuals with whom he might come into contact; his existence threatens the entire governmental system of reliance, trust, and shared values, of which he is a part.

What are the implications of this idea of corruption for an approach to corruption as an international social and governmental phenomenon—the focus of this volume? First, any prescription for combating corruption must include the moral and emotional dimensions of this concept as it is popularly perceived. The profoundly moral, religiously steeped, and absolute nature of corruption as evil frames what is an unquestionably powerful and emotionally evocative idea. We are not outraged about corrupt politicians because their existence in office proves a lack of efficiency or government transparency; we are outraged because of the evil, the arrogance, the flagrant disregard of deeply entrenched social norms that their tenure exhibits. Whether one agrees or disagrees with the invocation of popular moral outrage about corruption in a particular instance, account must be taken of the power and function of such moral outrage in popular attitudes.[44] Smith, in his contribution to this volume, discusses how moral decay and corruption are seen as cause and effect by ordinary Nigerians. He writes that "Nigerians' sense that their state and society have become increasingly amoral—with elites pursing wealth and power without regard for the consequences, and ordinary people seeking money by all means available simply to survive—contributes to a popular perception that law and order have given way to corruption at every level."[45] Indeed, corruption, infused with moral outrage, "has become the dominant discourse of complaint in the postcolonial world, symbolizing people's disappointments with democracy and development and their frustrations with continued social inequality."[46] He quotes the statement of French anthropologist Jean-Pierre

Olivier de Sardan that "'[a]t the everyday level, there is scarcely a conversation without hostile or disgusted references to corruption.'"[47]

If governments or reformers fail to respond to such popular emotions, their refusal can fuel forces of social and governmental instability. For instance, in an article, written in 1992, Brooke recounted the weak response of Venezuelan President Carlos Andrés Perez to corruption allegations and the dangers of a military coup that the situation presented.[48] Citizens threatened to take the situation into their own hands:

> Convinced that the Government is not serious about punishing corruption, a shadowy civilian commando group started attacking "corrupt politicians. . . ." The commandos, who say they share the ideals of the Bolivarian Revolutionary Movement, shot and wounded a pro-Government labor leader, knifed a former director of a state social security institute and threw a hand grenade at the house of the wife of a former President.
>
> Much of the broad popular support for Colonel Chàvez's first coup attempt was based on his assertion that he was moving "against corruption." A shantytown resident who would give only his first name, Freddy, spoke for many . . . when he noted approvingly that Colonel Chàvez "said he would hang all the corrupt politicians in the National Stadium."[49]

There was no further coup attempt; but popular sentiment of this kind paved the way for the election of Chàvez as president of Venezuela six years later.

The usual prescriptions for combating corruption—such as the establishment of open democratic governance, clear distinctions between public and private sources and roles, economic liberalization, improved law enforcement, accountable leaders, reduced bureaucratic discretion, and so on—may be essential; but they are generally remarkable for their avoidance of moral content.[50] One could respond that the principle of equality that undergirds democratic governance, or the idea of the rule of law that motivates more effective prosecution of bribe-takers, is the vindication of certain moral values; but these kinds of incidental moral content as a part of good government solutions are a far cry from the images of evil, depravity, and religious condemnation that popular attitudes toward corruption invoke.

In addition, the popular idea of corruption as moral failure may not be incorrect. The erosion of moral values may, in fact, play a critical role in the establishment and the flourishing of this phenomenon in many settings. It is an elementary truth is that a foundation of shared moral and civic values is critical to the maintenance of civil society and effective democratic governance. Corruption, as a breakdown of civic values in favor of personal and clan self-seeking, directly implicates this foundation. As Johnston writes, "it is not enough [when combating corruption] simply to identify aspects of an ideal market-democracy model that developing societies seem to lack."[51] We must, in addition, identify and foster the shared moral basis that is presupposed by ideas of democratic civil societies and participatory governments.[52] If diagnoses of and prescriptions for corruption ignore the underlying moral dimension of this phenomenon, they may fail to grasp either the complete root of the problem or the critical pieces of the solution. Such initiatives may also fail to express the urgency of the situation where a country is battling systemic corruption. Exhortations about the need for open government, the limitation of bureaucratic discretion, and improved law enforcement do not convey a sense of immediate crisis and governmental danger in the way that exhortations about corruption, moral decay, and evil do.[53]

The utility of the common idea of corruption should not, however, obscure its dangers. With the moral and emotional content of this idea comes the distinct risk of excess in the identification of corrupt targets, in the treatment of offenders, and in the ascription of the ills of the world to the workings of corruption. Impelled by the idea of corruption as evil, "[p]ublic anger at some exposed villainy of this sort is apt to be both blind and exacting."[54] If a person who is accused of corruption is seen as a monster, "contaminated" by the virus of evil, the ability to enforce adherence to the legal procedures and protections that are required by the rule of law becomes difficult. In addition, although corruption is unquestionably destructive to societies and governments, it is not—as Jomo K.S. points out in this volume—the only or (in many situations) even the primary cause of governance failure, poverty, or other ills.[55] Viewing corruption in emotionally evocative and cataclysmic terms may propel it to the status of "universally causative evil," a status that it does not deserve.

Conclusion

Defining corruption is notoriously difficult to do. Nevertheless, definitions of governance issues matter. Society's definitions or operative understandings of corruption help to identify what it believes to be the reasons for corruption's existence, and predetermines what it believes to be the effective and critical elements for corruption's cure.

Understandings of corruption that are advanced by academic theorists capture important pieces of the idea of corruption. Public corruption generally involves, in the predominant understandings, the violation of law, the breach of prescribed duties, the subversion of the public interest, and the violation of other broad normative standards. Corruption may also involve—in a more particularized sense—betrayal, secrecy, inequality, and private rent-seeking by public actors. However, as useful as these understandings are, something is missing. All such understandings fail to capture what is the deeply emotive quality and loathsomeness of corruption's core. Corruption, in its popular conception, is more than the breaking of rules or even self-seeking by public actors to the detriment of others. It is an expressly moral notion that challenges belief in a shared moral fabric. It expresses the transgression of some deeply held and asserted universal norm.

When one attempts to understand the phenomenon of corruption, and the public response to it, the power of this popular conception must be recognized. It must be recognized because it is a critical part of public attitudes toward corruption, and because it reminds theorists and practitioners that corruption often has deeper moral foundations. This view tells us that until we come to grips with the moral dimensions of this problem, our prescriptions for attacking this phenomenon will miss the essence of what popular attitudes may correctly recognize as the underlying problem, and the composition of the distinctly "corrupt" core.

Notes

1. The effects of cultural practices on corruption norms are discussed in several chapters in this volume. See, for example, Sarah Dix and Emmanuel Pok, "Combating Corruption in Traditional Societies: Papua New Guinea," chapter 9 in this volume; Robert Legvold, "Corruption, the Criminalized State, and Post-Soviet Transitions," chapter 8 in this volume; Daniel Jordan Smith, "The Paradoxes of Popular Participation in Corruption in Nigeria," chapter 11 in this volume.

2. John T. Noonan, *Bribes* (New York, 1984), 702. For cultural studies that have drawn similar conclusions, see, for example, Dix and Pok, "Combating Corruption in Traditional Societies," in this volume and Legvold, "Corruption, the Criminalized State," in this volume. At times, the cultural complexities involved in corrupt and non-corrupt distinctions are difficult for the external observer to fathom. For instance, Smith observes that the Nigerian people, who often simultaneously engage in condemning corruption, even while participating in it, are "increasingly caught up in corruption." See Smith, "The Paradoxes of Popular Participation," 288.

3. James C. Scott, *Comparative Political Corruption* (Englewood Cliffs, 1972), 3.

4. See, for example, John Gardiner, "Defining Corruption," in Maurice Punch, Emile Kolthoff, Kees van der Vijver, and Bram van Vliet (eds.), *Coping with Corruption in a Borderless World: Proceedings of the Fifth International Anti-Corruption Conference* (Deventer, 1993), 21, 26. See also Michael Johnston, *Political Corruption and Public Policy in America* (Monterey, 1982), 8.

5. Scott, *Comparative Political Corruption*, 5.

6. See David H. Bayley, "The Effects of Corruption in a Developing Nation," in Arnold J. Heidenheimer (ed.), *Political Corruption: Readings in Comparative Analysis* (New York, 1978), 521, 522; Arnold J. Heidenheimer, "The Context of Analysis," in his *Political Corruption: Readings in Comparative Analysis,* 3, 4; Joseph S. Nye, "Corruption and Political Development: A Cost-Benefit Analysis," *American Political Science Review,* LXI (1967), 417, 419.

7. For the idea that corruption involves "self-seeking," "personal enrichment and the provision of benefits to the corrupt," see Susan Rose-Ackerman, *Corruption and Government: Causes, Consequences, and Reform* (New York, 1999), 14, 9. For the view that corruption involves "private gain by dishonest dealings," see Gunnar Myrdal, "Corruption as a Hindrance to Modernization in South Asia," in Heidenheimer (ed.), *Political Corruption: Readings in Comparative Analysis,* 229, 232. "*Political corruption* is a general term covering all illegal or unethical use of governmental authority as a result of considerations of personal or political gain." See George C.S. Benson, Steven A. Maaranen, and Alan Heslop, *Political Corruption in America* (Lexington, 1978), xiii. As Bunn suggests in this volume, this breach-of-duty approach can be extended to include activities by private citizens that constitute a breach of public trust. See Matthew Bunn, "Corruption and Nuclear Proliferation," chapter 6 in this volume.

8. See Nye, "Corruption and Political Development," 417; Colin Leys, "What Is the Problem About Corruption?" *Journal of Modern African Studies,* III (1965), 215–217.

9. See Syed Hussein Alatas, *Corruption: Its Nature, Causes and Functions* (Aldershot, 1991), 2; Robert Klitgaard, *Controlling Corruption* (Berkeley, 1988), 24; Mark Philp, "Contextualizing Political Corruption," in Arnold J. Heidenheimer and Michael Johnston (eds.), *Political Corruption: Concepts & Contexts* (New Brunswick, 2002) (3rd edition), 41, 42.

10. H. A. Brasz, "The Sociology of Corruption," in Heidenheimer (ed.), *Political Corruption: Readings in Comparative Analysis,* 41, 42.

11. Vladimer Orlando Key, Jr., *The Techniques of Political Graft in the United States* (Chicago, 1936), 387.

12. See Daniel Lowenstein, "Political Bribery and the Intermediate Theory of Politics," *University of California Los Angeles Law Review,* XXXII (1985), 784, 830.

13. Robert Williams, "Corruption: New Concepts for Old?" *Third World Quarterly,* XX (1999), 503, 510.

14. See, for example, Denis Osborne, "Corruption as Counter-Culture: Attitudes to Bribery in Local and Global Society," in Barry Rider (ed.), *Corruption: The Enemy Within* (Boston, 1997), 9, 28; Ibrahim F. I. Shihata, "Corruption—A General Review

with an Emphasis on the Role of the World Bank," in Rider (ed.), *Corruption: The Enemy Within*, 255, 260.

15. Williams, "Corruption: New Concepts for Old?" 505. See also Robert C. Brooks, "Apologies for Political Corruption," in Heidenheimer (ed.), *Political Corruption: Readings in Comparative Analysis*, 501, 507.

16. See Carl J. Friedrich, "Political Pathology," *Political Quarterly*, XXXVII (1966), 70, 74; Barry Hildress, "Good Government and Corruption," in Peter Larmour and Nick Wolanin (eds.), *Corruption and Anti-Corruption* (Canberra, 2001), 1, 5.

17. Heidenheimer, "The Context of Analysis," 6 (emphasis added).

18. See Samuel P. Huntington, *Political Order in Changing Societies* (New Haven, 1968), 61; Bayley, "The Effects of Corruption in a Developing Nation," 528–529; Nathaniel H. Leff, "Economic Development through Bureaucratic Corruption," in Heidenheimer (ed.), *Political Corruption: Readings in Comparative Analysis*, 510, 516.

19. Scott, *Comparative Political Corruption*, 3–4.

20. See Bruce L. Benson, "A Note on Corruption by Public Officials: The Black Market for Property Rights," *Journal of Libertarian Studies*, V (1981), 305; Bruce L. Benson and John Baden, "The Political Economy of Governmental Corruption: The Logic of Underground Government," *Journal of Legal Studies*, XIV (1985), 391.

21. Benson and Baden, "The Political Economy of Governmental Corruption," 393.

22. Robert O. Tilman, "Black-Market Bureaucracy," in Heidenheimer (ed.), *Political Corruption: Readings in Comparative Analysis*, 62.

23. See Benson and Baden, "The Political Economy of Governmental Corruption," 393–395.

24. Ibid., 392–393; Bayley, "The Effects of Corruption in a Developing Nation," 528; Leff, "Economic Development through Bureaucratic Corruption," 510.

25. Most contemporary scholars agree that these theories seriously underestimate corruption's other costs—particularly the costs involved in damage to the accountability and transparency of government. See, for example, Pranab Bardhan, "Corruption and Development: A Review of the Issues," *Journal of Economic Literature*, XXXV (1997), 1320, 1327–1330; Paolo Mauro, "The Effects of Corruption on Growth and Public Expenditure," in Heidenheimer and Johnston (eds.), *Political Corruption: Concepts & Contexts*, 339; Paul D. Hutchcroft, "The Politics of Privilege: Rents and Corruption in Asia," in Heidenheimer and Johnston (eds.), *Political Corruption: Concepts & Contexts*, 489, 493–495; Alice Sindzingre, "A Comparative Analysis of African and East African Corruption," in Heidenheimer and Johnston (eds.), *Political Corruption: Concepts & Contexts*, 379, 444–447. See also Michael Johnston, *Syndromes of Corruption: Wealth, Power, and Democracy*, (New York, 2005), 18. Such routine problems are in addition to those problems that corrupt states pose to international security and global welfare. See Legvold, "Corruption, the Criminalized State," chapter 8 in this volume.

26. See Rose-Ackerman, *Corruption and Government: Causes, Consequences, and Reform*, 2–5; Klitgaard, *Controlling Corruption*, 19–23.

27. See Rose-Ackerman, *Corruption and Government: Causes, Consequences, and Reform*, 2, 9.

28. Ibid., 3.

29. Ibid., 22–23.

30. Philp, "Contextualizing Political Corruption," 42 (emphasis added).

31. For interesting analyses of these classical understandings see, for example, Carl J. Friedrich, *The Pathology of Politics: Violence, Betrayal, Corruption, Secrecy, and Propaganda* (New York, 1972), 130–131; J. Peter Euben, "Corruption," in Terence Ball, James Farr, and Russell L. Hanson (eds.), *Political Innovation and Conceptual Change* (New York, 1989), 220, 223–242.

32. See, for example, Friedrich, *The Pathology of Politics*, 127–141; Maryvonne Génaux, "Early Modern Corruption in English and French Fields of Vision," in Heidenheimer and Johnston (eds.), *Political Corruption: Concepts & Contexts*, 107–117.

33. Samuel Johnson, *A Dictionary of the English Language* (London, 1826), 154.

34. Williams, "Corruption: New Concepts for Old?" 504.

35. See, for example, Heidenheimer, "The Context of Analysis," 4; Wilmer Parker III, "Every Person Has a Price?" in Rider (ed.), *Corruption: The Enemy Within*, 87.

36. See, for example, Shihata, "Corruption—A General Review with an Emphasis on the Role of the World Bank," 262; Alatas, *Corruption: Its Nature, Causes and Functions*, 13; Walter Lippmann, "A Theory about Corruption," in Heidenheimer (ed.), *Political Corruption: Readings in Comparative Analysis*, 294, 295; Ronald Wraith and Edgar Simpkins, *Corruption in Developing Countries* (New York, 1964), 11–13; Friedrich, *The Pathology of Politics*, 28.

37. Stephen Hutcheon, "Eighteen to Face Court Charges Over $3 Billion Beijing Fraud," *Sydney Morning Herald* (4 April 1996), 10.

38. Edward A. Georgian, "Corruption's Many Tentacles Are Choking India's Growth," *New York Times* (10 November 1992), A1.

39. John Hall, "Oiling a Sleezy Machine," *Cincinnati Post* (9 January 2006), A10.

40. Smith, "The Paradoxes of Popular Participation," chapter 11 in this volume.

41. Klitgaard, *Controlling Corruption*, 23.

42. Colin Leys, "New States and the Concept of Corruption," in Heidenheimer (ed.), *Political Corruption: Readings in Comparative Analysis*, 216 and 341.

43. See, for example, Edward C. Banfield, *The Moral Basis of a Backward Society* (New York,1958), 83–101; Jeremy Boissevain, "Patronage in Sicily," in Heidenheimer (ed.), *Political Corruption: Readings in Comparative Analysis*, 138, 139. Robert Legvold describes a corrupt state as one in which "state activity has been 'privatized': that is, where either those in power or those with leverage over those in power use state agency to advance their private interests at the expense of the broader public good." See Legvold, "Corruption, the Criminalized State," 197.

44. See Smith, "The Paradoxes of Popular Participation," chapter 11 in this volume.

45. Ibid.

46. Ibid.

47. Ibid., quoting J. P. Olivier de Sardan, "A Moral Economy of Corruption in Africa?" *Journal of Modern African Studies,* XXXVII (1999), 25, 29.

48. See James Brooke, "Venezuela Still Edgy: Will There Be Coup No. 3?" *New York Times* (3 December 1992), A3.

49. Ibid.

50. See, for example, Johnston, *Syndromes of Corruption,* 2, 7, 9, 19, 22, and 26; Rose-Ackerman, *Corruption and Government,* 68, 87; Klitgaard, *Controlling Corruption,* 52–97; World Bank, *Helping Countries Combat Corruption: Progress at the World Bank Since 1997* (Washington, D.C., 2000), 54–66. The efficacy of these prescriptions is contested. See, for example, Jomo K. S., "Good Governance, Anti-Corruption, and Economic Development," chapter 18 in this volume.

51. Johnston, *Syndromes of Corruption,* 2.

52. For case studies exploring the role of foundational moral values in corruption prevention, see, for example, David Stasavage, "Causes and Consequences of Corruption: Mozambique in Transition," in Alan Doig and Robin Theobald (eds.), *Corruption and Democratisation* (London, 2000), 85–86; Susan Rose-Ackerman, "Corruption in the Wake of Domestic National Conflict," chapter 4 in this volume.

53. Because of its ability to invoke moral certainty and an acute sense of urgency, the idea of corruption has been used to express a variety of evils, such as the dangers of nuclear proliferation and the violation of human rights. See Matthew Bunn, "Corruption and Nuclear Proliferation," chapter 6 in this volume; Lucy Koechlin and Magdalena Sepúlveda Carmona, "Corruption and Human Rights: Exploring the Connection," chapter 12 in this volume.

54. Robert C. Brooks, "The Nature of Political Corruption," in Heidenheimer (ed.), *Political Corruption: Readings in Comparative Analysis,* 56.

55. See Jomo K.S., "Good Governance, Anti-Corruption and Economic Development," chapter 18 in this volume.

NATHANIEL HELLER

3 | Defining and Measuring Corruption: Where Have We Come From, Where Are We Now, and What Matters For the Future?

The importance in measuring corruption, and by extension, good governance (one of its antidotes), is not simply an esoteric academic debate left to development economists, political theoreticians, and statisticians. It has become, rather, a central issue to the broader field of good governance and anti-corruption reform, as a country's performance in such reforms has become increasingly linked to foreign aid flows.

While former World Bank President James Wolfensohn's famous 1996 "cancer of corruption" speech marked a watershed in acknowledging corruption as a central development issue, the challenge of measuring corruption and anti-corruption performance leapt to the forefront during the "Monterrey process." Major multilateral development organizations and governments met in 2002 at Monterrey, Mexico, to agree on practical steps for implementing the Millennium Development Goals: high-level objectives aimed at reducing poverty and accelerating development by 2015 in the world's poorest countries. The basic bargain agreed on at Monterrey moved corruption measurement to the front and center of the debate: if developing countries performed well on anti-corruption and good governance assessments, they would be rewarded with increased aid from the developed donor countries.[1]

This decision implied that the international community now needed consistently to measure corruption levels and countries' anti-corruption and good governance performance to determine those countries that would respond to the carrot of increased aid. The establishment of the U.S. Millennium

The author wishes to thank a number of colleagues at Global Integrity for their insight and feedback on this chapter, including Julia Burke, Marianne Camerer, Raymond June, Stephen Roblin, and Jonathan Werve.

47

Table 3-1. *Select Timeline of Major Corruption and Governance Metrics*

Index Name	Origin
Economic Intelligence Unit's Index on Democracy	Early 1970s
Freedom House's annual Freedom in the World Survey	1972
Polity Country Reports	1974
Transparency International's National Integrity Systems studies (NIS)	1994
Transparency International Corruption Perceptions Index (CPI)	1995
World Bank Institute's Worldwide Governance Indicators (WGI)	1996
Afrobarometer	1999
Business Environment and Enterprise Performance Survey (BEEPS)	1999–2000
International Research and Exchanges Board (IREX)'s Media Sustainability Index (MSI)	2000
World Bank's Doing Business Indicators	2003
Global Integrity's Integrity Indicators	2004
Open Budget Index (a project of the International Budget Project)	2006
Index of African Governance	2007

Description

The index provides a snapshot of the current state of democracy for 165 states and 2 territories and includes 5 categories: electoral process and pluralism; civil liberties; the functioning of government; political participation; and political culture. Data are drawn from third-party surveys and assessments.

The Freedom in the World survey evaluates the state of global freedom as experienced by individuals in countries. The survey measures freedom according to two categories: political rights and civil liberties. Centralized scoring committees outside of the country generate the scores for each country.

The Polity project examines the characteristics of governing institutions in countries, envisioning a spectrum of governing authority that spans from fully institutionalized autocracies through mixed authority regimes to full democracies. Coding of countries is performed by trained researchers outside of the country.

The NIS applies a holistic approach by assessing the key institutions, laws, and practices that contribute to integrity, transparency, and accountability. The NIS offers analysis on the extent and causes of corruption in a given national context as well as the adequacy and effectiveness of national anti-corruption efforts. Local experts are employed to generate the qualitative analysis.

The CPI ranks 180 countries according to their perceived levels of corruption. The rankings are determined by aggregating third-party expert assessments and opinion surveys.

The WGI report governance indicators for more than 200 countries and territories over the period 1996–2007 across 6 dimensions of governance, including control of corruption. Data are generated by aggregating third-party surveys and expert assessments in a similar fashion as the CPI.

The Afrobarometer measures the social, political, and economic atmosphere in Africa. Original household surveys are conducted in more than a dozen African countries and are repeated on a regular cycle.

BEEPS surveys more than 4,000 firms in 22 transition countries on a wide range of interactions between firms and the state.

The MSI analyzes the state of independent media in 76 countries across Africa, Europe, Eurasia, and the Middle East. It assesses how media systems change over time and across borders. Local experts are employed to score countries.

Doing Business assesses the ease of doing business across 178 economies through expert assessments performed by local in-country lawyers. Among other data generated, it assesses the time and cost to meet requirements to start a business, business operations, taxation, and closure of a business.

An Integrity Indicators scorecard assesses the existence, effectiveness, and citizen access to key governance and anti-corruption mechanisms through more than 300 discrete indicators. It examines issues such as transparency of the public procurement process, media freedom, asset disclosure requirements, and conflicts of interest regulations. Scorecards take into account both existing legal measures on the books and *de facto* realities of practical implementation in each country. Indicators are scored and blindly reviewed by in-country experts.

The index rates countries on how open their budgets are to the public and is intended to provide citizens, civil society, and legislators with the information needed to gauge a government's commitment to budget transparency. Local teams of in-country experts score each country's indicators.

The Index of African Governance ranks sub-Saharan African nations according to governance quality (focusing on governance "outputs") and assesses national progress in five areas: safety and security; rule of law, transparency and corruption; participation and human rights; sustainable economic opportunity; and human development. Data are currently aggregated from third-party surveys and assessments and collected in-country by index researchers.

Challenge Corporation (MCC), which explicitly links major aid packages (upward of $500 to $700 million) to country performance on a range of quantitative metrics, including anti-corruption performance, is the most ambitious effort to do so in the wake of Monterrey.

However, the field of corruption measurement has not moved nearly as quickly as the advent of the "aid-for-good governance" bargain that Monterrey helped to launch. While the demand for rigorous data and information on corruption has increased dramatically from the late-1990s, much of the field remains unchanged from its early days. The potential for misleading diagnostics, ill-informed aid decisions, and disillusionment with the anti-corruption movement looms large should this situation remain unaltered.

This chapter traces the history of the corruption measurement field in broad brushstrokes from its earliest days to present day efforts. In so doing, this chapter draws out lessons learned that can inform next-generation measurement efforts to avoid the negative outcomes suggested above.

The Early Days

Although the academic literature on corruption dates back several decades, the specific topic of how to measure corruption, anti-corruption performance, and good governance came into focus in the late-1970s through the work of some of the modern-day pillars in the field, including Klitgaard, Johnston, and Rose-Ackerman.[2] Their early work provided to "corruption" a definitional and conceptual clarity, by applying to it a political-economy analysis. Corruption was viewed as fundamentally rational rent-seeking behavior more likely to occur where transparency and oversight were low, discretion was high, and accountability mechanisms weak. This framework not only made intuitive sense but could be applied to a variety of sectors, countries, and cultures. It largely remains the foundation of much of the ongoing analytic and programmatic work in the anti-corruption community.

Despite this conceptual clarity, the early work struggled to gain traction on how systematically to track corruption as a measurable phenomenon. As Johnston and his colleague Heidenheimer would later write in their third edition of *Political Corruption*:

> For some groups of scholars, the global corruption landscape has come to be even more radically transformed. This is exemplified by the observation that where, in the 1980s, most transnational corruption comparisons were largely impressionistic, the 1990s saw the dispersion of

methodology which seems to allow objective quantification of corruption incidence and perception in various national settings. But these breakthroughs were accomplished in the face of bypassing crucial conceptual hurdles, such as the definition of basic terms. Moreover, they reflected a range of interests and outlooks that, while bringing new energy to the study of corruption, also tended to "flatten out" the variations among cases, rather than probing more subtle historical, cultural, and linguistic issues. In a way the dominant measurement efforts become focused on examining the extent to which various test tubes were more or less full than others, while ignoring variations in their shapes, and in what they contained.[3]

This prescience of the *conceptual gap* in the corruption measurement field—that methodologies were being developed without a clear sense of *what* they were actually measuring—would continue to haunt practitioners and academics in the coming years and come into sharper focus in the post-Monterrey era.

The "dispersion of methodologies" that Johnston and Heidenheimer flagged referred primarily to Transparency International's well-known Corruption Perceptions Index (CPI) and, later, to the World Bank Institute's Worldwide Governance Indicators (WGI). In the mid-1990s, development economists began to leverage business firm surveys and other opinion polls as proxies for corruption measurement to explore correlations and causality between corruption and various dependent variables such as economic growth and foreign direct investment. Such results seemed to suggest that lower levels of corruption were linked to greater growth and investment levels.[4]

The creators of the CPI, and later the WGI, tried to capture as many third-party "voices" as possible—as many proxies and signals of corruption that, when aggregated, pointed toward countries or sectors of the economy more or less likely to experience corruption. The WGI was particularly explicit in its use of the unobserved components model as an intellectual basis for aggregating as many similar surveys, polls, and expert opinions of corruption-like questions as possible. Since corruption cannot easily be seen directly or observed empirically, the authors argued that the WGI must rely instead on indirect observations that, when aggregated, can suggest the value of the desired variable.[5]

Both indices remain the standard bearers for aggregate rankings of corruption or governance and utilize third-party surveys that are related to the "basket" of corruption issues. Their primary attraction is their near-global coverage.

But these first-generation attempts to "measure" corruption presented obvious challenges. How could one capture the myriad nuances and unique instances of corruption in a single tool or single number? Was not the phenomenon too complex in any country to be boiled down to a ranking of absolute values? Some critics expressed concern for the conceptual issues that Johnston and Heidenheimer had raised. As Heywood wrote in 1997 about the CPI,

> In spite of their somewhat disingenuous remark that 'their perceptions [the CPI] may not always be a fair reflection of the state of affairs, but they are reality' . . . the index provides no evidence to indicate that those polled are operating with the same concept of corruption; nor, indeed, does it make a compelling case for privileging the views of those working for multinational firms [survey respondents] and institutions.[6]

Later, in the post-Monterrey era, both the WGI and CPI came under fresh criticism and rigorous deconstruction for their lack of conceptual clarity and the dangers in using either index for cross-country comparisons or for tracking changes in country performance over time. The fundamental criticism was that since both indices rely entirely on third-party data that may be, depending on the original source or survey, only tangentially related to corruption *per se,* the aggregate results were suspect in their definitional clarity. This chapter does not summarize such debates, but suffice it to say that there is a growing skepticism concerning both measurements' validity and practical use.[7]

This inability to observe corruption directly—acknowledged by both the producers and the critics of first-generation measurement tools—ultimately lead to second-generation measurement tools, which explicitly avoided attempts to measure corruption and instead sought to measure its opposites: good governance, anti-corruption, and accountability mechanisms. Such second-generation assessments sought to analyze, and quantify where possible, the existence and effectiveness of key anti-corruption and good governance mechanisms, with the hope that insights into those institutions and practices would suggest where corruption was more or less prevalent.

Among the second-generation tools were Transparency International's National Integrity Systems studies, purely qualitative political-economy analyses of anti-corruption country systems; the Global Integrity country assessments and Global Integrity Index, which both qualitatively and quantitatively analyze anti-corruption frameworks; the Open Budget Index and country assessments, initiatives of the non-profit International Budget Partnership that map and quantify transparent budget procedures in countries around the world; the donor community's Public Expenditure and Financial Accountability (PEFA) assessments, which examine a country's public financial management practice; and other country-specific qualitative governance assessments generated by the Inter-American Development Bank, the World Bank, and various bilateral donors. At the same time, second-generation household and firm surveys regarding experiences with corruption were launched, including the World Bank's Doing Business surveys and the Business Environment and Enterprise Performance Survey (BEEPS), jointly developed by the World Bank and the European Bank for Reconstruction and Development (EBRD).

All second-generation initiatives sought to complement first-generation aggregate surveys with rigorous, in-depth data (and qualitative narrative) on the existence and effectiveness of various anti-corruption practices and habits in countries and sectors. The use of on-the-ground experts to generate original data and information, rather than relying on third-party surveys or polls, is a primary feature of many of these initiatives. While this approach was far more labor intensive and costly than relying on pre-existing third-party data, progress was made in closing the conceptual gap that had plagued first-generation measurement tools.

Second-generation measures are increasingly touted as improvements on first-generation corruption and governance measurement approaches (the Global Integrity Index, for example, was described by the World Bank's 2006 *Global Monitoring Report* as an example of "good practice methodology for governance indicators"). However, such measures are limited in their geographical scope (not covering nearly as many countries due to cost and logistical constraints) and their irregularity, which creates problems for tracking changes over time. While measuring anti-corruption mechanisms and their implementations tends to yield more "actionable" indicators that suggest specific policy reforms, it does not necessarily indicate those reforms that are "action-worthy" or necessarily what are the right steps for governments, donors, or development practitioners.[8] This broader challenge of integrating both measures of governance or corruption "inputs" and governance or corruption "outputs" is discussed in more detail below.

Today: The State of the Art

The growing debate concerning the limitations of first-generation measurement tools, and the counterclaim that second-generation tools should not be relied on exclusively, given their geographic constraints and lack of naviga-bility toward "action-worthy" reforms, has helped to tease out a growing body of work that highlights the strengths and weaknesses of existing measure-ment tools. This chapter identifies four key dimensions that provide some important distinctions for users of the available measurement tools (both first- and second-generation).[9] This debate serves also as a useful segue into a discussion of the types of next-generation tools that are needed to fill exist-ing gaps in the field.

Scale and Scope of Governance and Corruption Indicators

What do indicators of governance and corruption measure or assess? This question would seem to be an obvious one to answer, but far too often users overlook this fundamental issue, as Johnston and Heidenheimer noted.

This core question has been difficult to answer largely because there is no consensus on the definition of "governance" or "corruption" among academ-ics, aid donors, development practitioners, and grassroots activists. There is wide variation in the meanings of the concept, as the evaluation of governance and corruption has broadened to include human rights, democracy, civil soci-ety, accountability, business transparency, fiscal accountability, and the rule of law. This expansion has led virtually every generator of an indicator to call its assessment a measurement of "governance" or "corruption," with little dis-cussion of the theoretical underpinnings for such claims.

The absence of standard meanings of governance or corruption risks draining the concepts of specificity, making them "catch-all" terms.[10] Without such definitions, it is difficult to identify what is being assessed with any pre-cision (for instance, institutions, rules, corruption, or results) making indi-cators less effective in providing operationally relevant data to users. This ineffectiveness is especially true for composite indices, which subsume several data sets into one (or more) governance indicator(s), making them arguably meaningless.[11]

Rule-Based vs. Outcome-Based Indicators

Although definitions of governance and corruption vary, corruption meas-urement tools (and parallel governance measurement tools) have clustered around two conceptual measurement frameworks: the existence and quality of institutions, rules, and procedures (governance or anti-corruption "inputs") or what those mechanisms lead to in practice (governance or anti-corruption "outputs" or "outcomes").[12] Unlike crime prevention or the qual-ity of health care, where empirical measurements such as crime rates and mortality or life expectancy rates can be used to measure outputs and the number of police on the street and doctors in hospitals can be used to measure inputs, governance and corruption are nebulous topics.[13] This fuzziness reflects in part a continued conceptual gap between three schools of thoughts: one that views governance as the institutions and rules that manage societal affairs and a second that views governance as an output of the political and social systems in a country. A third argues that governance is performance—the delivery of critical political goods to citizens.

Governance outputs remain largely reliant on proxies rather than empirical statistics (no one believes that the number of corruption cases brought to trial serves as an appropriate measurement of "good governance" or even "anti-corruption" outputs). Household and business firm surveys of experiences with bribery and corruption, as well as interviews with respondents discussing experiences with public service delivery and trust in government, come closest to measuring directly governance outcomes and corruption outputs. Those who define governance as a government's performance in delivering political goods to its citizens look to more explicit public service delivery statistics for measures of governance outputs: miles of roads, the number of health care clinics per capita, and teacher-student ratios, to name a few.

Governance and corruption measurement tools that primarily assess inputs have the benefit of providing clear information on key benchmarks—such as the existence and strength of official laws, regulations, and institutions—that are important to the architecture of good governance and anti-corruption. There are however relatively few examples of indicators of governance that focus exclusively on inputs. Notable examples include IREX's Media Sustainability Index, which rates the quality of independent media in thirty-eight countries, based on five criteria such as legal norms, professional standards, and supporting institutions. Another example of an input measure is George Mason University/University of Maryland's POLITY IV country reports, which collect information on the character of political regimes over time. Although both indices are not "governance" assessments explicitly, they do touch on elements of "good governance" considered crucial in any context (a free and fair media and basic democratic forms of government) and code countries by a set of standard and transparent criteria, without exploring the actual performance, or output, of those systems.

On the opposite end of the scale are indicators that largely measure outputs—that is, the processes, outcomes, and effectiveness of those same rules and legal frameworks. One such measure that attempts to do so is the Index of African Governance, which addresses such questions as whether and how citizens have benefited from increased government expenditures on health services and the percentage of school-aged girls who have completed primary school and gone on to secondary school. Another is Freedom House's annual Freedom in the World survey, which, in more than 190 countries, assesses political and civil liberties based on questions that gauge the degree of freedom of the media (e.g., are journalists harassed, imprisoned, or killed), among other indicators. Similarly, the Economic Intelligence Unit's Index on Democracy focuses on measuring outputs of democracy based on five categories: electoral process and pluralism; civil liberties; the functioning of government; political participation; and political culture. The World Bank's Doing Business indicators, which evaluate the legal and regulatory environment for business operations in a country, generate data that capture the number of days and average costs to perform various licensing and regulatory requirements.

Most available measurement tools fall somewhere in between measuring inputs and measuring outputs, and it could be argued that even the above-mentioned examples belong to a different or hybrid category. Some input-focused assessments go beyond simple *de jure* indicators to combine and capture the quality of *de facto* implementation. For instance, the Decent Work indicators in the International Labour Association's Gaps in Basic Workers' Rights measure the gaps between labor conventions and rights and their implementation and adherence. Global Integrity's Integrity Indicators assess the strengths and weaknesses of countries' public sector anti-corruption mechanisms using data and information on the legal anti-corruption framework, as well as its practical implementation. The International Budget Partnership's Open Budget Index explores the legal framework for transparent and accountable public budgeting processes in countries, as well as the shortcomings of those rules and laws in practice.

These more robust measurement tools can be thought of as "input-plus" indicators, though they still fall short of measuring true outputs. "Output-plus" indicators also exist; for example, the World Bank Institute's WGI combines both input data (the Global Integrity data, for instance) as well as output data (e.g., the number of journalists killed in countries each year).

Both rule-based and outcomes-based indicators have their strengths and weaknesses. Indicators of corruption and governance that focus on rules and inputs have the advantage of providing clear, straightforward information about the existence and strength of laws and regulations. They are also more naturally "actionable" by governments, citizens, and aid donors. Following on the example above, governments and citizens in a country cannot simply choose, as a matter of policy and practice, to lower the crime rate (an output).

They can instead choose to put more police on the streets or toughen penalties for offenders (inputs) with the hope that those inputs will lead to the desired output (less crime). That said, outcomes-based indicators can at times be unpacked to yield disaggregated data that are more "actionable" than their composite score. Both the CPI and WGI, for instance, are made up of dozens of source polls, surveys, and expert assessments that are often more accessible as guides for policymaking than are actual CPI or WGI scores.

Methodology

In addition to providing users with an understanding of what corruption measures are actually measuring, another important distinction between the various governance and corruption indicators is the methodological techniques that the creators of such tools have adopted to generate their products. The key differentiator is the types of data sources that are used. These methodological techniques are not merely technical footnotes to be glossed over; they instead have a dramatic impact on the resultant measures' strengths and limitations.

The most crucial methodological distinction is whether the indicator or toolkit is based on *composite* or *original* data. Toolkits that rely on original data gather new data for the explicit purpose of generating their respective index or assessment and can be particularly powerful because they unbundle euphemistic concepts such as "governance" or "corruption" into concrete issues where policy trade-offs can be weighed. Examples of this approach are the Global Integrity Index, the Open Budget Index (both are made up of scores generated by their local in-country experts), POLITY (scores are assigned directly by its researchers), the many original surveys of business experts on their perceptions of corruption, as well as original household surveys exploring perceptions and experiences of citizens. Beginning in 2008, the Index of African Governance is also generating original data via a network of on-the-ground researchers in Africa.

Composite indicators, on the other hand, aggregate and synthesize information from third-party data sources. They do not gather or generate their own data and instead rely on data from others, employing aggregation techniques to generate their own results or scores from those component sources. Composite indicators of corruption remain the most widely used measurement tools because of their near-global coverage; they are also typically first-generation toolkits. Among the most prominent aggregate measures are the World Bank's WGI and Transparency International's CPI.[14] Although they lack original data, these indices' component data can at times be unpacked to identify possible priorities for governance reform efforts (as noted above).

Both original and aggregate measures have their strengths and their weaknesses. Aggregate indicators can be useful in summarizing vast quantities of information from several sources, and in so doing, can limit measurement errors from individual indicators. Potentially, these measures can also increase the accuracy of measuring a concept as broad as corruption or governance.[15]

As critics have noted, the process of aggregating many component variables into a single score or category risks losing the conceptual clarity that is crucial to using governance and corruption measurement tools properly.[16] If users cannot understand or unpack the concept that is being measured, their ability to draw out informed policy implications is severely constrained. Original data-based indicators, when designed properly, can greatly help to identify potential points of intervention in the context of governance and corruption reform programs. Nevertheless, there is always a degree of subjectivity and ambiguity built into the classification and "coding" (assigning of scores) of original data-based measurement tools. For instance, the researchers working on country scores for the POLITY database follow strict criteria for assigning scores but are susceptible, as any of us would be, to some degree of unintentional bias or inconsistency. The same applies to local in-country experts working to assign scores for international non-governmental organizations (NGOs), such as Global Integrity or the International Budget Partnership.

The more troubling weaknesses of original data-based assessments occur when scores are assigned with little to no explicit scoring criteria. One example of this can be found in the Afrobarometer Survey, a widely used household survey that assesses African citizens' opinions on their government's performance and macro-economic issues. One question in the 2006 survey was, "On the whole, how would you rate the freeness and fairness of the last national election, held in [20*XX*]?" Respondents were offered the following choices: 1) Completely free and fair; 2) Free and fair, but with minor problems; 3) Free and fair, with major problems; 4) Not free and fair; 5) Do not understand question; and 6) Don't know.

Without criteria to define those responses, such as what are "minor" and "major" problems or what does "free and fair" mean, it is difficult to know precisely what attitudes and emotions respondents are reflecting in their response (indeed, the entire field of political psychology seeks to answer those very difficult questions).

Internal vs. External Stakeholders and Measures

Interest in working with local experts, as opposed to relying on outsiders for their opinions and ratings, is a recent trend in the field of corruption and governance measurement. This shift underscores the growing recognition that corruption and governance measurements need to be more relevant for stakeholders in a country. While international donors and investors have been the key external constituency that uses governance and corruption indicators to make aid and capital allocations, existing indicators, especially aggregate and perceptions-based assessments, have often proven to be less helpful to internal stakeholders (i.e., national governments and local grassroots advocacy groups). A single corruption "ranking" does little to assist a reform-minded minister or grassroots advocate when pushing forward often difficult and highly technical governance reforms.

The emphasis on making corruption and governance indicators more useful to national actors has been accompanied by increasing efforts to promote local "ownership" of such assessments. National ownership is based on the premise that such measures should be internally driven by local stakeholders (not foreign aid donors and non-governmental groups) and should be based on consultations with a broad range of national participants such as the government, civil society, and business associations. This inclusive, bottom-up and locally generated approach is important, proponents argue, for making governance assessments locally relevant, legitimate, and trustworthy.

The most well-known example of a nationally owned governance assessment is the Africa Peer Review Mechanism (APRM), a tool used by member states to assist each other in developing, preparing, and implementing effective programs of action to improve economic, political, corporate, and social governance. Member states facilitate the development of the national program of action, sharing best practices and supporting each other in capacity building and constructive peer dialogue and persuasion. Supporters of the APRM approach note that if nothing else, such a nationally driven or nationally owned assessment process forces recalcitrant governments to at least engage (if at times only superficially) in a dialogue around corruption and governance issues that might otherwise not occur.

Local "ownership" of governance and corruption assessments, however, is not without its problems, and the APRM process has come under significant criticism. As Hyden notes, there are significant challenges to aligning governance and corruption assessments with local needs on the conceptual, institutional, political, and operational levels.[17] The conceptual vagueness of the concepts of governance and corruption makes it difficult to determine the most appropriate models for indicators. Nationally owned assessments are also subject to self-censoring and the "whitewashing" of scores, given that government has a seat at the table and in some contexts may have political motivation to bias the data positively. From a logistical standpoint, nationally owned assessments are typically lengthy, drawn-out affairs that take years, rather than months, to complete. APRM's slow progress (and government interference in some countries) has frustrated many observers who had hoped that nationally driven governance and corruption assessments would represent the next wave of measurement tools. As of this writing, the jury is still out.

Moving Forward: Possibilities for the Future

Despite the increasing number of initiatives to measure corruption, governance, and anti-corruption performance and the growing consensus that no single tool is the answer, little systematic headway has been made on how to operationalize next steps in the field. A competing and growing collection of governance indicators and corruption measures continue to flourish, and, despite important distinctions between them, many users—both in and outside of government and donor agencies—are increasingly convinced that such a proliferation is harmful to the practical work of governance and anti-corruption reform.

Global Integrity interviewed more than two dozen practitioners in government, donor agencies, grassroots NGOs, and development contractors to explore how, when, and whether officials were using existing corruption and governance measurement tools; these interviews are included in the volume, *A User's Guide to Measuring Corruption,* that Global Integrity produced on behalf of the United Nations Development Programme (UNDP).[18] What Global Integrity learned during the course of and from those interviews is revealing.

Several key officials spoke to the issue of the *"labeling problem"*: the broad definitional scope of "governance" and "corruption" that makes the concepts mean everything and nothing. The vast and overwhelming range of "governance" and "corruption" assessments and indicators has led to tremendous frustration over the extent to which the information produced is "actionable" (or not) and amenable to policy intervention (or not).

Another issue that emerged from the interviews centered on the second conceptual category identified above: *what is being measured in indicators/measurement tools.* The desire for actionable data was raised again as users decried how most indicators—whether they focused on inputs, outputs, or both—seldom provided contextual information on the political-economic causes of the problems.

Respondents also had much to say about the *methodology* of existing governance indicators, the third conceptual distinction noted above. While perceptions-based surveys continue to be the most commonly used in the governance and corruption landscape, many respondents expressed frustration with these surveys' limited application to potential solutions, as well as the surveys' employ of subjective measures that practitioners felt were out of step with reality. Several respondents cited the usefulness of qualitative assessments, or a combination of quantitative and qualitative tools, to add context and depth to a country's analysis.

Respondents energetically observed the final typology explored above: *internal vs. external stakeholders.* Many interviewees expressed a desire for a greater use of local knowledge, internal assessments, and national ownership to cultivate government "buy-in." Indeed, they argued, such indigenous and internally generated tools may be more effective in assessing political-economic incentives to change—including political will—which several users identified as a major gap in existing governance and corruption assessments.

The longer the corruption measurement field continues to lag behind its users' complaints (a gap repeatedly identified by the users discussed above), the greater the risk that governments, aid donors, and practitioners will abandon any hope of making evidence-based decisions and revert to "best-guess" efforts for anti-corruption reforms. Even second-generation measurement tools have come under fire for failing to provide policymakers with truly "actionable" information that can be translated into specific policies. As the World Bank recently wrote in an independent internal evaluation of its own Doing Business indicators:

The DB [Doing Business] indicators have motivated policymakers to discuss and consider business regulation issues. Its active dissemination in easy-to-understand language permits widespread press coverage and generates interest from businesses, nongovernmental organizations (NGOs), and senior policy makers. DB has had less influence on the choice, scope, and design of reforms. Most Bank Group staff and country stakeholders interviewed for this evaluation report that they draw on a range of analytical material to determine the nature, sequence, and direction of reforms; the DB indicators have limited use in this regard. As a cross-country benchmarking exercise, DB cannot be expected to capture the country specific considerations involved in prioritizing, sequencing, and designing policy reforms. Each year DB spotlights countries that have demonstrated the largest gain in the overall ranking and an improvement on at least three indicators. Such an approach, while transparent, does not capture the reforms' relevance and their potential impact on the binding constraints to the investment climate in the country.[19]

Given the political and financial stakes, this lack of progress seems a discouraging outcome. More than ever, there must be a serious exploration of next-generation tools that can keep up with the growing demand for corruption and governance indicators. A concurrent investment in time, expertise, and financial resources is also necessary to enable such a step forward.

First, the growing demand for locally generated assessments is going to require financial investments as well as capacity-building to support local data-gathering institutions, whether governmental statistics offices, private survey companies, or local NGOs and research institutions. Even basic approaches such as household and firm surveys that explore experiences with corruption require careful planning, questionnaire development, and post-survey interpretation. The donor community can help to accelerate such home-grown measurements in developing countries by pooling financial and technical resources into a common fund or technical assistance mechanism. Unfortunately, no single actor currently has the mandate to drive such a coordinated effort, and while the UNDP has begun to take a lead role in herding Western donor cats who are interested in supporting anti-corruption and governance assessments, such an effort remains in its infancy.

Second, the field must push quickly into generating more highly disaggregated measurements of corruption. In plain terms, empty single-number rankings that do not assist with prioritizing policy choices are increasingly being ignored. The sum total of practitioner experience during the past two decades, combined with the growing criticism of single-number country rankings, suggests that the era of "name and shame" corruption indices may be coming to a close. The simple fact that so few users are able to take such indicators and put them to any practical use suggests that a change of course is needed. Understanding and measuring corruption levels in, for example, the extractive industries sector in a given region; particular states and provinces within a country; or the infrastructure or public utilities sectors represent the bleeding-edge of the research agenda. New initiatives such as the Extractive Industries Transparency Initiative and the Water Integrity Network suggest that there is growing interest in moving quickly into sector-specific measurement.

Third, there is a growing awareness that qualitative political-economy analyses should be relied upon as frequently as are quantitative measures of corruption. Regardless of how advanced the econometric tools are, it is difficult to imagine them ever fully capturing the nuances of how, when, and why corruption occurs in a given society. While qualitative tools lack comparability across countries, they can diagnose political chokepoints within a system that prevent the implementation of reforms. The most impressive new work in this area is emerging from aid donors themselves, notably the UK's Department for International Development's Drivers of Change studies generated in dozens of developing countries and similar assessments carried out by the Dutch and Swedish governments.

Fourth, in future measurement tools greater attention must be paid to leadership and political will as key ingredients to effective anti-corruption efforts—phenomena that must be captured or assessed. To date, the field has been dominated almost entirely by institutional analysis, the principal-agent-client model, and more generalized political theory sprinkled with anecdotal case studies. Few creators of measurement tools have attempted to tackle the issues of political will and leadership, and because of this, we have little understanding of what motivates elites and leaders to undertake (or shy away from) the tough anti-corruption reforms that are sorely needed. Combining or integrating such new measures with next-generation political-economy analyses could prove a powerful combination.

One of the most promising efforts in this context is the nascent Leaders, Elites, and Coalitions Research Programme under the auspices of the Global Integrity Alliance (no relationship to Global Integrity). The program is embarking on an ambitious data-coding exercise to define a taxonomy of leadership and then, through case studies, classify various examples of leadership to identify best practices for encouraging and sustaining "pro-development" coalitions of elites and leaders in countries.[20] The initiative, which grew out of a World Ethics Forum conference in Oxford in 2006, remains in its infancy and, after benefiting from initial financial support from the World Bank, faces a long road of internal capacity-building before it can have a significant impact on the debate. (It lacks, for instance, any full-time, dedicated staff or secretariat.) But its potential to identify trends and replicable success stories where leadership has played a key role in stimulating anti-corruption reform efforts is a tantalizing prospect.

Future measurement breakthroughs that have the greatest potential for impact are those that bridge the gap between theory and practice—those that are grounded in a solid theoretical framework but have been tested, debunked and adjusted, and tested again in the field. The foundation for those break-throughs has been laid through the work of the first two generations of corruption and governance metrics. The challenge now is to accelerate the development of new, third generation toolkits before attention shifts away from the anti-corruption and good governance agendas.

Notes

1. United Nations General Assembly Resolution 55/2 III–13, *United Nations Millennium Declaration* (2000).

2. Robert Klitgaard, *Controlling Corruption* (Berkeley, 1988); Michael Johnston, *Political Corruption and Public Policy in America* (Monterey, 1982); Michael Johnston, "The Political Consequences of Corruption: A Reassessment," *Comparative Politics,* XVIII (1986), 459–477; Susan Rose-Ackerman, *Corruption: A Study in Political Economy* (New York, 1978).

3. Arnold J. Heidenheimer and Michael Johnston (eds.), *Political Corruption: Concepts and Contexts* (New Brunswick, 2002), xii.

4. Stephen Knack and Philip Keefer, "Institutions and Economic Performance: Cross-Country Tests Using Alternative Measures," *Economics and Politics,* XII (1995), 207–227; Paolo Mauro, "Corruption and Growth," *Quarterly Journal of Economics,* CX (1995), 681–712; and later: Stephen Knack (ed.), *Democracy, Governance, and Growth* (Ann Arbor, 2003).

5. Daniel Kaufmann, Aart Kraay, and Pablo Zoido-Lobatón, "Governance Matters," *World Bank Policy Research Working Paper* No. 2196 (Washington, D.C., 1999), 1–61.

6. Paul Heywood, "Political Corruption: Problems and Perspectives," in his *Political Corruption* (Oxford, 1997), 9.

7. Christine Arndt and Charles Oman, *Uses and Abuses of Governance Indicators* (Paris, 2006); Daniel Kaufmann, Aart Kraay, and Massimo Mastruzzi, "Growth and Governance: A Reply," *Journal of Politics,* LXIX (2007), 555–562; Stephen Knack, "Measuring Corruption in Eastern Europe and Central Asia: A Critique of the Cross-Country Indicators," *World Bank Policy Research Working Paper* No. 3968 (Washington, D.C., 2006), 1–64; Marcus Kurtz and Andrew Schrannk, "Growth and Governance: Models, Measures and Mechanisms," *Journal of Politics,* LXIX (2007), 538–554.

8. Daniel Kaufmann and Aart Kraay, "Governance Indicators: Where Are We, Where Should We Be Going?" *World Bank Research Observer,* XXIII (2008), 1–43.

9. Much of this discussion draws on the volume UNDP and Global Integrity, *A Users' Guide to Measuring Corruption* (Oslo, 2008).

10. Goran Hyden, "The Challenges of Making Governance Assessments Nationally Owned," paper presented at the 2007 Bergen Seminar on "Governance Assessments

and the Paris Declaration," organized by the UNDP Oslo Governance Centre and the Chr. Michelsen Institute, Bergen, 24–25 September.

11. Arndt and Oman, *Uses and Abuses,* 72.

12. Hyden, "Challenges of Making Governance Assessments Nationally Owned," 2.

13. This is deliberately an overly simplistic paradigm for describing measures of crime and health care inputs and outputs; dozens of other crucial socioeconomic factors impact crime and health care to a large extent.

14. The 2008 Index of African Governance utilized both aggregate data and data obtained in-country. The in-country research supplemented the aggregate data for thirty-six of the forty-eight sub-Saharan African countries assessed in 2008. See Robert I. Rotberg and Rachel M. Gisselquist, *Strengthening African Governance: Ibrahim Index of African Governance, Results and Rankings 2008* (Cambridge, MA, 2008), available at http://belfercenter.ksg.harvard.edu/project/52/intrastate_conflict_program.html?page _id=223 (accessed 20 April 2009).

15. Kaufmann and Kraay, "Governance Indicators," 13.

16. Arndt and Oman, *Uses and Abuses,* 90.

17. Goran Hyden, a political scientist, is the co-author of the World Governance Survey.

18. UNDP and Global Integrity, *A Users' Guide,* 33.

19. World Bank, *Doing Business: An Independent Evaluation* (2008), xvi–xvii.

20. Leaders, Elites and Coalitions Research Programme, *Concept Note for Peer Review* (London, 2008).

SUSAN ROSE-ACKERMAN

4

Corruption in the Wake of Domestic National Conflict

Nation-states emerging from conflict are particularly susceptible to corruption. Many of the factors that create corrupt incentives in *any* society are likely to be present in post-conflict environments. The cumulative effect of these factors may be greater than the independent effect of each one. Although corruption is a potential problem in all post-conflict states, the nature of the conflict and the conditions under which the conflict ended help to determine the types of corruption that emerge. Although there are broad similarities across all corrupt environments, including post-conflict situations, there are also differences, which can be traced to the conflict itself and the way in which the conflict was resolved.

To demonstrate these points, this chapter first outlines the nature of corrupt opportunities and their interaction with post-conflict conditions. Next, it provides a taxonomy of post-conflict situations that draws on case studies of Guatemala, Angola, Mozambique, Burundi, and Kosovo. This section shows how the sources of post-conflict corruption differ depending upon the roles of former combatants, the existence of natural resource rents, the presence of organized crime, and the involvement of international actors. The chapter concludes with reform proposals that are consistent with the case studies and are tailored to the particular problems of weak, post-conflict states.

Corrupt Opportunities

Corrupt opportunities that arise in the wake of domestic national conflict mirror those in other high-corruption environments. The underlying incentives

This chapter draws on Susan Rose-Ackerman, "Corruption and Government," *Journal of International Peacekeeping*, XV (2008), 328–343; Rose-Ackerman, "Corruption and Post-Conflict Peace-Building," *Ohio Northern University Law Journal*, XXXIV (2008), 405–443.

are universal, but particular variants arise from efforts to rebuild the state, the society, and the economy. The nature of conflict and the resulting peace deal provide important pre-conditions for subsequent corruption. Research on corruption identifies several risk factors.

First, corrupt incentives are created by weak state institutions operating with unclear and poorly enforced rules to distribute benefits or impose costs. These incentives are enhanced if officials are poorly paid and trained and if the country has a poorly functioning judiciary that lacks independence. Such conditions frequently prevail in post-conflict societies. Further to exploit corrupt opportunities, officials may create or threaten to create delays as a means of extracting bribes. This can be an especially effective strategy in the emergency conditions that prevail in the immediate aftermath of violent conflict.

Second, large, one-of-a-kind infrastructural projects are convenient loci of payoffs for high-level officials. Often, a conflict has destroyed most of the infrastructure; therefore, there is pressure to initiate reconstruction projects quickly, without strong financial controls. In the case of very poor countries, there may have been little infrastructure to destroy, but post-conflict aid may be used to help the country catch up.

Third, corruption is a risk when substantial resources are available to the state apart from internal taxation. These may take the form of natural resource rents, but in post-conflict periods they also frequently involve large influxes of emergency and development aid. These resources create incentives for individuals to appropriate them for personnel use. The individuals who skim the rents may be public officials, domestic or international contractors, or outsiders whose responsibilities may include technical expertise and anti-corruption monitoring.

Fourth, corrupt enrichment often co-exists with legal opportunities for profit. This makes it possible for some to disguise corrupt gains as legitimate profits. The corrupt cannot easily be distinguished from the honest, successful entrepreneurs; frequently, the same people play both roles.

Fifth, organized crime may have become entrenched during the conflict through smuggling, arms dealing, etc. Its membership may grow, and it may consolidate power in the aftermath of the conflict, enlisting former combatants into its ranks and undermining law enforcement efforts through corruption or something close to a merger with state organizations.

All five risk factors are found to some degree in any weak state with infrastructural needs, externally provided funds, and prevalent organized crime. However, the conflict itself may have exacerbated the problem if it has bred a culture of secrecy and impunity where self-dealing was easy to conceal. Even if corruption were not pervasive during the conflict, the conflict's end may lead to a period of disorganization and weak state control. Governments may not be transparent and accountable, especially if those who gained financially from the conflict are in power and seek both to preserve past gains and benefit from the rebuilding effort. Formerly armed groups converted into political parties may view the state as a source for private gain. Even if a person wishes to report a corrupt offer, there may be no effective way to do so that does not invite harassment or worse.

Sometimes the relationship between private wealth and public power does not involve outright corruption in the form of monetary payoffs. Rather the problem is crony capitalism or state capture. State capture implies that the state largely serves the interests of a narrow group of businesspeople and politicians, sometimes with criminal elements mixed in. Elites are frequently able to capture the political and economic benefits of reconstruction. If they can maintain their power bases into the later post-conflict period, they position themselves to benefit because there are no other credible sources of power and because institutional constraints are weak.

The nature of the peace deal matters, particularly in determining whom corruption benefits and whom it harms. Does the old regime continue in power either because it has crushed the opposition or arranged a brokered deal that favors the incumbents? Alternatively, have the former fighters taken power with a mandate to clean house? If so, do they use this mandate simply to prosecute the old rulers, or do they apply high ethical standards to themselves? Political leaders buy off powerful private actors with patronage, and powerful private actors—including criminal groups and wealthy business interests—buy off weak politicians with money or promises of future jobs and business ventures. The political system may be in a corruption trap where payoffs lead to expectations of future payoffs.[1] In such cases, the effectiveness of government programs and the impact of foreign aid and lending suffer. Even if those with good political connections are also good economic managers, there is a long-term risk that they will exploit their dominant positions to squeeze out potential competitors. At the opposite extreme, a brokered peace deal that requires power sharing may create its own problems. The division of state power allows more hands to reach into the pot. Each group may feel pressure to provide benefits to its supporters, thus exhausting the pool of rents. Furthermore, if power-sharing means that those in government feel that their tenure is shaky or incomplete, they may try to take what they can for short-term gain.

A Taxonomy of Post-Conflict Corruption

Drawing on the work of a group of knowledgeable students, I studied the cases of Guatemala, Angola, Mozambique, Burundi, and Kosovo.[2] Table 4-1

Table 4-1. *Summary Information on Case Study Countries*

	Guatemala	Angola	Mozambique	Burundi	Kosovo
Population (million)	13.0 (7/08 est.)	12.5 (7/08 est.)	21.3 (7/08 est.)	8.7 (7/08 est.)	2.1 (2007 est.)
GDP ($bill PPP, 2007 est.)	67.45	80.95	17.82	6.39	4.0
GDP/pc ($PPP) (2007 est.)	5,400	6,500	900	800	1,800
% poor	56.2 (2004 est.)	70 (2003 est.)	70 (2001 est.)	68 (2002 est.)	37 (2007 est.)
Gini	55.1 (2007)	n.a.	47.3 (2002)	42.4 (1998)	30 (2005/2006)
Main Exports	Agricultural products	Oil, diamonds	Agricultural products, aluminum	Agricultural products	Mining, metal, and leather products
Date of Independence and Colonial or Dominant Power	1821 Spain	1975 Portugal	1975 Portugal	1962 Belgium	2008* Serbia
Date of Peace Accords	1996	2002	1992	2000	1999
Conflict Duration (yrs.)	36	27	15	38 (intermittent)	4
Parties to Conflict	Government of Guatemala, URNG	MPLA (ruling party), UNITA	FRELIMO (ruling party), RENAMO	Tutsi (former rulers, Hutu	Kosovar Albanians (with NATO help), Serbia
Nature of Peace Accords	Elections, Truth Commission, limited amnesty for political crimes	Electoral democracy with UNITA as a political party but with MPLA dominance	Democracy with RENAMO as a political party with UN financial assistance	Election in 2005 with quotas in parliament, defense forces, cabinet for Hutu and Tutsi	UN protectorate to be followed by the EU Multi-party elections
Role of Organized Crime	Important actors in illegal drug trade	Not recorded.	Not recorded.	Not recorded.	Smuggling during conflict; some role at present
Post-conflict Governments	Dominated by parties in power during conflict	Election won by MPLA; UNITA is represented in parliament	Elections won by FRELIMO; RENAMO has regional and parliamentary representation	Hutu victory subject to Tutsi quota; risk of renewed violence from a Hutu rebel group	Multi-party elections with elected officials, mainly Kosovar Albanians

Source for economic and population data: U.S. Central Intelligence Agency, *The World Factbook*, available at www.cia.gov/library/publications/the-world-factbook/ (accessed 28 April 2008).

*Contested by Serbia and Russia. Kosovo has been a province of Serbia, not a colony.

provides basic background data on the countries, the nature of their conflicts, and their aftermaths.

To characterize the essence and extent of corruption in these cases, the most important dimensions appear to be the government in power during the conflict, the level of destruction and displacement, the form of the peace deal, underlying economic and social conditions, and the role of outsiders (including other states, international institutions, and organized crime factions).

First, with the possible exception of Mozambique, the countries emerging from civil war had been governed by regimes that did not represent the interests of the majority. During the armed conflict, the majority of the population had little political power, although, of course, not all of those without power actively supported the rebels.

Second, civil wars leave behind physical destruction, internal displacement, and widespread loss of life. In the cases discussed here, all faced the task of rebuilding infrastructure and reintegrating into society both former fighters and displaced persons.

Third, peace comes in different ways. Some cases represent brokered peace deals in which weakened or exhausted rebels agreed to a truce that gave them a stake in the post-conflict state, but with no political control. Guatemala, Angola, and Mozambique are in that category. In Burundi and Kosovo, in contrast, the dominant ethnic group, formerly not in power, gained control of the government. Under the Burundi peace accords, the minority Tutsi, formerly in power, were guaranteed a continued role in the new democracy through quotas and other measures. In Kosovo, ethnic Kosovars, including former fighters against Serbia, took control of the government under a United Nations Protectorate.

Fourth, a country's economic base helps structure both the conflict and the post-conflict environment, and here the cases show substantial variation. Guatemala, Burundi, and Mozambique are largely agricultural economies dependent on exports of agricultural goods. Angola's economy is largely based on natural resource rents, although most of the population is engaged in agriculture. Kosovo has a low per capita income by European standards, and its natural resources were not exploited during the conflict.

Fifth, the level and distribution of income may be a consequence of past corruption and self-dealing, but it can also help determine the nature of present-day malfeasance. Income is very unevenly distributed in Guatemala and Angola, in contrast to Burundi, Mozambique, and Kosovo, which are more uniformly poor.

Sixth, other states influenced the intensity and duration of the fighting, helped broker the peace, and provided financial and human resources to aid peace-building. Angola, mainly because of its oil wealth, became a pawn in the Cold War. Mozambique's civil war was financed by its African neighbors. The Guatemalan conflict played out on the Cold War stage as the United States was determined not to have another Cuba in its backyard. In these cases outside involvement fueled conflict and withdrawal of support helped end it. Burundi's citizens suffered more from international neglect rather than active intervention as the world failed to halt the violence in Burundi and Rwanda. Kosovo struggled under Serbian dominance for many years, and its location inside Europe led NATO to intervene militarily and the European Union (EU) to participate in the peace-building effort.

Finally, organized crime may gain a foothold during the conflict and can take advantage of the state weakness that occurs with the end of fighting. This scenario appears to be a particular problem in Guatemala.

In all cases, the conflict and its aftermath both created corrupt incentives and gave domestic and international actors excuses to overlook corruption. Incentives were created by the weakness of domestic institutions, on the one hand, and by the influx of relief and rebuilding funds, on the other. Institutional weakness is, in part, simply a reflection of the lack of accountability of the pre-war states, but it was exacerbated by the wars' destructive impact on state functioning. Moreover, in the post-conflict period, international organizations, charged with maintaining a fragile and uneasy peace, emphasized internal stability over initiatives to build democratic and accountable public institutions. External funds and supplies created a pool of benefits available for theft. The aftermath of the war and the risk of renewed fighting were sometimes used by domestic politicians as an excuse for the lack of financial controls and the consequent leakage of funds. Emergency conditions that require a quick response were used by international donors as a further excuse for ignoring financial integrity. Furthermore, besides failing to promote the financial integrity of the local government, international officials often invoked extraordinary circumstances to justify their operations under very loose and flexible rules, which made supervision almost impossible and corruption likely.

Hence, there are common features of post-conflict situations that are well-known to generate corrupt incentives. These are overlaid in the individual cases with distinctive features of the post-conflict environment and of underlying economic and social conditions. Given these background conditions, I consider how the corrupt pressure points differ in the cases discussed below.

Guatemala

Corruption is a serious problem in Guatemala.[3] Impunity, a remnant of the armed conflict, hampers its effective prosecution.[4] Poverty and underdevelopment are both a cause and a consequence of corruption, but the lack of accountability in the wake of the conflict has allowed corruption to become entrenched. Weak and corruptible institutions have permitted organized crime to thrive, while the co-opting of state institutions and public officials has further undermined post-conflict state building.

During the war between 1960 and 1996, the army controlled all aspects of the state's administration, and there was little distinction between state resources and the resources of those in power.[5] In the immediate aftermath of the fighting, the old elite remained in power and had little interest in controlling corruption or in questioning the wealth of those who benefited financially during the conflict.[6] Officials' embezzlement of public funds has further compounded Guatemala's high level of inequality.[7]

Since the signing of the peace agreement in 1996, politicians have sought to pose as corruption-fighters in an effort to attract support and to undermine the opposition. Recent presidents have pursued charges against the outgoing administration and against opposition leaders, but at the same time, some in their own administrations have been viewed as corrupt.[8] Although corruption at the very top of the government appears to be a less serious problem than it was in the immediate post-conflict period, it remains a major issue at lower levels. Even if many of the prosecutions of top officials were politically motivated, to the extent that they actually uncover corrupt activities, they should have a deterrent effect on future office holders.

Such an optimistic assessment of the benefits of corruption prosecutions is, however, problematic given Guatemala's poorly functioning judicial and law enforcement systems.[9] The police are widely viewed as corrupt, and, in 1997, the World Bank named the judiciary as Guatemala's most corrupt institution.[10] Hence, legitimate prosecutions of corruption are unlikely to succeed, and false accusations undercut the political opposition. These weaknesses are, in part, a legacy of the violence. During the thirty-six-year conflict, the weakness of the justice system, which lacked independence, apparently amplified and reinforced the violence.[11] The relative lack of rule of law creates incentives for personal deal-making and bribes. Twenty-five percent of judges and 87 percent of public prosecutors acknowledged that they had been pressured by superiors or influential parties.[12]

Corruption and self-dealing are not a problem only at the top of government. Corruption and other types of malfeasance have limited the implementation of policies that were designed to benefit those who supported the guerilla movement or who are simply poor and disadvantaged. The Guatemalan Truth Commission recommended reparations as a way to restore the dignity of the victims of the armed conflict and guarantee that the violence would not be repeated.[13] The State of Guatemala, however, has yet to institute thoroughly a functioning reparations program. Some funds appear to have been diverted corruptly through inflated operating costs and make-work jobs, but the more fundamental problem is the continued influence of the old elite that has little interest in aiding those who supported the guerillas.[14] Here the problem is not corruption *per se*. Rather, funds designed to aid the victims of civil war were diverted to hurricane victims and Civil Defense members.

Organized crime groups, particularly those involved in the drug trade, have taken advantage of Guatemala's fragile institutions and weak legal environment to operate with little constraint and even to collaborate with some who possess political and economic power as well as with sections of the police.[15] Some armed groups who were involved in the conflict continue operating through criminal networks. The weakness of the political parties and the failure to purge the old security apparatuses "make it easier for organized criminal gangs rooted in clandestine counterinsurgency structures to maintain and extend their political influence in the post conflict period."[16] There is some evidence that death squad networks active during the conflict switched to illegal criminal activity after the peace accords were signed. These networks have flourished because of the weak institutional structure, and they then resist the development of more effective law enforcement and judicial institutions, "both to protect their members (some of whom were implicated in human rights violations during the conflict) and to ensure their continuing ability to operate freely."[17]

Although Guatemala's legal code outlaws corruption, those who attempt to combat corruption do not typically fare well. Attacks on human rights advocates are common. Lawyers and members of civil society who work to end impunity and prosecute the crimes of the past are frequently targeted for attacks, many of which can be traced to those who violated human rights during the war.[18] Often, the same scare tactics are used against those working to combat criminal gangs and embezzlement.[19]

Guatemala thus illustrates a case where the peace accord left the old elite in power, with few effective checks on their behavior and little effort to limit the development of links between criminals, ex-combatants, and state officials. The cycle of impunity feeds into the cycle of corruption. With the passing of time, some progress has been made against corruption at the top of the government, but the growing role of organized crime may undermine such initiatives. The lack of strong law enforcement and judicial institutions feeds into the criminal networks in a "vicious cycle in which weak institutions create opportunities for the spread of corrupt networks, which in turn seek to further weaken institutional capacity to combat corruption."[20] The vexed question raised by this case is whether the international community should have made a concerted effort to buy off and neutralize the political power of the old elite in the immediate post-conflict period, or whether it would have been better to hold them more rigorously to account. The old elite maintained power and continues to have little interest in vigorous law enforcement efforts that could threaten their position. An alternative with more required power sharing with the former guerillas might, however, have led to a scramble for private gain, as in Burundi, that could have been equally as destructive. Organized crime, fueled by the drug market in the United States, is a key factor in post-conflict Guatemala, and it has taken advantage of the fledgling government that emerged.

Angola

Angola is similar to Guatemala in that a protracted and destructive civil war ended in a brokered peace deal that left the old elite in power. This group had little interest in the creation of transparent and accountable institutions.[21] The former rebels organized as a political party but have little political influence; they won only 20 percent of the popular vote in the 2008 parliamentary election. The main difference, however, is the ruling group's access to a tremendous source of wealth in the form of off-shore oil production and, to a lesser extent, diamonds. Thus, a central issue is the management of these resources in the wake of conflict and the lack of transparency concerning the inflows and outflows of oil revenues. Angola is awash in funds but fails to use them effectively to benefit the bulk of its citizens. Angola ranked forty-four out of forty-eight in the 2008 Index of African Governance.[22] Because of the rise in oil prices, its GDP growth rate was 14 percent in 2006, but it has a highly unequal distribution of income and wealth.[23]

Although corruption in Guatemala facilitates the drug trade and provides impunity to the wealthy and powerful, in Angola corruption diverts the stream of petroleum rents into private bank accounts. A report in 2003, soon after the civil war ended, found that in Angola thirty-nine individuals were worth between $50 and $100 million, and another twenty were worth at least $100 million, for a total of at least $3.95 billion. All seven at the top of the list were present or past government officials.[24]

As in Guatemala, the Angolan civil war provided a cover for personal enrichment but on a much larger scale than in Guatemala, given the available resource rents. Political leaders often thinly disguise their theft of state resources. After the conflict ended, a widespread rebuilding program began, and government budgets remained large.[25] However, transparency did not improve. The IMF documents the high level of "unexplained" expenditures from 1997 to 2002, which totaled $4.22 billion over the period or about 9.25 percent of GDP each year.[26] The state-owned oil enterprise, Sonangol, appears to be at the center of the corruption involving extra-budgetary operations, especially through its off-the-books borrowing practices.[27]

After the end of the fighting, with no military threat present, the entrenched government passed several laws that criminalized and restricted information. Particularly noteworthy is the State Security Act that criminalized possession of documents that the government considers sensitive, even if lawfully obtained by those outside the government. Penalties can be imposed on both public officials and recipients of the information, and the law has extra-territorial reach.[28] With such restrictions on information, the government has found it easy to reward supporters, often permitting some of the oil wealth to flow by indirect methods into private bank accounts.[29] Most of the beneficiaries were "a nexus of families that are closely linked to the centers of power through marriage, business relations, political connections and high positions in the security forces and administration. At their kernel is the presidential family itself."[30]

Angola, although nominally democratic, is essentially controlled by the same elite group that was in power during the civil war. Thus, the details of the institutional structure are not very important to an understanding of post-conflict conditions. Angola's case demonstrates the way that natural resource endowments can fuel corruption, with few benefits trickling down to the population at large. The basic argument for this "resource curse" is that a resource-rich state does not need to depend on its citizens to accumulate government revenues but can use resource rents to finance the state. Furthermore, with large amounts of money flowing into state coffers and, corruptly, into the private bank accounts of the political elite, talented people select into public office, where they get rich; they ignore the private sector. Angola, however, provides an extra twist on this story. First, during the civil war, the losing guerilla group had access to a natural resource—diamonds—that was easy to transport and trade.[31] These resource rents along with outside help from sympathetic nation-states helped to sustain the conflict. Second, the security threat provided a cover for the winning political and economic elite to enrich themselves from oil rents. They claimed that large military expenditures were needed, appropriated a portion of the funds, and then justified their secrecy regarding the use of funds on national security grounds. Once the fighting ended, national security continued to be used as an excuse to limit transparency and even to increase penalties for leaking information. For the most part, those in power during the fighting now remain in control of the government. Hence, they have no interest in a retrospective accounting. The level of malfeasance and unjust enrichment that took place during the fighting has helped to fuel the government's interest in keeping information limited, as in Guatemala, but on a much grander scale.

At present, given the international focus on anti-corruption, Angola is taking some steps toward reform. The IMF reports some progress in Angola's systems of financial management but notes the need for improvement.[32] Of particular concern is the continuing lack of transparency in the accounts of Sonangol, which are still excluded from the government accounts. Despite urging from the IMF, the government has not applied to join the Extractive Industries Transparency Initiative, an international civil society effort that requires transparency regarding payments made to and received by the Angolan government.[33] The Angolan authorities claim that "oil companies have positively assessed Angola's bidding practices."[34] This hardly seems a sufficient justification as transparency is valuable not simply to generate fairer bidding processes, but also to permit more public oversight of the size and use of government revenues.[35]

The country lacks the capacity to administer complex systems of procurement, data gathering, transparency, and accountability. It is carrying out a massive rebuilding task with weak administrative and judicial capacity and obsolete statutes.[36] However, if corruption remains a major source of inefficiency in allocating and monitoring the rebuilding effort, then those involved have little incentive to create the kinds of capacities and financial controls urged by the IMF. The problem is not solely capacity but also political will. Although not without its own problems, the Kosovo case, discussed below, illustrates that one solution is to use expatriate monitors or advisors with expertise and the authority to act. The Angolan government, however, would be unlikely to accept such outside assistance. Foreign exchange from oil and diamonds gives its government leverage to resist external pressures, at the same time as its weak political system limits the efficacy of domestic protest.

Mozambique

Mozambique's transition out of conflict appears secure, having occurred more than fifteen years ago.[37] Although Mozambique remains poor, it is often pointed to as a relative success in post-conflict state building. Thus, it is an especially important case for the study of post-conflict corruption.

As in Guatemala and Angola, in Mozambique a long-time incumbent political group retained power after the end of conflict and still maintains a dominant position. However, the character of the incumbents appears different from those in Guatemala and Angola. Hence, corruption, although a serious problem, is not as deeply entrenched in Mozambique's political system. Furthermore, neither organized crime nor resource rents sustain the incumbent regime. Rather, as in the cases of Burundi and Kosovo, foreign aid provides crucial resources, and this aid is sometimes conditioned on reforms that improve state functioning. Hence, the role of aid and lending organizations is much more important here than in Guatemala and Angola.

By the time that United Nations (UN)-sponsored peace negotiations began, neither party had the capacity to defeat the other militarily.[38] The UN made sufficient funds available to achieve its priorities, which were: "the disarmament, demobilization, and reintegration into civilian life of government and RENAMO [rebel] combatants."[39] It supported the transformation of RENAMO into a political party and provided special assistance to ex-combatants.[40] Democratic elections were held in 1994.

In discussing corruption and other under-the-table payoffs, it is important to distinguish between activities that were part of the initial transition to peace and those that are systemic aspects of the long-term transition process.

First, some payoffs were closely tied to the process of transforming REN-AMO into a political party. The UN created and managed several trust funds to provide financial support for RENAMO's transformation and participation in elections.[41] The leadership benefited personally from these funds and made increasing demands after the peace agreement. There was no detailed accounting for the use of the funds *ex post,* although donors did impose some constraints *ex ante* on their disbursement.[42] The top UN official who dealt with Afonso Dhlakama, the RENAMO leader, "constantly stressed the importance of RENAMO's trust fund, from which the group's leader was receiving over $300,000 a month for 'expenses.'"[43] A second trust fund benefited all parties running for office. These funds were also disbursed with little accountability so that everyone involved in politics received payments. One official stated that ". . . to ensure political stability and peace, the [UN] 'forgot' those funds . . . because there had been a 'price of peace' for RENAMO, so it was fair to have it also for those non-armed opposition political parties."[44]

Second, systemic corruption is also a problem in spite of Mozambique's good record of economic growth and its relative success in carrying out reforms in the post-conflict period.[45] The end of conflict occurred as Mozambique was making a shift from a post-independence socialist model toward a capitalist economy.[46] Corruption apparently flourished in this environment both because of greater opportunities for licit and illicit enrichment due to the shift in the economic model, and the new corrupt opportunities created by the need to rebuild the country with foreign aid funds. Now aid inflows are large and rising in Mozambique, totaling about 15 percent of its GDP.[47]

These sources of corruption were exacerbated by the weakness of state institutions set up to control the developing market economy and the use of public funds. Unlike Angola's high-level kleptocracy, corruption in Mozambique is disorganized and "anarchic." As in the case of Burundi, discussed below, each corrupt official seeks personal enrichment, and the result is multiple demands for payoffs that can be costly in both time and money for anyone seeking to obtain a benefit or to avoid a cost controlled by public officials.[48]

Old methods of control through FRELIMO, the ruling party, have broken down, and effective impersonal rule-based systems do not exist. The move to a market economy was not comprehensive and was encumbered by the country's history. Customs, business regulation, police and the judicial system, and the distribution of foreign aid appear to be especially corruption prone. For example, in the customs service in the late nineties, anarchy and delay prevailed in a highly corrupt environment.[49] However, no exact measurements are available.

These weaknesses were exacerbated, as in Guatemala and Angola, because the ruling party had little interest in truly independent monitoring institutions. Furthermore, as a poor country, Mozambique has low levels of professional capacity, so even with a strong commitment to reform it would have faced capacity constraints.[50] Nevertheless, there has been moderate progress in the development of monitoring institutions. However, most institutions, including the judiciary and the police, are at an early stage of reform, and it will be important to assess their effectiveness going forward, especially because FRELIMO's dominant political position does not seem likely to end in the near future.[51]

Corruption in Mozambique is intimately tied to the country's transition to a market economy, with weak institutions and high aid dependency. A combination of moral suasion and the lack of opportunities as a result of government policy, civil war, and a weak economy kept corruption in check during the period of civil war. Key features of the post-conflict situation are: first, the weak and untested nature of public institutions in spite of (or maybe because of) continuity in leadership; second, the influx of foreign aid that continues to provide major funding. These funds are used for private gain, but they also are required for state functioning and have supported some of the new accountability methods. The conditions imposed by international institutions appear to have had a major impact on Mozambique's development, but these institutions are still too weak to withstand the corrupt incentives that arose from their creation.

As both are former Portuguese colonies in sub-Saharan Africa, it is instructive to compare Angola and Mozambique. Both moved to a state-planned economy after independence in 1975 through nationalizing the properties formerly owned by Portuguese settlers; both experienced long-lasting, devastating civil wars, which began shortly after independence and were fueled by outsiders based on international (Angola) and regional (Mozambique) rivalries; and both today face the problems of an inefficient bureaucracy and judicial system. Nevertheless, the two cases also have important differences. First, Angola is resource rich, especially in oil and diamonds; Mozambique is not a resource-rich country. Second, although harmful to its people and to the economy, Mozambique's civil war did not last as long as Angola's. Third, with the support of the UN, the Mozambique peace agreement was successfully followed by general elections. Three presidential and legislative elections have been held in Mozambique (1994, 1999, and 2004). Angola carried out a UN-supported election in 1992 in which results were not recognized by one of the factions, plunging the country back into civil war. The next election was in 2008. Fourth, in Angola the peace agreement was made after a military defeat of one of the factions, UNITA, while in Mozambique the rebel group retained some bargaining power during peace talks. Fifth, in Mozambique, although corruption remains a problem, there has been a largely successful effort to improve the country's budget procedures and its public financial management. In Angola the government is flush with oil and diamond revenues and does not need outside support. Hence, it can successfully resist reforms that could lead to more transparency and accountability in public finances. Mozambique stands in sharp contrast to Angola and its case suggests that even weak institutions when combined with the oversight of outside donors have some value.

Thus, in Mozambique the UN played a positive role in bringing the conflict to a close. It was able to achieve disarmament before the first democratic elections. This goal was achieved, in part, by providing financial support to rebel leaders to ensure their participation in the political process and by assisting former combatants. The World Bank and the IMF, beginning before the end of the conflict, helped to smooth the transition to a market economy and to democracy with aid and advice. This assistance appears to have had many positive effects, but one side effect was a rise in corruption as market opportunities increased. Those who funded the transition did not take sufficient account of the weakness of state institutions designed to regulate the market and control corruption. This case raises the question of whether it is possible to buy off former combatants with up-front payments at the same time as a transition to a market economy and democracy seeks to control corruption.

Burundi

In Burundi the rebels achieved some measure of success under the peace accords, but the peace remains fragile.[52] Burundi is a small, extremely poor, landlocked, African country that has suffered from widespread violence that began soon after its independence from Belgium. Its transition from civil violence began in 2000 when the Arusha Accords were signed, followed by elections in 2005. The accords provide constitutional protections for the minority Tutsi who were formerly the dominant political group. The constitution reserves 60 percent of the assembly for Hutu, and 40 percent for Tutsi.[53] The 2005 elections for the national assembly followed the constitutional provisions, and although the presidential election was marred by violence and irregularities, President Pierre Nkurunziza, a Hutu, won a decisive electoral victory.[54]

The accords stipulate that corruption is grounds for presidential and legislative impeachment and that "embezzlement, corruption, extortion and misappropriation of all kinds shall be punishable in accordance with the law. Any state employee convicted of corruption shall be dismissed from the public administration following a disciplinary inquiry."[55] However, against the background of an insecure, brokered peace and a power-sharing democratic government, corruption flourishes.[56] Most people link post-conflict corruption to the weakness of the state and the destruction of the economy during the decades of violence and insecurity.[57] In Burundi, the long-running crisis gave birth to a system of impunity.[58] A recent report listed poverty as the most important factor accounting for Burundi's corruption; followed by impunity; bad governance, especially lack of transparency; lack of political will to combat corruption; and traditional practices favoring corruption.[59]

Corruption and rent-seeking in Burundi also have historical roots. Since decolonization, ethnic and regional groups have manipulated state structures for their own benefit. In particular, portions of the minority Tutsi ethnic group managed to extend the favored position that they held during the colonial era into post-colonial control over most state resources.[60] Public corporations were used to collect and distribute rents to the political elite.[61] The Tutsi-dominated military enriched themselves through the customs sector, advantageous land holdings, and private taxation of citizens.[62] Much of the enrichment occurred through the state's legal mechanisms, however, rather than through illegal payoffs. Crony capitalism gave an unfair advantage to one group and a disadvantage to the population at large through appropriation of state resources.

The advantages held by the privileged elite helped feed the violence, and it gave the formerly disadvantaged a justification for appropriating state resources for private gain in the post-conflict period. In the three previous cases discussed, the lack of a change in the group in power fueled corruption, whereas in Burundi the change in the power structure gave the Hutu an excuse to enrich themselves to compensate for prior losses. The Burundi case shows how the division of power can itself fuel a particularly destructive type of corruption in the absence of effective control measures or ethical constraints.[63]

The contestation over state power weakened the state. A by-product of the quota system is competition for private gain. According to a local anti-corruption NGO, "The weakness of the state has increased corruption. Under the authoritarian regime, corruption was repressed. . . . The crisis led to a weakness of state power and an increase in civil disobedience."[64] With the end of a conflict the old elite networks no longer operate, and there are more opportunities for illicit personal enrichment.[65] Those in power do not feel secure. Hence, many tend to grab what they can while they can.

The two-way relationship between poverty and corruption makes it harder to establish a stable peace. As Terrance Nahimana, a civil society leader, points out, "If people are healthy and wealthy today, then it will be easier to make an arrangement about the crimes of the past. It is harder to accept the present when one is hungry and sees others driving around in fancy cars."[66] As USAID states, "in Burundi's post-conflict situation, therefore, corruption not only harms recovery and reconstruction, but risks re-igniting the social conflict that has characterized so much of the country's history."[67] The weak economy makes a credible anti-corruption policy difficult.

One can then ask whether international pressure and financial aid helped or hindered the transition in Mozambique. These factors have had an extremely influential role in Burundi's history, turned on and off depending upon the political situation.[68] Trade embargos pressured the government but also "stimulated development of a strong illicit economy benefiting those with access to political power and military protection."[69] International aid was conditional on acceptance of the peace agreement and thus played a decisive and positive role in pressuring the different factions to negotiate and reach an agreement.[70]

Recognizing the need to correct the underlying conditions that favor corruption, international donors are now working with a new Burundian government that has made the fight against corruption one of its stated priorities. Its focus is the adoption and exercise of anti-corruption laws, the reform of the public procurement system, and the strengthening of institutional structures.[71] However, accomplishments so far have been limited, partly because the judiciary and the police are weak and often corrupt themselves, but it is also because the newly created anti-corruption institutions are untried and have their own limitations. Neither the executive nor the legislature has been active in concrete anti-corruption efforts.[72] The new constitution set up the framework for an Anti-Corruption Brigade and an Anti-Corruption Court.[73] Although officers have been appointed to both of these institutions, they had not yet begun to function in 2008.[74] There are two large problems. First, the process for choosing personnel was not transparent; the political parties had a role in choosing the selected individuals. Second, although the law allows for the punishment of mid-level functionaries, it does not provide for the punishment of high-level ministers.[75] Furthermore, watchdog NGOs are few in number and subject to intimidation.[76] There are no protections for those reporting corruption. "People are afraid to report certain crimes because it puts them at risk. The population is still armed, and a corrupt individual may kill the person that reports them."[77] "In this context, public officials are always afraid of change" and seek the means to protect themselves against "an uncertain future."[78]

Much of the corruption in Burundi is linked to its poverty and its weak institutions. These conditions have been made worse by the recent conflict, but the corruption itself is of a type common in many poor countries. What makes the case distinctive is the power-sharing incorporated into the peace accords that builds in a divided governmental structure in an effort to make a return to violence unappealing. As a result, the state has been unable or unwilling to create a set of clear and well-enforced rules or to limit patronage and self-dealing. Formal power sharing limits the scope for competitive politics across ethnic lines. Thus, the political compromises that helped to end the fighting make corruption particularly intractable, especially in the presence of an influx of aid.

Kosovo

Kosovo provides a final variant on the theme of corruption in post-conflict situations.[79] It is a relatively positive case in that the newly democratic institutions have led to competitive elections where corruption allegations have hurt incumbents. Kosovo is small, with a population of almost 2 million, of whom 90 percent are of Albanian background. Kosovo has no guaranteed source of foreign exchange from natural resources such as oil, and although part of Europe, its situation is in some ways closer to that of Guatemala, Burundi, or Mozambique: the war was destructive, the economic situation is poor, and local institutions are weak.[80]

Kosovo is like Burundi in that Albanian Kosovars, allied with the former fighters, now largely control the elected government inside Kosovo but have limited discretion under UN (UNMIK) and EU auspices.[81] The main structural difference is that the Serbian minority, although granted some protections, has no formal representation through quotas and, in practice, has little power.

Corruption in Kosovo is related both to its immediate past and to the influx of funds for rebuilding and humanitarian efforts. Although often beneficial, the use of outsiders as guarantors and monitors to control malfeasance has sometimes backfired; advisors from the UN authority or other bodies have sometimes participated in corruption themselves.

Surveys show that perceptions of corruption are high for many state institutions, but individuals reportedly experience low levels of corruption in their daily lives.[82] The power authority, the privatization agency, and the Kosovo Central Administration rank as most corrupt. When the respondents were asked about their personal experience with corruption, however, only 6 percent of Kosovar Albanians and 7 percent of Kosovar Serbs stated that bribes were solicited from them in exchange for access to public services. The statistics show a steady downward trend since the peak in March 2005 when the percentage of actual corruption reported by respondents reached 23 percent.[83]

The gap between perceptions and experience may capture the distinction between high-level corruption and low-level payoffs that directly affect ordinary citizens. Media reports affect perceptions, and if such reports are to be believed, corruption is a serious problem at the top of the Kosovo government. Furthermore, the inability of the law enforcement and justice authorities to prosecute thoroughly and adjudicate cases of corruption enhances public distrust. Most prosecutions involved low-level bureaucrats.

The Milosevic regime's denial of public services to the majority Albanian population made corruption a necessary condition of daily life. In practice, the public services that were officially denied to Kosovar Albanians were for sale. This entrenched a culture of corruption in Kosovo, limited its moral stigma, and increased public tolerance of corruption. After the establishment of the UN protectorate, the gap left by the Milosevic regime was to some extent filled by criminals who presented themselves as members of the Kosovo Liberation Army. The sense of impunity felt by these people was fed by the Kosovars' general distrust of the judiciary, which in large part consisted of judges and prosecutors who served under the unpopular Yugoslav justice system—the regime against which most of these "heroes" had fought.[84]

Present day perceptions of corruption also reflect the inefficiency and ineffectiveness of various public institutions since the end of the conflict, which may or may not be due to corruption.[85] It is impossible to disentangle perceptions of corruption from simple inefficiency and waste, but corruption does appear to be part of the story for both the power authority and the privatization agency.[86] Other cases of corruption and official misconduct detected by the Office of the Auditor General were not followed up either by UNMIK or by local law enforcement authorities.

However, on the positive side, allegations of corruption and mismanagement, widely publicized in the media, were effectively utilized by the opposition parties, which in 2005 launched an aggressive campaign to discredit the ruling coalition. Moreover, the coalition parties also came under immense pressure from the international community. When the international community authorized talks for the settlement of Kosovo's status, these internal problems became especially salient as Kosovo sought to justify its claim for statehood. During this period, the opposition focused on several incidents that were effective in discrediting the main figures of the governing coalition. These scandals led to a political upheaval with the election of Agim Ceku as prime minister. He had led the Kosovo Liberation Army through the end of the conflict. As a professional soldier not affiliated with any political party, his nomination was an effort by coalition partners to boost the government's credibility.

Nevertheless, in spite of the political salience of corruption, reform will not be easy given the post-conflict legacy of weak institutions. However, a series of institutional improvements reflect the collaboration between the UN and local professionals to implement reforms that might otherwise have been politically difficult. Those reforms include judicial and prosecutorial changes, and the creation of audit and anti-corruption agencies.[87]

Kosovo's unresolved political status significantly exacerbated the extent of corruption in Kosovo's institutions between 1999 and 2006. Unclear lines of accountability and the lack of a precise division of responsibilities between local and international institutions made it very hard to hold public officials accountable. Hence, the early years under this system of government were characterized by high levels of corruption. A qualitative change occurred when the process for the resolution of Kosovo's final status began. Politicians and the society in general, under scrutiny from the international community, had an incentive to show that they were capable of establishing and maintaining a society based on the rule of law. Moreover, the opposition parties recognized the mounting civic dissatisfaction with the corrupt practices of the first three governments and capitalized on this discontent by prioritizing the fight against corruption. This produced results in the 2007 elections, and the newly elected government has proposed a revised anti-corruption strategy that went before the legislature in late 2008.[88]

Despite a rocky inception, Kosovo is beginning to control corruption through a combination of enhanced democratic accountability and outside influence. Although the first round of leaders may have operated with impunity, the press reported corruption scandals freely; these reports affected public opinion, and this disclosure led to the resignation and the removal of the implicated politicians. Weaknesses in the operations of prosecutors and the judiciary, however, are only now being addressed.

The presence of outsiders with both legal and financial clout has been a mixed blessing especially because some UNMIK-appointed individuals ended up succumbing to corrupt opportunities themselves. However, UNMIK does appear to have had a positive impact on democratic reform and on the creation of accountability and oversight institutions. Now that Kosovo is independent, UNMIK is expected to be replaced with an EU mission (justice, police, and customs) that will have a narrower mandate, building on the lessons learned from UNMIK.[89]

Kosovo politicians recognize that the fight against corruption is an issue that can help get them elected. Because the Kosovar Albanians are in control of the government, except in the few Serbian-dominated areas, elections can be fought on the grounds of policy and personal integrity, not ethnic allegiances. Furthermore, the peace-building process included efforts to improve institutions of oversight and control that, although imperfect, do function. Corruption has become a topic of public debate and criticism, and those who commit improprieties are punished at the polls.

Conclusion and Reform Proposals

Given these disparate but interlocking cases, what can one learn about the control of corruption in states emerging from domestic conflict? The goal is a well-functioning system in which violence is seldom intertwined with politics and where allegations of corrupt self-dealing lead to political consequences. In such a system, revelations of corruption may tip the balance against incumbents who are implicated in the wrongdoing. In contrast, if democracy is entwined with endemic corruption and public order is less well established, elections can be an opportunity for violence against opponents, individualized payoffs to voters, and corrupt payoffs to politicians.

Much has been made of the importance of "political will" and moral leadership at the top in establishing effective governments in post-conflict settings, but strong leadership and good morals are not sufficient. Political will by itself can breed autocracy. Too much moralizing risks degenerating into empty rhetoric—or worse, witch hunts against political opponents. Policy must address the underlying conditions that create corrupt incentives, or it will have no long-lasting effects.

Peace-building strategies must avoid triggering vicious spirals. Giving monopoly power to a few prominent people to jumpstart the economy may produce a society that is both lacking in competition and unequal. Early stage decisions can lock in this power for a small elite whose vested interests hold back efforts to increase competition and enhance fairness. Although it may be risky and difficult to counter corruption in post-conflict peace-building, if the problem is allowed to fester, it can undermine other efforts to create a stable, well-functioning state with popular legitimacy. Conversely, an open-ended free market solution in a state that lacks basic government capacity can lead to widespread competitive corruption as individuals and firms seek to evade the laws, "reinterpret" the laws in their favor, or simply avoid their strictures.

In post-conflict situations, policy recommendations that concentrate only on macro-economic aggregates are pointless. No growth can occur unless institutions are restored to a minimal level of competency. Corruption is a symptom that state and society relations are dysfunctional, undermining the legitimacy of the state and leading to wasteful public policies. Good policies are unlikely to be chosen or to be carried out effectively without honest institutions.

The five cases outlined herein provide a range of experiences with corruption in state building after civil war and widespread domestic violence. In Guatemala, Angola, and Mozambique the old elite retained power after the conflict. In Guatemala and Angola those elites were widely viewed as corrupt during the conflict. In Guatemala in the post-conflict period the elite benefited from links with organized crime involved mainly in the drug trade. In Angola the sources of wealth are oil and, to a lesser extent, diamonds, which benefit top officials and well-connected families through a series of opaque financial arrangements. In both countries these sources of wealth help keep entrenched corrupt networks in place and limit the development both of competitive

politics and of transparent and effective oversight and law enforcement institutions. These are cases where the lack of political will at the top limits anti-
corruption efforts, even given international pressures.

Mozambique had an increase in corruption after peace was achieved, but
this did not arise from the prior corruption of those in power. Rather it came
from the increase in opportunities created by the end of hostilities and by the
turn to a market economy, both within the context of a weak state. The use of
donor funds to pay off the former rebels and ease RENAMO's transition to a
political party may have been an effective way to end the violence, but it also
provided a way to use public money for private gain that may have made subsequent anti-corruption efforts less credible.

The empirical issue that was raised by the case of Mozambique was
whether its payments to RENAMO were a worthwhile price to pay for peace,
or whether the former rebels were simply bluffing for private gain. Did the
UN's strategy of buying peace, even if successful, lay the foundation for
entrenched corruption? How should the international community weigh the
benefits of a brokered end to violence against the risk of creating an environment of impunity? Such payments seem a necessary, if unpleasant, policy in
some cases, but the UN should structure such payments so that they do the
least damage. The emphasis should be on lump-sum payments, not arrangements that permit recipients to demand a share of the revenues from some
ongoing public enterprise or tax.

In Burundi and Kosovo, former anti-regime fighters gained control of the
government with formal power sharing in Burundi and Albanian dominance
in Kosovo. The former has led to a weak state with widespread competition
for illicit, private gain. The latter has begun to produce competitive politics
within the Albanian population that penalizes corrupt officials at the polls.
Kosovo is also beginning to establish oversight institutions that, although
beset by start-up problems, seem to play a positive role. Burundi has few such
institutions and is unable to provide many constraints on corrupt actors. The
country's poverty limits the available options.

Thus, corruption was and is part of the post-conflict situation in all of
these cases, but two distinct situations seem to be most troubling. The first is
the entrenchment of an old elite with access to significant rents, as in Angola
and Guatemala. At least in Angola with a reformed government, the rents
from oil and diamonds could theoretically be put to good use inside the state.
This is not true for organized crime proceeds in Guatemala, which depend
upon the corrupt use of the police, the customs authorities, and the army. The
second situation is a formal power-sharing deal among multiple groups where

politicians have no incentive to use corruption scandals as a way to achieve power. Rather, as in Burundi, the corruption of one group with a guaranteed share of power simply encourages other groups that are part of the brokered peace deal to seek personal enrichment as well. Mozambique and Kosovo are more hopeful cases. In the former, corruption appears to be a feature of the transition so that the main concern is avoiding a vicious spiral originating in particular conditions of the post-conflict transition. In the latter, in spite of high-level corruption scandals, some involving UN personnel, combating corruption does seem to be of political and public salience, with competitive elections providing a check on private malfeasance in a way that is lacking in the other cases.

These cases suggest some comprehensive lessons. First, peace agreements should incorporate measures to limit corruption. Negotiators might have the leverage to push through anti-corruption reforms, such as establishing an anti-corruption court, that might not be feasible later.

Second, as far as possible, peace negotiation processes should not be viewed as a way to divide the rents of state control among the different factions. Transitional governments are frequently constrained by the need to reach a compromise among various groups. The compromise may end the violence but may entrench or create corrupt structures. If well-resourced, international peacekeepers may be able to create a space in which reform can occur.[90]

Third, anti-corruption efforts need some early and visible victories and must fit the capacities of the country. Start simple. For example, be sure primary systems of financial control inside agencies are in place before creating secondary bodies such as anti-corruption commissions.[91]

Fourth, international aid can create incentives for corruption and hence needs to be audited and controlled. However, aid that is too strictly conditioned impedes the state from developing its own agenda and can hamper the consolidation of power.[92] One option for international actors is to use trust funds to administer aid programs with the ultimate goal of turning over such programs to the government. For example, the Afghan Reconstruction Trust Fund, operated by the World Bank, channels funds from twenty-four countries to the Afghan government.[93] In Mozambique, a trust that funds political parties accepts foreign donations.[94]

Fifth, as in Mozambique, international bodies can help to buy off rebels who can threaten a return to violence or dislodge corrupt incumbents. Doing so may involve arranging exile for former leaders or helping to incorporate them and their followers into the new state as political parties. Deeply corrupt leaders, however, should be exiled, not incorporated into the government.[95]

Sixth, international donors can help to review the training and integrity of law enforcement officers, military personnel, judges, and prosecutors. If these groups carry over from the old regime, they may be disinclined or unable to prosecute the corruption of that regime. Training and ethnic balance are especially important as this sector must ultimately be able to investigate and prosecute corruption charges in an even-handed manner. International aid can also help integrate former rank and file combatants with financial aid and training.

Seventh, local people must be involved in oversight, and safe havens need to be provided for whistleblowers. Protection for whistleblowers is especially important if societal violence is still prevalent. However, self-help vigilantes should be replaced with regular police. The armed forces' and other security services' ability to participate in legal businesses, to engage in illegal businesses, and to accept kickbacks should all be restricted.

Eighth, institutions of oversight need strengthening in most post-conflict states, but this may be a difficult task in the face of personnel with limited training. Nevertheless, both financial aid and foreign personnel can help to create bodies to administer a freedom of information law, to audit and monitor government spending, and to strengthen the independence of prosecutors and courts. The goal, of course, is to improve the capacity and independence of domestic actors so that foreign assistance can be cut back.

Finally, at the global level, organizations should work to develop stronger international controls on money laundering so as to make it difficult to export corrupt gains. Similarly, voluntary international initiatives, such as the Extractive Industries Transparency Initiative, represent promising experiments that deserve support as well as independent analyses of their effectiveness. Even in a resource-rich country such as Angola, such initiatives may have an effect if supported by multi-national investors.

Strong leadership from the top is needed as a post-conflict state moves toward the goal of a more legitimate and better functioning government and sidelines those who have used the state as a tool for private gain. International assistance can, in principle, help, but it needs to be tailored to avoid exacerbating the underlying problems created by the mixture of corruption and threats of violence from those inside and outside the government.

Notes

1. Alex J. Boucher, William J. Durch, Margaret Midyette, Sarah Rose, and Jason Terry, *Mapping and Fighting Corruption in War-Torn States* (Washington, D.C., 2007), 11–23.

2. See Tiri's website at www.tiri.org for additional cases (accessed 8 February 2008).

3. This section is based on a memo prepared by Jael Humphrey, Yale University. More details are in Rose-Ackerman, "Corruption and Post-Conflict Peace-Building," 411–421. Transparency International's 2007 Corruption Perceptions Index gives Guatemala a score of 2.8 out of 10.

4. Accion Ciudadana, *La Corrupción en Guatemala* (Guatamala City, 1999), 12.

5. Edelberto Torres, Accion Cuidadana, *El Sistema Nacional de Integridad en Guatemala* [The National Integrity System in Guatemala] (Berlin, 2001), available at www.transparency.org/content/download/1650/8371/file/guatemala.pdf (accessed 30 September 2008).

6. Giorleny D. Altamirano, "The Impact of the Inter-American Convention against Corruption," *Inter-American Law Review*, XXXVIII (2006–2007), 487–548, 538–539.

7. Rachel Sieder, Megan Thomas, George Viskers, and Jack Spence, *Who Governs? Guatemala Five Years After the Peace Accords* (Washington, D.C., 2002), available at www.hemisphereinitiatives.org/whogoverns.pdf (accessed 30 September 2008).

8. Global Advice Network, Business Anti-Corruption Portal, *Guatemala Country Profile,* available at www.business-anti-corruption.com/normal.asp?pageid=321 (assessed 22 July 2008).

9. Sieder and others, *Who Governs?* 32; U.S. Department of State, *Background Note: Guatemala* (2008), available at www.state.gov/r/pa/ei/bgn/2045.htm (accessed 30 September 2008).

10. Sieder and others, *Who Governs?* 39.

11. Maria Gonzalez de Asis, "Borrador Guatemala Reforma Judicial y Corrupción," Draft Guatemala Judicial Reform and Corruption (Washington, D.C., 1998), available at www.worldbank.org/wbi/governance/guatemala/pdf/guat_judrefcorr.pdf (accessed 30 September 2008).

12. Sieder and others, *Who Governs?* 35.

13. Guatemalan Commission for Historical Clarification (CEH), paragraphs 7 and 21.

14. Carlos Menocal, "Fondo de victimas de la guerra usado para Stan: Monto estaba por irse a fondo comun, debido a falta de ejecucion," *Prensa Libre* (20 March 2006), available at http://prensalibre.com/pl/2006/marzo/20/137330.html (accessed 30 September 2008); Network in Solidarity with the People of Guatemala, "Prioritize War Victims over Former Paramilitaries" (2004), available at www.nisgua.org/get_involved/speakers_tour/profit/tour_actions/Prioritize%20War%20Victims.pdf (accessed 30 September 2008); CEH, *Guatemala,* paragraph 28; Julieta Sandoval, "Pago a ex PAC con bonos del Tesoro," *Prensa Libre* (4 November 2004), available at http://prensalibre. com/pl/2004/noviembre/04/100860.html (accessed 30 September 2008).

15. U.S. Department of State, Bureau of International Narcotics and Law Enforcement Affairs, *International Narcotics Control Strategy Report, Country Reports 2007* (2007), available at www.state.gov/p/inl/rls/nrcrpt/2007/vol2/html/80887.htm

(accessed 30 September 2008); U.S. Department of State, *International Narcotics Control Strategy Report 2003: Canada, Mexico, and Central America* (2004), available at www.state.gov/p/inl/rls/nrcrpt/2003/vol1/html/29833.htm (accessed 30 September 2008); U.S. Department of State, Bureau of Western Hemisphere Affairs, *Background Note: Guatemala* (2007), available at www.state.gov/r/pa/ei/bgn/2045.htm (accessed 30 September 2008).

16. Sieder and others, *Who Governs?* 11.

17. Ibid.

18. Amnesty International, *Guatemala: Human Rights Activists Under Renewed Attack in 2005*, AI Index: AMR 34/007/2005 (2005), available at http://web.amnesty.org/library/Index/ENGAMR340072005 (accessed 30 September 2008).

19. Global Integrity, *2006 Country Report: Guatemala* (2006), available at www.globalintegrity.org/reports/2006/GUATEMALA/timeline.cfm (accessed 30 September 2008).

20. Sieder and others, *Who Governs?* 11.

21. The section on Angola was researched by Rodrigo Pagini de Souza, Yale Law School. More details are in Rose-Ackerman, "Corruption and Post-Conflict Peace-Building," 421–428; Tony Hodges, *Angola: Anatomy of an Oil State* (Bloomington, 2004), 21; Human Rights Watch, *World Report 2001*, available at www.hrw.org/wr2k1/africa/angola.html (accessed 30 September 2008).

22. Robert I. Rotberg and Rachel M. Gisselquist, *Strengthening African Governance: Ibrahim Index of African Governance, Results and Rankings 2008* (Cambridge, MA, 2008), available at http://belfercenter.ksg.harvard.edu/project/52/intrastate_conflict_program.html?page_id=223 (accessed 20 April 2009).

23. CIA, *The World Factbook—Angola* (2008), available at www.cia.gov/library/publications/the-world-factbook/print/ao.html (accessed 30 September 2008).

24. Economist Intelligence Unit, *Angola: Country Report* (2003), in Human Rights Watch (HRW), *Some Transparency, No Accountability: The Use of Oil Revenues in Angola and its Impact on Human Rights*, XVI (2004), 43.

25. HRW, *Some Transparency, No Accountability*, 44.

26. International Monetary Fund (IMF), *Angola Staff Report for the 2002 Article IV Consultation* (Washington, D.C., 2002), 31–33; IMF, *Angola: Selected Issues and Statistical Appendix* (Washington, D.C., 2003), 107–108, in HRW, *Some Transparency, No Accountability*, 33, 44–45.

27. An audit by KPMG in 2002 found a discrepancy of 2.0 to 2.6 billion dollars between the oil revenues claimed by the Ministry of Finance and those deposited in the Central Bank. KPMG, *Current Assessment of the Angolan Petroleum Sector: Inspection Report by KPMG for the Ministry of Finance, Government of Angola [Oil Diagnostic Report]* (Luanda, 2002). The report, performed under an IMF contract, was never formally released, but HRW obtained a copy (HRW, *Some Transparency, No Accountability*, 21–23, 27).

28. HRW, *Some Transparency, No Accountability*, 47–48.

29. Hodges, *Angola*, 131–138.

30. Ibid., 140.

31. Philippe Le Billon, "Buying Peace or Fueling War: The Role of Corruption in Armed Conflicts," *Journal of International Development,* XV (2003), 413–426; Hodges, *Angola,* 2.

32. IMF, *Angola: Staff Report for the 2007 Article IV Consultation* (Washington, D.C., 2007).

33. Information on the EITI is available at www.eitransparency.org (accessed 30 September 2008).

34. IMF, *Angola,* 10.

35. Of the seven companies surveyed, "only Chevron Texaco disclosed details of a payment with the agreement of the Government of Angola." Save the Children, *Beyond the Rhetoric: Measuring Revenue Transparency* (2005), 23, available at http://archive.revenuewatch.org/reports/pwyp032805c.shtml (accessed 30 September 2008).

36. IMF, *Angola,* 4–5, 14.

37. I thank Rodrigo Pagini de Sousa, Yale University Law School, for research on this case and Caroline Gross for comments on an earlier draft.

38. A. Mark Weisburd, *Use of Force: The Practice of States Since World War II* (University Park, 1997), 199; Pamela L. Reed, "The Politics of Reconciliation: The United Nations Operation in Mozambique," in William J. Durch (ed.), *UN Peacekeeping, American Politics, and the Uncivil Wars of the 1990s* (New York, 1996), 301–302; Michael Wesley, *Casualties of the New World Order: The Causes of Failure of UN Missions to Civil Wars* (New York, 1997), 87–88, 92, 95.

39. Malyn Newitt, "Mozambique," in Patrick Chabal and others (eds.), *A History of Postcolonial Lusophone Africa* (Bloomington, 2002), 185–235, 222.

40. James Dobbins, Seth G. Jones, Keith Crane, Andrew Rathmell, Brett Steele, Richard Teltschik, and Anga Timilsina, *The UN's Role in Nation Building: From the Congo to Iraq* (Santa Monica, 2005), 100, 104.

41. Adriano Nuvunga and Marcelo Mosse, *Reconstruction National Integrity System Survey* (Vancouver, 2007), 11–14, available at www.tiri.org/images/stories/NIR%20Countries%20%20Researches/Mozambique/Reconstruction%20National%20Integrity%20System%20Survey%20Mozambique.pdf (accessed 30 September 2008). As RENAMO's negotiator stated on 16 June 1992, there is "no democracy without money." Quoted in Nuvunga and Mosse, *Reconstruction,* 11.

42. Reed, "The Politics of Reconciliation," 285.

43. Ibid., 301.

44. Dr. Armindo Correia, former general secretary of the Electoral Administration Technical Secretariat, quoted in Nuvunga amd Mosse, *Reconstruction,* 15.

45. Clara Ana de Sousa and José Sulemane, "Mozambique's Growth Performance," in J. Ndulu Benno, and others (eds.), *The Political Economy of Economic Growth in Africa, 1960–2000, Volume 2: Country Case Studies* (Cambridge, 2008), 167–195.

46. M. A. Pitcher, *Transforming Mozambique: The Politics of Privatization, 1975–2000* (New York, 2002), 236–264.

47. IMF, *Country Report No. 07/258* (Washington, D.C., 2007), 5, 20.

48. Michel Cahen, "Nationalism and Ethnicities: Lessons from Mozambique," in Einar Braathen, Morten Bøås, and Gjermund Sæther (eds.), *Ethnicity Kills? The Politics of War, Peace, and Ethnicity in Sub-Saharan Africa* (New York, 2000), 163–187; David Stavasage, "Causes and Consequences of Corruption: Mozambique in Transition," in Alan Doig and Robin Theobald (eds.), *Corruption and Democratisation* (Portland, 2000), 65–97, 65–66.

49. Stavasage, "Causes and Consequences," 70–75. See also Marcelo Mosse, *Corruption and Reform in the Customs in Mozambique* (Vancouver, 2007), available at www.tiri.org/images/stories/NIR%20Countries%20%20Researches/Mozambique/ Mozambique%20Customs%20Case%20Study.pdf (accessed 30 September 2008).

50. Nuvunga and Mosse, *Reconstruction*, 22–23.

51. Ibid., 24, 33–81.

52. Jael Humphrey researched this section, including interviews in December 2007 and January 2008. International Crisis Group, "Burundi: Finalising Peace With the FNL," *Africa Report 131* (Brussels, 2007).

53. Romana Schweiger, "Late Justice for Burundi," *International and Comparative Law Quarterly*, LV (2006), 653, 654; Matthias Goldmann, "Does Peace Follow Justice or Vice Versa? Plans for Postconflict Justice in Burundi," *Fletcher Forum of World Affairs*, XXX (2006), 137; Kristina A. Bentley and Roger Southall, *An African Peace Process: Mandela, South Africa, and Burundi* (Cape Town, 2005), 32–43.

54. Filip Reyntjens, "Briefing: Burundi: A Peaceful Transition After a Decade Of War?" *African Affairs*, CV (2006), 117–135.

55. United States Institute for Peace, "Arusha Peace and Reconciliation Agreement for Burundi," Protocol II, Article 10 (2000), available at www.usip.org/library/pa/ burundi/pa_burundi_08282000_pr2ch1.html (accessed 30 September 2008).

56. Interview between Jael Humphrey and Pierre Claver Mbonimpa, founding president, Association Burundaise pour la Protection des Droits Humains et des Personnes Détenues (APRODH), in Bujumbura, Burundi (18 December 2007); Interview between Jael Humphrey and five of the twelve members of the executive committee including Gabriel Rufyiri, president, Observatoire de Lutte Contre la Corruption el les Malversation Economique (OLUCOME), in Bujumbura, Burundi (18 December 2007).

57. Interview between Jael Humphrey and Terrance Nahimana, president, Cercle d'initiative pour une vision commune (CIVIC), in Bujumbura, Burundi (18 December 2007).

58. OLUCOME interview (18 December 2007).

59. International Alert Gradis, *Le Phénomène de la Corruption au Burundi: Revolte Silencieuse et Resignation* (Bujumbura, 2007), 26.

60. Not all Tutsi shared equally. A group of Tutsi from one clan maintained a virtual monopoly over military and political power. International Crisis Group, "A Framework for Responsible Aid to Burundi," *Africa Report 57* (Brussels, 2003), 6.

61. Janvier D. Nkurunziza and Floribert Ngaruko, "Why Has Burundi Grown So Slowly? The Political Economy of Redistribution," in J. Ndulu Benno and others (eds.), *The Political Economy*, 51–85.

62. Bentley and Southall, *An African Peace Process*, 179–180.

63. Nkurunziza and Ngaruko, "Why Has Burundi Grown So Slowly?" 75. Interview between Jael Humphrey and a senior UN Human Rights official, in Bujumbura, Burundi (21 December 2007).

64. OLUCOME interview (18 December 2007).

65. UN Human Rights official interview (21 December 2007).

66. Nahimana interview (18 December 2007).

67. USAID, *Fighting Corruption and Restoring Accountability in Burundi* (Arlington, 2006), 3.

68. Bentley and Southall, *An African Peace Process*, 50.

69. Ibid., 7, quoting Rubin Lund and Hara Lund, "Learning from Burundi's Failed Democratic Transition, 1993–1996," in Council on Foreign Relations (ed.), *Cases and Strategies for Preventive Action* (Washington, D.C., 1998), 68, 80.

70. Bentley and Southall, *An African Peace Process*, 82, 116.

71. International Alert Gradis, *Le Phénomène*, 7, 26.

72. U.S. Department of State, Bureau of Democracy, Human Rights, and Labor, *Country Reports on Human Rights Practices: Burundi 2006* (Washington, D.C., 2007) [hereinafter *Burundi*], available at www.state.gov/g/drl/rls/hrrpt/2006/78722.htm (accessed 30 September 2008).

73. The minister of good governance, the highest official in charge of combating corruption, has changed twice this year. Ndayimirije and UN Human Rights official interviews (21 December 2007).

74. Ndayimirije interview (18 December 2007).

75. Ibid.

76. Gabriel Rufyiri, president of OLUCOME, was detained for four months in 2006 on defamation charges after he denounced government corruption. He was eventually released and acquitted (U. S. Department of State, *Burundi*).

77. Ndayimirije interview (18 December 2007).

78. Michael Masabo, *Country Review of Legal and Practical Challenges to the Domestication of the Anti-Corruption Conventions in Burundi* (Bujumbura, 2006).

79. This section was informed by research help from Dastid Pallaska, Yale University Law School. More details are in Rose-Ackerman "Corruption and Post-Conflict Peace-Building," 428–439.

80. Richard Sannerholm, "Legal, Judicial and Administrative Reforms in Post-Conflict Situations: Beyond the Rule of Law Template," *Journal of Conflict and Security Law*, XII (2007), 65–94, 70–71.

81. Comprehensive Plan for the Kosovo Status Settlement S/2007/168/Add, available at www.unosek.org/docref/Comprehensive_proposal-english.pdf (accessed 30 September 2008), 52–60.

82. United Nations Development Programme, "Kosovo Early Warning Report 17, April–June 2007" (New York, 2007), 30.

83. Ibid.

84. The American Bar Association (ABA) Rule of Law Initiative, *The Legal Profession Reform Index for Kosovo* (Washington, D.C., 2007), 3–8.

85. European Agency for Reconstruction "From Reconstruction to Reform, European Commission Support to the Energy Sector" (2006), available at www.ear. europa.eu/sectors/main/sec-energy.htm (accessed 30 September 2008).

86. In 2003, one of KEK's top managers, a UN-appointed official, was convicted in his native Germany of misappropriating €3.9 million from the KEK budget. Kosovar Stability Initiative, "Reconstruction Survey" (Prishtinë, 2007), 31.

87. ABA Rule of Law Initiative, *The Legal Profession Reform Index,* 3; UNMIK Regulations 2005/52, "On the Establishment of the Kosovo Judicial Council" (New York, 2005); UNMIK Administrative Instruction 2006/18, "Implementing UNMIK Regulation 2006/25 on a Regulatory Framework for the Justice System in Kosovo" (New York, 2006); Comprehensive Proposal for Kosovo Status Settlement, Annex IV Justice System, Article 3. Administrative Direction 2006/15 "On the Establishment of the Kosovo Special Prosecutors Office" (New York, 2006); U.S. Department of State, *2006 Country Reports on Human Rights Practices, Kosovo* (Washington, D.C., 2007), available at www.state.gov/g/drl/rls/hrrpt/2006/78837.htm (accessed 30 September 2008).

88. Mentor Borovci, "Challenges to Implementation of Anti-Corruption Activities in Kosovo: Kosovo Anti-Corruption Agency" (powerpoint presentation), available at http://europeandcis.undp.org/governance/parac/show/2785BD56-F203-1EE9-B79AD DA8D8DE4B1D (accessed 30 September 2008).

89. The planned transfer is being delayed by Russian and Serbian objections in the UN. "Kosovo's Future: Divided Rule," *Economist* (29 May 2008), 55. On 17 February 2008, the Kosovo Assembly adopted a Declaration of Independence. Countries that have recognized Kosovo's declaration are available at www.kosovothanksyou.com (accessed 30 September 2008).

90. Madalene O'Donnell, "Corruption: A Rule of Law Agenda," in Agnès Hurwitz and Reyko Huang (eds.), *Civil War and the Rule of Law: Security, Development, Human Rights* (Boulder, 2006), 225–260.

91. Ibid.

92. Mick Moore, "Death without Taxes: Democracy, State Capacity and Aid Dependence in the Fourth World," in Mark Robinson and Gordon Whites (eds.), *The Democratic Developmental State: Politics and Institutional Design* (New York, 1998), 84–121.

93. Lorenzo Delesgues and Yama Torabi, *Reconstruction National Integrity System Survey Afghanistan 2007* (Tiri, 2007), 17.

94. O'Donnell, "Corruption," 249.

95. Le Billon, "Buying Peace or Fueling War," 423.

KELLY M. GREENHILL

5

Kleptocratic Interdependence:
Trafficking, Corruption, and the
Marriage of Politics and Illicit Profits

On 23 April 2008, United States Attorney General Michael Mukasey offered a stark and foreboding assessment of the rising threat from international organized crime, asserting that the new global criminals are "more sophisticated, they are richer, they have greater influence over government and political institutions worldwide . . . and [they] are far more involved in our everyday lives than many people appreciate. . . . [Consequently], we can't ignore criminal syndicates in other countries on the naïve assumption that they are a danger only in their homeland, whether it is located in Eurasia, Africa, or anywhere else."[1]

Mukasey's troubling portents echo a growing chorus of prognostications regarding the unprecedented (and transnational) dangers associated with criminality today.[2] But, how fundamentally new and different is "organized crime" in today's increasingly globalized world?[3] How extensive are the ostensibly expanding links between international organized crime and domestic, state-based corruption? How significant a threat do such links pose, and under what conditions? Finally, why—since, as the conventional wisdom suggests, corruption and criminality are most likely to thrive where governance is weakest—are the majority of the world's significant transnational criminal networks actually based in more highly functioning states?

Even today, the connections between international criminal organizations, and between them and their host governments, in the post–Cold War period remain poorly understood. A decade and a half ago Williams suggested that

The author thanks Peter Andreas, Johann Graf Lambsdorff, Corbin Lyday, Ben Oppenheim, Robert Rotberg, and participants at a pair of workshops, sponsored by the American Academy of Arts and Sciences and the Program on Intrastate Conflict and Conflict Resolution at Harvard's Kennedy School of Government for valuable comments and suggestions on earlier versions of this chapter. The author also thanks Jarrod Niebloom for research assistance.

the difficulties facing analysts were two-fold. First, there were little reliable data upon which to draw. This problem was exacerbated by the fact that the relevant connections and relationships were developing and mutating so rapidly that they were outstripping observers' abilities to identify and explain them. Second, there were few extant models upon which to draw in conceptualizing the nature of these illicit linkages.[4] This chapter does not claim to have solved the data problem.[5] However, by drawing upon a cross-national sample of scholars' and practitioners' insights and observations regarding the world's most significant transnational criminal organizations and their domestic and international alliances, this theory-building chapter offers a new model that aims to sharpen our understanding of the nature of the aforementioned connections and their implications.[6]

Specifically, this chapter posits that the available, albeit case-specific, evidence suggests that the nature of the changes we have witnessed in the post–Cold War world are more quantitative than qualitative. In the aggregate, the problem of international organized crime (and associated corruption) *is* likely bigger and more threatening. But the nature of international organized crime is not fundamentally new or different.[7] Moreover, while the links between transnational criminal organizations (TCOs) and corruption are real and substantial, their effects across countries are highly variable, both in degree and in consequence. In the most egregious cases, the relationships between criminals and corrupt officials may assume an advanced form of what this author terms "kleptocratic interdependence"—namely, a set of profit- and power-driven, self-reinforcing domestic and international relationships between criminal groups and government officials. In its most basic form, criminals provide financial succor to receptive (would-be) political leaders, who, once in power, in turn strive to protect those providing their largesse. These activities concomitantly serve to strengthen and enrich both the criminals and the corrupt politicians, helping them to consolidate their power while heightening their mutual dependency.[8] In more advanced forms, TCOs may actually share the functions of sovereignty with the state. It is these relationships and their consequences upon which this chapter focuses.

These symbiotic and strategic interrelationships are likewise not new. However, in our new so-called "flattened" world, they unfortunately provide TCOs with novel economic and political opportunities to exploit as well as with a prominence that allows them to threaten both national and international security in myriad ways.[9] Again, this is not to say that the threat that TCOs pose, and, by extension, what is needed to combat them, is novel or unique. This statement may strike an informed reader as self-evident. Yet it is a point worth reiterating because there is a persistent, if misguided, tendency to treat transnational crime as a kind of monolithic global conspiracy. Doing so can be "particularly appealing because it suggests—implicitly at least—that a threat to international security may be emerging that is a worthy successor to the challenge posed by the Soviet Union during the Cold War."[10] When this threat is coupled with claims about the "unprecedented dangers" posed by terrorism, it can be particularly alluring, if equally misguided. This chapter, therefore, also differentiates between the nature and gravity of the threats that these relationships pose to weak and transitional states and those that they pose to more highly functioning democracies—the headquarters of choice for many prominent international criminal organizations.

The Origins of Kleptocratic Interdependence

Though organized crime has existed for centuries, the perception that it represents a security threat, and particularly an international threat, is a relatively new phenomenon. Instead, organized crime has traditionally been seen as a domestic problem that afflicted a relatively small number of states such as Italy, the United States, and Japan.[11] This recent perceptual shift may be largely attributed to the increased scale and scope of illicit activities perpetrated by TCOs. TCOs' growth and expansion are widely argued to be a consequence of their successful acquisition of the means and systems historically monopolized by nation-states, but deregulated by globalization, de-territorialized by the rise of free trade areas in Europe and North America, and democratized by the end of the Cold War and the collapse of the Soviet Union.

Broadly defined, TCOs comprise "structured groups that exist for an extended period of time, the members of which act in concert with the aim of earning profits or controlling markets, internal or foreign, by means of violence, intimidation or corruption, both in furtherance of criminal activity and in order to infiltrate the legitimate economy."[12] TCOs can be found in a wide variety of countries and may manifest themselves in myriad disparate guises.[13] From the infamous and rigidly hierarchical Italian and American mafias to lesser-known groups that have arisen in post-Soviet republics and other transitional states, TCOs differ greatly in structure and functionality, as well as in the various economic, political, and social conditions under which they develop. Nevertheless, virtually all tangible objects, commodities, and services in TCO transactions are likely to have significant economic value.[14] Illicit activities commonly attributed to TCOs include the production and trafficking of illicit drugs, illegal weapons transfers, human trafficking and migrant smuggling, vehicle theft and smuggling, organ trafficking, money laundering, and tax evasion—in short, an array of illegal commercial activities that fall well outside the legitimate economy.[15]

Yet TCOs cannot operate in a vacuum, nor can they operate exclusively in the illicit realm. TCOs, particularly those involved in illicit trafficking, require the assistance, or at least the tacit acquiescence, of actors within legitimate governmental and economic systems in order to function effectively and efficiently (e.g., to avoid detection of cross-border illicit and illegal flows; to forestall arrests and undermine legal cases, when apprehensions do occur; to launder profits so that they can be transferred into the licit economy and invested; and to legitimate their activities). Moreover, even that which composes the "illegal market" within a country can materially affect a criminal group's security and profitability.[16] Consequently, to minimize risk and simultaneously maximize profit, corruption is an invaluable tool for TCOs.[17]

The World Bank defines corruption as "the abuse of public office for private gain," which translates into "charging an illicit price for a service of using the power of office to further illicit aims."[18] However, public office can be abused for private benefit even if no bribery occurs through patronage and nepotism, the theft of state assets, or the diversion of state resources. Regardless of corruption's specific nature, it effectively "blurs the line" between states and TCOs. Corruption offers criminal groups the means to penetrate markets with relatively low transaction costs and then to exploit those markets largely unregulated, while presenting public officials with compelling inducements to further TCOs' illicit aims.[19]

Transnational trade- or trafficking-related corruption tends to manifest itself in two distinct forms: 1) as a failure to control illicit trade; and 2) as direct participation in this trade. In its simplest form, a failure to control is a crime of *omission,* in which state officials neglect to fulfill their supervisory duties. This type of corruption may be found at three different levels of law enforcement: the police or military, the judicial, and the penal. At the police or military level, "consent" is granted to the organization freely to carry out its illicit activities; in some cases, traffickers will pay officials to abandon their borders, posts, and bases. On both the judicial and penal levels, actors are rewarded for downgrading, undermining, or dismissing criminal cases, as well as for forestalling or discouraging legislation and regulation that might interfere with trafficking activities such as the prosecution and punishment of traffickers and those in their employ.

Of greater interest in this chapter, however, are the cases of direct participation in corruption. In contrast to crimes of *omission,* in cases of direct participation, compromised state officials engage in crimes of *commission,* whereby the corrupted both collaborate with, and are intimately tied to, criminal organizations. For example, in both Colombia and Tajikistan, government officials have been closely linked to drug smuggling, in Afghanistan the former anti-corruption chief was imprisoned for heroin distribution.[20] Corruption by direct participation is related to, but not synonymous with, what Green and Ward call "corruption as an organizational goal," whereby "illicit gain becomes in [and of] itself a goal of a state agency and the pursuit of profit determines the agency's decisions."[21] Accordingly, direct participation in corruption is often characterized by the involvement of state officials in some coordinating capacity with TCOs (e.g., officials operate "hand-in-glove" with TCOs and may even hold leadership roles within these organizations). In such situations, corruption will actually tend to *determine* state goals by shaping the rules or policies that state agencies enact or implement.

Some observers employ the term "state capture" to refer to corruption that "rather than purchasing discretionary administrative decisions such as the award of a particular contract, induces legislators or judges to change the legal 'rules of the game.'"[22] By extension, cases of "total state capture" refer to the "fusion of private or party-owned or associated firms with elements of state structure."[23] Within the context of the TCO–governmental relationships discussed herein, not only is there a fusion of the public and private, but there is also some measure of fusion between the licit and the illicit. Such situations can be found in both—what Legvold calls elsewhere in this volume—"criminal" and "criminalized" states.[24] Peruvian writer Mario Vargas Llosa characterized the Mexican political system under the Partido Revolucionario Institucional (PRI), for instance, as "criminal activity [that] occurred because there was no way to stop it or even much desire to do so, at least among the elites, so corrupt practices ensured that criminal activities flourished for those in and out of government."[25]

Corruption by direct participation is of special concern, because public officials compromised in this way maintain a dual ability to control and to direct (quasi-) state institutions and the illegal entities such institutions are theoretically meant to combat. The ability of those involved in these relationships to maintain and to extend corruption to the rest of the state is much greater.[26] As a parliamentary deputy in Kyrgystan complained: "only the bureaucrats live well—giving no material benefit to the country but keeping tight controls over all state mechanisms."[27] In the more distant past, James Madison likewise observed, "The accumulation of all powers, legislative, executive and judiciary, in the same hands may justly be pronounced the very definition of tyranny."[28] This is not to suggest that corruption by omission is unimportant, only that the potential scope, if not the scale, of the consequences of such crimes may be more circumscribed than those of commission.[29]

Moreover, the perception that corruption by direct participation is pervasive tends to have the added negative effect of undermining public faith in institutions as well as public willingness to combat corruption. As Neild notes, in the realm of corruption, transparency cuts two ways. "It is helpful if the media and public is critical of corruption and able to call effectively for reform; it is unhelpful if it causes the behavior of a rotten ruler or rulers to be imitated by the people of the country so that corruption and cynicism spreads."[30] Consider, for instance, the damaging effects of the public cynicism associated with the quip, "Don't steal! The government does not like competition"—which one can find on posters plastered throughout the notoriously, deeply, and chronically corrupt country of Guatemala.[31]

As suggested at the outset, what makes corruption by direct participation particularly problematic is that it can give rise to the phenomenon I call "kleptocratic interdependence." In contrast to Godson's principally, internally focused "political-criminal nexus (PCN)," kleptocratically interdependent relationships may be domestic or international in nature—or both simultaneously.[32] Kleptocratic interdependence is characterized by four key features: 1) a division of political, functional, and social control between state and non-state actors, i.e., the sharing of some of the sovereignty functions traditionally viewed as residing with the state; 2) a privileging of private gain over public good—although, in cases where states are particularly weak or poorly run, the public may in fact benefit from the existence of such relationships; 3) an absence or dearth of legal and juridical accountability; and 4) some measure of fusion between the licit and illicit economic realms—although what each of these comprise will vary across cases.[33] Such relationships arguably date back at least as far as the golden age of piracy and privateering, when states and sub-state rulers outsourced (domestically and internationally) many of the functions traditionally viewed as residing within the purview of the state, such as the extrajudicial provision of security or military force, in exchange for personal gain.[34]

The term kleptocratic interdependence has obvious roots in our understanding of the nature and conduct of kleptocracies, i.e., governments "characterized by rampant greed and corruption," which privilege the personal wealth and political power of government officials and the ruling class at the expense of the population.[35] However, one might most usefully think of this phenomenon as a malevolent stepchild of Keohane and Nye's "complex interdependence," which emphasized the significance of the myriad, and growing number of, complex transnational connections between states and societies.[36] In kleptocratic interdependence, by contrast, the focus is obviously somewhat different, although some of the key dynamics are analogous, if far less benign in consequence. One key feature of complex interdependence, for instance, is "the use of multiple channels of action between societies in interstate, transgovernmental, and transnational relations."[37] Correspondingly, in kleptocratic interdependence, corrupt officials not only "forge new alliances with traditional 'thieves-in-law'," but also, according to Handelman, "co-opt their methods, their organizations, and in some cases their personnel."[38] Likewise, in both phenomena, the relative balance of power between the parties to these alliances will shift over time and across issue area.[39] In the most extreme cases, they simply become one—as in cases of state capture or state criminalization. As political analyst Piontkovsky noted, it would be misleading to call Russia corrupt. Corruption is what happens "when businessmen offer officials large bribes for favors. Today's Russia is unique. The businessmen, the politicians, and the bureaucrats are the same people. They have privatized the country's wealth and [have] taken control of its financial flows."[40]

Ultimately, the strength of a criminal group is contingent upon its capacity to develop a network of relationships with members of other groups—be they entrepreneurs, politicians, bureaucrats, other criminals, etc. These relationships "may be defined as the chance to obtain illicit advantages in defeating competitors (for example, in the market: securing contracts, and in the political arena: buying votes) and attaining monopoly positions."[41] The function of the monopoly is to accumulate resources to invest in illicit markets, but also to gain the consent necessary to infiltrate legitimate society.[42] Why do these imperatives often give rise to self-reinforcing, kleptocratically interdependent relationships, as opposed to other kinds of alliances, such as temporary marriages of convenience? Why, in other words, in the face of seemingly obvious potential principal-agent problems and incentives to defect, do these relationships arise and then tend to persevere?

When and Why Kleptocratic Interdependence Grows and Persists

One compelling reason is the straightforward issue of power and what it can buy. Reliable officials in positions of power can be particularly valuable allies of TCOs. Consequently, TCOs have powerful incentives to contribute financial and other support to ensure that their "friends" get elected. Once installed—assuming the relationship is proving beneficial for both parties— TCOs have still more powerful inducements to ensure that their allies remain safely ensconced in their positions or that they seek an even higher office.[43] The Sicilian mafia, for instance, "has had very close links with the Christian Democratic Party and has infiltrated government at the local, regional and, to a degree, national levels."[44] In fact, according to a 2003 estimate, 40 to 75 percent of Christian Democrat deputies elected between 1950 and 1992 were openly supported by the Cosa Nostra.[45] There is likewise evidence that the U.S. mafia assisted the Democratic Party during the 1960 election season, arranging illegal votes that secured the election of John F. Kennedy.[46] These examples are hardly unique. As former Mexican secretary of agriculture and tourism, mayor of Mexico City, and wealthy PRI stalwart, Carlos Hank Gonzalez allegedly put it: "'A politician who is poor, is a poor politician.' Entering politics in Mexico was regarded as an effective way of gaining wealth, and a successful, wealthy politician is more likely to be admired than scorned."[47] Meanwhile, in Thailand, this kind of interdependence became so pervasive that "in many cases, political parties would consult with these godfathers in order to determine who should be nominated as their candidate." [48] Further, for a variety of rational reasons (e.g., transaction cost-reductions associated with "extending the shadow of the future") and psychological reasons (e.g., the lure of sunk costs) the longer such relationships profitably persist, the more likely the relevant parties will seek to extend them still further into the future.[49]

While TCOs can use their relationships with politicians to protect themselves, government officials and entities can likewise use their involvement with organized criminal groups to solidify their hold on power. The Milosevic regime in the former Yugoslavia, for instance, used corruption and drug smuggling to finance Serb paramilitaries, while for a time the Indonesian armed forces were believed to have raised at least half of their operational costs from illegal activities, including oil and drug smuggling and the protection of illegal logging—also a noteworthy source of income for the police.[50] For its part, during his tenure as leader of Peru, Alberto Fujimori's administration allegedly used the hundreds of millions of dollars it raised through embezzlement as well as "murder, kidnapping, and narcotics trafficking" to corrupt others in the government and beyond, to subvert democracy, and to establish its grip on power.[51] In fact, throughout Latin America, it is well known that many public officials have been offered the option of *plato o plomo* ("money or lead," or as others have translated the term, "bribe or bullet").[52]

Alliances such as these were likewise critical in the political and economic success stories of at least several of the so-called Asian tigers. For example, the rapid growth and political and economic recovery of post–World War II Japan is owed in part to its uneasy alliance with the country's traditional organized crime groups, the *yakuza* ("the violence group"). With the blessing of the American occupation forces, the organized crime syndicate helped to make available goods that were in short supply at war's end. As allies of the political "rightists," the syndicate helped to undermine support for the left (potential Communists) and undertook some of the "enforcement-related" duties usually reserved for the state.[53] These relationships did not end with the occupation, either. As Kaplan and Dubro put it, for decades afterward:

> At the police level, there was a strong response to gang power, and crackdowns and arrests were frequent. But high officials, particularly those in the right wing of the LDP, were less concerned with the day-to-day rackets of the *yakuza*, and often more interested in making alliances with them. . . . The gangs played an essential role in the creation of several immense fortunes and helped others in shaping political careers that reached, in some cases, to the very top.[54]

Taiwanese leaders similarly benefited from their relationships with the so-called Chinese "Triads" during the country's post-war period. As one observer put it when discussing the close relationship between the Triads and the ruling KMT: "Crime provided an official cause for state control of local areas, a control enforced through the unofficial alliance of government and local, criminal ('black society') gangs." In fact, according to a 2000 story in *Asia-Week*, the original members of the Taiwan triads were sons of KMT officers who fled the mainland after China fell to Mao:

> The KMT regulars were not popular in Taiwan, where many natives considered them an invading force. Children like [eventual Taiwanese billionaire] Sheen [Ching-jing] were ready targets for the animosity. Weak and scrawny, Sheen formed a gang with other 'mainlanders' for protection. Over time, similar groups, often started by the sons of KMT military fathers, morphed into Taiwan's biggest and most notorious crime syndicates.[55]

In short, power provides a compelling and long-standing incentive for the formation and sustenance of these symbiotic relationships.[56]

A second reason is that kleptocratic interdependence is self-perpetuating the direct participation of government officials in TCOs tends to increase the potential for these organizations to expand the size and scope of their criminal enterprises. As TCOs' wealth and power increase, they are then—at least theoretically—better able to spread their illicit largesse still more broadly as well as expand and consolidate their criminal empires. For instance, while 80 percent of the cocaine and 30 percent of the heroin that is introduced into the United States emanates from Colombia, in 1991 a Colombian constitutional amendment was passed, blocking the extradition of Colombian drug traffickers to the United States.[57] (Although, it should be noted, this amendment has since been overturned.) Moreover, TCOs that are figuratively speaking "in bed" with political authorities may also find their positions enhanced by officials' prosecution of potential competitors. As then attorney general in the Italian Supreme Court of Appeals, Giuseppe Guido Lo Schiavo wrote, "It has been said that the mafia despises the police and the magistracy, but it is incorrect." Rather, the mafia "has always had respect for the magistracy and for Justice. It has submitted to its sentence, and has not obstructed the judge in his work. In the pursuit of bandits and outlaws it openly sided with the force of law and order."[58]

In addition to the first two factors, corruption by direct participation has the further perfidious effect of heightening TCOs' own protection by increasing the incentives for corrupt officials to shield those who could compromise them. For example, in Peru, the bribe-dispensing Secret Police Chief Vladimiro Montesinos Torres videotaped his bribes, as proof of the recipients' complicity.[59] Once compromised, politicians are subject to potential blackmail and coercion, which can make decisions to shift one's stance on corruption or repudiate one's relationship with a particular TCO problematic.[60] As Lambsdorff has observed, the fact that an illicit deal has been concluded makes both parties co-dependent, for either could denounce the other; this factor further binds them together and mitigates the need for enforcement mechanisms.[61] For example, as one report about Georgia has noted, criminal leaders "take a ride in the cars belonging to senior officials in the Georgian authorities, give business advice to businessmen and, if arrested, enjoy support from the bureaucrats."[62] In other words, as crime becomes more entrenched, compromised political elites become progressively less likely to fight it.

This result is reinforced by the fact that corruption, and criminalization more broadly, may be understood in some circles "as coping mechanisms for people in societies and economies that are not working effectively." Indeed, organized crime may be viewed as "a form of entrepreneurship, providing economic opportunities, a basis for capital accumulation, and multiplier [of] benefits that would otherwise be absent in economies characterized by slow economic growth or even decline."[63] Within states where wages are low and conditions particularly dire, low-level corruption by omission serves as a kind of income augmentation, and shadow economies as a critical means of subsistence. For instance, in discussing the importance of the mafia in both Italian and Russian society, Allum and Siebert note that "these groups are an integral part of these countries' civil society, a presence there to control, 'to keep an eye' on 'everything' and 'everyone,' so that they can make money undisturbed; in some cases, they appear more efficient than the state, as an alternative state, which provides what the state is unable to provide—jobs, protection, goods, and services."[64]

Organized crime may even supplant the state in providing funding for research and non-profit enterprises. Indeed, a St. Petersburg gangster, Anatolii Vladimirov, reportedly made a large donation to an impoverished astronomy research institute in the city. In return, the scientists named an obscure star "Anvlad" after their benefactor.[65] As Williams starkly put the dilemma faced by many: "the presence of these phenomena, particularly on a large scale is a critical indicator that other things are going wrong. The difficulty, of course, is that they exacerbate the conditions that gave rise to them in the first place, thereby rendering the underlying problems even more resistant to solution."[66]

Take, for instance, the issue of taxation and state revenue. When less economic activity is conducted in the legitimate, taxable economy, states are forced to raise taxes on the remaining licit economy to try to recoup lost income and cover their budgetary costs. In a vicious cycle, state's efforts to boost their tax bases push more businesses into the illicit realm (via fraud, tax evasion, etc.) to circumvent inflated tax rates. And, by extension, states with reduced treasuries are still less equipped to combat organized crime and illicit trafficking.[67]

The Political Geography of TCOs and Kleptocratic Interdependence

Evidence suggests that tendencies toward ever-greater TCO accretion of power and penetration are especially likely in contested or institutionally compromised states. Indeed, some states become so corrupt and infiltrated that they are known as "criminal" or "bandit" states.[68] TCOs have, for instance, been exceedingly adept at exploiting weak state capacity in conflict zones, such as Sierra Leone, Guinea-Bissau, and the Democratic Republic of the Congo, where political authority is contested or formal institutions have collapsed. TCOs have also been adept in still unstable post-conflict settings, such as Bosnia-Herzegovina, Angola, and Kosovo, where authority has not been firmly reestablished.[69] For example, the FBI has reported that Balkan organized crime groups, particularly those composed of ethnic Albanian families, have expanded since the mid-1990s into Italy, Germany, Switzerland, Great Britain, Scandinavia, and the United States. Indeed, by 2003, the EU had declared Balkan organized crime one of the greatest criminal threats that the EU faced, estimating that Balkan TCOs controlled upward of 70 percent of the heroin trade and were rapidly gaining market share in human smuggling, prostitution, and car theft.[70]

Moreover, the existence of family, clan, and gang ties may further cement loyalties between TCOs and government officials.[71] In the case of the Italian mafia, for instance, the failure of the government to provide necessary goods and services led to what Paoli terms a "double morality." While, on one hand, Italians greatly respected their relationships with family, relatives, friends, patrons, and clients, on the other hand, they felt no responsibility to the state, which to them was "abstract."[72] In addition, the shared identities of many TCOs' constitutive members tend to keep them based in one central location, while simultaneously allowing for capital, transportation, cross-border mobility, and other byproducts of globalization to maximize illicit profit far from their home bases. Specifically, such ties tend to serve as a kind of "organizational glue," allowing for dissemination by way of cells that are dispersed among other nation-states where criminal activity takes place. For example, the regional ties that comprised Cali, North Valle, Coasta, and Medellin in Colombia; the regional and organizational ties that bind the Sicilian, Comorra, and 'Ndrangheta Italian mafias; the ethnic and language identities among post-Soviet Chechen, Georgian, Russian, Azeri, and Abkhazi groups, as well as those that unite the geographically dispersed Turko-Kurdish groups, who cooperate extensively with the "Albanian" groups; and the familial and cultural connections between the Chinese, Hong Kong, and Taiwanese Triads.[73]

In fact, evidence suggests that kleptocratically interdependent relationships are increasingly global—partnerships that Williams has referred to as "strategic alliances."[74] Global alliances between TCOs (and TCOs and governments) promise multiple benefits: they "enable partners to share financial and operating risks and costs; to garner benefits associated with economies of scale and operating synergies; to exploit existing (and trusted) trading channels and networks; and to increase market share."[75] Because TCOs are profit-maximizing and risk-reducing entities, it makes sense that they would seek out such partnerships, particularly in cases where individual groups share the common problems of circumventing law enforcement and national regulations. Moreover, low barriers to entry for new "businesses," coupled with the fluidity and speed of international travel and communications, have helped "create an entrepreneurial free-for-all with potentially high payoffs that outweigh the risks associated with law enforcement and regulatory efforts." As a result, small-time businesses and individual entrepreneurs flourish alongside their larger and more expansive counterparts.[76] To be clear, far from all international organized crime is conducted by organized, standing entities; as this chapter stated at the outset—much of what is referred to as "organized crime" is actually quite disorganized.[77] That said, the threat posed by these strategic alliances—and particularly those that have also succeeded in penetrating or capturing states—should not be dismissed.

For a sense of the global scale and variety of these alliances, consider the following examples. As soon as the Soviet Union fell, criminal leaders from Moscow and the Baltics began holding "summits" with members of the Italian mafia as well as with members of South American drug cartels.[78] As a result, Italian and Russian criminal networks have since forged cooperative relationships, while Colombian and Russian criminals have forged guns-for-drugs deals. There have likewise been reports of Colombians taking part in money laundering in Russia and Ukraine.[79] In other words, Russian bureaucrats are not only "in bed" with Russian criminals—whose illegal commercial enterprises are "multi-national"—but they are holding "slumber parties" with their counterparts elsewhere in the world. The Russians are hardly alone. Colombian-Sicilian connections have reportedly resulted in alliances between Colombian cocaine suppliers and Sicilian groups that "possess local knowledge, well-established heroin distribution networks, extensive bribery and corruption networks, and a full-fledged capability for money laundering." Likewise, Nigerian trafficking organizations have allegedly exchanged heroin for cocaine with Colombians. Not only has this trade assisted Colombians in developing their own heroin market, but it has also provided opportunities for Nigerians to sell cocaine in Western Europe.[80]

Within Western Europe, Turkish organized crime groups were traditionally hierarchical and homogeneous. But in recent years they have reportedly forged "enduring partnerships" with other organized crime groups in Europe. In particular, collaboration between Turkish and Albanian groups "has proved beneficial in exploiting large segments of the European market, in many different fields of illegal business."[81] And in North America, an alliance between Mexican and Chinese criminal organizations has purportedly resulted in what the *Los Angeles Times* described as "a clandestine corridor linking the villages of Fujian, the shores of Mexico and Central America, and suburban safe houses in heavily Chinese enclaves of the San Gabriel Valley."[82] An inference that can be drawn from this example—among myriad others—is that "when trafficking routes and methods of proven effectiveness are available not only is the product virtually irrelevant," but also "these organizations are willing to engage in any kind of alliance that facilitates their illegal enterprise."[83]

Moreover, apropos of the latest trend in globalization, when the *yakuza* faces the problem of an aging membership and a lack of young recruits, it reportedly subcontracts to Chinese gangs.[84]

While these alliances may be global in reach, TCOs still have home bases. So where are the major players based? Not necessarily where one would think. While virtually no country is free from organized crime, and almost every country has produced criminals who belong to or work for such groups, ten countries have produced what are generally considered the largest and strongest of such organizations. See Table 5-1.

Conventional wisdom suggests that criminality and corruption should be most acute in the world's most poorly governed countries. Yet what Table 5-1 makes clear is that—with the exception of groups operating out of Nigeria—today's most powerful and well-known TCOs appear to be based in more highly functioning states.[85] In fact, six of the nine (recognized) principal TCOs are based in democracies, while the rest are within so-called hybrid regimes.[86] Seven of the ten garner the highest ranking on the UN's Human Development Index, and only one (Nigeria) currently qualifies (by UN standards) as a failed state, although more than a few others bear close observation.[87] Data are highly varied in terms of bribe taking and regulatory environment. However, it is worth noting that TCOs are not based in countries that rank at the bottom of the Corruption Perceptions Index (CPI) or the Bribe Payers' Index (BPI) (lower rankings indicating more corruption). At the same time, however, they are not based in countries near the top of those indices either. With the exception of the United States, the same is true for the Ease of Doing Business Index. (Indeed, some would argue that the United States' high ranking on the index makes it an especially auspicious location as a TCO home base.)[88] Furthermore, when the list includes the top fifteen to twenty most powerful and well-known TCOs, Nigeria still remains a significant outlier.[89]

In sum, the problem of TCO-governmental alliances is not limited to a particular region, culture, or state of development. That the majority of the most significant TCOs appear to be firmly ensconced and even "headquartered" in highly developed states that are at least somewhat well governed makes it clear that the profit motive is a key determinant of their choice of locations. (The roles played by historical precedent and the significance of identity ties further reinforces these choices.) Among other things, better-developed infrastructure and higher standards of living among one's local customer base (read "more disposable income") make such states desirable headquarters. In short, TCOs, particularly those that can depend upon protection from friends in high places, will readily accept the higher risks of

Table 5-1. *Comparative Indicators for the "Headquarters" of What Are Widely Regarded as the World's Most Significant Transnational Criminal Organizations (TCOs)*

Home Country	Albania	China[a]	Columbia	Italy	Japan	Mexico	Nigeria	Russia	Turkey	U.S.
Major Group Name	Mafia	PRC; HK; T (Triads)	Cartels	Sicilian Mafia or Cosa Nostra; Calabrian 'Ndrangheta Neapolitan Camorra; and Sacra Corona Unita of Apulia	Yakuza or Boryokudan	Cartels		Mafia	the Turks	American Mafia or Cosa Nostra
Failed States Index (2007)[b]	111 (Warning)	PRC Tied at 62 (Warning)	33 (Warning)	156 (Moderate)	164 (Sustainable)	102 (Warning)	17 (Alert)	Tied at 62 (Warning)	93 (Warning)	160 (Moderate)
Economist Democracy Index (2007)[c]	5.91	PRC (2.97); HK (6.03); T (7.82)	6.40	7.73	8.15	6.67	3.52	5.02	5.70	8.22
UN Human Development Index (2005)[d]	68 (High)	81 (Medium); HK (21-High)	75 (Medium)	20 (High)	8 (High)	52 (High)	158 (Low)	67 (High)	84 (Medium)	12 (High)
World Bank's "Ease of Doing Business" Index[e]	136	83	66	44	12	53	108	106	57	3
Infrastructure Index (2001)[f]	NA	(PRC) 34.19; Others NA	58.64	NA	NA[g]	52.98	36.86	NA[h]	59.82	81.01
Corruption Perceptions Index (2007)[i]	104	Tied at 72; HK (14); T (Tied at 34)	68	41	17	Tied at 72	147	143	Tied at 64	20
Bribe Payers Index (2007)[j]	NA	29; HK (18–19); T (26)	NA	20	11	17	NA	28	27	9–10

a. "PRC" here refers to China; "HK" refers to Hong Kong; and "T" refers to Taiwan.
b. Scores are 1–177; 177 is best.
c. Scores are 1–10; 10 is best.
d. Scores are 1–177; 1 is best.
e. Scores are 1–178; 1 is best.
f. Scores are 1–100%; 100% is best.
g. Surely approaching 100, however (e.g., UK=100).
h. But former Asian republics average about 60.
i. Scores are 1–179; 1 is best.
j. Scores are 1–39; 1 is best.

operating in states with greater institutional capacity in return for greater rewards. This being said, however, as Patrick rightly notes: "the relationship between transnational organized crime and weak states is parasitic."[90] Hence, all things being equal, TCOs will naturally be drawn to environments where the rule of law is absent or imperfectly applied, law enforcement and border controls are lax, regulatory systems are weak, contracts are spottily enforced, public services are unreliable, corruption is endemic, and the state may be subject to capture. Capacity gaps such as these provide "functional holes" that criminal enterprises can exploit. Thus, poor governance has made Africa, in the words of the UN Office on Drugs and Crime, "an ideal conduit through which to extract and/or transship a range of illicit commodities, such as drugs, firearms, minerals and oil, timber, wildlife, and human beings."[91]

Nevertheless, profits are paramount for TCOs. In today's globalized economy, realizing high returns is contingent upon criminal organizations' abilities to tap into global markets both to sell illicit commodities and to launder the proceeds. The capacity to do so successfully is in turn predicated on access to a variety of financial services, modern telecommunications, and transportation infrastructure; all of which explain why South Africa and Nigeria have become magnets for transnational and domestic organized crime, as well as why Togo has not.[92]

Furthermore, as Table 5-2 demonstrates, when actually compared, countries that appear to have little in common historically, politically, and economically, may be similar when it comes to their experiences with kleptocratic interdependence and corruption.[93]

What similarities do come through include: 1) most of the world's highly significant TCOs have roots that date back a century or more; 2) the level of kleptocratic interdependence is (historically) quite high, even in places where the CPI and BPI rankings are relatively low; 3) global demand for a variety of goods has catalyzed significant growth in the majority of these groups since the 1970s and 1980s; and 4) progress toward combating TCO penetration made in one part of the world (Japan, Italy) appears to be echoed by a slide toward greater dysfunctional interdependence elsewhere (Russia, Albania).[94] This discrepancy suggests there may be no global trends on this front to which we can point, other than the fact that the size, scale, and scope of these groups' product lines and profitability seem only to be rising.[95]

Implications and Conclusions

As most, albeit not all, TCOs are more concerned with profits than politics, the majority are unlikely to undermine systems that they are able to exploit

Table 5-2. *Transnational Criminal Organizations (TCOs)*

TCO	Size/Membership	Age; Growth of Entity or Entities
Albanian Mafias	15 families	Reportedly since 1500s; grew significantly in the 1980s, after allying with Italians, and as a consequence of the 1999 Kosovo war (plus the 1997 collapse of Albania)
Chinese Triads	Six triads; 100K+ members (But there are also distinct, less organized groups, e.g., Big Circle Boys)	17th century; grew significantly with LDP and external support post-WWII; global growth made possible by significant migration in the 1990s
Colombian Cartels	Previously two very powerful, diverse cartels (Medellin and Cali); today, more fractured	1960s; with growth of drug prohibitions and global increase in demand for marijuana, and later, cocaine
Italian Mafia	Approximately 350 families	19th century
Japanese Yakuza	Approximately 60–85K members	17th century; allegedly began as three distinct groups, which later evolved and mutated; supported by U.S. and LDP post-WWII
Mexican Cartels	Several distinct kinship-based cartels	1970s–1980s with growth of drug demand and trade; growth also benefited greatly from alliance with Colombians; although Mexican organized crime is centuries old
Nigerian Groups	Tribal, kinship-based	Since independence (1914); have blossomed since the 1980s
Russian Mafia	Approximately 100–200 groups	Organized crime pre-dates 1917 Revolution, but grew significantly in 1950s and 1960s, as a result of alliances with elites; it exploded post–Cold War
The Turks	Approximately 12 groups and Turko-Kurdish clans.	Centuries old: Turko gangs of smugglers across Caucasus and Ottoman Empire; steady growth since the 1970s; exploded in the 1990s
American Mafia	25 "families"	Mid- to late 19th century

Specialty or Specialties	Degree of Kleptocratic Interdependence	Global Reach/Alliances
Diverse; but especially drugs, people, and arms	All-time high	Active in EU (it is "the new Colombia of Europe") and the U.S.; FBI says these groups might supplant the U.S. Cosa Nostra
Diverse; especially counterfeiting and drugs	Uncertain, but experts say they could become "the most dangerous" 21st century TCO. Evidence points to increasing ties to PRC officials (money, too)	Five based in Hong Kong and Taiwan, one in PRC; penetration wherever there is a significant diaspora
Mostly drugs, but also kidnapping and other human-focused crimes	Previously very high; at present, probably medium to high, but somewhat uncertain	Worldwide trade; allied with Italian, Russian, and Mexican mafias. Once, deep penetration throughout Central/South America
Very diversified; but not prostitution or kidnapping	Low to medium (declining since mid-1990s; still high in local areas)	Worldwide (at least 40 plus countries), with myriad alliances
Diverse; especially drugs, extortion, fraud, gambling, pornography, and prostitution	Formerly very high; declining since the mid-1990s, with heightened enforcement, relative LDP weakening and the end of the Cold War	Present throughout the world (especially South Korea, Australia, and Hawaii), but most sales and activities are domestic
Especially human and drug trafficking; also murder for hire	High under the PRI; declining somewhat, especially under Calderon	Extensive ties to Colombians and Chinese
Diverse; especially drugs, fraud, and money laundering	High, but lower than under Abacha	Reportedly active in 80 countries, including the U.S.
Very diversified	All-time high	Worldwide; although this is disputed
Diverse; especially drugs, people, pirated goods, and counterfeit documents	High; though enforcement increasing in 2000s, (especially post-2005)	Active in EU and central Asia; ties to Albanian and other Balkan groups; active too in European diaspora
Diverse; but especially drugs, gambling, fraud, and pornography	Generally low; but medium-high in local areas	International ties, but most sales and activities are domestic

and abuse for their own purposes. Outside of smuggling nuclear or other WMD-related materials, there is little prospect that TCOs will pose an existential threat to advanced, highly functioning democracies. That said, there are real and profound reasons for concern about the burgeoning relationships between transnational crime and corruption. Organized crime does result in the victimization of individuals and also can serve to undermine a "nation's social fabric." It can also impede the free flow of goods, money, and people across borders by requiring onerous inspections and record keeping designed to impede crime, and, from a broader economic perspective, it represents a significant dead-weight loss to the societies afflicted by it.

States that are relatively secure also have interests in ensuring that more vulnerable states do not become destabilized and threaten to undermine the neighbors of such vulnerable states—for instance, giving rise to a regional war in the Balkans. In other countries, such as Colombia, criminal activities can finance insurgencies that threaten social stability, even if the movements' prospects of successfully seizing power are slim. Finally, in countries transitioning from authoritarian rule, rampant organized crime can undermine support for the new political system, leading to disaffection among the population and even, in some circles, nostalgia for the old system (e.g., Russia and Iraq).

Kleptocratically interdependent relationships do not develop overnight. There often must exist a "window of opportunity" for a criminal group—which may have dominance over a particular territory or ethnic community—to gain the officials' (or even, the state's) recognition as a valuable potential partner. This transition from gang predation to state-TCO symbiosis tends to occur if and when the criminal group has developed a mutually beneficial relationship with officials within the legitimate governance structure (or the state as a whole), especially in the context of enhanced enforcement and the redefinition of what constitutes the illegal market. For instance, the American mafia developed such a relationship with U.S. government officials during the time of prohibition (combining the threatening use of force with payments supplied to state officials), and the Japanese Liberal Democratic Party developed such a relationship with the *yakuza* in the immediate aftermath of World War II. Conflict, be it military, political, or ethnic, can likewise facilitate the coupling of organized crime and corruption as can the failure of states and collapse of empires—a common occurrence in the post–Cold War period.

At the same time, it is worth noting that many of the same transformations that have "facilitate[d] the globalization of crime, including revolutions in transportation and communication, also greatly facilitate the globalization of crime control."[96] While the end of the Cold War opened up a host of opportunities for enterprising criminals, it concomitantly reduced the leverage of crime bosses who had served as anti-Communist allies, making domestic and international actors willing to pursue them in ways that were not deemed possible amid the global ideological struggle that existed during the Cold War. Further, there appears to be a growing willingness of authorities in corruption-ridden states to cooperate with others, most notably the United States, in efforts to combat organized crime, generally, and to apprehend and punish drug lords, more specifically. For one thing, states—especially since 9/11—have been increasingly willing to extradite their own criminals, a policy switch that not only benefits the states directly but also gives the states favor with foreign governments; for instance, in 2006, Mexico extradited sixty-three drug dealers to the United States—a record number.[97]

How successful these efforts will ultimately prove is an open question, as historically decapitating the leadership of one criminal entity has often led to the ascendancy of another.[98] Although a detailed examination of these propositions is beyond the scope of this chapter, history also demonstrates that: 1) concerted pressure and external support, coupled with 2) a shift in the domestic leadership structure and the relative power of political parties, and 3) an increase in support for such efforts by the public can weaken, if not necessarily eliminate, kleptocratically interdependent relationships and diminish the power of TCOs within a state.[99] As Harris notes, continued TCO success "is dependent on the acquiescence and sometimes the complicity of stronger and more powerful players in the international arena." Thus, if and when their usefulness begins to evaporate (as with the end of the Cold War) and when they begin to "constitute a threat to the interests of more powerful players," through violence or threatening to bring down a government, "they may be eliminated as significant political players and if necessary killed."[100] Recent developments in Japan, Italy, and the United States offer some evidence for these propositions as well as some reason, albeit limited, for hope.[101]

Notes

1. U.S. Department of Justice, "Remarks Prepared for Delivery by Attorney General Michael B. Mukasey on International Organized Crime at the Center for Strategic and International Studies" (23 April 2008), available at www.justice.gov/ag/speeches/2008/ag_speech_080423.html (accessed 1 May 2008).

2. Such fears are widely expressed both in policy circles and in the popular press. In fact, before the terrorist attacks of 9/11/01, transnational organized crime topped the list of many countries' twenty-first-century security threats. See Moisés Naím,

Illicit: How Smugglers, Traffickers, and Copycats are Hijacking the Global Economy (New York, 2005); Misha Glenny, *McMafia: A Journey Through the Global Criminal Underworld* (New York, 2008).

3. One important caveat is in order. Even assuming transnational organized crime is burgeoning, it may nevertheless represent only a small percentage of the total volume of illicit cross-border economic activities, most of which are likely undertaken by "disorganized criminals," rather than organized groups.

4. Quoted in Phil Williams, "Transnational Criminal Organizations: Strategic Alliances," *The Washington Quarterly*, XVIII (1995), 57–72, available at www.sgrm.com/strategic.htm (accessed 10 November 2007).

5. For one thing, as Naylor rightly notes, there is no way to prove that there is more criminal activity than before, or to prove that the percentage of illegal profits has increased compared to legal profits. See R. T. Naylor, *Wages of Crime: Black Markets, Illegal Finance, and the Underworld Economy* (Ithaca, 2002). To make matters still worse, "many governments are reluctant to inform us about the true extent of the phenomenon inside their borders and tend to interpret requests for data and information, even from international institutions, as a gross violation of their sovereignty." From Fabio Armao, "Why is Organized Crime So Successful?" in Felia Allum and Renate Siebert (eds.), *Organized Crime and the Challenge to Democracy* (London, 2003), 28.

6. See as well the excellent edited volume, Nikos Passas (ed.), *Transnational Crime* (Aldershot, 1999); and Roy Godson (ed.), *Menace to Society: Political-Criminal Collaboration Around the World* (London, 2003).

7. For a similar viewpoint, see Stergios Skaperdas, "The Political Economy of Organized Crime: Providing Protection When the State Does Not," in Amihai Glazer and Kai A. Konrad (eds.), *Conflict and Governance* (Berlin, 2003), 170 ("It is indeed evident that such connections have increased under the influence of . . . a more globalized economy. However, there does not appear to be a qualitative shift in the way organized crime groups do business and the degree of economic and political control than traditionally exerted."); and Peter Andreas and Ethan Nadelmann, *Policing the Globe: Criminalization and Crime Control in International Relations* (Oxford, 2007). It must be reiterated, however, that good data on illegal activities and illicit economies are notoriously hard to come by; indeed, even the authors who used this figure acknowledge that it is highly suspect. Cited in H. Richard Friman and Peter Andreas, "Introduction: International Relations and the Illicit Global Economy," in Friman and Andreas (eds.), *Illicit Global Economy and State Power* (Boulder, 1999), 2. For a detailed discussion of the difficulties associated with deriving good estimates of illicit activities, and the significant policy implications thereof, see Peter Andreas and Kelly M. Greenhill, "Introduction," in Andreas and Greenhill (eds.), *Cooking the Books: The Politics of Numbers in Crime and Conflict* (forthcoming).

8. While decidedly distinct, this process resembles the process of state formation, as hypothesized by Mancur Olson, whereby stationary bandits develop symbiotic and routinized, but nevertheless extractive, relationships with the people in a particular

territory. See Mancur Olson, *Power and Prosperity: Outgrowing Communist and Capitalist Dictatorships* (New York, 2000).

9. For instance, they violate national sovereignty; undermine democratic institutions even in states where these institutions are well established; threaten the process of democratization and privatization in states in transition; and further complicate combating thorny problems such as nuclear proliferation and terrorism. See Williams, "Transnational Criminal Organizations." On the "flattening" of the world, see Thomas Friedman, *The World Is Flat: A Brief History of the Twenty-First Century* (New York, 2005).

10. Williams, "Transnational Criminal Organizations." See also Michael Woodiwiss, "Transnational Organized Crime: The Global Reach of an American Concept," in Adam Edwards and Peter Gill (eds.), *Transnational Organised Crime: Perspectives on Global Security* (London, 2003), 13–20. In fact, U.S. Senator John Kerry was quoted as saying that "organized crime is the new communism, the new monolithic threat," in R. T. Naylor, "From Cold War to Crime War: The Search for a New 'National Security' Threat," *Transnational Organized Crime,* I (1995), 37–56. (Consider, moreover, that the journal in which Naylor published Kerry's quote was only founded in 1995.)

11. "International Crime," in Patrick Clawson (ed.), *Strategic Assessment 1997: Flashpoints and Force Structure* (Washington, D.C., 1997), available at www.ndu.edu/inss/Strategic%20Assessments/sa97/sa97ch16.html (accessed 4 November 2008).

12. Agreement on an exact definition of what constitutes or is a TCO has long been controversial. Herein, this author adopts the spirit of the UN definition employed in the draft convention on transnational organized crime. "UN Convention against Transnational Organized Crime," available at www.odccp.org/palermo/convmain.html (accessed 18 February 2008).

13. They are so widespread that one observer has quipped that Vatican City may be the only state that is free from them; Skaperdas, "The Political Economy of Organized Crime," 163–164.

14. Edward Morse, "Transnational Economic Processes," in Robert Keohane and Joseph Nye, *Transnational Relations and World Politics,* XXIII (1971), 47. See also Table 5-2 in this chapter.

15. Allan Castle, "Transnational Organized Crime and International Security," *University of British Columbia Working Paper* No. 19 (Vancouver, B.C., 1997), 10.

16. For instance, the simple economic law of supply and demand means that the criminalization of activities and goods will tend to increase their profitability, which tends to redound to the benefit, rather than the detriment, of TCOs. See, for example, Andreas and Nadelmann, *Policing the Globe.*

17. While TCOs also employ the threat and use of violence as barriers to entry and as a way to protect market share, coercion is rarely sufficient to guarantee sustained cooperation, as it is solely predicated on negative incentives and fear. For one thing, the incentives to identify and embrace non- or less coercive alternatives are strong. Moreover, as Schelling notes, "by force alone we cannot even lead a horse to drink. Any

affirmative action, any collaboration, almost anything but physical exclusion, expulsion, or extermination requires that an opponent or a victim *do* something, even if only to stop or get out. . . . Brute force can only accomplish what requires no collaboration." Thomas C. Schelling, "The Diplomacy of Violence," in his *Arms and Influence* (New Haven, 1966), 8.

18. Robert Klitgaard, cited in Louise Shelley, John Picarelli, and Chris Corpora, "Global Crime, Inc.," in Maryann Cusimano Love (ed.), *Beyond Sovereignty: Issues for a Global Agenda* (New York, 2007), 146. For a classic, comprehensive treatment of the causes and consequences of corruption, see Susan Rose-Ackerman, *Corruption and Government: Causes, Consequences and Reform* (New York, 1999).

19. Michael Rolston, "Globalizing a Traditional Cottage Industry: International Criminal Organizations in a Global Economy," available at http://globalization.icaap.org/content/special/rolston.html#_ftn2 (accessed 1 May 2008).

20. Several years ago, the Tajik ambassador to Kazakhstan was arrested while in possession of 62 kilograms of heroin and $1 million cash. A few days later, Tajikistan's trade representative in Almaty was arrested when another 24 kilograms of heroin was found in his home. The confiscated heroin was discovered to have come from Afghanistan and was reportedly bound for Siberia and Russia's Pacific coast region. From Stephen Handelman, "Thieves in Power: The New Challenge of Corruption," in Steven Otfinoski (ed.), *Nations in Transition* (Washington, D.C., 1999), 47; Justin Huggler, "Afghan Anti-Corruption Chief is a Drug Dealer," *The Independent* (10 March 2007).

21. Penny Green and Tony Ward, *State Crime: Governments, Violence and Corruption* (London, 2004), 16.

22. Ibid.

23. International Crisis Group, *Macedonia's Public Secret: How Corruption Drags the Country Down* (Brussels, 2002).

24. In this volume, Robert Legvold defines "criminal states" as those "not merely where criminal activity has penetrated widely within the state, but where the core activity of the state is criminal," whereas "criminalized states" comprise those in which corruption is endemic, although "state's core activity may not be corrupt, but the *process* by which the state acts is." Robert Legvold, "Corruption, the Criminalized State, and Post-Soviet Transitions," 196.

25. Quoted in James Robinson, "The Paradox of Liberalization: How Democratization and Neoliberal Reform Destabilize Developing Countries: The Case of Mexico," unpublished paper (San Diego, 2006), 2.

26. See, for example, Ricardo Soberón Garrido, "Corruption, Drug Trafficking and the Armed Forces: An Approximation for Latin America" in his *Crime in Uniform: Corruption and Impunity in Latin America* (Amsterdam, 1997), available at www.tni.org/detail_page.phtml?&page=reports_drugs_folder3_soberon (accessed 4 November 2008).

27. Igor Grebenshchikov, "Central Asian Leaders Think Alike," available at www.iwpr.net/index.pl?archive/rca/rca_200103_45_4.eng.txt (accessed 10 December 2007).

28. Quoted in John McMillan and Pablo Zoido, "How to Subvert Democracy: Montesinos in Peru," *Journal of Economic Perspectives,* XVIII (2004), 70.

29. Although, this is arguably an empirical question, subject to testing.

30. Robert Neild, *Public Corruption: The Dark Side of Social Evolution* (London, 2002), 13.

31. Green and Ward, *State Crime*, 11.

32. One might, loosely speaking, conceive of kleptocratic interdependence as a synthesis of Roy Godson's PCN and Phil Williams's "strategic alliances" (discussed in this chapter), and the analysis contained herein has benefited greatly from the insights offered by both. See Godson (ed.), *Menace to Society,* especially 1–26; and Williams, "Transnational Criminal Organizations." One clear domestic example was the profound penetration of the Colombian government by drug cartels in the early 1990s. However, the cartels also reached far beyond their home base and cultivated ties to political leaders and top-level officials in a number of Central American and Caribbean countries, for example, in Panama, the Bahamas, Antigua, the Turks and Caicos Islands, and Cuba. Their purported aim was the enhancement of logistics and money flows, for example, "to obtain landing and refueling facilities, docking facilities, storage sites, permission to operate cocaine laboratories and various financial and money laundering services." They were likewise rumored to have contributed funds to the 1994 presidential campaigns of Ernesto Perez Balladares in Panama and Ernesto Zedillo in Mexico, and paid $6 million to ensure the victory of Ernesto Samper in Colombia in 1994. From "International Crime," *Strategic Assessment 1997,* available at www.ndu.edu/inss/Strategic%20Assessments/sa97/sa97ch16.html (accessed 1 December 2007).

33. Political control is loosely tied to *who* gets to make decisions; functional control, to *what capabilities to impose order and use force* are available to those relevant actors; and social control, to *what (and whose) norms* dictate behavior. These terms (but not their meanings) have been derived from Deborah Avant's compelling exploration of the rise of private military firms. See Avant, *The Market for Force: The Consequences of Privatizing Security* (New York, 2005), 40–42.

34. On the nature of earlier historical examples, see Lindsay S. Butler, *Pirates, Privateers, and Rebel Leaders of the Carolinas* (Chapel Hill, 2000); Janice Thomson, *Mercenaries, Pirates, and Sovereigns* (Princeton, 1994). In a more contemporary context, the relationships between states and private military firms share some of these characteristics as well. See Avant, *The Market for Force,* especially 40–142; Peter W. Singer, *Corporate Warriors* (Ithaca, 2003). A more recent example is that of China in the 1920s, a period in which control of the country was uneasily, but profitably, shared between the government and warlords. See Olson, *Power and Prosperity,* 6–10.

35. See, for instance, Johann Graf Lambsdorff, *The Institutional Economics of Corruption and Reform* (New York, 2007), 81–108; and Olson, *Power and Prosperity.*

36. Robert Keohane and Joseph Nye, *Power and Interdependence* (New York, 1977).

37. Ibid.

38. Handelman, "Thieves in Power: The New Challenge of Corruption," 45–54. According to Handelman, "One vivid example of this comes from Ukraine. In a controversial tape recording, former Ukranian President Leonid Kuchma is heard discussing with his aides how to apply pressure on a prominent banker and a rebellious

member of parliament. 'Everyone who works for us should pay money for his *krisha*,' Kuchma says, using the Russian criminal jargon for the 'roof' of protection and extortion rackets favored by the underworld. Kuchma has refused to authenticate the tapes, which his former security guard disclosed."

39. See Keohane and Nye, *Power and Interdependence*.

40. Andrei Piontkovsky, "Putinism: Highest Stage of Robber Capitalism," *Russia Journal*, issue 47 (2000).

41. Armao, "Why is Organized Crime So Successful?" 29.

42. Ibid.

43. See Olson, *Power and Prosperity*, 103–104.

44. Phil Williams, "Transnational Criminal Organizations and International Security," in John Arguilla and David Ronfeldt (eds.), *In Athena's Camp: Preparing for Conflict in the Information Age* (Santa Monica, 1997), 331.

45. Cited in Letizia Paoli, "Broken Bonds: Mafia and Politics in Sicily," in Godson, ed., *Menace to Society*, 40.

46. Robert J. Kelley, "An American Way of Crime and Corruption," in Godson, ed., *Menace to Society*, 109.

47. Robinson, "The Paradox of Liberalization," 2.

48. Somrüdee Nicro, "Thailand's NIC Democracy: Studying from General Elections," *Pacific Affairs*, LXVI (1993), 176.

49. On the cooperation inducing effects of iteration, see David Kreps and others, "Rational Cooperation in Finitely-Repeated Prisoner's Dilemma," *Journal of Economic Theory*, XXVII (1982), 245–252; Robert Telsor, "A Theory of Self-Enforcing Agreements," *Journal of Business*, LIII (1980), 27–44. On how sunk cost considerations can affect behavior, see Daniel Kahneman and Amos Tversky, "Prospect Theory: An Analysis of Decisions Under Risk," *Econometrica*, IIIL (1979), 313–327.

50. Green and Ward, *State Crime*, 13.

51. McMillan and Zoido, "How to Subvert Democracy," 72.

52. Elaine Shannon, *Desperados, Latin Drug Lords, U.S. Lawmakers, and the War America Can't Win* (New York, 1988), 21.

53. The United States reportedly also allied with French Corsican gangsters to disrupt Communist strikes and "break the back of the French Communist Party" during this same period. See Alfred McCoy, *The Politics of Heroin* (New York, 1991); cited in David E. Kaplan and Alec Dubro, *Yakuza: Japan's Criminal Underworld* (Berkeley, 2003), 44.

54. Kaplan and Dubro, *Yakuza*, 31–82, 62.

55. "Tycoon with a Triad Past," *CNN/TIME Asiaweek*, XXVI (14 April 2000); see also "Triads in Taiwan: the Dragon Rears an Ugly Head," available at http://michaelturton.blogspot.com/2005/05/triads-in-taiwan-dragon-rears-ugly.html (accessed 1 May 2008).

56. South Korea also reportedly represents "a striking 'success story'" in the use of corruption to serve governmental goals during its period of military rule and significant economic growth from 1961 through 1987, although it is less clear what role TCOs played in this context. Green and Ward, *State Crime*, 13.

57. U.S. Congress, Senate Committee on Foreign Relations, *Corruption and Drugs in Colombia: Democracy at Risk* (1996), v, vii, 104–147; John McCullough Martin and Anne T. Romano, *Multinational Crime: Terrorism, Espionage, Drugs and Arms Trafficking* (New York, 1992), 135.

58. Cited in Paoli, "Broken Bonds," 33.

59. McMillan and Zoido, "How to Subvert Democracy," 70–72.

60. Ibid. Moreover, not to put too fine a point on it, but defecting from a relationship with a TCO can result in the ultimate penalty—death. That said, assassinations could discourage others from forming alliances with that TCO in the future.

61. Johann Graf Lambsdorff, "Making Corrupt Deals in the Shadow of the Law," *Journal of Economic Behavior and Organization*, XLVIII (2002), 221–241.

62. Cited in Phil Williams, "Criminalization and Stability in Central Asia and South Caucasus," in Olga Oliker and Thomas Szayna (eds.), *Faultlines of Conflict in Central Asia and the South Caucasus* (Santa Monica, 2003), 81.

63. Ibid., 93.

64. Allum and Siebert, *Organized Crime*, 2. See also the excellent analysis of the Italian mafia by Diego Gambetta, *The Sicilian Mafia: The Business of Private Protection* (Cambridge, MA, 1993).

65. Clawson (ed.), *Strategic Assessment 1997*, available at www.ndu.edu/inss/Strategic%20Assessments/sa97/sa97ch16.html (accessed 4 November 2008).

66. Williams, "Criminalization and Stability," 93.

67. Shelly, Picarelli, and Corpora, "Global Crime, Inc," 152.

68. See also the chapter by Robert Legvold in this volume.

69. Stewart Patrick, "Weak States and Global Threats: Fact or Fiction?" *Washington Quarterly*, XXIX (2006), 39.

70. "Testimony of Grant D. Ashley, Assistant Director, Criminal Investigative Division, Federal Bureau of Investigation, Before the Subcommittee on European Affairs, Committee on Foreign Relations, U.S. Senate, 'Eurasian, Italian, and Balkan Organized Crime'" (30 October 2003), available at www.fbi.gov/congress/congress03/ashley103003.htm (accessed 5 August 2008); Terry Frieden, "FBI: Albanian mobsters 'new Mafia,'" *CNN.com* (18 August 2004), available at www.cnn.com/2004/LAW/08/18/albanians.mob/index.html (accessed 17 April 2009).

71. See Williams, "Transnational Criminal Organizations."

72. Because of their identity-based ties: "[m]afiosi protected persons and property in their communities, repressed the most serious threats to the established order, countered behavior in conflict with sub-cultural norms, and mediated conflicts within the local society and the relations between that society and the outside world." Quoted in Paoli, "Broken Bonds," 31. These findings echo somewhat those of Edward Banfield who, during his fieldwork in southern Italy in the 1950s, found that when living under conditions of extreme duress and uncertainty many villages had difficulty forming ties beyond their family units—ties that Banfield contended were necessary precursors to economic development and modern society. Edward Banfield, *The Moral Basis of a Backward Society* (Glencoe, 1958).

73. Shared skill sets and criminal records can also serve as the requisite organizational glue. However, such ties tend to be weaker than ethnic and clan ties and are thus more likely to rely on (the threat of) coercion to ensure loyalty, and, not coincidentally, they are also more susceptible to fracturing over time than identity-based ties. See Rensselaer Lee and Francisco Thoumi, "Drugs and Democracy in Colombia," in Godson, ed., *Menace to Society,* 80; Allum and Siebert, *Organized Crime,* 8; and Williams, "Transnational Criminal Organizations."

74. Williams, "Transnational Criminal Organizations."

75. Refik Culpan and Eugene A. Kostelak Jr., "Cross-National Corporate Partnerships: Trends in Alliance Formation," in Refik Culpan (ed.), *Multinational Strategic Alliances* (New York, 1993), 116.

76. Williams, "Transnational Criminal Organizations."

77. Peter Reuter, *Disorganized Crime: The Economics of the Visible Hand* (Cambridge, MA, 1983). See also R. T. Naylor and Margaret E. Beare, "Major Issues Relating to Organized Crime: Within the Context of Economic Relationships" (1999), available at www.ncjrs.gov/nathanson/organized.html#fdoc (accessed 10 October 2008).

78. Stephen Handelman, "The Russian 'Mafiya,'" *Foreign Affairs,* LXXIII (1994), 83–96.

79. Williams, "Transnational Criminal Organizations."

80. Ibid.

81. Ioannis Michaletos, "Turkish Organized Crime," *Worldpress* (12 November 2007), available at www.worldpress.org/Europe/2987.cfm (accessed 10 October 2008).

82. Sebastian Rotella and Lee Romney, "Smugglers Use Mexico as Gateway for Chinese," *Los Angeles Times* (21 June 1993), A3; cited in Michaletos, "Turkish Organized Crime."

83. See Friman and Andreas, *Illicit Global Economy and State Power*; Williams, "Transnational Criminal Organizations."

84. William Grimes, "Wiseguys and Fall Guys, Welcome to Globalization," *New York Times* (11 April 2008).

85. For governance indicators and rankings, see also Daniel Kaufmann, Aart Kraay, and Massimo Mastruzzi, *Governance Matters 2007: Worldwide Governance Indicators 1996–2006* (Washington, D.C., 2007). In addition, while they are smaller, criminal organizations based on Korean, Filipino, Thai, Burmese, Pakistani, Israeli, and Jamaican national bases also have begun to cause serious worry for law enforcement officials.

86. Counting the majority of the Triads as based outside of the PRC. See Table 5-2 in this chapter.

87. By some measures, Nigeria is not a failed state. See, for instance, Robert I. Rotberg and Rachel M. Gisselquist, *Strengthening African Governance: Ibrahim Index of African Governance, Results and Rankings 2008* (Cambridge, MA, 2008), available at http://belfercenter.ksg.harvard.edu/publication/18541/strengthening_african_governance.html (accessed 25 February 2009).

88. See Skaperdas, "The Political Economy of Organized Crime."

89. See Kaufmann, Kraay, and Mastruzzi, *Governance Matters*; Stewart Patrick,

"Weak States and Global Threats: Fact or Fiction?" *Washington Quarterly,* XXIX (2006), 27–53.

90. Patrick, "Weak States and Global Threats," 38–39.

91. Phil Williams, "Transnational Criminal Enterprises, Conflict, and Instability," in Chester Crocker, Fen Osler Hampson, and Pamela Aall (eds.), *Turbulent Peace: The Challenges of Managing International Conflict* (Washington, D.C., 2001), 97–112; UN Office on Drugs and Crime (UNODC), *Why Fighting Crime Can Assist Development in Africa: Rule of Law and Protection of the Most Vulnerable* (Vienna, 2005).

92. Patrick, "Weak States and Global Threats," 39.

93. See also Kimberley Thachuk, "Corruption: The International Security Dimension," available at http://usinfo.state.gov/eap/Archive_Index/Corruption_The_Inter national_Security_Dimension.html#chuck8 (accessed 4 November 2008).

94. Please contact this author for the list of sources used in compiling these data.

95. Nevertheless, as Patrick notes, links between TCOs and state weakness appear to vary by "product sector." For instance, what are widely regarded as the most poorly governed states dominate the annual list of countries that the U.S. designates as "major" drug-producing and transiting nations. Nearly 90 percent of global heroin, for example, comes from Afghanistan and is trafficked to Europe via poorly governed states in Central Asia or along the "Balkan route." Myanmar (Burma) is the second largest producer of opium and a key source of methamphetamine. Likewise, although good data are hard to come by, weak states similarly appear to dominate the list of countries designated as the worst offenders in human trafficking. See Patrick, "Weak and Global Threats," 39. See also U.S. Department of State, "Presidential Determination on Major Drug Transit or Major Illicit Drug Producing Countries for Fiscal Year 2006," *International Country Narcotics Strategy Reports* (Washington, D.C., 2005); UNODC, *2005 World Drug Report* (Vienna, 2005); and U.S. Department of State, *Trafficking in Persons Report* (Washington, D.C., 2005).

96. Andreas and Nadelmann, *Policing the Globe,* 248.

97. "Mexico Extradites an Unprecedented Number of Drug Lords to US," *USA Today* (20 January 2007); James C. McKinley, Jr., "Drug Lord, Ruthless and Elusive, Reaches High in Mexico," *New York Times* (9 February 2005).

98. For instance, there is some evidence to suggest that in the aftermath of the destruction of the Medellin cartel and the assaults on the Cali cartel, the Norte del Valle cartel has stepped into the breach. See "Cartel Infiltrates Colombian Military," *United Press International* (8 September 2007); Winifred Tate, "Accounting for Absence: The Colombian Paramilitaries in U.S. Policy Debates," in Andreas and Greenhill (eds.), *Cooking the Books,* 6.

99. See Neild, *Public Corruption,* 202–203.

100. Robert Harris, *Political Corruption: In and Beyond the Nation State* (London, 2003), 176.

101. For a detailed examination of the elimination of threats posed by the TCOs run by South-East Asian drug baron Khun Sa and Colombian drug lord Pablo Escobar, see Harris, *Political Corruption,* 180–188.

MATTHEW BUNN

6 | *Corruption and Nuclear Proliferation*

Corruption is a critical, under-recognized contributor to nuclear proliferation. With the possible exception of North Korea, corruption was a central enabling factor in all of the nuclear weapons programs of both states and terrorist groups in the past two decades. Indeed, corruption is likely to be essential to most cases of nuclear proliferation. Unless a state or group can get all the materials and technology needed for its nuclear weapons program from some combination of its own indigenous resources; outside sources motivated only by a desire to help that nuclear program; or outside sources genuinely fooled into providing technology that they believe is for another purpose, illicit contributions from foreign sources motivated by cash will be central to a nuclear program's success. New steps to combat corruption in the nuclear sector, and in security, law enforcement, and border control agencies that are responsible for preventing nuclear theft, technology leakage, and smuggling are essential to strengthen the global nonproliferation regime.

Of course, since corruption and proliferation are both secret activities, no precise measure of the frequency of proliferation-related corruption is available. No one knows if the documented cases represent nearly all of the cases that have occurred, or only the tip of the iceberg. This chapter uses a brief summary of the global black-market network led by Pakistan's Abdul Qadeer (A. Q.) Khan to illustrate the broader phenomenon; it lays out a taxonomy of different ways in which corruption can contribute to proliferation (or slow it, in some cases); and it offers the outline of an approach to reduce the dangers that are posed by corruption-proliferation linkages.

Defining Corruption

Transparency International defines corruption succinctly as "the misuse of entrusted power for private gain."[1] This misuse of power applies not only to corrupt public officials, but also to private employees with entrusted power: a company official who gives a lucrative contract to one supplier rather than another in return for kickbacks is clearly corrupt. Access to sensitive nuclear weapons–related technology and information also represents entrusted power. Selling that entrusted information or technology for private gain, knowing that it probably will be used to contribute to a nuclear weapons program in a foreign state, is a corrupt act—as the term is used in this chapter—even if the sellers manage to carry out their activities in locations where the laws are so weak that the sellers are not violating local law. Many of the corrupt participants in recent proliferation cases fall into this category; they did not hold public office, but rather used their access to key information, equipment, or materials (which had been entrusted to them by states, or firms acting on behalf of states) to earn millions of dollars from illicit transfers.

By this definition, for example, Peter Griffin, a British citizen, who was a key supplier of uranium enrichment centrifuge technology to Pakistan knowing full well that Pakistan would use this technology to produce nuclear weapons, would be considered corrupt, even though he did not hold public office, and even though he has long argued (perhaps correctly) that at the time of his activities, the export control laws that were in place were so weak that his activities were not illegal.[2] On the other hand, the firms that sold centrifuge-related equipment to Iraq in the apparently genuine belief that it was going to be used in the oil industry would not be considered corrupt, though they certainly had inadequate procedures in place to manage sensitive technologies. Between these extremes, there is the gray area where individuals may be able to convince themselves that nothing is amiss with a high-technology purchase, even when there are glaring signs of proliferation intent—which is the reason why many countries' export control laws limit exports that the exporter "knows *or has reason to know*" will be used for illicit weapons programs.[3]

By this definition, people who spied—that is, provided entrusted information—for cash would be considered corrupt, but people who spied or transferred sensitive technology and materials because they believed in the cause of those who they were helping would not. In the case of major transfers of information, equipment, and materials for nuclear weapons, however, this definition does not provide a limitation. While there have been ideological rationalizations involved in technology transfers, all of the major transfers considered in this chapter appear also to have involved substantial amounts of money that has gone into the pockets of corrupt participants. Transfers that are made on these scales are rarely done for free.

An Illustrative Case: The A. Q. Khan Network

As is now widely known, Pakistan's Khan led a global black-market nuclear technology network that operated for two decades. It marketed uranium enrichment centrifuge technology to Libya, Iran, North Korea, and possibly to others. The network also provided items such as a detailed nuclear bomb design (to Libya, and possibly to others) and instructions on casting uranium metal into the hemispheres that are useful for bomb components (to Iran, and possibly to others).[4] Corruption was fundamental to everything that the network did.

The operation began when Khan, who had been employed at a firm that was a subcontractor for the European enrichment consortium Urenco, left the Netherlands for Pakistan with centrifuge designs, photographs, a list of key suppliers, and a web of personal contacts. His initial theft of the centrifuge designs appears to have been motivated primarily by nationalism, and hence should not, by the definition above, be considered an act of corruption. However, the act was certainly illegal, and Khan's personal ambition played a role. Once back in Pakistan, Khan eventually convinced Prime Minister Zulfiqar Ali Bhutto that Pakistan would need to corrupt a wide range of suppliers to get covert, illegal supplies for its centrifuge program and, therefore, that Khan would have to control personally "large sums of money" with the freedom to "spend it without anyone looking over [his] shoulder."[5]

This arrangement, which continued in various forms for decades, succeeded in its intended purpose. Using this cash and Khan's network of contacts among European centrifuge technology suppliers, Khan and his Pakistani colleagues succeeded in corrupting many suppliers and buying key components and materials such as maraging steel (a difficult-to-make specialty steel with the high strength that is needed for fast-rotating enrichment centrifuges). Friedrich Tinner, Henk Slebos, Gotthard Lerch, Gerhard Wisser, Daniel Geiges, and Peter Griffin were among the most important of those who provided sensitive information and technology in return for cash—each individual's acts clearly meeting any reasonable definition of corruption. (Many of these individuals, however, have never been jailed, were jailed only briefly, or were not jailed until years after the network had been disrupted, either because of a lack of evidence that could be produced in open court or because the export control laws in the countries where they were operating were so weak that their exports were not illegal at the time.)

The large flows of cash to Khan, with little accountability, also led to corruption in Pakistan. As the years went by, Khan, despite having a modest government salary, became well-known for his wealth and power.[6] Moreover, Khan reportedly used large sums of cash to pay off a range of military personnel and government officials (including a succession of officers that were charged with security at the A.Q. Khan Research Laboratories, Pakistan's main facility for enriching uranium for its nuclear bomb program), to subsidize dozens of reporters for favorable coverage, and even to create prizes that were then awarded to Khan. Decades later, when President Pervez Musharraf established the National Accountability Bureau to help address corruption in the Pakistani government, the bureau developed a remarkable 700- to 800-page dossier on Khan's corruption. The documents reportedly confirmed that Khan owned at least nine houses in Pakistan and London that were worth millions of dollars; controlled bank accounts that contained some $8 million in several countries; and also owned a hotel in Timbuktu, named after his wife, to which a Pakistani Air Force cargo plane had delivered a load of furniture. In addition, the papers detailed a range of corrupt transactions, in which Khan had personally skimmed 10 percent from procurement contracts for the A.Q. Khan Research Laboratories or had arranged to purchase far more of certain expensive items than the laboratory needed, apparently selling the rest for profit. (The laboratory—which includes the enrichment plant that produced the highly enriched uranium [HEU] for Pakistan's bomb—was renamed in Khan's honor.) Despite such overwhelming evidence, the bureau decided not to bring a case against Khan because he was so powerful, and the corrupt network that he had established penetrated so far within the Pakistani establishment that attempting to prosecute him might have brought down the National Accountability Bureau.[7]

Having successfully corrupted European and other suppliers to get what they needed for Pakistan's program, Khan and his co-conspirators then turned their network into an export enterprise, supplying centrifuge technology and other nuclear weapons–related technologies to Iran, Libya, and North Korea (to name the documented cases).[8] There are continuing controversies over the extent to which any or all of these transfers were authorized by the Pakistani government or high-level officials other than Khan; officially, the Pakistani government asserts that no senior officials except Khan were involved. Since the operation included steps such as removing entire centrifuges from the Khan Research Laboratories and flying them to foreign countries on Pakistani military aircraft, accepting the assertion that the operations were unauthorized leads to the conclusion that security failed on an epic scale, representing a remarkable level of success for Khan in corrupting others to take part in this scheme.[9] In all likelihood, there was a combination of authorization and corruption that penetrated deeply into the Pakistani military and security establishment. There are strong suggestions, for example, that the initial transfers to Iran were authorized by General Aslam Beg, then the chief of army staff, less so for cash than to build a strategic anti-Western alliance.[10] Ultimately, the high-level positions of those who probably participated in the network raise the question of "state capture"—corruption so deep that on some key issues, the corrupt participants can control the policy of the state.[11]

Whatever the case, it is clear that corruption was an essential element of this entire operation. Many of the same corrupted suppliers who had provided technology and equipment to Pakistan then did the same for the network's other clients, and they and Khan reportedly earned millions of dollars in the process. Gotthard Lerch, for example, reportedly initiated the network's first dealings with Iran in the 1980s, arranging for the network to provide centrifuge designs and components in return for $10 million, of which Lerch pocketed $3 million.[12] Ultimately, individuals or firms in some twenty countries participated in what was truly a global network. Most of these participants were corrupted, knowingly providing technologies that would contribute to nuclear proliferation for cash. Admittedly, some may have been genuinely unaware of the real end use of what they were providing. For example, managers of the Scomi plant in Malaysia, which was making key centrifuge components for Libya's program, claim that they believed that the parts that they were making were for the oil industry.[13]

In the end, foreign intelligence services managed to penetrate the network (turning at least one of the corrupted participants, Urs Tinner, son of one of Khan's original suppliers). Foreign governments seized a ship that was filled with centrifuge parts that was headed for Libya. The Libyan government, in the process of giving up its nuclear and chemical weapons programs, provided detailed information on its dealings with the network. Musharraf forced Khan to make a televised confession and placed him under house arrest. Khan, however, remains a revered national hero in Pakistan and was released from house arrest with no charges against him in early 2009. Only a few of the other Pakistani participants were ever detained, and, as far as is publicly known, none are still in custody. Only a few of the participants that are located elsewhere have spent time in jail; most remain free.

A Taxonomy: Corruption-Proliferation Linkages

The proliferation programs of states and of terrorist groups are generally different, given the far greater technical and financial resources that a state can bring to bear, and states' and terrorists' different goals. Typically, a proliferating state wants an arsenal of safe, reliable weapons that can be delivered by missile or aircraft and that can be stored for a long time, to act as a deterrent. A terrorist group, by contrast, may be satisfied with one or two crude, unsafe, unreliable weapons that fit in a minivan.

In particular, proliferating states typically seek the technology to make their own nuclear bomb material (though they may also seek ready-made bomb material as a complementary short-cut). In recent years, easy-to-hide uranium enrichment centrifuges have been the technology of choice for the determined nuclear cheater.[14] Because the export of this technology from states that had it to potential proliferant states was generally banned, corrupting people to convince them to sell illicitly is fundamental to these programs. States have also sought nuclear weapon designs, nuclear weapon manufacturing technology, and more. A typical procurement transaction might involve several stages, each of which might require cash to grease the skids. These stages can include:

—Convincing an individual or firm to provide sensitive technology, equipment, or materials;

—Bypassing or gaining approval from whatever internal review process may exist at the firm;

—Bypassing or gaining approval from whatever export control system the country may have; and

—Bypassing or gaining approval from customs and border control officials.

For terrorists, by contrast, making their own nuclear bomb material is simply out of reach.[15] Unfortunately, however, if terrorists succeeded in getting plutonium or HEU, making a crude nuclear bomb, while a substantial challenge, is not as difficult as many believe, and is within the plausible capability of a sophisticated terrorist group.[16] Aum Shinrikyo and al Qaeda, the two terrorist groups whose efforts to get nuclear weapons have been the most substantial and well documented to date, both sought to get either stolen nuclear weapons or stolen nuclear materials that could be used to make a bomb and to recruit or otherwise acquire the expertise that was needed to make a bomb.[17] In both cases, a key approach was to offer large sums of cash to people who might have had access to such items to get them to agree to provide them. Aum Shinrikyo, for example, reportedly attempted to arrange a meeting in Russia with then-Minister of Atomic Energy Victor Mikhailov, to offer him $1 million for a nuclear warhead—a clumsy approach that certainly would not have worked.[18] Aum Shinrikyo's "Construction Minister," Kiyohide Hayakawa, traveled repeatedly to Russia, buying a wide range of weapons and technologies (including a military helicopter, which was shipped to Japan for the cult's use). One of Hayakawa's notebooks from these trips includes the notation "how much is a nuclear warhead?" followed by several possible prices.[19]

As in the case of a state, a procurement effort by a subnational group that is seeking a nuclear weapon or the materials to make one would typically proceed in several stages, all of which might be facilitated by corruption. The stages involve:

—Convincing an individual or group to steal the desired items (or to help others to do so, for example, by turning off alarms or providing detailed information on security arrangements); or

—Convincing an individual or group to sell already-stolen items; and

—Bypassing or gaining approval from customs and border control officials.

An examination of the relevant cases suggests that the two most important types of proliferation-related corruption include technology experts who corruptly provide sensitive technology (especially centrifuge technology) to states, and nuclear staff or security and border officials who participate in or facilitate theft and smuggling of nuclear materials, possibly for terrorist groups. Below is a brief taxonomy of the different stages of proliferation efforts that are carried out by states or subnational groups in which corruption may play an important role.

Corrupt Provision of Sensitive Information, Technology, or Equipment

Corrupt provision of sensitive information, technology, or equipment appears to be the most common form of proliferation-related corruption, and it has been a factor in every state nuclear weapons program in recent decades. Iraq's extensive successes in corrupting suppliers in Europe, the United States, and elsewhere have been well documented; in many respects they parallel Pakistani successes. Individuals and firms in Europe, the United States, and elsewhere provided a wide range of centrifuge designs, components, flow-forming machines for manufacturing centrifuges, etc. Some of these firms and individuals apparently were unaware of the purposes for which their technologies would be used, but others actively helped to forge end-user certificates, falsify

export forms, and the like. Two corrupt individuals played particularly crucial roles in Iraq's program: German engineer Bruno Stemmler provided
detailed centrifuge design drawings, stolen centrifuge components, and extensive personal assistance to Iraq in return for just over $1 million; Karl-Heinz
Schaab provided more advanced centrifuge designs, techniques for manufacturing key components, machines for testing and balancing centrifuges, and
on-site technical help that accelerated the Iraqi program "by many months, if
not years," in return for millions of dollars.[20] Iran, Libya, and North Korea all
convinced suppliers to provide them with controlled technologies in return
for large sums of cash. The suppliers, in most cases, knew full well that the
technologies would be used for nuclear weapons.

Further, people who have critical proliferation-sensitive knowledge that
have left the agencies, firms, or institutes where they acquired that knowledge pose a particularly difficult control problem that is not addressed by
many current non-proliferation programs.

Many of the most important corrupt technology suppliers fall into this
category. When Stemmler was introduced to the Iraqis, he was "embroiled in
a conflict" with his employer and looking to leave, having already been forced
out as head of the company's isotope separation lab "in a manner that left him
embittered and angry."[21] He left the firm, apparently stealing extensive documentation and nuclear components in the process, and sold his knowledge to
the Iraqis. Schaab, recruited for the Iraqi effort by Stemmler, had left the same
centrifuge firm of his own accord, also "bitter" about how he had been treated
there.[22] While Gotthard Lerch was working for Leybold-Heraeus in Germany
when he began supplying Khan, he was forced to resign after the government
questioned his dealings with Pakistan; he moved to Switzerland in 1983 and
continued to supply the Khan network for two decades from there.[23] This
history suggests that it is time to reconsider current policies that ignore personnel who have left their institutes or firms in programs intended to redirect
weapons scientists to civilian work and that impose few constraints on individuals who previously had authorized access to highly sensitive technologies.

In some cases, the corrupt suppliers in these transactions were individuals; in others entire firms or institutes were involved. A prominent example
is H+H Metalform GmbH, in which Iraq secretly bought a major share, and
that provided a wide range of centrifuge-related technologies and materials.[24] Similarly, Iraq secretly acquired the British precision machine tool firm
Matrix Churchill, which became a central element of Iraq's illicit procurement program.[25] In another troubling case, even after the 1991 imposition of
United Nations sanctions that banned all transfers of long-range missiles or

components, Iraq succeeded in convincing Russian institutes to provide a wide range of missile technologies to Iraq, including missile guidance equipment that was taken from dismantled Russian strategic submarine-launched ballistic missiles (SLBMs) and was tested and certified as functioning properly by one of Russia's key missile institutes.[26] As this act was in direct violation of Russian export control laws and UN sanctions, to which Russia was a party, in return for cash to the institutes (and perhaps to individual managers there), this transaction was clearly corrupt. These cases may represent a situation in which a few corrupt individuals at a firm convinced the rest of the firm to move ahead with a particular transfer, thereby putting the reputation of the entire firm at risk.

Corrupt Provision or Theft of Sensitive Materials

Provision of materials is closely related to provision of information, equipment, and technology. In the case of nuclear weapons programs, the materials in question may be materials that are needed to manufacture equipment that produces nuclear bomb material (such as the high-strength maraging steel for centrifuges that was mentioned above), or they may be the nuclear bomb materials. (The key materials that can be used to fuel the nuclear chain reaction in a nuclear bomb are plutonium or HEU.[27])

Corrupt provision of materials such as maraging steel has been a factor in (at least) the Pakistani, Iraqi, and Iranian nuclear programs. The Iraqi purchase of 100 tons of maraging steel—estimated by Mahdi Obeidi, the purchaser, as enough for 10,000 centrifuges, capable of producing material for 15 nuclear bombs a year—was so clearly understood as corrupt by all participants that some of the key discussions took place in a strip club in Paris.[28]

There have been numerous cases (primarily in the 1990s) of authorized insiders stealing plutonium or HEU with the intention of selling it on the black market. By the definition above, these individuals would be considered corrupt, since they were misusing entrusted access to these materials in the hopes of private gain. The public record, however, does not yet include successful cases in which potential buyers corrupted existing insiders at facilities where plutonium and HEU existed and convinced them to steal it for them—that is, cases where the theft took place at the instigation of a known buyer. In at least one case, intelligence agents posing as buyers may have provoked a theft of nuclear material in this way: in 1994, the 363 grams of plutonium seized at the Munich airport from a flight that came from Moscow was the result of a sting operation by German intelligence (though the public record is not clear on whether the sting provoked the theft or the thieves already had the material when the sting began).

More recently, there was a clear attempt to corrupt insiders to steal bomb material. During 2003, proceedings in a Russian criminal case revealed that a Russian businessman had offered $750,000 for stolen weapons-grade plutonium for sale to a foreign client, and he had made contact with residents of the closed nuclear city of Sarov, home of one of Russia's premier nuclear weapons laboratories, to try to secure a deal.[29] Two Sarov residents received $50,000 up-front from the Nizhny Novgorod businessman, Boris Markin, with the promise of the rest to come when the plutonium was delivered. Fortunately, the two were scam artists with no access to plutonium. Oddly, though his effort to get stolen plutonium was a grave crime under Russian law, when the two men made off with his down payment, Markin went to the local branch of the Federal Security Service (FSB, from its Russian title, the successor to the KGB) and charged the two with fraud—perhaps fearing his client, whose money he had spent, more than he feared the Russian security services.[30] As the investigation was underway, Markin was hit by a car and killed. While Russian investigators concluded that his death was an accident, with no relation to the case; suspicions remain. Although no actual plutonium was stolen, this incident is particularly troubling in that it demonstrates the existence of Russian businessmen with substantial sums of cash and connections to clients abroad seeking to buy weapons-grade plutonium and knowledgeable enough to begin making contact with residents of closed nuclear cities to do so.[31]

Groups such as al Qaeda have made repeated efforts to buy already-stolen nuclear material, though there is not yet public evidence that they have actively attempted to corrupt individuals to carry out such theft. In the early 1990s, for example, al Qaeda sought to purchase what it believed to be HEU from a smuggler in the Sudan, though this transaction appears to have been a scam. As recently as 2003, U.S. intelligence received "a stream of reliable reporting" that al Qaeda operatives in Saudi Arabia were negotiating for the purchase of three Russian nuclear warheads.[32] Indeed, efforts to corrupt people who might be able to provide nuclear weapons or materials have been fundamental to all of the known terrorist efforts to acquire nuclear weapons to date.[33]

Corrupt Assistance in Sensitive Materials Thefts

Of course, corrupt insiders might not carry out a theft of potential nuclear bomb material, but instead might only assist in the theft—leaving a back door open, turning off a crucial alarm, providing information about security system weaknesses and exactly which material to take, etc. In a 1993 case at the Sevmorput Naval Shipyard, for example, Dmitry Tikhomorov, an employee at the yard, told his brother, a retired naval officer, about security weaknesses there, assisting his brother in stealing 4.5 kilograms of uranium enriched to approximately 20 percent U–235.[34] In the United States and in a number of other countries, the "design basis threat" that nuclear security systems are required to protect against includes the possibility of an insider providing this sort of assistance to thieves.[35]

Such corrupt assistance can take many forms and can require many levels of knowledge on the part of the corrupted individuals. In Russia, for example, the largest nuclear weapons facilities are located in "closed cities," with a fence around the entire city that is guarded by armed troops. No one may enter the city without approval from Russian authorities, and everyone going in or out is checked by the guards. A U.S. study based on interviews with residents of one of these cities, however, found that the cost of bribing a guard to gain access to the city without being checked amounted to a few dollars or a bottle of vodka.[36] In mid-2006, Russian President Vladimir Putin fired the Ministry of Interior's (MVD) Major-General Sergei Shlyapuzhnikov, who was the deputy commander of the MVD department that was charged with law and order in the closed cities; according to the Russian state newspaper, he was fired for organizing smuggling in and out of those cities and handing out passes that allowed people and vehicles to enter and leave without being checked.[37] By allowing unchecked passage, such corrupt officials could create major pathways for nuclear theft and smuggling without realizing that they were contributing to anything more than low-level smuggling of cigarettes and pirated CDs.

Corrupt guards at nuclear sites pose a particular risk. In 2003, Igor Goloskokov, then the chief of security at Seversk (formerly Tomsk-7), one of Russia's largest plutonium and HEU facilities, warned that the MVD troops that were guarding the site were poorly paid, poorly trained, and frequently corrupt, becoming "the most dangerous internal adversaries."[38] This situation is of particular concern since a survey of a wide range of thefts from guarded facilities found that the guards were frequently among the thieves.[39] Corruption in the military and security services that are charged with guarding nuclear stockpiles is widespread in Russia and in Pakistan and has included corrupt assistance to terrorists.[40]

Corrupt Hiring that Provides Access to Sensitive Technology or Materials

There are many institutions in many countries where jobs are for sale. This circumstance can create major opportunities for those seeking to access a site's technology or materials to infiltrate the institution by buying their way in. When a hire means money into the hiring official's pocket, there is a strong incentive not to do an in-depth background check. In one study, for example, U.S. researchers, working with Russians living in the closed nuclear city of Ozersk, home of the Mayak Production Association, one of Russia's largest plutonium and HEU processing facilities, were able to develop rough estimates of the cost of purchasing a wide range of jobs at the Mayak complex.[41]

Corrupt Financing of Sensitive Transfers

Many of the transfers of sensitive nuclear weapons–related technology that are described above involved the exchange of millions or tens of millions of dollars. The witting or unwitting participation of major banks in financing the transactions was essential. In many cases, the banks, where accounts and wire transfers were used, had no knowledge of the illicit transactions and cannot be considered corrupt. Other banks, however, were clearly complicit. Iraq's program established a special relationship with the Atlanta branch of the Banca Nazionale de Lavoro (BNL), a bank that is owned by the Italian government, with branches all over the world. BNL handled billions of dollars in Iraqi funds and financed a wide range of illicit purchases. Atlanta branch manager Christopher Drogoul and five other employees were subsequently charged with conspiracy, wire fraud, and related crimes.[42] Similarly, the Bank of Credit and Commerce International (BCCI)—a bank renowned for its deep corruption—played a central role in financing the activities of the Khan network.[43]

Corrupt Approval of Sensitive Transfers

In some cases, individuals or firms that provide sensitive technology, equipment, or materials simply smuggle it across borders without seeking any type of permission. In other cases, corrupt participants falsify documentation to get shipments through customs or export control processes. On occasion, the officials charged with reviewing and approving or rejecting high-technology exports may be bribed to approve illicit shipments. In the case of the transfers of Russian ballistic missile guidance to Iraq, for example, at one stage a Russian customs official reportedly raised questions about the low declared value of a set of boxes that contained missile guidance equipment, but he approved the shipment in return for a bribe.[44] It seems likely that the frequency of this type of corruption is far greater than is known.

Corrupt Approval of Border Crossings

Customs and border control officials in many countries are notoriously corrupt. The responsibility to oversee what can and cannot be brought across a border, often at remote posts, with little oversight, creates opportunities for corruption to flourish. The possibility that contraband can get past borders in return for a modest bribe poses a fundamental problem for efforts to block illicit transfers, whether of nuclear materials, nuclear technologies, or drugs and other contraband.

In the case of preventing nuclear smuggling, donors have long recognized that there may be little value in providing radiation detection equipment to officials if those using it can easily be bribed to ignore an alarm.[45] In a significant case in 2006, stolen HEU had reportedly been smuggled from Russia to Georgia with the aid of a corrupt border official who was a relative of the principal smuggler, Oleg Khintsagov.[46]

Similarly, in late 2004, Russian authorities revealed that they had launched an investigation into a smuggling ring that was apparently run by customs inspectors at the Russia-Finland border checkpoints of Torfyanovka and Brusnichnoye. In 2003, the smugglers allegedly allowed 1,356 cargo trucks to pass through the checkpoint without paying the requisite duties, costing the state a total of $30 million in uncollected fees. Andrej Andreyev, the head of the Torfyanovka checkpoint, was fired as a result of the ongoing investigation. Although this ring does not appear to have been involved in nuclear smuggling, such an organized ring of corrupt customs officials can create important opportunities for smuggling nuclear materials or technologies.[47]

Corrupt Protection of Proliferation Activities and Networks

Organized crime groups and criminal networks regularly infiltrate police forces, or they corrupt members of the police around the world, allowing these groups to be warned of impending searches or arrests. In some cases, judges are corrupted to protect criminal networks as well. It is not clear from the public record whether proliferation networks have paid for such protection. It seems likely that Khan's extensive corrupt network in Pakistan provided important warnings and protection that allowed some of the network's illegal activities in Pakistan to continue longer than they otherwise would have.

Corrupt Interference in Non-Proliferation Programs

Over the years, the United States and other countries have spent billions of dollars on programs to fix some of the weaknesses that corrupt proliferation participants have exploited—helping states upgrade security for nuclear stockpiles, strengthen export controls, and more. Corruption has certainly slowed and interfered with these efforts—not surprising, as non-proliferation programs have been implemented in some of the world's most corrupt countries, from the former Soviet Union to Pakistan.

The most infamous case is that of Evgeniy Adamov, Russia's former minister of atomic energy. In 2008, Adamov was convicted of taking part, with others, in stealing 62 percent of the shares (a value of some $31 million) of a joint venture that was involved in implementing the U.S.-Russian HEU Purchase Agreement.[48] U.S. prosecutors have charged Adamov with stealing $9 million from U.S. funds that had been provided to upgrade nuclear safety at Russian reactors. The U.S. officials who oversee that program have pointed out that the nuclear safety work that they paid for was completed, so if Adamov stole money, it was from the people who did the work and did not get paid as much as they should have, not from the United States.[49] Corruption was reportedly a commonplace feature of Adamov's activities during his tenure at the ministry.[50]

Adamov's case is by no means an isolated one, however. Corruption is endemic in key ministries with which foreign non-proliferation programs have had to work. As one example, Russian sites must get approval from Rosatom (the institution that replaced the Ministry of Atomic Energy, which is now a state corporation) for U.S.-funded contracts to upgrade nuclear material security and accounting systems. These approvals are often delayed at headquarters for months at a time. But the headquarters' official charged with approving these contracts told an expert from one Russian site that they could be approved in a week or two if he paid an expediting fee of a few percent of the contract value to a private firm (owned by people close to the official making the suggestion).[51]

In another instance where at least suspicions of corruption slowed down non-proliferation cooperation, in the early 1990s, the United States and Russia disagreed over the design for a massive, secure storage facility for material from dismantled nuclear weapons, which was to be built at Mayak. The institute that designed the building refused to provide the design and allow the project to begin until it had been paid $1 million that it was owed for its work, and the Ministry of Atomic Energy claimed to have no money to pay it. The U.S. Department of Defense (DOD), which was funding the project, refused to pay, arguing that Russia's willingness to do so was an indicator of whether Russia was serious about paying its agreed share for the cost of the project. After months of delay, the U.S. Department of Energy (DOE) agreed to pay to avoid continued delays. The question then arose of how the money should be transferred. Victor Mikhailov, Adamov's predecessor as minister of atomic energy, provided a bank account in an off-shore banking haven in Europe and suggested that the money be sent there. Given the chaos in the Russian banking system at the time, it is quite possible that this was a legitimate ministry bank account, but Mikhailov's suggestion did not meet "the smell test," and ultimately, the U.S. government dispatched U.S. officials to carry cash directly to the design institute.[52]

Corrupt Permissions that Allow Control Weaknesses to Continue

In many cases, weaknesses that might be exploited by those seeking nuclear materials or technology would be expensive to fix, which creates a potential incentive to use bribery to avoid having to fix them. In Russia, for example, nuclear security inspectors for Rostekhnadzor, the agency charged with regulating security and accounting for non-military nuclear material, are paid only a few hundred dollars a month. If they find a significant violation of nuclear security or accounting rules, the cost of fixing those violations in many cases is hundreds of thousands or millions of dollars. The potential incentive to bribe the inspector to overlook the problem is obvious. In 2008, a Russian MVD colonel was reportedly arrested for soliciting thousands of dollars in bribes to overlook violations of security rules in the closed nuclear city of Snezhinsk.[53] While this appears to be the only case of bribery of this type of official in the public record, bribery of virtually all other types of inspectors is commonplace in Russia.

Domestic Corruption as an Obstacle to Proliferation Success

As with any other large-scale project that a government undertakes, corruption can also interfere with nuclear, chemical, or biological weapons programs. While there is no evidence that Khan's extensive corruption slowed the Pakistani nuclear weapons program, it certainly made it more costly. In Iraq, under Saddam Hussein, corruption permeated virtually every major program. While corruption related to the oil-for-food program helped to finance illicit procurement after the 1991 war, corruption and empire-building by the technical leaders of the weapons program may also have distorted and slowed the effort. Covering some 35,000 m^2, for example, the immense nuclear weapons development and testing facility at Al Atheer appears to have been far larger than many reasonable estimates of the need.[54]

Corruption and Proliferation: What Is The Role of Organized Crime?

Corruption and large, established organized crime organizations are often conceived of as integrally linked. But in the case of nuclear proliferation, it appears that there are many cases of corruption that do not involve anything resembling traditional Mafia-style organized crime groups.

Clearly, the Khan network and the illicit procurement networks that were put together by Iraq, Iran, and others represent organized operations that relied heavily on corrupting potential suppliers and were, in some of their activities, criminal. Yet there is little evidence in the public record that traditional organized crime groups played any substantial part in these proliferation activities. These proliferation networks focused on corrupting a rarefied world of experts in advanced technologies who typically had little to do with the ordinary criminal world.

With respect to the smuggling of nuclear and radiological materials, there is an ongoing debate about the past and potential future role of organized crime. On the one hand, the known cases of smuggling of plutonium or HEU have generally not involved organized crime. Indeed, they have often involved what might be called comically disorganized crime—thieves who stole nuclear material with no particular idea about how to find a buyer, incompetent middlemen who had no idea what to charge for nuclear material or how to move it, and so on.[55] A detailed analysis of both nuclear cases and the much larger number of cases involving radiological materials suggests that only about 10 percent of the total number of cases appear to involve some type of organized crime, even when that is broadly defined as any enduring group whose primary purpose is to generate illegal profits.[56] There are strong arguments that traditional organized crime groups, deeply penetrated into the societies in which they operate and with large investments in legitimate stocks and real estate, may have little incentive to help terrorists destabilize their home societies or to engage in nuclear activities that are likely to bring the full fury of their home states down upon them.

On the other hand, there are reasons to suspect that the role of organized crime may be larger—or may become larger in the future—than these statistics and arguments suggest.[57] First, there may be a selection bias in the public record: it may be that the known cases have little involvement of organized crime because the thieves and smugglers who *are* associated with organized crime are less amateurish and do not get caught. Second, there are cases that suggest a linkage. In the early 1990s, for example, there was a case involving tons of HEU-contaminated beryllium that were smuggled from Russia to Lithuania, which clearly involved organized crime.[58] Similarly, a low-enriched uranium (LEU) fuel element, containing a small amount of U-235 that was stolen from a research reactor in Kinshasa, wound up in the hands of the Sicilian Mafia, where it was eventually seized in an Italian police operation.[59]

Third, organized crime's presence around nuclear facilities and along key transit routes may provide opportunities for buyers to make connections to potential nuclear thieves and to move their material without detection. Shelley and Orttung have reported cases that they describe as involving organized crime groups paying smugglers to transport nuclear materials.[60] Established smuggling routes for other contraband and corrupted border officials may provide opportunities for would-be nuclear smugglers to cooperate with organized crime groups to move their material without detection, possibly without the organized crime groups even being aware that nuclear material is the contraband that is being smuggled. A substantial fraction of Afghan heroin, for example, is known to go through Russia en route to Europe, creating opportunities for criminal and terrorist operatives from Russia, Afghanistan, and Pakistan to build relationships and to make contacts that may contribute to undetected nuclear smuggling. Two Uzbek smugglers were arrested in Kazakhstan in 2002 with a large cache of heroin and 1.5 kilograms of uranium oxide—this is at least one case where these activities merged.[61]

Shelley and Orttung have also found indications of substantial penetration of the closed nuclear city of Ozersk by organized crime (smuggling narcotics into the city by bribing the poorly paid guards, for example). Moreover, they note that under Russian law, criminals from the city were allowed to return to the city after serving their prison time and that the number of released criminals returning to Ozersk has increased markedly.[62] Such organized crime activity in a town that houses thousands of people who have access to a facility with tens of tons of plutonium and HEU clearly poses the risk that organized crime groups could make the connections needed to get involved in nuclear theft and smuggling.

Moreover, an argument can be made that newer organized crime groups that originate in conflict zones thrive on chaos, work with terrorists, and may be less restrained in dealing with nuclear or radiological materials.[63] Indeed, in the case of both the Afghanistan-Pakistan region and Colombia, drug trafficking and other criminal activities are so closely linked with terrorism that it is difficult to define the distinction between terrorist groups and organized criminal groups. The 2008 seizure of documents that indicated that the Revolutionary Armed Forces of Columbia (FARC) was considering a deal to buy and resell uranium is troubling, as it highlights that a professional group, with established smuggling operations, was potentially interested in engaging in nuclear smuggling.[64] At the same time, the documents also highlight the amateurish nature of so many nuclear smuggling cases, as the seized memorandum describes without question a $2.5 million-per-kilogram price for what turned out to be depleted uranium (a material that is essentially useless for either nuclear weapons or radiological "dirty bombs" and can readily be purchased for prices 10,000 times less).[65]

In short, the evidence available to date suggests (though it does not prove) that organized crime's involvement in nuclear smuggling has been limited. But it also provides grounds for being concerned that this restricted involvement may change in the future.

Countering the Proliferation-Corruption Linkage

Given this history, the obvious question is what steps would be most effective in reducing the dangers that are posed by corrupt individuals who participate in proliferation. Klitgaard has famously argued that corruption equals monopoly power plus discretion in using this power, minus accountability: C=M+D-A. According to this model, the obvious recommendations to control corruption are to decrease monopoly and discretion and to increase accountability.[66] Along similar lines, Huther and Shah have outlined an economic model in which potentially corrupt individuals rationally calculate the likely benefits from corruption and the probability and consequences of being caught, and are corrupt whenever the expected benefits are greater than the expected costs.[67] The obvious recommendations, using this model, are approaches that reduce the income that can be earned through bribes and increase both the probability of being caught or the penalties for being caught. But other scholars argue that a broader approach is needed, taking into account moral perceptions about corruption, differences in national cultures, and how deeply corruption has penetrated into a particular national system; the history of successes and failures in combating corruption suggests that what may work in one context may not work as well in another.[68]

Elements of the history that I have described suggest that at least some aspects of proliferation-related corruption may be different from other corruption, and may require a different response. While the states that have sought nuclear weapons in the last fifteen years—North Korea, Iran, Iraq, Libya, and possibly Syria—are all among the world's most corrupt countries, a large fraction of the corrupt suppliers of these efforts came from some of the world's *least* corrupt countries—such as Germany, Switzerland, Britain, and the United States. Hence, programs to reduce overall corruption in a particular country, by themselves, may do little to reduce the risk of proliferation-related corruption. This situation can be explained in part by the weakness of commonly perceived norms against proliferation in these countries (especially those in Europe) in the 1970s and 1980s, when many of the key technology suppliers first began to participate. At that time, the understanding that the spread of nuclear weapons was a deadly threat to the international community was not nearly as widespread as it is in the twenty-first century; export control laws in Europe were weak and poorly enforced, European governments were actively promoting high-technology exports, and they were seeking to smooth away obstacles to such job-generating activities. Many of the participants in these networks appear to have convinced themselves that there was little harm in what they were doing, little chance of being caught, and that if they were caught, there was little chance of serious consequences. To reduce the risks of corrupt participation in proliferation networks in the future, all of these perceptions must be changed.

The pervasive secrecy that surrounds the technologies and materials of nuclear, chemical, and biological weapons makes the usual anti-corruption prescriptions of greater public openness, transparency, and freedom of information far more difficult to implement in the case of proliferation-related corruption. Another common prescription—reducing the discretion available to officials—is also not generally appropriate in this case, as all those involved in guarding nuclear, chemical, and biological stockpiles, or in stopping proliferation conspiracies, must be creative in responding to unexpected circumstances and not only use their rule-books.

To counter the proliferation-corruption linkage, I suggest a multi-pronged strategy that is based on strengthening non-proliferation norms in key sectors; improving controls over sensitive technologies; increasing the probability that proliferation-related conspirators will be caught; increasing the expected consequences of being caught for proliferation-related corruption; making it difficult to overcome proliferation controls without a large and complex corrupt conspiracy; and establishing targeted anti-corruption programs in key sectors.

Strengthening Non-Proliferation Norms in Key Sectors

Studies of compliance with safety rules indicate that the probability of compliance with a rule is high among staff who believe that the rule is important, even if there is a low probability that non-compliance will be detected.[69] Much the same is likely to be true for proliferation-related corruption. Indeed, it seems likely that the critical reason why so little nuclear theft occurred in the former Soviet Union in the mid-1990s, when security for nuclear stockpiles was alarmingly weak and nuclear workers were desperate for additional income to feed their families, was the intense patriotism and devotion to duty of the vast majority of former Soviet nuclear workers.[70] By contrast, the corrupt participants in the Khan network overwhelmingly convinced themselves that the consequences of what they were doing were either minor or positive—that deterrence would be served by more countries having nuclear weapons or that if they did not sell these technologies others would.[71] Convincing the staff who might be corrupted at key points in the proliferation chain—and particularly those with the access to sensitive technologies and materials required to initiate such a transfer—that proliferation is a critical danger to their countries and to the world could make a substantial difference in reducing the danger of proliferation-related corruption.

In this respect, proliferation-related corruption may be far easier to counter than other forms of corruption. Even in countries where the national culture condones widespread corruption, there is generally a strong moral norm against helping other countries (or worse yet, terrorist groups) get nuclear, chemical, or biological weapons—and this culture can be built upon. This norm is strong in Russia and the other states of the former Soviet Union.

The following steps should be taken to strengthen non-proliferation norms in key sectors.

Required Training on the Proliferation Threat

Governments should: a) identify all individuals who have access to and knowledge of proliferation-sensitive technologies and materials, and b) require these individuals to participate in at least yearly briefings on the danger of proliferation, the impact proliferation could have on their country or firm, the reality of ongoing black-market attempts to acquire these technologies, the penalties for participating in proliferation, and cases where corrupt participants suffered severe punishments for their participation. At facilities with plutonium or HEU, these briefings should include not only individuals with direct access to the material but guards and others who have enough knowledge of the security system to help thieves to overcome it. At the same time, it is crucial to carry out such training in ways that do not give insiders new ideas for corrupt sales. Some of the nuclear material thieves of the 1990s, for example, were motivated by press reports of the large sums that buyers were willing to pay for potential nuclear bomb material.[72] Governments should regularly assess the effects of these training programs on targeted staff's proliferation attitudes and adjust the training approaches accordingly.

Programs to Strengthen Security Culture

Governments should require each firm or institute working with proliferation-sensitive technologies or materials to establish a program to promote a strong security culture among its staff, focused on a clear understanding of the threat, on knowledge of and willingness to comply with the security rules, and on an understanding of the need to keep an eye out for and be willing to report on suspicious incidents and activities.[73] The United States and Russia have undertaken a joint effort to promote a security culture at Russian sites with plutonium and HEU, but there is a great deal more to be done at these sites and elsewhere around the world. The series of incidents that have taken place at Los Alamos over the decades, and the 2007 incidents in the U.S. Air Force, which led Secretary of Defense Robert Gates to ask for the resignation of both the secretary of the Air Force and the Air Force chief of staff, make clear that further steps to strengthen nuclear security culture are needed in the United States as well.[74] Finding ways to change ingrained cultures at a wide range of nuclear-related institutions throughout the world remains an extraordinary policy challenge.[75]

Building Non-Proliferation Professional Norms

An understanding of the threat posed by the proliferation of nuclear, biological, and chemical weapons, and the personal responsibility of each person who has access to technologies that are relevant to such weapons, should become a normal part of training and professional development in these fields. Professional societies should include non-proliferation pledges in their codes of ethics and professional behavior.

Improving Controls over Proliferation-Sensitive Technologies

One of the most troubling aspects of either the nuclear theft cases of the 1990s or the history of the black-market nuclear technology networks is how weak the controls were that the conspirators had to overcome. In one case in 1993, for example, an individual walked through a gaping hole in a fence at a naval base, walked to a small shed, snapped the padlock with a metal bar, entered the shed, took several kilograms of enriched uranium, and retraced his steps, without setting off an alarm or encountering a guard. No one noticed until hours later—and then only because he had been careless and had left the door of the shed partly open and the broken padlock lying in the snow. The Russian military prosecutor in the case concluded that "potatoes were guarded better."[76]

Clearly, such vulnerabilities should not be allowed to exist. Governments must put in place effective, worldwide controls over proliferation-sensitive technologies and materials. Fortunately, substantial steps in this direction have already been taken. Security for nuclear weapons, plutonium, and HEU in the former Soviet Union has improved dramatically in the last fifteen years, and nuclear security upgrades have been undertaken in many other countries since the 9/11 attacks. After the proliferation leakage of the 1970s and 1980s, many countries in Europe and elsewhere have greatly strengthened their export control systems.

In 2004, partly in response to the Khan network, the UN Security Council unanimously approved UN Security Council Resolution 1540, which legally obligates every UN member state to "take and enforce effective measures to establish domestic controls to prevent the proliferation of nuclear, chemical, or biological weapons and their means of delivery," including "appropriate effective" security and accounting for any such stockpiles that they may have; "appropriate effective" border controls and law enforcement to prevent "illicit trafficking and brokering of such items;" and "appropriate effective" export controls, transshipment controls, and controls on financing such transactions, with appropriate penalties for violations. UNSC 1540 also requires every member state to adopt and enforce "effective" laws that prohibit non-state acquisition of nuclear, chemical, or biological weapons and any efforts to assist non-state actors in obtaining such weapons.[77] Unfortunately, most states have taken few, if any, actions to meet their UNSC 1540 obligations, and the major powers have taken only the most modest actions to make use of this new non-proliferation tool. Most of the steps that need to be taken to improve controls over proliferation-sensitive technologies around the world can be seen as simply implementation of states' existing UNSC 1540 obligations.

The following steps should be taken to strengthen controls over proliferation-sensitive technologies.

Establishing Effective Security and Accounting Worldwide

All nuclear weapons and weapons-usable nuclear material worldwide should be secured to standards that are sufficient to defeat the threats that terrorists and criminals can pose, in ways that will work, and in ways that will last. There is no doubt that such stockpiles must be protected against theft by corrupt insiders, as well as by outsiders with insider assistance. In particular, effective global standards for nuclear security are urgently needed; since UNSC 1540 already requires all states to provide "appropriate effective" security, the United States and other leading nuclear powers should seek to define the essential elements of an appropriate, effective system and work to help (and to pressure) all countries with nuclear stockpiles to put those essential elements in place.[78] As part of this global nuclear security effort, the number of locations where such materials exist and the scale of transport of them should be drastically reduced, making it possible to achieve higher security at a lower cost. The nuclear material needed for a bomb is small and difficult to find; security measures to prevent such materials from being stolen are critical, as all subsequent layers of defense are variations on looking for needles in haystacks. While substantial progress in improving nuclear security has already been made, there is a wide range of additional steps that still need to be taken to achieve effective and lasting nuclear security worldwide.[79]

Improving Protection against Insider Theft

Given the corruption problem—and other means by which those seeking nuclear bomb material might convince insiders to help them—improved security against insider thieves is particularly important. Governments should ensure that no one is allowed access to nuclear weapons, separated plutonium, HEU, or information about how these materials are guarded, without a thorough background check and ongoing monitoring for indicators of suspicious activity. The number of people who have access to such materials should be kept to an absolute minimum. Such weapons and materials should be stored in high-security bunkers or vaults whenever they are not in use; access to such bunkers and vaults should only be possible for a small number of carefully screened individuals. The "two-person rule" or "three-person rule" should be maintained, so that no one is ever alone with such items.[80] Areas where such materials are processed should be continuously monitored by guards or security cameras. All windows, ventilation shafts, and other means to get such materials out of the buildings, without going through the monitored exits, should be blocked, and those blocks should be regularly inspected. Monitored exits should include radiation detectors that will set off an alarm if anyone were carrying out plutonium or HEU.

Rigorous nuclear material accounting and control systems should be put in place that would ensure that any theft of nuclear material would be detected quickly (or while it was still in progress) and localized to the area where it occurred. Regular "red team" exercises should be conducted, with insiders pretending to be nuclear material thieves, to test whether intelligent insider adversaries can find vulnerabilities in the security system. Governments should reconsider existing policies that require facilities only to be able to protect against a single insider, rather than an insider conspiracy; a substantial fraction of thefts of valuable non-nuclear items from guarded facilities around the world are perpetrated by groups that include more than one insider.[81]

Effective, Worldwide Border, Export, and Transshipment Controls

These levels of control will never be as effective as security measures at the source can be, and putting these types of controls into place worldwide will pose even greater challenges than those posed by securing global nuclear stock-piles against theft. Leading nuclear technology states typically have put in place stronger export controls after experiences with the Iraqi and Pakistani procurement networks. But few countries can claim that they already have in place genuinely effective controls at all of their borders, on any attempts at illicit exports of proliferation-sensitive technologies, and on the transship-ment of sensitive technologies through their countries. Although UNSC 1540 creates a binding legal obligation for more than 190 member states, and the Khan network had key nodes in states no one had worried would contribute to nuclear proliferation (such as Malaysia and Dubai), donor states that help countries improve their export and border controls, such as the United States, still have programs focused on only a fraction of the world's countries. Nev-ertheless, for the countries on which they have focused, efforts such as DOE's International Export Control Cooperation program and the U.S. State Depart-ment's Export Control and Border Security (EXBS) program have contributed substantially to improved export controls; similar efforts should be under-taken for more states. Here, too, an international effort is needed to lay out the essential elements of appropriate effective systems in each of these areas and work to help (and to pressure) states to put those essential elements in place. In the nuclear area, states should give the International Atomic Energy Agency (IAEA) the mandate and resources to help to develop interpretations of the particular steps that are required to meet the UNSC 1540 obligations, to review states' performance, and to coordinate assistance to states.[82]

Strengthening Industry Education and Internal Compliance Programs

Governments must ensure that each firm or institute with proliferation-sensitive technology fully understands existing export control laws, prolifer-ation threats, proliferators' use of front companies and false end-use declara-tions, and the like. Each firm or institute with proliferation-sensitive technology should establish an in-depth internal compliance program to review not only the legality but the wisdom of proposed exports. Govern-ments should approve legislation that makes it possible to hold a designated officer at each firm or institute personally accountable for that organization's exports—providing a strong incentive to ensure that the organization com-plies with relevant laws. But governments should seek to help firms and insti-tutes carry out these responsibilities, focusing more on a partnership than on an adversarial approach. Such partnerships should include steps to encourage firms and institutes to provide information to governments about suspicious inquiries, companies that may be operating as fronts for proliferators, and the like without fear of negative consequences, and steps to encourage government officials to provide any information and assistance that may help firms and institutes improve their internal compliance programs. Governments or industry associations should help to share the best practices of those firms that have established exemplary internal review programs.[83]

Reducing the Risks Posed by Retired Individuals with Sensitive Knowledge

From Bruno Stemmler to Gotthard Lerch and beyond, many of the corrupt participants in recent proliferation conspiracies had left the firms or institutes where they had originally received access to sensitive knowledge. Little attention has been given to the proliferation risks posed by such individuals outside the officially sanctioned system of controls. Improving controls at established firms and institutes will not solve the problem posed by people who are no longer at those places. Retired experts may pose particular proliferation risks, as they have time available and may be more vulnerable to economic desperation. Governments should establish lists of *all* individuals that have been granted access to particular areas of nuclear, chemical, and biological weapons technologies, whether they are still working in officially sanctioned firms and institutes or not, and should regularly monitor their current location and status—even after their formal clearances have expired. Pension programs should be designed to ensure that people who have particularly sensitive knowledge have enough to subsist without becoming financially desperate. Programs should be established to provide non-proliferation briefings to these individuals, and to attempt to draw them into the broader scientific community and its norms. Scientist redirection programs could be broadened to include retired individuals, for example, by providing tax reductions to firms that hire anyone who was a weapons scientist in the past.

Making the Conspiracies Needed for Success More Complex

The danger of corruption is reduced when more people at more separate locations have to participate for the corrupt act to succeed. If a single paid-off guard is enough, the risk is high, but if three or four guards in different parts of a facility would have to participate for a theft to succeed, the risk is far lower.

Steps that should be taken to raise the barriers to proliferation-related conspiracies include:

Requiring the "Two-Person" or "Three-person" Rule

Making sure that no one is ever alone with a nuclear weapon or the materials to make one is an important first rule that countries such as the United States and Russia have had in place for many years. In a discussion in 2005, I asked a retired Russian officer who had been a senior commander of the 12th Main Directorate of the Ministry of Defense, the force that guards Russia's nuclear weapons, whether he was worried that the endemic corruption and theft in the Russian military would penetrate into that force. This provoked the blackest of humor: pointing out that the 12th maintains the two- or three-person rule, he smiled and said that as a result, most generals prefer to work with conventional weapons, where there are more opportunities to make money. Simple technological options—such as locks that require two people to turn their keys or type in their codes at the same time, several meters apart from each other, to gain access to a vault or bunker—can help enforce the two- or three-person rule and should be used.

Ensuring that Radiation Detectors Are Monitored at More Than One Location

There is always a possibility that a guard, who observes a radiation detector at some remote border crossing, or at the exit of a nuclear facility, would look the other way when the alarm goes off, or turn off the detector, in return for a bribe. Hence, to the extent practicable, all such detectors should be rigged so that both alarms and the functioning of the machine are monitored not only by an on-site guard, but by someone else some distance away as well, making it much more difficult to bribe both watchers. The U.S.-sponsored "Second Line of Defense" program, for example, helps countries install radiation-detection equipment at key ports and border crossings and often rigs these systems so that they will be monitored not only by on-site personnel but also by others off-site, such as at a regional headquarters. As of early 2006, however, the program had not yet obtained the funding that is needed to incorporate this approach consistently, wherever its radiation detectors were to be installed.[84]

Remotely Observing Personnel at Key Locations

To ensure that the systems for nuclear material protection, control, and accounting (MPC&A) that are put in place with U.S. assistance are being used appropriately and maintained, the United States and Russia have established the MPC&A Operations Monitoring (MOM) project, in which security cameras observe key locations at a few selected facilities—such as the guards at the point where staff pass through radiation detectors when exiting the facility—and transmit these images to officials elsewhere (such as to the site's security managers).[85] This approach helps to detect and deter corrupt behavior at these key points and should be adopted more broadly at nuclear facilities worldwide.

Increasing the Probability of Being Caught

Clearly, that the Khan network operated successfully for some twenty years, with scores of participants (individuals and firms) in some twenty countries, illustrates that the probability that corrupt proliferators will be caught has been too low to deter them.

In addition to the improved controls over sensitive technologies described above, several other measures should be taken to increase the probability that nuclear smuggling or black-market nuclear networks will be detected.

Expanding International Police and Intelligence Cooperation

Efforts to stop corrupt proliferation rings must be every bit as global, intelligent, and adaptive as the rings themselves. The disruption of much of the Khan network involved successful cooperation between intelligence and police agencies in several countries, particularly the United States and Britain. Governments should substantially expand the cooperation between law enforcement and intelligence agencies that are focused on nuclear smuggling and black-market nuclear technology networks.[86] This effort should include cooperative, in-depth analyses of international black-market nuclear technology networks and nuclear smuggling rings, looking at particular cases, the motivations and methods of the participants, the possible interconnections between these networks (or between these networks and organized crime or terrorist groups), and how links are forged.[87] This international cooperation should also run additional stings and scams to catch participants in this market, collect intelligence on market participants, and increase the fears of real buyers and sellers that their interlocutors may be government agents. Furthermore, these efforts should be well-publicized to increase fears of such operations among potential buyers and sellers. Intelligence agents from the United States and other leading nations should also work with the semi-feudal chieftains who control some of the world's most dangerous and heavily smuggled borders to convince them to let their contacts know if anyone tries to move nuclear contraband through their domains.[88]

Strengthening Police and Intelligence Agencies' Ability to Monitor Proliferation-Related Trafficking in Key Countries

In many countries, police and intelligence agencies have little ability to understand, for example, that the precision-machined parts that are made at a particular factory in their country are for another country's uranium enrichment centrifuges. Through programs such as the International

Counterproliferation Program (ICP) at the U.S. Department of Defense, the United States and other donor countries have been providing proliferation-related training to law enforcement and border control officials in a number of countries. But there is much more to be done to strengthen police and intelligence capabilities to counter proliferation around the world. At a minimum, all potential source states and likely transit states should have units of their national police force trained and equipped to deal with nuclear smuggling cases, and other law enforcement personnel should be trained to call in those units as needed.

Establishing Well-Publicized Incentives to Inform on Proliferation Conspiracies

Most of the confirmed cases in which stolen weapons-usable nuclear material was successfully seized, or black-market nuclear technology transfers were successfully interdicted, involved having one of the conspirators or someone whom they tried to involve in the effort inform on the others. The success in convincing Urs Tinner to inform, for example, was crucial to the success in disrupting the Khan network.[89] Additional steps should be taken to make such informing more likely—including anonymous hotlines or websites that are well-publicized in the nuclear community, and rewards for credible information.

Systems-Level Approaches to Interdicting Nuclear Smuggling

The United States and other countries have invested a great deal of money to install radiation detectors at key ports and border crossings around the world. Such detectors have a real, but limited, role to play in reducing the risk of nuclear terrorism. The length of national borders, the diversity of means of transport, the vast scale of legitimate traffic across these borders, the small size of the materials needed for a nuclear bomb, and the ease of shielding the radiation from plutonium or especially from HEU all operate in favor of the terrorists. Neither the detectors now being put in place nor the Advanced Spectroscopic Portals planned for the future can offer much chance of detecting and identifying HEU metal with modest shielding—though they likely would be effective in detecting plutonium or strong gamma emitters such as Cs-137 that might be used in a so-called "dirty bomb."[90] Few of the past successes in seizing stolen nuclear material have come from radiation detectors; indeed, in many cases it is more likely that traditional counterterrorism approaches and border controls will detect the smugglers than that detectors will detect the nuclear material that they are smuggling. To gain the maximum benefit from investments in the prevention of nuclear smuggling requires a systems-level approach that looks not just at how well an individual detector may perform but at what options adversaries have to defeat the system—by choosing other routes, bribing officials to get past detectors, hiding nuclear material in difficult-to-search cargoes, etc.—and what options the defense might have for countering those adversary tactics.[91] Extensive "red teaming" should be used to ensure that a wide range of ideas that intelligent adversaries could pursue have been explored. Based on such an analysis, the United States and other leading governments should develop a strategic plan that goes well beyond detection at borders; detailing what police, border, customs, and intelligence entities in which countries should have what capabilities by when; and what resources will be used to achieve those objectives.

Interdicting Other Elements of Nuclear Terrorist Plots

Governments should also undertake an intense international effort to stop the other elements of a nuclear plot—the recruiting, fundraising, equipment purchasing, and more that would be required. Because of the complexity of a nuclear effort, these efforts would offer a bigger and more detectable profile than many other terrorist conspiracies. The best chances to stop such a plot lie not in exotic new detection technologies but in a broad approach to counterterrorism—including addressing the anti-American hatred that makes recruiting and fundraising easier, and makes it more difficult for governments to cooperate with the United States.[92]

Strengthening the International Atomic Energy Agency's (IAEA) Efforts

The IAEA has established a small unit to collect and analyze information on black-market nuclear technology networks.[93] Among other activities, this unit, known as the Nuclear Trade and Technology Analysis (TTA) unit, has established relationships with many companies that have key centrifuge-related technologies, and has convinced them to provide information on any suspicious inquiries that they receive. But this group has few staff, little money, and little authority. Moreover, to date the purpose of this analysis is only to support the IAEA's safeguard assessments of countries' nuclear programs by providing information on what they may be shopping for; ideally, such information should also be used to warn countries and companies about potential illicit front companies and networks and to help to plug leaks. Governments should give the IAEA the resources, authorities, information, and expanded mission necessary to maximize this group's effectiveness. Governments should also consider establishing similar groups focused on chemical, biological, and missile technologies.

Increasing the Expected Consequences

Many of the corrupt participants in black-market technology networks or nuclear smuggling have received remarkably light punishments. Yuri Smirnov, who stole 1.5 kilograms of weapons-grade HEU in 1992, in the first well-documented case of theft of weapons-usable material, received three years of probation—hardly a sentence likely to deter other nuclear thieves.[94] Stemmler, a key contributor to Iraq's centrifuge program, died of natural causes without being convicted. Schaab, another notorious participant in Iraq's centrifuge program, was convicted of exporting centrifuge rotors without a license and received a fine of DM 20,000 and a suspended sentence. Later, when the full extent of his activities became clear, Schaab was convicted of treason and received a fine of DM 80,000 and a five-year term, but because he was cooperating with the German authorities and had been in jail pending trial, he was released as soon as he was convicted.[95] The British government dropped charges against Griffin, one of the Khan network's key suppliers.[96] Khan, as noted above, was under only house arrest, and was released in early 2009.

Part of the problem is that the laws that relate to such crimes in many countries are weak. Remarkably, under Article 226 of the Russian criminal code, the penalty for stealing an assembled nuclear weapon is only five to ten years. The penalty for smuggling weapons of mass destruction is the same as the penalty for smuggling drugs: three to seven years.[97] In either case, however, the Russian authorities are also able to use treason statutes, for which the penalties are more severe. Many countries have laws with even lower penalties—or may not even have laws that prohibit various types of proliferation-sensitive exports, or *attempts* to carry out nuclear theft or proliferation-sensitive exports.

Given the scale of the potential consequences, all countries should put in place laws that make real or attempted theft; smuggling; or unauthorized possession of nuclear weapons, plutonium, or HEU (or chemical or biological weapons) crimes with penalties comparable to those for murder or treason. This step would be consistent with the Convention on Physical Protection of Nuclear Material and the International Convention for the Suppression of Acts of Nuclear Terrorism, both of which require all parties to pass "appropriate penalties" for nuclear theft and related crimes, taking into account their "grave nature." Stiff penalties should also be put in place for those who participate in black-market proliferation networks. At the same time, care should also be taken to avoid a perverse effect—in which people refuse to report such crimes, or juries refuse to convict, because of a perception that the penalties are disproportionate.[98]

Ultimately, consciously helping terrorists or proliferating states obtain nuclear, chemical, or biological weapons—or attempting to do so—should be considered an international crime with universal jurisdiction (meaning that a perpetrator could be prosecuted wherever he or she were caught), similar to piracy or hijacking.[99] The first steps in this direction are already being taken. The Convention on the Physical Protection of Nuclear Material and the nuclear terrorism convention both require all parties to put in place laws under which they either take jurisdiction to prosecute offenders caught on their territory (even if the crime had been committed elsewhere and the offenders were from another state) or to extradite them. But it is not clear how many countries have in fact passed laws that give them criminal jurisdiction if a nuclear thief, smuggler, or would-be nuclear terrorist from elsewhere were apprehended on their territory. Much remains to be done to move toward universal jurisdiction for such crimes.

Establishing Anti-Corruption Programs in Key Sectors

There can be little doubt that a pervasive atmosphere of corruption and insider theft increases the risk for theft of nuclear weapons and materials. Although corrupt technology suppliers such as Stemmler, Schaab, and Lerch came from low-corruption countries, it also seems clear that pervasive corruption increases the risk for the corrupt sale of proliferation-sensitive technology and equipment.

Hence, in addition to the programs to build non-proliferation norms in key sectors that were described above, governments should also pursue targeted anti-corruption programs for particularly proliferation-sensitive firms, institutes, and agencies. These would certainly include all firms or institutes handling nuclear weapons, plutonium, or HEU; nuclear weapons designs and manufacturing technologies; or enrichment and reprocessing technologies. It would also include border control and customs officials, nuclear guards, and export control agencies.

The particular anti-corruption programs that will be most effective are likely to vary from one context to another.[100] Higher salaries, to reduce the need for corrupt supplementary income, are certainly needed in some countries for nuclear guards, technicians with access to plutonium and HEU, customs and border control officers, export control license reviewers, and nuclear security inspectors—though it should be kept in mind that men like Stemmler and Schaab were already well-to-do, not desperate and underpaid (and Khan still more so). A variety of approaches to accountability should be put in place, including an independent inspector general (with access to all the needed information and facilities) for each critical agency involved in managing and controlling proliferation-sensitive technologies with the mission and resources to root out corruption and provide accountability for performance. Laws and institutions to protect and encourage whistleblowers should be established. Selling of jobs that include access to nuclear materials or technologies could be addressed through rules requiring that job openings be posted, open competitions held, and hiring decisions made by groups rather than individuals—combined with regular independent reviews of the reasons why particular candidates were hired. Governments should institute anti-corruption training programs for border control and customs forces, export control agencies, nuclear facilities, and others who might play important roles in proliferation-related corruption. All of these steps should be regularly assessed to see if they appear to be having the desired impact in changing attitudes and behavior.

Corruption among nuclear guards poses a particular problem, which must be dealt with through a thorough professionalization of these forces. In Russia, for example, nuclear weapons are guarded by the kind of force they should be guarded by—a reasonably well-paid, well-equipped, and well-trained professional force of volunteer soldiers. Most of those with access to nuclear weapons are officers. By contrast, sites with plutonium and HEU are primarily guarded by poorly paid and poorly trained conscripts with little idea of the importance of what they are guarding, among whom corruption is endemic.[101] Russia and other countries should shift to a system of well-paid, well-trained, well-equipped professional guard forces for all nuclear facilities.

Strengthening the Role of the Legislature, the Media, and Non-Governmental Organizations

In the United States and in a few other countries, investigations by the national legislature, the media, and non-governmental organizations (NGOs) have had a tremendous impact in revealing weaknesses in nuclear security, export controls, and similar measures, and putting pressure on governments to correct them.

Legislatures in every key country where proliferation-sensitive technologies exist should establish oversight committees charged with looking into the adequacy of their countries' controls, the dangers of proliferation-related corruption, and steps to address these dangers. Legislatures should insist on receiving the access to classified information necessary to pursue these questions. In many countries, this change will be a step-by-step process; but an initial successful investigation can go a long way to establish a legislature's role in these areas. Governments and non-government experts should work to educate legislators in key countries on these critical issues.

While secrecy is an immense constraint, the media and NGOs do have important roles to play. Efforts should be made to educate reporters and to support NGOs that are focused on these issues in key countries, building a global network of concerned citizens who hold their governments accountable to stop corrupt proliferation networks.

Conclusion

Corruption is a central, unrecognized theme of the story of nuclear proliferation. Corruption has been a critical enabling element of the nuclear weapons programs in Pakistan, Iraq, Libya, and Iran. North Korea appears to have developed its plutonium production program largely with indigenous technology, but it appears that corruption likely played a central role in its uranium enrichment program, for which the technology was supplied by the Khan network. The attempts that al Qaeda and Aum Shinrikyo made to get nuclear weapons also relied on the central strategy of corrupting potential sellers and thieves.

Indeed, corrupt suppliers are essential to any state or to a subnational attempt to get nuclear weapons, unless the state or group in question can:

—Develop its needed technologies on its own;

—Convince states to decide consciously to supply them; or

—Convince individuals, firms, or institute suppliers to provide the needed technologies or materials by means other than cash.

Hence, better protection against corrupt proliferation conspiracies is central to strengthening the global effort to stem the spread of nuclear weapons. There is an urgent need to strengthen non-proliferation norms in key proliferation-sensitive sectors; improve protection for sensitive technologies from corrupt insiders; increase participants' perceptions of the probability and consequences of being caught; and combat corruption in firms, institutes, and agencies where corruption could contribute to proliferation.

None of these steps will be easy. Those who benefit from corruption will resist efforts to constrain it. Only through sustained leadership at high levels of many governments, which brings together a broad coalition of concerned parties—and a focus on the real danger that is posed by proliferation—can there be hope for success. As with other aspects of non-proliferation, the political atmosphere in which states could be convinced to take additional action would be improved if the nuclear weapons states were seen to be negotiating in good faith toward nuclear disarmament.

Notes

1. See, for example, Transparency International, "Frequently Asked Questions About Corruption," available at www.transparency.org/news_room/faq/corruption_faq (accessed 7 September 2007).

2. See, for example, Griffin's assertion that "there's no bloody evidence" that he ever did anything illegal, a statement made after the British government dropped charges against him. See "U.K. Drops Investigation Into Khan Network Supplier," *Global Security Newswire* (14 January 2008). See also the interview with Griffin in Steve Coll, "The Atomic Emporium: Abdul Qadeer Khan and Iran's Race to Build the Bomb," *The New Yorker* (7 August 2006), available at www.newyorker.com/archive/2006/08/07/060807fa_fact_coll?currentPage=1 (accessed 14 September 2008).

3. See, for example, U.S. Export Administration Regulations, Part 772, Definitions of Terms.

4. For accounts of the Khan network, see, for example, International Institute for Strategic Studies, *Nuclear Black Markets: Pakistan, A.Q. Khan and the Rise of Proliferation Networks: A Net Assessment* (London, 2007); Douglas Frantz and Catherine Collins, *The Nuclear Jihadist* (New York, 2007); Adrian Levy and Catherine Scott-Clark, *Deception: Pakistan, the United States, and the Secret Trade in Nuclear Weapons* (New York, 2007); Gordon Corera, *Shopping for Bombs: Nuclear Proliferation, Global Insecurity, and the Rise and Fall of the A.Q. Khan Network* (New York, 2006).

5. See the account of this meeting in Frantz and Collins, *The Nuclear Jihadist*, 67–68.

6. For a typical account, see Ibid., 252–256.

7. For a published account of this episode, see Ibid., 253–257. I have supplemented this published account with personal discussions with Hassan Abbas, the National Accountability Bureau investigator assigned to review the dossier, who recommended against pursuing a case against Khan despite his manifest corruption. Abbas' book on Khan, the Pakistani bomb, and its proliferation is forthcoming.

8. One Iraqi intelligence document records an offer for centrifuge technology from a man who said he was representing Khan, which Iraq apparently did not have time to follow up on before the 1991 war. For a discussion of this offer and a translated copy of the Iraqi intelligence memo that reports it, see David Albright and Corey Hinderstein, "Documents Indicate A.Q. Khan Offered Nuclear Weapons Designs to Iraq in 1990: Did He Approach Other Countries?" (Washington, D.C., 4 February 2004), available at http://isisonline.org/publications/southasia/khan_memo.html (accessed 8 September 2008).

9. Khan's wife defends him in an article, pointing out that security at the Khan Research Laboratories was provided by a unit of 500–1,000 personnel commanded by a brigadier general. If the activities were not authorized, some portion of the security force would have to have been either fooled or corrupted. See Hendrina Khan, "Stabbed in the Back," *Spiegel Online International* (11 August 2008), available at www.spiegel.de/international/world/0,1518,571356,00.html (accessed 7 September 2008).

10. Hassan Abbas (personal communication, December 2007 and January 2009).

11. For a discussion of state capture that is focused on former communist countries, see Joel S. Hellman, Geraint Jones, Daniel Kaufmann, and Mark Schankerman, "Measuring Governance, Corruption, and State Capture: How Firms and Bureaucrats Shape the Business Environment in Transition Economies," *Policy Research Working Paper* 2312 (Washington, D.C., April 2000).

12. Frantz and Collins, *The Nuclear Jihadist*, 156–161.

13. Raymond Bonner and Wayne Arnold, "'Business as Usual' at Plant That Tenet Says Was Shut," *New York Times* (7 February 2004).

14. Syria's recent covert construction of a plutonium production reactor is an important exception. For a discussion of the concealment strategies Syria used, see David Albright and Paul Brannan, "The Al Kibar Reactor: Extraordinary Camouflage, Troubling Implications" (Washington, D.C., 12 May 2008), available at www.isis-online.org/publications/syria/SyriaReactorReport_12May2008.pdf (accessed 7 September 2008).

15. See, for example, Matthew Bunn and Anthony Wier, "Terrorist Nuclear Weapon Construction: How Difficult?" *Annals of the American Academy of Political and Social Science*, DCVII (2006), 133–149. Aum Shinrikyo, however, failed to recognize the difficulty of enriching uranium, and at one stage purchased a sheep farm in Australia and stole documents related to laser isotope enrichment—probably the most technologically demanding method for enriching uranium that was ever devised—with the idea that they would mine their own uranium and enrich it themselves to make a bomb. This effort, in essence, conforms to the common pre-9/11 prediction that people who want to commit murder on a nuclear scale are too confused in their thinking to succeed in doing so. See Matthew Bunn and Anthony Wier, with Joshua Friedman, "The Demand for Black Market Fissile Material," in *Nuclear Threat Initiative Research Library: Securing the Bomb* (Cambridge, MA, 2005), available at www.nti.org/e_research/cnwm/threat/demand.asp (accessed 14 September 2008).

16. Bunn and Wier, "Terrorist Nuclear Weapon Construction," 133–149.

17. Bunn and Wier, "The Demand for Black Market Fissile Material," available at www.nti.org/e_research/cnwm/threat/demand.asp (accessed 27 February 2009).

18. Ibid.

19. See, for example, discussion in U.S. Congress, Senate, Committee on Government Affairs, Permanent Subcommittee on Investigations, *Global Proliferation of Weapons of Mass Destruction: A Case Study on the Aum Shinrikyo: Staff Statement* (Washington, D.C., 1995), available at www.fas.org/irp/congress/1995_rpt/aum/index.html (accessed 14 September 2008). For an overview of Aum Shinrikyo's nuclear efforts, see Bunn and Wier, "The Demand for Black Market Fissile Material."

20. For an account of Stemmler's role, see, for example, Mahdi Obeidi and Kurt Pitzer, *The Bomb in My Garden: The Secrets of Saddam's Nuclear Mastermind* (Hoboken, 2004), 90–92. See also "Iraq's Acquisition of Gas Centrifuge Technology: Part I: H+H Metalform—Funnel for the Iraqi Gas Centrifuge Program" (Washington, D.C., 2003), available at www.exportcontrols.org/centpart1.html (accessed 8 September 2008). For a detailed discussion of Schaab's role, see "Iraq's Acquisition of Gas Centrifuge Technology: Part II: Recruitment of Karl Heinz Schaab" (Washington, D.C., 2003), available at www.exportcontrols.org/centpart2.html (accessed 8 September 2008). See also Obeidi and Pitzer, *The Bomb in My Garden,* 120–124. The "many months" assessment is from Obeidi, the leader of the Iraqi centrifuge program. The International Institute for Strategic Studies described Schaab as "the most notorious" engineer who helped Iraq's centrifuge program, and who "probably bears more responsibility for the spread of centrifuge enrichment technology than anyone outside the Khan network." International Institute for Strategic Studies, *Nuclear Black Markets,* 47–49.

21. See "Iraq's Acquisition of Gas Centrifuge Technology: Part I: H+H Metalform—Funnel for the Iraqi Gas Centrifuge Program."

22. See "Iraq's Acquisition of Gas Centrifuge Technology: Part II: Recruitment of Karl Heinz Schaab."

23. See Frantz and Collins, *The Nuclear Jihadist,* 155–156.

24. For a discussion, see "Iraq's Acquisition of Gas Centrifuge Technology: Part I."

25. See Institute for Science and International Security, "Matrix Churchill Group" (Washington, D.C., 2003), available at www.exportcontrols.org/matrixchurchill.html (accessed 8 September 2008). See also International Institute for Strategic Studies, *Nuclear Black Markets,* 46.

26. Vladimir Orlov and William C. Potter, "The Mystery of the Sunken Gyros," *Bulletin of the Atomic Scientists,* LIV (November/December 1998), available at http://cns.miis.edu/research/iraq/gyro/index.htm (accessed 14 September 2008), 34–39.

27. John P. Holdren and Matthew Bunn, "Technical Background: A Tutorial on Nuclear Weapons and Nuclear-Explosive Materials," in *Nuclear Threat Initiative Research Library: Securing the Bomb,* available at www.nti.org/e_research/cnwm/overview/technical.asp (accessed 14 September 2008).

28. Obeidi and Pitzer, *The Bomb in My Garden,* 100.

29. "Russian Court Sentences Men for Weapons-Grade Plutonium Scam," trans. BBC Monitoring Service, *RIA Novosti* (14 October 2003); "Russia: Criminals Indicted for Selling Mercury as Weapons-Grade Plutonium," trans. U.S. Department of Commerce, *Izvestiya* (11 October 2003).

30. "Russia: Criminals Indicted for Selling Mercury as Weapons-Grade Plutonium," trans. U.S. Department of Commerce, *Izvestiya* (11 October 2003).

31. A summary of multiple Russian press reports can also be found in "Plutonium Con Artists Sentenced in Russian Closed City of Sarov," *NIS Export Control Observer* (November 2003), available at http://cns.miis.edu/pubs/nisexcon/pdfs/ob_0311e.pdf (accessed 8 September 2008), 10–11.

32. George Tenet, *At the Center of the Storm: My Years at the CIA* (New York, 2007), 275–276.

33. For a discussion of the al Qaeda and Aum Shinrikyo cases, see Bunn and Wier, "The Demand for Black Market Fissile Material."

34. For a detailed account of this case, see Oleg Bukharin and William Potter, "Potatoes Were Guarded Better," *Bulletin of the Atomic Scientists,* LI (May/June 1995), 46–50.

35. Corruption is, of course, only one of the methods that nuclear thieves might use to convince insiders to participate; blackmail is also a dangerous possibility, potentially turning trustworthy insiders into co-conspirators. In Northern Ireland, for example, one bank's security system required two senior bank officers to turn keys at the same time to open the vault. A gang, apparently associated with a splinter of the Irish Republican Army, kidnapped the families of two of the bank's senior officers. The officers opened the vault and allowed the gang to make off with millions of pounds in banknotes. See Chris Moore, "Anatomy of a £26.5 Million Heist," *Sunday Life* (21 May 2006).

36. Louise Shelley and Robert Orttung, then at American University (personal communication, September 2005). For a published account of other results from this study, see Robert Orttung and Louise Shelley, *Linkages between Terrorist and Organized Crime Groups in Nuclear Smuggling: A Case Study of Chelyabinsk Oblast,* PONARS Policy Memo No. 392 (Washington, D.C., 2005), available at www.csis.org/media/csis/pubs/pm_0392.pdf (accessed 14 September 2008). A more detailed account of this work has not yet been published.

37. "The President Issued a Decree To Dismiss Deputy Chairman of the MVD Department in Charge of Law and Order in Closed Territories and Sensitive Sites, Major General Sergey Shlyapuzhnikov," trans. Anatoly Dianov, *Rossiyskaya Gazeta* (2 June 2006).

38. Igor Goloskokov, "Refomirovanie Voisk MVD Po Okhrane Yadernikh Obektov Rossii (Reforming MVD Troops to Guard Russian Nuclear Facilities)," trans. Foreign Broadcast Information Service, *Yaderny Kontrol,* IX (Winter 2003), available (in Russian) at www.pircenter.org/data/publications/yk4-2003.pdf (accessed 14 September 2008).

39. Robert Reinstedt and Judith Westbury, *Major Crimes as Analogs to Potential Threats to Nuclear Facilities and Programs* (Santa Monica, 1980).

40. For corruption in the Russian military, see Tor Bukkvoll, "Their Hands in the Till: Scale and Causes of Russian Military Corruption," *Armed Forces and Society,* XXXIV (2008), 259–275. For cases involving terrorism, see the discussion in Simon Saradzhyan and Nabi Abdullaev, "Disrupting Escalation of Terror in Russia to Prevent Catastrophic Attacks," *Connections* (Spring 2005).

41. Louise Shelley and Robert Orttung, then at American University (personal communication, September 2005). This was only one element of a broad range of corruption and penetration by organized crime that the researchers found at Ozersk (formerly Chelyabinsk-65). For a published account of other results from this study,

see Orttung and Shelley, *Linkages between Terrorist and Organized Crime Groups in Nuclear Smuggling.*

42. See Institute for Science and International Security, "BNL" (Washington, D.C., 2003), available at www.exportcontrols.org/bnl.html (accessed 8 September 2008).

43. See Frantz and Collins, *The Nuclear Jihadist,* 141–142; International Institute for Strategic Studies, *Nuclear Black Markets,* 30. For more on BCCI generally, see James Ring Adams and Douglas Frantz, *A Full-Service Bank: How BCCI Stole Billions Around the World* (New York, 1992).

44. Orlov and Potter, "The Mystery of the Sunken Gyros," 35.

45. U.S. Congress, Government Accountability Office (GAO), *Combating Nuclear Smuggling: Corruption, Maintenance, and Coordination Problems Challenge U.S. Efforts to Provide Radiation Detection Equipment to Other Countries,* GAO-06-311 (Washington, D.C., 2006), available at www.gao.gov/new.items/d06311.pdf (accessed 14 September 2008).

46. See Michael Bronner, "100 Grams (And Counting): Notes From the Nuclear Underworld" (Cambridge, MA, June 2008), available at http://belfercenter.ksg.harvard.edu/files/100-Grams-Final-Color.pdf (accessed 8 September 2008); Lawrence Scott Sheets, "A Smuggler's Story," *Atlantic Monthly* (April 2008).

47. Vladimir Kovalyev, "Customs Inspectors Accused of Smuggling From Finland," *Moscow Times* (22 October 2004).

48. See David Nowak, "Adamov Gets 5 1/2 for Stealing $30 Million," *St. Petersburg Times* (22 February 2008). Adamov's sentence was later suspended, and he was released.

49. Interview with DOE official (August 2005).

50. Interview with official who worked closely with Adamov during his time as minister of atomic energy (September 2005).

51. Interview with a Russian site expert (July 2005).

52. Based on author's participation in these discussions.

53. "An Employee of the Department of Classified Facilities of the MVD Was Arrested in Snezhinsk: What Incriminates the 'Silovic,'" trans. Jane Vayman (29 May 2008), available at www.ura.ru (accessed 8 September 2008).

54. For a brief description of al Atheer, with overhead photographs, see "Al Atheer/al-Athir" (Washington, D.C., no date), available at www.globalsecurity.org/wmd/world/iraq/al_atheer.htm (accessed 8 September 2008).

55. For example, Yuri Smirnov stole 1.5 kilograms of 90 percent enriched HEU from the Luch Production Association in Podolsk in 1992, with no plan for how he was going to sell it. Acquaintances of Smirnov's were car battery thieves and suggested that their buyer in Moscow might also be willing to buy Smirnov's HEU. Smirnov was arrested with the battery thieves when they were at the train station, waiting to go to Moscow. See the interview with Smirnov in PBS, "Frontline: Loose Nukes: Interviews"(1996), available at www.pbs.org/wgbh/pages/frontline/shows/nukes/interviews/ (accessed 14

September 2008). For an overview of the "amateurish" nature of the known incidents in recent years and the lack of organized crime involvement in most cases, see Sonia Ben Ouagrham-Gormley, "An Unrealized Nexus?: WMD-Related Trafficking, Terrorism, and Organized Crime in the Former Soviet Union," *Arms Control Today* (July/August 2007), available at www.armscontrol.org/act/2007_07-08/CoverStory.asp (accessed 8 September 2008).

56. See International Institute for Strategic Studies, "Illicit Trafficking in Radioactive Materials," in *Nuclear Black Markets,* 132–134. This chapter, largely drafted by Lyudmila Zaitseva, is as of this writing the best publicly available overview of the known data on nuclear and radiological smuggling. For an earlier account that provides excellent anecdotal descriptions of corrupt participants at various stages of nuclear smuggling, see Lyudmila Zaitseva and Kevin Hand, "Nuclear Smuggling Chains: Suppliers, Intermediaries, and End-Users," *American Behavioral Scientist,* XLVI (February 2003), 822–844.

57. For recent assertions that organized crime groups *are* deeply involved in nuclear and radiological trafficking, see Louise Shelley, "Trafficking in Nuclear Materials: Criminals and Terrorists," *Global Crime,* VII (August 2006), 544–560; Louise Shelley and Robert Orttung, "Criminal Acts: How Organized Crime is a Nuclear Smuggler's New Best Friend," *Bulletin of the Atomic Scientists,* LXII (September/October 2006), 22–23.

58. This shipment involved 4.4 tons of beryllium, including 140 kilograms that was contaminated with a very small amount of HEU. For a description of the organized crime role, see Tim Zimmerman and Alan Cooperman, "The Russian Connection," *US News and World Report* (23 October 1995), 56–67.

59. What the mafia would have wanted with it, given the small amount of non-weapons-usable material that it contained, remains something of a mystery. See, for example, discussion in Sara Daly, John Parachini, and William Rosenau, *Aum Shinrikyo, Al Qaeda, and the Kinshasa Reactor: Implications of Three Case Studies for Combating Nuclear Terrorism* (Santa Monica, 2005), available at www.rand.org/pubs/documented_briefings/2005/RAND_DB458.sum.pdf (accessed 14 September 2008).

60. Shelley and Orttung, "Criminal Acts: How Organized Crime is a Nuclear Smuggler's New Best Friend," 22–23.

61. International Institute for Strategic Studies, *Nuclear Black Markets,* 133.

62. Orttung and Shelley, *Linkages between Terrorist and Organized Crime Groups in Nuclear Smuggling,* 161. See also Shelley, "Trafficking in Nuclear Materials," 555–556.

63. For an extended version of this argument, see Louise Shelley, "The Unholy Trinity: Transnational Crime, Corruption, and Terrorism," *Brown Journal of International Affairs,* XI (Winter/Spring 2005), 101–111.

64. For a discussion of other FARC activities, see Jessica C. Teets and Erica Chenoweth, "To Bribe or to Bomb: Do Corruption and Terrorism Go Together?" chapter 7 in this volume.

65. See, for example, Kelly Hearn, "FARC's Uranium Likely a Scam," *Washington Times* (19 March 2008).

66. Robert Klitgaard, *Controlling Corruption* (Berkeley, 1991).

67. Jeff Huther and Anwar Shah, "Anti-Corruption Policies and Programs: A Framework for Evaluation," *World Bank Policy Research Working Paper* No. 2501 (Washington, D.C., 2000).

68. See, for example, Anwar Shah and Mark Schacter, "Combating Corruption: Look Before You Leap," *Finance & Development* (December 2004), 40–43; Omar Azfar, "Disrupting Corruption," in Anwar Shah (ed.), *Performance Accountability and Disrupting Corruption* (Washington, D.C., 2007), 255–283.

69. James Reason, *Managing the Risks of Organizational Accidents* (Aldershot, U.K., 1997), 145. In this particular study, the chance that women would violate a rule that was perceived as "compliance important, usually legally required, but chances of detection low to moderate" was only 3 percent. The probability of noncompliance was dramatically higher if either: a) compliance with the rule was perceived as "relatively unimportant" or b) the "personal benefits of violating are high and direct"—both are circumstances that seem to have applied to the corrupt European participants in the Khan network.

70. For a discussion of security for nuclear stockpiles in the former Soviet Union in the 1990s, with photographs, see Matthew Bunn, *The Next Wave: Urgently Needed New Steps to Control Warheads and Fissile Material* (Washington, D.C., 2000).

71. See, for example, the interviews in Coll, "The Atomic Emporium."

72. See, for example, interview with Yuri Smirnov in PBS, "Frontline: Loose Nukes: Interviews."

73. For a set of recommendations for the assessment and strengthening of security culture in organizations, see International Atomic Energy Agency, "Nuclear Security Culture: Implementing Guide," *Nuclear Security Series* No. 7 (Vienna, 2008). For a good account of nuclear security culture in Russia in particular, see Igor Khripunov and James Holmes (eds.), *Nuclear Security Culture: The Case of Russia* (Athens, GA, 2004).

74. A detailed account of the inadvertent movement of six nuclear weapons, along with a review of organizational issues that contributed to this incident, can be found in Defense Science Board, Permanent Task Force on Nuclear Weapons Surety, *Report on the Unauthorized Movement of Nuclear Weapons* (Washington, D.C., 2008), available at www.fas.org/nuke/guide/usa/doctrine/usaf/Minot_DSB-0208.pdf (accessed 14 September 2008). For a remarkably harsh official critique of the security culture at Los Alamos and elsewhere in the Department of Energy system, see President's Foreign Intelligence Advisory Board, *Science at Its Best, Security at Its Worst: A Report on Security Problems at the U.S. Department of Energy* (Washington, D.C.,1999), available at www.fas.org/sgp/library/pfiab/ (accessed 14 September 2008).

75. Matthew Bunn, *Securing the Bomb 2008* (Cambridge, MA, 2008), 159–160, available at www.nti.org/securingthebomb (accessed 10 January 2009).

76. Bukharin and Potter, "Potatoes Were Guarded Better," 48.

77. United Nations Security Council, "Resolution 1540," S/Res/1540 (New York, 28 April 2004). Two subsequent resolutions have extended the term of the committee that

has been established to oversee implementation. For a range of documents related to UNSC 1540 and the implementation committee's work, see "1540 Committee," available at www.un.org/sc/1540/ (accessed 8 September 2008).

78. For a discussion attempting to define the nuclear security and accounting measures that are required to comply with UNSC 1540, see Matthew Bunn, "'Appropriate Effective' Nuclear Security and Accounting— What is It?" presentation to Joint Global Initiative/UNSCR 1540 Workshop on "'Appropriate Effective' Material Accounting and Physical Protection," Nashville, TN, 18 July 2008, available at http://belfercenter.ksg.harvard.edu/files/bunn-1540-appropriate-effective50.pdf (accessed 14 September 2008).

79. See Bunn, *Securing the Bomb 2008.*

80. The two-person rule is maintained for all U.S. nuclear weapons at all times. Russian officers that are associated with the 12th Main Directorate of the Ministry of Defense (known by its Russian acronym as the 12th GUMO), which is responsible for guarding Russia's nuclear weapons, report that they go further and maintain a three-person rule so that no group smaller than three people is allowed access to a nuclear weapon.

81. In the United States, for example, the Department of Energy is now spending more than $1 billion a year on security, much of which is going to improved protection against outsider attacks that might involve large numbers of adversaries with heavy armament, helicopters, shaped-charge explosives, military training, insider information on the security system, and more. But the insider threat that facilities must defend against includes only one non-violent individual. The rationale for this approach is the belief that the established process for background checks and personnel reliability monitoring will reliably prevent people, who would use violence to carry out a nuclear theft or join in a conspiracy to carry out nuclear theft, from becoming insiders in the first place. U.S. assistance with security upgrades in other countries is also typically designed only to protect against a single insider.

82. See International Institute for Strategic Studies, *Nuclear Black Markets,* 161–162.

83. The German firm Leybold-Heraeus, for example, was deeply embarrassed by the large amount of the company's technology that UN inspectors found in Iraq. The company, now known as Oerlikon Leybold Vacuum, established an in-depth internal review program for all exports that had resulted, by 2004, in the company turning down over €20 million in business. David Albright, a critic of poor export controls and company participation in illicit proliferation, has described Oerlikon's program as a model that other companies should emulate. See briefings by Ralph Wirtz of Oerlikon and Albright (as well as the briefing by Matti Tarvainen, head of the IAEA's program to track illicit nuclear trade), in *Finding Innovative Ways to Detect and Thwart Illicit Nuclear Trade,* Carnegie International Nonproliferation Conference, 25 June 2007, transcript available at www.carnegieendowment.org/events/index.cfm?fa=event Detail&id=1029 (accessed 8 September 2008).

84. U.S. Congress, GAO, *Combating Nuclear Smuggling,* 16–18.

85. For a brief discussion of the MOM project, see U.S. Congress, GAO, *Nuclear Nonproliferation: Progress Made in Improving Security at Russian Nuclear Sites, but the Long-Term Sustainability of U.S.-Funded Security Upgrades Is Uncertain,* GAO-07-404 (Washington, D.C., 2007), 26–28, available at www.gao.gov/new.items/d07404.pdf (accessed 14 September 2008). For earlier accounts, see U.S. Department of Energy, *National Nuclear Security Administration, Strategy Document: MPC&A Operations Monitoring Project* (Washington, D.C., 2002); Kathleen N. McCann and others, "The National Nuclear Security Administration's (NNSA) Material Protection, Control, and Accounting (MPC&A) Operations Monitoring (MOM) Project," in *Proceedings of the 43rd Annual Meeting of the Institute for Nuclear Materials Management,* Orlando, Florida, 23–27 June 2002 (Northbrook, 2002).

86. For discussions arguing, similarly, for a greater emphasis on post-theft intelligence and police interventions to reduce the threat of nuclear terrorism, see, for example, Rensselaer Lee, "Nuclear Smuggling: Patterns and Responses," *Parameters: U.S. Army War College Quarterly* (Spring 2003), available at www.carlisle.army.mil/usawc/parameters/03spring/lee.pdf (accessed 14 September 2008); Rensselaer Lee, *Nuclear Smuggling and International Terrorism: Issues and Options for U.S. Policy,* RL31539 (Washington, D.C., 2002).

87. A remarkable proportion of the analysis that is done on nuclear smuggling today is done at the level of overall statistics, rather than by in-depth analysis of individual cases and their implications. For a discussion of this point, see, for example, Shelley, "Trafficking in Nuclear Materials: Criminals and Terrorists," 547.

88. Though these individuals may be highly corrupt, it may be possible to motivate them to help to stop shipments dangerous enough to motivate governments to take action that would interfere with their normal smuggling operations. See William Langewiesche, "How to Get a Nuclear Bomb," *Atlantic Monthly,* CCXCVIII (December 2006), 80–98. While many of the specific factual assertions in this article are incorrect, this suggestion makes a good deal of sense.

89. Frantz and Collins, *The Nuclear Jihadist,* 247–249.

90. See, for example, Thomas B. Cochran and Matthew G. McKinzie, "Detecting Nuclear Smuggling," *Scientific American* (March 2008).

91. See, for example, Matthew Bunn, "Designing a Multi-Layered Defense against Nuclear Terror," paper presented at The Homeland Security Advisory Council Task Force on Weapons of Mass Effect, Washington, D.C., 13 June 2005, available at http://belfercenter.ksg.harvard.edu/publication/17189/ (accessed 14 September 2008). See also Michael Levi, *On Nuclear Terrorism* (Cambridge, MA, 2007), 6–9; 87–123.

92. For a discussion of the various stages of a nuclear terrorist plot, what available information suggests about how likely each plot is to succeed, and steps that can be taken to reduce those probabilities of success, see Matthew Bunn, "A Mathematical Model of the Risk of Nuclear Terrorism," *Annals of the American Academy of Political and Social Science,* DCVII (September 2006), 103–120. For a different approach that also focuses on many elements beyond only securing nuclear stockpiles, see Levi, *On Nuclear Terrorism.*

93. For a brief overview, see Matti Tarvainen, "Procurement Outreach in Revealing Proliferation Networks," transcript available at www.carnegieendowment.org/events/index.cfm?fa=eventDetail&id=1029 (accessed 8 September 2008).

94. See, for example, William C. Potter, "Nuclear Smuggling From the Former Soviet Union," in David R. Maples and Marilyn J. Young (eds.), *Nuclear Energy and Security in the Former Soviet Union* (Boulder, 1997), 139–160.

95. For accounts of Stemmler and Schaab, see "Iraq's Acquisition of Gas Centrifuge Technology: Part I" and "Iraq's Acquisition of Gas Centrifuge Technology: Part II."

96. See "U.K. Drops Investigation Into Khan Network Supplier."

97. See *Report of the Russian Federation on the Implementation of Resolution 1540* (2004), S/AC.44/2004/(02)/14 (New York, 2004).

98. For an interesting account of how lower penalties that have a higher likelihood that they will be imposed may work better, see Azfar, "Disrupting Corruption," 256–257.

99. For an excellent discussion of the potential power of such an international criminalization approach in the case of chemical and biological weapons, see Matthew Meselson and Julian Robinson, "A Draft Convention to Prohibit Biological and Chemical Weapons under International Criminal Law," *Fletcher Forum of World Affairs,* XXVIII (Winter 2004), 57–71, available at http://fletcher.tufts.edu/forum/archives/pdfs/281pdfs/Meselson.pdf (accessed 14 September 2008).

100. See, for example, Azfar, "Disrupting Corruption."

101. Goloskokov, "Reforming MVD Troops to Guard Russian Nuclear Facilities."

JESSICA C. TEETS *and* ERICA CHENOWETH

7

To Bribe or to Bomb:
Do Corruption and
Terrorism Go Together?

Colombia consistently ranks as one of the more corrupt countries in the world; it ranked 3.8 out of 10 on the 2008 Corruption Perceptions Index. Incidentally, Colombia has suffered decades of terrorist attacks conducted by one of the most enduring terrorist groups in the world—the Fuerzas Armadas Revolucionarias de Colombia (FARC). Conventional wisdom suggests, and U.S. policy subscribes to the belief, that corruption and terrorism coexist in a mutually reinforcing relationship.[1] Such a conclusion seems intuitive given conditions in Colombia and elsewhere, where corruption and terrorism seem to coincide. This relationship, however, has always been a matter of speculation; it has not yet been systematically assessed. This chapter explores the connection between corruption and terrorism to determine whether and how corruption increases terrorist activity.

Assuming that corruption and terrorism do go together, there exist two potential explanations for this relationship in the literature. According to one perspective, terrorists may develop within or attack corrupt states because they resent the government's inconsistent application of the rule of law. This *motivational* explanation contends that poor governance increases terrorists' motivations to attack or organize. The motivational approach predicts that terrorists attack corrupt governments out of frustration. Moreover, when the government adopts practices that undermine public confidence in the state's legitimacy, terrorist groups can exploit this mistrust by providing public goods to society to win its sympathy and support. This approach explains why Hamas remains popular in the Palestinian Territories in light of Fatah's corruption and inability to provide public goods. Thus, according to this theoretical approach, corruption has a direct relationship to terrorism. Corruption motivates groups to pursue terrorist tactics and motivates the public to support such groups.

According to a second logic, corruption does not directly cause terrorism. Rather, it indirectly increases the ability of groups to carry out attacks. Corrupt states create opportunities for terrorist organizations because of an inability or unwillingness to enforce the rule of law, which reduces the costs of operating within such territories. In addition, the presence of corruption allows for the creation of a criminal infrastructure that groups use for funding, weapons, transport, and forged documents, thereby strengthening terrorist organizations.[2] This criminal infrastructure supports illicit trade in arms, people, and drugs, and creates three conditions of which terrorist groups take advantage: 1) a signal to potential terrorists that the state does not have the capacity to enforce the rule of law; 2) an infrastructure in money laundering, secretive transportation, and forged documents; and 3) a flow of materials and independent funding by which terrorists can conduct their activities, thereby lowering the costs to terrorists of operating from within these countries. In contradistinction to the motivational approach, the *facilitation* explanation argues that corruption and terrorism coexist, but that the relationship between the two is indirect rather than direct. This approach predicts that terrorist attacks will emanate from states with high levels of corruption, but not necessarily target those states directly.

This chapter explores the relationship between corruption and terrorism to determine whether such a relationship exists and, if so, whether the motivational or facilitation approach better explains the relationship. Using quantitative data on terrorist activity, we tested whether corruption motivates or facilitates terrorism. We developed several models that test the effects of corruption rankings, money laundering, drug trafficking, and arms imports on the emergence of homegrown terrorist groups and the production of terrorist attacks against other countries. To investigate the motivational and facilitation hypotheses, we conducted these tests on a sample of 30 countries from 1980–2001, and 169 additional countries from 1995–2001. Our findings support the facilitation approach, in that higher levels of corruption in a country increase the number of terrorist attacks originating from that country. More indirectly, countries that facilitate illicit drug trade, money laundering, and major arms imports also produce an increased number of transnational terrorist attacks. In addition, corrupt countries with vast arms imports are likely to produce transnational terrorist attacks. Interestingly, the presence of money laundering increases the number of homegrown terrorist groups while the presence of an illicit drug trade decreases the number of these groups. To account for this puzzling finding, we posit that the interests of drug traffickers and terrorists are often antithetical to one another. If a connection exists between drug revenue and terrorist groups, the strongest group may discourage competing groups from forming.

The findings herein are less supportive of the motivational approach, revealing that terrorists are able to exploit resources within corrupt countries, but that corrupt countries are not necessarily victims of terrorism. Nor do they create new homegrown groups. As the brief case study of the FARC included in this chapter illustrates, the facilitation approach suggests that corruption not only produces more favorable conditions under which terrorists conduct attacks, it also produces externalities that the international community must address through targeted policy programs.[3]

This chapter reviews the theoretical relationships between corruption and illicit trade, illicit trade and terrorism, and corruption and terrorism. The chapter then discusses the quantitative analysis used to test these relationships, and it explores the case of Colombia to highlight the interaction between corruption and terrorism. Last, the chapter offers theoretical and policy conclusions derived from the authors' findings.

Corruption, Illicit Trade, and Terrorism

The broad range of activities composing corruption and the differing legal interpretations of corruption across countries contribute to the difficulty of easily defining the term "corruption." Moreover, the perspective of the scholar plays a role in whether she utilizes an economic, moral, or legal definition. In this chapter, we use Rose-Ackerman's definition of corruption due to its breadth and relatively uncontroversial acceptance among scholars. Rose-Ackerman defines corruption as "using public goods or capacity for private benefits."[4] This definition of corruption is public-office centered and concentrates on "behavior which deviates from the normal duties of a public role because of private-regarding (personal, close family, private clique) pecuniary or status gains; or violates rules against the exercise of certain types of private-regarding influence."[5] In addition, this definition looks at both administrative corruption, as represented primarily by the misappropriation of government property, and political corruption.[6]

Scholarship regarding the consequences of corruption is divided between positive and negative effects, but the preponderance of evidence clearly rests with the scholars who view corruption as having mostly negative economic and political effects. According to the "positive corruption" arguments, corruption might alleviate security concerns by allowing citizens to bypass ineffective or overburdened state institutions and channel political demands through informal avenues.[7] As Scott states, drawing on the case of ethnic Chinese businessmen in Thailand who were barred from formal office-holding but were influencing political decisions via bribery, "Corruption thus frequently represents an alternative to coercion as a means of influence."[8] In addition, Nye finds that corruption may bridge potentially violent societal cleavages among elites or between elites and the rest of society.[9] In these ways, scholars argue that corruption offers alternatives to violence.[10] The presence of corruption creates alternative avenues for interest articulation during and after the decision-making process. These avenues in turn allow for the non-violent expression of dissent and the ability of groups to 'buy' their favored policy (or at least the non-enforcement of the offensive policy).

Most research, however, emphasizes the negative consequences of corruption. This research finds that corruption decreases growth, investment, and entrepreneurship, and weakens the legal capacity of the state—thus generating more opportunities for crime and illicit trade.[11] The findings in this chapter also support the negative consequences argument.

The study of terrorism is likewise split along two general lines. Some scholars focus on the motivations of individuals and groups to adopt terrorism to express their political grievances, whereas others use a structural approach that assumes that terrorism will emerge wherever the costs of adopting terrorism are low. Other scholars attempt to combine these two perspectives.[12]

First, among those who favor motivational aspects of the phenomenon, scholars have surveyed a wide array of possible causes, from individual-level alienation to cross-cutting socioeconomic grievances.[13] Among the most common explanations is that individuals or groups adopt violence against unjust state adversaries who have either abused their power or applied the rule of law unfairly.[14] According to this logic, repressive states should experience the highest level of terrorism, whereas states that are restrained vis-à-vis their constituents should experience the lowest level of terrorism. Some studies expand upon this perspective, suggesting that government provisions of public goods such as security, social welfare, education, and political freedoms reduce the motivation for groups to use terrorism against the state.[15]

Second, an opportunity-based approach assumes that all individuals or groups would resort to violent means given a common set of incentives and constraints. Crenshaw discusses terrorism as a rational choice behavior, a simple political strategy with calculated cost and benefit considerations.[16] Specifically, where expressing political grievances is difficult but using violent forms of expression is easy, one should expect to see more terrorism.[17] Some scholars have found, for example, that states that observe civil liberties constrain themselves when fighting terrorists, thereby making terrorism easier in such countries.[18] The findings in this chapter support an opportunity-based approach, where terrorists use an existing criminal infrastructure supported by corruption. This infrastructure reduces the costs of terrorism, but does not necessarily create the frustration that motivates such acts.

The Relationship between Corruption and Terrorism

As discussed briefly above, extant literature specifies several processes through which corruption could motivate or facilitate terrorism. The motivational approach argues that corruption creates public distrust and dissatisfaction with the government, resulting in violent mobilization against the state as well as political vacuums that terrorist organizations can exploit to gain public support. Several scholars argue that pervasive corruption might create an environment where terrorist organizations gain public support and sympathy through supplying public goods that the government no longer supplies.[19] Case studies examining the widespread public support of Hezbollah and Hamas contend that the pervasive corruption in Lebanon and the Palestinian Territories has created an environment where the inability of the state to meet basic needs gives these groups an opportunity to act as a substitute for the state.[20] These groups then provide comprehensive public goods such as education and health care that engender widespread public support for these organizations. With public support, these groups have access to recruits, funding, and legitimacy that makes combating them difficult. In the case of Hamas, the group was able to translate its widespread public support into electoral power. The motivational approach expects to see corrupt states as the most common targets of domestic and foreign terrorism due to perceptions that the states' policies are unjust. Therefore, the cases of Hezbollah and Hamas support a motivational argument, although it is clear that these groups have had additional grievances beyond ruling party corruption and illegitimacy.[21]

Emerging from this discussion are several testable hypotheses. When specifying the hypotheses, we used the target selection of the terrorists to infer their motivations. In other words, if groups attack states against which they hold grievances, one should expect to see terrorists targeting the most corrupt states. In terms of domestic terrorism, one would expect more domestic terrorist groups to emerge within corrupt states rather than transparent states. Hypotheses 1 and 2 relate to the motivational approach.

H_1: *Increasing corruption has a positive effect on the number of terrorist attacks targeting a country.*

H_2: *Increasing corruption has a positive effect on the emergence of domestic terrorist group(s).*

While most research does not find a direct causal relationship between corruption and terrorism, corruption may play a key role in altering the set of constraints imposed upon potential terrorists, thereby serving as a facilitating factor. Under the facilitation approach, an indirect relationship is hypothesized.

H_3: *Countries with easy access to materials and existing criminal infrastructure will produce more terrorist activity.*

The opportunity costs of conducting activities in such states are lower than in states where control of corruption and illicit materials is robust; therefore, corruption facilitates terrorist activity. The existing empirical support for each of these arguments is outlined below.

Corruption Signals Low Costs

Corruption weakens legal enforcement, which creates an environment enabling many different types of criminals to carry out activities.[22] In countries where corrupt states perpetuate the perception that the government cannot or will not maintain the rule of law, terrorists may see such corruption as a signal that they can conduct their own operations with impunity. Over time, states build reputations that would-be terrorists observe in calculating the costs of conducting their operations.[23] Lawlessness within such countries announces to terrorists that existing criminals find the costs of maintaining illegal activities low or easily surmountable. Once they have established havens within such countries, corruption allows groups to exploit the existing infrastructures of illicit trade networks to maintain their chain of materials and supplies, thereby reducing the costs of terrorist operations.

Access to Materials

Inflows of arms, illicit drugs, and illicit money create pools of resources for terrorists. As of 2008, the United Nations (UN) estimates that more than 500 million small arms and light weapons are circulating in the world, and while an estimated 50 to 60 percent of this trade is legal, many weapons end up in illicit markets. For example, there are approximately 10 million illicit weapons in Afghanistan, an estimated 7 million in West Africa, and about 2 million in

Central America. According to UN studies, illicit trafficking in small arms plays a major role in the violence that permeates many societies, and more important for the purposes of this chapter, excessive flows of illegal small arms destabilize governments, encourage crime, and foster terrorism.[24]

The supply chain for drug trafficking, similar to arms trafficking, depends heavily on corruption or the inability to enforce laws within the host country.[25] While there is no consensus on the total amount of international financial flows associated with the illicit drug trade, the UN estimates that it reaches $400 billion a year. Given that drug production and trade is illegal in almost every country, the drug trade in a country depends on the ability of those involved in the trade to bribe or intimidate government officials of that host country. This process must occur along the supply chain, from farmers growing drug crops, to processing facilities, to transportation within and outside the country, and finally, the circulation of profits.[26] Without the ability to bribe or otherwise compel government officials into allowing drug production and trade, there are multiple points in this process where the trade might be halted.

Some argue that terrorist organizations, and perhaps the governments that harbor and support them, engage in drug dealing or profit from such dealings.[27] One such instance is the case of a Midwestern methamphetamine and methamphetamine-precursor trafficking organization, some of whose personnel were nationals of Middle Eastern countries funding terrorist organizations such as Hezbollah and Hamas.[28] Analysts note that only a small amount of these revenues would end up as profit for a terrorist group. In particular, groups that live by "taxing" or facilitating the production of raw drug crops, which is where terrorist groups are most likely to be involved, are dealing with drugs at the point in the supply chain where their value is lowest.[29] However, as many analysts pointed out after the 9/11 attacks, the estimated cost to carry out the attacks was between $500,000 and $2 million. Using Kleiman's estimate that $2 million represents less than one hour's worth of revenue in the illicit market for cocaine in the United States, or about 1 percent of the annual value of the coca leaf that generates cocaine for the U.S. market, then it is clear that the transfer of funds from drug trafficking into terrorist organizations does not have to be substantial to be significant.[30]

Despite the theoretical possibility of funding apertures, systematic empirical evidence of such leaks is sparse.[31] Many scholars have questioned the logic of this linkage arguing that while transnational criminal organizations and terrorist groups often adopt similar methods, they are inherently striving for divergent ends.[32] As one study argues, "With the exception of Colombia, rarely do the large established crime organizations link with terrorist groups, because their long-term financial interests require the preservation of state structures."[33] These scholars contend that crime is primarily an economically driven enterprise, while terrorism is generally rooted in political pursuits.[34] Thus, many analysts insist that terrorist funding primarily comes from donors, and secondarily from criminal activities such as extortion, theft or robbery, and illicit-market (including drug) transactions. Moreover, these organizations vary enormously in their ability to solicit contributions or illegally generate funding.[35] For example, because al Qaeda is financed by the bin Laden family fortune or by fund-raising in Saudi Arabia, its dependence on drug revenues is slight.[36] By contrast, drug revenues are undoubtedly important, perhaps central, to the financing of both the FARC in Colombia and of the paramilitary forces opposing the FARC, as they were to the *Sendero Luminoso* ("Shining Path") in Peru.[37] Spanish authorities report that the 2004 terrorist attacks on the Madrid train system that killed nearly 200 people and injured 1,400 more were financed largely by sales of hashish (a marijuana derivative) and ecstasy (MDMA).[38] While some groups directly engage in drug trafficking as a way to fund terrorist activities, this does not seem to be a common practice. In fact, groups vary in their funding sources, and most groups rely heavily on donations or coerced payments through ransom or theft. One area of potential research is to classify groups by funding sources to determine how more effectively to combat terrorism. Groups that depend on illicit trade would be adversely affected by international cooperation to reduce trafficking. However, the majority of groups receive their funding from other sources, both legal and illegal, which makes targeting drug revenue streams difficult.

Criminal Infrastructure Exploitation

The facilitation approach also predicts that terrorists are able to exploit pre-existing criminal infrastructures. Terrorist groups may exploit the infrastructures established by drug traffickers, such as arms smuggling, money laundering, and transportation networks. According to this argument, the existence of large illicit markets facilitates terrorist activity by supporting infrastructures comprised of money launderers, "cloned" cell phone providers, and suppliers of false identification documents.[39] Another possibility is that terrorist material and personnel might be disguised as part of the illicit drug trade, just as illicit drugs have been known to move disguised as other smuggled materials (e.g., diamonds). Unwitting accomplices and complicit officials may be less reluctant to participate in what they perceive to be drug dealings than terrorist activity.[40]

Existing infrastructures may also reinforce expectations about how corrupt government officials behave with regard to bribery. As Kleiman suggests, "Once corruption becomes embedded in the practice of an agency, it may not remain restricted to its original domain; an army commander accustomed to taking bribes from drug traffickers may be less resistant to bribes from terrorist groups."[41] While this argument is plausible and supported by case studies, one could also argue that corrupt officials might accept bribes from groups that they consider "economic," while they would be wary of accepting bribes from terrorist groups that might attack governments. The costs of being found complicit in terrorist activity are much higher than that of a global drug trade. Given the secretive nature of corruption and terrorism, this relationship is a difficult one to parse.

Although in theory illicit trade creates the infrastructure for smuggling capabilities and the funding that terrorist organizations could use, significant empirical evidence is lacking. For example, after the 9/11 attacks, U.S. officials speculated that terrorists might be using the same money-laundering services that support illicit drug transactions, but evidence showed that they were using a separate set of institutions related to international remittances.[42] While the narco-terrorism literature suggests that terrorists might utilize infrastructures created to traffic drugs or directly engage in drug trafficking to fund their activities, there exists little evidence of these claims outside of Colombia, Turkey, Peru, Sri Lanka, and Afghanistan. In those cases where a drug trade exists, one finds that if a terrorist organization forms these activities might become linked, such as the PKK in Turkey, the FARC in Colombia, and the Shining Path in Peru. However, drug and terrorist organizations have antithetical goals—profits and politics respectively—which do not create an environment for a sustainable partnership. In addition, for many factions, drugs are antithetical to group morals. For example, the Taliban's supreme leader Mullah Omar stated that "[i]n the long term our objective is to completely cleanse Afghanistan [of drug production]. But we cannot ask all those whose living depends entirely on the opium harvest to switch to other crops. . . . At any rate, one thing is certain: we will not allow opium and heroin to be sold in Afghanistan itself. If non-Moslems wish to buy drugs and intoxicate themselves, it is not our job to protect them."[43] This fundamental conflict between group ethics and funding sources means that even if the possibility of drug trade exists, these groups would want to use this funding source in a limited and secretive way. Therefore, any linkage between illicit drug trade and terrorism is limited to countries with an existing drug trade, and is either a short-term alliance between competing groups or is used as a temporary funding source. Few cases of sustained narco-terrorism exist in the literature, beyond Afghanistan and several Colombian groups.

Thus, while past research on illicit trade does not find that corruption causes such trade as a result of resentment toward the offending state, it does link pervasive corruption to the weakening of regulations and legal enforcement, which, in turn, creates an environment for illicit trade and trafficking. In this chapter's brief examination of this relationship in two areas of illicit trade—arms and drug trafficking—we find that corruption enables the key stages of illicit trade, namely supply, transportation, and laundering of revenues.

Several expectations can be identified that would confirm a facilitation approach. Hypothesis 3 posits that terrorists conduct their activities within corrupt states to attack other states. In addition to testing this specific relationship, we also expect that arms imports, drug production, and money laundering should facilitate terrorist activities within corrupt states. These expectations are identified in the three variants of hypothesis 3.

H_{3a}: *Increasing corruption has a positive effect on the number of terrorist attacks emanating from a country.*

H_{3b}: *Arms imports have a positive effect on the number of terrorist attacks emanating from corrupt countries but no effect on the number of terrorist attacks emanating from transparent countries.*

H_{3c}: *Drug production and money laundering have positive effects on the number of terrorist attacks emanating from the country.*

In the following section, we further explore this relationship through statistical analysis and trace the process of corruption that facilitates terrorism in the case of Colombia.

Research Design

To test the hypotheses emerging from the discussion above, we conducted tests on a sample of 30 countries from 1980–2001, and 169 additional countries from 1995–2001. The unit of analysis is the country year. Due to missing data, the total number of observations is close to 1,000.

We used three alternative dependent variables for theoretical reasons as well as robustness. The first dependent variable is the number of attacks originating from within the country in question. Second, we included an alternative dependent variable: the number of attacks targeting a country in a given year. These data were aggregated from the ITERATE data set, which includes transnational terrorist attacks from 1968 to 2004.[44] ITERATE uses open source media accounts of terrorist attacks as a way to measure the number of transnational terrorist attacks originating from within a country (both targets and origins). Third, we measured the number of new terrorist groups, which includes the number of new homegrown terrorist groups emerging within a country in a year. These data were collected and coded in Chenoweth 2007 based on profiles of terrorist groups in the Terrorism Knowledge Base at RAND-MIPT.[45]

Corruption is measured using Transparency International's Corruption Perceptions Index (CPI), which ranks 180 countries by their perceived levels of corruption from 1995 to 2007. Scores are determined by experts and opinion surveys, and range from 1 "most corrupt" to 10 "least corrupt."[46] Many criticisms are leveled at the CPI, but these data are still useful for several reasons.[47] Although the data are problematic due to perceptual biases, they provide the only reliable measure of corruption to date. Despite the different sources for the CPI and other existing corruption surveys, Shang Jin Wei has found that pairwise correlations among the indices are very high. For example, the correlations between the Business International and CPI indices and between Business International and Global Corruption Report indices are 0.88 and 0.77, respectively. These high correlations suggest that statistical inference on corruption is not very sensitive to the choice of corruption index.[48] Although many scholars question whether perceptions of corruption depend on culture, we argue that legislation across countries defines corruption in similar ways and regulates against certain acts, such as bribery. In fact, Lambsdorff tested the correlation between the Gallup International Survey, which surveys the general public, and the other surveys on corruption and found high correlations. He argues that the perceptions of what activities constitute corruption are more universal than previously thought.[49] The seven surveys that measure corruption worldwide also are highly correlated with each other, allowing scholars more confidence in the universality of these measures.

To assess the specific mechanisms by which terrorists could access illicit materials, we developed several dummy variables for the number of arms, amount of illegal money, and the drug production among sample countries. We constructed dummy variables for these measures due to data availability—most of these measures are found in lists of "top" or "major" countries. The dummy variable for arms imports is coded "1" if the country has been among the top 50 arms importers in the world from 1980 to 2007, and "0" if otherwise.[50] The variable identifying major drug-producing countries is coded "1" if the country was on the U.S. Department of State's list of "major drug producers," and "0" if otherwise.[51] Third, the variable called "money" is coded "1" if the country is on the U.S. Department of State's list of "priority countries" for money laundering, and "0" if otherwise.[52] If the facilitation hypothesis is correct, we expect all three variables to have positive effects on the number of terrorist attacks originating in a country.

Several control variables were also included. We control for the state's capacity to control its territory using the Correlates of War National Capabilities Index.[53] This variable is available from 1800 to 2001, and is intended to be a proxy for the government's resources and capacity to maintain the legitimate use of force.

To control for the confounding effects of previous terrorist attacks on the likelihood of future terrorist attacks, we included a lagged measure of the number of transnational attacks emerging from the country in the previous year. This variable serves as a control for the contagion effects of terrorism as well as autocorrelation within the temporal unit.

Our estimation method utilizes zero-inflated negative binomial (ZINB) models with the country year as the unit of analysis. ZINB estimation is appropriate because there are two different "types" of zero counts in our estimations. For example, in some years, Country A may experience zero terrorist attacks because it never has and never will experience terrorist attacks. Country B, on the other hand, may experience zero terrorist attacks despite experiencing them in previous years, which is theoretically a distinct phenomenon. The ZINB model allows us to distinguish between Countries A and B in estimating the effects of the independent variables on both the *propensity* of different countries to produce terrorist attacks (the inflate model), as well as the *number* of terrorist attacks and groups among relevant countries (the count model).

The inflate model shows us which factors move a country from a non-event (i.e., no terrorist groups or attacks) to an event—the probability of experiencing an event over the entire period. The count model analyzes the magnitude of these factors in countries that have had an event—the effects of these factors on the total number of events in each country in each year. The ZINB model helps to isolate the cause of the event, as well as factors that increase the magnitude of events. This separation allows us to distinguish between causal and intensification variables to make more accurate policy recommendations.

Empirical Results: Support for the Facilitation Approach

To assess the motivational approach, we designed tests for hypotheses 1 and 2, which focus on the effects of the CPI score on the number of transnational terrorist attacks targeting a country (Model 1), and the number of new home-grown terrorist groups emerging within the country (Model 2). If hypotheses 1 and 2 are correct, we should expect to see a negative relationship between the CPI score and terrorism.

Model 1 demonstrates the effects of the CPI score on the number of transnational attacks experienced by a country. The inflated model reports that the level of corruption has no effect on the probability that a country will ever be the target of transnational terrorist attacks, while government capabilities reduce the probability that states will be the target of transnational attacks. The count model also demonstrates that the level of corruption has no effect on the number of attacks against a country, suggesting that terrorists single out neither corrupt nor transparent states as targets. A state's capabilities reduce the number of attacks, and a history of being the target of transnational terrorist attacks increases the number of transnational attacks against a country the following year.

Therefore, Model 1 finds little support for hypothesis 1, which represents the motivational approach, although the model does not account for domestic terrorism. We also tested hypothesis 2, which predicts an increase of homegrown terrorist groups within corrupt countries; this increase is likewise represented in Table 7-1. Model 2 tests the effects of corruption using the number of new homegrown terrorist groups emerging within the country as the dependent variable. The inflated model reports that the level of corruption has no effect on the probability that a country will become a first-time host for new homegrown terrorist groups. Government capabilities have consistent effects, decreasing the probability that new terrorist groups emerge within a state. The count model shows, however, that neither corruption nor government capabilities affect the number of new homegrown groups in countries with these groups. A history of sustaining transnational terrorist attacks has a positive effect on the number of new homegrown groups. Thus, we find no support for hypothesis 2.

The results in Table 7-1 suggest that corrupt states are no more or less likely to experience homegrown terrorism directed at the state, which the motivational approach predicts. Because the motivational approach receives little initial support, we next tested hypothesis 3a, which predicts that the CPI score should have a negative effect on the number of terrorist attacks emanating from a country. Table 7-2 reports the findings.

As we see in the inflated portion of Model 3, the level of corruption has no effect on the probability that a country will be the originating country of a transnational terrorist attack. Government capabilities decrease the proba-

Table 7-1. *Tests of the Motivational Approach*

	Model 1		Model 2	
	DV: Number of transnational attacks targeting country		DV: Number of homegrown terrorist groups emerging from within the country	
Count Model				
CPI score	−.03	(.02)	.00	(.05)
Capabilities	−.13***	(.04)	−.05	(.12)
History of attacks	.12***	(.01)	.02**	(.01)
Constant	1.25***	(.24)	−.99*	(.53)
Inflate Model				
CPI score	.14	(.13)	.18	(.17)
Capabilities	2.50***	(.62)	.97***	(.34)
Constant	−19.73***	(4.68)	−6.88**	(3.21)
N	984		984	
Nonzero observations	548		144	
Zero observations	436		840	
LR chi^2	308.90		8.03	
Probability > chi^2	.0000		.0453	

Notes: Zero-inflated negative binomial model with standard errors reported in parentheses. Note that the signs on the coefficients in the inflated model are reversed during interpretation.
***$p < .01$, **$p < .05$, *$p < .1$.

bility that states will be the origin of transnational attacks. States with high capabilities are least likely to be the source of transnational terrorism. According to the count model, the CPI score reduces the number of attacks, as do a state's capabilities, while a history of sustaining transnational terrorist attacks increases the number of transnational attacks emanating from within a country. Taken as a whole, Model 3 tells us that the strongest states are the least likely producers of transnational terrorist attacks; among those countries that do produce transnational terrorist attacks, corruption increases terrorist attacks, which confirms the facilitation approach represented by hypothesis 3a.

The results in Tables 7-1 and 7-2 shed light on the complexity of the relationship between corruption and terrorism. Corruption does not motivate terrorism because of grievances against corrupt states, but rather it facilitates terrorism. This finding lends some support to the expectation that corruption lowers the barriers to terrorist attacks, probably because obtaining illicit materials to conduct attacks is more difficult in less corrupt or transparent countries.

Table 7-2. *Test of the Facilitation Approach*

	DV: Number of transnational attacks originating from country	
Count Model		
CPI Score	−.03**	(.02)
Capabilities	−.13***	(.04)
History of attacks	.11***	(.01)
Constant	1.27***	(.24)
Inflate Model		
CPI Score	.16	(.14)
Capabilities	2.44***	(.62)
Constant	−19.34***	(4.67)
N	984	
Nonzero observations	543	
Zero observations	441	
LR chi²	304.74	
Probability > chi²	.0000	

Notes: Zero-inflated negative binomial model with standard errors reported in parentheses. Note that the signs on the coefficients in the inflated model are reversed during interpretation.
***$p < .01$, **$p < .05$, *$p < .1$.

Due to preliminary support for the facilitation hypotheses, we next examine the mechanisms that would bolster the facilitation approach. To do this effectively, we constructed several tests of the effects of arms imports, money laundering, and drug production on the propensity of a state to produce transnational terrorist attacks. Hypotheses 3b and 3c predict that each of these variables should have a positive effect on the number of terrorist attacks produced. The effects of these conditions are reported in Table 7-3.

In Model 4, we tested the effects of being a major arms importer, a major illicit drug producer, and a country involved in money laundering on the propensity to produce transnational terrorist attacks. State capabilities and the presence of money laundering decrease the probability of being a country of origin for terrorist attacks. Among existing host countries, money laundering, arms imports, and drug production *increase* the number of transnational terrorist attacks originating in the country. Therefore, the presence of money laundering potential does not cause a country without a prior history of originating attacks to suddenly have attacks, but in countries with an attack history, money laundering, illicit drug trade, and arms imports increase the

Table 7-3. *Effects of Arms Imports, Drug Production, and Money Laundering on Terrorism*

	Model 4		Model 5	
	DV: Number of transnational terrorist attacks originating		DV: Number of new homegrown groups	
Count Model				
Country is among top 50 arms importers, 1980–2007	.57**	(.28)	.13	(.42)
Country is among top illicit drug producers, 1980–2007	1.54***	(.37)	−1.22**	(.54)
Country is among "priority countries" for money laundering, 1980–2007	1.15***	(.31)	2.17***	(.45)
Capabilities	.12	(.11)	.14	(.15)
Constant	−1.69**	(.80)	−2.75***	(.91)
Inflate Model				
Country is among top 50 arms importers, 1980–2007	2.74	(2.03)	−1.11	(.96)
Country is among top illicit drug producers, 1980–2007	−15.27	(778.06)	−13.86	(533.29)
Country is among "priority countries" for money laundering, 1980–2007	2.65*	(1.40)	1.59	(1.10)
Capabilities	2.35**	(.99)	.85***	(.26)
Constant	−19.64**	(8.80)	−5.13**	(2.15)
N	759		603	
Nonzero observations	165		68	
Zero observations	594		535	
LR chi^2	62.29		21.91	
Probability > chi^2	.0000		.0002	

Notes: Zero-inflated negative binomial model with standard errors reported in parentheses. Note that the signs on the coefficients in the inflated model are reversed during interpretation.

***$p < .01$, **$p < .05$, *$p < .1$.

number of these attacks originating from the host country. These results again support the facilitation hypothesis.

In Model 5, we found that state capabilities also have a negative effect on the probability of being a host to homegrown terrorist groups. In terms of the number of homegrown groups shown in the count model, we found that money laundering has a positive effect on the number of new groups, whereas drug production has a negative effect. The results in Model 5 suggest that the presence of money laundering facilitates the creation of more groups through access to financing sources, while drug production within a country discourages the development of homegrown terrorist groups. Money laundering generates the most elastic resources—cash—that terrorists can use. Drugs, while lucrative, are less elastic and flexible when it comes to obtaining weapons, traveling, and paying salaries to operatives. Furthermore, drug producers and terrorist groups might find their long-term goals incompatible as terrorists seek to impose instability where drug producers depend on stable consumer markets.[54] Drug revenue in a country with terrorist organizations helps to discourage the formation of other terrorist groups due to competition. The strongest group may want to monopolize drug revenues and discourage the formation of competing groups.

Finally, we tested the interaction between corruption and resource inflows that could be useful to terrorists. Our assumption in testing this interaction is that terrorists should be especially interested in obtaining arms, which is more likely in corrupt countries that are also major importers of arms. Table 7-4 reports findings of the differential effects of major arms imports on the number of transnational attacks emanating from within corrupt, semi-corrupt, and less corrupt countries.[55]

Model 6 reveals that among corrupt countries, being a top fifty arms importer has a positive effect on the probability that a country will be the origin of transnational terrorist attacks, but has no effect on the *number* of transnational attacks originating from that country. The number of attacks is negatively influenced by government capabilities and positively influenced by a history of terrorist attacks.

Among semi-corrupt states, the inflated portion of Model 7 shows that being a top fifty arms importer has no effect on the probability of being the origin of terrorist attacks, while government capabilities have a negative and significant effect. In the count model, only a history of transnational attacks has a significant effect on the number of terrorist attacks that semi-corrupt states produce.

Finally, Model 8 tested these effects among transparent countries. The inflated model reports that being a major arms importer has no effect on the number of transnational terrorist attacks produced by these states, while state capabilities have a significant and negative effect on the probability. In the count model, arms imports have no effect on the number of attacks produced, while state capabilities decrease the number of attacks.

Taken together, we can interpret Models 6, 7, and 8 in the following way. First, corrupt countries with major inflows of arms are more likely to be producers

Table 7-4. *Effects of Arms Imports on Terrorism, by Levels of Corruption*[a]

	Model 6		Model 7		Model 8	
	DV: Number of transnational attacks originating from country					
	Corrupt Countries[†]		Semi-Corrupt Countries[‡]		Transparent Countries[‡‡]	
Count Model						
Country is among top 50 arms importers, 1980–2007	−.00	(.33)	.20	(.14)	.58	(.42)
History of attacks	.04***	(.02)	.10***	(.01)	−.00	(.03)
Capabilities	−.29**	(1.10)	−.05	(.05)	−.33**	(.16)
Constant	2.74	(1.85)	.63**	(.31)	1.99**	(.97)
Inflate Model						
Country is among top 50 arms importers, 1980–2007	−3.21**	(1.56)	−16.85	(3,620.51)	.61	(.76)
Capabilities	−.47	(.33)	2.49***	(.74)	.88***	(.34)
Constant	−2.55	(1.85)	−18.78***	(5.59)	−5.45**	(2.21)
N	135		626		107	
Nonzero observations	74		371		38	
Zero observations	61		255		69	
LR chi^2	17.97		229.66		9.39	
Probability > chi^2	.0004		.0000		.0245	

Note: Zero-inflated negative binomial model with standard errors reported in parentheses. Note that the signs on the coefficients in the inflated model are reversed during interpretation.

a. We were unable to estimate the effects of drug production and money laundering in a similar way because of data limitations. Because of missing data, the number of observations in each category (i.e., corrupt, semi-corrupt, and transparent) was too small to make robust inferences ($n = 31$, 189, and 45, respectively) except in the semi-corrupt category. Moreover, there are no observations of major drug-producing transparent countries, so the drug production variable drops out of all models. Future iterations of the study should increase the observations and use more fine-grained data to address these problems.

†: Transparency International rankings up to the 33rd percentile; ‡: Transparency International rankings between 33rd and 89th percentiles; ‡‡: Transparency International rankings in the 90th percentile.

***$p < .01$, **$p < .05$, *$p < .1$.

of transnational terrorist attacks than "non-corrupt" arms importers. In general, government capabilities reduce the probability and number of terrorist attacks regardless of corruption levels. The combination of corruption and the inflow of arms generate externalities with regard to terrorism, since corrupt arms importers are the most common hosts of transnational terrorist attacks against other states. This finding lends further support to the facilitation hypothesis.

These relationships, however, are mainly correlational. To demonstrate how facilitation mechanisms operate, the illustrative case of the FARC in Colombia is briefly explored below.

Case Study: Narco-Terrorism in Colombia

The FARC emerged out of civil warfare in Colombia, but did not develop into a strong domestic or international actor until the 1980s when drug cartels and terrorist groups in Latin America engaged in *de facto* strategic alliances. Terrorist and criminal groups in the 1980s primarily entered into cooperative relationships for operational purposes. For example, cocaine cartels based in Medellin and Cali regularly hired FARC and M19 guerrillas to provide security for their plantations.[56] The FARC has since taken over much of the drug trade and is now one of the world's wealthiest terrorist groups, with more than 90 percent of the FARC's income stemming from the drug trade, extortion, and kidnapping.[57] The drug trade remains its biggest earner with annual profits in the range of $600 million. The FARC's total expenditure in 2004—$282 million spent on weapons, training, explosives, bribes, and other items—pales in comparison to its income of approximately $1.36 billion for that same year.[58] These resources are then deployed as bribes to secure arms, training, protection from security forces, and immunity from law enforcement so that the FARC may continue its efforts to control Colombia.

The FARC uses domestic and international bribery to facilitate its efforts in both the drug trade and the civil war. Corruption in Colombia existed before the FARC and helped facilitate the drug cartels' trafficking; however, the FARC uses bribery much more extensively than the cartels: "Bribery is an essential strategy for them [FARC] to secure maximum profit and ensure minimum disruption of their business activities by law-enforcement operations."[59] Using bribery to facilitate its activities, the FARC operates in money laundering, arms imports, and transportation through its respective existing infrastructures.

Domestically in Colombia, the FARC bribes both law enforcement and customs officials to protect its business operations. The FARC "purchases" intelligence from the police and security forces, using bribery to protect its operations. For example, the group maintains extensive intelligence networks that inform it of the activities of the police and military, many of whom it ultimately co-opts. As Thachuk describes, "Police are paid to provide information on planned raids, when arrests will occur, and how investigations will proceed. Prosecutors are bribed not to prosecute, judges not to convict, and penal officials not to detain criminals and terrorists who do end up in jail."[60] Nagle confirms this use of bribery: "The FARC has also actively sought to corrupt and intimidate government officials into assisting the FARC in carrying out various objectives, and to infiltrate local and regional government. . . . The intelligence network is comprised of taxi drivers, domestic servants, and corrupt officials in government, military, and the national police."[61]

In addition to corruption among central customs and security forces, 13.1 percent of the nation's municipal mayors have direct links to the insurgency and another 44 percent collaborate in some form with the insurgency.[62] Through a combination of bribery and intimidation, therefore, the FARC influences 57.1 percent of the nation's mayors, who attend clandestine meetings, implement policies that are favorable to the insurgency, and on occasion even divert government funds to the guerrillas.[63]

The existing criminal infrastructure established by the cartel has greatly expanded the FARC's resources, as has funding from the drug trade. The presence of corruption allows the FARC to secure its illegal business, with, as some reports suggest, salaries for collaborators that are often double that given to government soldiers. In fact, the FARC's expenditure on bribery is more than $12 million each year.[64] This case illustrates the role of corruption as a facilitating factor for terrorist formation, expansion, and attacks. However, this case also demonstrates that we cannot speak of corruption as only a domestic factor, just as we no longer can speak of terrorism as a purely domestic one. While the FARC has not conducted attacks outside of Colombia, it has engaged in documented bribery in other states to obtain materials for its attacks in Colombia.

As Greenhill and Bunn point out in their respective chapters on international criminal networks, domestic corruption also enables terrorist groups to utilize existing criminal networks easily to transport materials.[65] For example, the FARC exchanges drugs for weapons and cash with organized crime groups in Chechnya, Russia, Ukraine, and Uzbekistan, and reports indicate that as much as 90 percent of the ammunition used by the insurgents may come from Venezuelan army stocks sold to them by corrupt officials in that country.[66] This demonstrates how corruption can affect terrorists' abilities to exploit small arms imports for their activities at home and abroad.

Corruption facilitates not only the purchase of materials for criminal and terrorist organizations, but also their transport. For example, in the case of the FARC cooperation with corrupt Russian military figures, organized crime bosses, and diplomats during 1999–2000, bribery of customs officials was used to move regular shipments of up to 40,000 kg of cocaine to the former Soviet Union in return for large shipments of Russian and Eastern European weaponry. According to U.S. intelligence officials, this major Russo-Colombian smuggling operation reportedly worked as follows: 1) Russian-built IL-76 cargo planes took off from various airstrips in Russia and the Ukraine laden with anti-aircraft missiles, small arms, and ammunition; 2) The planes, roughly the size of Boeing 707s, stopped in Amman, Jordan, to refuel. There, they bypassed normal Jordanian customs with the help of corrupt foreign diplomats and bribed local officials.[67]

While this chapter does not provide a detailed case study of the FARC, this brief analysis illustrates the process whereby corruption facilitates terrorism both domestically and internationally. States with criminal infrastructures in drug trafficking, arms trade, and money laundering provide resources easily utilized by terrorist groups. Indeed, it is difficult to imagine the FARC's survival if such infrastructures, patterns of bribery, and illegal funding did not exist.

Despite the importance of corruption and the subsequent creation of a criminal infrastructure that reinforces corruption, there are signs that the disparate logics of drug trafficking and terrorism are difficult to maintain in one organization. First, the FARC spends a good deal of its resources on the drug trade, leading some to suggest a growing rift in the FARC between those who want to concentrate on drug trafficking and those who want to focus on insurgency.[68] Second, the 2008 rescue of hostages in Colombia illustrates the disintegration of the FARC's military structure. While it is unclear from the available examples of narco-terrorism whether these alliances can be maintained, the use of drug trafficking by terrorist groups is worrying, given these groups' ability to dramatically expand their operations through bribery.

The case of the FARC demonstrates how corruption is more a facilitator of terrorist activity than a motivator of terrorist activity. The FARC came into being as a revolutionary Communist group opposed to the Colombian regime long before the drug trade was linked to its terrorist activity. Subsequently, the FARC has used corruption within Colombia and the resultant criminal infrastructure to expand its influence. Involvement in the drug trade helped the FARC operatives to raise more money, recruits, and materials to enhance their strength and reach. But corruption was not the direct motivator for their terrorist activity; rather, the FARC came into being to oppose the Colombian government on ideological grounds.

Implications of Our Research

Although the results herein are somewhat intuitive, they arise from the first systematic exploration of the links between corruption and terrorism and suggest specific policy implications. While corruption does not directly cause terrorism, it does serve to facilitate terrorist activities. Although both corruption and terrorism are difficult issues to resolve, our findings show that corruption, like terrorism, is not the problem of just one country but of all countries. Thus, this international problem needs international solutions. The following policy suggestions do not address the many root causes of corruption or terrorism, but rather they target the ways in which corruption facilitates terrorist activity.

First, countries with high levels of corruption, the presence of illicit trade, and existing terrorist groups should be identified as the highest priority. As our research shows, the combination of these factors creates an increase in terrorist activity. Second, the international community must focus on the global supply chain for illicit trade such as drugs and arms. International cooperation is necessary to ensure that goods are being monitored and do not end up in the hands of terrorist groups. For example, the FARC arms shipments from Russia were routed through Jordan, where they could have been stopped before reaching Colombia if customs officials had had the technology and mandate to communicate and cooperate globally with anti-terrorism programs.

The international community needs to establish strict controls on arms inflows into highly corrupt countries. Although these controls might be difficult to enforce, arms flowing into such countries are likely to assist terrorists in launching attacks against neighboring states, making these controls vital to security. For example, according to Transparency International ratings, Iraq ranks third to last in the world with regard to corruption, followed only by Myanmar (Burma) and Somalia. Despite these low rankings, arms inflows to Iraq have increased from $46 million to $244 million between 2004 and 2007.[69] Because of poor governance in Iraq, the more arms that flow into the country, the more likely terrorists are to obtain them and use them against foreign actors. While many argue that arms imports are necessary to maintain stability in Iraq, our findings suggest that stability needs to be established in Iraq through good governance before arms will be useful to diminish the terrorism problem. Moreover, supplying Iraq with arms is likely to generate externalities in neighboring countries because terrorists can conduct their planning and operations against foreign states within Iraq. Neighbors such as Turkey may have difficulties with cross-border terrorists, thus contributing to regional instability.

Last, the international community should invest in increasing state capacity in high-threat countries by training customs and law enforcement officials, implementing international bounty rewards for "catching" illicit shipments, and investing in technology that allows for more transparency and communication along the international supply chain. Although these policy suggestions are not comprehensive solutions, they allow for better coordination of international anti-trafficking and anti-terrorism efforts.

Notes

1. We define terrorism as the threat or use of force against noncombatants by a non-state actor in pursuit of a political goal. In this study, we operationalize terrorism using the number of terrorist attacks as well as the number of new terrorist groups that emerge within a country. For a thorough discussion of competing definitions of terrorism and their implications, see Bruce Hoffman, *Inside Terrorism* (New York, 2006).

2. David Lieb, "Ashcroft Derides Corruption as 'Sanctuary to the Forces of Terror,'" *Kansas City Star* (18 February 2004); Barry Rider, "Organized Crime and Terrorism: Tracking and Attacking the Assets of Economic Crime and Terrorism" (20 June 2002), International Chamber of Commerce Commercial Crime Services Annual Lecture, available at www.iccwbo.org/iccbjfh/index.html (accessed 25 April 2008).

3. Bartosz H. Stanislawski, "Transnational 'Bads' in the Globalized World: The Case of Transnational Organized Crime," *Public Integrity*, VI (2004), 155–170.

4. Susan Rose-Ackerman, *Corruption: A Study in Political Economy* (San Diego, 1978).

5. Joseph Nye, "Corruption and Political Development: A Cost-Benefit Analysis," *American Political Science Review*, LXI (1967), 416.

6. Enrico Columbatto, "Discretionary Power, Rent Seeking and Corruption," *International Centre for Economic Research Working Paper* No. 24–2001 (Torino, 2001), available at www.icer.it/docs/wp2001/EC24-01.pdf (accessed 25 April 2008); see also Arvind Jain (ed.), *Economics of Corruption* (Boston, 1998). Many activities that economists would classify as "rent seeking" are also included in this definition. In this chapter, we differentiate rent seeking from corruption in that while rent seeking might be politically and economically harmful, it is not necessarily illegal.

7. Samuel Huntington, *Political Order in Changing Societies* (New Haven, 1968); James Scott, "The Analysis of Corruption in Developing Nations," *Comparative Studies in Society and History*, XI (1969), 325–341; Robert I. Rotberg (ed.), *State Failure and State Weakness in a Time of Terror* (Washington, D.C., 2003); Robert I. Rotberg and Rachel M. Gisselquist, *Strengthening African Governance: Ibrahim Index of African Governance, Results and Rankings 2007* (Cambridge, MA, 2007).

8. Scott, "The Analysis of Corruption," 321.

9. Nye, "Corruption and Political Development," 420.

10. Ibid.; see also Ting Gong, *The Politics of Corruption in Contemporary China: An Analysis of Policy Outcomes* (Westport, 1994).

11. See Vito Tanzi, "Corruption Around the World: Causes, Consequences, Scope, and Cures," *IMF Staff Papers,* XLV (1998); Susan Rose-Ackerman, "Corruption and Development," in Joseph Stiglitz and Boris Pleskovic (eds.), *Annual World Bank Conference on Development Economics 1997* (Washington, D.C., 1998), 149–171; Antonella Della Porta and Alberto Vannucci, *Corrupt Exchanges* (New York, 1999); Paolo Mauro, "Corruption and Growth," *Quarterly Journal of Economics,* CX (1995), 681–712; Shang Jin Wei, "Corruption in Economic Development: Beneficial Grease, Minor Annoyance, or Major Obstacle?" *World Bank Policy Research Series* 2048 (1998), available at www.worldbank.org/wbi/governance/pdf/wei.pdf (accessed 25 April 2008); Daniel Kaufmann, "Corruption: The Facts," *Foreign Policy,* CVII (1997), 114–132.

12. Quan Li, "Does Democracy Promote or Reduce Transnational Terrorist Incidents?" *Journal of Conflict Resolution,* XLIX (2005), 278–297.

13. See Ted Robert Gurr, *Why Men Rebel* (Princeton, 1970); Mark Irving Lichbach, "Deterrence or Escalation? The Puzzle of Aggregate Studies of Repression," *Journal of Conflict Resolution,* XXXI (1987), 266–297; Karen Rasler, "Concessions, Repression, and Political Protest in the Iranian Revolution," *American Sociology Review,* LXI (1996), 132–152; Jeff R. Goodwin, *No Other Way Out: States and Revolutionary Movements, 1945-1992* (New York, 2001); Roger D. Peterson, *Understanding Ethnic Violence: Fear, Hatred, and Resentment in Twentieth Century Eastern Europe* (New York, 2002).

14. See, for instance, Brian Martin, *Justice Ignited: The Dynamics of Backfire* (Lanham, 2007).

15. Brian Burgoon, "On Welfare and Terror: Social Welfare Policies and Political-Economic Roots of Terror," *Journal of Conflict Resolution,* L (2006), 176–203.

16. See Martha Crenshaw, *Terrorism in Context* (University Park, 1995).

17. Joseph K. Young and Laura Dugan, "Veto Players and Terror," paper presented at International Studies Association, San Francisco, 26–29 March 2008.

18. Li, "Does Democracy Promote or Reduce Transnational Terrorist Incidents?" 281–283.

19. Eli Berman and David D. Laitin, "Religion, Terrorism and Public Goods: Testing the Club Model," *National Bureau of Economic Research Working Paper* No. 13725 (Cambridge, MA, 2008); Pierre-Emmanuel Ly, "The Charitable Activities of Terrorist Organizations," *Public Choice,* CXXXI (2007), 177–195.

20. Herbert Kitschelt, "Origins of International Terrorism in the Middle East," International Policy Analysis Unit (2003), available at www.fes.de/ipg/ONLINE1_2004/ARTKITSCHELT.HTM (accessed 31 October 2008).

21. Ahmed Rashid, *Jihad. The Rise of Militant Islam in Central Asia* (New Haven, 2002).

22. Tamara Makarenko, "Terrorism and Transnational Organised Crime: The Emerging Nexus," in Paul Smith (ed.), *Transnational Violence and Seams of Lawlessness in the Asia-Pacific: Linkages to Global Terrorism* (Honolulu, forthcoming).

23. James D. Fearon, "Rationalist Explanations for War," *International Organization,* XLIX (1995), 379–414; James D. Fearon, "Signaling versus the Balance of Power and

Interests: An Empirical Test of a Crisis Bargaining Model," *Journal of Conflict Resolution,* XXXVIII (1994), 236–269; Barbara F. Walter, "Building Reputation: Why Governments Fight Some Separatists But Not Others," *American Journal of Political Science,* L (2006), 313–330; Barbara F. Walter, "Information, Uncertainty and the Decision to Secede," *International Organization,* LX (2006), 105–135; Barbara F. Walter, "Does Conflict Beget Conflict? Explaining Recurring Civil War," *Journal of Peace Research,* XLI (2004), 371–388.

24. United Nations Conference on the Illicit Trade in Small Arms and Light Weapons, "Under the Gun: Controlling Illegal Firearms Trade," *UN Chronicle* (1 March 2001); Susannah Dyer and Geraldine O'Callaghan, "Combating Illicit Light Weapons Trafficking: Developments and Opportunities," *British American Security Information Council Research Report,* XCVIII (1998), available at www.basicint.org/pubs/Research/ 1998combatingillicit.pdf (accessed 25 April 2008).

25. Peter A. Lupsha, "Drug Lords and Narco-Corruption: The Players Change but the Game Continues," *Crime, Law and Social Change,* XVI (1991), 41–58.

26. Peter Andreas, "The Political Economy of Narco-Corruption in Mexico," *Current History,* XCVII (1998), 160–165.

27. Richard Clutterbuck, "Cocaine, Terrorism, and Corruption," *International Relations,* XII (1995), 77–92.

28. Associated Press, "U.S. Drug Ring Tied to Aid for Hezbollah," *New York Times* (3 September 2002), A16.

29. Mark A.R. Kleiman, "Illicit Drugs and the Terrorist Threat: Causal Links and Implications for Domestic Drug Control Policy," CRS Report for Congress (20 April 2004).

30. Ibid., 4.

31. For a discussion of the limited nature of these ties, see Renssalear W. Lee, "Soviet Narcotics Trade," *Society,* XXVIII (1991), 46–52; Jean-Claude Salomon, François Haut, and Jean-Luc Vannier, *Two Typical "Degenerate Guerilla Groups": The Liberation Tigers of Tamil Eelam and The Kurdistan Workers' Party* (Paris, 1996).

32. Louise I. Shelley and John T. Picarelli, "Methods Not Motives: Implications of the Convergence of International Organized Crime and Terrorism," *Police Practice and Research,* III (2002), 305–318.

33. Louise Shelley, "The Unholy Trinity: Crime, Corruption, and Terrorism," *Brown Journal of World Affairs,* XI (2005), 101–111.

34. Sometimes, of course, economic and political goals overlap, as is the case with narco-terrorists in Afghanistan and Latin America. Generally, however, political objectives are what distinguish terrorists from ordinary criminals and drug lords.

35. James Adams, *The Financing of Terror* (New York, 1986); Andrew Silke, "Drink, Drugs and Rock 'n' Roll: Financing Loyalist Terrorism in Northern Ireland - Part Two," *Studies in Conflict and Terrorism,* XXIII (2000), 107–127.

36. For a description of fundraising by the Tamil Tigers, see Robert I. Rotberg (ed.), *Creating Peace in Sri Lanka* (Washington, D.C., 1999).

37. Asa Hutchinson, Testimony before the U.S. Senate Committee on the Judiciary, "Narco-Terror: The Worldwide Connection Between Drugs and Terrorism," 107th Congress, 2nd session (13 March 2002), available at www.dea.gov/pubs/cngrtest/ct 031302p.html (accessed 25 April 2008); see also Hugh Poulton, *Top Hat, Grey Wolf and Crescent: Turkish Nationalism and the Turkish Republic* (New York, 1997); Henri Barkey and Graham Fuller, *Turkey's Kurdish Question* (New York, 1998).

38. Dale Fuchs, "Spain Says Bombers Drank Water from Mecca and Sold Drugs," *New York Times* (15 April 2004), A3.

39. Patrick Clawson and Rensselaer W. Lee, *The Andean Cocaine Industry* (New York, 1996); Martin Rudner, "Misuse of Passports: Identity Fraud, the Propensity to Travel, and International Terrorism," *Studies in Conflict and Terrorism*, XXXI (2008), 95–110.

40. Kleiman, "Illicit Drugs and the Terrorist Threat," 1, 7.

41. Ibid.

42. Many analysts contend that informal, *hawala* money-transfer networks might be used. See Douglas Frantz, "U.S.-Based Charity is Under Scrutiny," *New York Times* (14 June 2002), A1.

43. Observatorie Geopolitique des Drouges, *The World Geopolitics of Drugs: Annual Report 1997–1998* (Paris, 1998), 97, available at http://bbsnews.net/research/ogd99_6en.pdf (accessed 25 April 2008).

44. Edward Mickolus, *ITERATE: International Terrorism: Attributes of Terrorist Events* (Vienna, 2006).

45. RAND-MIPT, "Terrorism Knowledge Base," available at www.tkb.org/ (accessed 25 November 2005).

46. Transparency International, "Corruption Perceptions Index" (2008), available at www.transparency.org/policy_research/surveys_indices/cpi (accessed 25 April 2008). In addition, composite scores are available for several dozen countries from 1980 to 1992. These older data are included in our study and are available from the Internet Center for Corruption Research at www.icgg.org/corruption.cpi_older indices.html (accessed 25 April 2008).

47. See Nathaniel Heller, "Defining and Measuring Corruption: From Where Have We Come, Where Are We Now, and What Matters for the Future?" chapter 3 in this volume.

48. Wei, "Corruption in Economic Development," 8.

49. Johann Graf Lambsdorff, "Corruption in Comparative Perception," in Jain (ed.), *Economics of Corruption*, 81–110.

50. See Stockholm International Peace Research Institute (SIPRI), "Arms Transfers Database" (2007), available at http://armstrade.sipri.org/arms_trade/values.php (accessed 25 April 2008).

51. U.S. Department of State, Bureau of International Narcotic Law Enforcement Affairs, *International Narcotic Control Strategy Report 2008* (2008), available at www.state.gov/p/inl/rls/nrcrpt/2008/vol1/html/100775.htm (accessed 25 April 2008).

52. Ibid.

53. J. David Singer, "Reconstructing the Correlates of War Dataset on Material Capabilities of States, 1816–1985," *International Interactions,* XIV (1987), 115–132; National Material Capabilities Dataset, v3.02, available at www.correlatesofwar.org/COW2%20Data/Capabilities/nmc3-02.htm (accessed 25 April 2008).

54. Shelley, "The Unholy Trinity," 101–111; Kleiman, "Illicit Drugs and the Terrorist Threat," 1, 7.

55. Using Transparency International rankings, we define "corrupt" countries as those up to the 33rd percentile; "semi-corrupt" countries as those between the 33rd and 89th percentiles; and "transparent" countries as those ranking in the 90th percentile.

56. Max Manwaring, "Non-State Actors in Colombia: Threat and Response," U.S. Army War College, Strategic Studies Institute Report (Carlisle, PA, 2002), available at www.strategicstudiesinstitute.army.mil/pdffiles/pub16.pdf (accessed 16 October 2008).

57. Jeremy McDermott, "Colombian Report Shows FARC is World's Richest Insurgent Group," *Jane's Intelligence Review* (19 August 2005).

58. Justine Rosenthal, "For-Profit Terrorism: The Rise of Armed Entrepreneurs," *Studies in Conflict and Terrorism,* XXXI (2008), 481–498.

59. Felia Allum and Renate Siebert, *Organized Crime and the Challenge to Democracy* (London, 2003).

60. Kimberley Thachuk, "Corruption: The International Security Dimension," NDU Symposium, Washington, D.C., 20–21 February 2002.

61. Luz Nagle, "Colombian Asylum Seekers: What Practitioners Should Know About the Colombian Crisis," *Georgetown Immigration Law Journal,* XVIII (2003), 441.

62. J. P. Sweeney, "Tread Cautiously in Colombia's Civil War," *Heritage Foundation Backgrounder* No. 1264 (Washington, D.C., 1999).

63. Tamara Makarenko, "On the Border of Crime and Insurgency," *Jane's Intelligence Review* (18 December 2001); Jane's Terrorism and Insurgency Centre, "FARC and the Paramilitaries Take Over Colombia's Drug Trade," *Jane's Intelligence Review* (1 July 2004), both available at http://jir.jenes.com/public/jir/index.html (accessed 25 November 2008).

64. Chris Dishman, "Terrorism, Crime, and Transformation," *Studies in Conflict and Terrorism,* XXIV (2001), 43–58.

65. See Kelly Greenhill, "Kleptocratic Interdependence: Trafficking, Corruption, and the Marriage of Politics and Illicit Profits," chapter 5 in this volume; Matthew Bunn, "Corruption and Nuclear Proliferation," chapter 6 in this volume.

66. George Franco, "Their Darkest Hour: Colombia's Government and the Narco-Insurgency," *Parameters,* XXX (2000), 83–93.

67. Bruce Michael Bagley, "Globalisation and Latin America and Carribean Organised Crime," *Global Crime,* VI (2004), 32–53.

68. Thachuk, "Corruption."

69. In 1990 U.S. dollars; see SIPRI, Arms Transfers Database (2007).

ROBERT LEGVOLD

8

Corruption, the Criminalized State, and Post-Soviet Transitions

Scarcely anyone doubts that Russia and the majority of post-Soviet states are among the most corrupt in the world. Only a scattering of African and Latin American states can claim as much, and even then not with the same across-the-board regional sweep.[1] In Transparency International's (TI) 2008 rankings, 8 out of the 12 post-Soviet states were clustered in the bottom 35 of the 180 states rated.[2] A host of additional studies, surveys, and anecdotal evidence come to roughly the same conclusion. Since Russia, with its eleven time zones, nearly a third of the world's gas, and close to half of the world's nuclear weapons, and the other eleven countries that occupy the vast space and house the immense resources of the former Soviet Union, are not Antarctica or a set of small, remote, hopelessly weak states, but the critical hinterland of Europe, Asia, and a turbulent Islamic south, presumably this unpromising claim ought to be of significance for the rest of us. But why?

Obviously corruption on this scale creates large distortions in normal economic and political activity and makes life difficult for a lot of Russians, Kazakhs, and Ukrainians. But need this be of real concern to outsiders? In other contexts, corruption is thought to impede economic development (although some argue that the relationship is the other way around, and, in fact, that international aid agencies' preoccupation with fighting corruption actually thwarts development).[3] The parallel in the case of the post-Soviet states is the pernicious link between corruption and economic reform, and, therefore, sustainable economic growth. If wide-spread corruption prevents a large and potentially prosperous country such as Russia or Ukraine from taking the steps that will ultimately free it from the dead weight of the past, it can rightly be argued that the economies of many other countries will lose as well. Or, if it is thought that corruption-inhibited political reform will leave these countries more authoritarian than democratic, again, the effects, particularly, on neighboring states, are likely to be unhappy.

In this chapter, however, the argument is bolder and more direct. It is that corruption at the level enveloping most of the post-Soviet states, in particular Russia, poses a direct threat to the world outside—a threat not merely to international welfare, but to international security. There is a corollary: If corruption in and among the post-Soviet states poses this kind of threat, then it no longer deserves to be treated as a secondary issue and given passing attention by all but those who have a special professional interest in the subject. It should be front and center when thinking about the core security challenges facing the international community, and a key concern for major powers when designing their foreign policies toward Russia and the region.

Corruption in Russia and surrounding states influences, for the worse, most of the crucial facets of the international security agenda: issues of war and peace, including regional conflict; global terrorism; and the proliferation of weapons of mass destruction (WMD). No less important, corruption is a burden when facing issues of global welfare: the risk of failed or failing states; the abuse of human and minority rights; threats to health; the flow of "contaminants," such as drugs, trafficked humans, and illegal arms; and the damage done to national economies by illicit trade, money laundering, and transnational crime.

Concepts and Causal Arrows

As is evident throughout the essays in this volume, conceptual problems begin with the word itself. Not that perfectly serviceable definitions do not exist. The standard dictionary definition is "the inducement of a political official by means of improper considerations to commit a violation of duty." Fair enough, but what then are "improper considerations" and what constitutes a "violation of duty?" Social scientists have tried to remove this ambiguity with ever more elaborate formulations. Some would define corruption as "behavior which deviates from the formal duties of a public role because of private-regarding (personal, close family, private clique) pecuniary or status gains; or violates rules against the exercise of certain types of private-regarding influences."[4] In all cases, however, the meanings that analysts attach to the word fail to capture the meanings that different peoples in different societies at different times attach to actual behavior. One person's corrupt action is another's socially acceptable transaction. To some what seems a blight on economic and political progress for others serves as an inevitable, even necessary, aspect of change in chaotic and uncharted periods of transformation.[5] Add to this conceptual ambiguity the shaky nature of the data that are used to measure corruption and the analytical challenge grows exponentially. As a result, even the basic questions are not easily answered: How bad is the problem? Are things getting better or worse?

Without gainsaying these difficulties, here they are set aside. First, because despite imprecision in the data on corruption in Russia and the region, no one—insider or outsider, analyst or victim—doubts that corruption exists there on a grand scale. Second, there is no question that in virtually all of the post-Soviet states, with the questionable exception of Georgia, corruption is growing, not receding. This chapter offers instead conceptual distinctions to help one think about the specific nature of corruption in the post-Soviet region.

The first of these distinguishes among categories: the criminal state, the criminalized state, and public corruption. The criminal state, as used here, refers to places not merely where criminal activity has penetrated widely within the state, but where the core activity of the state is criminal; that is, where the state depends overwhelmingly on the returns from illicit trade to finance itself and, therefore, not only protects, but, in fact, conducts the bulk of the business. None of the twelve internationally recognized post-Soviet states—and certainly not Russia—fall into this category. But several of the so-called *de facto* mini-states left in the wake of separatist struggles within the post-Soviet states—Abkhazia and South Ossetia in Georgia, Transdniestr in Moldova, and Nagorno-Karabakh in Azerbaijan—fit this description.

Russia, Ukraine, and the other post-Soviet states belong in the middle category: the criminalized state. Corruption in their case is too extensive and, above all, too entwined with the state to treat it as in the category of public corruption; that is, states where bribery works with some agencies or where "bad apples" among public officials turn up more than sporadically, but where core institutions remain uncontaminated.[6] The concept of the criminalized state, in contrast, implies a qualitatively different level of corruption, one in which the state itself is suffused with corruption. The state's core activity may not be corrupt, but the *process* by which the state acts is.

Of the various formulas invented to represent this phenomenon, the notion of "state capture," introduced by officials at the European Bank for Reconstruction and Development (EBRD) and the World Bank, is one of the most helpful.[7] State capture occurs when, in contrast to mere bribe-making, to secure access to a good or an exception to existing rules, interested parties exploit the malfeasance of officials to change the rules (laws, judicial rulings, or bureaucratic regulations). Rather than state officials and bureaucrats extorting business firms or ordinary individuals, powerful individuals or groups use material rewards or physical threats to reshape the state. Alternatively, the criminalized state can be thought of as one where much, if not most, state activity has been "privatized"; that is, where either those in power or those with leverage over those in power use state agency to advance their private interests at the expense of the broader public good.[8]

One can also distinguish between systemic and non-systemic corruption, systemic corruption being broader than the criminalized state. Because systemic corruption entails wide swaths of civil society together with the state, not simply a state suborned by powerful but select private stakeholders, it can be both more extensive and more deeply rooted than the criminalized state. I say "can be" because in the literature systemic corruption often simply refers to the debasing of the state by a bureaucracy or a wide swath officialdom that is up for sale, but without indicating at what point a canker in the state becomes its very essence. Take, for example, the contrast between the Soviet Union, on the one hand, and Russia and other post-Soviet states, on the other: to categorize corruption in both cases as systemic without noting where corruption metamorphoses into the criminalized state obscures the sad reality distinguishing the present from the past.

Divided further into centralized or decentralized systemic corruption, the concept captures important differences among the post-Soviet states. As used by Stefes, when systemic corruption is centralized, the state controls the "networks of corruption," deciding who gets what, when, and how; when decentralized, networks of corruption have free rein, and they—often in chaotic and violently competitive fashion—define the shape, scale, and impact of corruption.[9] A related contrast is between locally based and nationally based corruption, that is, whether the heart of the problem is the wayward conduct of government at the center or, alternatively, more commonly in the regions and towns. Those who stress the distinction between centralized and decentralized systemic corruption contend that decentralized corruption is more difficult to contain and redirect or correct as well as more threatening to political stability. The same can be said of corruption centered on local and regional governments. In the post-Soviet states, however, corruption thrives at both levels, and there is often a symbiotic relationship between the two. Many of the more important players in the private sector act on both levels or do their business with local political officials who have entrée at the national level. Or national figures have private interests in the regions that benefit from what the traffic will bear locally. In other cases where the two domains are separate, usually because national authorities have only a weak writ over local politics, the center would have trouble attacking corruption, even if it wished to, because it lacks adequate leverage.

These notions suffer much the same conceptual ambiguity as the concept of corruption itself, but they have the utility, even as rough hewn tools, of creating qualitative distinctions missing from broad quantitative indicators. They also provide at least primitive guideposts, allowing one to focus on the sources of the problem, if only by revealing essential aspects of its nature. Hence, they serve as a starting point for wrestling with the question of what it will take to see change in these societies, and, by extension, what policies on the part of others can have an effect, if any.

Contours

Pick the measure, and by it Russia and most of its post-Soviet neighbors will score badly. It is not merely their shoddy showing in Transparency International's widely cited rankings or the fact that from 2005 to 2008, with the exception of Georgia, their standing in all cases slid—often by 15 places or more (Russia from 126 to 149).[10] By another standard, in an effort to assess how strong a country's institutions are for fighting corruption, of the nine post-Soviet countries included in the 2007 Global Integrity Index rankings, only Kazakhstan has an overall score placing it in the "moderate" category. The other eight all fall in the "weak" or "very weak" category (Armenia and Tajikistan).[11] In this case, Georgia is among those that have slipped a full category from moderate to weak. No matter which survey—the Business Environment and Enterprise Performance Survey, the World Economic Forum's Executive Opinion Survey, the IMD's World Competitiveness Yearbook, or the World Bank's Country Policy and Institutional Assessment—most of the post-Soviet states, including Russia, end up toward the bottom, and where there is progress, rarely is it in mitigating the more serious forms of corruption, such as state capture.[12]

Before digging further into what may gradually come to seem to the reader one grim statistic piled on another, until the situation begins to look unredeemable, two qualifications deserve noting. First, while corruption in Russia and the other post-Soviet states is at a qualitatively different level from corruption in the Russian past or from what one sees in most other societies and, indeed, that now exists on a scale that poses a threat to the outside world, this does not mean the problem is insoluable. Nor even less does it diminish the remarkable change that has occurred in many of these societies—change that has made life better and richer for a sizable portion of their populations.

The other qualification confesses the obvious. The story that follows is told with facts and figures, but, as anyone who works in the murky world of measuring corruption knows, the data are disturbingly imprecise. They are not a last word, but a loose approximation of the problem—some looser than others. The data suggest rough magnitudes, and only by adding them together do the contours of the threat emerge.

This being said, more telling than cross-country statistical rankings are the manifestations of corruption—the forms that it takes, the scale that it reaches, and the place that it occupies. Stefes, who has written the most thorough comparative study of corruption in Armenia and Georgia, reports that under the prior Shevardnadze regime, mafia groupings, protected by public officials, cornered 30 percent of Georgian banking revenues, 40 percent of hotel and restaurant income, and 40 percent of the construction industry.[13] In Armenia 60 percent of the country's industrial infrastructure was "sold" for $800,000.[14] In Georgia a high percentage of foreign aid and loans was embezzled by senior officials in the Ministry for Fuel and Energy, including $380 million, roughly half the foreign aid given to refurbish the energy sector.[15] In Armenia, between 1991 and 1998, Telman Ter-Petrosian, the brother of the president, was said to control "construction and other industries." The ministers of internal affairs and defense controlled "the import and distribution of food and oil products," while "several other ministers" grew rich by embezzling humanitarian aid. Under Ter-Petrosian's successor, the brothers Serge and Aleksandr Sargsian—the former, Armenia's current president—have a lock on the gas and fuel market, and "are the main exporters of scrap metal."[16] In almost all cases, these spheres of the economy are said to be rife with corruption.

Before the Rose Revolution, working-level officials in the Georgian tax department "paid around $20,000 to get their jobs"; an Armenian wanting a traffic police officer's post, $3,000–$5,000; a judge's position, about $50,000; and "ministerial appointments could cost between $200,000 and several million USD, depending on the 'profitability'" of the portfolio.[17] In the case of the Armenian traffic officer, his monthly pay is $35–$50 a month. "He," Stefes explains, "can make an additional $500 a month through bribes but needs to pay his superior about $10 a day to keep his job," thus recouping "his initial investment in about two to three years."[18]

The system worked much the same way in Georgia, and it does so in most of the post-Soviet states, varying only in the cost of a given position or a given service. In Russia in 2005, to elude the military draft, a Moscow resident expected to pay $5,000; a resident of central Russia, $1,500.[19] Bribes to get into Russia's most prestigious universities have ranged from $30,000–$40,000;

into second- and third-tier institutions, much less.[20] When bribery exists not only on this scale, but according to established schedules of payment known to a broad customer base, one distinguishing feature of the criminalized state is in place.

In the case of Ukraine, one 2007 survey found that 67 percent of Ukrainians confessed to "corrupt transactions" in dealing with government officials.[21] "In the last two to three years, around 2,500 Ukrainian enterprises have allegedly been raided," (as in, stolen through the courts).[22] And despite the hopes engendered by the Orange Revolution and the modest improvement in the months after, in 2007 the World Bank reported that between 2005 and 2006 according to governance indicators, including corruption, Ukraine had fallen from the 35th percentile to the 28th.[23] The Atlantic Council study that assembled these signposts stresses how much of Ukraine's corruption amounts to what the World Bank–EBRD authors call state capture in all three branches of government, including, in particular, the legislative branch. "The price of passing a bill," it says, citing "some investigative journalists may be as high as a few million dollars."[24] It is not surprising then that 52 percent of Ukrainians think that "corruption is justified in most situations to get things done."[25] This sentiment doubtless marks popular attitudes in most post-Soviet states and represents, if not the criminalized state, then, at a minimum, systemic corruption.

In the Russian case, an Information Science for Democracy (INDEM) survey, the most in-depth study that has been done to date on corruption, contends that from 2001 to 2004, Putin's first term in office, what it classes as "business corruption" (the price of doing business, as opposed to the petty and sometimes not-so-petty bribes that the average person pays to get through life) increased nine-fold.[26] If measured against federal budget revenues, the returns from corruption were a third less in 2001; by 2005 they were reported to be 2.6 times larger.

The INDEM survey, unlike any other done among the post-Soviet states, measured both extortion and the willingness to yield to it in "everyday corruption." Everyday corruption includes everything from arranging medical treatment to getting a passport or driver's license, from securing a favorable court ruling to obtaining a title to property. According to the survey's results, in 2004 the total for everyday corruption remained at roughly $3 billion (up slightly from $2.8 billion in 2001), but paled in comparison to business corruption, which was estimated at $316 billion, nine times the figure in 2001. Within these broad parameters, the survey uncovered significant secondary phenomena. For example, at the level of everyday corruption, the results indicated that while public officials pushed harder for bribes in 2004 than in 2001, in general the public was less willing to pay them (the only exception was in the willingness to bribe to avoid military conscription).[27] When explaining why the public bribed, the most often cited reason (54–56 percent) was that the individuals involved knew in advance that they needed to do so—one more manifestation of systemic corruption.

The INDEM data on business corruption did not include either the pressure for bribes or the willingness to pay, but it did stress the exponential increase in the size of the bribes paid (the average bribe increased from $10,200 to $135,800 over the four years) and the annual amount paid in bribes (from $22,900 to $243,750). The study also measured which branch of government exacted the largest share of the pie, with the executive trumping the others several times over (being the choice in 2004 by more than 76 percent of the respondents, compared to 6.2 percent for the legislative and 4.8 percent for the judicial). That said, the latter two branches had gained a point or two on the executive branch in the intervening four years, although the percentage of those saying "it was difficult to say" had increased from 2 percent to 12.4 percent, which was interpreted as meaning that it was too risky to say.

Causes

Corruption in Russia and the other post-Soviet states arises, as it does in any state, in the nexus between opportunity and risk. When public officials have discretion over the distribution of benefits sought by private citizens or costs that they wish to avoid, the temptation to welcome or demand a bribe arises. When the risks entailed in offering or taking a bribe are lower than the payoff, the temptation often prevails.[28] Risk depends on the odds that the transgression will be detected, the magnitude of the penalty if it is, and the likelihood of the penalty actually being imposed. Thus, one-half of the cost-benefit analysis at the heart of corruption comes back to the strength, probity, and predictability of political institutions. The other half features the reward side: first, how valuable is the favor, award, permission, or punishment over which a public official presides, or how valuable can it be made by manipulation; second, how exclusive is his or her control over it; third, in how many facets of economic and social life do bureaucrats or politicians have benefits to confer or penalties to apply; and, fourth, how many bureaucrats or politicians are involved in the act.

The matrix that these calculations yield makes room for several useful contrasts. Some of the contrasts are at the level of bribe frequency and size. Susan

Rose-Ackerman makes the point that if punishment is harsh, swift, and sure, political agents or would-be bribers are normally deterred, and instances of corruption shrink, but those that remain are likely to involve larger bribes, reflecting a higher risk premium.[29] Conversely, where most bribes are small but common, enforcement may be spotty or toothless.

Various combinations among the multiple factors, however, create the basis for a typology at the systemic level. In countries where the spheres in which public officials have benefits to grant or punishments to inflict are limited and so too are the benefits or punishments within their control; where penalties and their certainty are great, because institutions and mores ensure both; and where organization, resources, and technique permit a high rate of detection, corruption is not a serious blight on the political and economic systems. Their closest approximations are the countries at the top of Transparency International's rankings. Most fall somewhere in between. The line dividing those countries that suffer from attention-deserving public corruption and those burdened by systemic corruption is more blurred. Presumably it lies somewhere between cases in which the regulatory framework, anti-corruption measures, and tradeoffs against the costs of enforcement leave the country exposed to sporadic, at times sensational, instances of corruption, versus cases where many, if not most, parts of government are contaminated, because government has a wide range of favors to dispense, particularly in forms prone to illicit bargains, enforcement is lax even if anti-corruption legislation is in place, and a "culture of corruption" has taken root. That is, people accept corruption as in the nature of things and the only way to transact business.

The post-Soviet states, however, reside further down the spectrum. These countries suffer from the worst version of the matrix: weak states with bloated, semi-autonomous bureaucracies; elaborate overlapping but contradictory regulatory frameworks; political agents at multiple levels of government with either excessive discretionary power or a capacity to manufacture it; half-formed or easily subverted institutions that observe or implement law only on some days; an unusual degree of concentrated but unconsolidated wealth in the hands of political leaders at both the national and regional levels; and a culture of corruption in the broader population. It is a poisonous mix, limning the criminalized state while predicting the obstacles to dismantling it.

Still, to catalogue a dismal configuration is not to explain its reason for being. The route to the criminalized state in the post-Soviet era has been cleared by the cumulative impact of three phenomena: the Soviet legacy, the transition (from one economic order to another), and the more recent trend toward political il-liberalism. One influence has been added to another creating a powerful, albeit far from uniform, impulse to the deformed models that these states have become.

None of the new states that have risen from the ruins of the Soviet Union, of course, emerged *de novo*. All bore the imprint of a system shot through with elements of corruption. It is fair to say that corruption in the Soviet Union was systemic; that is, it was a regular and essential feature of political and economic life, not simply an episodic or marginal deviation from standard norms. At the most mundane level, scarcely any of life's simple activities—such as getting one's apartment plumbing fixed, or a room added to the dacha, or a better position on the waiting list for an appliance in short supply—transpired without a few bottles of vodka or some other welcome gift, including head-turning sums of money. The practice was called *blat,* and every Soviet citizen knew the word as well as when and how to engage in it. So commonplace was it that few thought of it as anything other than the norm. Similarly, nearly all Soviets at one point bought a pair of jeans, a CD, a pair of knockoff Nikes, or sometimes considerably more expensive items, *naleva,* that is, on the black market. Because by the 1970s the second or shadow economy was estimated to constitute close to 25 percent of GDP and involve more than 80 percent of the population in buying or selling, all of it illegal, corruption in this form was, indeed, systemic.[30]

The second economy flourished in the Soviet Union because of scarcity, and scarcity was the product of a physically planned economy that denied consumers the goods that they wanted. It also generated a third level of corruption that arose from over-taut planning. Factory managers faced the unrelenting pressure to achieve assigned production targets—targets that rose if met—while constantly menaced by bottlenecks and delays in the supplies needed to turn out their products. As a result, they often directly sought out suppliers and cut illegal deals to short circuit the process, and they put people, called *tolkachi* (or "pushers"), on their payroll to head up the effort.

Never mind that the authorities tolerated to a considerable extent the masquerade, because, as noted by Western analysts, it smoothed the functioning of an economy that otherwise would never have managed to get things when and where needed. By the rules of the system the abuse was corruption and, when egregious, punished, but so widespread that it added immensely to what made corruption in the Soviet Union systemic. It also frequently became damaging or, worse, utterly dysfunctional. It was damaging when a manager could pay off an official to look the other way when targets were not met or met with defective goods. It was dysfunctional when party officials, sometimes senior party officials, simply faked production results, as when over

time virtually the entire *apparat* of the Uzbek communist party and government falsified their republic's cotton yields worth an estimated $6.5 billion,
leading to the arrest and prosecution of many hundreds of officials in the
mid-1980s, including every national minister except one.[31]

The effects of over-taut planning and scarcity, in turn, were magnified by
the pathologies of an authoritarian system in decline. Patron-client relationships flourish in settings where power is concentrated upward and political
success depends on networks of mutual support. When the values that once
gave the system integrity faded and cynicism or, at best, self-seeking set in,
these relationships became natural channels for corruption, each a potential
mini-pyramid distributing up through the network's hierarchy the gains
extracted at ground-level. Or, when formed at the very top around a senior
official or his or her family members, they siphoned into private hands large
chunks of state resources.

While scarcity and clientelism, when combined with the moral decay arising from long-lost ideological idealism, led to widespread corruption
throughout the system, the Soviet Union never became a criminalized state;
although it can be argued that some of the republics during certain periods
(e.g., Georgia and Uzbekistan) did.[32] Legislators were not for sale, not least
because they had little power to legislate, and the authoritarians who did, for
the most part, did so to keep the system going, not to fill their pockets. Leonid
Brezhnev's son-in-law may have stolen on an impressive scale, but few thought
Brezhnev or his colleagues on the Politburo were plundering the state. In part
they had less incentive to do so, because they, like others atop the party and
government ranks, already enjoyed privileges unavailable to the public (special stores with access to scarce foreign goods, exclusive health and resort
facilities, chauffeured automobiles, and elegant apartments and dachas, etc.).
At times a local official or a court could be bought, but for the most part they
operated within the norms of the system; alas, norms that sanctioned great
political injustice when faced with dissent. The second economy, while illegal
in its very nature, operated alongside, not inside, the state. Officials again
crossed the line, and more than a few availed themselves of its opportunities,
but their misdeeds were surreptitious, not the daily fare of the bureaucracies
within which they operated.[33]

Hence, the Soviet Union provided a base for the criminalized state, but not
its essence. That required the collapse of the Soviet Union, and the chaotic
transition from one economic order to another. Beyond the leavening effect of
disintegrating rules and institutions, the other crucial impulse to the criminalization of the state was the appearance of private property; private property

on a grand scale. Suddenly everything that had been the state's patrimony for centuries—land, natural resources, factories, and markets—was up for grabs, and the rush, as one scholar put it, to "steal the state" was on.[34]

Because the authority and formal institutions of the state dissolved but not the informal networks or special access of those who populated it, public officials and, above all, the managers of factories, firms, and resource-extracting complexes were well-placed to manipulate the transfer of property, and then either to strip assets or to use dubiously acquired ownership in one sector, for example, banking, to accumulate holdings in other still more undervalued holdings, such as oil or metals. Much of this plundering occurred not in a violation of law, but in a vacuum of law. The insider deals, stacked auctions, and deceived stake holders constituted abuses that in a normal regulatory environment would have been defined as corruption. But the real burgeoning of corruption took place afterward.

At the top of the heap, those who had amassed fortunes by cornering key properties (including a fair number of Gosplan, party, Komsomol, defense, and interior officials) perpetuated their success by suborning legislators and regulators into passing laws or implementing regulations that obstructed potential competitors or, at times, by hiring a cheaper, more lethal solution. When necessary these officials did not hesitate to use the tax authorities or the courts to crush the owners of the property that they coveted, and then they simply seize their holdings. Meanwhile, these practices were repeated a thousand times over, as they seeped down through the society, and took hold in localities. The dramatic instances may have been the head of the State Statistics Committee and twenty of his subordinates arrested in 1998 for doctoring data to allow large firms to evade taxes, or the payoffs spirited into Swiss bank accounts by the head of the Kremlin property department for contracts given to Mabetex, a foreign construction firm—and the protection he then received from the Russian government. But what created the dense fabric of corruption were local officials happily collaborating with predatory business interests, indifferent to the law and property rights, and ready to share in the spoils. In addition, scores of officials throughout the lower reaches of government came to treat extortion as normal compensation for sanctioning business in their area. And in too many cases, local officials or enterprise directors simply stole what they could, such as Georgian officials in the town of Ninotsminda, who pilfered hundreds of telephone lines to be sold on the Turkish scrap metal market, leaving 25,000 residents with three.[35]

As Varese notes, "When a centrally planned economy comes to an end, the result is a dramatic increase in the number of property owners and in transactions among individuals with property rights," and, hence, in "opportunities to engage in criminal activities."[36] The incentives to bribe, steal, and extort grow as well. Both propositions, however, miss a more subtle effect. The sudden opportunity to accumulate property, when property rights are not yet secure, transforms surviving institutions and, even more, informal mechanisms into vessels of corruption. Take the long-lived Russian tradition of *krugovaya poruka*: a notion that, tracing back to Muscovy, meant "collective responsibility" for the group. Historically it was an administrative device employed by the tsarist state to extract resources and keep order at the local level. In Stalin's day it became the resort of the political and professional elite struggling to avoid being sucked into the machinery of repression. But in the upheaval of the last twenty years it has turned into the ubiquitous form by which bureaucrats collude with fellow bureaucrats to skirt the law, high rollers arrange and then conceal their illicit deals, and political leaders create teams who guard their power and add to their wealth.[37]

Privatization amidst institutional chaos and missing or feckless legislation also subverts the remnants of structures intended to sort out the excesses during the transition from one economic order to the next. A court system inherited from the Soviet era, unlearned in the nature of law in a capitalist system, presented with a welter of ambiguous, mutually contradictory new legislation, lacking accountability to the public, underpaid, and denied access to adequate information in deciding cases, not surprisingly has turned out to be a weak barrier against abuse, and often its facilitator.[38] Most surveys show that the majority of Russians and Ukrainians do not expect to get a fair decision in court or, if fair, even fewer believe that it will be enforced, and half of the third who believe that they can get a fair decision assume that it will be through bribing. What is true of the judiciary is equally true of government bureaucracy, particularly regulatory agencies. The Soviet bureaucracy was a sullen, red-tape-ridden affair, greased with more than the occasional bribe. But its successor, filled largely with the same people only now with many others added, has made rent-seeking the major mode of operation. Bureaucrats could not have done so if the licensing, customs, registration procedures, tax codes, and fire and health inspections devised to deal with property in the hands of many private owners had not yielded the means.

As the effects of the transition from one economic order to another add greatly to the weight of legacy, the more recent trend toward political illiberalism in all but one or two post-Soviet states appears to have made transitional ills worse. One needs to be careful here: the basis for arguing that the move away from democratic practice contributes to the criminalized state is flimsier than for either the weight of history or the effects of privatization. A positive correlation exists between the stages by which most of the post-Soviet states have veered from a democratic path in the last seven or eight years and their steady slide in the cross-country corruption rankings. But this correlation only *suggests* a relationship; it does not *prove* it.

If a causal relationship is sought, it is usually argued that increased authoritarianism (diminished press freedom, weakened parliaments, stifled political opposition, etc.) destroys the transparency, external oversight, whistle-blowing, and competing anti-corruption programs necessary to fight corruption. One piece of evidence, however, does seem to suggest a close relationship. Soon after Putin came to power in 2001, the Duma passed the 2001 judicial reform act designed to correct many of the flaws in the old system; the same year new laws designed to reduce bureaucratic rent-seeking (by reducing opportunities and incentives) were passed. That since then corruption in Russia has grown, not shrunk, would seem logically to imply that broader political trends have strengthened the criminalized state, allowing it not merely to carry on, but to subvert measures intended to curb it.

Consequences

Much of the harm from corruption featured in the literature focuses on what happens within a country. The emphasis is on the connection between corruption and poverty or on the impediments corruption places on economic development. In the case of the post-socialist states, attention shifts to the related matter of corruption's implications for reform, including its negative effect on the synergies between political and economic reform—or alternatively to the positive impact of reform on corruption. These do constitute crucial dimensions of the problem, but they are not the only ways that corruption—particularly in the form of the criminalized state—matter. The effects also cross borders and radiate into the wider international community, threatening both international security and international welfare, the concern of this book.

The argument has become almost commonplace that, as the 2003 *Transition Report* of the EBRD puts it, "a strong link" exists "between the depth of democracy and the level of economic reform."[39] "Only countries that have established high levels of political and civil liberties and the effective rule of law have made significant progress in the . . . crucial area of institution-building or 'second phase' reforms." (First phase reforms are seen as price and trade liberalization and small-scale privatization, and have been achieved in countries with "less liberal political regimes.") Corruption impedes important elements of political liberalization, such as judicial impartiality, administrative reform, and secure property rights. The state then ends up absent or, worse, an obstacle where it is most needed in helping to build market institutions. Government becomes a shield for, rather than a constraint on, "vested interests" that block change threatening "their gains from only partial reforms and distorted markets."[40] And, in specific respects, such as obstructing the growth of small and medium-size enterprises, according to most surveys conducted among businessmen, corruption and its corollary, anti-competitive practices, outrank taxes and business regulations as barriers.

If the role of corruption in impeding economic and political reform is generally accepted, the same cannot be said about two other linkages: corruption as a drag on economic growth and corruption as a cause of political instability. Among the post-Soviet states no obvious connection stands out between levels of corruption and annual GDP performance. Some countries toward the bottom of TI's CPI have had substantial growth rates over the last decade. On the other hand, some that rank higher, such as Moldova, have enjoyed far lower rates of growth, but so have some of the most corrupt, such as Uzbekistan. The difference obviously has much more to do with the economic and trade advantages that one country enjoys when compared to another. Those endowed with oil and gas have done better than those without. So have countries with larger and more balanced economies, such as Ukraine, versus those with mono-cultural economies, such as Moldova.

On the other hand, quite possibly corruption, if not a barrier to growth, does produce sub-optimal growth. Proving a counterfactual, however, is no easy task, and certainly not one this chapter is capable of addressing.[41] A second effect, however, seems still more plausible: while corruption may not prevent growth, it likely does pose an obstacle to sustainable growth. It may do so in several ways: by fostering rentier capitalism; by impeding economic diversification; by slowing structural reform; and by feeding on itself and swelling until it leads to major market distortion.

The link to political instability is even more cloudy. Some argue that much of what gets labeled corruption either eases the frictions of the transition from one economic order to another or helps to generate jobs and economic activity, and, therefore, contributes to political stability. Two authors, looking at the Chinese case, contend that "transitory-corruption" during the early phases of economic reform, as opposed to "steady-state corruption," can actually facilitate "permanent, desirable institutional change," by essentially turning bureaucrats into sponsors of private business and, when these are successful, then siphoning them into management and out of the state sector.[42] Clifford Gaddy, too, would distinguish between "good" and "bad" corruption. "Good corruption," he says, "greases the wheels and broadens support for the system."[43] He has in mind "rent sharing for the purpose of social stability (providing jobs and incomes), or for state interests." It is, he suggests, borrowing from the Russian journalist Yuliya Latynina, roughly similar to the distinction from Soviet days between "stealing from the firm" and "stealing for the firm."

Without denying the merit of either argument, however, one can entertain doubts stirred by more baleful effects. Where corruption discredits government and saps its legitimacy in the eyes of average citizens, or alienates them and destroys their will to sacrifice for it, or even to comply with its norms, political stability cannot be served. Nor is there any question that popular perceptions of widespread corruption served as one of the major catalysts for all three of the so-called color revolutions (in Georgia in 2003; Ukraine, 2004; and Kyrgyzstan, 2005). When the streets are mobilized, by definition political stability has departed. Moreover, to the extent that outsiders—Russia and, to a degree, the Western powers—define these as moments of instability, and insert themselves, invariably they are made more so, and with an international resonance. At this point the threshold between the internal and external world has been crossed.

Normally when people think of how corruption in Russia or any of the other countries that were part of the Soviet nuclear establishment matters to those of us outside, rumors of smuggled highly enriched uranium (HEU) getting into the wrong hands come to mind. Stories such as that of Oleg Khintsasgov, a two-bit smuggler arrested by Georgian security agents in 2006, after slipping through Russian-Georgia border controls with 100 grams of uranium enriched to 89 percent pure (weapons grade material) in a plastic sandwich bag hidden in "his tattered leather jacket," are attention-getting.[44] These stories matter because, as of 2007, Russia was thought to possess more than 1,050 metric tons of HEU, capable of yielding "20,000 simple nuclear weapons or more than 80,000 sophisticated weapons," a good deal of it used as naval reactor fuel or in civilian research reactors, and some in laboratories, much of it poorly secured.[45] If for no other reason, the significance of systemic corruption and, worse, the criminalized state, is altogether different when present in a country possessing accessible fissile material as well as chemical and biological weapons.

While the nuclear threat gives corruption in the post-Soviet region the deepest resonance in the outside world, it only begins the parade of hazards and harms. In general, these dangers fall into two categories: damage to international welfare and threats to international security, and the line dividing one from the other quickly blurs. Only by totaling the effects in each category, and then considering their combined impact, does one begin to get a sense of how substantial and central corruption in Russia and the neighboring states is to the core dynamics of international politics.

The menace they pose starts with the infusion that Russia and the others make to the flow of "contaminants:" drugs, disease, trafficked humans, arms, and contraband. Russia's share of estimated illicit trade is but a fraction of that of the chief offender, China.[46] Still, $21 billion, Russia's annual estimated portion, is scarcely a pittance alongside China's supposed $79.5 contribution.[47] Even before one gets to the lethal elements in this commerce, Russian corruption makes its mark. When it comes to the counterfeit and piracy market, at $6 billion Russia's total is but 10 percent of China's. Even so, this puts Russia alongside China as one of the two countries that are highest on the "priority watch list" in the Office of the United State Trade Representative's "Special 301" Report.[48] "The U.S. copyright industries," the report says, "estimate that they lost in excess of $1.4 billion in 2007 due to copyright piracy in Russia."[49]

To put the problem in perspective, it is true that while Chinese and Russian counterfeiting and piracy may be as high as 20–25 percent of the U.S. market, the lost revenue, estimated at $200–250 billion, is less than 2 percent of GDP ($13.84 trillion in 2007). Nonetheless, this total represents a considerable burden on legitimate business and significant job losses (estimated at 750,000).[50] The same can be said for Japan and Europe, the two areas that follow the United States as the principal targets of this trade. Nor is it irrelevant to national and international welfare, when tainted or fake pharmaceuticals reach these markets.[51]

Far more pernicious, however, are the other components of illicit trade, and here Russia and its neighbors figure still more prominently. Start with human trafficking: one study suggests that in the decade between 1995 and 2005 as many as 500,000 to 850,000 women may have been trafficked out of Russia.[52] In Ukraine, a country with a little more than a third of the population of Russia, from 1991 to 1998, an estimated 500,000 women were victimized.[53] More shocking, in Moldova, parallel estimates in the first decade after the collapse of the Soviet Union were 200,000–400,000 women, which, if true, is close to 10 percent of the female population.[54]

Add to the human trafficking Russia's new role in the multi-billion-dollar-a-year trade in wildlife and animal parts (a volume considerably larger than estimated illegal arms sales). Although Russia's share in this area, again, does not compare with China's, because China is a major market for wildlife derivatives, such as bear paws and gallbladders, wild ginseng, Siberian tiger skins and bones, as well as Amur leopards—nearly all of them endangered species—and these exist in the Russian far east near the Chinese and North Korean borders, the partnership between Russian poachers, corrupt Russian police officers, and Chinese criminal gangs thrives.

Lest the impression be that the enslavement of women to prostitution and the trade in endangered species pose only a problem for our consciences and not really a threat to global welfare, let alone international security, it is worth noting how some of the money earned gets spent. In Bangladesh, those eager to profit from the trade in rare wildlife include groups like Harkat-ul-Jihad-al-Islami, which is linked to al Qaeda, and Jama'atul Mujahideen Bangladesh, led by a figure once close to Bin Laden's World Islamic Front for the Jihad Against the Jews and Crusaders.[55] "In the last fifteen years," Glenny writes, "the Caspian Sea's sturgeon population has fallen dramatically. In 2004 just 760 tons of sturgeon were caught by the Caspian nations, down from 26,000 tons in 1985."[56] Illegal fishing is largely responsible for the plundering that has pushed this ancient species to the point of extinction, and doubtless a portion of the earnings helps to arm violent Islamic groups in the north Caucasus. Similarly income from the Macedonian brothels in which young Moldovan, Ukrainian, and Russian women are imprisoned has gone to the Kosovar Albanian guerilla group, the Kosovo Liberation Army, and to the allied National Liberation Army in Macedonia.

The most obvious threat to global welfare from illicit trade in and out of the post-Soviet region comes from the drug trade. Afghanistan, since the overthrow of the Taliban, has emerged as a more dominant supplier of heroin to the global market, and Central Asia serves as an ever more important conduit into Europe, China, and Russia. According to the United Nations Office on Drugs and Crime (UNODC), in 2007 Afghanistan cultivated 193,000 hectares of opium poppies, more than double the acreage in the Taliban era and more than 21 times that after the Taliban cracked down on cultivation in 2000.[57] From this, Afghanistan produced 8,200 tons of opium, making it "practically the exclusive supplier of the world's deadliest drug (93 percent of the global opiates market)."[58] The porous borders of Tajikistan and its northern neighbors and the easily co-opted police and border officials in these countries combine to make this region the overland hub not only for the flow of opium to the outside world, but also a rapidly expanding volume of processed heroin.

In this web, Russia is both victim and abettor. Fifteen billion dollars in revenue is said to be from drug trafficking in a Russian black market worth supposedly $21 billion.[59] While Russia and Ukraine are transit points in the final leg of Afghan heroin headed to the Baltic states and the rest of Europe, they, with increasingly devastating consequences, are also a destination. Figures for heroin users, the drug of choice in Russia, vary wildly, but the 2007 World Drug Report of the UNODC suggests that as of 2000–2001 the number may have been 1.5 million (2 percent of the population ages 15–64), a number that has risen since then, because Russia and Central Asia, along with Iran, are among the few areas of the world that have recorded growing heroin consumption.[60]

Heroin use is directly tied to increasing HIV/AIDS rates in Russia, Ukraine, Central Asia, and China, where in all instances more than 70 percent of HIV cases are from shared drug needles. While the National Intelligence Council's (NIC) earlier near pandemic projections for HIV-infection rates in Russia and four of the world's most populous states turn out to be greatly exaggerated, the problem of increasing infections is serious and has the potential to spread beyond national borders.[61] UNAIDS estimates that 940,000 Russians are HIV-positive, 80 percent of whom have a history of needle drug use. In Ukraine the figure is thought to be 1 percent of the total adult population.[62]

The adverse welfare effects from illicit trade are matched, if not trumped, by its effects on national and international security, and it is in this realm that the special and extreme forms of corruption prevailing in Russia and the other post-Soviet states weigh most heavily. The less dramatic measure of the problem resides in the gross statistics. Best estimates place the volume of illegal arms washing around the globe at $10 billion, not a large figure when compared with the drug trade or trafficking in counterfeit goods, but this former trade involves a good deal of misery and mayhem. Much of this owes to the commerce in small arms and light weapons valued at $2–3 billion a year.[63] As Patricia Lewis, the director of the United Nations Institute for Disarmament Research, reports, out of 640 million small arms abroad in 2006, approximately 40–50 percent were "illegally held" and 25 percent were "obtained through illicit trade."[64] The numbers, however, tell nothing of the doubled-sided evil this traffic entails. For most of it fuels the violent ethnic and intra-societal conflicts marking war in the post–Cold War period. The UN Department for Disarmament Affairs reported that of the forty-nine major conflicts fought in the 1990s, forty-seven were waged with small arms. Each year between 300,000 and 500,000 people die by small arms and light weapons, mostly civilians, and many women and children.[65] As the team preparing for the third biannual UN meeting on curbing this trade stresses, "Small arms and light weapons destabilize regions; spark . . . and prolong conflicts; obstruct relief programs; undermine peace initiatives; exacerbate human rights abuses; hamper development; and foster a 'culture of violence.'"[66] The other half of the sad tale returns full circle to illicit trade in its ugliest dimensions, because the trade in illegal small arms and light weapons is largely financed by drug, diamond, wildlife, timber, and human trafficking. The Revolutionary Armed Forces of Colombia (the FARC), for example, was said to generate $500 million through drug operations, a fair share of which was spent on weapons.[67]

Re-enter the Russians—at least, Viktor Bout, who in the years after the collapse of the Soviet Union managed to become the world's most notorious illegal arms merchant, until he was arrested in Thailand in 2008. Bout ran guns for the FARC (including surface-to-air missiles and armor-piercing, anti-tank weapons) as he had done for agents of violence in conflicts from Afghanistan to South Africa, Rwanda to Sierra Leone. Bout is not the Russian government, but he would never have been able to build his fleet of 60 Soviet-era transport aircraft and a staff of 300 pilots, nor would he have had the same access to the massive inventories of Soviet military hardware that were spread around the post-Soviet space, were it not for the readiness of officials in many countries and many bureaucracies, including Russia, to look the other way for the right reward. In 2000, U.S. intelligence officials described these operations as "literally an industry" involving parts of the Russian military and intelligence services, organized crime, and corrupt Russian and Jordanian officials (Jordan being a key transit point), with most of the arms going to the FARC but some to Hezbollah as well.[68] Large IL-76 cargo aircraft carried arms out of Russia and Ukraine and returned with shipments of up to 40,000 kilograms of cocaine for the Russian and European market. Nor does the fact that Russia is not high on the lists of countries engaged in the world market for small arms and light weapons trade (the United States is) explain away Russia's role in the supply of illicit arms—small, light, and heavy.[69]

Three factors converge to make Russia and, indeed, much of the post-Soviet region critical in this deadly sphere. First, the collapse of the Soviet Union left staggering quantities of arms spread among the twelve new, chaotically governed post-Soviet states. Even the smaller countries inherited enormous stocks of arms and munitions, much of the armament unsuited to the reduced, modernized militaries they needed, and under only weak and desultory government control—indeed, much of it still in the hands of military commanders at left-over Soviet-era bases.

The second factor then followed: a poorly supervised military, in disarray, suddenly without resources—and sitting atop the fragmenting remnants of the world's largest arsenal—went into business. Turbiville has detailed the complex array of mechanisms and agencies by which officers up to the most senior levels of command collaborated with business and criminal groups to funnel everything from small arms and ammunition to helicopters and fixed-wing aircraft to all comers, including drug cartels.[70] Not only are military figures involved, but a more far-flung web of players has also entered the game. Serio describes a bank set up to finance the sale of fighter jets abroad, a bank underwritten by the Solntsevo crime group, aided by "high-ranking officials" from the Russian Foreign Intelligence Service and military intelligence (GRU), with a Moscow city official as deputy director, and under the control of a former KGB officer who had long been involved in smuggling gold and precious gems in collaboration with "Uzbek crime bosses." The ex-KGB agent had managed to wangle a license to sell arms on the international market at the same time that he had acquired a key role in the export activity of a major military aircraft manufacturer.[71]

The cascade of fugitive arms was heaviest in the 1990s when Russia's, Ukraine's, and Kazakhstan's control over arms exports was the most decentralized and poorly policed and the military most destitute. But a third factor has left the problem only partially curbed: namely, a lack of transparency in the management of arms sales. The Small Arms Trade Transparency Barometer ranks countries according to the timeliness, clarity, and comprehensiveness by which they report arms sales. On a 15-point scale, Russia receives 6.5—better than Bulgaria's and North Korea's 0, but still at the bottom of the pack.[72] The lack of transparency is almost certainly tied either to the inability of the Russian authorities adequately to track even officially licensed sales or the unwillingness of formidable sectors within the military and in Rosoboronoexport, the massive state agency in charge of arms exports, to have their activities too closely scrutinized. Moreover, signs that corruption in the Russian military was again on the rise in the Putin era gave the defense establishment little incentive to cooperate with any who might argue for greater openness and accountability.[73]

Given the scale and range of arms in Russia, Ukraine, and some of the other post-Soviet states, small arms and light weapons may be the least significant portion of the flow to dangerous destinations. From 2001 until the fall of Baghdad in 2003, Iraqi embassy personnel spirited out of Russia high-tech equipment, such as radar jammers, GPS jammers, night-vision devices, avionics, and missile components on weekly flights to Baghdad, enabled by bribes to Russian customs officials.[74] There was also the lieutenant colonel in the Rocket and Artillery Armaments Service of the Siberian Military District arrested for selling AK-74 automatic weapons and grenade launchers to a private Russian arms dealer. Or there is the case of General Matvei Burlakov, commander of the Soviet Western Group of Forces in East Germany, and later deputy minister of defense, who was eventually sacked for criminal activity, some of which apparently involved the disappearance of armored vehicles, MiG aircraft, and tons of ammunition from depots under his command.[75]

The heights to which corruption reaches can at times be stunning. For example, when former Ukrainian President Leonid Kuchma's bodyguard, Nikolay Melnichenko, fled Ukraine in 2000 he carried with him tape recordings, later authenticated by the U.S. government, of Kuchma discussing with the director of Ukraine's arms export agency a deal to smuggle four Kolchuga passive radar stations to Iraq through a Jordanian intermediary.[76] Such stories are legion, but represent only a fraction of the deals done since the collapse of the Soviet Union.

In a criminal mini-state, like the breakaway territory of Transdniestr, gun running is not merely a lethal form of corruption, but a key activity of the state. According to Naím, Transdniestr not only exports "vast quantities of Soviet shells and rockets . . . [but] newly manufactured machine guns, rocket launchers, [and] RPGs," produced in "at least six sprawling factories."[77] For the discerning buyer, Transdniestr's authorities also have available mines, anti-aircraft missiles, and Alazan rockets that can carry radiological payloads. All of this export activity takes place under the enterprising eye of President Igor Smirnov's son, who conveniently heads both Sheriff, a shadowy monopoly arms exporting company, and the country's customs service.

The post-Soviet space, however, not only supplies the outside world with arms, drugs, disease, trafficked humans, wildlife, and counterfeit goods, it, in specific cases, also illustrates how corruption converges with other factors to ignite and then prolong violent intrastate conflict. As the Soviet Union collapsed in the early 1990s, separatist struggles produced war in five regions (Abkhazia and South Ossetia in Georgia, Transdniestr in Moldova, Nagorno-Karabakh in Azerbaijan, and Chechnya in Russia). The causes of these conflicts were complex and diverse, but in all cases funding was important, and this came predominantly from the "shadow and criminal economies."[78] Zürcher, a scholar who has produced the most sophisticated study of these conflicts, calls those who organized and led them "entrepreneurs of violence," and he stresses that one of the first things that they do is "create an economy" integrated into "transnational networks of trade and investment," but in which "trafficking of drugs and weapons . . . kidnapping and extortion, and . . . taxing the shadow economy" are key.[79] Moreover, he argues, "If government officials receive a share of the revenues from the market of violence," as many did, "or are themselves acting as warlords, they have an interest in prolonging the violence at low levels."[80] The same can be said for the rebel side as well.[81]

Corruption's malign effects in Russia and other post-Soviet states extend much beyond what has been touched upon here. Nothing has been said of its relationship to terror, and cases such as that in 2004, when bribes of $170 and $34 enabled two suicide bombers to board two different planes and, once aloft, blow them both up at almost the same time, killing ninety passengers.[82] No mention has been made of how Russian banks launder money through Abkhazia by working with money-transfer businesses, such as Contact, Golden Crown, and VIP Money Transfers.[83] And no attention has been given to the distortions and impediments on investment introduced by the scale of corruption surrounding Russia's energy giants, particularly Gazprom, where kickbacks on pipeline contracts range between 45 and 75 percent.[84]

Before moving on, however, a key distinction needs to be emphasized, lest the significance of Russia's and the other post-Soviet states' contribution to the world's ills from these illicit activities be misunderstood. The point is not that Russia or any of its neighbors constitute the key to ending, for example, the role of small arms in violent conflicts. Were Russian arms to cease flowing tomorrow, the problem would remain, because the perpetrators of violence usually buy or seize their arms within their own societies or, if supplied from abroad, they deal with middle men who pilfer arms from legitimate sources and operate far from the point of origin. Rather the danger is in the cumulative effect of so many noxious flows emanating from one region and exacerbating incrementally so many global problems.

Cures

It would be unrealistic in the extreme—not to mention arrogant—to minimize how difficult it is to reduce, never mind eliminate, corruption in any society. None would see the United States as fundamentally corrupt; it cannot be said to suffer systemic corruption; nor has it ever been a criminalized state. Still, the illicit drug market in the United States is said to exceed $65 billion, nearly three times larger than the next closest country (Mexico at $23 billion). As the world's largest arms merchant, more than once it has been victim to fraudulent arms deals, such as the "Demavand project," which illegally delivered F-4 fighter planes, more than 2,000 anti-tank missiles, and parts for 235 Hawk missiles to Iran in the 1980s.[85] To believe that the country—at least segments of society—is merely an innocent object of these scourges, and not an agent would be naïve. Countries still struggling to escape from the rubble of a brittle, backward empire's collapse; countries with half-formed institutions and the dead weight of unreconstructed bureaucracies; countries unaccustomed to the norms and regulatory frameworks of modern market economies, but overwhelmed by the license that they permit cannot be expected to move smartly forward into a corruption-free future. The surprise is not in the way they have stumbled, but that their failings were so little anticipated by the major Western powers, and then so little a part of their core agenda when dealing with these states, even now.

Humility deserves a place for two other reasons, both of which are essential preliminaries to a consideration of a strategy for addressing the challenge to international welfare and security posed by Russia and the other criminalized post-Soviet states. First, the crucial sources of the problem are not only obvious (i.e., wayward officials, weak property rights, poor law enforcement, criminal groupings or even "entrepreneurs of violence," and the like), but profound. A large portion of illicit trade grows out of poverty. The women trapped in the dehumanizing brothels of the Balkans, Israel, and along Europe's trucking routes do not come from the upwardly mobile young women in Moscow, St. Petersburg, and Kyiv. The couriers willing to smuggle caviar or uranium are not the well-heeled lords at the top of the operation. And the poachers of endangered species in eastern Siberia are not members of corporate mafias, but rather their foot soldiers or modest free-lancers.

Similarly, the failure of national leadership in most of these countries to make much of a dent in the problem owes not only to a lack of will on the leaders' part or an acceptance of the wealth accumulation going on among their senior supporters and ministers—although these are important factors—but also to the weakness of the states over which these leaders preside. Even the most authoritarian regimes find themselves bestride hierarchies either unresponsive to their commands or easily circumvented by entrenched groupings and informal networks.

Second, corruption when systemic, and especially when embodied in the criminalized state, should not be thought of as a loose array of criminal activity, each form with its distinctive characteristics, demanding specialized solutions, and the concern of different government agencies, NGOs, and international fora. Rather, corruption in the criminalized state is an integral phenomenon, where the sum of the parts creates something far more corrosive for core political and economic institutions and far more damaging to the outside world than the parts taken separately. This means that a state that wants to deal seriously with dismantling the criminalized state, as well as foreign governments and international organizations that want to help, must have a strategy that is far more ambitious, with a wider scope, than anything developed thus far.

The challenge in strategic terms is to unbind and then mitigate the three fundamental sources of the criminalized state: corruption's long historical pedigree in Russia; the pathologies of the transition from one economic order to another; and the more recent drift away from liberal reform in nearly all of the post-Soviet states. Because corruption has never been absent from Russian society in the last half millennium, to assume that Russian, Ukrainian, or any other set of post-Soviet leaders, even of the strongest will, could tear it up by its roots would be simpleminded. But political leadership could make a conscious effort to weaken what Russia's new president, Dmitri Medvedev, calls an attitude of "legal nihilism," the tendency of the average Russian to regard law as rubbery and often irrelevant. "The reason is simple:" writes a U.S. lawyer who practices law in Russia, "Russian law still tends to protect the rights of citizens from the state less than it serves to impose the will of the state on the citizens ... when state interests are not involved, Russians enjoy considerable freedom despite what the law forbids, but when state interests are involved, they enjoy diminished freedom despite what the law permits. A right thus enforced is degraded into a mere revocable license, and a fixed obligation into a merely contingent liability."[86]

The problem's roots, of course, run far deeper, specifically to Russia's long and continuing divorce from the rule of law. When Medvedev outlines his plans for attacking corruption (discussed below), including the legal nihilism that he deplores, he, wittingly or not, is touching on Russia's recent experiment with more authoritarian approaches. Russia is neither alone or extreme in the drift toward il-liberalism among the states of the former Soviet Union. In all of these states, that leaders carry out and tolerate others' abuses of civil and property rights, of due process, and of an open public sphere only reinforces the public's indifference to law and, by extension, its lax attitude toward corruption. The concrete steps to tame corruption explored below are essential. They represent the best chance for rolling back the criminal excesses unleashed in the transition from the wreckage of the Soviet Union to new political and economic orders. Yet to assume that most of them will come to pass or that those that do will have much effect without change at this more fundamental level would be delusional. Returning to the larger framework introduced earlier, in the end, what matters most and first is dismantling the criminalized state. Addressing corruption's other dimensions—including systemic corruption—can only be a subsequent and far longer-term enterprise.

The path forward, however, is no great mystery. Neither, alas, is it any easier. It starts with concrete steps to deal with the most conspicuous forms of corruption. The Atlantic Council study on corruption in Ukraine, for example, recommends that a widely discredited judiciary be skirted and a special chamber created, "staffed by a new generation of judges and focused specifically on fighting corruption involving high and mid-level officials."[87] The study suggests the addition to this chamber of an independent "National Investigative Bureau," modeled after the FBI, well-funded and equipped, and under proper oversight. To deal with legislative corruption, the study's authors advocate the coordination and consolidation of anti-corruption legislation, reducing the scope of parliamentary immunity, and limiting the private sector activities of parliamentarians, while clarifying conflict of interest standards. All public officials, they suggest, should be obliged to submit detailed declarations of assets and incomes and then be subject to investigation, if their "everyday life-styles" are conspicuously incommensurate. An independent inspector general's office, with wide-ranging investigative and audit powers, should exist in every ministry and major government office, presided over by someone selected outside the ministry or government office. To deal with extensive money laundering, the study recommends the creation of an "investigative unit" attached to Ukraine's Central Bank. All of these are sensible recommendations and fit equally well Russia and the other post-Soviet states.

They are also consistent with what in the general literature constitutes the widely accepted elements of an anti-corruption strategy. Addressed to the root causes of corruption, they take as their point of departure the need to reduce the incentives and opportunities officials have for engaging in corruption, while increasing the penalties for transgressions, the likelihood of detection, and the certainty that penalties will be implemented. Thus, the advice normally begins with civil service reform—higher salaries for officials, equal or better than they can command in the private sector; transparency when hiring; penalties that more than match (or recoup) the gains from bribery, and applied to both parties; corruption-free internal control mechanisms; and mechanisms for external oversight.[88]

In the case of Russia and most of the other post-Soviet states, administrative reform, the phrase Russians use, poses a far more fundamental challenge. Enhancing and disciplining the bureaucracy must go hand in hand with shrinking it. Soviet bureaucracy was vastly oversized, inefficient, and obstructive. It has grown larger in the post-Soviet era. Tellingly, when two scholars ran a model testing five explanations for corruption levels across Russian regions: 1) level of economic development, 2) endowment in natural resources, 3) size of government, 4) imbalances between the power of the state and the business sector, and 5) accountability—the element with greatest statistical significance was the number of bureaucrats (size of government).[89] Were a similar study done comparing post-Soviet states, the results are likely to be the same.

Decreasing corruption's other elements involves reducing the spheres of activity where corruption flourishes and limiting the discretion that officials have over benefits in those spheres that remain. In the post-Soviet case, this task merges with the challenge of scaling back the overall size of the bureaucracy. Reducing arenas of corruption entails limiting and streamlining regulatory procedures, eliminating government controls over prices, exports, and investments, as well as shifting public services, if well-delivered, to the private sector (provided it is competitive and transparent). Limiting the discretion of officials involves minimizing the points at which they have the authority to act on a case-by-case basis, ensuring that petitioners are not left without recourse, and designing a credible appeal process.

Of the post-Soviet states, only Georgia has recorded measurable progress in undoing the criminalized state. In TI's CPI, it moved from 133rd in 2004 to 68th in 2008. According to the World Bank's *Doing Business 2008,* Georgia's ranking in nearly all categories improved markedly from 2005 to 2008 (in "starting a business" from 59 to 10; "doing business" from 112 to 18; "dealing with licenses" from 152 to 11, and "trading across borders" from 149 to 64).[90] Georgia's success has been accomplished by taking many of the steps outlined above. Since the Rose Revolution, government bureaucracy has been whittled down from eighteen to thirteen ministries, and the staff, reduced by 25 percent.[91] A year and a half into Mikheil Saakashvili's presidency, the parliament adopted legislation that reduced the number of required business permits from more than 900 to fewer than 160.[92] In fact, across a broad spectrum of measures, Georgia, as evaluated by the Council of Europe's *Groupe d'Etats contre la corruption* (GRECO), has improved with remarkable speed and comprehensiveness.[93] In June 2005, the president announced "The National Anti-Corruption Strategy," and the Ministry on Reform Co-ordination (MRC) was given responsibility for issuing a public biannual report on its implementation. In turn, each ministry and government agency must report to the MRC on the progress it has made in fulfilling the Action Plan, and, for this purpose, each now has within it an internal unit attached to the Office of the Inspector General tasked with auditing the ministry and investigating any indication of malfeasance. The units can act based on their own initiative or on the basis of complaints from citizens, information from other governmental units, or reports in the mass media.

An independent department within the prosecutor general's office has responsibility for pursuing all corruption cases in Georgia. The process of hiring its senior staff includes an interview with a panel of representatives from NGOs, government bodies, and "respected people," as well as "measures to ensure integrity such as polygraph testing."[94] The department, according to the Anti-Corruption Network (ACN) report, "enjoys good cooperation with the Ministry of Interior, the Financial Monitoring Service, the Assets Declaration Bureau within the Ministry of Justice and the Chamber of Control." The Chamber of Control, in turn, is an independent body that supervises the legality of the use of state property, including the use of state funds by local government, and that reports bi-annually to the parliament. In 2005, it sent 378 reports of irregularities to the prosecutor general's office.[95] Overall during 2004–2005 more than 1,000 criminal cases were investigated by this special department, and a number of high-level officials were indicted, including the head of the Railway Department, the director general of the Power Engineering Regulatory Commission, the former heads of the Tax Department and of the Large Tax Payers Inspection, the director of the Customs Department, and director general of one of the large telecommunication companies.[96]

Georgia has installed legislation that protects whistleblowers. It has sharpened and tightened regulations on conflict of interest for public officials, including the employment of relatives. It has instituted strict requirements for the financial declarations that officials must submit to the tax authorities, including assets as well as income, along with requirements for compliance reporting. It has severely limited the ability of civil servants to move from government posts into private enterprises or into organizations that were previously under their supervision. It has criminalized money laundering; specified the range of banking, currency exchange, brokerage, insurance, notary, securities, and non-banking depository companies that must report suspicious transactions; and created the Financial Monitoring Service attached to the National Bank of Georgia to oversee these processes. Most notably, Georgia has raised significantly the salary of public officials across the board, improved their training, and sought to raise their status in the eyes of the public. In what has been the most celebrated case, the Georgian government abolished the old civilian police system, recruited a new force, virtually from scratch, that is well-paid and well-outfitted, and overnight transformed a thoroughly bribe-driven service into a professional organization that is respected by the public.

Impressive as all this is, in any one dimension important deficiencies remain, and these are spelled out in detail in the evaluation reports of GRECO and ACN. Much still has to be done to cleanse the customs service, a crucial channel for corruption. Evidence exists that kickbacks to those close to senior levels of government have not ended. And, in the process of clamping down on large-scale corruption and seizing illegitimately acquired property, due process has often been set aside.

But Georgia does appear to be evidence for the lessons learned in Asia— the only post-Soviet state to offer even a hint of being so. In Asia in the postwar period, of four states particularly marked by corruption, two eventually broke the cycle and escaped from systemic corruption. Two did not.[97] The Philippines was one that did not, although over the Marcos, Aquino, and Ramos eras it amassed seven anti-corruption laws and thirteen anti-graft agencies, more than any other Asian state. In contrast, in Singapore, after the People's Action Party came to power in 1960, leadership made fighting corruption a priority, developed a comprehensive strategy embodied in the Prevention of Corruption Act of 1960, and empowered the Corrupt Practices Investigation Bureau (CPIB) to enforce this act. The CPIB was given the power to search and arrest as well as to investigate "any bank account, share account or purchase account" suspected of being in violation of the Prevention of Corruption Act. The bureau was also placed in the prime minister's office, and made independent of the police, a step seen as critical to its success. After 1971, Hong Kong followed the same model with comparable success.

Georgia appears to fit the Singapore and Hong Kong models, at least in terms of the start made, but the lessons for the other post-Soviet states, particularly the larger ones, are not entirely clear. The first lesson from the Georgian case that is shared with the two Asian success stories features the importance of forceful leadership from the top—the factor discussed in Rotberg's chapter in this volume.[98] Both Saakashvili and Zurab Zvania, the first prime minister after the Rose Revolution, had served in government during the Shevardnadze period, the first as minister of finance and the second as speaker of the parliament; both were seen as honest and both left their posts in protest over the prevailing levels of corruption. They led a revolution that was as much sparked by a public revulsion against corruption as by the manipulation of recent parliamentary elections. And they, both out of conviction and political imperative, staked the legitimacy of their new government on doing something effective to correct a thoroughly corrupt environment. Moreover, their determination to move Georgia into Europe and its two key institutions, NATO and the European Union (EU), gave them added incentive to follow through.

Ukraine, at the time of the Orange Revolution, had two of the same "advantages:" that is, public anger over corruption was an important factor animating the revolution, and the leadership of the Orange Revolution wanted to speed Ukraine's integration into European institutions. But, unlike Georgia, the leaders of the Orange Revolution had neither the will nor the capacity to launch a comprehensive, focused, high-priority campaign to deal with the problem. Elsewhere—in Russia, Belarus, Kazakhstan, and the rest of Central Asia—all three impulses (a leadership ready to lead, an aroused public, and the beckoning of EU membership) are simply missing. Moreover, undoing systemic corruption in a city-state such as Hong Kong or Singapore, or even in a country of fewer than 5 million people, the size of West Virginia, poses less of a challenge than it does in countries as large as Russia, Ukraine, and Kazakhstan, with ramified political geographies, vastly larger administrative structures, and infinitely greater opportunities to engage in a far wider range of corrupt activities.

In Russia, Dmitri Medvedev came to office promising a major new effort to battle corruption, and within four months had produced a "National Plan for Counteracting Corruption," including a broad legislative program that he wanted enacted by the end of the year.[99] It was, he said, intended to bring Russian legislation into compliance with the UN Convention against Corruption and the Council of Europe's Criminal Law Convention on Corruption, both of which Russia had ratified in 2006. The plan lays out a four-pronged attack: first, to provide a clear definition of corruption and measures to prevent corrupt actions, including public and parliamentary oversight; second, stiffer standards for those entering state service and tighter review of their declared assets and life style; third, efforts to raise the qualifications of judges and other legal personnel; and, fourth, a series of steps to increase transparency in state transactions by making them electronic, to reduce hurdles confronting small- and medium-sized businesses, and to punish officials who "limit or eliminate competition" among businesses. Within these outlines, the plan does incorporate a number of measures that, were they effectively implemented, would be a significant advance, such as standards for sorting out conflicts of interest for state officials, ensuring a genuinely competitive procedure for hiring public officials, installing units in state agencies to monitor and report corruption, and establishing a central body to ensure compliance with the UN and Council of Europe conventions.

Doubts, however, die hard, and for three reasons. First, this is scarcely the first time that a Russian leader has declared a war on corruption or that the parliament has undertaken major anti-corruption legislation. The first two such bills passed in 1995 and 1997, only to be vetoed by Boris Yeltsin. A third in 2002 never made it past the first reading. And the Council for Fighting

Corruption formed on the eve of the 2004 presidential election was dissolved soon after. Second, significant loopholes are likely to remain. For example, existing Russian law leaves it to the discretion of a superior whether an offend- ing subordinate is punished, and it is not clear that this added opening to cor- ruption will cease. Nor is it clear that, in the end, the law will make it a crim- inal offense when there is a "significant increase in the assets of a public official that he or she cannot reasonably explain in relation to his or her lawful income," since when ratifying the UN Convention against Corruption, the Russians excused themselves from this provision. And the list goes on.

The third reason, however, reaches to the very heart of the problem. Even if the program brought to and passed by the parliament meets the standards of the UN and Council of Europe conventions, the cornerstone of the crim- inalized state will remain. For while a corruption-saturated bureaucracy and officialdom constitutes the body of the criminalized state, the venal, self- seeking clans at the top are its brain. Until President Medvedev and those on whom he depends are willing or, indeed, are in a position to take on these powerful clusters, each of which jealously guards its massed wealth and ver- tical power structures, often in competition with one another, the new pres- ident's plans will only scratch the surface. Although Medvedev recognizes that the problem is broad, indeed, systemic, and says so, without steps to make key players at senior levels part of the solution, rather than as now the ultimate source of the problem, his campaign, as Elena Panfilova puts it, will end up fighting "those who commit corruption" rather than corruption itself—fighting the "consequences, [and] specific individuals" rather than fighting "the causes."[100]

Panfilov, the head of Russian Transparency International, fully compre- hends the nature of the problem, and what she grasps, other Russians do as well. She is aware of the Asian cases cited above, and she uses the Singapore and Hong Kong examples to underscore the importance of creating strong inde- pendent agencies to monitor and prosecute corruption.[101] But while she stresses the need for sound anti-corruption legislation and effective enforce- ment mechanisms, she also starts at a more fundamental level. Unless politi- cal corruption, by which she means fraudulent elections and purchased offices, ceases, little chance exists that politicians who have arrived by this route will have much interest in curbing corruption in its other forms. She—and by no means she alone—goes further to argue that a free press acting as a watchdog and a civil society strong enough to engage the subject are key if leaders truly desire to dismantle the criminalized state. Medvedev says as much, too. But then we are brought back to the larger issue of Russia's general political course, and the unanswered question is whether Medvedev really understands the price paid for constraining an open society and genuinely wants to move in the other direction. Even if he wishes do so, the question that looms still larger is whether he has the political resources and leverage to counter the powerful currents flowing against him.

Moreover, as the Georgian case illustrates, progress in attacking the forms of corruption that impede economic reform and retard growth does not eliminate the effects of systemic corruption that cross borders and harm global welfare and international security. Much of the thrust of Georgia's national anti-corruption campaign is directed at business corruption and street-level everyday corruption, but does not necessarily choke off the cross-border smuggling of arms, drugs, humans, and other dangerous contraband that thrives in the separatist territories and eases its way abroad thanks to customs officials beyond Georgian control or those who are not yet purged of bad habits.[102] Much of what the Georgians have done has served well to weaken the criminalized state, and weakening the criminalized state remains the essential step in coping with the threat that corruption in Russia and the other post-Soviet states poses to the outside world. Still, the problem remains far broader, requiring a more comprehensive strategy within these states and in the wider international community, particularly among the major players.

Implications for U.S. Policy and the Role of the International Community

In the end, an anti-corruption strategy that is up to the challenge posed by the post-Soviet states goes much beyond the conventional measures described above—ambitious as they are. Such a strategy can only be constructed and executed with the cooperation of the United States, Europe, and Japan. For example, an equally important way to deal with the peril of smuggled nuclear materials is to take away the object rather than to disrupt the mode. That is, to blend down HEU to low-enriched uranium (LEU) unsuitable for nuclear weapons. The United States and Russia have a 1993 agreement to cooperate in converting 500 metric tons of Russian HEU by 2013, but that still leaves 550 metric tons in Russian stocks, some of it under less than fully secure controls. These two countries have failed to accelerate, let alone expand, these efforts, because of an unwillingness to provide the necessary funding, a reluctance to drive down the price of LEU on the commercial market for domestic nuclear fuel, and an excessive notion of what each needs to keep in reserve for its nuclear weapons program.[103]

Denying the wherewithal to those who would traffick in small arms offers a parallel case. The Program of Action (PoA) adopted by the 2001 UN Conference on Illicit Trade in Small Arms and Light Weapons urges countries to create national agencies to coordinate policies on small arms trade within their governments, to identify and destroy stocks of surplus weapons, to mark guns when manufactured to allow tracing, to take inventory of state-held arms, to keep careful records of gun production, to issue end-user certificates for the export and transit of guns, to regulate the activity of private arms brokers, to strengthen the enforcement of arms embargoes, to stimulate the involvement of civil society organizations in efforts to thwart small arms proliferation, and to report regularly to the UN on implementation. While more than 191 countries signed on to the PoA, few have come close to fulfilling these goals. In the post-Soviet region, the Central Asian and South Caucasus states have scarcely tried. Russia and Ukraine have tinkered with legislation that introduced a number of these controls, but then did little to ensure implementation, and failed entirely to file reports on the progress made against illicit trade in small arms.[104] The United States has been among the best in tightening its formal rules and procedures, notwithstanding a gaping hole in its performance because of the massive loss of small arms and light weapons during the Iraq war. But the United States joined Russia and China in fighting a stronger regime that turns voluntary commitments into treaty obligations, and then went beyond these two countries in its opposition to specific steps, such as constraining transfers to non-state actors (contending that it would hamper "the rights of the oppressed to defend themselves against tyrannical and genocidal regimes"), establishing controls over small arms ammunition, and tightening restrictions on civilian arms possession. Much can be done to stem the flow of illicit arms from the post-Soviet region, but only if the U.S. and Russian governments make it happen.

Trade policy constitutes another resource, if an anti-corruption strategy is conceived broadly. In this case it becomes a tool for fighting the effusion of counterfeit goods and piracy. Bring Russia, Ukraine and the others into the World Trade Organization (WTO) and they are then subject to the Agreement on Trade-Related Aspects of Intellectual Property Rights (TRIPS), negotiated in the 1984–1996 Uruguay Round. They will then be obliged not only to meet TRIPS standards on copyright, trademark, industrial design, patents, and trade secrets, but to comply with its enforcement requirements. The agreement spells out specific rules for obtaining evidence, injunctions, and damages; the rights of courts to dispose of or destroy pirated or counterfeit goods; and the imperative that trademark counterfeiting and copyright piracy be criminalized. True, as the China case underscores, negotiating the transition period and settling the specific terms of accession need to be well-crafted, but even in this case TRIPS has been a vital means of getting at the single largest source of counterfeiting and piracy.

Spelling out what these terms should be goes beyond the task undertaken in this chapter, which is to signal the scale of the challenge and to suggest a way to think about a broad and basic strategy for addressing it. The same can be said of the concrete measures needed to attack each area of illicit trade, from nuclear-grade weapons materials to human trafficking, from illegal arms sales to the trade in endangered species. These steps are not difficult to locate. For example, Bunn, in this volume, lays out a comprehensive set of actions designed to sever the link between corruption and the risk of nuclear, chemical, and biological weapons proliferation. Heineman, in his chapter, describes what must be done to make the 1997 OECD convention on bribery effective, a task that transfers the burden back on to the United States and the European states, for they, particularly the Europeans, have preserved loopholes in the regime that leave the temptation intact.[105] And, for virtually every specific area, highly expert NGOs have elaborate, specific ideas of what needs to be done. Concrete ideas are not the problem; mobilizing governments to give them life is. The argument is that until governments, including that of the United States, recognize how high the stakes are, and move corruption from the shadows to the center of their policies for the post-Soviet states, practical measures, no matter how well-conceived, will remain largely a dead letter.

Thinking of an anti-corruption strategy in more expansive terms opens the door to mobilizing a vast array of resources. For virtually every form of corruption flourishing in the post-Soviet states, there exist multiple fora and conventions addressed to the problem. Russia, for example, is one of thirty-four members of the Financial Action Task Force (FATF), established by the G-7 in 1989 to combat money laundering. Member countries have accepted the principle of multilateral monitoring and peer review, and each year are assessed on their progress in implementing what are called the "Forty Recommendations" and "Nine Special Recommendations." Russia, however, exempts international transfers through Abkhazia from financial monitoring, and this, as noted earlier, is an important money laundering channel. There is also MONEYVAL, which does much the same under the auspices of the Council of Europe and in collaboration with FATF. Armenia, Azerbaijan, Georgia, Russia, and Ukraine are all members. And in 2004, with Russian initiative and the support of the International Monetary Fund (IMF), the World Bank, and FATF, the Eurasia Group (EAG) was created as a regional version of FATF for Belarus, China, Kazakhstan, Kyrgyzstan, Russia, Tajikistan, and Uzbekistan.

It would be Pollyannaish to pretend that any of these mechanisms and dozens like them function smoothly or fully, or to deny that governments often honor them more in the breach. Each of them, however, has the potential to be tightened and rendered more effective, and here they are introduced simply as a collective element in an anti-corruption strategy designed to deal with the full magnitude of the challenge posed by the criminalized post-Soviet state. Any one of these tools may only touch a fragment of the problem, but taken as an ensemble they constitute a useful element in a comprehensive anti-corruption strategy, employed on the inside and pushed from the outside.

Out of this analysis comes a final set of over-arching propositions. First, to repeat a central proposition, corruption in Russia and the other post-Soviet states is a large, multi-layered problem that is neither epiphenomenal nor secondary, but one that cuts to the heart of political and economic trends in these countries and that directly impinges on core issues of global welfare and international security. Thus, the different manifestations of corruption should be neither conceived of nor treated in isolation, much as political leadership in these countries may prefer, or much as leadership elsewhere may think fits their own attention span and resources. Rather, these many different dimensions of the problem should be recognized for the synergies among them and addressed on a scale and with a comprehensiveness that does justice to their combined effect. That, in turn, requires a strategy that integrates a wide range of approaches, instruments, and institutions, rather than settling for the piecemeal, dispersed, and uncoordinated efforts that today mark the actions of nearly all of the post-Soviet governments and, without exception, governments on the outside. In this spirit, not only within Russia and the other post-Soviet states, but within the United States, the EU, and Japan, there should be a central agency where the problem's many parts are brought together and responses integrated.

That said, while at a macro or strategic level the challenge needs to be conceived, measured, and targeted in this integrated and comprehensive fashion, at the micro or tactical level, it makes sense to proceed sequentially, focusing initial efforts on problems where the obstacles to success are fewer. For example, forms of illicit trade that do not directly implicate senior leadership, such as drug and human trafficking, may be easier to attack than those, such as money laundering, the arms trade, and manipulated investments, that cut closer to the interests of many in power. Not only is the leadership in Russia,

Ukraine, and other post-Soviet states likely to see it as in the national interest to lessen these scourges, but the aid of the outside community is essential if success is to be achieved.

Second, the solution to corruption on the grand scale plaguing the post-Soviet states must emerge within these countries. Little will change until leaders come to power determined to rid their countries of the criminalized state. International institutions and other countries can nudge these states in this direction, and greatly aid the process once started, but, given the tamper-resistant character of the criminalized state, its undoing must come from the inside. This does not mean that U.S. efforts and those of others are pointless. Indeed, the argument for struggling to find ways of denting, even in limited degree, different aspects of corruption in Russia, Ukraine, and the other post-Soviet states is not that modest steps may be all that is possible, but that successful cooperation, even if modest, may be the best way to build a basis for more ambitious next steps.

Third, and finally, for the United States, members of the EU, and Japan, the effort to address corruption in the post-Soviet states impinges on the entirety of their policy toward these states. If the issue of the criminalized state and its consequences merit mainstream attention and deserve a more prominent place among U.S., European, and Japanese priorities when dealing with the region, then a successful strategy will depend on the quality of the overall policy into which it is integrated. For those states, such as Ukraine, Moldova, Georgia, Armenia, and Azerbaijan, that want to draw closer to Europe and benefit either from entry into or cooperation with the EU and NATO, the focus on destroying the criminalized state should be as integral to general U.S. and European policy as is encouraging steps to bring their militaries into conformity with NATO standards or pushing for fair and free elections.

Russia poses a different challenge and none greater than for the United States. Even before the dramatic events of August 2008, when Russia unleashed the fury of its military power on Georgia, the U.S.-Russian relationship had deteriorated badly, making a constructive dialogue and cooperation on almost any issue difficult. After the Russian-Georgian war, the United States faced a basic choice: whether to give highest priority to impressing on Moscow the unacceptability of using military power so brutally in disputes with neighbors, even if at the price of meaningful cooperation in nearly any other area, or to manage the rise of a prickly and assertive Russia by engaging it. If the United States goes down the first path, drawing lines in the sand and edging toward a policy of neo-containment, Russia will respond in kind, and the relationship will continue the downward spiral of the last several years. In this case, little room will remain for developing, let alone implementing, a coherent and comprehensive strategy addressed to the dangers that corruption in Russia poses for the security and welfare of others. If the alternative path is selected, finding a way to engage Russia on critical issues—both those that unite and those that divide the two countries—will be more challenging than at any time since the Cold War. Still, were the two sides to succeed, the task would then be not only to develop the kind of comprehensive U.S. strategy that is urged in this chapter, but to proceed in ways likely, even if only tentatively, to encourage Russian cooperation. In the most general terms this means first, choosing a vocabulary by which the two sides can have a constructive dialogue and second, focusing on solutions that the Russians see as in their self-interest to embrace.

Notes

1. Here as elsewhere the three Baltic states are excluded, because, since joining the EU and NATO, their profiles are very different.

2. Transparency International, "Corruption Perceptions Index" (2008), available at www.transparency.org/layout/set/print/policy_research/surveys_indices/cpi/2008 (accessed 2 December 2008).

3. See Jomo K.S., "Good Governance, Anti-Corruption, and Economic Development," chapter 18 in this volume.

4. This is Joseph Nye's widely employed definition from Nye, "Corruption and Political Development: A Cost-Benefit Analysis," in Arnold J. Heidenheimer (ed.), *Political Corruption: Readings in Comparative Analysis* (New Brunswick, 1978), 566–567. For an extensive exploration of the definitional problems, see John Gardiner, "Defining Corruption," in Arnold J. Heidenheimer and Michael Johnston (eds.), *Corruption: Concepts and Contexts* (Piscataway, 2001) (3rd edition), 25–40. And, in this volume, note the definitions used by Susan Rose-Ackerman, Daniel Jordan Smith, and others.

5. As Richard Cooper asked during an authors' meeting: "When our ancestors offered an animal or human sacrifice to the gods, was it a bribe and, therefore, corruption?"

6. My assumption is that most of the countries in this third category populate the middle quartiles of Transparency International's rankings.

7. See Joel Hellman, Geraint Jones, and Daniel Kaufmann, "Are Foreign Investors and Multinationals Engaging in Corrupt Practices in Transition Economies," *Transition* (2000), 4–7. The fullest elaboration of the concept is in the same authors' "Seize the State, Seize the Day: State Capture, Corruption and Influence in Transition," *World Bank Policy Research Working Paper* No. 2444 (Washington, D.C., 2000), available at www.worldbank.org/wbi/governance/pdf/seize_synth.pdf (accessed 28 October 2008).

8. What distinguishes the "privatized" criminal state from the normal give and take between special interests and political decision-makers is a key qualification introduced by James Scott: Interactions "breaching the formal norms of office." See James C. Scott, *Comparative Political Corruption* (Englewood Cliffs, 1972), 5.

9. Christoph H. Stefes, *Understanding Post-Soviet Transitions: Corruption, Collusion and Clientelism* (New York, 2005). Stefes treats "state capture" as essentially a manifestation of decentralized systemic cooperation, but that seems to this author to underestimate the intimate connection between political authority and private actors regardless of the degree of centralization.

10. And for all of these countries their rating on the ten-point Corruption Perceptions Index (CPI) scale was under 3; Uzbekistan's, 1.8. (As all students of TI and other similar ratings underscore, variations in rankings from one year to the next are not meaningful because the comparison set is not constant, and where it is, one country's apparent deterioration simply may be another country's improvement. But to drop fifteen places or more over a relatively short period suggests a very real deterioration.)

11. The report is available at http://report.globalintegrity.org/globalindex/results.cfm?printVersion (accessed 2 December 2008).

12. For the most thorough evaluation of a broad range of corruption rating efforts for the twenty-seven post-socialist states (East European as well as post-Soviet), see Stephen Knack, "Measuring Corruption in Eastern Europe and Central Asia: A Critique of the Cross-Country Indicators," *World Bank Policy Research Working Paper* No. 3968 (Washington, D.C., 2006).

13. Stefes, *Understanding Post-Soviet Transitions,* 90. Stefes cites G. Glonti and G. Lobzhanidze, *Thieves-in-Law: Professional Crime in Georgia* (in Russian) (Tbilisi, 2004).

14. Ibid., 95.

15. Ibid.

16. Ibid., 97–98.

17. Ibid., 100.

18. Ibid., 101.

19. Steven Lee Myers, "Pervasive Corruption in Russia is 'Just Called Business,'" *New York Times* (13 August 2005).

20. News articles laying out the anecdotal evidence appear regularly. For a good example, see Peter Finn, "Taking on Russia's Ubiquitous Bribery: President Has Pledged to Undo 'a Way of Life,'" *Washington Post* (14 July 2008).

21. Jan Neutze and Adrian Karatnycky, "Corruption, Democracy, and Investment in Ukraine," *Atlantic Council Policy Paper* (October 2007), 6.

22. Ibid., 13.

23. Ibid., 5. The actual figures were 34.5th percentile and 27.7th percentile, respectively.

24. Ibid., 19.

25. Ibid., 1, here citing a May 2007 Millennium Challenge Corporation "National Baseline Survey."

26. INDEM Foundation, "Corruption Process in Russia: Level, Structure, Trends" (2005), 1, available at www.indem.ru/en/publicat/2005diag_engV.htm (accessed 2 December 2008). The survey was conducted in six representative regions: Kostroma, Novgorod, Chuvash, Volgograd, Sverdlov, and Khabarovsk.

27. Perhaps this change should not be surprising. Susan Rose-Ackerman has argued that the willingness to bribe depends on whether the bribing official has a monopoly position or, for a number of the categories under "everyday corruption," the victim has multiple options. See her chapter, "The Political Economy of Corruption," in Kimberly Ann Elliott (ed.), *Corruption and the Global Economy* (Washington, D.C., 1997), 40–41.

28. Rose-Ackerman lays all this out admirably in "The Political Economy of Corruption," 38–41.

29. Ibid., 40.

30. Gregory Grossman, "The 'Second Economy' of the USSR," *Problems of Communism,* XXVI (1977), 25–40; William A. Clark, *Crime and Punishment in Soviet Officialdom: Combating Corruption in the Political Elite 1965–1990* (Armonk, 1993).

31. This case also involved Brezhnev's son-in-law, Yuri Churbanov, who, in 1988 under Gorbachev, was sentenced to twelve years in prison for accepting $150,000 in bribes as a junior official in the Ministry of Interior; the bribes were payoffs for enabling the Uzbeks to conceal their long-standing fraud. See Bill Keller, "Brezhnev Son-in-Law Gets 12-Year Term," *New York Times* (31 December 1988), available at http://query.nytimes.com/gst/fullpage.html?res=940DE1D61731F932A05751C1A96E 948260 (accessed 29 October 2008).

32. In the Uzbek case, in the latter years under Sharif Rashidov (the first secretary of the Uzbek communist party from 1959–1983), not only was literally the entire government and party hierarchy complicit in falsifying cotton production, leading the central government to purge virtually all senior officials in 1986, but protection rackets, large-scale theft, and the selling of positions in universities, institutes, and government were widespread. Akhmandzan Adylov, the director of the Papski cotton combine in Ferghana Valley, was an extreme but symptomatic case. He ruled over a labor force of 30,000 in what was effectively a "mini-sovereign state" and lived on an estate filled with peacocks, lions, and concubines.

33. Some serious students of corruption in the Soviet Union would see the distinctions drawn here as too lenient, too dismissive of how pervasive corruption was. See, for example, Konstantin M. Simis, *USSR the Corrupt Society: The Secret World of Soviet Capitalism* (New York, 1982). Others who have closely studied organized crime in the post-Soviet period and its relationship to generalized corruption, and compared the present to the past, do acknowledge the qualitative difference. See, for example, Joseph D. Serio, *Investigating the Russian Mafia* (Durham, 2008), 26, 146–147, 249.

34. Steven Solnick, *Stealing the State: Control and Collapse in Soviet Institutions* (Cambridge, 1998).

35. Stefes, *Political Transitions and Systemic Corruption,* 94.

36. Federico Varese, *The Russian Mafia: Private Protection in a New Market Economy* (New York, 2002), 1.

37. This is well described in Alena V. Ledeneva, *How Russia Really Works: The Informal Practices that Shaped Post-Soviet Politics and Business* (Ithaca, 2006), 91–106.

38. The phenomena have been described in many places, but one succinct source is Erik Berglöf, Andrei Kunov, and others, *The New Political Economy of Russia* (Cambridge, 2003), 67–97. Much of the problem centers on the *arbitrazh* courts. The complex factors at work in this instance are thoroughly explored in Varese, *The Russian Mafia*, 42–54.

39. European Bank for Reconstruction and Development (EBRD), "Transition Report 2003: Integration and Regional Cooperation" (2003), available at www.21i.net/index.html?page_id=271&node=85&level=2&l=1 (accessed 10 April 2009).

40. EBRD, "Transition Report 1999: Ten Years of Transition" (1999), available at www.ebrd.com/pubs/econo/4050.htm (accessed 10 April 2009).

41. Addressing the contrary argument of those who maintained that corruption can actually facilitate growth (by cutting through bureaucratic red-tape, opening contracts to the well-off rather than the well-connected, etc.) is not necessary, because, at best, their argument would only apply to cases of "public corruption," not of "systemic corruption," let alone the criminalized state. The argument has been made by Colin Leys, "What Is the Problem about Corruption," *Journal of Modern African Studies*, III (1965), 215–230, and James C. Scott, "Analysis of Corruption in Developing Nations," *Comparative Studies in Society and History*, XI (1969), 315–341.

42. Susanto Basu and David D. Li, "Corruption in Transition," *William Davidson Institute Working Paper* No. 161 (Ann Arbor, 1998).

43. See his testimony before the Subcommittee on Domestic and International Monetary Policy, Trade and Technology of the House Committee on Financial Services (17 October 2007).

44. Lawrence Scott Sheets, "A Smugglers's Story," *Atlantic* (April 2008), 60–70.

45. This is an estimate from the Union of Concerned Scientists in their factsheet on "HEU in the United States and Russia" (2007), available at www.ucsusa.org/global_security/nuclear_terrorism/military-stockpiles-of-highly-enriched-uranium-heu.html (accessed 2 December 2008).

46. If the data on corruption within countries are problematic, those on illicit trade are considerably more so. Peter Andreas argues that many of the popularly circulated statistics on trafficking in drugs, humans, and endangered species come close to being picked out of thin air and are, at best, the product of unverifiable sources and methods. Andreas, however, offers no alternative way of understanding the scale of various forms of illicit trade, which he acknowledges is a serious problem. See his "Numbers Games: (Mis)measuring Illicit Flows and Policy Effectiveness," Paper prepared for the International Studies Association, San Francisco, 26–29 March 2008. In using the data that follow, this author is aware that they are at best suggestive approximations.

47. These figures come from "Havocscope Black Market Indexes," which in turn draws on reports from government and press agencies (such as the U.S. Department of State's Bureau of International Narcotics and Law Enforcement Affairs and RIA-Novosti), as well as from trade associations (such as the Association of American Publishers, the Motion Picture Association, and the International Federation of Phonographic Industry). The data are available at www.havocscope.com (accessed 2 December 2008). One should note that trade associations do have an incentive to make the data as dramatic as possible in order to underscore the scale of the problem that they face.

48. Office of the U.S. Trade Representative, *2008 Special 301 Report,* available at www.ustr.gov/assets/Document_Library/Reports_Publications/2008/2008_Special_301_Report/asset_upload_file553_14869.pdf (accessed 2 December 2008). The priority watch list also includes Argentina, Chile, India, Israel, Pakistan, Thailand, and Venezuela, but these are treated as less urgent cases. The next level down is the "watch list," which contains most of the remaining post-Soviet states. Ukraine improved from 2006 to 2007 by moving from the priority watch list to the watch list.

49. Ibid., 34. Andreas makes the valid point that a figure like this is misleading by suggesting that the buyer of a counterfeit item at a fraction of its legal market price would have paid its legal market price absent the counterfeit item. See Andreas, "Numbers Game," 8.

50. The job loss figure is widely circulated, particularly by the National Chamber Foundation. See its report, "What Are Counterfeiting and Piracy Costing the American Economy" (2005), available at www.uschamber.com/NR/rdonlyres/esjjx6nnnpwvswfix tkolx4huoxllo7q526ifotwrwfre3vctawib7rkbj7ywc6muwoj4nv7mxdu3m3pix53lfjtgve/ WhatAreCounterfeitingandPiracyCostingtheAmericanEconomy.0805.pdf (accessed 2 December 2008).

51. Russia and the other post-Soviet states, it appears, are not major offenders in the manufacture of fake pharmaceuticals, but China is. See Ted C. Fishman, "Manufake-ture," *New York Times* (9 January 2005).

52. Louise I. Shelley and Robert W. Orttung, "Russia's Efforts to Combat Human Trafficking: Efficient Crime Groups Versus Irresolute Societies and Uncoordinated States," in William Alex Pridemore (ed.), *Ruling Russia: Law, Crime, and Justice in a Changing Society* (Lanham, 2005), 167–182.

53. The estimate is from the International Organization for Migration, cited in Donna M. Hughes, "The 'Natasha' Trade: The Transnational Shadow Market of Trafficking in Women," *Journal of International Affairs,* LIII (2000), 628–629.

54. Preston Mendenhall, "Sold as a Sex Slave in Europe," *MSNBC.com* (June 2001), available at www.msnbc.msn.com/id/3071965/print/1/displaymode/1098 (accessed 2 December 2008). The figure is plausible, because one expert study reports that illegal emigrants into Europe from Moldova over this period was between 600,000 and one million, 70 percent of whom were women. See Jana Costachi, "Preventing Victimization in Moldova," *Global Affairs,* VIII (2003), 30. Costachi was at the time the director of the Center for Prevention of Trafficking in Women.

55. Adrian Levy and Cathy Scott-Clark, "Poaching for Bin Laden," *The Guardian* (5 May 2007).

56. Misha Glenny, *McMafia: A Journey through the Global Criminal Underworld* (New York, 2008), 47.

57. United Nations Office of Drugs and Crime, "Afghanistan Opium Survey 2007" (August 2007), 3.

58. Ibid., iv. The production figure in 2001 was 1,600 tons.

59. U.S. Department of State, Bureau of International Narcotics and Law Enforcement Affairs, "International Narcotics Control Strategy Report" (March 2007), available at www.state.gov/p/inl/rls/nrcrpt/2007/vol1/html/80860.htm (accessed 2 December 2008).

60. United Nations Office of Drugs and Crime, "2007 World Drug Report," 55.

61. The report entertained the possibility that by 2010 the number of HIV-infected persons in Nigeria, Ethiopia, Russia, India, and China would grow from "around 14 to 23 million currently to an estimated 50 to 75 million." In Russia, the number swelled from 1–2 million to 5–8 million. See National Intelligence Council, "The Next Wave of HIV/AIDS: Nigeria, Ethiopia, Russia, India, and China (Summary) ICA 2002-04D" (September 2002), available at www.mindfully.org/Health/2002/AIDS-HIV-Next-WaveCIASep02.htm (accessed 2 December 2008).

62. Interview with Peter Piot, executive director of UNAIDS, "Central Asia: UNAIDS Chief Says Disease Spreading at Record Pace," Radio Free Europe/Radio Liberty (27 March 2008), available at www.rferl.org/featuresarticle/2008/03/4f57503a-0807-4495-a3a6-cfdd73d3d47a.html (accessed 2 December 2008).

63. Michael T. Klare, "Curbing Trade in Small Arms: A Practical Route," *U.S. Foreign Policy Agenda,* VI (2001), 20–22, available at www.ciaonet.org.monstera.cc.columbia.edu:2048/olj/fpa/fpa_jun01.pdf (accessed 2 December 2008).

64. United Nations Department of Public Information, "Press Conference by the United Nations Institute for Disarmament Research," available at www.un.org/News/briefings/docs/2006/060630_Lewis.doc.htm (accessed 2 December 2008).

65. There is no commonly accepted definition of small arms and light weapons. Generally the former refers to revolvers, rifles, sub-machine guns, and assault rifles. The latter to grenade launchers, portable anti-tank missiles and rocket systems, mortars of calibers less than 75mm, and so-called MANPADS (man-portable air defense systems). See also Michael Klare and Robert I. Rotberg, *The Scourge of Small Arms* (Cambridge, MA, 1999).

66. "Program of Action (PoA) to Prevent, Combat, and Eradicate the Illicit Trade in Small Arms and Light Weapons, in All Its Aspects" (July 2008), available at http://disarmament.un.org/cab/salw.html (accessed 2 December 2008).

67. Rachel Stohl, "The Tangled Web of Illicit Arms Trafficking," in Gayle Smith and Peter Ogden (eds.), *Terror in the Shadows: Trafficking in Money, Weapons, and People* (Washington, D.C., 2004), 23. For a discussion of the FARC, see Jessica C. Teets and Erica Chenoweth, "To Bribe or to Bomb: Do Corruption and Terrorism Go Together?" chapter 7 in this volume.

68. Sue Lackey with Michael Moran, "Russian Mob Trading Arms for Cocaine with Colombian Rebels," *MSNBC.com* (9 April 2000), available at www.msnbc.msn.com/id/3340035/print/1/displaymode/1098/ (accessed 2 December 2008).

69. A highly competent survey of the small arms and light weapons picture in Russia, both civilian and military, including export rates and illicit trafficking can be found in Maxim Pyadushkin, with Maria Haug and Anna Matveeva, "Beyond the Kalazhnikov: Small Arms Production, Exports, and Stockpiles in the Russian Federation," *Small Arms Survey Occasional Paper* No. 10 (Geneva, 2003).

70. Graham H. Turbiville, "Weapons Proliferation and Organized Crime: The Russian Military and Security Force Dimension," *INSS Occasional Paper* No. 10 (Washington, D.C., 1996), 1–29.

71. Serio, *Investigating the Russian Mafia,* 200.

72. "Small Arms Trade Transparency Barometer 2007," in *Small Arms Survey 2007* (Geneva, 2007), available at www.smallarmssurvey.org/files/portal/issueareas/transfers/transfers_pdf/barometer/B_07.pdf (accessed 30 October 2008).

73. See Tor Bukkvoll, "Their Hands in the Till: Scale and Causes of Russian Military Corruption," *Armed Forces and Society,* XXXIV (2008), 259–275.

74. Iraq Survey Group Final Report, available at www.globalsecurity.org/wmd/library/report/2004/isg-final-report/isg-final-report_vol1_rfp-08.htm (accessed 1 March 2009).

75. Turbiville, "Weapons Proliferation and Organized Crime," 10.

76. The Center for Public Integrity, "Kuchma Approved Sale of Weapons System to Iraq," available at www.publicintegrity.org/articles/entry/411/ (accessed 2 December 2008). An audio version of the original tape and an English translation are available at this site.

77. Moisés Naím, *Illicit: How Smugglers, Traffickers, and Copycats are Hijacking the Global Economy* (New York, 2005), 57–58.

78. Christoph Zürcher, *The Post-Soviet Wars: Rebellion, Ethnic Conflict and Nationhood in the Caucasus* (New York, 2007), 6.

79. Ibid., 60.

80. Ibid., 61.

81. For an excellent analysis of the way the volume of black- and gray-market arms surged and then influenced these conflicts, see Spyros Demetriou, "Politics from the Barrel of a Gun: Small Arms Proliferation and Conflict in the Republic of Georgia (1989–2001)," *Small Arms Survey Occasional Paper* No. 6 (Geneva, 2002).

82. "Russian Airplane Bombings of 24 August 2004," *Wikipedia.org,* available at http://en.wikipedia.org/wiki/Russian_aircraft_bombings_of_August_2004 (accessed 2 December 2008).

83. See Mikheil Tokmazishvili, "Money Laundering and Money Corporation Relations in Abkhazia" (2006), available at www.traccc.cdn.ge (accessed 8 August 2008).

84. For the story inside Gazprom, see Mikhail Kroutikhin, "Energy Policymaking in Russia: From Putin to Medvedev," *NBR Analysis,* XIX (2008), 23–33, available

at http://nbr.org/publications/analysis/pdf/vol19no2.pdf (accessed 2 December 2008).

85. Stuart Diamond, with Ralph Blumenthal, "Huge Illegal Deal on Arms for Iran Was Known to U.S.," *New York Times* (2 February 1987).

86. William R. Spiegelberger, "The Rituals of Power," unpublished manuscript (July 2008).

87. Neutze and Karatnycky, "Corruption, Democracy, and Investment in Ukraine," 31.

88. Rose-Ackerman, "The Political Economy of Corruption," 46–55, explores these steps together with the full suite of measures in an anti-corruption strategy—as well as the complex tradeoffs in choosing how the different elements are combined.

89. Phyllis Dininio and Robert Orttung, "Explaining Patterns of Corruption in the Russian Regions," *World Politics*, LVII (2005), 500–529.

90. World Bank, "Doing Business 2008 Georgia," Doing Business Project, available at www.doingbusiness.org (accessed 2 December 2008). The report contains the rankings for 178 countries.

91. Stefes, *Understanding Post-Soviet Transitions*, 168.

92. Ibid., 167.

93. Group of States Against Corruption, "Evaluation Report on Georgia" (December, 2006), 23, 31. It is instructive to compare the assessment of the GRECO Evaluation Team's report on Georgia with the parallel evaluation of Ukraine in the same year. Ukraine comes close to a model of a country with an extensive but empty shell of anti-corruption measures. Even that, however, is better than Russia and Belarus, which had not submitted to evaluation.

94. Anti-Corruption Network for Eastern Europe and Central Asia (ACN), "Georgia: Update on National Implementation Measures," in *Istanbul Anti-Corruption Action Plan for Armenia, Azerbaijan, Georgia, Kazakhstan, the Kyrgyz Republic, the Russian Federation, Tajikistan and Ukraine* (Paris, 2006), 4, available at www.oecd.org/dataoecd/10/11/38009260.pdf (accessed 30 October 2008).

95. Group of States Against Corruption, "Evaluation Report on Georgia," 14.

96. ACN, "Georgia: Update on National Implementation Measures," 4.

97. For the details, see Jon S.T. Quah, "Responses to Corruption in Asian Societies," in Heidenheimer and Johnston (eds.), *Political Corruption: Concepts and Context*, 525–529. The successful states were Singapore and Hong Kong. The unsuccessful states were the Philippines and Indonesia, although Quah also treats Pakistan as part of the latter category.

98. See Robert I. Rotberg, "Leadership Alters Behavior," chapter 13 in this volume.

99. The national plan is available in Russian at http://kremlin.ru/text/docs/2008/07/204857.shtml (accessed 2 December 2008).

100. "High Stakes in Russia's Corruption Battle," interview with Elena Panfilov, *Open Democracy.net* (28 July 2008), available at www.opendemocracy.net/Russia/article/high-stakes-in-Russias-corruption-battle (accessed 2 December 2008).

101. Ibid.

102. Alexander Kukhianidze, "Organized Crime and Smuggling through Abkhazia and South Ossetia," in Sami Nevala and Kauko Aromaa (eds.), *Organized Crime, Trafficking, Drugs* (Helsinki, 2004), 87–101.

103. A good discussion of the issue is in Union of Concerned Scientists, "Military Stockpiles of Highly Enriched Uranium (HEU)," available at www.ucsusa.org/global_ security/nuclear_terrorism/military-stockpiles-of-highly-enriched-uranium-heu.html (accessed 2 December 2008).

104. Biting the Bullet Project, *Reviewing Action on Small Arms 2006: Assessing the First Five Years of the UN Programme of Action* (2006), 50–51; 108–110.

105. See Ben W. Heineman, Jr., "The Role of the Multi-National Corporation in the Long War against Corruption," chapter 14 in this volume. For a good account of how this affects the behavior of Western businessmen in Russia, see William R. Spiegelberger, "Russian Roulette: Doing Business in Russia in Compliance with Anti-Bribery Laws and Treaties," *Journal of Law and Business,* II (2006), 819–841.

SARAH DIX *and* EMMANUEL POK

9

Combating Corruption
in Traditional Societies:
Papua New Guinea

Corruption is rampant and largely unchecked in the Pacific island nation of Papua New Guinea (PNG).[1] Grand corruption has many faces in PNG: nepotism, administrative corruption, and state capture. Systemic nepotism, including ghost workers on a payroll and political favor-based hiring, has cost the state millions of dollars in just one province, as seen in the case of the Southern Highlands provincial administration. Administrative corruption reportedly takes place in a formalized system of commissions on real or rigged procurement contracts, out of court settlements, and other payments made by the state to private actors. State capture is evident to most observers in the forestry and petroleum extraction industries, which are dominated by select foreign interests licensed by the state.

Petty corruption exists, but it appears to be more opportunistic and less widespread than grand corruption. The majority of the 6 million Papua New Guineans live in traditional societies, with more than 800 sociolinguistic groups. Given that 85 percent are subsistence farmers, most Papua New Guineans do not have cash on hand to pay bribes, although they may trade in other goods and favors. Moreover, as evidenced by the paucity of schools, community health clinics, and roads in much of the country, many rural villagers have minimal or no interaction with the government, and thus have little opportunity or need to pay bribes on a day-to-day basis.

That said, every five years many political candidates in this constitutional parliamentary democracy are known for buying blocks of voters at election time, by negotiating for an entire village's vote. In urban areas, traffic police

The authors thank Diego Miranda, Ron May, and Fiona Hukula for their comments and contributions.

239

collect fines without giving receipts when their supervisor is not present. To get a phone line installed or repaired, people pay the state-owned phone company cash or beer. Sometimes this is given as a bribe (in order to get the service) and sometimes as a tip (after the installation).

To explain why corruption persists despite the existence of arguably adequate anti-corruption laws and institutions, analysts and the public commonly cite widespread public tolerance of corruption as the cause.[2] According to this perspective, that which Westerners consider to be corruption is acceptable in PNG, as a modern expression of Melanesian "traditional custom." That is to say, corruption is a function of PNG's culture, one that is not attuned to modern institutions. While this view acknowledges that other factors such as state weakness, poor governance, and the lack of institutional capacity are present, its emphasis on the pervasiveness of a corruption-abiding culture makes it difficult to imagine how reform-minded policymakers could bring about change.[3]

However, this chapter argues that while Papua New Guineans do draw culturally embedded lines between acceptable and unacceptable behavior, this culturally relative demarcation does not mean that Papua New Guineans are indifferent to or generally approve of scams, graft, or bribes—especially when they do not perceive direct benefits for themselves or their social network. Although there are public examples of a community's and clergy's protection and forgiveness of individuals indicted in scams (like the National Provident Fund in 1999), it does not necessarily follow that these supporters would overlook such transgressions in another community.[4] The number of complaints lodged with the Ombudsman Commission in its regional offices, as well as in its head office, demonstrates that even without whistleblower protection, a considerable number of citizens do acknowledge corruption, and do not regard it as acceptable.

As this chapter argues, the way political leaders have used certain components of traditional culture—namely, the kinship system and deference to "big men"—help to explain the persistent and increasing corruption in PNG.[5] This is not to say that culture is an excuse for corruption, or that reformers should attack culture to reduce corruption. Rather, this chapter points to the need to reduce the apparent conflict between kinship or social network obligations and public service.[6] To achieve this reduction, this chapter argues, policymakers need strategically to recast existing national institutions in ways amenable to local-level, traditional institutions now at risk due to the leaders' perversion of the *wantok* system and because of the overwhelming pressure of big men that is entrenched in politics at the national level.

The first section of this chapter analyzes the legal framework and institutional developments in PNG, showing how these institutions are, on paper, up to the task of confronting corruption. It then contrasts their expected effectiveness with their rather weak performance over the years, particularly in the realm of grand corruption. The second section considers the aspects of traditional culture that leaders have invoked to legitimize corruption. The lack of constraints on leaders at the national level is contrasted to the traditional checks that may be found at the local level.

This chapter then highlights the need to enhance social accountability through measures to "thicken" civil society, that is, to broaden and deepen social networks and organizations. It also argues for increasing the public's formal access mechanisms to national, provincial, and local governments. In conclusion, the chapter posits that reform-minded leaders should articulate the objectives that the Western-influenced institutions should achieve—such as justice or security—in line with functions that traditional institutions have provided in PNG over several millennia.

"Good Enough" Laws and Institutions

Corrupt acts in PNG have continued to flourish despite adequate laws and institutions that have been designed to combat such acts.[7] A formal code of conduct governs all elected parliamentarians as well as senior executives of government and quasi-government institutions at the national and subnational levels.[8] Violations of the leadership code are reported to the Ombudsman Commission, an independent, constitutionally established office that administers the code. Like other citizens, leaders may also be prosecuted for bribe-taking, fraud, exerting undue influence, and misuse of tendering under the criminal code.[9] The 1989 Audit Act, the 2005 Proceeds of Crime Act, the 2005 Public Finance Management Act, and the 2007 Electoral Reform Act add to the legal framework that can be used to fight corruption.[10]

The Ombudsman Commission consists of three ombudsmen (including the chief) who equally exercise the committee's constitutional powers. Each operates his or her own investigations independently, and no ombudsman has the power to oversee operations of another's investigations.[11] The Ombudsman Commission may initiate investigations as well as respond to complaints or referrals, question decisions and decision-making, and consider defects in laws. The commission refers matters to the public prosecutor, or refers directly to the Leadership Tribunal, and reports to parliament.[12]

A key anti-corruption institution is the Office of the Auditor General, which is a permanent constitutional authority that inspects, audits, and reports on the "control of and transactions with or concerning the public monies of PNG."[13] The prime minister chairs a parliamentary Auditor General Committee, which appoints the auditor general. The auditor general audits the government on an annual basis, and reports his findings to the parliamentary committee and to parliament.

A police Fraud Squad investigates high-profile cases of corruption. Also within the police, as of 2008, there is a Financial Intelligence Unit (FIU) that includes a forensic accountant.[14] Other key anti-corruption actors are the attorney general and solicitor general, along with the courts, the electoral commission, and parliamentary oversight committees such as the Public Accounts Committee (PAC) and the Parliamentary Committee on Provincial Government Suspensions. Also of note are special commissions of inquiry, which can be initiated by the government to investigate particular scandals. Examples are the landmark investigation on the forestry industry in 1987, the inquiry into the engagement of Sandline International in 1997, the National Provident Fund in 1999, the privatization and sale of PNG Banking Corporation in 2003, and the Finance Department inquiry in 2008.

Overall, the types of corruption most often cited and discussed by the media as of 2009 have been cases of grand corruption, encompassing financial mismanagement and public tenders, as well as electoral fraud, particularly the buying of block votes (or exchanging pigs and beer for them). Below is an analysis of the performance of two of the main institutions that are directly responsible for these areas of corruption: the Ombudsman Commission and the auditor general.

Poor Institutional Performance and Legitimacy

The Ombudsman Commission is arguably the most important and respected anti-corruption institution. Review of its reports as well as external assessments and studies show that, since 1975, it has acted independently and has, in a number of instances, been assertive in fighting corruption and public sector mismanagement. A case in point is the chief ombudsman's 2008 referral of the prime minister to the justice system for years of non-compliance with annual reporting requirements.[15] While critics argue that this move was long overdue, it was still bold.[16] Given the steady flow of complaints about corruption and the demand for ombudsman services, there is a good case to be made to expand the ombudsman's presence in all the provinces, instead of having only four regional offices.

However, the ombudsman commission's actions are constrained by various factors, including that its jurisdiction ends when a suspected corrupt leader leaves office, allowing those being investigated to avoid scrutiny by stepping down. Furthermore, resources allow for only up to nine cases per year to be investigated. Even when a leader is referred to the Leadership Tribunal, the current maximum period of preclusion from office that the tribunal can impose is only three years. In criminal cases, the Ombudsman Commission may refer leaders to the public prosecutor to pursue the criminal matter in the National Court.

The landmark report on corruption in the forestry sector in the early 1980s, which failed to result in any prosecutions, illustrates that detailed ombudsman commission reports may be ignored.[17] Worse, alleged culprits remain active in the public sector, and in a number of cases these leaders have effectively competed in the electoral arena. Taking a benign view of these legal limitations, one might recommend improving the Ombudsman Commission's funding, staff incentives, training, and management. Yet, given the commission's inability to directly prosecute in the National Court, the unenforceability problem remains unaddressed by such an approach.

It has been proposed that the commission's decisions could be enforced through referral to the National Court, without the need for approval from the public prosecutor. This proposal is problematic for two reasons. First, there is the political climate as of 2008. Parliament moved to take power away from the Ombudsman Commission, not expand it.[18] This restriction of power was achieved in 2008 by requiring new standards for evidence in commission investigations. As of this ruling, the evidence has to be almost as strong as evidence in a criminal case in a court of law. If the commission's reports lacked teeth before, under this decision, they will lack cases as well. To propose, then, that parliament should expand the commission's reach and grant it power to prosecute criminally leaders is unlikely to get far on its own, without strong allies. This is not to say that an expansion of power should not be proposed, but if it is to be achieved, one would need to build a coalition of support among policymakers or leverage support from civil society and the private sector. This support is not at hand as of early 2009.

Second, even if the rules were changed to give the Ombudsman Commission more power, neither the commission nor the court could actually enforce the commission's decisions. Enforcement ultimately depends on the legitimacy of the commission (and the court), and this authority is in short supply for Western institutions in PNG. In the case of the commission, on the one hand, it does have a positive reputation for integrity among domestic and international stakeholders. The public continues to submit a number of complaints. But, on the other hand, the commission has a track record of writing reports that have been disregarded, repeatedly, for the past thirty years. Even if granted more power, without legitimacy the commission and its reports may continue to be disregarded. An approach to reduce this risk would be for the commission initially to choose targets, such as corruption by foreign companies, that would be likely to receive domestic public support. As for more politically challenging cases, the commission could address them within socially acceptable norms to maximize the impact of its recommendations.

As mentioned above, the auditor general's office is another key anti-corruption institution. The auditor general's constitutionally mandated appointment and his legislated powers are broad in scope. The Audit Act of 1989 "requires" the auditor general to examine management frameworks and control structures that address efficiency and effectiveness, legal compliance, and "waste and extravagance."[19]

In practice, however, the auditor general's impact is challenged by a number of constraints, particularly its geographically widespread mandate. By his own account, the auditor general will never have the resources to cover all regions and their establishments: 28 national departments, their agencies, and their representations in 19 provinces; 19 provincial governments and their business arms; more than 450 local level governments and their business arms; more than 350 financial statements by authorities and commercial agencies; and 19 provincial treasuries with additional district treasury offices, hospitals and boards, educational institutions, and hundreds of trust accounts.[20] Compounding matters is the lack of qualified staff, which is especially acute in the finance field.

An additional major constraint is the fact that the auditor general refers to the Parliamentary Accounts Committee (PAC). Despite having its funds cut off and other attempts to undermine its work, the PAC stands out for having tenaciously investigated ninety-five government agencies and departments in 2007. The PAC concluded that not one agency or department had complied with the Public Financial Management Act over the PAC's five-year term.[21] However, nothing has come of the report and its recommendations have not been followed. Not only does this reflect the lack of the PAC's weight, such non-action also limits the potential impact of the auditor general insofar as it relies on reporting to the PAC for further action.

Institutional Developments

The forming of the National Anti-Corruption Alliance (NACA) is an illustration of significant inter-agency, institutional development; through NACA, different law and justice sector agencies—including the three above—collaborate and share expertise to investigate and prosecute high-profile cases. Its first case was launched in 2006: an investigation of close to 300 "ghost" employees on the Southern Highlands provincial administration payroll. As a result of the investigation, these employees were removed from the payroll and referred to the justice system for prosecution. The investigation also caught two big fish, a former Southern Highlands governor and a parliamentarian.[22] In 2008, NACA began another case to investigate a goods and services tax (GST) rebate fraud that involved a syndicate of persons (tax payers, tax agents, and revenue collectors). It is estimated to have cost the state more than $4 million as of late 2008.

While law and justice agencies collaborate on inter-disciplinary investigations through NACA, on an individual level, most of these institutions do not function as well as they are intended to. Donors and government both point to the anti-corruption agencies' lack of capacity and resources. The NACA pilot case, for example, was successful by all accounts. But the alliance was coordinated by a one-person office with a limited budget, allowing NACA to carry out only one case at a time. Worse, in 2008, members of parliament cut off the Public Accounts Committee's (PAC) funding in order to stymie a major inquiry into the large sums of money available to members of parliament. The PAC's probe had raised fundamental questions about resource allocations, which are determined in the national budgeting process.

Notwithstanding limited funding and the consequent constrained reach of PNG's anti-corruption institutions, in certain cases the ingenuity of courageous public officials and their advisors has resulted in startling findings of corruption and detailed recommendations. Even in those exemplary cases of agency effort, however, their findings, recommendations, and even judicial sentences have been ignored or overturned by the political powers that be. It is not farfetched to foresee, in light of the analysis above, that the stonewalling of such cases could easily be followed by a further reduction of funding for insubordinate institutions.

Since poor funding and understaffing reduce the performance of anti-corruption institutions, such institutions would clearly benefit from more funding and training. However, as the PNG chapter of Transparency International has wryly observed, sectoral performance has not improved significantly despite years of substantial financial and technical advisory support.[23] The legislative and executive branches are seen by the public and media as corrupt and lower levels of the judiciary are also regarded as tainted.[24] In this light, one needs to consider the political reasons why anti-corruption institutions are not as effective as they could be.

The PNG Way?

Why are the recommendations and findings of the three main anti-corruption institutions unenforceable? Why does the political system get away with it? As this next section elucidates, the subversion of traditional culture by political leaders is to blame for this "unexpected" outcome. Yet only a restatement of (modernly interpreted) traditional culture, not its annihilation, offers a workable and sustainable response to these outcomes.

Although the PNG public sector has clear rules and standards for behavior, public officials face competing demands from kinship groups to share the benefits and wealth that are under their control.[25] Indeed, many Papua New Guinean leaders advance culture or tradition (specifically, its modern interpretations) as a justification for corrupt behavior. An obvious solution to this apparent conflict between ethical behavior and custom is to legalize culturally acceptable practices and remove or reduce opportunities for officials to exercise discretionary authority.[26]

At the same time, however, the authors of this chapter suggest that such an undertaking must be done in a way that recognizes and draws on traditional concepts or symbols such as sharing, transparency, community assets, *wantok,* and big men. At the national level, one could identify and strengthen culturally sensitive checks and balances that are able to replicate what, in the past, occurred at the local level in PNG: control over the behavior of leaders. Otherwise, those within kinship networks will quickly find ways to get around the rules by connecting officials whose sole authority has been removed, but who can regain power by an elaborate system of exchange with others. The ineffectiveness of more than thirty constitutional reforms in the last thirty years is testimony to Western institutions' lack of legitimacy in the eyes of traditional society. Simply stated, these institutions are not embedded in PNG society, as they have failed to find a place in the cultural framework in which this society operates.

The traditional Melanesian big man managed community assets and made decisions in consultation with elders. He bestowed pigs and feasts to members of his community and exchanged gifts of shells with others in his kinship network. Because he lived in the community, his assets were fairly transparent and he was trusted. This was not, of course, a flawless system, as opportunities were plenty for big men to exploit the power delegated to them. But they were trustees more than authoritative leaders, and the power could be taken back.[27] In general, they took care not to accumulate excessive wealth or otherwise abuse their power, at the risk of being driven out or shamed before the community in which they lived. The big man would participate in rituals of gift giving and exchange with his *wantok* or kin around him. In the absence of modern state institutions, the stability of the *wantok* required husbandry by big men and, in turn, the welfare of big men depended on their ability to cement the stability of their *wantok*.

Today, the *wantok* and big men traditions manifest themselves in PNG's political arena as a system by which elected leaders and bureaucrats use public office as an opportunity to accumulate wealth and therefore status, and by which these officials' *wantoks* expect the spoils of office to confer direct benefits. There are important regional differences; abuse of the system for personal gain is more culturally acceptable in the Highlands and less so in the Sepik region, for example, where anyone who has wealth is suspect. In any case, framing their power in culturally acceptable terms such as feasts and exchanges may lend legitimacy to contemporary leaders who seek to augment their power by wealth, patronage, and an electoral support base.

Yet, unlike in the villages where the system of governance had as a counterpart some checks and balances—above all, the close scrutiny of a local big man's actions by his *wantok*—today there seem to be few constraints for national big men. Such leaders are living far from the direct scrutiny of a village, in Port Moresby, but can use important state resources to sustain their positions in their villages. Corruption, inefficiency, and mismanagement, in general, are likely consequences of this imbalance.

The Big Man

Big men are leaders in the political units that they represent. In traditional PNG society, big man status was gained through inheritance (pre-colonial) or earned from deeds (colonial). To be a big man in the past century in the PNG Highlands, for example, one had to have a lot of wealth, in the form of pigs, land, and wives. This system meant that men had to work hard to produce their wealth, to gain people's trust, and the favor of would-be wives and their families. There are anecdotal accounts of corruption where a big man took a pig or another item of value from a community member and never paid the person back. But this was not common as political units were small, and what a big man did was seen and heard by others in the village.[28] The big man status was treasured, and given the likelihood and consequences of being caught, one did not risk ruining one's reputation or being socially punished by other means.

In contrast, today the big man's status is often achieved through attainment of elected office, education, money, or other modern, material indicators that are in some cases inherited, but more often than not require entrepreneurship in the private or public sectors. In the Highlands tradition, if a man is wealthier than others around him, he claims to be a big man. But if he is well-educated and has a good job, these factors also make him a big man. Getting recognized as a big man in one's social base has driven people to go out of their way to accumulate as much wealth as possible to attain such status.[29] Increasingly, as PNG grows nationally integrated, the state has provided opportunities for gaining not only political power but wealth to a degree that largely exceeds that which was previously achievable at the local level. Yet, there is nothing in this national arena to control this behavior, and both the likelihood of being caught and consequences for exploiting one's power are not great.

In the electoral arena, in particular, big man status allows politicians, particularly members of parliament in many provinces, to act essentially unchecked by any national level counterpart. The tradition of *wantok* provides these politicians with a paralegal network through which they can control their districts (through block voting), and the *wantok* legitimizes, so to speak, behavior that ultimately diminishes the power and relevance of other traditional institutions. Most district-level institutions and resources are controlled by members of parliament, either directly or indirectly. As a result, members of parliament are expected to represent their constituents, yet their discretionary funds are typically not directed to provincial administrations or constituents in general, but rather to smaller groups: the members' *wantoks*.

The Wantok System

Although corruption in PNG is similar to corruption in other developing countries with weak states, one might consider the Melanesian *wantok* system that underlies corruption in PNG to be distinct at the turn of the twenty-first century. *Wantok* literally means "one talk" or speaking the same language. In practice it refers to tight, reciprocal social networks or what anthropologists call segmentary societies. Segmentary societies have been universal in human history, and are still a strong, stable form of social organization.[30]

The larger linguistic groups in PNG have a number of distinct *wantok* systems within them.[31] The *wantok* system that existed before modernization and democratic rule is seen today as having helped family relationships prosper, and as having assisted those in need. *Wantok,* in short, was a kinship-based, safety-net system that provided traditional people with a sense of identity that predated (and likely still overshadows) any other supra-identity.

The concept of *wantok* has gone beyond its traditional boundaries. Particularly in urban or transnational settings, a *wantok* may also be a multi-linguistic, multi-ethnic social or professional network. With the modernization and nationalization of politics in PNG came the growth of the public sector and capital, and new leaders, as well as their *wantoks*, quickly exploited the system to facilitate corruption, especially through nepotism and political patronage. If a person knows someone who is in a position to influence the hiring and firing of individuals in an organization, it is an opportunity for an unqualified person to be hired, while a qualified person can be fired. *Wantokism* also facilitates the efficient block-purchase of votes and complicity in procurement and public works kickback schemes.

Of course, *wantokism*, as it has been illustrated thus far, is not different from informal networks elsewhere in the world. The difference in PNG, though, lies in the sanctification of these networks' activities under the veil of tradition, without the existence of any culturally valid mechanism to reveal the trick or to punish the resulting unethical behavior.

Traditionally, *wantokism* was rooted in custom, guided by natural laws, and informally enforced by the village. Principles such as honesty, loyalty, trust, kindness, and helping people in need were at the center of this custom. *Wantok* was a means to ensure that custom was fulfilled and enforced. In other words, *wantokism* was an operationalization of custom. Even today, for example, when paying a "bride price" in the village, the bride's *wantok* reimburses the groom's family for half the cost.

In 2009, one sees practices such as nepotism, cronyism, misuse of public facilities, widespread abuse of power, misuse of public properties, and negligence of duties and responsibilities being excused under the rubric of custom. In court, although pleas of "custom" are not accepted as a justification for corrupt acts themselves, custom is accepted in certain cases as a mitigating factor when the judge hands down a sentence.[32]

By appropriating the definition of *wantokism* to serve their ends, national policymakers have not only undermined the performance of the state—to the extent that some observers are concerned that PNG may be a failed state—but are subverting traditional forms of doing politics at the local level as well.[33] The consequence of the perversion of the big man and *wantok* traditions are the purchase of voting blocks, the centralization of all districts' decisions in the hands of a few, nationally controlled cronies, and the slow, but relentless, erosion of traditional forms of authority by cash-plenty national politicians.

Social Accountability

Standard mechanisms of horizontal accountability—an intrastate system of checks and balances—do not effectively control political power in PNG.

Likewise, the vertical accountability mechanism of elections has not proven to be effective in PNG.[34] A solution to this absence of accountability is collective action by citizens to hold the government accountable for enforcing the laws as well as improving public sector performance.[35]

In this chapter, the authors argue that there is a need, if PNG is to improve accountability, to develop social-control mechanisms. Although the *wantok* system has created strong social capital, one might say that it has discouraged collective action.[36] Social control would not only serve to sanction politicians and bureaucrats, it also has the potential to activate and give teeth to the ineffective horizontal mechanisms such as the judiciary or parliamentary commissions.[37] For example, citizen score cards or participatory tracking and monitoring systems could serve to enhance government performance. This could also build public confidence, which could enhance the institutions' credibility, and in turn, its effectiveness.

Above all, the authors of this chapter see a role for social accountability to remedy the lack of an effective, legitimate, and therefore enforceable check on corruption at the national level. With a parliament that is dominated by the executive, who can check the prime minister? And who can check members of parliament, some of whom have achieved an impressive 100 percent noncompliance with financial reporting regulations in 2007, but still managed to get another year of slush funds at a higher amount in 2008?

To the extent that there are, as of early 2009, effective anti-corruption mechanisms in place, they are only at the local or provincial levels. Take, for example, village courts and alternative dispute mechanisms. If one bears in mind that these institutions may be subject to the same problems that plague other institutions in PNG, then these courts should be better resourced, developed, and expanded so that they can be more effective. But two critical points come out of this example. First, the community-based courts and other local mechanisms are not equipped to control the member of parliament who is their provincial governor, the member of parliament who represents the different districts within each province, or the member of parliament from another province whose semi-private graft reduces the pool of resources that should be available to all provinces.

Second, the underfunding of informal and formal subnational institutions has been exacerbated by the profound 1995 so-called "indigenous" reform that caused a power shift from the subnational to national government.[38] Although the village courts faced challenges prior to the reform, the reform effectively dried up funding and other resources to provinces, which explains why village courts were significantly constrained until funding began to increase in 2005.[39]

To revive the village courts, one must address the underlying national–sub-national dynamics that squeezed the courts in the first place.

Indeed, the trend is toward continuing the centralization of power and funds. In 2008, parliament voted to increase the amount of discretionary funds (so-called slush funds) allocated each year to each member of parliament. The equivalent in the United States would be for members of the House of Representatives to control, collectively, more than 10 percent of the national budget, with each representative receiving the same amount of money, irrespective of the needs of the district that he or she represents.

Furthermore, while the idea in PNG is for the member of parliament to use those funds to benefit his or her constituents, in effect few members of parliament use them to contribute to province-wide expenditures, concentrating instead on cementing their power in the district that they represent. This focus on the local district is a catch-22 in that members of parliament argue that the funds should be under their control because provincial administrations are not capable of handling them, but the very lack of funds leaves these administrations without the resources to offer reasonable compensation, build capacity, and provide needed services.

Anti-Corruption Reform Efforts

As of 2009, anti-corruption reform is afoot in PNG, but policies and action plans have yet to address the underlying power structures that perpetuate the status quo, in this case, corruption. Anti-corruption advocates have reviewed PNG's integrity pillars and are familiarizing themselves with a lengthy menu of international practices through workshops and meetings.[40] Discussions favor a holistic and coordinated inter-agency approach to strengthening these existing pillars.

At a 2008 round-table discussion with a handful of elected leaders that are interested in fighting corruption, the sentiment was that leaders create or pervert the systems.[41] As the government's leaders pointed out, good leadership makes a difference, as seen in the province of Madang. And as the opposition leaders noted, bad leadership aggravates corruption, as seen in Southern Highlands province. According to both sides, the solution requires better and more moral leadership, and enforcement of existing (Western) laws, without much consideration for changing the underlying incentives for corruption.

Several key documents have emerged. One such document is the draft anti-corruption strategy for 2007–2012, developed by the current director of NACA while he was working within the prime minister's office. This strategy prioritizes political, legislative, and administrative reforms. Another document is the National Law and Justice Policy and Plan of Action, which has been implemented as of late 2008. This policy plan "recognizes the limitations of the state institutions and promotes the expansion of crime prevention and restorative justice approaches based upon the culture and traditions of PNG communities. It promotes initiatives such as mediation, alternative dispute resolution, village courts, and crime prevention strategies."[42] Along these lines, a new bill on community courts has been drafted.[43]

A third key document that is being followed up on by the Fraud Squad is the result of a 2005 review by the Justice Advisory Group for the law and justice sector's National Coordinating Mechanism. This report's overarching recommendation is to implement a national plan of reform. Similar to the plan of action above, this reform plan suggests strengthening village courts and providing support to existing civil society groups that advocate against corruption.

In other sectors, anti-corruption reforms have been attempted but not institutionalized. For example, there was a much-praised anti-corruption reform in the fishery sector. However, a 2008 audit by a Big Four accounting firm illustrates that this reform has not been sustained over time. Historical experience suggests that while change is possible in PNG at the sectoral level, reforms risk being undermined when information on their performance and compliance is not readily available to the public. As is argued in the next section, institutionalization of reform in PNG fundamentally requires the development of a "thick" civil society able to inform, monitor, and challenge the government when necessary.

The Power of Civil Society

Social control can enable civil society and the media to hold governments accountable by making multiple demands of the rule of law and due processes. Strengthening civil society has become a common mantra for those eager to see governments held accountable in developing countries. Not surprisingly, the 2005 Justice Advisory Group Report in PNG emphasized the need to support civil society organizations that are fighting corruption. Likewise, the Australian aid agency, which provides and monitors close to one quarter of PNG's national budget, recognizes its importance in the fight against corruption and provides significant funding to various civil society initiatives in PNG, including those that do research and raise awareness.

External aid has primarily supported existing organizations by providing funds for civic education, advocacy campaigns, or public awareness-raising. But in addition to being informed, citizens need to actively participate in public decision-making and demand services from the government.[44] Strengthening the political clout of the poor in civil society has the potential to make reforms more effective.[45]

Moreover, the authors of this chapter argue that the state, the private sector, as well as donors and likeminded non-governmental organizations (NGOs) may explicitly facilitate the "thickening" of civil society. This action includes, but is more than, building leadership or other capacities of established NGOs in the governance sector. To do so requires policies and programs that create incentives for leaders and systematically remove obstacles to the establishment and growth of a wide variety of sustainable organizations that can complement and perhaps compete with the predominantly Port Moresby–based NGOs.

In a country with an estimated 57 percent adult literacy rate and only 55 percent of children enrolled in primary school, where an entire generation in the autonomous province of Bougainville has been left out of school altogether, a critical building block to an informed and engaged civil society is long-term investment in formal and informal education.[46] Such investment must encompass strategies that build a common language and social linkages across and beyond *wantoks,* promote citizens who are more critical and informed consumers, and enable communities directly to engage in government processes and advocate for themselves.

Simultaneously, the development of civil society requires the explicit facilitation of the growth and proliferation of organized groups: grassroots women's groups, faith-based groups, self-help groups, lending and savings groups, umbrella groups, and others that bring people together with a common purpose. National NGOs have proven to be a critical actor in generating debate, communicating information to citizens, serving as watchdogs, encouraging citizens to bring legal claims or complaints against the state, and drafting legislative proposals. But at the provincial and grassroots levels, there is also a need for community-based organizations to coordinate and present claims against the state and obtain feedback from citizens on more local issues.

PNG's Transparency International chapter (TI–PNG), the Institute for National Affairs, and the Media Council are perhaps the most communicative and developed organizations that are contributing to the fight against corruption, and more broadly, bringing about better governance.[47] These organizations certainly deserve further support. TI–PNG has set up a network of community groups across the country that effectively disseminate information through the media. TI–PNG has also proposed an initiative to provide low-cost cell phones to rural teachers so that they can easily report what is happening at the local level to journalists, government, and non-profit watch-dogs. Given the significant challenges of linking people in this country who speak more than 800 distinct languages, greater access to low-cost communication would significantly facilitate citizen access to information and their ability to organize and demand better governance.

Civil society need not be organized directly around only anti-corruption efforts for it to have an impact on corruption. For example, church groups are common throughout PNG, and the National Council of Churches' organizing framework for these groups includes not only spiritual activities but also community, social, and economic activities. The council has found that women who are hesitant to take leave from family duties to organize collectively do come together for bible study and then find the capacity, within this group, to discuss domestic violence or HIV/AIDS. In time these discussions, with a church leader's support, could encourage members to seek information and access to government services and share information with their community about this access and the government's performance. As the experiences of Latin America (and particularly of Brazil during the 1970s and 1980s) illustrate, the pressure of these small groups is often necessary, if not sufficient, for the liberalization of a political arena that was previously dominated by less-than-democratic governments.[48]

In addition to faith-based groups, the environmental movement is fairly active in PNG. Some organizations have made a direct connection between environmental issues and corruption. For example, the Environmental Law Centre facilitates rural landowners' legal claims and also galvanizes support for national anti-corruption reforms. One organization's involvement in a neighborhood campaign to increase safety in a Port Moresby slum could lead to a drive to register children for school and could activate group members to decide to take literacy classes or to be more engaged in the governmental processes around them.[49] At the very least, this engagement would be likely to provide mechanisms of social accountability, and thus would allow individual citizens or members of organized civil society to participate in monitoring, budgeting, or other activities from which they were previously alienated.

Many of these "thousand flowers" could (or would wish to) make a difference in corruption. More likely than not, citizens, acting individually, would produce inefficient mechanisms for promoting better service delivery. Nevertheless, citizens' collective presence would facilitate collective action, and thus provide what PNG is in 2009 painfully lacking: an entity able effectively to contest the government's otherwise unilateral policy imposition.

Conclusion

The post-colonial system of democratic governance has eroded the strength of pre-colonial and colonial "traditional" systems of control over those in power. Yet, at the same time, it has given contemporary leaders new forms and arenas of power to exploit, and more resources to embed these leaders in the new system, without the parallel development of culturally accepted checks.

Some examples of traditional checks on governors were credible threats to violators and use of shaming or even sorcery, such as casting spells on transgressors who believed in these spells' powers. While such checks would have contained the scale and incidence of bad governance at the local level in the past, with the modernization and nationalization of PNG politics, these mechanisms have been unable to cope with the influx of wealth, urban migration, and evangelism. There is nobody at the national level, other than transplanted and poorly integrated Western institutions, to control the behavior of the powerful.

This constraint-free environment has allowed big men the discretion not only to act as uncontested predators at the national level, but it has provided these men with resources to weaken traditional checks and balances at the local level as well. Examples of such modifications are the 1995 reform that shifted power from provinces to the center, and effectively debilitated local administration and village courts, with only a few exceptions; current efforts to meddle with local elections; and the attempts to abolish provincial government altogether.

If corruption is to be controlled, new control mechanisms are needed that are able to confront the leaders and force them to operate within socially acceptable and beneficial boundaries. Yet, such reform requires, paradoxically, re-casting existing national institutions in terms that are acceptable to the 800-plus traditional societies within PNG. Such a reform also requires the expansion of contextually derived, social accountability mechanisms, along with other checks, that function nationally and subnationally in the way that other controlling features did in previous periods, at the village level.

An unexploited feedback mechanism exists between the needs of a traditional society that is at risk of being defined, at the village level, by the will of national big men, and the needs of national formal institutions that are attempting to gain legitimacy and popular support to limit what is, as of 2009, an unconstrained executive. To take advantage of this feedback mechanism, these institutions need to do, with modern, formal means, what traditional institutions informally attempted: control the behavior of big men who, unconstrained, would otherwise tear apart the fabric of society.

Notes

1. Data on corruption in PNG are scant and unreliable. To put this statement into context: the last household survey in PNG was done over twenty years ago, the consumer price index has not been updated in years, and the national statistician position at the census bureau has long been vacant. The authors of this chapter, in 2009, are carrying out a national survey of experiences with corruption. According to Transparency International's Corruption Perceptions Index, on a scale of 10 (highly clean) to 0 (highly corrupt), PNG scored a 2 in 2007 and 2008, which suggests an increase in perceptions of corruption since 2006. Scores from previous years suggest a decrease in perceptions in 2006 and 2004 and an increase in 2005. The changes in score could be in part a result of the addition of new sources in 2004 and 2006. PNG's country ranking has seemingly worsened over time, but it is problematic to compare country ranking from one year to another because the countries included in the study have changed each year since PNG first participated in 2003. In any case, TI's index does not measure people's experience with corruption, but rather, businesspersons' and country analysts' perceptions of it.

2. See, for example, Joe Kanekane, "Tolerance and Corruption in Contemporary Papua New Guinea," *National Research Institute Discussion Paper* No. 47 (Port Moresby, 2007), 23–26.

3. See, for example, Hengene Payani, "Bureaucratic Corruption in Papua New Guinea: Causes, Consequences and Remedies," in David Kavanamur, Charles Yala, and Quinton Clemens (eds.), *Building a Nation in Papua New Guinea: Views of the Post-Independence Generation* (Honolulu, 2005), 91–105.

4. *State* v. *Iori Veraga,* N2921 (2005).

5. See David Kombako, "Corruption as a Consequence of Cultural and Social Idiosyncrasies in a Developing Society," *National Research Institute Discussion Paper* No. 47 (Port Moresby, 2007), 27–38.

6. This conflict is discussed in Sinclair Dinnen, *Law & Order in a Weak State: Crime and Politics in Papua New Guinea* (Honolulu, 2001).

7. See Global Integrity Report at http://report.globalintegrity.org/Papua%20New%20Guinea/2007/scorecard (accessed 15 January 2009).

8. *Organic Law on the Duties and Responsibilities of Leadership* [Papua New Guinea] (16 September 1975), available at www.unhcr.org/refworld/docid/3ae6b54d10.html (accessed 11 February 2009).

9. Sections 87, 88, 92 and 97 of the Papua New Guinea Criminal Code.

10. The Audit Act (1989) adds to section 214 of the constitution by expanding the mandate and autonomy of the PNG Auditor General's Office. Under the Proceeds of Crime Act, money laundering and conspiracy to commit organized crime are illegal. The Public Finance Management Act legislates procedures regarding the Consolidated Revenue Fund and the Trust Fund, which are often under scrutiny in grand corruption cases. And the Electoral Reform Act provides for the integrity of elections.

11. The chief also manages the office and the division of work between the members.

12. At the request of the Ombudsman Commission, a Leadership Tribunal (court) is convened by the chief justice.

13. Papua New Guinea Constitution, sec. 214.

14. The FIU was created according to the 2005 Proceeds of Crime Act.

15. "Somare Snaps at Watchdog," *Post-Courier Online* (4 July 2008), available at www.postcourier.com.pg/20080704/frhome.htm (accessed 11 December 2008).

16. The referral was made on the eve of the chief ombudsman's retirement, and was immediately challenged before the court by the prime minister.

17. Asia Pacific Action Group, *Barnett Report: The Summary of the Report of the Commission of Inquiry into Aspects of the Timber Industry in Papua New Guinea* (Port Moresby, 1990).

18. Chief Ombudsman Ila Geno's keynote speech at the National Research Institute (28 April 2008).

19. Independent State of Papua New Guinea, *Audit Act 1989.* No 1 of 1989.

20. George Sullimann, "The Role of the Auditor-General," *National Research Institute Discussion Paper* No. 47 (Port Moresby, 2007), 39–43.

21. Todagia Kelola, "Government Arms Not Complying with Act," *Post-Courier* (18 April 2007), 5.

22. "Police Arrest Hami Yawari," *Post-Courier Online* (22 August 2008), available at www.postcourier.com.pg/20080822/news.htm (accessed 11 December 2008).

23. Transparency International, "Judicial Reform in PNG in Need of Political Will," in *Global Corruption Report 2007* (New York, 2007), 263–266.

24. See Albert Ayius and Ronald May (eds.), *Corruption in Papua New Guinea: Towards an Understanding of Issues* (Port Moresby, 2007). Also see Henry Okole and David Kavanamur, "Political Corruption in Papua New Guinea: Some Causes and Policy Lessons," *South Pacific Journal of Philosophy and Culture,* VII (2003), 7–36; Justice Sector Advisory Group, *Fighting Corruption and Promoting Integrity in Public Life in Papua New Guinea* (Port Moresby, 2005).

25. See the Papua New Guinea Leadership Code (National Public Service Code of Business Ethics and Conduct) as per the Public Services Management Act of 1995.

26. Susan-Rose Ackerman, *Corruption and Government: Causes, Consequences and Reform* (New York, 1999), 39–68 and 91–109.

27. Francis Fukuyama, "State-Building in the Solomon Islands" (memo, 9 July 2008).

28. The traditional political unit was smaller than any of the 800 linguistic or ethnic groups. See Dinnen, *Law & Order in a Weak State,* 175.

29. Not surprisingly, with the cultural diversity within the country, there is considerable variation on what a big man is. This portrayal may be more applicable to the Highlands than, for example, the Sepik region where a big man may face social pressure to be humble or at least not flaunt his wealth. For a more nuanced analysis of the

big man, see Bill Standish, *The 'Big-man' Model Reconsidered: Power Stratification in Chimbu* (Port Moresby, 1978).

30. Fukuyama (memo, 9 July 2008).

31. The main ethnic groups are Melanesian, Papuan, Negrito, Micronesian, and Polynesian.

32. While the PNG legal system does make provisions for custom, this does not mean that everything that is customary is acceptable. For example, while marriage custom is respected, practices such as domestic abuse are not condoned.

33. See discussion in Alphonse Gelu, "PNG A Failed State," *Post-Courier* (14 March 2007).

34. Ray Anere and Nicole Haley, *Election 2007 Domestic Observation Report,* Inter-Departmental Election Committee and Electoral Support Program (Port Moresby, 2008).

35. John Ackerman, "Social Accountability in the Public Sector: A Conceptual Discussion," *Social Development Paper* No. 82 (Washington, D.C., 2005). See also Anwar Shah (ed.), *Performance Accountability and Combating Corruption* (Washington, D.C., 2007).

36. Fukuyama (memo, 9 July 2008).

37. Enrique Peruzzotti and Catalina Smulovitz (eds.), *Enforcing the Rule of Law* (Pittsburgh, 2006).

38. Kelly Edmiston, "Fostering Subnational Autonomy and Accountability in Decentralized Developing Countries: Lessons from the Papua New Guinea Experience," *Public Administration and Development,* XXII (2002), 221–234.

39. The province of East New Britain's exceptionality may be attributable to greater resources and strong donor involvement following the natural disaster.

40. Peter Larmour and Manuhuia Barcham, "National Integrity Systems in Small Pacific Islands," *Public Administration and Development,* XXVI (2005), 174–186; Albert Mellam and Daniel Aloi, "National Integrity System Transparency International Country Study Report: Papua New Guinea, 2003," *Discussion Paper* No. 89 (Port Moresby, 2003).

41. National Research Institute's Leadership Summit on Good Governance, Parliament House, Port Moresby, 4–5 August 2008.

42. Government of Papua New Guinea, National Law and Justice Policy and Plan of Action 2005.

43. A bill on community courts was drafted in 2008. If enacted, it would strengthen village-level courts, which have extensive jurisdiction in matters arising from custom.

44. Maxine Pitts, *Crime, Corruption and Capacity in Papua New Guinea* (Canberra, 2002).

45. Merilee Grindle, "Good Enough Governance: Poverty Reduction and Reform in Developing Countries," *Governance,* XVII (2004), 525–548.

46. UNESCO Institute of Statistics, "UIS Statistics in Brief," available at http://stats. uis.unesco.org/unesco/TableViewer/document.aspx?ReportId=121&IF_Language=eng &BR_Country=5980 (accessed 11 December 2008).

47. Peter Larmour, "Transparency International and Policy Transfer in Papua New Guinea," *Pacific Economic Bulletin,* XVIII (2003), 115–120.

48. Arturo Escobar and Sonia Álvarez (eds.), *The Making of Social Movements in Latin America* (Boulder, 1992).

49. For a dynamic view of urban settlements, see Michael Goddard, *The Unseen City: Anthropological Perspectives on Port Moresby, Papua New Guinea* (Canberra, 2005).

ROTIMI T. SUBERU

10

The Travails of Nigeria's
Anti-Corruption Crusade

Since Nigeria's transition from military to civilian rule in 1999, the country has witnessed an unprecedented official campaign against political corruption. Whereas previous attempts to combat this endemic and systematic malaise were largely ad hoc, arbitrary, rhetorical, ineffectual, or counterproductive in nature or impact, the post-1999 anti-corruption campaign has involved the establishment or revitalization of three national anti-corruption agencies, namely, the Code of Conduct Bureau (CCB) and Code of Conduct Tribunal (CCT); the Independent Corrupt Practices and Other Related Offences Commission (ICPC); and the Economic and Financial Crimes Commission (EFCC). These agencies have spearheaded the unprecedented investigations, indictments, prosecutions, convictions, and dismissals of key public figures, such as the vice-president of the federation, the head of the national police force, the leadership of the National Assembly, federal ministers, and state governors for their corrupt behavior or abuse of office, thereby enhancing (albeit modestly) the country's global integrity and transparency indices.[1]

Yet, political corruption remains rife, endemic, persistent, and lethal in Nigeria. As claimed by Human Rights Watch in a report on Nigeria's fraudulent and violent 2007 elections: "the conduct of many public officials and government institutions is so pervasively marked by violence and corruption as to more resemble criminal activity than democratic governance."[2] Indeed, far from signaling the onset of an anti-corruption revolution in Nigeria, the record of the country's anti-corruption crusade since 1999 may illustrate the constraints and contradictions that can vex and stymie such campaigns in societies where corruption is entrenched within the political elite and anti-corruption bodies are not effectively insulated from manipulation by this elite.

This chapter looks at corruption from the top down and, therefore, complements the grassroots approach that Smith adopts in his chapter for this volume.[3] Ordinary Nigerians may be "active participants in the social reproduction of corruption," but the principal perpetrators are elite politicians at national and subnational levels.[4] The petty corruption that takes place ubiquitously in Nigeria is conspicuously trivial compared to the monumental corruption that is orchestrated at the upper reaches of the country's society and polity.

Indeed, a politico-institutional perspective on corruption in Nigeria provides a more proximate and somewhat less cynical and complacent analysis of this problem than the cultural and structural perspectives adopted by Smith and many other observers of Nigeria. The social reproduction of corruption argument is crucially valuable to highlight the cultural underpinnings of political corruption in Nigeria. Such foundations include the blurring of public and private roles, the sons-of-the-soil syndrome, and widespread expectations of gift giving, nepotism, and favoritism. This culture of corruption is structurally rooted in the country's ethnic fragmentation (reflecting its relative artificiality and infancy as a post-colonial state), economic underdevelopment, and attendant statism (the sweeping control of the state over the economy). Such statism has been profoundly aggravated by Nigeria's emergence as a major oil exporter since the 1970s. By placing enormous amounts of money at the disposal of governmental officials and political leaders, the country's oil wealth has fuelled political corruption and undermined transparency efforts. This wealth has also effectively aborted the fiscal nexus of accountability between state and society that is entailed by public taxation of the population, as distinct from governmental expropriation of natural resource rents. Yet, whatever may be its underlying structural foundations or cultural ramifications, the pervasive incidence or persistence of high-level political corruption clearly points to the absence of effective horizontal and vertical institutions of accountability that can expose, punish, and thus deter corruption.

Because such institutions are crucial but often lacking, this chapter focuses on the nature and roles of Nigeria's anti-corruption agencies, the impediments that have undermined their effectiveness and credibility, and the prospects for more effective anti-corruption reforms. Following an overview of the evolution of Nigeria's anti-corruption agencies, the chapter outlines the pervasiveness of corruption in Nigeria, identifies five key impediments to the effectiveness of the organizations that are designed to combat the problem, and concludes with a summary of the main findings and their implications.

The Evolution of Nigeria's Anti-Corruption Institutions

When it obtained its independence from Britain in 1960, Nigeria inherited British penal and criminal codes, in the North and South respectively, which included sections on corruption and the abuse of public office. Among other provisions, these sections criminalized certain corrupt activities, including false claims, extortion, the unlawful purchase of property, theft or misappropriation of the "property of the State," the soliciting or taking of gratification in respect of an official act, and other forms of abuse of office and breach of official trust by public servants. The codes prescribe substantial punishments for these infractions. For instance, under section 315 of the penal code, whoever "being in any manner entrusted with property . . . in his capacity as a public servant . . . commits criminal breach of trust in respect of that property shall be punished with imprisonment for a term which may extend to fourteen years and shall also be liable to a fine."

These codes have never been effectively enforced. Instead, Nigeria's political leaders as well as the "police, the prosecutors, and the courts all joined in the general perversion of public office to private ends, and the corrupt acts that the codes prohibited became endemic throughout Nigeria in every branch and institution of government at every level: local, state, and federal."[5] Such pervasive corruption has become a major driver of political instability in Nigeria, as ostensibly corrective military officers have overthrown conspicuously corrupt civilian political elites only for other soldiers to remove such officers for the same malfeasance. In this way, the campaign against corruption became a "rhetorical centerpiece" of successive Nigerian governments.[6]

Nonetheless, the rhetorical strictures against corruption by rival political elites did produce several formal attempts to address this scourge. Such efforts include, for example, General Yakubu Gowon's 1966 criminal justice decree that sought to clarify and strengthen the country's statutory anti-corruption provisions; the establishment in 1975 of a Public Complaints Commission to investigate and redress complaints of unlawful behavior by public officers; the incorporation of the CCB and CCT into successive Nigerian Constitutions since the 1979 basic law for the Second Nigerian Republic (1979–1983); and the establishment of special panels that investigated, sentenced, and recovered public property from corrupt public officers, including several former military and civilian governors, in 1975 and 1984, respectively. Other important examples include the promotion of elaborate public education programs, ranging from the largely rhetorical Ethical Revolution policy of the Shehu Shagari civilian administration in the Second Republic to the draconian War

Against Indiscipline and Corruption (WAIC) of Mohammed Buhari's military administration (1984–1985); and the appointment in 1989, during the aborted transition to a Third Nigerian Republic, of a National Committee on Corruption and other Economic Crimes, which provided the inspiration for the inauguration, more than a decade later, of the ICPC and EFCC.[7]

The most systematic effort to combat political corruption in Nigeria's post-independence history began in 1999, with the transition from military rule to the Fourth Nigerian Republic and the inauguration of Olusegun Obasanjo (Nigeria's former military ruler from 1976 to 1979) as civilian president. Obasanjo's principal anti-corruption initiative during his two constitutional terms (1999–2007) revolved around the activities of the two anti-corruption agencies that he statutorily established, namely, the ICPC and EFCC. Along with the preexisting, constitutionally entrenched CCB and CCT, the ICPC and EFCC constitute the country's present institutional arsenal for combating high-level political corruption.

The CCB and CCT

Originally established under the 1979 Nigerian Constitution, the CCB and CCT are the country's oldest anti-corruption agencies. They are also the only anti-corruption bodies to be specifically mentioned in the Nigerian Constitution. The CCB and CCT are mandated to enforce a constitutionally prescribed code of conduct for public officials, including the periodic declaration of assets, the prohibition of foreign bank accounts, and the avoidance of conflicts of interest. Largely ineffectual before the establishment of the ICPC and EFCC, the CCB and CCT have become more active in investigating and reporting the false declaration of assets, the fraudulent acquisition of properties, or the illicit operation of foreign accounts by public functionaries, especially by state governors.

The ICPC

Established under the Corrupt Practices and Other Related Offences Act of 2000, the ICPC is empowered to "receive and investigate complaints from members of the public on allegations of corrupt practices and . . . prosecute the offenders." The ICPC is also required to initiate and supervise the review of public practices and procedures that aid malfeasance and to educate and mobilize the public against bribery, corruption, and related offences. Between 2000 and 2005, the ICPC prosecuted 49 cases, involving 104 individuals; established Anti-Corruption and Transparency Monitoring Units (ACTUs) in 145 government agencies; and launched numerous anti-corruption enlightenment and mobilization programs in public and private organizations across the country.[8]

The EFCC

Established in 2004 with the prodding of the G-7-based Financial Action Task Force (FATF) on Money Laundering, the EFCC is by far the most effective (and controversial) anti-corruption agency in Nigeria's history. Its purpose is to prevent, detect, investigate, and prosecute any cases of economic and financial crimes in Nigeria. Under the youthful and energetic leadership of its pioneer chair, Nuhu Ribadu, a lawyer and serving police officer, the EFCC had, by 2006, investigated more than 2,000 cases; made more than 2,000 arrests; prosecuted more than 300 cases, achieved 88 convictions, and recovered more than $5 billion in stolen assets and monies.[9]

Obasanjo's selective use and partisan manipulation of the EFCC in the months leading up to the rigged 2007 elections, however, "destroyed much of the institution's credibility and effectiveness as both a deterrent and a mechanism of accountability."[10] What is more, after the elections as the EFCC moved to prosecute former governors (who had lost their constitutional immunity from prosecution after serving their terms in office), the EFCC came under intense political scrutiny designed to cripple the agency and frustrate the prosecution of the former governors. Consequently, Ribadu was removed by the post-Obasanjo administration of President Umaru Yar'Adua in 2007. Farida Waziri, a lawyer and retired police officer, who was alleged to be a "consultant" to some of the high-profile politicians that the EFCC was attempting to prosecute for corruption, replaced him.[11] This brazen political reshuffling in the EFCC effectively aborted, or at least severely compromised, one of the boldest institutional efforts to combat the malaise about endemic corruption in Nigeria.

Endemic Corruption

Although there are no systematic estimations of the extent to which corruption exists in Nigeria, few will disagree with Soyinka, Nigeria's Nobel Prize–winning writer and irrepressible social critic, that the country "has become a byword for the most breathtaking scam in high places, for endemic corruption, a contempt for accountability and transparency, and the abuse of national resources in the pursuit of personal and party power consolidation."[12] According to ICPC Chairman, Justice Emmanuel Ayoola, some $500 billion, or more than two-thirds of Nigeria's oil earnings, have been stolen from the country's coffers since 1960.[13] This amount includes the estimated $3.6 billion that General Sani Abacha personally looted from the national treasury during his brutal reign as Nigeria's military dictator from 1993 to 1997. Although corruption has probably been more intense under military rule in Nigeria, civilian rule has witnessed more extensive revelations of official malfeasance, because of the obvious greater civil and political freedoms afforded by non-authoritarian rule. To focus on the more recent experience of party politics in Nigeria, the following sections highlight a selection of major reports of political corruption at the federal, state, and local levels since the country returned to civilian rule in 1999.

The Federal Government

The executive, legislative, and judicial branches of the Nigerian federal administration are incontrovertibly enmeshed in corruption, including mutual recriminations of malfeasance. In 2006, for instance, President Obasanjo accused Vice-President Atiku Abubakar of using the multi-million dollar Petroleum Technology Development Fund (PTDF), which was under Atiku's supervision, to fund the business operations of Vice-President Atiku's friends. A committee within the Nigerian Senate pronounced Atiku guilty of aiding the diversion of monies from the PTDF. But Atiku responded with several damning allegations against Obasanjo's misuse of the same fund. Such accusations included the authorization of the payment of "250 million naira of public funds" to Obasanjo's "personal lawyer," as well as "the scandalous lending of billions of naira of PTDF money" to a bank from which the president subsequently obtained "a personal loan of 200 million naira" in an implicit "trade-off" for the lending.[14]

Several federal cabinet ministers were indicted for corruption after 1999. In 2003, for instance, Sunday Afolabi, Mohammed Shata, and Hussaini Akwanga, the two former erstwhile ministers and the latter permanent secretary in the Ministry of Internal Affairs, were charged with taking bribes for a $214 million government contract with the French firm Sagem SA, involving the ultimately unsuccessful National Identity Cards Project.[15] Nigerian federal ministers and officials also reportedly received $182 million from Halliburton and $14 million from Siemens as bribes for the award of contracts in Nigeria's gas and telecommunications sectors, respectively.[16] In 2005, Education Minister Fabian Osuji was dismissed for giving a bribe of $400,000 to Senate President Adolphus Wabara (who was also forced to step down as Senate president) in a bid to get the National Assembly to approve more funds for the Education Ministry.[17] A month later in the same year, the housing minister, Alice Osomo, was fired for authorizing the sale of hundreds of government properties at below market value to top officials.[18] Similarly in a statement in 2008 to a Senate committee probing a lands allocation scandal in the Federal Capital Territory (FCT), Nasir el-Rufai revealed that, as minister of the FCT, he approved the allocation of prime plots in the territory to his brothers, nieces, in-laws, and three spouses, and to the president's private company, Obasanjo Farms.[19] And in 2008, the Minister of Health Adenike Grange and other key officials from the ministry were charged with siphoning more than $1 million from the ministry's budget through fictitious and frivolous contracts.[20]

As it is the case with the federal political executive and ministries in Nigeria, the country's national legislature is extensively and intensively enmeshed in corrupt practices. Described by one prominent columnist as a "consortium of certified crooks," members of the National Assembly have featured prominently in the breach of public trust and the misappropriation of national resources.[21] Salisu Buhari and Evans Enwerem, respectively the first Senate president and Speaker of the House of Representatives under the 1999 constitution, were forced to resign for forgery and perjury.[22] Enwerem's successor, Chuba Okadigbo, was indicted and impeached in 2000 for awarding inflated procurement contracts in the National Assembly to companies linked with assembly members.[23] Similarly, Patricia Etteh, the first Speaker of the House under Yar'Adua, was forced to step down as speaker, following her indictment for the awarding of inflated, multi-million dollar contracts for the renovation of two official residences (her own and that of the deputy speaker) and the purchase of twelve cars.[24]

Compared to the federal executive and legislature, the Nigerian judiciary is relatively less tainted by massive corruption. The Supreme Court, in particular, has attracted some praise for its relative professionalism, neutrality, integrity, and credibility in adjudicating intergovernmental, electoral, and other political disputes, despite sustained and brazen attempts by the politicians to co-opt and corrupt the judiciary. Although the independent Supreme Court has remained a beacon of integrity, the lower tiers of the country's judiciary are often "corrupt, inept, and politicized."[25] The courts have been periodically implicated in scandalous activities, including bribe-taking and the pronouncement of spurious, apparently corruptly induced, judgments. An example of such a judgment is the "curious" and unconstitutional "perpetual injunction," issued by the Federal High Court in Port Harcourt, restraining the EFCC from pursuing corruption charges against former "Rivers State Governor Peter Odili [who] presided over the theft and mismanagement of several billion dollars in oil revenues during eight years in office."[26] Judicial corruption has, moreover, affected key administrative institutions that were designed to promote professionalism and transparency in the justice sector. In 2008, for instance, Justice Timothy Oyeyipo, the administrator of the National Judicial Institute (NJI) and former chief judge of Kwara State, was removed from the NJI for diverting an estimated 1.4 billion naira of the institute's funds into a secret account.[27]

A high-profile case of corruption in a law enforcement institution in Nigeria involved police Inspector General Tafa Balogun, who was convicted in 2005 of stealing more than $121 million from the police budget.[28] Corruption is also rampant in Nigeria's other quasi-military and military-affiliated institutions, including the customs, immigrations, and armed services. In early 2008, for instance, the federal government officially acknowledged that the country's "military officers" provided assorted firearms from the Nigerian armory to militant groups that were involved in hostage-taking and oil-bunkering in the Niger Delta.[29]

State Governments

The most spectacular cases of corruption in Nigeria since 1999 have involved the state governors. Under Nigeria's oil-centric federal system, the country's thirty-six states statutorily receive 24 percent of monies in the "federation account," which comprises all major centrally collected revenues. The states also effectively control another 20 percent of federation account revenues that are earmarked for the country's 774 constitutionally designated local government areas. Between 1999 and 2007, thirty-one governors were indicted or brought under investigation by the country's three anti-corruption bodies for various breaches of the public trust, including embezzlement, money laundering, false declaration of assets, maintaining foreign bank accounts in contravention of the code of conduct for public officers, and the illegal acquisition of properties in Nigeria and abroad.

One governor, Diepreye Alamieyeseigha of Bayelsa State, was sentenced in 2007 to two years in jail after pleading guilty to charges of corruption and money laundering, including the defrauding of Bayelsa State of 241 million pounds and the illicit acquisition of eleven properties in Nigeria and South Africa.[30] Other governors serving between 1999 and 2007 that were formally charged with comparable acts of corruption include Joshua Dariye of Plateau State, Peter Fayose of Ekiti, James Ibori of Delta, Lucky Igbinedion of Edo, Orji Kalu of Abia, Chimaroke Nnamani of Enugu, Jolly Nyame of Taraba, and Saminu Turaki of Jigawa.

Dariye was indicted for looting "about N1.5 billion belonging to Plateau State" and corruptly disbursing "N1.1 billion to seven beneficiaries," including the ruling Peoples Democratic Party (PDP).[31] Fayose was found "guilty of siphoning state funds into personal bank accounts and receiving kickbacks."[32] EFFC investigations of Delta's finances "uncovered several questionable payments to companies, associates, and aides of Ibori, running into billions of naira . . . in the most brazen and monumental case of looting [of a] State treasury by any chief executive."[33] Furthermore, among the 103 counts that the EFCC leveled against Ibori was his attempted $15 million bribe for EFCC officials to drop the case against him.[34]

Igbinedion was arraigned on "a 142 count charge of stealing, corruption, and abuse of office" involving about "N2.9 billion, belonging to Edo State," including federal "statutory allocations" to local governments in the state.[35] Following a controversial plea bargain he struck with the EFCC at the Enugu High Court in early 2009, Igbinedion pleaded guilty to the offence of false declaration of assets and was fined 3.5 million naira and made to forfeit three properties.[36] Kalu, according to the EFCC's 107-count charge against him, "used the machinery of Slok, his private company, to launder about N3 billion . . . of Abia [S]tate funds."[37] Nnamani illegally maintained "20 secret bank accounts" in the United States and "abused his office by diverting public funds" worth "about N5.4 billion" to "acquire no fewer than 172 assets which include radio stations and higher [educational] institutions" in Nigeria.[38]

Among other charges, Nyame allegedly received "gratification of N80 million in 2005 from a contractor," "pocketed" N32.3 million from a budget dedicated to "preparations for the visit of President Obasanjo to Taraba [S]tate," and "allocated the sum of N250 million for the purchase of stationery for government offices out of which he . . . diverted about N180 million for his personal use."[39] The EFCC indicted Turaki for laundering "N33.6 billion in one year [2006]" and "stealing $20 million within the same period."[40]

Although Alamaisegha, Dariye, and Fayose were impeached for corruption, only Alamaisegha was formally convicted and sentenced, while Igbinedion was allowed "to escape with a slap on the wrist [which] can only encourage more people to loot the public till."[41] Meanwhile the judicial proceedings against the remaining seven indicted governors were, by early 2009, paralyzed by the political emasculation of the EFCC and deliberate judicial torpidity. Worse than such maneuverings, no visible progress was made in the cases of more than twenty other former governors indicted or under investigation by the ICPC, CCB, and EFCC. Rather, Nnamani and Turaki, among several other governors and politicians linked with corruption, won elections that put them in the Nigerian senate in 2007.

Local Governments

To reiterate, Nigeria's 774 local governments statutorily receive 20 percent of centrally distributed oil revenues, in comparison with the 56 percent and 24 percent by the central and the state governments, respectively. A significant proportion of the statutory allocations to the localities is hijacked by the federal and especially by the state governments "for their own use—without any legal justification," and often in an opaque, arbitrary, and openly corrupt manner.[42] For example, President Obasanjo in 2006 unconstitutionally orchestrated the payment of 7.4 billion naira of local government statutory allocations into a Police Equipment Fund (PEF), which was subsequently "shockingly converted" from an official presidential committee into a scandal-infested non-governmental organization under the control of the president's brother-in-law, Chief Kenny Martins.[43] Such brazen expropriation of local finances from the top reinforced a culture of financial impunity at the local government level, where corruption "assumed astronomical proportions," permeating "the entire fabric of the system."[44]

Jones Aluko, a scholar and former local-level administrator has documented the various strategies by which local government chairmen, councilors, career officers, and traditional rulers perpetrate corruption in Nigerian localities. Such corrupt acts include: regular awards of inflated, frivolous, or fictitious construction or renovation contracts; reckless extra-budgetary spending on trivialities such as travelling allowances, hospitality, and gifts; the siphoning of public funds through the abandonment, non-execution, or poor execution of approved projects; the use of the security vote, an opaque budget line under the discretionary control of the local government chairman to channel public funds into private pockets and diverse forms of patronage; the direct embezzlement and theft of council funds and properties, including generators, refrigerators, furniture, and drugs; the diversion of user fees from local stalls and motor parks into private pockets; and politicization and corruption of staff recruitments through the subordination of the formal merit-based standards to personal, patronage, communal, and other informal considerations.[45]

Indeed, a 2007 Human Rights Watch report on local government corruption in Rivers State highlights several examples of gross misallocation and outright theft of local-level funds in the state that included, for example, the illegal allocation to the chair of Khana's local government in 2005 of salary and allowances worth $376,000, which "w[ere] nearly half the total amount allocated for the wages and allowances of Khana's 325 health-sector workers"; the allocation in 2006 to the chair of Tai's local government of a security vote of $300,000, which exceeded the council's total capital budgets for either health or education; and the illegal awarding during 2005–2006 by the chairman of Opobo Nkoro's local government of $91,000 worth of construction contracts to himself.[46]

As a result of widespread corruption, Nigerian local governments, even more than the state and federal administrations, have acquired a reputation as "huge drain pipes of waste," patronage, and embezzlements.[47] Indeed, as claimed by EFCC chairwoman Farida Waziri, "Local governments have become so far removed from the lives of the people to a point where some chief executives of local councils no longer reside in the domains they were elected to administer. They drive to the council headquarters in their jeeps from the state capitals or the Federal capital Territory, pay salaries and share other monies and disappear until it is time to share the next subvention."[48]

Yet, except for a 2002 conviction obtained by the ICPC against local government Chairman Emmanuel Egwuba and the often politically motivated probes and arbitrary sacking of elected local government councils by (equally venal) state governments, corruption at the local government level has persisted virtually unchecked since 1999. Neither the intensification of the crusade against corruption as a rhetorical pastime of the Nigerian political leadership, nor the establishment of the ICPC and EFCC as novel anti-corruption agencies has done much to stem the tide of corruption at the local level or at the upper tiers of the Nigerian federal system.

Problems with Nigeria's Anti-Corruption Institutions

The effectiveness of Nigeria's anti-corruption agencies and campaigns has been stymied by at least five interrelated political or institutional impediments.

The Absence of Political Insulation

A major debilitating feature of Nigeria's anti-corruption agencies (and of other sensitive bodies, including the electoral administration) is their appointment, supervision, and funding by the "very politicians whom they [are] supposed to regulate."[49] The president, subject to confirmation by the Senate, appoints the members of the CCB, ICPC, and EFCC. What is more, according to section 3 (2) of the EFCC Act:

A member of the Commission may at any time be removed by the President for inability to discharge the functions of his office (whether arising from infirmity of mind or body or any other cause) or for misconduct or if the President is satisfied that it is not in the interest of the Commission or the interest of the public that the member should continue in office.[50]

In addition, the administrative secretaries of these agencies are direct appointees of the president, and the bodies are funded mainly through the federal government budget, which is approved by the National Assembly. Although they are not formally subject to the direction or control of any external person or authority in the discharge of their functions, these agencies have invariably been hobbled by their institutional dependence on the governing class in general, and the presidency specifically. The proximity of the EFCC to the presidency, in particular, has facilitated its political desecration and emasculation, and tarnished its credibility as an autonomous and non-partisan instrument of accountability.

A more judicious institutional design would have been to entrust the appointment and operational direction of the anti-corruption agencies to an autonomous council of civil society organizations or to the independent judiciary. While the president, subject to confirmation by the Senate, also formally appoints the Nigerian federal judiciary, the justices are not unilaterally removable by the chief executive. More important, the original nominations and recommendations for appointment to the bench are made by two non-partisan constitutional bodies, specifically, the Federal Judicial Service Commission and the National Judicial Council. Both bodies are dominated by serving or retired jurists and are headed by the chief justice of the federation. This substantial political insulation has largely prevented the judiciary, unlike the anti-corruption bodies, from completely plunging into political impotence or partisan disrepute.

Conflicted, Uncommitted, or Subversive Political Leadership

Nigeria's recent anti-corruption campaign owes a lot to the personal zeal and commitment of Obasanjo, a former chair of Transparency International's Advisory Council. In his inaugural speech as civilian president in 1999, Obasanjo described corruption as "the greatest single bane of our society," adding that no "society can achieve anything near its full potential if it allows corruption to become the full-blown cancer it has become in Nigeria." "Rampant corruption," he vowed, will be "stamped out," and there "will be no sacred cows."[51] Indeed, Obasanjo went ahead to promote several anti-corruption initiatives, including the establishment of the ICPC and EFCC, the introduction of the Budget Monitoring and Price Intelligence Unit (BMPIU) or the "due process" mechanism in the federal administration, and the ratification of the Extractive Industries Transparency Initiative (EITI). Yet, Obasanjo's anti-corruption policy was partly rhetorical, plainly conflicted, and increasingly politically motivated.

While he supported the establishment and development of the ICPC and EFCC, for instance, Obasanjo increasingly turned these bodies into instruments of political vendetta against his opponents within and outside the PDP, especially his estranged deputy, Atiku. At the same time, Obasanjo hardly lived up to his professions of total and undiluted opposition to corruption. Rather, he quickly reneged on a promise publicly to declare his assets, failed to confirm the appointment of an acting auditor-general of the federation, schemed corruptly (but unsuccessfully) to set up his third term run for the presidency, facilitated the rigging of the 2007 elections, and cultivated or maintained intimate political ties to notoriously corrupt political "godfathers" such as the Uba brothers (Chris and Andy) of Anambra State and Lamidi Adedibu of Oyo State. More specifically, Obasanjo was repeatedly linked to various abuses of the public trust, including unconscionable land grabs in Abuja, opaque acquisitions of huge personal shares in major corporate enterprises, the authorization of questionable privatizations and public contracts, and the brazen extortion of money from federal government contractors and public institutions to fund his personal library project.[52]

President Yar'Adua's approach to the problem of corruption has been similarly conflicted and ultimately even more fatal for the anti-corruption campaign. In his inaugural address in 2007, Yar'Adua acknowledged the flaws of the 2007 elections and pledged his commitment to electoral reform, the rule of law, and corruption control. Thereafter, in a nationally unprecedented act of transparency, Yar'Adua publicly declared his financial assets, an example that was eventually (if reluctantly) followed by Vice-President Goodluck Jonathan, but not by other members of the federal cabinet. Yet, Yar'Adua ultimately succumbed to pressures from Ibori and other corrupt former governors, who actively funded or supported his presidential campaign, to thwart the EFCC's anti-corruption campaign.

First, the administration announced that the EFCC and ICPC should "initiate criminal proceedings with the consent and approval" of the minister of justice and attorney general of the federation, Michael Aondoakaa, a politician and former legal counsel to some politicians under investigation by the

EFCC.[53] The attorney general's attempted usurpation of the independent prosecutorial powers of the anti-corruption agencies was generally regarded as abusive and excessive, especially as his office already enjoys the controversial constitutional power of *nolle prosequi*, which allows him to authorize the discontinuation of any ongoing criminal prosecution. Second, in the face of widespread public opposition to this attempt to bring the anti-corruption agencies under the direct control of Aondoakaa, the Yar'Adua administration reaffirmed the prosecutorial autonomy of the agencies but then moved stealthily to ease the highly effective Ribadu out of the EFCC by asking him to proceed on a mandatory course for senior police officers. This ousting was followed by a purge of many of Ribadu's closest associates in the EFCC, and by Ribadu's demotion (from the rank of assistant inspector-general of police to deputy commissioner) and his subsequent dismissal from the police force for alleged insubordination. Third, Aondoakaa promoted the appointment (by the president) of Waziri, a fellow ethnic Tiv from Benue State, as Ribadu's successor. Finally, Aondoakaa continued his policy of shielding high-profile politicians from prosecution for corruption by refusing to honor Nigeria's obligations, under the Mutual Legal Assistance Agreement with Britain, to assist the British government in combating financial and economic crimes committed abroad by Nigerian public officers, including ex-Governor Ibori.[54]

Indeed, if the anti-corruption postures of Obasanjo and Yar'Adua were conflicted, the attitude of much of the political class betrayed a lack of enthusiasm for, or a determination to subvert, the campaign against corruption. In particular, the National Assembly and several state governors launched systematic legal and political challenges designed to ensure the obliteration or incapacitation of the anti-corruption agencies. Specifically, the National Assembly tried to enact a new anti-corruption law that would have weakened the investigating and prosecuting powers of the ICPC (following investigations by the commission in 2002 of the leadership and several members of the assembly over allegations of corrupt practices). The state governments, for their part, challenged the constitutionality of the ICPC in the Supreme Court. Supported by Ben Nwabueze, a leading constitutional scholar and former federal minister of education, the state governments claimed that the central government's establishment of a federation-wide anti-corruption body was contrary to the states' autonomy under the country's federal system.[55] This claim was made in spite of the overwhelming funding of the states by centrally collected revenues, as well as the explicit constitutional mandate for the federal government to establish and regulate authorities in the federation to achieve certain fundamental objectives, including the abolition of "corrupt practices and the abuse of power."[56] Although the attempted statutory emasculation or constitutional invalidation of the ICPC by the National Assembly and the state governments were ultimately unsuccessful, they underscored the intensity of political opposition to the anti-corruption campaign.

Lack of Critical Human, Technical, and Financial Resources

The ambivalent or hostile attitude of the political class to the anti-corruption campaign has left the anti-corruption bodies under-resourced in financial, technical, and human terms. The CCB and CCT, for instance, are moribund because they suffer from "paucity of funding," "inadequate office accommodation," "low staff strength," and "derelict and dilapidated infrastructures."[57] Similarly, the 2000–2005 progress report of the ICPC lamented:

> Inadequate funding is a major constraint. . . . An examination of the pattern of proposed budgets and actual amounts approved and released shows that year in and out, releases fall grossly short of proposals. . . . The untimely release of the approved funds also constitutes an impediment to the execution of the Commission's programs. [All] operational departments and units are grossly understaffed. . . . The Commission's library lacks the relevant materials to sufficiently meet the actual needs of the staff, lawyers and non-lawyers alike. . . . Most staff of the Commission are yet to receive adequate basic and specialist training required for good performance of their job. . . . Investigators are also constrained in the retrieval of documentary evidence due to lack of capacity-enhancing equipment such as a forensic laboratory. . . . Non-computerization of . . . official records and case files hampers information storage and retrieval and oftentimes leads to delay in information sharing.[58]

These resource gaps have often required the intervention of international donors: "ICPC's 30-minute television program 'Fighting Corruption,' which was cancelled in 2002 due to paucity of funds, was renewed in 2003 with partial funding from an international donor agency."[59] The EFCC alone has received more than $37 million from the European Union and other external donors for projects such as the establishment of a training and research institute, a financial intelligence unit, IT infrastructure, a forensic laboratory, and a crime data center.[60] While it has been critical in salvaging the anti-corruption program from abysmal failure, this external assistance has invariably raised questions regarding the local ownership and long-term sustainability of the program.

The Alienation of Civil Society

Despite their vulnerability to the corruption and fragmentation that plague the country, Nigerian civil society groups and organizations have been in the forefront of the campaign to promote transparency and accountability. These groups include Transparency in Nigeria (TIN); Integrity; Zero-Corruption Coalition (ZCC); Human Rights Law Services (Huri-Laws); Academic Staff Union of Universities (ASUU); Catholic Commission for Peace, Justice, and Development; Civil Liberties Organization (CLO); the Nigerian Labor Congress (NLC); activists within the Nigerian Bar Association (NBA); and Nigeria's numerous private media organizations.

Among other anti-corruption initiatives, these organizations have proposed and drafted new legislation, including a whistleblowers law and a Freedom of Information (FOI) Act, designed to promote accountability and transparency in Nigeria. Indeed, following sustained advocacy and lobbying by civil society, the National Assembly passed a FOI bill in 2007. However, the bill suffered a major setback when Obasanjo withheld his assent and the assembly could not override his veto until the end of its constitutional term in May 2007. Obasanjo's decision reflected widespread suspicion within the Nigerian political class that a FOI bill would impede the preservation of politically sensitive state secrets, undermine national security, and give Nigeria's already irrepressible and sometimes sensational media further license to embarrass and harass public officers. For Nigeria's civil society organizations, however, the non-ratification of a FOI bill is symptomatic of the government's insincerity in its anti-corruption campaign, since "the unacceptable level of graft in the polity is traceable to the ability and capacity of public officers and their accomplices to cover their tracks by denying the public access to official records."[61]

Nigerian civil society was further alienated from the official anti-corruption campaign by serving or retired functionaries' domination over anti-corruption agencies, with little or no representation for independent interests or organizations within the society; by Obasanjo's selective and vindictive prosecution of the anti-corruption crusade, including the use of the EFCC to undermine the credibility and competitiveness of the 2007 elections; by Yar'Adua's displacement of Ribadu from the EFCC; and by the EFCC's subsequent failure effectively to continue or pursue corruption charges against several politicians.

Ribadu's removal, humiliation, and persecution provoked broad condemnation from the Nigerian public. "Instead of reinforcing the autonomy of an organization that is clearly dedicated to probity and political integrity," wrote Soyinka in his reaction to the removal, "notice has been sent to all four corners of the nation and to the international community that, at the slightest threat to the hegemony of corrupt rule, the credibility of even the most laudable institutions will be eroded."[62] "Ribadu," according to Fawhinmi, Nigeria's leading civil rights lawyer, "waged a war against corruption, graft, stealing and money laundering . . . in the corridors of power. In return, the regime of Yar'Adua decided to wage an unrelenting war against the anti-graft war."[63] Nigerian civil society groups were especially concerned that Ribadu's exit would end the EFCC's prosecutions and investigations of high-profile politicians. For example, the ZCC stated in 2008 that it was "concerned that some former and current public officers who have been indicted for corruption and whose cases have been fully investigated have not been charged to court."[64]

The Absence or Weakness of Complementary Reforms

Nigeria's 1999 transition from autocracy to democracy and the civilian administration's subsequent creation of new anti-corruption institutions, as well as the enunciation of associated governance reforms, were not accompanied by critically required complementary changes. Rather, the inadequacy or incompleteness of Obasanjo's reform agenda were underscored by the continued impotence of public audit institutions, the abortion of the freedom of information legislation, the absence of significant progress in police sector reforms, the non-enforcement of political campaign financing regulations and, most crucially, the political subordination of electoral administration, leading to the monumental corruption in the electoral processes in the states and nationally.

One area of continuity with the impunity of Nigeria's authoritarian past is the constitutional immunity from prosecution (although not investigation) for corrupt practices that serving political chief executives enjoy. President Yar'Adua, among others, has singled out this immunity as an undesirable feature of the current constitutional framework and a primary candidate for future constitutional reform. Another glaring example of the lack of complementary, democratic anti-corruption reform involves the role of the Code of Conduct Bureau, which is constitutionally required to make declarations of officials' assets "available for inspection by any citizen of Nigeria on such terms as the National Assembly may prescribe."[65] Yet, precisely because the National Assembly has failed to enact the required complementary legislation, the bureau has continued to deny public access to these records. Furthermore, in the absence of the required act, the bureau has established "onerous provisions that tend to discourage members of the public from making enquiries about declaration of assets made by public officers."[66]

The severest instance of non-reform in Nigeria, however, involves the electoral administration, which continues to be characterized by the corrupt manipulation of politically recruited, but so-called independent, electoral commissions at national and state levels. As of early 2009, corrupt politicians have been able to use their appointments and control of the electoral administration to deny voters a voice in the electoral process, to acquire illicit access to state resources, and to suborn or subvert key institutions, including the legislature and judiciary. As long as the basic electoral process for installing or replacing political office-holders remains mired in fraud, abuse, and impunity, so long will political corruption remain an endemic and intractable feature of Nigerian governance.

Conclusion

The momentum of anti-corruption reform engendered by Nigeria's 1999 transition from military to civilian rule underscores democracy's institutional potential to promote political accountability and transparency and rein in elites' malfeasance. But Nigeria's democracy remains deeply flawed and corrupted. Nigeria's new anti-corruption agencies have achieved only limited (but nevertheless significant) success largely because they have not been adequately protected from the corrupt political class that they are designed to restrain, and because their establishment has not been accompanied by complementary institutional reforms.

Although it is unrealistic to expect the country's current corrupt civilian elite to alter the existing institutional underpinnings of its power, it is possible to envisage a constituency for change and reform of civil society, the political opposition, enlightened factions of the ruling party (for example, the so-called integrity group in the current Nigerian National Assembly), and external development partners. Moreover, given the destabilization of and violent conflict in regions of Nigeria that are engendered by corruption (especially in the restive, oil-rich Niger Delta), incentives for stronger anti-corruption reforms can come from the collective stakes that Nigeria's political and civil society should have in preventing the collapse of democracy, the return of the military, or the disintegration of the state.

As recognized by the Anti-Corruption Reforms Committee of the 2005 National Political Reform Conference, Nigeria's "foundation and superstructure have become permeated by corruption to such an extent that this evil has become a threat to its very existence."[67] The committee proposed or reiterated the following reform measures, among others, for strengthening the country's anti-corruption campaign: the publication of public officers' declarations of assets, the removal of the constitutional immunity for political chief executives, the nomination of members of anti-corruption agencies by civil society groups (Nigeria Labor Congress, Nigerian Bar Association, Institute of Chartered Accountants, Academic Staff Union of Universities, etc.), the coordination and harmonization of the activities of the anti-corruption agencies as well as provisions for their adequate funding, and the streamlining and facilitation of current processes for the litigation and adjudication of corruption offences. Along with electoral reforms, through the political insulation of the electoral administration, which should be modeled after the country's relatively independent judiciary, these institutional reform measures can help to restrain and reverse the malaise of political corruption that plagues Nigeria.

Notes

1. Nigeria's Corruption Perceptions Index (CPI) score improved from 1.6 in 1999 to 2.7 in 2008. Its ranking on the index also improved from 98th out of 99 countries in 1999 to 121st out of 180 in 2008. Similarly, Nigeria's overall global public integrity index improved from "weak" in 2004 to "moderate" in 2006. See Transparency International, CPI reports, 1996–2008, available at www.transparency.org (accessed 26 January 2009); Global Integrity, "Nigeria," available at www.globalintegrity.org/reports/2006/nigeria/index (accessed 11 May 2008).

2. Human Rights Watch, *Criminal Politics: Violence, "Godfathers" and Corruption in Nigeria* (New York, 2007), 1.

3. Daniel Jordan Smith, "The Paradoxes of Popular Participation in Corruption in Nigeria," chapter 11 in this volume.

4. Ibid., 284.

5. Philip Ostien and M. J. Umaru, "Changes in the Law in Sharia States Aimed at Suppressing Social Vices," in Philip Ostien (ed.), *Sharia Implementation in Northern Nigeria: Sanitizing Society* (Ibadan, 2007), 15.

6. Human Rights Watch, *Chop Fine: The Human Rights Impact of Local Government Corruption and Mismanagement in Rivers State, Nigeria* (New York, 2007), 94.

7. See Okechukwu Oko, "Subverting the Scourge of Corruption in Nigeria: A Reform Prospectus," *New York University Journal of International Law and Politics*, XXXIV (2001–2002), 397–473.

8. See Independent Corrupt Practices and Other Related Offences Commission (ICPC), *Progress Report, September 2000–July 2005* (Abuja, 2005), ii.

9. Nuhu Ribadu, "Interim Investigation Report on Cases of Financial Misappropriation and Money Laundering Against Some States and Local Governments," Text of a Presentation to the Nigerian Senate, Abuja, 27 September 2006, 3.

10. Human Rights Watch, *Criminal Politics*, 49.

11. "New EFCC Boss, Waziri, Stood Surety for Akume; Accused of Being Consultant to Ibori, Marwa, Others," *Sunday Tribune* (1 June 2008), available at www.tribune.com.ng/01062008/news/news3.html (accessed 31 May 2008).

12. Wole Soyinka, "Exit Ribadu," available at www.nigerianmuse.com/opessays (accessed 24 May 2008).

13. See Tony Akowe, "ICPC Boss: Officials Falsify Assets Declaration," *The Nation* (14 May 2008), available at www.thenationonlineng.com (accessed 14 May 2008); Segun Olatunji, "Banks Aid Looting of Public Treasury, Says ICPC," *Punch* (14 May 2008), available at www.punchng.com (accessed 14 May 2008).

14. Azimazi Momoh Jimoh, "Atiku Alleges Massive Looting of PTDF Funds," *The Guardian* (19 December 2006), available at http://ngrguardainnews.com (accessed 4 September 2008).

15. Lilian Ekeanyanwu, Shina Loremikan, and John Ikubaje, *National Integrity Systems TI Country Study Report Nigeria 2004* (Berlin, 2004), 16.

16. See Akanimo Sampson, "Halliburton: How Government Officials Were Bribed With $182m," *The Nation* (6 September 2008), available at www.thenationonlineng.com (accessed 6 September 2008); "Nigeria Probes Siemens Bribe Case," *BBC News* (21 November 2007), available at http://news.bbc.co.uk/2/hi/africa/7105582.stm (accessed 6 September 2008); Musikilu Mojeed, "Why We Re-engaged Siemens-FG," *Punch* (22 August 2008), available at www.punchng.com (accessed 22 August 2008).

17. See *Global Integrity 2006 Country Report Nigeria* (Washington, D.C., 2006), 6.

18. Ibid.

19. Anza Philips, "The Other Side of Abuja Land Grab Story," *Newswatch* (12 May 2008), 30–31.

20. Tobs Agbaegbu, "Why a Trap Was Set for Grange," *Newswatch* (7 April 2008), 22–24.

21. Tatalo Alamu, "As El-Rufai Unravels," *The Nation* (18 May 2008), available at www.thenationonlineng.com (accessed 18 May 2008).

22. *Global Integrity 2006*, 4–5.

23. Ibid., 5.

24. "Nigeria Speaker Goes in Graft Row," *BBC News* (30 October 2007), available at http://news.bbc.co.uk/2/hi/africa/7069654.stm (accessed 21 September 2008).

25. Oko, "Subverting the Scourge," 471–472.

26. See Godwin Ijediogor, "Farida Waziri: Challenge of Sustaining Anti-Graft Momentum," *The Guardian* (2 August 2008), available at www.guardiannewsngr.com

(accessed 2 August 2008); Human Rights Watch, "Nigeria: Firing of Anti-Corruption Chief Would Boost Abusive Politicians" (1 January 2008), available at http://hrw.org/english/doc/2008/01/01/nigeri17671_txt.htm (accessed 10 May 2008).

27. Lanre Adewole, "N1.4bn Found in Judges' Secret Account-N185m Contract Awarded to Fake Firm-Judge Others Face Trial," *Nigerian Tribune* (18 August 2008), available at www.tribune.com.ng/18082008/news/news1.html and http://nm.online nigeria.com (accessed 21 September 2008).

28. Human Rights Watch, *Chop Fine*, 95.

29. See Bertram Nwannekanma, "Falana Writes Yar'Adua, says Okah's Trial a Cover-Up," *The Guardian* (4 June 2008), available at www.guardiannewsngr.com (accessed 4 June 2008).

30. Davidson Iriekpen, "EFCC Set to Auction Alamieyeseigha's Assets," *This Day* (14 August 2007), available at www.nfiu.gov.ng (accessed 8 September 2008).

31. Andrew Airahuobhor, "Dariye Returns," *Newswatch* (11 March 2007), available at www.newswatchngr.com/editorial/allaccess/special/10311115157.htm (accessed 21 September 2008).

32. Senan Murray, "Fears Over Nigeria Emergency Rule," *BBC News* (19 October 2006), available at htttp://news.bbc.co.uk/go/pr/fr/-/2/hi/Africa/6065706.stm (accessed 11 September 2008).

33. Dayo Aiyetan, "Allegations of Corruption Against Ex-Governor James Ibori," *Tell* (23 November 2007), available at www.waado.org/nigerdelta/delta_state_govt/Tell_magazine_ibori.htm (accessed 10 May 2008).

34. Human Rights Watch, "Nigeria," 1–2.

35. Andrew Airahuobhor, "Wanted for Fraud," *Newswatch* (21 January 2008), 30–32.

36. "EFCC and Igbinedion's Trial," *Punch* (9 January 2009), available at www.punchng.com (accessed 22 January 2009).

37. Oke Epia, "EFCC: How Kalu Stole N3b," available at www.nfiu.gov.ng (accessed 10 May 2008).

38. See Tobs Agbaegbu, "Nnamani's 20 Foreign Accounts," *Newswatch* (19 May 2008), 12–18; Andrew Airahuobhor, "EFCC Versus Nnamani," *Newswatch* (19 May 2008), 19–20; and Epia, "EFCC."

39. Epia, "EFCC."

40. Okey Muogbo and Lanre Adewole, "Ex-Gov. Nnamani Arrested; Turaki Weeps as Court Refuses Bail for Him; Kalu, Dariye Return to EFCC," available at www.nfiu.gov.ng (accessed 8 September 2008).

41. "EFCC and Igbinedion's Trial."

42. Human Rights Watch, *Chop Fine*, 14.

43. Abubakar Umar, "How Obasanjo and Co. Looted Nigeria in Eight Years," available at www.saharareporters.com/colabubakarumar1.php (accessed 21 September 2008).

44. Jones Aluko, *Corruption in the Local Government System in Nigeria* (Ibadan, 2006), 82, 87.

45. Ibid. Other such offenses involve the inclusion of ghost workers on council payrolls; the orchestration of "worthless," "unnecessary," or fictitious seminars, workshops, and consultancies as a means of looting the considerable amount of local revenues that are statutorily earmarked for the training and retraining of local government staff; the use of local government funds for political party operations and campaigns; and systematic collusion between external auditors and local government functionaries to conceal or destroy potentially incriminating evidences of graft and financial misappropriations.

46. Human Rights Watch, *Chop Fine,* 32, 36, 56.

47. Oscarline Onwuemenyi, "Tackling Corruption in Local Councils," *Punch* (31 August 2008), available at www.punchng.com (accessed 31 August 2008).

48. Ibid.

49. Larry Diamond, "Issues in the Constitutional Design of a Third Nigerian Republic," *African Affairs,* LXXXVI (1987), 216.

50. *Economic and Financial Crimes Commission (Establishment) Act* (4 June 2004), available at www.efccnigeria.org (accessed 17 April 2009), 3.

51. "Nigerian President Obasanjo's Inaugural Speech," *BBC News* (29 May 1999), available at http://news.bbc.co.uk/2/low/world/monitoring/356065.stm (accessed 4 September 2008).

52. Umar, "How Obasanjo and Co. Looted."

53. See Davidson Iriekpen, "Yar'Adua and EFCC: Between Rule of Law and Populism," *This Day* (14 August 2007), available at allafrica.com/stories/200708140378.html and www.nfiu.gov.ng (accessed 8 September 2008).

54. Femi Falana, "Ethics and Governance, the Rule of Law and Anti-Corruption: A Nigerian Dilemma" (9 December 2007), available www.saharareporters.com (accessed 17 April 2009).

55. See Ben Nwabueze, *How President Obasanjo Subverted Nigeria's Federal System* (Ibadan, 2007), 51–96.

56. Constitution of the Federal Republic of Nigeria 1999, sec. 15, schedule 2 (Part I), item 60.

57. National Political Reform Conference (NPRC), *Report of the Anti-Corruption Reforms Committee* (Abuja, 2005), 41–42, 46, 60.

58. ICPC, *Progress Report,* 120.

59. Ibid., 50.

60. Osita Nwajah, "Economic and Financial Crimes Commission: Frequently Asked Questions," *The Guardian* (18 September 2007), 17.

61. "The Beleaguered FOI Bill," *The Guardian* (6 May 2008), available at www.guradiannewsngr.com (accessed 6 May 2008).

62. Soyinka, "Exit Ribadu."

63. Gani Fawhinmi, "Why I Can't Accept Award of OFR," *The Guardian* (16 December 2008), available at www.ngrguardiannews.com (accessed 23 January 2009).

64. "Nigeria: Government is Paying Lip Service to Anti-Graft War Coalition" (3 August 2008), available at http://allafrica.com/stories/200808041109.html (accessed 6 August 2008).

65. Constitution, schedule 3 (Part I).

66. NPRC, *Report,* 60.

67. Ibid., 28.

DANIEL JORDAN SMITH

11

The Paradoxes of
Popular Participation
in Corruption in Nigeria

Nigeria has a widespread reputation as a corrupt country. Some years ago it appeared at the top of Transparency International's list of the most corrupt countries, and it continues to be regarded as a bastion of fraud, graft, and deceit. This image of Nigeria coincides with an era in which corruption is a common explanation for political and economic disappointments in Africa and in much of the developing world. In the language of cause and effect, corruption is often portrayed as an independent variable inhibiting the desired and supposedly dependent outcomes of democracy and development. The view that corruption is a problem in and of itself is prevalent and powerful. Despite this widespread perception, scholars have long recognized that corruption is as much a product of political and economic problems as it is their cause. While corruption is typically studied from the top down with a focus on the state, a perspective that privileges the everyday lives of ordinary people offers different and important insights. Looking at corruption from the bottom up reveals the complex ways in which this phenomenon is woven into the fabric of political and economic life—part and parcel of both the maintenance of social inequality and the struggles to respond to it. This chapter conveys the advantages of looking at corruption ethnographically, as a lens through which to understand processes of social change in Nigeria, and arguably in other societies as well.

For many years, my affection for Nigeria, my attachment to friends and colleagues there, and my intellectual orientation as an anthropologist prevented me from approaching corruption as an object of scholarship.[1] Writing about corruption in Africa runs the risk of perpetuating common Western misrepresentations of the continent. However, Nigerian citizens exhibit an intense preoccupation with their country's corruption, which suggests that simply countering negative images obscures important questions. Nigeria *is* rife with corruption, and no one is more aware of this reality than ordinary Nigerians. This chapter examines the various ways that Nigerians are fixated on and passionate about corrupt practices. Instead of trying to minimize the significance of Nigeria's notorious problem, I have increasingly realized that explaining corruption is central to understanding the very fabric of Nigerian society.[2]

Many of the ethnographic examples here come from southeastern Nigeria—the Igbo-speaking region. However, the kinds of everyday corruption that I describe are not unique to the Igbo or to the Southeast. Indeed, part of my argument is that corruption and the discourses that it produces are central to the way that Nigerians—and arguably people in many postcolonial contexts—experience and understand the relationship between state and society.

The central issue addressed in this chapter is how ordinary Nigerians can be, paradoxically, active participants in the social reproduction of corruption, even as they are also its primary victims and its principal critics. Understanding Nigerians' seemingly contradictory positions requires situating corruption in its political, social-relational, and moral contexts. For Nigerians, corruption can be, on the one hand, a survival strategy and a moral imperative, and, on the other hand, a political ruse to be condemned for its deception and venality. Corruption, in its many valences in Nigeria, is a potent stimulus for cultural production, both as a means for corruption's pursuit and as a method to combat its consequences. The contradictions of corruption both mirror and explain Nigerians' growing expectations of and frustrated aspirations for democracy and development.

Scholars have offered analyses that contribute to explaining why ordinary Africans participate in corruption that can be inimical to their own interests.[3] In a seminal article, Ekeh examined corruption in Africa in terms of "two publics," one moral and rooted in ties to kin-group and community of origin, and the other amoral, a legacy of institutions imposed under colonialism.[4] While Ekeh's notion of two publics is analytically useful, in practice the two publics overlap and interpenetrate (and I would go further to suggest that the domains of public and private intertwine as well). The realms of kinship and the state are mutually implicated in a political economy that is organized around patron-clientism, in which people rely on kin, on people of the same community of origin, and on other hierarchically organized social ties of affection and obligation for assistance. To understand the motives that underlie "corrupt behavior," it is essential to recognize that self-interest in Nigerian society (and in other African contexts) is intertwined with group interests and group identity. Rather than attributing these complex interconnections to some sort of primordial culture, and therefore assuming that processes of modernization will weaken such ties, I suggest that the salience of kinship's reciprocal obligations may be growing at the same time as Nigerians negotiate processes of development, rural-urban migration, and democratization within a context of pronounced political and economic instability. In such an environment, ordinary people perceive participation in corrupt activities as necessary to achieve their moral, political, and economic objectives, even as they simultaneously recognize its detrimental effects.

Nigeria's social context is central to explaining when and why Nigerians participate in corruption, but also to understanding what kinds of corruption are acceptable, and what kinds produce the popular discontent that fuels many salient contemporary social phenomena. Over the past few decades new forms of corruption have emerged that Nigerians widely view as illegitimate. This illegitimacy is most pronounced where Nigerians feel deceived by the post-colonial state's failure to deliver the expected benefits of development and democracy, at the same time that more traditional mechanisms of patron-clientism are perceived to be breaking down. In other words, as elites manipulate the intertwining of bureaucratic and kinship-based clientelism to maximize their wealth and power, the legitimacy of both idioms is undermined.

A patron-client system has long served as a buffer against the state's capriciousness by providing access to resources through familiar mechanisms of reciprocity. This system is widely perceived by ordinary Nigerians to have given way to a much more individualistic pursuit of wealth and power. The use of deceptive mechanisms for corruption has diffused throughout society, creating a popular sense of crisis about social morality, wherein Nigerians see the repercussions of corruption in everyday life as both caused by and contributing to the demise of morality. The perception that corruption is rooted in social amorality obscures the political and economic underpinnings of inequality, while paradoxically creating hope. At the same time that Nigerians see themselves as complicit in corruption, they also view themselves as the ultimate agents of change.

The Nigerian Factor

Throughout the 1990s, the community of Amibo struggled to become the last of eleven villages in Ubakala, a semi-rural area, to be connected to Nigeria's national electricity grid. Many families in Amibo had wired their houses for electricity over the prior decade, and the community had contributed money to erect poles to induce the National Electric Power Authority (NEPA) to extend service. Numerous village delegations had been sent to NEPA and to a series of military administrators and civilian governors. On each visit, these delegations deposited money with state officials as an incentive to mobilize assistance. Yet electricity was never provided. Community frustration contributed to accusations of corruption targeted at the government, but also directed inward. Politicians and bureaucrats who had collected the community's money were condemned for their venality. But many villagers who had contributed funds as part of collectively imposed levies suspected that perhaps their own kin had pocketed some of the community money, leaving too little for the payoffs to government and NEPA officials. When asked where he thought the problem really lay, a friend said, "Who can tell? In any case, it is 'the Nigerian factor.'" Ordinary citizens frequently describe corruption with this phrase, which indicates the perceived prevalence and intractability of the problem. Suspicions of corruption span the social spectrum, potentially implicating not only elite politicians, but also kinsmen in village communities.

In his trenchant book, *The Trouble with Nigeria*, Achebe notes Nigerians' penchant for complaining: "Whenever two Nigerians meet, their conversation will sooner or later slide into a litany of our national deficiencies."[5] Achebe laments that this national inclination is a sign of resignation and says that his book aims to challenge such complacency. Corruption is, indeed, so prevalent in Nigeria that ordinary citizens experience and express some degree of resignation. The very expression "the Nigerian factor" suggests that Nigerians have concluded that corruption is endemic; it defines the nation. Yet resignation is only one of the meanings behind Nigerian narratives of complaint. Even as Nigerians feel resigned, enticed, trapped, and compelled to participate in their country's ubiquitous corruption, they also feel angry, frustrated, dismayed, and betrayed.

Popular anger about corruption is common not only in Nigeria, but across Africa, as it is in many regions around the globe. In an excellent analysis of the dynamics of corruption across sub-Saharan Africa, Olivier de Sardan notes the extent of African discontent about corruption: "At the everyday level, there is scarcely a conversation without hostile or disgusted references to corruption."[6] In many ways, corruption has become the dominant discourse of complaint in the post-colonial world, symbolizing people's disappointments with democracy and development and their frustrations with continued social inequality. Yet even as they feel anger and discontent, ordinary Nigerians participate in forms of corruption that perpetuate their victimization.

Corruption, Patron-Clientism, and the Post-colonial State

In 2002 I was traveling on public transportation with an American student who had just arrived in Nigeria. As we approached a police checkpoint on the road from Port Harcourt to Owerri, the minibus slowed. Several vehicles had stopped ahead of us. A man behind me muttered "thieves," referring to the heavily armed policemen who blocked our way. When the vehicle ahead of us seemed to have been stopped for more than the usual few seconds, a woman on our bus said audibly, "Give them something so we can pass now." As we reached the head of the queue, our driver handed a policeman a banknote in a somewhat furtive manner, and we were again on our way. I had seen the transaction so many times over the years that I hardly noticed. But as soon as we had passed the checkpoint, my student asked in a whisper, "If everyone knows exactly what is happening, why do the driver and the policeman half-heartedly try to conceal it?" In retrospect, this question and the events that preceded it raised important issues about the relationship between ordinary citizens, corruption, and the state.

The half-concealed levy paid to a policeman at a roadside checkpoint represents an example of a recent transformation in Nigeria's political economy of patron-clientism that characterizes Nigerian citizens' relationship to their post-colonial state. In traditional systems of patronage, or at least as Nigerians romanticize them, exchanges between elites and common people were based on reciprocity and a sense of mutual obligation. Inequality was tempered by a moral economy in which the links between the haves and have-nots created mechanisms for accountability. In contemporary Nigeria, people of all social strata continue to navigate political and economic insecurity and inequality by relying on social networks of patronage that are rooted in such a system of reciprocity, whereby ties based on kinship, community of origin, and other associations provide access to the resources of the state. However, many Nigerians believe that elites have hijacked the patronage system and perverted it to serve their own interests. Further, the Nigerian state's alternative idiom of accountability, which is based on a social contract between the government and its people, is equally perceived by Nigeria's citizens as corrupt. Indeed, the integration of the system of patronage with the facades of bureaucracy and officialdom produced by the post-colonial state facilitates the corruption that is ubiquitous in Nigeria. Bayart has suggested that "The post-colonial state thus represents an historical mutation of African societies, taken over the long term: never before, it seems, has the dominant class managed to acquire such marked economic supremacy over its subjects."[7]

The conventional wisdom in Western society, exemplified in many donor-sponsored programs to promote democracy and "good governance" in Africa, opposes the realms of modern neoliberal democracy and traditional systems of kinship and patron-clientism. But in Nigeria, elites and ordinary citizens live simultaneously in both worlds. Indeed, although observers and analysts frequently make sense of this complexity by contrasting the two systems, or by describing Africans as "straddling" multiple social worlds, for most Nigerians these contrasting systems are experienced as one reality.[8] The Nigerian state is simultaneously a neoliberal institution claiming the full range of powers and responsibilities that are typical of modern nation-states, and a prize to be captured and shared according to the principles of patronage.[9]

The role that ordinary citizens play in the social reproduction of corruption, even as the vast majority is acutely aware that the system disproportionately benefits a few at the expense of the many, is inherent in a political economy of patronage. Elite politicians, government officials, and economic moguls—federal ministers, state governors, Nigerian National Petroleum Corporation managers, major construction and petroleum industry contractors, etc.—commonly reap many millions of dollars through corrupt acts. However, people at varying levels of society take advantage of inequality to benefit from corruption. It is almost a cliché that in African societies everyone is a patron to a lesser person and a client to a more powerful person.[10] As Olivier de Sardan notes, "Woe betide the man who knows no one, either directly or indirectly."[11]

In a country where the World Bank estimates nearly 60 percent of the population lives below the poverty line (estimated at less than $1 per person per day), most people do not benefit substantially from either the formal mechanisms of government or the more informal networks of patronage that constitute a significant proportion of the everyday political economy. But even ordinary citizens have daily experiences with corruption in their efforts to forge better lives for themselves and their families, as they confront and participate in forms of corruption in schools, hospitals, and a wide range of other efforts to obtain basic resources and services from the state. At the same time that Nigerians aspire to a modern lifestyle, they become increasingly caught up in corruption. While millions of poor Nigerians are largely excluded from the struggle for wealth and power that occurs at the nexus between the state and from the networks of patronage that vie to control it, even the poor are aware that it is through these social connections, and increasingly through corruption, that people access the state's resources and those of the national economy.

To be without a patron is to be without access to resources, but to be a patron is to be under great pressure to accumulate and to share wealth, including by means of corruption. Many of my friends in positions of relative power in Nigeria remark on and frequently complain about the pressures from kin, community members, friends, and associates to use the power of their offices or the benefits of their wealth to fulfill requests for help. Whether one is a school principal, a successful businessman, the director of a development NGO, a customs officer, or a motor vehicle licensing agent, the pressure to use one's position to benefit people in networks of personal association is intense. These expectations are particularly powerful in situations where patrons can leverage benefits and services from the state. That the state is central to the system of corruption should not be surprising given its importance as an employer and provider of services, but also given the sheer economic dominance of the state in a country where the principal source of wealth is petroleum, and oil revenues are directly controlled by the government.[12]

The particular history and current configuration of the country's petroleum-dominated political economy intensifies the importance of the state in Nigeria.[13] Oil was discovered in the Niger Delta in 1958, but it was not until the 1970s, when Nigeria joined OPEC and the Middle East crisis sent the price of oil skyrocketing, that the country was transformed into a "petrostate."[14] As the nation became increasingly dependent on oil as a source of revenue, rent-seeking behavior gradually replaced productive agriculture as the primary means to achieve wealth and prestige. The Nigerian state became the locus of competition for resources; a reality captured in the colloquial expression Nigerians use to describe the state: "the national cake," of which everyone wants a piece. During the oil boom, the government rapidly consolidated its control over the oil industry and centralized the distribution of revenues to lower tiers of government and society. The collapse of oil prices in the 1980s exposed the contradictions in Nigeria's largely non-productive petroleum economy, making who controlled the state and its increasingly scarce oil revenues the object of even more intense competition, feeding corruption and stoking discontent over the consequent poverty and inequality.

For Nigerians, the state and corruption are synonymous. Because they must navigate—indeed, participate in—corruption if they are to achieve even their most mundane and reasonable aspirations, most Nigerians realize that what Bayart describes regarding African post-colonial states more generally is particularly true in Africa's giant: "It would be an error to see all these dealings simply as the corruption of the State. They are, conversely, the State's fabric. . . ."[15] In Nigeria's petroleum-dominated political economy of patron-clientism, where corruption rules, it makes sense that "strategies adopted by the great majority of the population for survival are identical to the ones adopted by the leaders to accumulate wealth and power."[16]

Forms of Corruption

Defining corruption is difficult and has occupied a good deal of space in the social sciences literature, particularly in political science.[17] Most political science definitions include the state and typically emphasize the misuse of public office for private gain. For example, Nye's classic definition is widely cited: "Corruption is behavior which deviates from the formal duties of a public role because of private-regarding (personal, close family, private clique) pecuniary or status gains; or violates rules against the exercise of certain private-regarding influence."[18] In formulating his definition, Nye recognized that corruption also has much broader moral meanings: "a change from good to bad."[19] These vague and less technical aspects have mostly been ignored in political science. For political scientists who look at state corruption, Nye's strict definition and its many subsequent variants, which sidestep issues of morality, provide a parsimony that facilitates an appealing clarity.

For an anthropologist who looks at corruption ethnographically, from the bottom up, such parsimonious definitions obscure as much as they reveal. In Nigeria, the question of whether the misuse of public office for private gain constitutes corruption varies significantly depending upon the context. The social morality of behavior figures much more prominently into popular assessments of corruption than any technical definition. Ordinary Nigerians make decisions about so-called corruption in the context of deep loyalties to kin and community that often trump the relevance of bureaucratic rules and state laws. Social morality and notions of appropriate civic behavior remain rooted to a significant degree in institutions other than the state, in part because of the failure of the state to deliver its promised benefits. Nevertheless, rising expectations about the state, and about democracy and development, are part of a process in which the relationship between social morality and governance is changing. Rather than separating corruption and morality, it is necessary to sort out how they fit together in Nigeria.

Instead of imposing a definition of corruption on Nigeria, I am interested in the multiple ways that Nigerians employ the concept of corruption. As such, I use local categories and implied definitions to build an analysis that makes sense of corruption in light of what Nigerians do and say. Given that

Nigerians see corruption at work not only in public offices but also across a wide range of commercial exchanges and interpersonal relations, tying the definition of corruption strictly to affairs of the state is limiting. However, even as this anthropological account of corruption incorporates and interprets a range of local meanings, it will become clear that the emergence of the post-colonial state is central to Nigerian experiences of corruption, and that the expectations and disappointments generated by the state permeate Nigerians' collective imagination about corruption. Many of the narratives of discontent that appear moralistic and less directly about official corruption per se are, in fact, heavily influenced by experiences with and expectations of the state.

Based on an extensive comparative study of corruption in three West African countries (Benin, Niger, and Senegal), Blundo and Olivier de Sardan developed a useful typology of forms of corruption that maps reasonably well onto the Nigerian scene.[20] The seven basic forms they identify are: 1) commission for illicit services, 2) unwarranted payment for public services, 3) gratuities, 4) string pulling, 5) levies and tolls, 6) sidelining, and 7) misappropriation.[21] In Nigeria, people commonly pay extra money for basic services such as the issuance of licenses, passports, and birth certificates. Nigerians typically call a gratuity a "dash," and do not think of it in the same terms as a bribe. But as Blundo and Olivier de Sardan point out, a dash only makes sense in an environment where officials fail to do diligently their jobs without the demand for a bribe. In fact, many Nigerians recognize that dashes are frequently simply more sociable and socially acceptable ways to pay bribes.[22]

String pulling refers to using social and political influence to promote favoritism, offering preferential access to employment, education, and a range of other opportunities, particularly those allocated by the state. From experience, Nigerians commonly believe that resources and opportunities are awarded based, above all, on who you know. Levies and tolls are relatively stark forms of tribute that persons in power can extract from ordinary citizens. For example, police who collect illegal tolls from motor vehicle drivers at roadside checkpoints, vigilante groups that demand a security levy from local businesses, or bureaucrats who require pensioners to pay money in order to receive their pensions all fall into this category. In most cases, Nigerians view this type of levying as outright extortion. Sidelining refers to the use of public or company resources for private purposes; for example, using official vehicles for personal travel, running a private clinic in a public health facility, or using university resources to conduct a private consulting job. Misappropriation extends this practice further, whereby public materials are not simply used for private purposes, but expropriated entirely, usually in a manner more concealed than sidelined, as misappropriation is both more illegitimate and more obviously illegal.

Blundo and Olivier de Sardan's typology is preferable to more simplistic analyses that distinguish only between large-scale and petty corruption or between good corruption (that arguably facilitates development) and bad corruption (that arguably inhibits development). Their typology certainly captures and describes a wide range of forms of corruption that are prevalent in Nigeria, but as Blundo and Olivier de Sardan acknowledge, the boundaries between these forms are fluid, and the perceived legitimacy of practices depends on context, and particularly on the position of the people participating in or assessing the behavior. Such an approach is also state-centered and sidesteps key questions about the intersection between social morality and corruption. Some forms of corruption are almost always less legitimate than others. For example, the tolls collected by police at checkpoints are widely resented, whereas a patron pulling strings to assist a friend or relative is often seen as highly legitimate and even morally honorable.

A number of dimensions are salient to situate the particular forms of corruption in Nigeria as well as to understand their degree of acceptability. Whether a particular behavior is perceived as corrupt, and how corrupt a behavior is judged to be, depends on where the behavior falls along a number of intersecting continua. These continua include legality and illegality, legitimacy and illegitimacy, as well as scale (i.e., petty and massive), and whether an individual is a beneficiary or a victim. Social distance from acts of corruption is generally predictive of perceived illegitimacy, as people socially removed from corruption perceive it as corrosive. Perceptions in cases of closer proximity to the corrupt act depend heavily on whether a person is a beneficiary or a victim. While smaller-scale corruption is more widely tolerated, the most egregious forms of corruption are the least likely to be punished, because the most powerful people participate in them.

Leaders, Ordinary Citizens, and Corruption in Everyday Life

The debate in Nigerian popular discourse about corruption often focuses on whom to blame, and in particular how much corruption is the fault of leaders versus how much it is the fault of ordinary Nigerians. The dominant view in Nigeria is that the country's corruption is principally a leadership problem. Achebe articulates the "bad leaders" argument:

The trouble with Nigeria is simply and squarely a failure of leadership. There is nothing basically wrong with the Nigerian character. . . . If indeed there is any such a creature as "an average Nigerian" he is likely to be found at a point in social space with limited opportunities for corruption as we generally understand the word. Corruption goes with power; and whatever the average man may have it is *not* power. Therefore to hold any useful discussion of corruption we must first locate it where it properly belongs—in the ranks of the powerful.[23]

Whether or not they have read his book, average Nigerians largely share Achebe's view. The vitriol that Nigerians express against their leaders in everyday conversation affirms how much ordinary citizens blame politicians for the country's predicament. Indeed, as an observer, I sympathize with the view that Nigerian leaders bear much of the responsibility for the widespread corruption that stifles development, produces poverty, and reinforces inequality within Nigeria. But ordinary Nigerians, especially those whose life trajectories put them in contact with the state, whether through education, business, politics, or simply through the seeking of social services, are also well aware of their own complicity in perpetuating corruption. Nearly all of the thousands of Nigerians that I have listened to over nineteen years acknowledge that it is not just the country's leaders who are corrupt. Daily debates and conversations in marketplaces, offices, bars, and buses, as well as in Nigeria's vibrant media, excoriate not only the president and his cronies, but corrupt Nigerians at all levels of society. In my experience, to find a Nigerian who does not recognize his own culpability in reproducing Nigeria's corruption is the exception rather than the rule. The same person who rails against former dictator General Sani Abacha or former President Olusegun Obasanjo can, in a different moment, lament or laugh about his own involvement in corruption.

Corruption permeates nearly every facet of public life and many facets of private life. The language and metaphors of corruption have even penetrated people's understandings of their intimate interpersonal relationships. To explain corruption in Nigeria, it is necessary to understand that many average Nigerians who condemn corruption also participate in its social reproduction. Further, it is important to be able to distinguish, where possible, between the types of corruption that Nigerians undertake based on positive values associated with kinship, reciprocity, and loyalty, and those activities that Nigerians label as unacceptable. The ordinary Nigerians who participate in corruption often feel compelled to do so in the context of political and moral economies that seem to leave them little choice to do otherwise. Through examining the everyday workings of corruption in their most mundane forms—in bureaucracies, business, education, and health care and even in intimate personal relationships—it becomes possible to see how Nigerians can be both critics and complicit participants in corruption.

Access to Education

Formal education is a marker of modernity both for Nigerian people and for social scientists who use formal education to measure the extent of "modernization." In the sociological literature, the spread of formal education is frequently associated with a growing emphasis on individualism, the advent of the nuclear family and fertility transition, the emergence of "citizen" as an aspect of individual identity, and the rise of bureaucratic social organization. In Ubakala, the semi-rural community where I conducted field research in the mid-1990s, nearly all children attended primary school. More than three-quarters started, though many did not finish, secondary school. Parents routinely complained about the high costs of "training children," even as they did all they could to further their children's education. The burden of training children was partly offset because the costs of education were widely shared, as parents relied heavily on the support of their kin. People's experience with access to education in Nigeria reinforced a model of how the world works, which said: "a person needs connections, especially family connections, to succeed."[24] The following account of one girl's route to secondary school is typical of how Nigerians, in order to access opportunities for modern education, must negotiate and manage their networks of social relationships, especially networks of kinship, in processes that to outsiders would likely be labeled as corrupt.

CASE STUDY 1. Benjamin and Ifeoma are Igbos from Ubakala living in Lagos.[25] Benjamin struggles to make a small photocopying business profitable, while Ifeoma has a steady but low-paying clerical job at a bank. They have been married more than twelve years and have four children.

When their eldest daughter, Nneka, completed primary school, Benjamin and Ifeoma had aspirations that she would be admitted to a selective federal government secondary school, particularly one close to Umuahia, because it had a good reputation and Benjamin's relatives in Ubakala could assist in looking after their daughter.

Nneka was an excellent student, regularly finishing first or second in her class. She scored well on her secondary school admissions test, but not well enough to gain entrance to the federal school that her parents had chosen.

Soon after the scores came out, when it was clear that Nneka would not get automatic admission, Benjamin asked me if I would talk to the principal to see if Nneka could be admitted on her "discretionary list." He thought I might have some clout because I had then recently conducted a study in Umuahia secondary schools as part of my research and therefore knew officials in the Ministry of Education; I was affiliated with Abia State University and therefore had status in the world of higher education; and he thought I knew a lot of "Big Men" in Umuahia. I did not know the principal, but Benjamin hoped my influence would be great enough anyway.

I went to visit the principal. Essentially, I was asking her to grant Nneka admission based on who I was. She refused. When I reported the results of my visit to Benjamin and Ifeoma they did not seem surprised. Benjamin said: "She was afraid because you are a white. She just wanted to hide everything from you." Instead of the profound disappointment that I had expected, Benjamin and Ifeoma were upbeat. Since I had last seen them, Ifeoma discovered that her sister had a friend in the Federal Ministry of Education in Lagos. This woman said that she would try to get Nneka admitted through the minister's discretionary list. In the end, Benjamin and Ifeoma had to dash the woman in the ministry a few thousand naira (approximately $50, a considerable sum for average Nigerians) to secure Nneka a place.[26]

To believe Nneka's admission was based on an outright bribe would be a mistake, though clearly the dash was a necessary part of the process. Nneka's admission was, nevertheless, only possible because of Ifeoma's sister's connection. The money involved represented the social distance between the parties involved. The woman in the ministry almost surely would have refused any dash to help her own sister's daughter. Likewise, a complete stranger offering money to get on the minister's list would likely have been dismissed.

However, when Nigerians are *truly* angry about corruption they talk about cases where people do sell access to services only for the money. But in general, people are careful to circumvent state or bureaucratic rules only among those that they know and trust, partly out of fear that the rules will be used against them. Instances of corruption are far more likely when they are undertaken as the fulfillment of expectations and obligations to one's personal network of social relations—especially kinship and affinal relations. To accept money from a stranger to facilitate admission of a child who is not qualified based on her exam result is wrong: the rules of the state apply in such an impersonal case. To help your relation get admission when her scores were below the cut-off is expected and morally justified: the rules of kinship, community, and reciprocity apply when the stakes are personal or communal.

Contracts: Patronage and the State

Few events bring more excitement to a family and a community than the news that one of its own has been appointed to an important government position. To have a son or townsman placed in a high public office creates expectations of access to the most notorious and lucrative form of Nigeria's infamous corruption—a contract. Contracts are the mechanism through which specific jobs (e.g., the building of a road, the importation of equipment, the printing of identity cards, and the supplying of stationery) are awarded. While private companies in Nigeria sometimes hire contractors to complete various tasks, by far the biggest source of contracts of varying types is the government. Contracts are symbols of the system of patronage that dominates the Nigerian political and economic landscape, as coveted as they are reviled.

A contract is the most prominent symbol of patron-clientism in Nigeria in part because of the critical importance of oil in the country's political economy. With the oil boom in the 1970s, Nigeria's economy became much less diversified, and the dependency of state and local governments on the federal government deepened. Investments in agriculture declined because the influx of petrodollars created an illusion of instant and seemingly unending prosperity. By 1980, more than 95 percent of Nigeria's export earnings came from oil, that number constituting 55 percent of total government revenue.[27] Elites no longer depended on access to "surpluses generated by peasant producers but on oil rents redistributed through the state apparatus."[28] Central government control of and dependence on rents associated with the oil industry intensified the vertical hierarchy of patronage networks and the importance of government contracts as a source of wealth.[29]

When a contract is awarded through corruption in Nigeria, seemingly everyone knows exactly what is transpiring. Further, Nigerians assume that virtually every state-related decision or enterprise is corrupt. Ordinary citizens tell stories of corruption with a combination of lament, resignation, and humor. Discourses about contracts and corruption inundate local conversations about Nigerian business and politics. Such talk routinely swings between condemnation on the one hand, as people lament a road repair contract that has been abandoned or concluded without noticeable improvements, wonder how a country so rich in natural resources can be so poor, or speculate about how a new political appointee will distribute government resources to his own people; and conspiratorial anticipation on the other hand, as individuals survey their social networks for a connection to a new big man, plan a "courtesy call" to a new official, or prepare a bid on a contract in hopes that family, community, or political connections will give them the inside track. People share a sense that corruption has perpetuated poverty in a land of wealth, and that only the rich get richer. Nonetheless, everyone aspires to be rich.

Although Nigerians recognize and condemn, in the abstract, the patronage system that dominates the allocation of government resources, in practice people feel trapped. A university professor, and friend, who was appointed as state commissioner of agriculture, explained corruption to me in this way: "Even if I wanted to avoid the practice of awarding contracts on the basis of favoritism, I could not. My people would say that I am selfish and foolish. Who gets to such a position of power and then refuses to help his people? Only the worst kind of person." A man who enriches himself through emptying government coffers is, in his community, despised only if he fails to share that wealth with his people—through direct gifts to individuals and community development projects, but also through more ceremonial distributions such as lavish weddings for his children, spectacular burials for his parents, and extravagant chieftaincy installation ceremonies for himself. At such events his people enjoy his wealth; they "chop" (eat) his money.

Although their wealth must be shared, the pressure on big men to be corrupt goes beyond awarding contracts to their relatives and cronies. One also enriches oneself. To be a commissioner and not build a palatial house in the village would be to fail to fulfill the expectations of one's family and community. A big man in government or business can only distribute to and share with relatively few people the fruits of his office through official channels, but there are additional expectations that he should accumulate significant personal wealth—wealth that one's kinsmen and townsmen feel entitled to draw upon.[30]

The case studies of the awarding of contracts that are detailed below illustrate the ways in which local moralities intersect with state politics to create and reproduce a political economy grounded in patron-clientism. These examples involve relatively small-sized patrons and smaller-sized clients to support the overall argument that corruption is sustained precisely because people at all strata in Nigeria are invested in and, in some measure, benefit from the accumulation and distribution of public resources through informal private networks. The cases also highlight the importance of personal relationships, especially kin relationships, in negotiating a system in which patron-client ties become less dependable as social connections grow more distant.

CASE STUDY 2. Ike Nwodu is a married father of five who lives in Umuahia. One of his relatives directed the World Bank–funded Abia State Agricultural Development Programme from 1994 to 1995 and Ike was awarded a substantial contract—about 4 million naira (almost $50,000)—to supply locally fabricated machinery for palm kernel processing. Ike estimated that he would make close to a 500,000 naira profit ($6,250) for himself at the end of the contract, after supplying the equipment and giving his relative his share.

In Ike's case, his relative, the director, would receive about 400,000 naira. Igbos often spoke of "the 10 percent rule"—meaning that one is expected to give back 10 percent of the total amount of any contract to the person(s) who awarded it. In the 1990s, people began to complain that commissioners, director-generals, directors, and military administrators were demanding more than the customary 10 percent. One military administrator in Abia State earned the dubious nickname "Where My Own?" for his incessant demands for his share.

In response to widespread evidence that its funds were being misused, the World Bank ordered a probe of many of its projects and imposed a freeze on payments to all contractors. Ike had supplied the equipment and used his initial "mobilization fee" (money awarded, in theory, to help the contractor with start-up costs) to pay off his relative. At the time that the World Bank stipulated these investigations or freezes, Ike was waiting for the final payment to repay debts to his own suppliers and pocket his profit.

As a result of the probe, Ike's relative was fired and a new director was appointed. When the World Bank finally lifted the freeze on payment of outstanding debts to contractors and Ike went to collect, he found that the new director wanted his own share in order to authorize disbursement. The delay imposed by the World Bank had caused his own creditors to become annoyed, and this change in directors meant that almost all of Ike's profit was drained to pay off the new man. Ike vowed never again to seek a contract from an internationally funded project.

CASE STUDY 3. Godwin Okoro is in his late 40s, married with five children. Godwin is popularly known as "World Biz"—short for World Business—among his friends, a praise name coined during his past as a wealthier man. He hails from a local government area (similar to a county) that is the home of a former civilian governor. World Biz is married to a woman from the former governor's family, and during the former governor's tenure, World Biz parlayed his in-law relationship into a series of lucrative contracts.

Times became leaner during the military regime. His patron was long out of power. World Biz did not have a job, but still managed to make a living through small contracts. In 1996, World Biz campaigned for a particular candidate in his local government chairmanship elections. He borrowed money from me and others, assuring us that when his candidate won he would "be in money." He expected lucrative contracts in return for his mobilization of followers.

His candidate won the election, but for months afterward World Biz complained that the man was ungrateful. He made frequent visits to the chairman's office in hopes of a business deal. But the chairman refused, complaining about lack of funds, debts to pay that had been inherited from the last government, and increased state and federal scrutiny of local government spending. At first World Biz accepted the excuses and maintained hope. Eventually he concluded that the chairman had no intention of rewarding him. The chairman was an ingrate, World Biz said, and he did not "know politics." Within a few months the military again dissolved the local government councils. The chairman was out of office. Only weeks after that he died unexpectedly of a heart attack. World Biz said it was God's way of punishing him.

World Biz's expectation that he be rewarded was directly related to the fact that he had "delivered his people" in the chairmanship election. Given World Biz's propensity to exaggerate on his own behalf, there is no way of knowing how instrumental he was in securing the chairman's election. Regardless, World Biz had called upon a widely shared value in Nigerian politics that a man should be rewarded for delivering his people.

While there is no doubt that elite Nigerians disproportionally benefit from the country's current political and economic structures, these structures are sustainable only because they are supported by a complex moral economy in which those at the top fulfill obligations and duties to their followers and clients. In the first case, Ike's kinship tie was crucial for securing the government contract. When his relative was dismissed, Ike's contract was compromised. World Biz's experience with his local government chairman illustrates that patrons and clients do not always agree on the extent of obligations. World Biz's interpretation of the chairman's death demonstrates the strong belief in the moral economy of patron-clientism. That his marital ties to the last civilian governor proved more beneficial than the political ties to the elected official shows that one can be secure in ties created through marriage and kinship, more so than in those produced purely through political alliances.

Good Corruption and Bad Corruption

The community development union is perhaps the most important formal mechanism by which the Igbo-speaking people of southeastern Nigeria (particularly those who have migrated away from their rural villages) "deliver" or "share" the fruits of success with their kin and their communities of origin.

The importance of these unions in tying migrants to their natal communities and bringing material benefits to rural villages is well-documented.[31] These voluntary organizations, with ascriptive membership bases, focus their energies on developing or "getting up" rural communities.[32] Migrants who accumulate wealth in their endeavors away from the village are expected to contribute significantly to development efforts at home. Of course, wealthy "sons abroad" do not act purely out of loyalty to their natal communities; in the act of contributing they build their networks of clients and enhance their prestige. In the context of contemporary Nigerian politics, such ties and bases of support are essential to achieve political power. These dynamics contribute to the tremendous importance of place of origin in Nigerian politics.[33]

Processes of securing and delivering resources to rural communities through community development unions illustrate the shifting and situational definitions of corruption in the minds of Nigerians. The dynamics that underlie these unions also illustrate the processes by which common people put pressures on their successful kin that contribute to corruption. The following case study depicts the nature of such pressures and shows how differently corruption is judged depending on the context in which it occurs.

CASE STUDY 4. Odi Nwoke was in his twenties when he first migrated from Ubakala to Lagos before the Nigerian civil war. He built a successful printing business and over the years had become rich. Like most of Ubakala's successful migrants, he built a house in his village and came home several times a year to visit family and participate in important social events and ceremonies. He maintained active membership in the Ubakala Improvement Union and contributed to community development projects.

In the early 1990s, during one of the several transitions from military to civilian rule, a political patron who Odi had cultivated over the years selected Odi for a directorship in an Abia State government parastatal (an institution set up by government that is ostensibly independent from the government). This position enabled Odi to disperse significant business contracts and build his own fortune. At home in Ubakala, his appointment was celebrated and during his brief tenure of eighteen months Odi managed to enhance his position significantly in Ubakala through awarding favors, increasing his contributions to the Ubakala Improvement Union, and hosting lavish social ceremonies to which his kin and neighbors were invited.

In 1996, Odi left Lagos and retired to Ubakala. In part as a reward for his contributions to the community, he was voted in as an officer of the Ubakala Improvement Union. Immediately following Odi's election, Ubakala went through a period of political upheaval over the selection of a traditional ruler, or *eze*. Efforts to control the Ubakala Improvement Union were central in this political fight. Several months after his election, rivals accused Odi of misusing the union's funds. His accusers demanded that he be removed from office.

Judgments about whether Odi had misused union funds fell largely along lines of political cleavage in the community, but no one disputed that misusing union funds was a grievous offense. Odi had been celebrated and rewarded for the benefits that he delivered to the community through his position with the parastatal, even though most people assumed that resources had been accumulated through diverting "public funds" for "private use." Money allegedly stolen from the Ubakala Improvement Union, on the other hand, brought great condemnation and was used as a political weapon against Odi and his allies. In these two instances, the contrast in how Odi's corrupt behavior was judged illustrates the importance of social context in Nigerians' perceptions of the relationship between morality and corruption.

419: Corruption, Deception, and Social Morality

Despite the continued prevalence of ordinary Nigerians' participation in corruption and the pragmatic role that various corrupt practices play in how Nigerian citizens navigate the challenges of contemporary life, many forms of corruption are perceived as illegitimate. As indicated in Odi's case, similar instances of corruption can be accepted or condemned based on a person's social position (e.g., beneficiary or victim; distant observer or interested party). If "the Nigerian factor" is corruption, the primary mode of *illegitimate* corruption in Nigeria is "419." Named after the number in the Nigerian penal code for a specific form of fraud, 419 (pronounced four-one-nine) emerged in the 1980s during Nigeria's economic decline, when the country fell from the heights of the worldwide oil boom into a political and economic morass marked by military dictatorships, inflation, a rapidly devaluing currency, and widespread poverty and unemployment.[34] The original meaning of 419 is linked to a particular practice in which the perpetrators sent letters and faxes that relied on the symbols of Nigeria's petroleum-dominated political economy—official letterhead and signatures, Nigerian National Petroleum Corporation insignia, lines of credit, government contracts, etc.—to bait largely foreign targets into providing advance fees with the promise of a larger payoff. The scams relied not only on the trappings of the Nigerian state, but also its reputation for corruption, enticing people with the expectation that some of the millions of dollars siphoned off by corrupt officials could be obtained simply by providing a foreign bank account and advance fees. Apter has cogently described how 419 emerged as Nigerians became disillusioned with the state at the same time that the state itself, no longer awash in oil money, relied on the politics of illusion to maintain its eroding legitimacy.[35]

The original 419 scams have continued to flourish; they have even increased and expanded as the Internet has democratized access to technology during the same period as Nigeria's transition to democratic governance after many years of military rule. Even more significant than the continued practice of 419 scams through e-mail is that 419 has become an all-encompassing signifier in Nigerian discourse for any behavior that relies on dissimulation, illusion, or some other manipulation of the truth to facilitate gain or advantage. Indeed, nothing better illustrates the Nigerian definition of illegitimate corruption than the spectrum of activities and behaviors that are described as 419.

During my fieldwork in 2004, the Nigerian Labour Congress, an umbrella organization that represents many trade unions, called a national strike to protest government efforts to deregulate the price of gasoline, kerosene, and diesel, a policy that would result in significant increases in the cost of Nigeria's highly subsidized domestic fuel. National strikes over fuel prices have been common in Nigeria's recent history.[36] The strike in 2004 was widely observed, and after several days, during which the nation's economy was largely shut down, the government was forced to compromise, still raising fuel prices but keeping them well below the deregulated levels that had been proposed. In the period during and after the strike, the issue of corruption in Nigeria's oil economy, always a popular topic, reached its peak in everyday conversations.

Nigerians commonly believe that cheap domestic fuel is a national birthright, perceived as one of the few benefits that an otherwise corrupt and ineffectual government ought to be able to deliver to the masses in Africa's oil-producing giant. In one of the great ironies and tragic symbols of Nigerian underdevelopment, during the Obasanjo regime, from 1999 to 2003, Nigeria imported nearly all of its refined fuel from overseas, as the country's four broken-down oil refineries remained non-functional despite numerous huge government contracts to repair them. The popular belief, voiced in the idiom of 419, was that the country's political elite, led by the president, deliberately kept the country's refineries from being repaired so that they could profit from controlling the importation and distribution of fuel. One account of the domestic fuel situation, provided by a friend during a conversation as we waited in line for fuel at a crowded petrol station after the 2004 strike was called off, illustrates a widely held view:

[President] Obasanjo is just playing us 419. Government could easily repair the refineries but they leave them failing on purpose. I mean, in this country, with the billions generated from oil revenues, are you telling me that for several years they cannot even repair one refinery? No way. Obasanjo and the ex-military boys, they want it this way. They control the importation of fuel from abroad. They own the ships, the local marketing companies, the petrol stations. I understand some of them have even built refineries abroad. Can you imagine? While our refineries rot they have built their own abroad to profit from our suffering. It is not enough that they steal the oil revenues. They also sell our oil back to us at a profit. No. It's 419, it's 419.

Whether or not this account is entirely factual, it represents a common awareness that elites are getting rich at the expense of the masses and that 419—here, illusion created through deception—is the central strategy. While most people see elites as the biggest perpetrators of 419, people also share a common belief that 419 has filtered throughout Nigerian society, a perception illustrated in the discourse resulting from the fuel strike. For example, proprietors of local filling stations were accused of 419 for hoarding fuel as the strike approached, pretending that their stocks had run out in anticipation of higher prices after the strike. Even the urban street urchins who sell black market fuel in plastic jugs at the roadside when gasoline is scarce are accused of 419 because motorists suspect that they mix cheaper kerosene with more expensive gasoline to increase their small profits.

Implied in many common popular critiques of 419 is an understanding that politicians use the state to deceive ordinary people for the benefit of elites. Indeed, politics is perceived to be a primary arena for 419. Over the years Nigerians have realized that various programs implemented by military governments as part of the promise to return the country to civilian rule were elaborate ruses. No example is more telling than the 1993 presidential election, when then military dictator Ibrahim Babangida ultimately annulled the vote after dragging the country through an artificial process in which the military directed every step of the transition, including the creation of political parties, the writing of their manifestos, and the determination of eligible candidates. Babangida's cancellation of the election just days after the vote, which led to five more years of brutal dictatorship under Abacha, was viewed by many Nigerians as the ultimate 419, committed by the Nigerian leader who was most associated with the term.[37] Political 419 has not been the exclusive province of the military, however. The elections in 2003, conducted by a democratically elected government, were widely viewed as 419 by Nigerians who saw the huge victories for President Obasanjo's ruling People's Democratic Party as a process of elite-driven selection masquerading as a democratic election.

The concept and practices of 419 have extended to multiple spheres of contemporary life in Nigeria. Any new visitor to the country is bound to notice that literally thousands of houses and buildings in cities and towns across the country bear the message "This House Is Not for Sale." Ask any Nigerian the purpose of this message and he or she will tell you that it is to prevent 419. One popular form of 419 is to assume the identity of a real estate agent or a property owner trying to sell his house. In Nigeria's cities and towns, where the real estate market is tight, buyers can be induced to make down payments to secure a later purchase, and in some cases entire transactions have been completed before the buyer discovered that the deal was a scam. In Nigeria there is always the added fear that even if a house has been sold in a scam one might still lose it if the buyer has more money or better political connections than the owner.

Four-one-nine appears in contexts where one might not expect it to; indeed, that it does so is part of the reason that it is successful. When I first lived in Nigeria, young men in Lagos sometimes stood on the side of the road signaling to drivers that something was wrong underneath the drivers' cars. If a driver stopped, the man that had flagged him or her down would offer to check under the car, quickly creating a real problem that only a mechanic— his co-conspirator—could fix.

On a bus ride that I once took between cities in Nigeria, a passenger asked that we all pray for Jesus' "journey mercies," a practice common in the heavily Christian south. Indeed, buses are a popular venue for evangelism and I braced myself for proselytizing. But the man quickly shifted from talk of God to talk of illness and medicine, explaining that he was a renowned healer and that he had brought his medicines on board to help his companions on the journey. He explained that his plastic bottles full of red liquid treated malaria and typhoid and that the ones with yellow liquid treated an assortment of "woman problems" such as irregular menses and infertility; he even had different powders for toothaches and foot odor. Each time that he introduced a new medicine a man in the back of the bus shouted that he wanted it and asked the price. He paid enthusiastically and was given his medicine. Eventually, a few other passengers bought some too. After several stops the medicine peddler disembarked, presumably to continue his sales on a bus going the other way. His main customer also left at the same stop. Once they exited, the woman sitting beside me turned toward me and said, as I had been thinking, "It's 419. The fellow at the back eagerly buying all the medicine is his partner." She paused and added, with a sigh, "Nigeria. . . ."

Corruption and Its Discontents

Nigerians' sense that their state and society have become increasingly amoral—with elites pursuing wealth and power without regard for the consequences, and ordinary people seeking money by all means available simply to survive—contributes to a popular perception that law and order have given way to rampant corruption at every level. The concept of 419 and the breadth with which it is applied across social domains represent this collective conclusion that the country has spiraled out of control. The Pidgin English phrase *Nigeria na war-o* (Nigeria is a war) has become one of the most common expressions in everyday speech. No external critics are as harsh in the evaluation of Nigerian society as are Nigerians.

Nonetheless, implicit in Nigerians' anger and frustration about corruption is the recognition that matters could be and should be different. The perception of 419 as amoral is rooted in strong expectations about social morality, based, in part, on a traditional moral economy wherein reciprocity, kinship, and personal allegiance dictate forms of sociability and social obligation in which the welfare of others is privileged over individual interests. Or perhaps more accurately, individual interests are tied to protecting the welfare of others. In many ways, this moral economy remains powerful in contemporary Nigeria and even contributes to forms of "corruption" that Nigerians see as more or less legitimate. In some situations, Nigerians' discontents are projected backward to better times, in a nostalgia for an idealized past. But in their frustrations over the current state of affairs, many people also look forward to anticipated transformations. The ideals of democracy and development promulgated by the post-colonial state increasingly influence expectations about social morality. Concepts of probity and official accountability are fertilized even in a setting where they are frequently deployed duplicitously.

It is absolutely essential to recognize that Nigerians are ambivalent about corruption. Their acute dissatisfaction with the most amoral forms of corruption, commonly glossed as 419, is produced in relation to experiences with institutions and forms of human relationship that are *not* corrupt. Whether it is trusted friendships and family ties, upright and generous religious congregations and fellowship groups, or networks of informal business relationships that cooperate effectively based on high degrees of trust and internal self-regulation, all Nigerians have experiences with social forms that are honest and scrupulous. Even in the realm of formal institutions associated with the state, examples of people and organizations with a reputation for integrity are well known. Understanding these social currents that push against corruption is as important as explaining those that facilitate corruption.

Conclusion

Distortions are created and inequalities perpetuated when corruption in Nigeria is explained based on reified and simplistic notions of African culture. Such conceptions should be strongly contested. But it is irresponsible, both from a political and a scholarly point of view, to shrink from confronting the troubling conclusions about the relationship between corruption and culture that are evident in this ethnographic account. It is impossible to absorb the prevalence of corruption and the discontent that it produces in Nigeria without concluding that corruption has become heavily implicated in Nigerians' views of their culture.

Nigerians' ambivalence about corruption is explained by the realities that they face. To the extent that ordinary Nigerians are participants in corruption, as well as critics and victims, it is because they are pragmatic: the stakes for individuals in Nigeria are tied ideologically and materially to the social groups to which they belong. Thus, when individuals make choices that one might describe in terms of corruption, they do so with a sense that their own failures to acquire resources will drag others down, and with the knowledge that their own success will be evaluated in terms of its contribution to the larger group. Further, people are well aware of the intense scrutiny that they face from their families, communities, and other associates. When Nigerians speak of "the Nigerian factor," they are referring not only to corruption per se, but also to the pragmatic choices that individuals must make in the context of their obligations to deliver to their people whatever share of the national cake they can capture.

From this perspective, corruption does not appear so detrimental, and, indeed, if this were all there was to corruption, perhaps Nigerians would be much less discontented than they are. But as the concept of 419 suggests, corruption in contemporary Nigeria has far exceeded the boundaries that can be explained by ties of kinship, obligations of patronage, and duties to the communities and groups to which an individual belongs. Because 419 relies on deceptions that manipulate the facades of the state, the trappings of development and democracy, and the symbols of modernity, 419 stands for people's dissatisfaction with precisely these aspects of contemporary life in post-colonial Nigeria. As the institutions of kinship and patron-clientism have become increasingly stretched and strained with the rise of the state as the primary locus of national patrimony, and as people can no longer reliably depend upon reciprocity and sharing to deliver what they need, practices of 419 have become part of a pragmatic repertoire that large numbers of Nigerians use to exploit the contemporary political economic landscape. To ordinary Nigerians, the most troubling implication of "the Nigerian factor" is that 419 has become a way of life.

But the fact that most Nigerians are upset about, even obsessed with, the prevalence of 419 in their society suggests that countervailing moralities and life strategies are still dominant. The notion of 419 is an indigenous critique of the forms of corruption that the vast majority of Nigerians reject. Unfortunately, the degree to which ordinary Nigerians point fingers of accusation inward, quickly suspecting each other of 419, also deflects attention from the larger structural explanations for their suffering.

Notes

1. I lived in Nigeria for more than six years, and I have worked or conducted fieldwork there for extended periods of time over the last nineteen years. From a personal point of view, I long felt that focusing on corruption stereotyped and oversimplified the lives of people that I knew and cared about. From an intellectual point of view, I thought that writing about corruption ran the risk of perpetuating common Western misrepresentations of Africa. These issues remain of great concern to me.

2. I examined corruption in Nigeria in a recent book, *A Culture of Corruption: Everyday Deception and Popular Discontent in Nigeria* (Princeton, 2007). Many of the ethnographic examples in this chapter draw on material from this monograph. In addition to addressing the paradoxes of popular participation in corruption, the book explores the social consequences of popular discontent about corruption, arguing that this discontent helps explain many significant contemporary social trends in Nigeria.

3. Jean-Francois Bayart, *The State in Africa: The Politics of the Belly* (London, 1993); Giorgio Blundo and Jean Pierre Olivier de Sardan, "La Corruption Quotidienne en Afrique de l'Ouest," *Politique Africaine*, LXXXIII (2001), 8–37; Patrick Chabal and Jean-Pascal Daloz, *Africa Works: Disorder as Political Instrument* (Bloomington, 1999); Richard Joseph, *Democracy and Prebendal Politics in Nigeria: The Rise and Fall of the Second Republic* (New York, 1987); Jean Pierre Olivier de Sardan, "A Moral Economy of Corruption in Africa?" *The Journal of Modern African Studies*, XXXVII (1999), 25–52.

4. Peter Ekeh, "Colonialism and the Two Publics in Africa: A Theoretical Statement," *Comparative Journal of Society and History*, XVII (1975), 91–112.

5. Chinua Achebe, *The Trouble with Nigeria* (London, 1983), 2.

6. Olivier de Sardan, "A Moral Economy of Corruption in Africa?" 29.

7. Bayart, *The State in Africa,* 87.

8. Ekeh, "Colonialism and the Two Publics in Africa"; Bayart, *The State in Africa.*

9. Ibid.; Joseph, *Democracy and Prebendal Politics in Nigeria*; Charles Nelson, "PAT 101: Principles of Patronage," *Issues: A Journal of Opinion,* XXIV (1996), 45–51.

10. Warren d'Azevedo, "Common Principles and Variant Kinship Structures Among the Gola of Western Liberia," *American Anthropologist,* LXIV (1962), 404–420.

11. Olivier de Sardan, "A Moral Economy of Corruption in Africa?" 41.

12. Andrew Apter, *The Pan-African Nation: Oil and the Spectacle of Culture in Nigeria* (Chicago, 2005); Michael Watts, "The Shock of Modernity: Petroleum, Protest and Fast Capitalism in an Industrializing Society," in Alan Pred and Michael Watts (eds.), *Reworking Modernity: Capitalisms and Symbolic Discontent* (New Brunswick, 1992).

13. Apter, *The Pan-African Nation*; Watts, "The Shock of Modernity: Petroleum, Protest and Fast Capitalism in an Industrializing Society"; Terry Lynn Karl, *The Paradox of Plenty: Oil Booms and Petro-States* (Berkeley, 1997).

14. Apter, *The Pan-African Nation*; Michael Watts, "Oil as Money: The Devil's Excrement and the Spectacle of Black Gold," in R. Martin (ed.), *Money, Power and Space* (Malden, 1994). For a similar analysis of Venezuela's petro-state, see Fernando Coronil, *The Magical State: Nature, Money, and Modernity in Venezuela* (Chicago, 1997).

15. Bayart, *The State in Africa,* 89.

16. Ibid., 237.

17. See, for example, Arnold Heidenheimer (ed.), *Political Corruption: Readings in Comparative Analysis* (New York, 1970).

18. Joseph Nye, "Corruption and Political Development: A Cost Benefit Analysis," *American Political Science Review,* LVI (1967), 419.

19. Ibid.

20. Blundo and Olivier de Sardan, "La Corruption Quotidienne en Afrique de l'Ouest."

21. Briefly, commission for illicit services refers to a user's payment to officials who then grant access to unwarranted advantages to a user. For example, a contractor might provide money to a government official to ensure that he receives a job in a process supposedly based on competitive bids, or an importer might pay a customs official to underestimate the value of his goods to reduce a tariff. Unwarranted payment for public services involves an official forcing a user to pay for a service that is ostensibly provided for free, or inflating the cost of a routine service. A gratuity is also a kind of payment for services, but usually after the fact, and commonly couched in the idiom of a "thank you."

22. As I try to make clear, though, a dash is often a monetary symbol of a personal or social relationship rather than the naked exchange of money for some (illegal or improper) action or service, as is the case with a bribe.

23. Achebe, *The Trouble with Nigeria,* 1, 38. Italics in original.

24. Nelson, "PAT 101: Principles of Patronage."

25. All names in the case studies are pseudonyms.

26. As alluded to earlier in the text, from a Western viewpoint a dash appears to be a euphemism for a bribe. Policemen ask for dashes at checkpoints; customs officers expect them at the airport. But it can also simply be a gesture of generosity. An in-law can be given a dash after a visit, or a poor gardener might get a dash from his wealthy boss around Christmas-time.

27. Watts, "The Shock of Modernity: Petroleum, Protest and Fast Capitalism in an Industrializing Society."

28. Ibid., 36.

29. Joseph, *Democracy and Prebendal Politics in Nigeria.*

30. Chabal and Daloz, *Africa Works,* 42–43.

31. Josef Gugler, "The Son of the Hawk Does Not Remain Abroad: The Urban-Rural Connection in Africa," *African Studies Review,* XLV (2002), 21–41; Audrey Smock, *Ibo Politics: The Role of Ethnic Unions in Eastern Nigeria* (Cambridge, MA, 1971); Victor Uchendu, *The Igbo People of Southeast Nigeria* (Fort Worth, 1965).

32. Uchendu, *The Igbo People of Southeast Nigeria.*

33. Smock, *Igbo Politics*; Peter Geschiere and Josef Gugler, "The Urban-Rural Connection: Changing Issues of Belonging and Identification," *Africa,* LXVIII (1998), 309–319.

34. Apter, *The Pan African Nation*; Watts, "The Shock of Modernity: Petroleum, Protest and Fast Capitalism in an Industrializing Society."

35. Apter, *The Pan African Nation,* 226–236.

36. Ibid.

37. Ibid., 236–248; Larry Diamond, Anthony H. M. Kirk-Greene, and Oyeleye Oyediran, *Transition without End: Nigerian Politics and Civil Society under Babangida* (Boulder, 1997).

LUCY KOECHLIN *and* MAGDALENA SEPÚLVEDA CARMONA

12

Corruption and Human Rights: Exploring the Connection

The first paragraph of the Preamble to the United Nations Convention against Corruption (UNCAC) declares the state parties' concern "about the seriousness of problems and threats posed by corruption to the stability and security of societies, undermining the institutions and values of democracy, ethical values and justice and jeopardizing sustainable development and the rule of law."[1] Similarly, the Preamble to the Council of Europe Criminal Law Convention on Corruption emphasizes that "corruption threatens the rule of law, democracy and human rights, undermines good governance, fairness and social justice, distorts competition, hinders economic development and endangers the stability of democratic institutions and the moral foundations of society."[2] In other words, the international community recognizes that corruption directly threatens fundamental legal, as well as social, economic, and political, principles. This realization is not new. In 1789, the Preamble to the French Declaration of the Rights of Man and of the Citizen stipulated that "ignorance, oblivion, or contempt" of human rights "are the only causes of public misfortunes" and government corruption.[3]

It is intuitively and empirically plausible that there is a significant correlation between low levels of development, human rights abuses, and the spread of corruption.[4] How exactly this correlation is articulated is open to empirical survey and further analytical inquiry, but this chapter argues that the relationship between human rights and corruption is one that needs to be understood from the perspective of the vulnerable and poor. The protection and empowerment of the vulnerable and disadvantaged is a core objective of a human rights approach, and, given the developmental objectives of anti-corruption reforms, this objective is implicitly and explicitly central to anti-corruption agendas. While in practice human rights and anti-corruption approaches often operate in isolation from each other, both approaches strengthen the understanding of the interdependencies between corruption, discrimination, and accountability processes. One advantage of examining the links between corruption and human rights is that human rights standards, as established in major international treaties, impose obligations upon states. Focusing on specific human rights helps to identify who is entitled to make claims when acts of corruption occur and who has a duty to take action against corruption and protect those that are harmed by it.

As this chapter examines, in the case of Malawi, a human rights approach may help to empower claim holders to demand their rights in relation to corruption. Such an approach can also assist states (including all branches of government) and other public authorities to fulfill their human rights responsibilities at every level. Linking human rights to corruption might also facilitate increased public support for anti-corruption strategies. Despite strong rhetorical commitments to combat corruption, the political impact of anti-corruption programs in Malawi has been low. To increase political support for anti-corruption initiatives, it is necessary to build public pressure. Identifying the specific links between corruption and human rights may persuade key actors—public officials, parliamentarians, judges, prosecutors, lawyers, businesspeople, bankers, accountants, the media, and the general public—to take a stronger stand against corruption.

This chapter does not assume that a human rights framework provides the only or even the best tool of those that are available. Nonetheless, this chapter analyzes the potential of the human rights framework to have a positive impact in certain areas that are key to anti-corruption reforms. Such a framework amplifies and broadens accountability systems that are supported by anti-corruption reforms. Ultimately, the aim of the chapter is to call for a broader collaboration between the anti-corruption and human rights movements. For this purpose, the chapter first outlines central cornerstones of anti-corruption approaches. Second, the anti-corruption and human rights framework in Malawi is explored for a better understanding of the measures and issues that are facing countries and citizens. Last, the insights drawn from the case of Malawi are discussed with regard to the potential for an anti-corruption approach that is enriched with human rights principles and tools to increase the inclusion and protection of discriminated, poor, and vulnerable groups in anti-corruption reforms.

An Anti-Corruption Perspective

In recent years, many different measures of corruption have been developed, countering the myth that nothing can be done about corruption. In the following section, two different but highly influential international approaches are outlined, followed by a discussion of the shortcomings of key anti-corruption reforms and the relevance of including a human rights perspective in these reforms.

The International Anti-Corruption Framework

The problem of corruption has engaged the interest of national and international communities for the last two decades. It has been put on center stage by the development community, which has finally recognized that corruption is a major obstacle to sustainable development and reform efforts. This recognition is closely related to the emergence of the concept of (good) governance (i.e., the role of capable, accountable, and effective public institutions to deliver services to, respond to, and protect their citizens). Anti-corruption efforts include a broad range of measures, the most important of which are aimed at strengthening the rule of law; supporting meritocratic systems, ethical values, and adequate pay within the civil service; establishing specialized accountability agencies such as anti-corruption bodies to increase public awareness and to prevent, as well as (sometimes) enforce, anti-corruption principles; and, not least, generally fostering transparency and accountability processes within and across all sectors of society. In many developing countries, concern with corruption has led to a wave of national anti-corruption strategies, and on a regional and international level a host of conventions as well as voluntary initiatives have emerged, each addressing one component or several components of corruption.[5]

The most significant of these initiatives is the United Nations Convention against Corruption (UNCAC), which was adopted in 2003 and entered into force in 2005. It has since been ratified by more than 120 countries. UNCAC is the most extensive instrument against corruption, defining a wide range of mandatory as well as voluntary principles of and best practices for anti-corruption. As an international treaty, it is evident that the state is the main subject of the duties and responsibilities that are outlined. However, UNCAC makes clear that corruption needs to be addressed by all sectors, both nationally and internationally, to support "the participation of society and reflect the principles of the rule of law, proper management of public affairs and public property, integrity, transparency and accountability."[6] Major provisions regard the establishment of bodies responsible for coordinating preventive measures, efficient and accountable public sector management, civic participation, and extending the criminalization of corrupt practices.[7] Recognizing the capacity restraints of developing countries as well as the difficulties of tracing corruption in a globalized world, UNCAC also underlines the importance of international cooperation and information exchange in strengthening national and international efforts against corruption. UNCAC has become the most important internationally acknowledged frame of reference for best practice for combating corruption and serves as a frame of reference for most, if not all, contemporary, national anti-corruption strategies.

The most frequent critique raised against UNCAC is that many of its provisions are voluntary, not mandatory. Moreover, there is no monitoring mechanism in place yet that assesses the degree of governmental compliance, which makes it difficult for citizens to judge the extent of implementation. Tellingly, though, throughout the whole document no human right is explicitly mentioned, although many of the articles deal with relevant provisions: cases in point are the articles relating to public procurement and management of public finances, access to information (named 'public reporting'), or the participation of society.[8]

National Integrity Systems

UNCAC managed to put corruption on the map of the international community by setting a comprehensive set of standards for anti-corruption efforts. The anti-corruption measures anchored in UNCAC reflect the fact that corruption is not a one-dimensional phenomenon, but that it needs to be addressed by a variety of measures; such measures may be general in nature, but they need to be adapted to the relative national context. The importance of the institutional context for understanding and effectively combating corruption is epitomized in the National Integrity System (NIS) approach. The concept, coined by the most prominent non-governmental organization (NGO) engaged in the fight against corruption, Transparency International, stresses that the role of systemic reforms is to promote integrity, transparency, and accountability and thus to prevent corruption.

The fundamental premise of the NIS approach is that high levels of corruption result from the promotion of private interests over the public interest. In a society where power is monopolized, rules are at risk of being distorted in the interest of those in power, and power-bearers are held less responsible for their actions and decisions. In other words, the accountability mechanisms intended to check the power of public officials are inadequate, leading to widespread corruption and the subversion of the public interest. The establishment of stronger horizontal accountability processes and a balanced configuration of agencies and rules designed to check abuses of public power—a National Integrity System—is seen as a key way to change such cultures of corruption.

The NIS approach defines the most important "pillars" of integrity that can be adapted to the specific institutional setting of any country. These pillars include central public bodies, i.e., the executive, legislature, and judiciary; specific horizontal accountability bodies such as supreme audit institutions or anti-corruption agencies; as well as the private sector and civil society. The NIS seeks to conceptualize the interrelationships between accountability mechanisms and provide a framework to assess the extent and the causes of corruption and to profile systemic corruption risks in a given country.[9] Potentially, the NIS country surveys can provide useful tools for identifying entry-points for stakeholder dialogues about corruption or prioritizing anti-corruption measures in a country. In practice, however, they are underutilized by national and international actors, as they are too general and of varying quality for practitioners and scholars. A further critique is that, as in the UNCAC, human rights do not feature explicitly anywhere in the source book, and only rarely are they mentioned in the individual country surveys. This blind spot is highlighted by the fact that human rights commissions are not mentioned among the key integrity pillars, unlike, for instance, ombudsmen.[10]

Accountability Systems in Anti-Corruption Strategies

As can be gleaned from the section above, the anti-corruption community firmly promotes institutional and legal accountability mechanisms as keys to preventing corruption. As dysfunctional public institutions and skewed power relations are at the heart of corruption, accountability measures are aimed at strengthening the public sector as well as making it more responsive by supporting a coherent, comprehensive legal system; strong oversight institutions; and the participation of civil society. Such measures can include provisions for access to information, asset declaration or whistle-blowing; legal reforms such as the introduction of anti-corruption legislation that makes specific corrupt acts illegal and hence justiciable; or the establishment of new horizontal accountability bodies such as an anti-corruption agency. These systems are designed to safeguard the public interest and guarantee responsive public institutions, and they require a strong rule of law, a sound institutional design, as well as engaged citizens to sustain their vitality.

However, these reforms have been heavily criticized for their top-down, state-centered quality; they do not take into account the political context in which they operate, which accounts for the uneven results of anti-corruption reforms.[11] In other words, successful reforms may need to go beyond sound institutional design; indeed, it can be argued that reform is a more intricate, incremental, and complex process than is generally assumed. Corrupt practices are more than just a product of dysfunctional public institutions; they are intimately intertwined with prevalent social practices, especially in the political sphere: "[a]s an illicit form of social exchange, corruption is closely connected with (and not always easily distinguishable from) other types of informal exchange engaged in by political actors."[12] This insight is brought to life by the ethnographic, bottom-up perspective on corruption in Nigeria provided in this volume by Smith, who illustrates "the complex ways in which [corruption] is woven into the fabric of political and economic life—part and parcel of both the maintenance of social inequality and the struggles to respond to it."[13] Institutional reform may be a necessary but not a sufficient condition to change such exchange practices, to transform a culture of corruption into a culture of accountability.

The inclusion of a rights-based approach could prove useful to this transformation process, as the language and tools of human rights focus both on codified rights as well as on discriminatory and unequal social structures. Although anti-corruption agendas are based on the assumption that the rule of law and other formal accountability mechanisms will support a strong civil society and, presumably, percolate down to the citizens' level, there is no explicit reference to human rights in key anti-corruption documents. The NIS or UNCAC are cases in point.[14] This omission can be traced to the anti-corruption community; both on an activist as well as on a policy-making level this community does not conceive of human rights as instrumental in the fight against corruption. If at all, human rights are seen to be an outcome, not a method of anti-corruption intervention.

Malawi: Exploring the (Dis)junctures

The following section explores the anti-corruption and human rights framework in Malawi, a country that faces many developmental challenges, and a country that has endorsed a strong human rights framework as well as anti-corruption measures. However, these efforts have yet to come to fruition. The authors argue that neglecting to recognize and incorporate a human rights approach into the agendas of anti-corruption initiatives constitutes a serious weakness of anti-corruption efforts, as the incorporation of a human rights approach would enhance the spectrum and scope of accountability mechanisms, thereby bringing both reforms closer to the people.

Malawi's Commitments to Human Rights and Anti-Corruption

Malawi has voluntarily assumed several international obligations for the promotion and protection of human rights. Malawi is a state party to the International Covenant on Economic, Social and Cultural Rights (ICESCR), the International Covenant on Civil and Political Rights (ICCPR), and its Optional Protocol, the Convention on the Rights of the Child (CRC), the Convention on the Elimination of All Forms of Racial Discrimination (CERD), the Convention on the Elimination of All Forms of Discrimination against Women (CEDAW), and the Convention against Torture and Other Cruel, Inhuman or Degrading Treatment or Punishment.[15] At the regional level, Malawi has assumed obligations for economic, social, political, civil, and cultural rights by ratifying the African Charter on Human and People's Rights and the African Charter on the Rights and Welfare of the Child.[16] All of these human rights treaties impose on the state several obligations to respect, protect, and fulfill human rights. Within the framework of these treaties, Malawi is subject to several monitoring mechanisms. On the one hand, there are the supervisory mechanisms of the UN treaties called "treaty bodies" such as the Human Rights Committee; the Committee on Economic, Social and Cultural Rights; and the Committee on the Rights of the Child, as well as several so-called charter-based mechanisms, which are supervisory mechanisms that are not based on human rights treaties but rather on the UN Charter.[17] Under the UN framework, the charter-based mechanisms include the "Universal Periodic Review" (UPR) and the "special procedures," which are mechanisms of the Human Rights Council, which replaced the former Commission on Human Rights.[18] On the other hand, Malawi is also subject to regional human rights mechanisms such as the African Commission and Court on Human and Peoples' Rights.

At the domestic level, the Constitution of the Republic of Malawi gives great prominence to human rights. The constitution refers not only to civil and political rights but also to economic, social, and cultural rights, and the right to development.[19] For example, Article 30 prescribes that the state shall take all necessary measures for the realization of the right to development. Such measures shall include, among others, equal opportunity for all in their access to basic resources, education, health services, food, shelter, employment, and infrastructure."[20] Under the "Principles of National Policy" (Article 13), the state has an obligation to promote and protect the welfare of its citizens, specifically in terms of gender equality, health, nutrition, the environment, education, and the protection of various disadvantaged groups. Moreover, under the same article, a paragraph is devoted to "Public Trust and Good Governance," underlining the importance of accountability and transparency to foster trust in public institutions.

The constitution also establishes several important human rights bodies such as a Human Rights Commission (Chapter XI), an Ombudsman (Chapter X), and a National Compensation Tribunal (Chapter XIII). The "Malawi Human Rights Commission" (MHRC), started in 1996, has a broad mandate to promote and protect human rights.[21] According to the constitution, the "Commission shall be competent in every respect to protect and promote human rights in Malawi in the broadest sense possible and to investigate violations of human rights on its own motion or upon complaints received by any person, class of persons or body." The constitution gives the Human Rights Commission broad powers to investigate human rights violations upon its own initiative or upon complaints that it receives. The commissioners can comment publicly on any human rights issue and make recommendations to the executive and legislative branches. The Ombudsman is entrusted to investigate cases where it is alleged that a person has suffered an "injustice" and it does not appear that there is an available remedy. The National Compensation Tribunal is mandated to investigate and take legal action against government officials who are responsible for the abuses.

According to this constitutional framework, Malawi is equipped with an extensive legal and institutional foundation that guarantees core political and civil rights, as well as economic, social, and cultural human rights. Relevant constitutional oversight bodies oversee the realization of these rights and principles. The Republic of Malawi has also taken several measures to combat corruption at the international and domestic level. The most important one is, no doubt, the UNCAC, which Malawi signed in 2004 and ratified in 2007.[22] Malawi is also a member of the New African Partnership for Development (NEPAD), which stipulates a wide range of principles for economic, social, and political governance. More important, Malawi has also signed the Memorandum of Understanding for the African Peer Review Mechanism (APRM), which assesses and supports the implementation of NEPAD's provisions. The APRM identifies corruption as a significant cross-cutting issue and puts a strong emphasis on preventive measures.[23] At the domestic level, the constitution considers transparency, accountability, personal integrity, and financial probity as "fundamental principles" and requires the "introduc[tion] of measures which will guarantee accountability, transparency, personal integrity and financial probity and which by virtue of their effectiveness and transparency will strengthen confidence in public institutions." In conformity with these principles, the president gave his assent to the Corrupt Practices Act in 1995, and Malawi established an Anti-Corruption Bureau in 1998.[24] The bureau is a government department and its director and deputy director are appointed by the president. In addition, giving or receiving a bribe—whether to or from a Malawian or to or from a foreign official—is a crime under Section 90 of Malawi's penal code.

Citizens' Realities

In spite of Malawi's commitment to both human rights and the prevention of corruption on an international and domestic level, the social, political, and economic realities of Malawi have yet to change significantly. Whereas Malawi is ranked in the top quarter of sub-Saharan African countries in the Index of African Governance, reflecting its strong institutional framework, according to the 2007 Human Development Index, Malawi ranks 164th out of 177 countries. Malawi is considered one of the least developed countries, with relatively weak state institutions, facing major development challenges. Corruption is one of these challenges—Malawi ranked 115th out of 180 countries on the 2008 Corruption Perceptions Index (CPI), with its score of 2.7, which remained virtually unchanged from past years. This assessment is confirmed by the World Bank Institute's Governance Indicators, which, since 2003, has ranked the control of corruption in Malawi just above the 25th percentile.[25]

Therefore, in spite of an advanced constitution that has been in force for fifteen years and a political agenda that emphasizes the promotion and protection of human rights and the fight against corruption, in practice, most citizens remain disenfranchised and vulnerable to abuses of power by public officials. Although some core dimensions of the National Policy Priorities have certainly improved over the last decade, most citizens still do not have access to adequate nutrition, health, or education. The rural standard of living, which is postulated as a key success indicator of government policies in the constitution, is bleak; and gender equality is still at the stage of sensitization and awareness-raising.[26]

In other words, key economic and social rights that are mentioned in the constitution as well as relevant international standards that Malawi has subscribed to—such as the right to life, the right to education, freedom of expression, the right to an adequate standard of health, or the right to food—are not guaranteed by the state. Partly due to Malawi's weak economic base, partly due to a lack of political will, many of Malawi's obligations and corresponding human rights are neither being protected nor realized.

As Kayangolu argues, the "promotion of human rights as a means of social transformation can . . . be judged on the basis of what impact the promotion, protection and enforcement of the rights have had on the position of . . . disadvantaged groups."[27] Discussing contemporary land, labor, and gender relations in Malawi, he comes to the conclusion that "despite changes at the highest normative level," this transformation remains incomplete.[28] Current reports on key sectors confirm that the vulnerabilities of citizens have not improved significantly. On the contrary, reports reveal that policies that are targeted to aid the poor are not showing tangible effects. For instance, the Malawi Poverty and Vulnerability Assessment of 2006 reveals that there are continuing and considerable gaps between poor and non-poor in accessing education services, as well as access to health care.[29] Another area of grave concern is the situation of prisoners, whose right to life, a fair trial, health care, or adequate nutrition are routinely denied.[30]

The question of what factors affect the access to and utilization of services, such as health or education, especially from the perspective of marginalized citizens, requires closer attention. In none of the sector surveys, with the exception of prisons, was corruption mentioned explicitly as a factor impeding access to services. However, it is evident from other empirical surveys that, in a context of endemic corruption, the misappropriation of public funds and the abuse of positions of power impact the poor disproportionally by entrenching inequalities and the vicious circle of exclusion.[31]

The poor and vulnerable bear the brunt of social, economic, and political inequalities. Also, the gap between human rights and anti-corruption rhetoric and reality is a feature of the structural and material difficulties that these countries face, in terms of national income, physical and human resources, and infrastructure. These difficulties are not an excuse, however, for negating the internationally acknowledged, intrinsic value of human rights and the obligation of the state to respect, protect, and fulfill these rights. Moreover, the profiles of the sectors show that the realization of these rights is only prevented in part by structural difficulties; political priorities define the allocations of the available resources, and these political priorities are not sufficiently shaped by the needs and rights of the disenfranchised. The question is, then, to whom and through which mechanisms are the policymakers accountable.

Anti-Corruption and Accountability Systems

Chapter Three of Malawi's constitution postulates that "the authority to exercise power of State is conditional upon the sustained trust of the people of Malawi and that trust can only be maintained through open, accountable and transparent Government and informed democratic choice." Moreover, "the inherent dignity and worth of each human being requires that the State and all persons shall recognize and protect fundamental human rights and afford the fullest protection to the rights and views of all individuals, groups and minorities whether or not they are entitled to vote."[32]

Accordingly, the constitution provides a strong legal and institutional framework that protects citizens' rights and establishes a sophisticated system of horizontal accountability bodies.[33] These bodies include those mentioned above such as the Human Rights Commission and Inspectorate of Prisons. Not surprising, for a young and poor democracy, however, these accountability institutions, as well as the whole democratic framework, have yet to be consolidated.[34] The parliamentary culture in Malawi is still very uneven, not least as a result of a weak electoral commission and flawed election processes or of the lack of funds available for these committees to convene.[35] The justice system, while generally regarded as independent, suffers from meager human, financial, and physical resources, which seriously impede procedures of and access to justice. As a report on the justice system in Malawi describes, "the vast majority of people are not able to enforce their rights because they cannot access formal justice delivery institutions, including the courts. Poor people, especially women, are disproportionately impeded by the various physical, financial and linguistic barriers."[36] These barriers include the physical distance to the nearest court, the financial costs of court and lawyer fees, and the fact that English is the official language of the courts but not the first language of the majority of the population—a problem that is also salient to participation in and access to the proceedings of the National Assembly.

In the same vein, the capacity and visibility of the accountability bodies is patchy. A report by the British Department of International Development (DFID) on governance in Malawi concluded that its "accountability institutions suffer the same capability weaknesses as the rest of government": inadequate funding; weak legislative frameworks, terms, and conditions of service; weak capacity and human resources, as well as particular bureaucratic mindsets both within the executive as well as, at times, within the institutions themselves.[37] Notwithstanding their constitutional mandate, these accountability bodies are heterogeneous and diverse in their endowments as well as in the degree of their financial and operational independence.[38] Whereas, for instance, the Law Commission is a relatively strong and robust institution that, albeit under-resourced, is in a position consistently to exercise its mandate, other such bodies are practically non-existent or severely challenged because they lack operational independence.[39]

A prime example is the Malawi Anti-Corruption Bureau (ACB), which has received prominence through President Bingu wa' Mutharika's vow of "zero tolerance of corruption." Since its establishment the ACB has been strongly supported by various donor agencies financially, materially, and technically; hence, it does not suffer from a lack of capacity. In spite of the relatively comfortable funding situation, the ACB is deemed to be "weak" by the 2007 Global Integrity Report (although Malawi's anti-corruption legislation is classified as "very strong").[40] This assessment reflects the popular perception of the ACB, which says that the ACB suffers from a "high profile cases syndrome."[41] Since the ACB's establishment, the opposition and the media have persistently accused the ACB of being subject to political manipulation and preoccupied with political witch-hunts, rather than with corruption cases that concern the daily lives of citizens.[42] In spite of high rates of corruption in daily life, citizens' access to the ACB is low, and the ACB is not renowned for its responsiveness and openness: "Although the ACB has made it known that citizens can blow the whistle, it takes [a] long [time] for citizens to know or even verify if indeed the bureau has acted on their complaint. Most times the ACB does not. And it is not publicly known to."[43] The inertia of the ACB seems largely due to political interference in its operational work. An indication of how strong the political pressures may be is that the director of the ACB has been changed three times within the last several years, always under accusations by the government that he is incompetent or corrupt: "In Malawi, President Bingu wa' Mutharika's declared war on corruption received a significant boost after the Public Appointments Committee (PAC) of parliament appointed Alexious Nampota as the new anti corruption czar to lead the Anti-Corruption Bureau. President Mutharika has sacked two previous directors of the anti-corruption body over graft charges. He also clashed with members of the parliamentary appointment committee after they refused to confirm a previous nominee."[44] Indeed, such influence by the executive is legal, as according to Section 6(3) of the Corrupt Practices Act, the president is empowered to suspend the director of the bureau if he or she "considers it desirable to do so."[45]

Executive interference also raises its ugly head in other key institutions, a fact lamented by the Human Rights Commission in a report on accountability. The following quote from the directorate of the public prosecutions is particularly illustrative of the mindset that seems to pervade the executive's attitude toward constitutional bodies: "The most outstanding challenge that the office of the Director of Public Prosecutions faced was that for close to four months the office ran without the Director following the sudden removal of the then Director of the Public Prosecutions. Reacting to critics on the manner in which the DPP was removed, the state president indicated that the director of public prosecutions was lawfully removed. The president further informed the public that 'no office that has been appointed can be independent of the appointing authority.'"[46]

This quote is symptomatic of an attitude that seems to be entrenched in Malawi. Beyond the indisputable fiscal restraints and economic challenges with which the government is confronted,

> the gap between the state and society is also defined by what we would term 'political culture': in the mindsets of many government officials as well as in the population, the state and government are not here to serve the people, but to direct them, or, worse, serve the interests of the powerful. Bureaucracy as a means to frustrate instead of facilitate, the use of discretionary and arbitrary action, the pursuit of personal instead of national interests by politicians and civil servants alike are not conducive to the operationalisation and internalisation of values such as equity, participation and representation. . . . In a state where these bodies guarding the rights and obligations of state and society are, in the words of many people we spoke to, 'treated like children' by the executive, such long-term development perspectives will remain skewed.[47]

In spite of an advanced institutional and legislative accountability framework, fundamental flaws remain that weaken the effective functioning of these accountability bodies and systems. Some of these flaws, such as the terms and conditions of appointment, can be remedied relatively easily. However, the expansion of political and civil liberties and the establishment of an institutional framework of accountability are—albeit indispensible—not sufficient to create and sustain a culture of integrity, ensure civil and political rights, realize economic and social rights, and overcome a lethargic and unresponsive political will. To transform the political, economic, and social inequalities that are at the root of the corruption that causes and facilitates inequalities and discrimination in Malawi, additional pressure is needed. Such pressure stems from both horizontal and vertical accountability processes.[48] Anti-corruption reforms, even those aimed at empowering citizens to demand accountability from their government, such as Malawi's constitution, are institutional frameworks that provide the tools for more effective and accountable policies and politics; but they are only the vehicles, not the drivers. To "do politics" differently, to bring principles of transparency and accountability to life and give them political significance, takes a far greater surge in citizens' articulation and power.[49]

The ACB has conveyed this insight succinctly on its website: "In order for every person in Malawi to benefit from a decline in corruption, there needs to be fostered a climate which is hostile to corruption, whereby every person stands up and says that they will not tolerate corruption any longer. A massive change in attitude towards corruption is needed, and the current laissez-faire concern must be abandoned. People must tell their elected leaders and pressurise those employed in the public service and also private sector that they will no longer put up with abuses of their rights."[50]

Although political will and citizen empowerment are acknowledged as decisive factors in anti-corruption programs, policies that include such elements tend to shy away from the thorny and highly political issue of unequal power relations and the infringement of individual rights. Such policies fall short of addressing fundamental questions of protection of rights and access to resources. The same holds true for the human rights agenda, as Kanyongolo argues cogently in his case study on human rights in Malawi.[51] If these root causes are not addressed, the risk of institutionalizing inequalities becomes, like corruption and human rights abuses, endemic. In other words, institutional and legal reform alone is a necessary, but not a sufficient, condition for changing a political culture and democratizing rights and opportunities. As Landman and Schudel conclude, "long term cultural change, however, is much harder to instil as sedimented practices over time have become institutionalised and reified to such a degree that corruption becomes an acceptable form of 'doing politics' and human rights violations continue with impunity."[52]

Where Are the Anti-Corruption Efforts Going?

Despite all the institutional and legislative efforts to combat it, corruption not only remains a challenge in Malawi, it continues to flourish.[53] The international and national anti-corruption efforts have not achieved great effect to date. As indicated above, a remaining central problem is the attitude of the executive toward abuses of power, which will not be overcome by institutional reforms alone. As the review of Malawi's national readiness to participate in NEPAD states, one of the key issues facing governance in Malawi is what NEPAD terms "sound laws, refusal to obey. . . . Nearly all the experts interviewed . . . noted that what Malawi lacks is not law (although there are significant shortcomings that need focus), but disciplined implementation and leadership to command compliance with existing rules. The government has developed an internal culture of impunity in which regulations, laws and the constitution itself are routinely ignored and violations are rarely punished."[54]

Such a diagnosis is harsh, but it is one that has not fundamentally changed in the fifteen years that have passed since Malawi's adoption of a progressive constitution. As long as accountability bodies are "treated like children" and a culture of impunity is nurtured, justice will continue to be administered along power lines, and not by respect for laws, procedures, or citizens' rights—a situation that is compounded by the severe resource constraints with which Malawi is faced.[55]

Malawi is not unique in this regard. Every country with widespread levels of corruption—and they are the rule, not the exception, as Transparency International's World Map of the Corruption Perceptions Index confirms—grapples with its own structural as well as cultural factors that subvert both anti-corruption as well as human rights objectives.[56] At the same time, the human rights framework and relevant anti-corruption and accountability reforms have doubtlessly led to an expansion of the legal and moral basis upon which the rule of law and the rights of citizens can be claimed. As this chapter demonstrates, however, such an expansion needs to be filled with deeper political significance. Fighting corruption is essentially a political program that stands in for more accountability, transparency, legality, and, not least, equality. Evidently, the same holds true for human rights. As Uvin states forcefully, "the nature of the duties that are created by human rights claims is a deeply political and constantly shifting matter. . . . It is not about merely asserting the existence of legal claims and abstract categories . . . but about political struggles, in which codified human rights are tools that crystallize the moral imagination and provide power in the political struggle but do not substitute for either."[57]

It is precisely at this point that the integration of a rights-sensitive approach into anti-corruption initiatives can act as a conveyor belt between the formal legal-institutional framework and its transformation into social, economic, and political realities. Accountability in terms of legal as well as political obligations to explain and justify (in)action is pivotal to reforming dysfunctional state institutions and realizing citizens' rights.

Why Include a Human Rights Approach
in the Fight against Corruption?

While conventional wisdom seems to indicate that the fight against corruption and the more general goal of ensuring human rights share a common ground, often the strategies to end corruption and to promote and protect human rights run in parallel. Human rights and corruption should not be treated in isolation of each other. To date, however, few efforts have been made to find a common strategy that will reinforce the fight against corruption and the protection of human rights. Even fewer efforts have been undertaken to reach out to and actively include those parts of society that are further removed from the epicenters of policy-making. Combating corruption and ensuring human rights both require strong collective, coordinated efforts from different sectors in society. Further, in-depth analyses of the links between corruption and human rights are necessary to move beyond narrow approaches to both anti-corruption and promotion of human rights. Human rights can also inform anti-corruption strategies, by assessing the impact of specific corrupt practices on core human rights (such as access to basic resources). This process would doubtlessly amplify the transformative effect on the lives of the poor and provide a real alternative to the sweeping mainstream approaches to anti-corruption reforms such as those that Jomo critiques in this volume.[58]

In other words, a better understanding of these interdependencies may encourage organizations and agencies that work in the field of human rights more closely to collaborate with national and international anti-corruption agencies. Moreover, these interdependencies might persuade the organizations that they need to look beyond traditional coalitions to energize their movements.[59]

Building Political Will

As this chapter has illustrated, despite strong institutional and legislative frameworks to combat corruption, the impact of the anti-corruption programs in Malawi has been low. To fight corruption effectively, a strong political will is necessary. To increase political support it is necessary to build public pressure. Linking human rights to corruption may help to promote a culture of zero tolerance against corruption.

Identifying specific links between corruption and human rights may persuade key actors—public officials, parliamentarians, judges, prosecutors, lawyers, businesspeople, bankers, accountants, the media, and the public in general—to take a stronger stand against corruption. Governments are generally permeable to pressure from human rights groups. Applying human rights principles and norms may diminish the level of public tolerance of corruption and strengthen public support for anti-corruption measures, even in countries that are sensitive to references to human rights. More to the point, by using core economic, social, and cultural rights as a frame of reference—such as water, housing, health, or education—corrupt practices can be differentiated from one another and prioritized according to the degree that they impact the lives of the vulnerable. This method would enable bottom-up political mobilization and help bridge the gaps between officials' rhetoric and their political practices.

Empowering People and Raising Awareness

A crucial component of a human rights approach is to empower claimants and to clarify the obligations of duty bearers. Human rights standards, as established in major international treaties and domestic legislation, impose obligations upon states. A clear understanding of the practical connections between corruption and human rights may empower claim holders to demand their rights in relation to claims of corruption, and induce states (including all branches of government) and other public authorities to respect, protect, and fulfill their human rights responsibilities at every level.

A human rights approach can also provide additional accountability mechanisms to the fight against corruption. One of the advantages of linking acts of corruption with violations of human rights is the heightened awareness that one can challenge corruption through the numerous mechanisms that exist for monitoring compliance with human rights at the national (e.g., domestic courts and ombudsman office), regional (e.g., African Commission and Court on Human and People's Rights), and international (e.g., United Nations human rights mechanisms) levels. The possibility that victims of corruption can have recourse through human rights mechanisms such as those used by the International Covenant on Civil and Political Rights (ICCPR), Convention on the Rights of the Child (CRC), and the International Covenant on Economic, Social, and Cultural Rights (ICESCR) would give prominence to a corruption case and may force the state to redress the situation. Such mechanisms might also make corrupt officials more cautious of misusing their public power. Using human rights mechanisms may therefore have a deterrent effect on corruption.

A human rights approach may also raise people's awareness about the impact that corruption has on their individual rights. If corruption is perceived as a violation of human rights, people will be aware of the consequences that corruption has on individuals' interests and how detrimental even a minor corrupt practice may be for victims and the population generally. This knowledge might convert large sections of the citizenry into strong supporters of the fight against corruption.[60]

When looking at human rights' implications for corruption, it is possible to circumvent legalistic difficulties in the fight against corruption. For example, when a police force does not, in principle, have the power to prosecute a corruption case, connecting the case with a human rights violation might enable the prosecutors to act. Such a connection would also allow ombudsman offices to address cases of corruption as part of their constitutional duty to promote and protect human rights. In this way, accountability mechanisms become far more responsive and closer to citizens' realities.

Preventing Corruption

A weak human rights protection can create opportunities for corruption. Thus, the promotion and protection of human rights may also be a good strategy to prevent corruption.[61] While it is not the intention of this chapter to address this issue in detail, those human rights that are crucial to preventing corruption are mentioned below.

THE RIGHT TO FREEDOM OF EXPRESSION. The right to freedom of expression (including the rights to free and pluralistic media; assembly; and association) is essential to enable effective participation from citizens and to combat corruption. When governments do not interfere illegitimately with the free flow of information, there should be more opportunities to denounce cases of corruption. However, as people in the media can also be bribed, this right alone is not sufficient. Governments must also guarantee the plurality of the media as a tool to prevent corruption. Often, when there is no respect for freedom of expression, there are weak media that are unable to expose corruption, without risking lawsuits for defamation or libel.

THE RIGHT TO INFORMATION. Previously, this right was interpreted as an obligation upon governments not to interfere with the flow of information. It was not until 2002 that the African Commission on Human and People's Rights introduced the notion of a positive obligation more explicitly and in 2006 that the Inter-American Human Rights Court ruled unambiguously in favor of a right to access public information. Thus, from the human rights perspective, states should make administrative documents public when they could prove to be crucial for citizens' decision-making and for a social audit of the state's administration. The challenge of guaranteeing citizens' access to information, however, implies a series of reforms and positive measures that governments must undertake to make progress in the effective application of this right.[62]

POLITICAL RIGHTS AND ENCOURAGING PARTICIPATION. Citizens' low political participation creates conditions for impunity and corruption. Their effective exercise of their political rights would assist in the fight against corruption by counterbalancing the state's abuse of power that leads to corruption.

Participation is an essential principle of human rights. While access to national and international human rights accountability mechanisms is not free of impediments, the mobilization of citizens nonetheless acts as an effective tool for accountability. As demonstrated, corruption and human rights abuses are embedded in inequitable power relations; although institutional reforms can be implemented from above, the participation and engagement of citizens needs to be mobilized from the bottom. The integration of a human rights approach into anti-corruption efforts allows citizens to engage in areas where they are most affected by corrupt practices. A rights-based approach lends momentum to a redistributive and socially empowering agenda that resists the kind of authoritarian and discretionary tendencies that are the hallmark of a culture of impunity. The rights that are invoked belong to people(s), and not to the government, and hence the processes of asserting and claiming these rights gives civic spaces—such as constitutional rights— political and social meaning.[63]

Incorporating the Perspectives of Vulnerable and Disadvantaged Groups

Most important, a human rights approach incorporates the perspectives of vulnerable groups and disadvantaged groups—a perspective rarely included explicitly in anti-corruption approaches, in spite of its developmental thrust. A human rights approach is essentially about empowering vulnerable and disadvantaged groups, driven by cross-cutting principles of non-discrimination, participation, and accountability. A human rights approach emphasizes that vulnerable groups are not passive recipients in the fight against corruption but are crucial partners. These groups should not be consulted in a superficial manner solely to satisfy a bureaucratic requirement of participation.

The case of Malawi shows that even where an institutional framework is strong, state reform and horizontal accountability bodies alone are not robust enough and often not responsive enough to meet the demands and needs of marginalized groups. Several human rights obligations refer to the protection of the vulnerable and disadvantaged against abuses. Beyond the explicit inclusion of principles such as non-discrimination and protection of the poor and vulnerable, a human rights approach to anti-corruption expands both the normative framework as well as the legal tools at its disposal.[64]

Evidence-Based Strategies

While this chapter stresses the advantages of a human rights approach to anti-corruption, it is important to note that the human rights movement would also greatly benefit from a closer collaboration with the anti-corruption movement. The anti-corruption movement has developed a wide range of mapping tools and diagnostic instruments that allow for the systematic identification of corruption risk factors in specific sectors.[65] Anti-corruption approaches also use the statistical analyses from the information collected by governments and their methodologies for budget analysis. These diagnostic tools and methodologies can also contribute to human rights assessments. While human rights organizations are increasingly considering these tools, anti-corruption organizations have more experience using such instruments and can assist the former in development.

Conclusion

In principle, strategies to end corruption and to promote and protect human rights are likely to reinforce one another. Little work has been done to incorporate a human rights perspective in the fight against corruption. Individuals and organizations that promote and protect human rights and those that fight corruption tend not to work together.

Fortunately, this disconnect seems to be changing, as there are examples of the integration of both agendas.[66] Worth noting here is the recent mission of the African Commission on Human and People's Rights to Malawi, when in 2008 it met with the Anti-Corruption Bureau to discuss the human rights dimension of corruption in Malawi.[67] Nonetheless, further efforts need to be taken to enhance the collaboration and cross fertilization of these efforts.

This chapter attempted to demonstrate that while institutional and legislative frameworks may have strong provisions in place, such systems alone are not sufficient to transform political orders that are characterized by the widespread disenfranchisement of citizens. This chapter argues that it is necessary to go beyond conventional institutional and legislative approaches to make anti-corruption reforms less technical and more powerful in terms of political, social, economic, and legal transformation.

First, the integration of a human rights approach places corruption (or, more precisely, a specific corrupt practice) within a universal normative framework. Second, this normative framework obliges states and governments to respect, protect, and fulfill specific rights and, hence, obliges them to act when corruption affects compliance with these duties. Third, the universality of human rights and the relevant international human rights treaties both transcend the inadequacies of national jurisdictions as well as strengthen relevant national provisions, in terms of a normative discourse as well as in terms of international legal mechanisms.

While a detailed examination of the further links between corruption and human rights is necessary, a pragmatic starting point for stronger synergies between these initiatives is that a clear understanding of the links may favor closer collaboration between organizations and agencies working in the field of human rights and national and international anti-corruption agencies. This chapter tries to persuade these organizations of the need to look beyond traditional coalitions to energize their respective movements.

In practice the measures taken for fighting corruption rarely refer to human rights obligations. To some extent, it seems that anti-corruption experts are underutilizing a system that might improve the performance of certain areas of their anti-corruption strategies. Weak national governance and justice systems can be strengthened by recourse to international regimes, and, moreover, provide powerful, external tools for disenfranchised citizens to hold their governments to account and enforce responsiveness not only through classic (and often cumbersome) legal remedies, but through a mix of processes, such as diagnosis; awareness raising; cross-cutting coalition-building; international treaties; and dialogue and debate on a local, national, and international level.

However, it should be mentioned that while human rights supervisory mechanisms are more frequently making express references to corruption, there is still no systematic approach to addressing corruption. The lack of direct references to the link between corruption and human rights by international treaties and by institutions working respectively in anti-corruption and human rights is at odds with the multi-faceted links between corruption and human rights in practice.

Last, while this chapter argues that a closer collaboration between the anti-corruption and the human rights movements will bring several advantages, there are still several challenges that need to be addressed and overcome. The two movements have their own histories and have developed a distinct body of practices and range of methodologies. There are now specific international standards for anti-corruption as well as for human rights efforts. The incorporation of a human rights framework into anti-corruption strategies would require overcoming mutual skepticism, misunderstandings, and sometimes distrust between the two movements. Collaboration would require the human rights movement to develop new alliances and cooperation skills. NGOs will need to build alliances not only with states, private sectors, or other NGOs but also with other actors such as politicians, journalists, and development organizations. More than ever, when dealing with corruption, the human rights movement should reflect and reformulate its traditional repertory of practices and strategies. This reorganization will require transforming its arid and abstract legal language into an accessible language for other disciplines. A crucial challenge to placing individuals at the center of anti-corruption efforts is that those who are most in need of human rights protection may not be aware of their rights, in particular of their economic, social, and cultural rights. Rights-awareness training and confidence-building is crucial to both the human rights approach as well as to an enriched anti-corruption agenda.

Notes

1. United Nations Convention against Corruption (UNCAC), adopted by the General Assembly, Resolution 58/4 on 31 October 2003. In accordance with Article 68 (1) of the aforementioned resolution, the United Nations Convention against Corruption entered into force on 14 December 2005. For the full text of the convention see www.unodc.org/pdf/crime/convention_corruption/signing/Convention-e.pdf (accessed 2 May 2008).

2. "Criminal Law Convention on Corruption," 27 January 1999, *European Treaty Series* No. 173. The convention entered into force on 1 July 2002.

3. Déclaration des Droits de l'Homme et du citoyen du 26 août 1789: "considérant que l'ignorance, l'oubli ou le mépris des droits de l'homme sont les seules causes des malheurs publics et de la corruption des Gouvernements."

4. For a seminal contribution see Michael Johnston, *Syndromes of Corruption—Wealth, Power and Democracy* (New York, 2005); for empirical evidence see Daniel Kaufmann, *Human Rights and Governance: The Empirical Challenge* (New York, 2004),

available at www.worldbank.org/wbi/governance/pdf/humanrights.pdf (accessed 1 January 2009). Kaufmann strongly suggests that "components of governance, such as corruption, are a mediating link between first and second generation human rights issues, and a determinant of development outcomes" (p. 2). See also Daniel Kaufmann, "Human Rights and Governance: The Empirical Challenge," in Philip Alston and Mary Robinson (eds.), *Human Rights and Development: Towards Mutual Reinforcement* (New York, 2005). For further empirical correlations see Todd Landman and Charles J.W. Schudel, "Corruption And Human Rights: Empirical Relationships And Policy Advice," *International Council on Human Rights Policy (ICHRP) Working Paper* (Geneva, 2007), available at www.ichrp.org/en/projects/131?theme=8 (accessed 5 February 2009).

5. Some of the most important conventions are the African Union Convention on Preventing and Combating Corruption, the OECD-ADB Anti-Corruption Action Plan for Asia and the Pacific, the OAS Convention, the Council of Europe Civil and Criminal Law Conventions against Corruption, as well as the OECD Convention on Combating Bribery of Foreign Public Officials. Other important voluntary initiatives include the Extractive Industry Transparency Initiative (www.eiti.org), Partnering against Corruption (www.weforum.org/pdf/paci/PACI_PrinciplesWithoutSupport Statement.pdf), and the Defense Pact (www.defenseagainstcorruption.org). See also Rotimi T. Suberu, "The Travails of Nigeria's Anti-Corruption Crusade," chapter 10 in this volume.

6. See UNCAC, Article 5.1. See also Ben W. Heineman, Jr., "The Role of the Multi-National Corporation in the Long War against Corruption," chapter 14 in this volume.

7. See UNCAC, Article, 6, 7, 13, and Chapter 3, respectively.

8. See Article 9, 10, and 13, respectively. A simple word-count shows that the UNCAC encompasses 18,417 words, but the terms "political rights," "torture," "health," "food," or "wages" are not mentioned, and "rule of law" is mentioned only three times, whereas the term "corruption" is featured, not surprisingly, seventy-three times. For the complete word count table, including a comparison with relevant Human Rights Covenants, see Kaufmann, *Human Rights and Governance*, 41, available at www.world bank.org/wbi/governance/pdf/humanrights.pdf (accessed 5 February 2009). For a more recent discussion of corruption and human rights see Transparency International, *Human Rights and Corruption Working Paper* No. 5 (Berlin, 2008).

9. For more information on the NIS, on NIS country study reports, and the development of the NIS methodology see Transparency International's website at www. transparency.org/policy_research/nis (accessed 5 February 2009).

10. For an assessment of the NIS approach see Lucy Koechlin, "An Evaluation of National Integrity Systems from a Human Rights Perspective," *ICHRP Working Paper* (Geneva, 2007), available at www.ichrp.org/en/projects/131?theme=8 (accessed 5 February 2009).

11. For an early and trenchant critique see Morris Szeftel, "Misunderstanding African Politics: Corruption and the Governance Agenda," *Review of African Political*

Economy, XXV (1998), 221–240; for a more recent critical discussion see Alan Doig and Heather Marquette, "Corruption and Democratization—The Litmus Test of International Donor Agency Intentions," *Futures*, XXXVII (2005) 199–213; for a case-study that underlines this point see Sarah Dix and Emmanuel Pok, "Combating Corruption in Traditional Societies: Papua New Guinea," chapter 9 in this volume.

12. Penny Green and Tony Ward, *State Crime: Governments, Violence and Corruption* (London, 2004), 11. See also Patrice Chabal and Jean-Pascal Daloz, *Africa Works: Disorder as Political Instrument* (Oxford, 1999).

13. Daniel Jordan Smith, "The Paradoxes of Popular Participation in Corruption in Nigeria," 283.

14. There are exceptions, such as the document that the World Bank published on occasion of the fiftieth anniversary of the Universal Declaration of Human Rights. See World Bank, *Development and Human Rights: The Role of the World Bank* (Washington, D.C., 1998). However, this underlines the consequential approach to human rights, justifying why human rights are not explicitly incorporated into an anti-corruption approach: "By helping to fight corruption, improve transparency and accountability in governance, strengthen judicial systems, and modernize financial sectors, the Bank contributes to building environments in which people are better able to pursue a broad range of human rights" (p. 3). On this point see also Joseph M. Ackerman, "Human Rights and Social Accountability," *Social Development Papers* No. 86 (Washington, D.C., 2005).

15. The International Covenant on Economic, Social and Cultural Rights was adopted on 16 December 1966, entered into force 3 January 1976. An additional protocol that opened an international channel through which victims could complain about the violation of economic, social, and cultural rights was adopted by the UN General Assembly on 10 December 2008. The International Covenant on Civil and Political Rights was adopted on 16 December 1966, entered into force 23 March 1976. Its first additional protocol establishing the competence of the Human Rights Committee to deal with individual petitions was adopted and entered into force at the same time as the covenant. The Convention on the Rights of the Child was adopted on 20 November 1989 (entered into force 2 September 1990). Two additional protocols to this convention were adopted on 25 May 2000 on the rights on the sale of children, child prostitution, and child pornography; and on the involvement of children in armed conflict. Both protocols entered into force in 2002. The Convention on the Elimination of All Forms of Racial Discrimination was adopted 21 December 1965, entered into force 4 January 1969. The Convention on the Elimination of All Forms of Discrimination against Women was adopted on 18 December 1979, entered into force 3 September 1981. Its Optional Protocol conferring to the committee monitoring this treaty competence to deal with individual complaints was adopted on 10 December 1999 (entered into force 22 December 2000). The Convention against Torture and Other Cruel, Inhuman or Degrading Treatment or Punishment was adopted on 10 December 1984, entered into force 16 June 1987.

16. The African Charter on Human and People's Rights was adopted on 27 June 1981, entered into force 21 October 1986. The African Charter on the Rights and Welfare of the Child was adopted on 11 July 1990, entered into force 29 November 1999.

17. Each of the "core international human rights instruments" has established committees of experts to monitor the implementation of the treaty provisions by its States parties. By ratifying or accessing the core treaties named above, States parties agree to be bound by these committees. There are several examples in which "treaty bodies" refers to corruption. For example, in the case of Malawi, the Committee on the Rights of the Child has noted that "rampant corruption" impedes the implementation of the convention and has a particular impact "on children belonging to the most vulnerable groups." See United Nations, "United Nations Convention on the Rights of the Child," U.N. Doc. CRC/C/15/Add. 174, para. 5, 1989. Public Special Procedures are monitoring mechanisms of human rights that are endorsed to individual experts ("Special Rapporteurs," "Special Representatives," and "Independent Experts") since 1967, whose common mandate is the investigation and reporting of human rights situations either in a specific territory (country mandates) or with regard to phenomena of violations (thematic mandates). The list of existing special procedures is available at www2.ohchr.org/english/bodies/chr/special/index.htm (accessed 5 February 2009).

18. The UPR is a periodic review mechanism to evaluate the fulfillment of human rights obligations by all state members of the United Nations. To review how it works, see Human Rights Council (HRC), *Resolution 5/1,* 18 June 2007. This resolution was endorsed by the General Assembly Resolution 62/434 on 3 December 2007. See also HRC, "General Guidelines for the Preparation of Information under the Universal Periodic Review," *6/102* (27 September 2007). These are mechanisms that were established by the Human Rights Council to address either specific country situations or thematic issues in all parts of the world. These mechanisms are entrusted to examine, monitor, advise, and publicly report on human rights situations. Often "special procedures" refers to corruption from a human rights perspective. For example, the Special Rapporteur on the Right to Health has noted that when there is corruption in the health sector, the state is not complying with its obligation to achieve progressively the realization of the right to health established in Article 2 ICESCR. See Paul Hunt, "Report of the Special Rapporteur on the Right of Everyone to the Enjoyment of the Highest Attainable Standard of Physical and Mental Health," U.N. Doc. E/CN.4/2006/48, para 40, 3 March 2006. For more information on these mechanisms see www2.ohchr.org/english/bodies/chr/special/index.htm (accessed 1 January 2009). The Human Rights Council was established by General Assembly Resolution 60/251 on 15 March 2006.

19. The constitution entered into force on 18 May 1994. See, for example, Chapter V of the constitution. This chapter does not, however, delve into the right to development, preferring instead to refer to the more specific economic, cultural, and social rights. For a succinct synopsis and critique of the right to development, see Peter Uvin, *Human Rights and Development* (Sterling, 2004), 40–43; for a more extensive

discussion see the contributions in Bard A. Andreassens and Stephen P. Marks (eds.), *Development as a Human Right: Legal, Political, and Economic Dimensions* (Cambridge, MA, 2006).

20. See Chapter IV "Human Rights," Article 30 "Right to Development," of the constitution: "1. All persons and peoples have a right to development and therefore to the enjoyment of economic, social, cultural and political development and women, children and the disabled in particular shall be given special consideration in the application of this right. 2. The State shall take all necessary measures for the realization of the right to development. Such measures shall include, amongst other things, equality of opportunity for all in their access to basic resources, education, health services, food, shelter, employment and infrastructure. 3. The State shall take measures to introduce reforms aimed at eradicating social injustices and inequalities. 4. The State has a responsibility to respect the right to development and to justify its policies in accordance with this responsibility."

21. The commission began functioning in January 1996 but became fully operational on 26 December 1998. Its operation is determined by the *Human Rights Commission Act*, No. 27 of 1998. For further information on the MHRC see www.malawi humanrightscommission.org (accessed 5 February 2009).

22. See www.unodc.org/unodc/en/treaties/CAC/signatories.html (accessed 5 February 2009).

23. For further information see www.nepad.org/aprm/ (accessed 2 May 2008); for an initial assessment of Malawi, see Ross Herbert, *Malawi and the African Peer Review Mechanism: A Review of National Readiness and Recommendations for Participation* (Johannesburg, 2004).

24. *Corrupt Practices Act*, No. 18 of 1 December 1995.

25. Malawi is ranked 11 out 48 in the 2008 Index of African Governance. For further information on the methodology, see Robert I. Rotberg and Rachel M. Gisselquist, *Strengthening African Governance: Ibrahim Index of African Governance, Results and Rankings 2008* (Cambridge, MA, 2008). Consult Transparency International's website for details on all CPIs; see www.transparency.org/policy_research/surveys_indices/cpi/2007 (accessed 5 February 2009). The Worldwide Governance Indicators is an aggregate index that measures six different dimensions of governance, one of which is the control of corruption (for Malawi see http://info.worldbank.org/governance/wgi/mc_chart.asp# [accessed 5 February 2009]). The governance chart shows the percentile rank of each country on the selected governance indicator. In other words, the percentile rank indicates the percentage of countries worldwide that rate below the selected country. Higher values indicate better governance ratings. Malawi, for the control of corruption, ranks only just above the bottom quarter of all countries worldwide. For all rankings and data see http://info.worldbank.org/governance/wgi/index.asp (accessed 5 February 2009).

26. See the Republic of Malawi and World Bank, *Malawi Poverty and Vulnerability Assessment* (Washington, D.C., 2006). See also United Nations Development Programme

(UNDP), *Malawi Human Development Report 2005: Reversing HIV/AIDS in Malawi* (New York, 2005), available at http://hdrstats.undp.org/countries/ (accessed 5 February 2009). See Freedom House, "Freedom in the World: Malawi 2008," which states that "[d]espite constitutional guarantees of equal protection, customary practices perpetuate discrimination against women in education, employment, and business." See www.freedomhouse.org/inc/content/pubs/fiw/inc_country_detail.cfm?year=2008& country=7439&pf (accessed 5 February 2009). See also Malawi Human Rights Commission, *Mfulu: Malawi Human Rights Commission Bulletin* (Lilongwe, 2006).

27. Fidelis Edge Kanyongolo, "The Rhetoric of Human Rights in Malawi: Individualization and Judicialization," in Harri Englund and Francis B. Nyamnjoh (eds.), *Rights and the Politics of Recognition in Africa* (London, 2004), 70.

28. Ibid., 77.

29. Republic of Malawi and World Bank, *Malawi Poverty and Vulnerability Assessment*, 261. See the Lorenz Curves on school enrollment, income distribution, and public expenditure on p. 259. The report reveals a differentiated picture of government expenditure: "it was found that government spending in the health services is distributed with considerable equity across socioeconomic groups. Nevertheless, whilst the benefits from the provision of government health centers were equitable, the poor receive a considerably lower share of the benefits from the subsidy for the provision of government hospitals. The benefit incidence was largely explained by differences in the utilization of health services and the lower reported incidence of illness amongst the poor, rather than the distribution of the health subsidy" (p. 264).

30. See, for instance, Josh Ashaz, "Cruel Prison Conditions Damage Malawi Human Rights Record," *Nyasa Times* (5 November 2007). Ashaz states that congestion, overstaying, inadequate diet, substandard sanitation, lack of proper health care, and physical assault by guards are some of the major problems that prisoners in Malawi face. For a detailed discussion see Hillery Anderson, "Justice Delayed in Malawi's Criminal Justice System— Paralegals vs. Lawyers," *International Journal of Criminal Justice Sciences*, I (2006), 1–11. The Malawi Human Rights Commission, *2006 Executive Report on Human Rights Accountability in Malawi by the Three Arms of Government* (Lilongwe, 2007), 27. The report states: "Overcrowding in the prisons goes against Section 42 (1) of the Constitution which obliges the State to keep detained persons in conditions that are consistent with their dignity. Further this situation is an affront to the United Nations Standard Minimum Rules for the Treatment of Prisoners which Malawi voluntarily subscribed to by being a State party."

31. See for instance Edgardo Campos and Sanjay Pradhan (eds.), *The Many Faces of Corruption: Tracking Vulnerabilities at the Sector Level* (Washington, D.C., 2007); Jaques Hallak and Muriel Poisson, *Corruption Schools, Corrupt Universities: What Can be Done?* (Paris, 2007); Transparency International, "Corruption in the Education Sector," *Working Paper* No. 04/2007 (Berlin, 2007); Transparency International, *Global Corruption Report 2006: Corruption in the Health Sector* (Berlin, 2006).

32. The Constitution of the Republic of Malawi (1994, rev. 2004), "Chapter III Fundamental Principles," 13; emphasis added. This formulation echoes key tenets of the anti-corruption as well as the human rights agenda. The promotion of transparency, the "integrity, accountability and proper management of public affairs and public property" is emphasized in Chapter I of the United Nations Convention against Corruption. See, for instance, UNCAC, Article 13 "Participation of Society," which states that: "1. Each State Party shall take appropriate measures, within its means and in accordance with fundamental principles of its domestic law, to promote the active participation of individuals and groups outside the public sector, such as civil society, non-governmental organizations and community-based organizations, in the prevention of and the fight against corruption and to raise public awareness regarding the existence, causes and gravity of and the threat posed by corruption. This participation should be strengthened by such measures as: (a) Enhancing the transparency of and promoting the contribution of the public to decision-making processes. . . ." Equally, the Preamble of the International Covenant on Economic, Social and Cultural Rights underlines the "inherent dignity and . . . the equal and inalienable rights of all members of the human family."

33. Horizontal accountability bodies are "institutions of the state or of quasi state institutions that both check on each other and are mutually supportive of each other to make government work"; these bodies have both an oversight mandate upholding the rule of law and basic democratic values and act as conduits between state and society to ensure governmental responsiveness and accountability. See Joel D. Barkan and others, "Emerging Legislatures: Institutions of Horizontal Accountability," in Brian Levy and Sahr John Kpundah (eds.), *Building State Capacity in Africa: New Approaches, Emerging Lessons* (Washington, D.C., 2004), 211.

34. For an important contribution on democratic consolidations and human rights see David Beetham, *Democracy and Human Rights* (Cambridge, 1999).

35. See, for instance, Nixon S. Khembo (ed.), *Elections and Democratisation in Malawi: An Uncertain Process* (Johannesburg, 2005).

36. Fidelis Edge Kanyangolo, *Malawi: Justice Sector and the Rule of Law, A Review by AfriMAP and Open Society for Southern Africa* (London, 2006), 19–20.

37. Department for International Development, *Malawi Country Governance Report* (London, 2007), 3.

38. For an extensive discussion see Wiseman Chirwa and Lucy Koechlin, *Horizontal Capacity Assessment of the Oversight Institutions Named in the Constitution, the ACB, and Related Institutions in the Legislature, the Executive, and the Informal Justice Sector of Malawi,* Report for the Democratic Consolidation Programme (Lilongwe, 2006).

39. For instance, the Inspectorate of Prisons, which is a constitutional body charged with the monitoring and protection of the values and norms of the constitution as well as of international standards (see Section 169), has a mandate that has been impossible to fulfill in any way for lack of staff, budget, and an incomplete legislative framework.

40. See Global Integrity, *Global Integrity Scorecard: Malawi* (Washington, D.C., 2007), available at http://report.globalintegrity.org/Malawi/2007/scorecard (accessed 15 August 2008). For a comparative analysis of strengths and weaknesses of anti-corruption agencies, including those in Malawi, see Alan Doig, David Watt, and Robert Williams, *Measuring 'Success' in Five African Anti-Corruption Commissions—The Cases of Ghana, Malawi, Tanzania, Uganda and Zambia,* U4 Report (Bergen, 2005).

41. Dingiswayo Madise, "Challenges in the Fight Against Corruption in Malawi," paper presented at a meeting on Deepening the Judiciary's Effectiveness in Combating Corruption, UNECA, Addis Ababa, Ethiopia, 19–23 November 2007, 3.

42. See Freedom House, "Freedom in the World: Malawi (2008)," 3, available at www.freedomhouse.org/inc/content/pubs/fiw/inc_country_detail.cfm?year=2008& country=7439&pf (accessed 15 August 2008).

43. See Global Integrity, *Global Integrity Scorecard: Malawi,* 84.

44. Peter Clottey, "Malawi Appoints New Anti-Corruption Czar," *Voice of America Online* (15 November 2007), available at www.voanews.com/english/archive/2007-11/2007-11-15-voa1.cfm?CFID=232811297&CFTOKEN=92041180 (accessed 5 February 2009).

45. *Corrupt Practices Act,* Section 6(3), 1 December 1995.

46. Malawi Human Rights Commission, *2006 Executive Report on Human Rights Accountability in Malawi by the Three Arms of Government* (Lilongwe, 2007), 19–20.

47. Chirwa and Koechlin, *Horizontal Capacity Assessment of the Oversight Institutions,* 15; emphasis in original.

48. See also, for example, Rob Jenkins, "The Role of Political Institutions in Promoting Accountability," and Anwar Shah, "Tailoring the Fight against Corruption to Country Circumstances," both in Shah (ed.), *Performance Accountability and Combating Corruption* (Washington, D.C., 2007). The latter states that "Watchdog agencies have achieved success only in countries where governance is generally good, such as Australia or Chile. In weak governance environments, these agencies often lack credibility and may even extort rents. In Kenya, Malawi, Nigeria, Sierra Leone, Tanzania, and Uganda, for example, anticorruption agencies have been ineffective" (p. 246).

49. For an informed analysis based on graphic case-studies on how far removed and implausible the discourse on human rights is from the popular perspectives of impoverished Malawians, see Harri Englund, *Prisoners of Freedom* (Berkeley, 2006). An analogy can easily be drawn to anti-corruption discourses.

50. See the Malawi Anti-Corruption Bureau at www.anti-corruptionbureau.mw/acb_civic-edu-save.html (accessed 25 April 2008).

51. See Kanyongolo, "The Rhetoric of Human Rights in Malawi: Individualization and Judicialization," 64–82.

52. Landman and Schudel, "Corruption and Human Rights: Empirical Relationships and Policy Advice," 20.

53. See World Bank, *Malawi: Governance and Corruption Baseline Survey* (Washington, D.C., 2006); Afrobarometer, "Responsiveness and Accountability in Malawi," *Afrobarometer Briefing Paper* No. 31 (East Lansing, 2006).

54. Herbert, *Malawi and the African Peer Review Mechanism,* 2.

55. Arguing along the same lines is Kanyongolo, "The Rhetoric of Human Rights in Malawi," 64–82.

56. See www.transparency.org/policy_research/surveys_indices/cpi/2007 (accessed 5 February 2009). The results of the annual Corruption Perceptions Index are depicted graphically as a world map: well over half the world is steeped in shades of red—the deeper the red, the higher the level of corruption. "Culture" here is used as Clifford Geertz understands it: "culture is patterns of meanings and significance that underlie continual processes of communication and interpretation; in other words, how social practices are "woven into the fabric of political and economic life" (see Smith, "The Paradoxes of Popular Participation," chapter 11 in this volume). See Clifford Geertz, "Thick Description: Toward an Interpretive Theory of Culture," in his *The Interpretation of Cultures* (New York, 1973), 3–30.

57. Uvin, *Human Rights and Development,* 134–135.

58. Jomo K.S., "Good Governance, Anti-Corruption, and Economic Development," chapter 18 in this volume.

59. This section draws from the insights of this chapter, as well as from the research findings of the International Council of Human Rights Policy's (ICHRP) research project on corruption and human rights (see ICHRPs website at www.ichrp.org).

60. See www.anti-corruptionbureau.mw/faqs.html#8 (accessed 5 February 2009). It is interesting to note that the Anti-Corruption Bureau of Malawi's website has a section that responds to Frequently Asked Questions (FAQ) by public officers, one of which is "Why should I remain free of corruption?" The answer reveals the lack of a human rights approach within the consequences of corruption: "As a Public Officer you have been entrusted by the people of Malawi to serve them fairly and efficiently. Self-interest means that you cannot discharge your important duties properly and you will lose respect. In addition, corruption tarnishes the image of the public service. The new democratic Malawi wants to encourage development so that everyone can benefit. But, if the Nation gets a reputation for corruption then investors and entrepreneurs will not come here-they will take their money somewhere else so we will all suffer. If you go to prison because you have been convicted of corruption then you personally will suffer. But think also about other people whose welfare depends on you. They too will suffer just because of your greed. You must therefore look beyond self-interest and consider the implications of your acts. Corruption is evil and must be resisted under all circumstances. This is the challenge which faces you as a Public Officer." It might be interesting to explore whether or not emphasizing the human rights consequences for the acts of corruption could provide further encouragement to "remain free of corruption."

61. For empirical evidence, see Kaufmann, *Human Rights and Governance.*

62. Interestingly, since the Declaration of the United Nations Convention against Corruption, several crosscutting issues have emerged, albeit at times using different terms for the same objective. For instance, a prominent issue in the human rights community, namely access to information, is not contained verbatim in UNCAC.

However, partly overlapping objectives are pursued in Article 10 of UNCAC, which prefers the term "public reporting."

63. For a differentiated discussion on corruption and the "right to development" see David Beetham, "The Right to Development and its Corresponding Obligations," in Andreassens and Marks (eds.), *Development as a Human Right,* 79–95.

64. The principle of non-discrimination is of the utmost importance in international law. Various formulations of prohibition of discrimination are contained in, for example, the UN Charter (Articles 1(3), 13(1)(b), 55(c), and 76), the Universal Declaration of Human Rights (Articles 2 and 7), the ICCPR (Articles 2(1) and 26), and the CRC (Article 2). Some instruments are expressly aimed at addressing specific prohibited grounds for discrimination such as CERD and CEDAW, and other instruments aim at addressing the prohibition of discrimination in the exercise of one or several rights, such as ILO 111, which refers to discrimination in the exercise of the right to work (employment and occupation), and the UNESCO Convention against Discrimination in Education.

65. For a succinct overview of the strengths and weaknesses of corruption indices see Nathaniel Heller, "Defining and Measuring Corruption: From Where Have We Come, Where Are We Now, and What Matters for the Future?" chapter 3 in this volume.

66. A good example from development practice is provided by the Southern African Regional Poverty Network (SARPN), Oxfam International, and Concern Worldwide. They have developed an approach they term "Triple Threat," which denotes "the combined web of factors that reduce people's livelihood security: 1) Food Insecurity (Environmental), 2) Governance, and 3) HIV and Aids." See Southern African Regional Poverty Network, Concern Worldwide, and Oxfam International, *Strengthening Responses to the Triple Threat in the Southern Africa Region—Learning from Field Programmes in Malawi, Mozambique, and Zambia* (Geneva, 2007), 1. Drawing from field programs in Malawi, Zambia, and Mozambique, this report seeks to address livelihood insecurity by incorporating not only environmental factors and health issues, but also governance dimensions such as "lack of accountability or proper allocation and use of state resources" or "participation and the voice of citizens, including lack of civil rights and education" (p. 2). The responses developed for Malawi within this broader approach include both human rights awareness and advocacy as well as "classic" anti-corruption initiatives such as budget and expenditure tracking or capacity-building.

67. See African Commission on Human and People's Rights, "Press Statement at the Conclusion of the Promotional Mission of the African Commission on Human and Peoples' Rights to the Republic of Malawi" (Banjul, 2008), available at www.achpr. org/english/Press%20Release/Press%20Statement_end%20of%20mission_Malawi.htm (accessed 5 February 2009).

ROBERT I. ROTBERG

13

Leadership Alters Corrupt Behavior

The policeman who "charges" drivers for non-existent infractions, the customs official who "under-invoices" a shipment of tractor parts and splits the difference with an importer, the office-bound bureaucrat who gives permits for foreign currency to favored businessmen for "a consideration," and the high-ranking cabinet minister who prefers one supplier of fighter aircraft or naval frigates over another in exchange for serious "rents" are each behaving rationally by cheating their governments and the citizens that they are pledged to serve. They are all corrupt and corrupted, certainly, but by adopting a conscious strategy of self-enrichment through corrupt behavior they are merely following national norms that are sanctioned by leadership failures. They take their behavioral cues from their official superiors.

Lesser officials and politicians steal from the state and cheat their fellow citizens because of a prevailing permissive ethos. If their immediate superiors steal and cheat, lower-ranked civil servants and security personnel believe that they, too, have a license to enrich themselves corruptly. Farther up the scale, too, middle-ranking government officials of all kinds look to their heads of state and cabinet ministers to see what they can "get away with." Once it becomes known that certain kinds or all kinds of corrupt behavior are acceptable, then all self-interested maximizers (nearly all of us) will hardly want to miss good opportunities to secure and then to employ official positions for private gain. Whatever one's views of human nature and human fallibility, if the prevailing political culture tolerates corruption, nearly everyone will seek opportunities to be corrupt. Such political cultures are determined, especially in new nation-states, by leadership signals, leadership postures, and leadership failures of omission and commission.[1]

Conversely, where top leaders are uncorrupted and where top leaders act effectively and decisively against corruption by punishing misbehaving colleagues and relentlessly pursuing miscreants, a governmental culture of abstinence can be created that positively rewards honesty and integrity. That kind of culture is hardly the norm throughout the developing world, indeed throughout the entire world, but there are sufficient successes—a number of states where corruption has been eschewed—to support the notion that sincerely anti-corrupt leaders can influence the official behavior of entire leadership cohorts and of whole countries. What Lee Kuan Yew did in Singapore and Seretse Khama did in Botswana can be emulated everywhere if leaders choose to lead responsibly.

Unfortunately, the evidence for all of these assertions about human behavior—about the predominant influence that proactive and venal leadership has on the incidence and aggregation of corrupt practice—is largely anecdotal. The man on the beat says that he steals and cheats because everyone else does and that he does not want to be left out of a chance to supplement his meager salary. The cabinet minister in charge of public works or capital projects reports that he is expected, as the incumbent in such a position, to produce rents that can be shared with other cabinet ministers and possibly with his heads of government and of state.

Burmese generals posted to frontier sinecures where gem and opium smuggling is rife and interdiction possibilities and corrupt partnerships are easy are expected to share their returns with their superiors and with the ruling junta. Those who procure arms or otherwise arrange large contracts with foreign suppliers cannot pocket all of the ill-achieved wealth themselves; they are expected to enrich others within their official hierarchies.[2] How else can corrupt heads of state build local palaces and purchase mansions overseas? Where do the funds come from that are so blithely stashed in overseas banking havens by the likes of Sani Abacha of Nigeria, Mobutu Sese Seko of Zaire, and Robert Mugabe of Zimbabwe?

Admittedly, there is a hoary argument that corruption in Africa, at least, is merely an outgrowth of traditional forms of culturally sanctioned gift-exchanges. Or corrupt practices and corrupt varieties of nepotism can be said reasonably to reflect customary respect for kinship obligations that, yes, flout Western expectations but are traditionally approved. Loyalties in many new societies run to the clan or lineage, not to the proto-nation or any national commonweal. In other words, public values confront family values and the latter understandably triumph—even when large-scale venal corruption in public works construction projects can hardly be construed as effective gift exchange.

Corruption begets more corruption. If leaders permit corrupt practices to begin, tolerate even episodic personal enrichment, or wink and nod only once in a while, the flood gates will soon open. Breaches of norms, sliding norms, or the development of new norms are easily communicated throughout a political system as expectations loosen or tighten. Leaders cast large shadows. Civil societies may rail at corrupt practices, journalists may investigate and uncover scandals, and prosecutors may bring egregious offenders before courts, but the acceptability and the prevalence of corrupt practices depends more on leadership action than on formal mechanisms of accountability. This is not to deprecate mechanisms of accountability, but it is to say that such mechanisms are insufficient, absent strong leadership, to stanch the natural human tendency to put self interest over national interest and emulation over conscience.

This argument follows from another—that in new societies (the more corrupt ones) political culture and systems of value are created, along with political institutions, by effective leadership. Thus, if we examine the countries that rank at the top of Transparency International's (TI) annual Corruption Perceptions Index, we see that they are either long-established developed or industrial nations with political cultures and institutions that anathemize political corruption or they are a few newly emergent nations that have managed, thanks to responsible leadership, to create similar political cultures and institutions to match those of the developed nations.

Leadership precedes institutional safeguards and also precedes the successful workings of formal mechanisms of accountability. In other words, it is leadership attitudes and leadership actions that create climates in which cheating is seen to be anti-social and the strict punishment of corrupt behavior by judicial processes and by political arbiters (the public, parties, and funders) is applauded rather than deprecated (as in contemporary South Africa).

All of these statements are propositions. They appear commonsensical, but we have very few evidence-based affirmations of their veracity. There are no double-blind studies, and even the best existing examinations of corrupt practices are impressionistic. There have been too few attempts—for obvious reasons—to measure the incidence of societal corruption that are based on leadership positive or leadership negative interventions. For example, when President Kenneth Kaunda left the presidency in Zambia in 1991, no reliable measures existed of national levels of corruption either in kwacha or in incidents of large-scale venality. Thus, we cannot be sure that the reign of his successor, President Frederick Chiluba, and his policies and practices while in office from 1991 to 2001 contributed to the massive increase in corrupt practice that was noticed by TI's annual ratings (impressionistic as they are). The only hard evidence that we have is that Chiluba was convicted of graft—stealing $46 million from the Zambian people—in a British civil court and in 2009 was being prosecuted by Zambia on 169 counts of corruption, abuse of power, and theft. He was also awaiting sentence after being convicted in a separate case of theft (from a Zambian bank) by public servant involving $500,000. About the same time, Chiluba's wife Regina was jailed for 3.5 years for receiving and obtaining stolen properties and for receiving $300,000 in cash and goods that President Chiluba had pilfered from state house.[3]

Likewise, did Mobutu Sese Seko greatly ramp up corruption in Zaire from 1965, as seems plausible from his accumulation of enormous wealth—$10 billion or so—or did his venality simply build on existing post-Belgian and Cold War U.S. tolerance for leadership aggrandizement? Nigeria has been known to be corrupt since the bad old slave trading days of the eighteenth century, but did the civilian and military successors to General Yakubu Gowon (head of state from 1966 to 1975) accelerate the scale of corrupt practice so that Nigeria now ranks near the pinnacle of worldwide corruption according to TI? Or did successive Nigerian leaders build upon prevailing societal behavior? This chapter asserts that leadership creates and nurtures many kinds of behavior, especially corruption. But the very opposite could, at least theoretically, be true.

Scott's seminal early work on corruption suggests that "a regime that enjoys both a symbolic and a rational commitment from its people and has effective institutions to channel these beliefs can bring to bear a variety of powerful social sanctions and new loyalty patterns to reinforce new administrative norms." Legitimacy, sanctions, and patterns that flow from a regime's probity are more telling than legal sanctions and other methods of vigorous enforcement. Although Scott says nothing about leadership, per se, the "legitimacy of effectiveness" that he cites as an essential supplement of mere rational legitimacy could not have been achieved, especially in the Singapore that Scott remarks upon, except by responsible, determined leadership.[4]

Anecdotally, to use examples from Asia, scholars and observers of Burma note the great rise in corruption under the autarkic dictatorship of General Ne Win, 1962–1988, continued ever since by General Than Shwe's commanding juntas, the successive State Law and Order and the Peace and Security Councils. Likewise, in Indonesia, the Dutch and Japanese occupiers may have tolerated and stimulated corruption, but the great rise in corrupt practice came under the indigenous autocracies of Sukarno and Suharto, both of whom greatly and openly enriched themselves and their families (nuclear and extended). The same can surely be said of the monarchy in Cambodia and Hun Sen's current elected quasi-democracy. The Marcos regime in the democratic Philippines was notorious for renting out the state and its many opportunities for enrichment. In such circumstances, what is to discourage the ordinary Filipino, Cambodian, Indonesian, and Burmese from piling on— from seeking enrichment, even at the margin of society?

In 1960s Thailand, as Scott's research demonstrates, military leaders and the weakened monarchy enabled corrupt practices to flourish. In those days Thailand politics were controlled not by widespread urban and rural voters but by a narrow elite that was divided into power-seeking and power-wielding cliques. The latter comprised the units of political competition, the major stakes of which were "the distribution of high posts, financial opportunities, and government-controlled privileges." Corruption "inevitably" flowed from the "political necessity" of the clique-manipulated distributive process. Cabinet ministers in these cases owed their power, and thus were loyal and obligated, to the cliques that helped to propel them into power. They therefore, as in Africa for similar reasons, had to provide for their followers. They had to deliver perquisites and rewards—lower down in the system—as bureaucrats loyal to the same clique had likewise to respond.[5]

The arrangements that may have been peculiar to Thailand in the 1960s mirror what stimulated corruption almost everywhere in the developing world and still motivates much of the high-level corruption that undermines efficient allocations of priorities globally. Scott reports that a Thai administrator tended to view the powers and property of his office as "part of his personal domain—a domain to be used in the pursuit of private and/or clique gain."[6] The higher the official and the more secure his ties were to the prevailing elite, the more readily he was able to do what he wanted, enriching himself and his clique despite regulations and legal sanctions. Lower officials followed such examples and the system, then and later, flowed from the leadership's omissions and commissions.

In 2008, Singapore and Botswana ranked 4th and 36th, respectively, among the least corrupt worldwide in TI's rankings; Singapore just behind Denmark, Sweden, and New Zealand and ahead of Finland and Switzerland; and Botswana ahead of Puerto Rico, Malta, Taiwan, and South Korea.[7] The United States ranked 20th. Those high standings testify to the strength of the two small nation-states' antagonism to the incubus of corruption. Each now boasts a robust political culture, with institutions to match, that is antithetical to corrupt practices. Yet neither nation-state was born non-corrupt. The international entrepôt of Singapore under British colonial rule and after, within Malaya and Malaysia, was penetrated by Chinese triads and widely acknowledged to be a permissive, wild city where corruption was customary. Botswana was a much poorer, sleepier outlying province of the British Empire when it achieved independence; there was little to be corrupted and few settlements of more than modest size. Similar, small British outposts in Africa with brand spanking new governments and civil services rapidly discovered how their official positions could create boundless opportunities for enrichment well beyond their modest regular salaries. But not Botswana, almost alone of the more than forty sub-Saharan territories that became self-governing after 1960.

In both cases, Lee Kuan Yew and Seretse Khama, the respective first leaders of Singapore and Botswana, had, by force of will, to impose prohibitions on corruption and to demonstrate that corrupt practices would not be tolerated at any level—there could be no deviations from an absolute jihad against corruption for fear that every minor mishap would undermine both the overall anti-corruption crusade and the entire, imperiled, nation-building enterprise. Khama felt the same as Lee but had the easier task locally, given Botswana's early poverty and lack of traditional corruption. Lee's task was much more difficult since his administration (after 1959 and, especially, after 1965) battled deeply engrained expectations of corruption locally and throughout Southeast Asia.

To quote Lee, "The percentage, kickback, baksheesh, slush, or whatever the local euphemism is a way of life in Asia: People openly accept it as a part of their culture. Ministers and officials cannot live on their salaries. . . . The higher they are, the bigger their homes and more numerous their wives, concubines, or mistresses. . . ."[8] Lee also cites the enormously high cost for candidates of winning elections in Taiwan, Malaysia, Indonesia, and Japan as another contributor to corruption. Winners must recover their expenditures, so they naturally exploit their official positions for private gain. In Botswana, the ruling party covered election expenses.

When Lee's Singapore was expelled from the Malaysian Federation in 1965 he knew that his battle for political hegemony against the nearby external forces of Malaysia and Indonesia; the comparatively distant external influence of China; and the more dangerous internal communists, the triads, and other local opponents could not be won if his own and his new administration's legitimacy was fatally sapped by real or perceived charges of corruption. Nor could his imperiled nation-building effort afford to be compromised by charges of corruption. Otherwise his intrinsically difficult enterprise would fail to capture the political support of the then wildly divided and linguistically fractured Chinese, Malay, and Indian populations of Singapore. It would fail to attract the foreign direct investments that were essential if the city-state were to thrive. Corrupted, Singapore would not thrive and it would remain a haphazard enterprise adrift in the backwash of Malaysia and Indonesia.

Lee's is the toughest and best modern example of a leader who understood the dangers to society and governmental accomplishment of corruption. His was not a moral or ethical critique, but his strict puritanical stance against practices that were corrupt or appeared corrupt was fully political. In the 1950s, in Singapore, idealistic students and others had become communists, disgusted with the "venality, greed, and immorality" of many Asian leaders. Fighters for freedom had become "plunderers" of their new societies. Students in Singapore and elsewhere saw the communists as dedicated, selfless, and non-corrupt.[9] Lee diagnosed, further, that corruption must be dealt with from the top down and by example. If the probity of the top leadership were exemplary, lower ranks would be less often tempted, and certainly rarely feel entitled, to cheat. He thus chose to confront the scourge of corruption head on, by declaring zero tolerance for elected or appointed officials who were inclined to act inappropriately on behalf of friends or clients (or for their kin or cliques) and thus to accept illicit favors.

"It is easy," as Lee admits, "to start off with high moral standards, strong convictions, and a determination to beat down corruption. But it is difficult to live up to these good intentions unless the leaders are strong and determined enough to deal with all transgressors, and without exceptions."[10] Indeed, few of the leaders of the nation-states of the developing world had those high moral standards, much less a determination to beat down corruption. Many talked the talk, piously, but few did more than establish mostly ineffectual anti-corruption commissions. Few had Lee's clear-eyed approach. Few disciplined their closest associates and thus translated the lofty rhetoric of promised integrity into effective action.

Tan Kia Gan, Lee's close friend and one-time minister for national development, was a director on the board of the then national Malaysian airline in 1966 when he was unceremoniously removed by Lee from all of his appointed positions and ostracized. Lee suspected that Tan had accepted cash to favor one aircraft supplier over another, but there was insufficient evidence to prosecute him for corruption. Nevertheless, Tan was ousted and shamed.

Wee Toon Boon was minister of state in the Ministry of the Environment in 1975 when he accepted a free trip to Indonesia, an expensive bungalow, and loan guarantees—all from a housing developer who could benefit from government contracts. Lee sacked him, but in this case the evidence was strong enough for the courts to hear his case and sentence him to more than four years in jail.

In 1979, Phey Yew Kok, president of the National Trade Union Congress and a member of parliament for Lee's ruling party, was accused of taking funds from the Congress and investing them for himself. Phey jumped bail and vanished to Thailand before Lee could press charges.

Teh Cheang Wan was minister for national development in 1986 when he accepted two large cash payments, the first from a development company that wanted to retain land that had been earmarked for compulsory acquisition and the second from a developer who wished to purchase state land for private purposes. After his bribe-taking was discovered, Teh committed suicide rather than face disgrace.

Because these instances of Singaporean high-level corruption were treated in an exemplary fashion, similar breaches of trust became remarkably rare. Singaporeans quickly appreciated that the governing elite were not routinely (as elsewhere) taking advantage of their official positions to enrich themselves and that Lee and his associates meant what they said when ensuring a "clean administration." That Lee punished his colleagues for stepping out of line was remarkable in Asia and in the developing world. That robust message had its impact on lesser officials as well as on the ruling cadre.

It also helped that in 1995, Prime Minister Goh Chok Tong ordered an investigation of properties that were purchased at a discount by Lee's wife and son (subsequently the prime minister). The developer (Lee's brother was a non-executive director of the publicly listed company) had apparently offered the same discount to others. When property values rose, the property that Lee (through his wife) and Lee's son had purchased appreciated, casting suspicion on the transaction. Parliament, investigating, and the Singapore Monetary Authority, doing the same, exonerated the Lees, presumably demonstrating that the country's top leadership (Lee was then senior minister) continued to be incorruptible.

In earlier British times, Singaporean police were renowned for scandal. As late as 1971, 250 mobile squad police took money regularly from lorry drivers to overlook infractions. Hawker license inspectors and land bailiffs were also on the take. But once Lee's administration jailed them, and demonstrated that their superiors were not themselves on the take, incidents of corruption at middle and low levels in Singapore receded.

Lee's government refused to rely on example alone. It tightened regulations and also loosened evidentiary restrictions. It published very clear guidelines, so those tempted to take advantage of their official positions (and the public) would have no illusions regarding the exact consequences of improper behavior. Continuing to use the British-created Corrupt Practices Investigation Bureau as the instrument of enforcement, Lee had it report directly to him in the prime ministerial office. In order to ease the possibility of convictions in questionable cases, Lee persuaded Singapore's Parliament to tighten various laws in stages. The definition of gratuity was widened to include "anything of value." Investigators, under the amended laws, could arrest and search suspects and family members, scrutinize bank accounts, and obtain income tax returns. Judges could fully accept the evidence of accomplices. Indeed, other legal changes compelled any and all witnesses who were summoned by the Corrupt Practices Bureau to give testimony.

Along the way, Lee's government greatly increased the fines for corruption and for misleading testimony. Later, the courts were permitted to confiscate all benefits that were derived from corruption.

Lee was particularly pleased that he enabled the courts to consider as corroborating evidence of corruption that a suspect was living "beyond his means" or owned property that could not be afforded on his or her nominal salary. The government thus gave increasing powers to the Corrupt Practices Bureau; it was the watchdog, and in a society as tiny and tight as Singapore, persons with ostentatious life styles were quickly suspect. Even before he strengthened the Corrupt Practices Bureau, Lee sacked a government chief fire officer when, at a reception, the officer's "stunningly attractive wife" appeared "bedecked with expensive jewelry." Unfortunately for the fire officer, "her scintillating adornments caught the practiced eye of the prime minister. . . ."[11]

All of these legal shifts, together with the immense leadership demonstration effect, greatly helped Lee to keep Singapore "clean." But many Singaporeans would argue that it was more the pegging of official salaries to corporate earnings that enabled policemen on the beat, accountants in government service, and even cabinet ministers to avoid accepting bribes or other inducements. After the 1970s, when Singapore had begun to grow robustly and Lee was sure that he and his associates had brought prosperity to the emerging city-state, he spearheaded a drive to create for Singaporeans perhaps the highest civil service salaries in the world. In 1995, ministerial and senior public officer salaries were set at two-thirds the level of comparable private sector earnings, with automatic annual increases without parliamentary approval. Senior officers in the police force, for example, were soon earning far more than commissioners and chiefs in large American municipal systems. Excellent emoluments obviously helped to keep Singaporean officials on the straight and narrow.

It is possible to argue, as many have, that institutions combat corruption, not leaders. The experience of Singapore and Botswana, and the emerging case of Rwanda (plus almost all of the positive American, European, and other Asian cases), supports that proposition. But leadership actions greatly determine the kinds of political cultures that emerge in newly emergent or post-conflict nation-states, and it is only from the establishment of political cultures that enshrine values antithetical to corruption that effective institutions of accountability and oversight emerge. Additionally, leaders beget good governance, and the practice of good governance nurtures and enables robust institutions and strengthens rules of law. The latter do not emerge in a vacuum but only as a result of early and careful leadership attention or core values. Leaders create a positive ethos by force of will or example, as Lee did, sometimes drawing on pre-existing mores or distilling traditional values (as Khama did). Only then can institutions and a workable institutional framework emerge.[12]

Lee and Khama had to mandate and then ensure rule of law regimes that were fair and perceived to be fair. They had to equip these regimes with judiciaries that were even-handed and not controlled by state house. Their actions, and the signals that they sent to their close associates, were carefully monitored by emerging publics. If those signals had been found wanting, rule of law would have been as compromised as it has been in most developing-world countries. Likewise, real power had to be transferred to legislatures. Rubber-stamping would have compromised the nation-building endeavor and undercut the national attack on corrupt practice. Efficient allocation of resources had to occur as well. Otherwise corruption would have been a necessary force to fulfill goals—as in Thailand and other nations.

But was and is Singapore really free from the taint of corruption—thanks to Lee's vision, tutelage, leadership, legal shifts, and salary improvements? The city-state has always ranked high on TI's lists. Even skeptics and critics, including early pundits, accept that Singapore has been "virtually free of corruption."[13] Compared to African countries other than Botswana and Mauritius, and other Asian nations and the Oceanic island-states, Singapore has, since the 1970s, if not before, been in a class of its own because of its early focus on the dangers to the state posed by corruption and because of its success in creating a conformist society that has long favored stability and prosperity over open political participation and the enjoyment of broad civil rights and liberties.

Despite Singapore's high anti-corruption reputation and its appropriate rankings near the top of all such listings, nepotism—a form of corruption—seems to be rife in a small country where Lee remained in charge or nearly in charge until he could safely pass the prime ministership on to his son and main heir. His wife also held important nonpolitical positions. Lee's defense, naturally, is merit. His wife and son gained their roles because of their talent, not through Lee. In that sense, Lee enabled family members to enrich themselves. At the same time, there have never been accusations that either Lee or his family otherwise used their positions for profit. And, like Lee, his son and wife are inordinately competent.

Critics such as Francis T. Seow, however, argue that Lee used his position to abuse power and to punish critics. Seow, then solicitor general, instances (among others) a case where he agreed to hefty bail for a legal advisor to the then Malaysian Singapore Airlines—someone who was suspected of a minor criminal breach of trust and indiscreet political interference. Lee—with whom Seow anyway had a testy relationship—strongly objected and hastened Seow's departure from government service.[14]

Lee's harsh handling of the international and local media largely confirms these criticisms. He and his government have won innumerable libel and slander cases against publications and individuals. They have bankrupted local critics and forced many media operations to shut down. Lee, in other words, is hardly a paragon of virtue. But he (and the institutions that he has built) has kept modern Singapore free from the taint of corruption as it is commonly understood. That is a unique achievement in Asia and the developing world.

There are no comparable examples of effective attempts to battle the scourge of corruption in the post-Soviet space of Central Asia, in China, in India, or in much of modern Africa. (I know of no cases of leaders who genuinely sought to squelch corruption, using Lee-like methods, and failed.)

In one corner of mainland Africa, however, Botswana is a beacon of brightness, largely because of the leadership of Seretse Khama. However, Khama died young, after fourteen critical years (1966–1980) as president; he left no memoirs and was far less explicit regarding his leadership vision than was Lee. Nor do Khama's biographers say much about his attentiveness to the corruption problem.[15] Nevertheless, it is evident from those who resided in or visited Botswana during Khama's presidency that he was conscious of the need to prevent corrupt practices from taking root. Even though the Bechuanaland Protectorate (now Botswana) under British rule was never a corrupt or corrupted polity, Khama knew well the temptations of Africa—both the new black-ruled Africa and the next door white-ruled land of apartheid. He knew how destructive such loose practices were to a new country, as in 1960s Ghana, Nigeria, Senegal, and so on. He was determined from the very first days of his incumbency to follow Lee and deter corruption by setting a personal example and ensuring that his vice-president and his cabinet ministers joined him in fostering a proper tone for the embryonic nation. He was very clear that politicians and civil servants were not to view independence as a route to personal enrichment.

As Quett Ketumile Masire, Khama's vice-president and successor as president, later wrote, corruption wrecks "whole economies" and benefits the few at the expense of the majority. "We worked hard to avoid" corruption, he wrote, and then to punish it severely if discovered. "In the beginning we were a poor country with a very simple administration and few resources." It was therefore very easy, he reported, to operate transparently. From the British, Botswana inherited a legacy of "properly accounting for things." From traditional society, it inherited a tradition of open discussion in the community *khotla,* so citizens could complain easily about abuses.[16]

Khama lived modestly, without motorcades or other ostentation, and that approach—rare in Africa—helped to strengthen and make effective the overall anti-corruption message. No cabinet minister traveled by first class air, unlike their peers in the remainder of independent Africa. During the initial years after independence, cabinet ministers drove themselves in their own automobiles. There were few of the usual perquisites that came with office in the developing world. Masire, as vice-president, traveled in the rear of an aircraft to an important meeting in Ethiopia. By the time he exited the aircraft the red carpet had been removed and the welcoming party had decamped.

What Khama and his administration, and successive presidents in Botswana, communicated so well to their constituents throughout the vast country was that he and they were not in politics to gain wealth or power. They were in office to build a new nation somewhat more singular than most other contemporaneous African nations. For him, being the first president of Botswana provided an opportunity to implant alternative African values, to create an open society, and to develop a political culture of democracy. For him, leadership meant guardianship, on behalf of the people. He was in office to provide a strong moral and practical compass for the nation, and that meant the elimination of any germs of corrupt practice.

Of even more practical importance for anti-corruption than his vision of democratic leadership and his personal modesty was Khama's canny decision to refrain from giving too much power to any individual. Ministers could make no major decisions on their own. They had to involve other departments. For example, when Botswana decided to grant a mining lease for diamonds or coal, a number of ministries had to be consulted and the final decision was taken collectively by the country's cabinet. Khama specifically told an early minister of mines who wanted to exercise the authority invested in him by the Mines and Minerals Act that he could not. "No, this is not something for one man on his own; it is too important. Even if you think it is right, if anything goes wrong, you must share the responsibility with your colleagues. . . . And if the people later think it is wrong, then you will have others to help you defend why it was thought to be the right thing to do."[17] Khama insisted that ministers had to reveal all implications of any decision, whether administrative or financial. Full transparency was necessary at all levels.

Khama also created a professional civil service using the British model, which by its very nature, and by the model Khama inspired, had explicit checks and balances. Civil servants were protected by a Public Service Commission and, initially, by the *esprit de corps* of local and expatriate leaders within the civil service. Politicians complained that their civil servants were too influential. "But if we had not received such complaints," Masire indicated, "I think we would have been in trouble, since it would have indicated that politicians were exercising unreasonable discretion."[18] That discretion could easily have led to special favors, under-the-table deals, and abundant corruption.

Khama and Masire also saw to the prosecution of the few prominent Tswana ministers and officials who misappropriated funds or benefited illicitly from their position. One of those miscreants was President Khama's cousin, a senior civil servant. Another was a senior officer of the ruling political party. Allegedly, a third was President Masire's younger brother. In that case the report of a high-level commission that looked into the accusations was published for all to examine. In a fourth case, Masire terminated an assistant minister in and the permanent secretary of the Ministry of Local Government and Lands even though the assistant minister's criminal conviction was later overturned on appeal.

When Masire was president and governing, Botswana became more complex as wealth flowed from diamonds, tourism, and beef. Petty thievery quickly escalated into a few major cases of corruption, especially in the 1990s. Masire's answer was to create tough new legislation and to create an anti-corruption unit that was based on the successes of the Hong Kong Colony model. He also believed that the fact that his administration pursued all serious allegations "and did not try to hide the fact [that] they occurred" was critical to strengthening Botswana's democracy, and also to the new nation's economic growth trajectory.[19]

Masire recalls that he was often offered access to secret bank accounts in Switzerland. Locally, businessmen tried to entangle him in conflicts of interest by offering him shares in their motor dealerships or other businesses. At ministerial, vice-presidential, or presidential levels, Masire makes clear that "justice must not only be done but must be seen to be done."[20] Many other developing world presidents and prime ministers have uttered similar pieties. In Khama and Masire's cases, the heads of state were determined to avoid the shame and the inefficiency of corruption at all costs. They knew, too, that if the leaders stayed clean, the country (mostly) would.

There is a third case that conceivably demonstrates the conclusive importance of leadership for corruption's reduction, but the evidence is not yet fully arrayed. "Corruption," President Paul Kagame of Rwanda says, ". . . is clearly, very largely, behind the problems [that] African countries face. It is very bad in African or Third World countries. . . ." It is hard to change because, continues Kagame, ". . . it has become a way of life in some places." In Rwanda, the president of a state-owned bank was prosecuted for giving friends unsecured loans. Policemen were known to take small sums to overlook minor street offences.

Kagame, like Khama and Lee, believes that "You can't fight corruption from the bottom. You have to fight it from the top." He has prohibited the employment, in his government, of his relatives or any relatives of ministers. He has shamed and prosecuted cabinet ministers and friends for slipping off the ethical high road. "Nor," reports Kagame's biographer, "are the guilty quietly rehabilitated . . . as happens in nearby countries. They can never return to public life, because they are considered guilty of something even worse than dishonesty."[21]

According to the *Economist*, the Rwandan government has, in recent years, cracked down hard on corruption and imprisoned ruling-party officials for pilfering public funds. "The police are professional, even enforcing laws on litter to make Rwanda the cleanest country in Africa." As the *Economist* also implies, tough leadership, not pre-existing institutions, is helping to transform Rwanda from dirty to clean, from free-wheeling to conformist, and from distracted to single-mindedly efficient. In the 2008 Index of African Governance, Rwanda ranked 18th; a slightly higher score and a lower rank by one place than the year before. That high ranking (of forty-eight sub-Saharan African nations) testifies to improving scores in corruption, among other variables. For corruption, Rwanda moved upward in the year from 22nd to 16th among the forty-eight—a substantial improvement.[22]

Kagame's administration has hung the streets and offices of Kigali, the national capital, with posters opposing corruption: "He Who Practices Corruption Destroys His Country."[23] All public officials—more than 4,000—are required to file annual statements of their net worth, echoing one of Lee's methods. In many countries such statements would pile up in an obscure office. In Rwanda, the government ombudsman assiduously examines them for signs of ill-gotten profits and the misuse of public office.

These three cases of leadership antagonism toward corruption are suggestive but hardly conclusive. This tentativeness is not to suggest that other, more important, factors were at work that mattered more to Botswana's and Singapore's clear success, and the seeming embryonic success of Rwanda, in dampening corrupt tendencies among cabinet ministers, middle-ranking operatives, and petty officials. Rather, without a good method to test the enduring impact of a leader's actions on the daily behavioral choices made by bureaucrats, it is difficult to be sure that what appears to have resulted from the actions and determination of Lee, Khama, and Kagame, respectively, actually happened and happened in the manner that has been suggested in this chapter.

Equally, it seems likely that Mobutu and Ne Win's thefts of state resources and the depredations, defalcations, and peculations of the likes of Abacha, Mugabe, Omar Bashir in the Sudan, Daniel arap Moi in Kenya, Siaka Stevens in Sierra Leone, Charles Taylor in Liberia, and many others across all developing countries gave implicit unholy license to middle- and low-ranking officials. Indeed, Mugabe and Mobutu and many others permitted (even encouraged) their underlings to steal from the state in order to control them more easily. Mugabe's Central Intelligence Organization was charged with keeping "tabs" on the corrupt dealings of Mugabe's subordinates, the better to blackmail or intimidate them into submission. The silken web of deceit enveloped everyone who wanted to do what others were doing, and the tentacles of corruption thus encompassed all parts of society in Zimbabwe, as in the numerous other wildly corrupt countries of the developing world.

Once a pattern develops—once (as Lee says) leaders develop patrimonial followings that have to be buttressed with cash, jobs, and other perquisites—and once leaders have mistresses and concubines, corruption becomes accepted at all levels of a developing society. Nigerians have long been accustomed to the norm of corruption. The issue is not whether or not a parent greases the headmaster's palm to enroll a son or daughter in school, the question is how much?[24] It becomes easier to pay off a policeman at a roadblock in Thailand or Mozambique than it is to object and to battle for rights. It is easier in Liberia to rig a bidding process for access to vast iron ore deposits than laboriously to hold external players to account.[25] But can we be sure that, after a certain chronological point, new leaders can begin to alter the pattern of corruption? Or is it likely that only when nations are being built from the ground up that leaders can make a positive difference? That is, once the rot of corruption has spread widely, can it be reduced and then largely eliminated?

Impressionistically, again, there are a number of cases that indicate that a new leader can shift the prevailing ethos sufficiently to make corrupt practices more unthinkable than they had been under previous regimes. But those leadership demonstrations of a novel probity must also be accompanied by swift and certain accountability, discovery, prosecution, and punishment. Furthermore, the Lee and Kagame examples suggest that tough, even draconian, methods (with or without due process) are helpful in coercing officials to avoid temptation and eschew ostentation. Khama, however, proceeded to reduce corruption more by example and by exhortation. That approach was sufficient for Botswana where it might well not have been for the much more vibrant and criminalized Singapore.

Countries such as South Africa, Zambia, Cambodia, Afghanistan, and Timor Leste, to cite a sample, are capable even today of reducing (as in Rwanda) or accepting the stain of corruption. It depends on their leaders and their leaders' willingness to motivate the apparatus of the state to act sternly. Ordinary citizens, and middle- and low-level officials, are still receptive to signaling in a way that is hard to imagine in a nation such as Nigeria or Burma, where corrupt expectations are widespread. Zimbabwe is another interesting case; when Mugabe goes, a successor will be able to set a tone almost from scratch. Zimbabwe would then become a nation-state where the propositions set out in this chapter could be tested and, perhaps, validated.

Notes

1. Joseph S. Nye points out that in addition to the common vertical chain of corruption model, horizontal chains exist—as in China—which largely consist of leaders punishing groups or persons considered non-loyal (personal communication, 17 February 2009).

2. See Sarah Dix and Emmanuel Pok, "Combating Corruption in Traditional Societies: Papua New Guinea," chapter 9 in this volume.

3. *Southern Africa Report* (6 March 2009), 5.

4. James C. Scott, *Comparative Political Corruption* (Englewood Cliffs, 1972), 19. The importance of leadership action in combating corruption has also been noted by Peter John Perry, *Political Corruption and Political Geography* (Brookfield, VT, 1997), 121.

5. Scott, *Corruption*, 61–62.

6. Ibid., 65.

7. Transparency International, "Corruption Perceptions Index" (2008), available at www.transparency.org/policy_research/surveys_indices/cpi/2007 (accessed 29 October 2008).

8. Lee Kuan Yew, *From Third World to First; The Singapore Story: 1965–2000* (New York, 2000), 163.

9. Ibid., 157.

10. Ibid., 163.

11. Francis T. Seow, *To Catch a Tartar: A Dissident in Lee Kuan Yew's Prison* (New Haven, 1994), 20.

12. This paragraph benefited from conversation with Ben W. Heineman, Jr. See also Robert I. Rotberg, "Creating Robust Institutions: Preparing Secure Foundations," unpublished paper (Cambridge, MA, 2006).

13. Michael D. Barr, *Lee Kuan Yew: The Beliefs Behind the Man* (Richmond, UK, 2000), 126; T. J. S. George, *Lee Kuan Yew's Singapore* (London, 1973), 97; James Minchin, *No Man Is an Island: A Study of Singapore's Lee Kuan Yew* (London, 1986), 253. All three authors are otherwise extremely critical of Lee, his legal shortcuts, and his autocratic leadership.

14. Seow, *To Catch a Tartar*, 46–52. Subsequently, in 1988 when he was in private legal practice, Seow was arrested and held for seventy-two days in a detention center and subjected to harsh interrogation procedures that amounted to torture. He had allegedly contravened a provision of the Internal Security Act, but Seow suggests that Lee had taken affront because of his legal defense of political protestors. For the details and a sharp commentary, see Seow, 106 ff. and the thirty-page foreword by C. V. Devan Nair to Seow's book. Nair had been a close associate of Lee's and a freedom campaigner who had been imprisoned by the British colonial authorities. In the foreword, Nair calls Lee's behavior "loutish" and treacherous.

15. See Thomas Tlou, Neil Parsons, and Willie Henderson, *Seretse Khama, 1921–1980* (Gaborone, 1995).

16. Quett Ketumile Joni Masire, "Economic Opportunities and Disparities," in Stephen R. Lewis, Jr. (ed.), *Very Brave or Very Foolish? Memoirs of an African Democrat* (Gaborone, 2006), 239.

17. Quoted in Ibid., 240.

18. Ibid., 240.

19. Ibid., 241.

20. Ibid., 242.

21. Stephen Kinzer, *A Thousand Hills: Rwanda's Rebirth and the Man Who Dreamed It* (New York, 2008), 236.

22. "A Pioneer With a Mountain to Climb," *Economist* (27 September 2008); Robert I. Rotberg and Rachel M. Gisselquist, *Strengthening African Governance: Ibrahim Index of African Governance, Results and Rankings, 2008 [and 2007]* (Cambridge, MA, 2008), available at http://belfercenter.ksg.harvard.edu/project/52/intrastate_conflict_program.html?page_id=223 (accessed 21 April 2009).

23. All quoted in Kinzer, *A Thousand Hills,* 235–236.

24. See Daniel Jordan Smith, "The Paradoxes of Popular Participation in Corruption in Nigeria," chapter 11 in this volume.

25. President Ellen Johnson-Sirleaf's government attempted to right the wrong after the fact, but without managing to plumb the full depths of the new nation's corrupt dealings. See James Butty, "Liberian Government Moves to Curb Corruption in Awarding Foreign Investment Contracts," *Voice of America Online* (15 September 2008), available at www.voanews.com (accessed 13 February 2009).

BEN W. HEINEMAN, JR.

14

The Role of the Multi-National
Corporation in the Long War
against Corruption

Multi-national corporations (MNCs) play a significant role in economic globalization. The annual revenues of the largest companies—such as Exxon-Mobil's $405 billion in 2007—put them among the largest twenty-five nations if these total revenues were equated to GDP. The top 200 MNCs account for over 50 percent of the world's industrial output.[1] MNCs undertake a wide variety of commercial activities: they export from their home country and manufacture and assemble in foreign countries. They have moved "off-shore" activities that were previously conducted in their home countries.[2] They have then "outsourced" to third parties some of those "off-shored" activities, creating complex global supply chains. They are engaged in every form of commerce from production of heavy equipment to the distribution of consumer goods and the provision of financial services. They bid on major projects across the world. They employ tens, if not hundreds, of thousands of foreign nationals. And, increasingly, their share of revenues and profits from activities outside their home country is approaching—or exceeding—50 percent, with an increasing proportion of those foreign revenues and profits coming from emerging markets.

Because of their size, reach, and visibility, MNCs also have—or should have—a significant role in attacking global corruption. This is especially so for corporations that are headquartered in the developed world, which must rely, increasingly, on revenue growth and profitability in the developing world. For purposes of this chapter, corruption is defined as bribery, extortion, and misappropriation.[3] For analytic convenience, this chapter also focuses on MNCs that are headquartered in the developed world, while recognizing that MNCs headquartered in markets such as China and India are rivaling their developed world counterparts in size, strength, and reach.[4]

This chapter is prescriptive because there is still a tremendous gap between MNC anti-corruption rhetoric and action. This chapter seeks to address institutional and political constraints realistically but also to suggest courses of action that can improve anti-corruption performance. In so doing, this chapter looks at the role of MNCs in four settings:

—*With respect to the corporation itself,* focusing on the actions needed to create a "high performance with high integrity" global culture;

—*With respect to the developed world's efforts to stop foreign bribery by its own MNCs,* focusing on the mixed record of the Organization for Economic Cooperation and Development (OECD) Convention on Combating Bribery of Foreign Public Officials since its effective date in 1999;

—*With respect to the efforts of international organizations to combat corruption in the developing world,* focusing on the World Bank Group; and, finally,

—*With respect to the efforts of developing nations to combat corruption through economic growth and the construction of an institutional infrastructure* that constrains corruption through transparent, accountable, and durable public sector entities that govern economic, social, political, legal, and administrative affairs.

This chapter emphasizes the first issue. Motivating private entities to create truly effective internal anti-corruption cultures and anti-corruption programs must be the ultimate purpose of governmental action, which should seek not only to punish wrong-doers but to drive corporations toward durable and sustainable anti-corruption behavior.[5]

Since the mid-1990s, corruption in the developing world has been a prominent item on the global agenda.[6] Few people today repeat the old argument that corruption is an efficient corrective for overregulated economies. The true impact of corruption is now widely acknowledged: corruption distorts markets and competition, breeds cynicism among citizens, undermines the rule of law, damages governmental legitimacy, and corrodes the integrity of the private sector. It is also a major barrier to development: diversion of funds to corrupt parties and systematic misappropriation by kleptocratic governments harm the poor. But there are few signs that the range and extent of corruption has diminished.[7]

The forces that will start and sustain the building of truly transparent, accountable, and durable institutional infrastructures in the developing world are complex. Such forces are likely to vary by nation because each has its own unique history and culture and each is at its own phase in the development process, from failed and failing to fragile and rising. But most experts would agree that one important factor is an MNC community that is committed to anti-corruption. The pressures for corruption inside corporations—and in global capitalism—make such commitments an elusive ideal.

Fusing High Performance with High Integrity in the Multi-National Corporation

The twin goals of the contemporary multi-national corporations, and indeed global capitalism, should be high performance with high integrity. High performance is strong sustained economic growth that is based on provision of superior products and services; that provides durable benefits to shareholders and other stakeholders (such as employees, pensioners, creditors, customers, suppliers, and communities); and that balances risk-taking with risk management. High integrity has three elements: a tenacious adherence to the spirit and letter of formal rules, legal and financial; voluntary adoption of global ethical standards that bind the company and its employees to act in its enlightened self-interest; and employee commitment to the core values of honesty, candor, fairness, reliability, and trustworthiness. These values, which avoid the back-biting and turf-fighting that cripple organizations, should permeate internal and external relationships and guide the creation and delivery of products and services.

The fusion of high performance with high integrity is necessary because at the heart of performance lie fundamental forces that, if left unconstrained, cause corporate corruption. Top performing companies apply relentless internal pressure on their employees to hit basic financial goals for net income, cash flow, stock price, and other numerical targets.[8] Pressure begets more pressure. "Stretch targets" may put numbers on steroids and the "nice to hit" targets may become implicit "must dos." Making these numbers is key to compensation, bonuses, promotion, and even job security, and creates ubiquitous temptations to falsify accounts, cut corners, or worse. Far-flung global enterprises face external pressures that also create ever present and illicit temptations.[9] The mix of these external pressures with a firm's internal pressures can be an especially toxic brew.

In my book, *High Performance with High Integrity*, I outline eight key principles and associated practices that explain how these corrupting pressures can be countered and how an affirmative culture of integrity can be created in transnational companies.[10] Below, I briefly apply that analysis to the bribery and extortion that MNCs face across the globe, discussing those principles and practices with greatest importance for combating corruption.

The Policy and the Problem

An MNC needs to adopt a broad rule that its employees will not tender anything of value to obtain an improper advantage when representing the company's interests to governmental or political authorities, when selling goods or services in public or private settings, or when conducting financial transactions. This rule should be observed for major discretionary decisions and for the more routine decisions as well.

This rule should apply not only to all employees, regardless of nationality and regardless of a weaker national law, but also to third parties who are representing the MNC: consultants, agents, sales representatives, distributors, and contractors. It also should apply to "controlled affiliates," those commercial entities in which the MNC owns a majority of voting stock or controls by other means.[11]

This rule will apply in many different contexts. Direct cash payments to public or private actors are forbidden. But improper payments can occur in other, more clandestine ways: through requests for, or use of, third parties; by providing gifts and entertainment; through provision of travel and living beyond clear business purposes; through "charitable" and "political" contributions; and through use of partners, suppliers, and investors connected to public decision-makers (e.g. the prime minister's daughter who owns the supply of coal for the power station). Except for direct payments to government officials, these forms of improper payments may, however, also be proper.[12] Thus, decisions by the MNC about what is an improper or proper payment are often fact-bound. A strong anti-corruption program requires a robust integrity culture; clear guidelines; and a strong, centralized, high-level process to make sure hard cases are decided on the right side of the line.

The Solution: Creating a Uniform, Global Integrity Culture

Culture constitutes the shared principles (values, policies, and attitudes) and the shared practices (norms, systems, and processes) that influence how people feel, think, and behave. In a large organization, adherence to legal and ethical rules is critical, and a deterrence culture that is based on a fear of being caught and punished must be real. But for strong corporations that culture of deterrence must be supplemented—even supplanted—by an affirmative culture where employees want to do "the right thing." But such an affirmative culture turns on CEO *leadership* that forcefully articulates values and aspirations and on CEO *management* that deals with the complexity of bribery by driving systems, processes, and resources deep into business operations and that holds employees accountable. Without these operational realities, the aspirations are only that, and the corporate cliché of "tone at the top" is just window dressing.

The performance-with-integrity culture must be uniform across the globe. To be sure, MNCs must be sensitive to cultural variation as they do business in many different nations. But the core rules, systems, and processes that produce high performance and high integrity must never be compromised due to variation in local practices. This fundamental point is discussed more fully below. But a cautionary word is appropriate here. Siemens, the powerful German industrial conglomerate, has been wracked with a significant overseas bribery scandal in recent years. The company has identified more than $2 billion in questionable payments; has had its board chair, CEO, and key staff and operational leaders removed; has had to pay $850 million to internal investigators; has had to adjust its tax returns at a cost of more than $500 million (because expenses taken as legitimate turned out to be illegitimate); will likely pay fines of more than $1.6 billion in enforcement actions and is still facing investigation and possible prosecution in multiple jurisdictions around the globe.[13] One source of this towering problem was the "decentralization" of company values, which allowed local and regional officers to disregard the paper policy against improper payments and "adapt" improperly to corrupt local practices.

Principles and Practices

A first principle for "how" to create an effective anti-corruption program is that the CEO, and other business leaders, must provide consistent and committed leadership. They must put integrity first and not pass off responsibility for this complex set of issues to staff functions (finance, law, human resources), which have a vital, but supporting, role. The message must be unequivocal. When I was at General Electric (GE), the CEOs (Jack Welch and then Jeff Immelt) would, at the annual meeting of senior leaders, consistently state the following:

—The corporation is built on reputation and performance with integrity as its foundation.

—Each leader in this room will be held personally accountable.

—There will be no cutting of corners for commercial reasons; integrity must never be compromised to "make" the numbers.

—One strike and you are out. You can miss the numbers and survive. You cannot miss on integrity.

CEOs must then give this core message meaning through tough discipline of their generals, not just their troops. For example, a seasoned GE business leader in an emerging market willfully sidestepped the company's due diligence procedures when shifting distribution from GE employees to a third party. When an internal audit uncovered improper payments by the distributor, the leader was terminated without equivocation or weighing the pro's of past success. The executive had crossed a line that leaders should defend, not bend. The tough message at senior leadership meetings—one strike and you are out—was driven home by tough action.

An even more thunderous message is delivered when a senior executive is removed for a failure of omission, not commission. A salient example of this occurred when an Israeli general in charge of procurement for the Israeli Air Force and a GE aircraft engines marketing manager fraudulently misappropriated millions of dollars provided by the U.S. government to the Israeli government to purchase U.S. fighter planes. For this to occur, there was wrongdoing by many in GE; many others knew about the fraud but failed to take action to stop it. The matter was investigated; a settlement was reached with the government; individuals were disciplined; and systems repaired. The ultimate question was what to do with GE's military engines leader, who was not involved in the corrupt acts but had failed to create a culture of integrity because too many in the organization were indifferent to intolerable acts for too long. After much debate, the executive was asked to leave the company. The message was clear: there was no favoritism. Generals would be held to higher standards than troops and failure to create a performance-with-integrity culture was an offense requiring separation.

A second principle is to manage performance with integrity as a business process. The essence of management is dealing with complexity through systems and processes. And, with respect to implementing an anti-bribery policy involving many different kinds of improper acts across many different cultures, such complexity is daunting. Such a policy involves building an "integrity infrastructure" into relevant but discrete business processes: marketing, sales, manufacturing, sourcing, and governmental relations. This policy has three essential components, expressed by GE in the following way:

—Prevent ethics and compliance misses . . . and when prevention fails;

—detect misses as soon as possible . . . and once detected;

—respond quickly and effectively to investigate the facts, discipline individuals, and remedy systems both in the particular business unit and across the corporation. (Again, to quote a GE mantra, it involves everyone, everyday, everywhere.)

The key to this integrity infrastructure is to "risk assess" business processes that pose corruption problems and then to develop systems and processes for "risk abatement." At GE, business leaders were made responsible for this fundamental activity and were paired with "domain experts": individuals with special expertise in anti-corruption (financial experts, auditors, lawyers). Over time, GE developed detailed implementing guidelines used across the globe and across its different business divisions to provide direction on some of the most difficult problems. Several salient examples follow.

THIRD PARTIES. Third parties constitute one of the most dangerous problems: agents, consultants, sales representatives, and distributors, who stand between the company and the customer, can be conduits for improper payments. The risk abatement process requires written specifications at the outset defining the commercial context and the specific need. Before any engagement can occur this specification has to be expressly approved by senior management so accountability is clearly fixed. The next phase involves due diligence. One subject of this diligence is the third parties' resources and expertise (what do their financials look like; who are their personnel; what knowledge of and experience in the industry do they have; what is their formal business entity documentation). A second dimension of due diligence is assessing reputation. This assessment involves both interviews and public record checks (for example, cross matches with terrorist lists; assessment of conflicts of interest; views of others in the business, diplomatic, and media communities; and a review of police records).

The written contract with third parties should contain critical terms: specifications of the work; a fee within a reasonable range for the work done (1 or 2 percent, not 10 or 15 percent); a structure for payments in phases tied to deliverables or other concrete steps where possible; the exclusion of unknown sub-contractors (who could be conduits); payments in-country (not in Switzerland); training in GE anti-corruption policies and practices; audit rights; right to terminate unilaterally; and a certification that the third party understands the company's anti-corruption policy and will adhere to it. GE employees on the front lines were given special training on third parties to identify red flags that would be reported up the "integrity infrastructure line" (e.g., requests for cash, inflated invoices, requests for partners or suppliers that were not in the original contract; in general an "eyes wide open" requirement to identify suspicious circumstances).

Because third parties pose such a risk for corruption, GE also held "summits" in difficult regions, such as the Middle East and Asia, to cut across its lines of business and to make sure that there was consistency in the terms and conditions for retaining third parties, in the use of best practices that emerged from experience in the region, and in the techniques used for reducing the absolute number of third parties to the greatest extent possible.[14] One problem in reducing third parties is that in many nations, governments request that agents or consultants be used. Could GE be certain that there were not improper payments? No, but it took extraordinary steps and care in preventing them.

GIFTS, ENTERTAINMENT, TRAVEL, AND LIVING EXPENSES. Gifts, entertainment, travel, and living expenses collectively constitute another serious problem area. For public officials, governments may have strict written limitations that are not implemented or enforced. Or governments may have only vague rules. Again, for GE, a systematic process that was applied across the globe was vital to reduce risk. Governmental policies had to be clearly researched, understood, and communicated to GE employees and followed even if government enforcement was, at best, erratic. With respect to travel and living expenses, a legitimate business purpose had to be defined in writing and, as with third parties, approved in writing by a senior manager. With respect to gifts, both giving and receiving gifts of more than nominal amounts were prohibited.[15] Strict record-keeping and auditing, to ensure a clear history, were also required. And employees that were responsible for reviewing expenditures in these areas—like employees that deal with third parties—were trained to spot red flags such as vague statements of purpose; missing receipts and documents for reimbursement; missing lists of attendees; improper venues; and unauthorized expenses for spouses.[16]

REGULAR MANAGEMENT REVIEWS. Regular management reviews, directed by business leaders, demonstrate to employees the foundational importance of implementing performance with integrity as a business process. These management reviews build on controllership, other preventive actions, and on follow-up auditing. The place or form may vary, but deep leadership engagement is essential.[17]

A third principle is to adopt global standards beyond the requirements that are imposed by formal rules that bind the company and its employees. With respect to improper payments, GE had a broad policy that its employees and third parties should not bribe or give in to extortion whatever their nationality; whatever the local law; and whether in a public or a private setting.[18] This broad approach was born from the company's belief that "what is legal" is an initial question, but "what is right" is the ultimate question. GE agreed with all the reasons, noted above, why corruption was harmful. But one reason was of signal importance. Bribes corrupt the internal culture of the corporation. They are unlawful; they are improper; they are secret; and they require falsification of the books. If, as I believe, a great corporation—indeed any great organization—is built on the honesty, candor, fairness, trustworthiness, and reliability of its employees, then bribes are inimical to those values, are inimical to other elements of integrity (adherence to rules and ethical behavior), and cannot be tolerated. It was for these reasons that GE adopted the broad anti-bribery policy that went beyond the technicalities of varying rules in varying jurisdictions. As discussed below, GE recognized that there would be a cost to this position, but believed deeply that the benefits were much greater than the risks.

A fourth principle—fostering employee awareness, knowledge, and commitment—and a fifth principle—giving employees voices—are closely related. Especially in the complex area of improper payments, employees need to understand their obligations, to do things right when the rules are clear, to do the right thing by seeking advice when the situation is not clear—and when company learning and judgment must be applied. Corporations must not only articulate "the word," they must explain to their employees why these principles are important for a global company and deliver this message energetically in combination with business training. This commitment to training is especially important in emerging markets with employees who have come from companies and cultures that have different values than a performance-with-integrity MNC and where ingrained attitudes ("it does not matter"; "we will not be caught"; "the company tacitly approves") must be overcome.[19]

Especially with respect to improper payments, corporations need to ensure that employees have "voice" to report concerns about potentially illicit activities. Such voice is in contrast to the "culture of silence" that plagues many corporations and that causes improper acts to go unreported and unaddressed. The key mechanism for such a voice is an ombuds system that encourages employees to report such concerns, anonymously if necessary, to the ombudspersons in the businesses or at corporate headquarters; that can take reports in many different languages; that follows up on concerns promptly and professionally wherever the facts lead; and that has real consequences in terms of discipline. At GE, employees had a duty to report possible improper payments (and could be disciplined for failure to do so) and had a related duty never to retaliate (a firing offense). Such a system not only detects, it deters because people know that their peers will report improprieties. When professionally handled, such a system does not cause false reports and back-biting because cheap shots won't work.[20]

A sixth principle is to compensate the CEO and other top business leaders not just for performance but for performance with integrity, especially in the tough area of anti-corruption in emerging markets. On this principle, the board of directors has the lead role. It must define new specification and management development processes for the CEO and top business leaders so that the CEO is not just one with a commercial vision and personal integrity but a leader who has the experience, skill, and intensity to fuse high performance with high integrity deep within the organization. And, because measurements drive so much of the behavior in corporations, this ultimately means that the board must establish certain performance-with-integrity metrics that relate to some percentage of cash compensation (salary and bonuses) and equity awards (such as stock options) both for the CEO and for top profit and loss leaders.[21]

Benefits and Costs

The benefits of a strong, uniform, global anti-corruption policy, which has a real impact at the operational level, occur in three dimensions. Inside the company, bribery is, as noted, antithetical to the core values of honesty, candor, fairness, reliability, and trustworthiness. It is contrary to an employment system that is based on merit, not cronyism and corruption. Strong anti-corruption measures can create pride in a company and create a potent environment for hiring, retaining, and motivating employees.

In the marketplace, a strong anti-corruption policy avoids the catastrophic legal risk of a towering bribery scandal that periodically affects emerging markets and companies doing business there, as the Siemens case demonstrates. As the political pendulum swings, companies involved with corrupt governments may be exposed. On the positive side, a strong policy against bribes enhances a corporation's reputation as a "clean" company. It can, thus, be a differentiating factor with corrupt competitors by appealing to technocrats, who, even in difficult markets, want to do the right thing and protect their own reputations. And, in some cases, such a policy requires that the company exit a market when the corruption is so pervasive that it is impossible for the company to operate without being tainted.[22]

In the broader global society, an anti-corruption policy generates credibility for corporations with regulators and in public debates. Such a policy increases the opportunities for positive media coverage, which gives a company a positive reputation in the public eye. And, most important, such a policy can contribute to the development of the legitimate and durable growth of transparent and accountable institutional infrastructures in developing countries.

Fusing high performance with high integrity ultimately creates trust with all stakeholders—shareholders, creditors, employees, customers, suppliers, governments, and the media—which allows corporations to have tremendous freedom, notwithstanding the regulations of a mixed economy, to allocate capital, find new markets, invest in technology, and create innovations that drive societal growth. It is the strongest possible argument for the spread of global capitalism.

A "no bribes" policy, taken seriously, has the cost of lost business in certain circumstances. This loss is hard to measure. But GE, for one, felt that the benefits, briefly described above, far outweighed these costs. At the end of the day, this was not about balancing dollars and cents. Such a policy was a matter of judgment and common sense. This policy went to the fundamental question of what does the company stand for, which requires values, vision, and leadership, not only a calculator and a spreadsheet.

Rhetoric and Reality

A fundamental question is how many MNCs actually fuse high performance with high integrity. Unfortunately, it is not an easy question to answer. Most MNCs have an anti-corruption policy on paper. But, many still believe that doing business in societies with bribery, extortion, and misappropriation requires use of illicit means and abandonment of their own stated principles. Hypocrisy exists; some would say it is widespread or even rampant.[23]

Thus, the basic question remains: how to create a pervasive integrity culture that is so critical to ensuring a robust global anti-corruption program. While this culture ultimately should be based on an affirmative desire to "do the right thing," it may start as a deterrence culture to avoid legal or reputational risks. That requires the developed world to enforce anti-bribery laws against MNCs headquartered there. But, as is argued in the next section, the record of the developed world on this vital subject is mixed, at best.

Efforts to Stop Developed World MNCs from Bribing in the Developing World

The OECD Convention on Combating Bribery of Foreign Public Officials was adopted in 1997 and entered into force in 1999. The convention commits the ratifying parties to enact and enforce national laws that make foreign bribery by their corporations a crime. These member states include the world's leading industrialized nations, which are home to most of the major multi-national companies. The goal of the convention is to address the "supply side" of global corruption and create a level, bribe-free playing field for developed world corporations. Such a playing field is achieved through the implementation of serious sanctions by member states when foreign bribes are paid to procure business overseas, especially in the developing world. An additional goal of the convention is to deter multi-national corporations' wrongdoing and thus ultimately to encourage them to build robust anti-corruption programs and sustainable performance-with-integrity cultures.

For those corporations committed to global anti-corruption agendas, making the convention work is an important test. Of the many initiatives on the broad anti-corruption agenda, the effort to stop foreign bribery by corporations headquartered in the OECD states is the most clear-cut and straightforward. And, serious enforcement of this convention in the all the member states—the creation of a truly level playing field—is a matter of high importance for all MNCs that are sincerely dedicated to high performance with high integrity.

The Record and the Problem to Date

Unfortunately, more than ten years after its adoption, the OECD convention's record of enforcement is mixed at best. That record is a story of tension between an important global commitment against corruption and parochial national interests that ignore anti-bribery mandates in order to protect national trade champions and domestic jobs. It is a story of some progress but many setbacks on the troubled convention road from words to deeds. Consistent, sustained implementation of the convention will require a change in the politics of the OECD, the signatory nations, and their corporations to counter the entrenched and powerful politics of corruption. MNCs that are committed to anti-corruption measures must work with like-minded government officials in both legislative and executive branches, with political parties, with business associations, with NGOs (such as Transparency International), and with the media to help to remedy the convention's failings.

The adoption of the OECD convention was widely regarded as a major breakthrough, with thirty-four (as of early 2009, thirty-seven) leading industrial countries agreeing to make foreign bribery by their own corporations a crime under their national laws. Previously, foreign bribery was a crime only under U.S. law (the Foreign Corrupt Practices Act [FCPA]). Everywhere else it was not prohibited by domestic laws, and foreign bribes were treated as tax-deductible business expenses in many nations.[24]

The convention charged the Working Group on Bribery to provide follow-up monitoring of member state compliance. The first phase of this monitoring involved the review of each member state's national laws to determine whether they met the requirements of the convention.[25] The second phase monitored the actual enforcement of national laws, a much more complex undertaking requiring OECD teams to visit each country.[26]

The OECD has no legal power to compel signatories to take action. Its principal lever is peer pressure, exercised in the first instance through the Working Group. The OECD monitoring process produces detailed criticisms and recommendations and is impressive in its professionalism and thoroughness. However, the preparation of country reports is time consuming, and they are customarily long and highly technical. Although the purpose of the reports is to bring peer and public pressure by exposing national weaknesses, the OECD, as a consensual organization, does not customarily run media campaigns to "name and shame" its member states. The OECD has also refused to issue comparative annual reports that cover prosecutions and investigations brought by each member state and that evaluate the relative performance of each country's anti-corruption program.

To provide the comparisons that are lacking in the OECD monitoring effort, Transparency International publishes an annual report on enforcement that covers thirty-four OECD countries.[27] The key findings of the 2008 Transparency International report show that there is some enforcement in sixteen of thirty-four countries, including five of the eight largest exporters: France, Germany, Italy, the Netherlands, and the United States (which has the most active enforcement program by far).[28] This enforcement includes member state prosecutions of major MNCs such as Siemens, Total, Baker Hughes, Statoil, Alstom, Enelpower, and Alcatel. However, there is little or no enforcement of the convention in eighteen countries, including large exporters such as Japan and Britain. In addition, the independence of centralized prosecutorial authorities and the existence of necessary expertise and resources to handle complex foreign bribery cases also vary widely among nations.[29] There is, as of 2009, a serious lack of political commitment by over half of the parties to the convention, ten years after it was adopted. The symbols of the convention's mixed record are Germany and Britain. After years of tax deductibility of bribes and turning a blind eye to the practices of its powerful exporting industry, German authorities are now actively engaged, along with other nations, in investigating the towering Siemens global bribery scandal. For example, the Munich prosecutors announced in 2008 that they had expanded their corruption investigation to include four major divisions (power transmission, power generation, medical, and transportation) and 270 individuals. This announcement has led to many other complaints, to possible changes in Germany's prosecutorial behavior, and to a heightened awareness by Germany's industries (although it is hard to evaluate yet whether there has been an actual alteration of German business practices overseas).[30]

By contrast, the British government has not rewritten its anti-corruption laws, as requested by the OECD Working Group, and it has prosecuted only a single case of foreign bribery since it ratified the convention in 1999. Moreover, in 2006, Prime Minister Tony Blair announced that, for national security reasons, the British Government had stopped dead in its tracks the long-running investigation of bribery allegations involving British Aerospace Systems' (BAE) lucrative Al Yamamah contracts for the sale of British fighter planes to Saudi Arabia. According to news reports, payments totaling as much as several billion dollars may have been paid by BAE, Britain's largest defense contractor, to members of the Saudi royal family to secure past and present fighter orders, almost certainly with the knowledge of the British Government. The Serious Fraud Office, a supposedly independent prosecutorial authority, justified the termination of the Al Yamamah contracts on national security grounds (the Saudis had threatened the Blair government that they would cut off intelligence exchanges on terrorism if the investigation continued). The unilateral use of an unauthorized and unconstrained "national security" rationale raises the specter that other nations will halt sensitive investigations, using national security as a pretext, when their real motives are to promote national commercial champions and avoid worldwide embarrassment. (In mid-2008, the House of Lords reversed a lower court ruling that the termination was unlawful under British law; the Lords held that it was an appropriate exercise of discretion and further held that the convention was unenforceable in British courts because it had not yet been "incorporated" into British domestic law by legislation.[31])

Assessing the convention ten years after its adoption, Fritz Heimann, the former chairman of Transparency International—U.S.A., and I drew these conclusions:

—There have been important achievements at the governmental level, including passage of laws by virtually all member states, professional monitoring by the OECD Working Group, and significant enforcement in some nations. But, on the negative side of the ledger, there has been little or no enforcement in many OECD states and, even in many of the "enforcing" states, there have been few successful prosecutions or settlements.

—The success of the convention will remain uncertain until there is significant enforcement in many more countries and until the threat presented by the British assertion of an unconstrained national security exception has been overcome.

—The situation as of 2009 is unstable. If the laggards do not come aboard soon existing support for enforcement could erode, especially in a time of economic turmoil when trade and jobs are in peril.

—With so few successful prosecutions outside the United States, there is little reason to think that the convention has produced a sea change in the behavior of international business, forcing the adoption of robust corporate anti-corruption programs and durable changes in corporate culture.[32]

Actions Needed and the Role of the MNC

Future progress on the convention will require new, concrete actions by the OECD, by laggard national governments, and by indifferent MNCs. MNCs that are committed to anti-corruption have an important role in effecting change at all three levels.

OECD ACTIONS. Peer pressure on laggard governments must be elevated to the ministerial level through active involvement by the secretary-general, the OECD Ministerial Council, and by top-level officials from member governments. These persons must deal directly with ministers of the non-enforcing states.

The OECD Working Group must explicitly address "the national security" exception used by the British to stop the Saudi investigation, as such an exception does not appear in the convention. Indeed, Article Five of the convention explicitly prohibits enforcement decisions from being "influenced by considerations of national economic interest, the potential effect upon relations with another state, or the identity of the natural or legal persons involved." The working group needs to make clear that, under international law, broad national security exceptions must be express, and only narrow exceptions of "necessity" (self-defense or imminent harm) can be implied under very stringent conditions.[33]

The OECD must continue to fund a rigorous working group monitoring program that includes country visits. There should be annual reports that compare and contrast enforcement in different countries in order to hold nations more fully accountable and give monitoring greater persuasive power. The OECD should seek to include as signatories major exporters such as China, Russia, and India. This effort is already underway.[34]

NATIONAL GOVERNMENT ACTIONS. Governments that have taken the enforcement path, including France, Germany, and the United States, must actively exert peer pressure on other countries. Failure to enforce the convention must be treated as a priority diplomatic issue (rather than an afterthought in a G-8 communiqué). The "enforcing nations" should closely support efforts by the OECD secretary general. These nations must also utilize bilateral relationships with laggard governments. For example, the United States must push its close allies, but poor performers with respect to the OECD convention—Britain and Japan—to get off the dime.

Various parties within a country's political system will also have to make anti-corruption a political issue of priority to turn laggard nations into enforcers. Can the development agency partner with the foreign office to persuade the president or the prime minister that an anti-corruption enforcement is of vital importance to the nation's self-interest? Will an opposition party make this an issue, with the aid of the media and NGOs? Will a scandal that ripens like Siemens', rather than one that shrivels like Britain's, transform public and political attitudes? The transformation of national attitudes will depend in part on external pressures from the OECD and from international governments, but it will depend most heavily on attitudes among key actors within a society, including enlightened companies.

MULTI-NATIONAL CORPORATIONS ACTIONS. As discussed earlier, to fulfill the ultimate purpose of the OECD convention, individual MNCs should implement robust anti-corruption programs. These programs are key building blocks to achieving a high-performance-with-high-integrity culture, which helps a company to avoid catastrophic risk and to achieve affirmative benefits within the company, in the marketplace, and in the broader global society.

Beyond the acts of individual MNCs, international companies can act in concert. Most important, they need to put pressure on their own governments to enforce anti-bribery laws. It makes sense for U.S. companies, operating under an active FCPA enforcement regime, to pressure the U.S. government to use its influence in multilateral settings (with the OECD) and bilateral settings (with, for example, Britain and Japan). But there are few signs that MNCs in the developed world are prepared to push hard in their home nations for active and uniform enforcement of the convention. This failure raises questions about whether other coordinated corporate initiatives are anything more than feel-good paper exercises with limited impacts.[35]

Progress or Hypocrisy in the Developed World

At the end of the day, the basic problem with the OECD convention is that the OECD has no power of enforcement; it only has the power of consensual peer persuasion. But the peer nations are divided. National governments are also susceptible to the politics of trade promotion and jobs at home. Without external pressures or enlightened CEO leadership, few multi-nationals will change their behavior. Leadership at the OECD, among national governments, and within MNCs is necessary to replace the old politics of corruption and execute a strategy to stop foreign bribes.[36] Without such an approach, the necessary steps outlined above will not be taken.

Such leadership will depend on leaders' acceptance of two broad animating ideas that will redefine national and corporate self-interest and accelerate the anti-corruption agenda beyond the slow, piecemeal, and incomplete steps that have characterized the past ten years.[37]

First, in a global economy, developed nations and MNCs must see that it is directly in their economic and foreign policy interests to stop corruption in emerging markets and to help developing nations to build transparent, legitimate, and accountable institutions. This goal is necessary for developing countries to achieve sustainable economic growth that benefits developed nations and their companies. It is also necessary to address the needs of the bottom billion, to use the phrase of development expert Paul Collier, and to prevent these countries from posing foreign policy and national security threats to the developed world. Admittedly, this is a mid-to-long-term self-interest, and it can be trumped by "short-termism. But "self-interest" it is nonetheless.

A second, related idea is that other parts of the broader anti-corruption agenda—actions by developing nations to strengthen their institutions and their economies and actions by multilateral development agencies to assist that task—depend, in important part, on the developed world: to provide direct investment, export markets, technical assistance, and other kinds of aid, resources, and support. But the credibility, moral authority, and impact of these other approaches are undermined when the developed world does not seriously address foreign bribery committed by its own companies.[38]

International Efforts to Stop Corruption in the Developing World and the Role of the MNC

For the reasons stated immediately above, high-performance-with-high-integrity MNCs have a strong interest in supporting international efforts to attack corruption in the developing world. These efforts can take many forms, including international anti-bribery conventions such as the UN Convention against Corruption; national development and assistance programs such as USAID, the UK's Department for International Development and Japan's JE Import/Export Company; and international financing institutions (IFI's) such as the World Bank Group, the European Bank for Reconstruction and Development, and the Asian Development Bank.[39]

The ability of these institutions to advance development in emerging markets, to reduce poverty, and to counter corruption is an enormously complex and controversial subject, which is far beyond the scope of this chapter. I merely want to illuminate briefly the constructive role MNCs can play within these institutions. Beyond the general interest in sustained and lawful development, MNCs have a strong, direct self-interest in such a role because MNCs may wish to seek contracts in a fair and transparent manner from international development funders that disburse funds to nations in the developing world. I use the World Bank Group as an example, in part because it disburses more than $24 billion a year out of the approximately $100 billion spent by international institutions or developed world nations on aid or financing programs in the developing world.

The World Bank Group's (WB) Governance and Anti-Corruption Strategy (GAC strategy) has developed over the past ten years.[40] It has two broad goals.

The first is country capacity building so that individual nations may develop institutional, not just physical, infrastructures to durable, transparent, and accountable public sector economic, social, political, legal, and administrative entities. Such institutions are essential for effective governance, which can stimulate economic growth, reduce poverty, and combat corruption. The basic rationale for such an approach is that a nation's capacity for good governance and effective anti-corruption efforts are of central importance in contemporary theories of sustainable development.[41] In 2007, approximately 15 percent (about $4 billion) of WB funds were directed for the broad purpose of governance and anti-corruption capacity building.

The second goal of the GAC strategy is program integrity—preventing fraud and corruption in the disbursement of the bank's funds, whether directed at capacity building or other dimensions of development (e.g., improving education or health care). The reasons for program integrity are many: the bank's charter requires it as a matter of fiduciary duty; a similar duty applies to the bank's administration of "other peoples' money" (13 percent of the WB's loans or grants come from member state trust funds or development programs); illicit leakage of program funds obviously harms the intended beneficiaries—the world's poor; and the bank cannot have credibility in its capacity building goals unless it has credible integrity in its own programs. Indeed, program integrity efforts can serve as demonstrations of effective techniques that have wide applications in developing nations.[42]

Unfortunately, the 2007 Volcker Review Panel, which assessed the bank's anti-corruption efforts, concluded that WB's capacity building efforts are part of a long and complex process in each nation and that they have "often [been] characterized by false starts, overly broad and poorly rooted initiatives with limited influence." Similarly, with respect to program integrity, the panel concluded that "... the Bank's approach to corruption has been ad hoc and piecemeal ... too often commitment to program integrity has been lacking." Indeed, many on the WB's operational side (in the International Development Association [IDA] and the International Bank for Reconstruction and Development [IBRD]) have viewed program integrity with ambivalence or even hostility, in part because of controversy engendered by investigations of wrongdoing. In summary, the Volcker Review Panel called for more active leadership within the bank, not just from the president and the board, but also from the "Managing Directors, the Regional Vice Presidents, and Country Directors [who] must all understand and drive the entire governance program and the anti-corruption mission with it ... [in] both staff and operations throughout the organization ... [and that] emphasis cannot just be on country capacity building but on the vital, complementary objective of program integrity."[43]

The Volcker Review Panel called for a comprehensive approach to program integrity that integrated both headquarters' staff (finance, legal, audit, and human resources) and its operational personnel (e.g., in the IBRD and IDA) who design and implement country programs. Such a comprehensive program had elements similar to those in the anti-corruption programs of MNCs—prevention, detection, investigation, remediation, and evaluation.[44] In all of these areas, private sector expertise can materially assist WB program integrity efforts, either through business associations such as the International Chamber of Commerce, through NGOs drawing on business skills such as Transparency International, or through direct consultations with MNCs that are committed to anti-corruption programs.

Most important, program integrity must focus on preventing and addressing corruption in program designs with recipient nations, rather than waiting for formal investigations of the WB and member states after the corruption has allegedly occurred. Prevention, as discussed, involves systematic risk assessment and risk abatement. But, in the WB context, it entails trained project management that is directed at process mapping of projected money flows; procurement and contracting disciplines; use of "integrity pacts" between government and the private sector on specific public contracts; implementation and monitoring techniques; response to red flags; and formal auditing at various stages of the project. MNCs' knowledge and experience can also involve a variety of other steps in this broad project management process, including education and training, disbursement controls, complaint handling, transparency, root cause analysis, and best practice sharing. In general, such contributions can address all the principles and practices summarized in the section above, as they apply to the WB program integrity efforts because the management of money flows as a fiduciary across different nations, peoples, and cultures is directly analogous.

Although there are without doubt important lessons to be learned from MNCs, the WB is, of course, different from a corporation. First, the leadership of the bank must deal with a board comprised of representatives from nations around the globe. Within this complex governance structure, it must overcome the lax leadership of the past and force headquarters' staff. This governance structure must also then integrate those staff to act in concert with those of IBRD and IDA operations by comprehensively defining elements of the program integrity framework and making them operational; by assessing current capabilities and capacities in the WB and making necessary personnel changes; and by making key leaders accountable, through metrics and evaluations of program integrity that are tied to compensation and promotion.

Second, even if the bank could compose a focused effort that targets program integrity, as well as country capacity building, it must, of course, work with, or at least within, client nations that are the recipients of funds, that administer programs, or where problems cause the WB to find third parties that can carry out projects if the nation or its sectors are too corrupt. Such a program requires discussions that are difficult and actions regarding how to manage funds and make expenditures that will advance program goals, not line the pockets of the corrupt. This effort requires political and policy skills different from those that are possessed by MNC leaders. And these skills are especially challenged in nations with a high level of corruption and a low level of positive economic growth. But these obvious differences should not derogate from the MNCs' potential to provide advice from their experiences on best practices in the systems, processes, and disciplines that are necessary to effectuate program integrity and capacity building.

The Role of the MNC in the Developing World

The MNC's role in the World Bank's second strategy goal for its governance and anti-corruption initiative—capacity building in developing nations—is best considered in the broader context of how developing nations can effect change. Of all the difficult topics discussed in this chapter, this one is the most difficult (perhaps by far). And I leave it to others in this volume, and elsewhere, to confront this issue more thoroughly.

It is fair to say that "development" is now viewed as involving both economic growth and institution (or state) building from the different perspectives of development specialists, economists, business professors, and political scientists.[45] The path each nation will take will be heavily influenced by its own history and culture. The precise sequencing of economic growth and institution building will depend, but economic growth without institutions can lead to state capture or kleptocracy, and institution building without economic growth is not possible or durable. Nations or areas must want to start the development process—it cannot be forced from outside the country—but outside assistance, if desired, can be important. And, in lawless societies, anti-corruption measures that are not part of larger institution building will not work; they are an important part of durable, transparent, accountable public institutions but are not sufficient alone.

In light of this complex consensus, what can be said, in summary, about the role of MNCs? First, they may make an important contribution to economic development in a number of ways: exporting important goods and services that are used to build infrastructure; helping to develop natural resource production for global markets; providing foreign direct investment for manufacturing, assembly, and product development; establishing research and development centers; transferring technology; transferring global management practices; providing education and training; and utilizing local, third party suppliers as part of global supply chains.

Second, by fusing high performance with high integrity inside their organizations, MNCs can not only avoid contributing to the corruption in a developing nation, but they can serve as models for how business can be conducted. In China, for example, GE joined with the Chinese government to host meetings for Chinese businesses on how they can comply with environmental and anti-corruption laws. It is fair to say that GE's standing in that nation was due, in part, to its role as a practical business school for both performance and integrity.

Third, as noted, MNCs have a broader anti-corruption role with other institutions: through the developed world's governmental effort to prohibit foreign bribery by its corporations; through voluntary cooperative efforts in business associations; and through cooperation with IFIs, such as the World Bank (in improving program integrity) or the UN (in implementing the UN Convention against Corruption).

But fourth, these broader anti-corruption efforts must be supplemented by MNC efforts to build institutional and governance capacity in developing nations—working with IFIs or other international actors or working directly with the host nation. MNCs have a powerful interest in broad "rule of law" initiatives because business depends so much on property rights, contract enforcement, and a certain level of regulatory and legal predictability (in a nation of laws, not of men). This process may start with expanding the laws that are on the books. But, ultimately, it must focus on how to make laws effective in action. MNCs can address this issue by educating, training, and perhaps by making commercial law a beachhead for broader legal change. China has put a great number of laws on the books and is beginning to develop legal institutions, at least in the commercial area, that are somewhat removed from corruption and the influence of the communist party. But others would say that the structure is (to mix national metaphors) but a "Potemkin village," with a generation to go before it becomes effective, predictable, and reliable. This broader role in advocating for rule of law extends to the larger questions of state-building—not only the building of courts but also administrative agencies and financial management institutions (budget and finance)—which are such an important part of the development equation. Here MNCs can partner with others to provide relevant technical assistance.

Finally, beyond building institutional infrastructures, MNCs have a role to play in the broad public policy debates in emerging markets about the fundamental balance between equity and efficiency, growth and sustainability, energy use and environmental protection. It is in their enlightened self-interest to help establish "public goods" in these developing nations that a corrupt government or pure market forces cannot create but that are essential to durable development. In doing so, MNCs must be non-partisan; they must advocate for principles, but not support parties. They must focus on accurate, credible facts and analysis. MNCs must seek a balance between legitimate competing interests, especially between private interests that can drive economic growth, and public interests to protect social justice and other social goods. Without all of these broad societal efforts, the chances that anti-corruption efforts will succeed are limited.[46]

In the end, one might ask whether this broad, multi-faceted role that I have suggested for MNCs in the long war against corruption is too idealistic or naïve. I began this chapter by recognizing that there are powerful internal and external forces within the global corporation that promote corruption. But I also explained that an MNC that combines high performance with high integrity can realize benefits inside the company, in the marketplace, and in the global society by operationally fusing these foundational goals. Ultimately, developing nations that can achieve economic growth and build institutional

infrastructures are of profound long-term benefit to MNCs because they provide a sound environment for sustainable economic activity. Just as it is in the
corporation's enlightened self-interest to fuse high performance with high
integrity, so too is it in the MNC's interest, in all the ways that I have suggested,
to add its resources, expertise, and commitment to the building of social, economic, political, legal, and administrative institutions that are transparent,
accountable, and durable and in which there is but an irreducible minimum
amount of corruption.

MNCs are not sufficient for economic growth and institution building in
the developing world. But they may be necessary—and are at least important—and at the very least should do no harm. If they act in their enlightened
self-interest, they, in sum, have a significant role in shortening the long war
against corruption.[47]

Notes

1. Manfred B. Steger, *Globalization* (New York, 2003), 48–49. In 2002, Steger noted
that there were 50,000 firms that could be termed "transnational" because they had
subsidiaries in a number of nations and that together these transnational companies
accounted for more than 70 percent of world trade. If one equated sales with GDP, 51
of the 100 largest economies as of 2002 were corporations, while 49 were nations.

2. For example, MNCs provide elements of product and service development
such as raw materials, components of goods, ingredients of food, and medicine; they
also provide a wide variety of services (from information technology to call centers,
from financial analysis to legal analysis and reading medical images).

3. There are other forms of international crime (terrorism, drug trafficking, illicit
arms trade, money laundering, piracy and counterfeiting, and abuse of women and
children). But I focus on the first meaning, while I recognize that I do so for analytic
convenience and that bribery, extortion, and misappropriation are connected in the
real world to other kinds of crime and corruption such as money laundering, illicit
drug traffic, illicit traffic in deadly weapons, and organized crime in general.

4. I will consider the role of the MNC in many facets of corruption: the supply side
(bribes) and the demand side (extortion or misappropriation); grand corruption (e.g.,
involving high-level officials with discretion over major governmental decisions) and
petty corruption (e.g., involving low-level officials who demand payments for the
performance of routine duties); and both public and private sector corruption. While
"domestic" corporations in each nation are also implicated in corruption, my focus is
on entities that are engaged in cross-border commerce.

5. This essay is based, in part, on my work for nearly two decades as senior vice
president for law and public affairs of one of the world's largest MNCs (GE) and my

involvement with Transparency International, the world's foremost anti-corruption non-governmental organization. In 2007, I was also privileged to serve on the Volcker Review Panel, which studied anti-corruption efforts at the World Bank Group; this intense experience along with GE's perspective on the World Bank and other IFIs informs my observations on the subject of corruption. Finally, as senior officer of an MNC, who spent time in many different developing nations, and as an interested amateur in development (though far from an expert), I have some concluding comments on the broader role of MNCs in development. See Paul A. Volcker and others, "Independent Panel Review of the World Bank Group Department of Institutional Integrity" (Washington, D.C., 13 September 2007). This chapter is also based on my prior writing in this area. See Ben W. Heineman, Jr., *High Performance with High Integrity* (Cambridge, MA, 2008); Ben W. Heineman, Jr., "Avoiding Integrity Landmines: An Inside Look at How GE Worked to Build a Culture That Sustains Both High Performance and High Integrity," *Harvard Business Review,* LXXXV (2007), 100–108; Ben W. Heineman, Jr. and Fritz Heimann, "The Long War Against Corruption," *Foreign Affairs,* LXXXV (2006), 75–86; Ben W. Heineman, Jr. and Fritz Heimann, "Arrested Development: The Fight Against International Corporate Bribery," *National Interest,* XCII (2007), 80–87. I am indebted to my colleagues at GE, to Mr. Heimann, to my colleagues at Transparency International, and to the members and staff of the Volcker Review Panel.

6. There is, of course, no shortage of corruption in the developed world, but legal systems are often—though not always—capable of uncovering corruption and prosecuting it according to the rule of law. Regardless of its other issues, the Bush Administration, for example, had a decent record on the prosecution of corporate crime and a good record in the enforcement of the Foreign Corrupt Practices Act.

7. The World Bank Institute estimated in 2004 that public officials received more than \$1 trillion in bribes each year. This figure does not include the amount that public officials stole through embezzlement and misappropriation.

8. Other financial goals include: return on investment, return on equity, product launch targets, sales targets, and productivity increases.

9. Many non-U.S. markets—from Russia to Brazil, from the Middle East to Asia—suffer from weak rule of law, endemic corruption, and pervasive conflicts of interest. Yet these same markets are a crucial source of growth for MNCs. Employees in these markets often come from a different tradition that tolerates practices, such as bribes, that are contrary to performance with integrity. Similarly, doing business with a government is often essential, and extortion and misappropriation are clear and present dangers in places where the rule of law is tenuous at best. Unconstrained, these external pressures, too, can corrupt capitalism.

10. Heineman, *High Performance with High Integrity,* 25–99.

11. An MNC must encourage its affiliated but non-controlled companies to adopt the MNC's policies, principles, and practices.

12. Consultants or agents may be necessary; travel and living expenses may be directly related to the legitimate promotion of goods and services or to the execution of a contract; political or charitable contributions may be lawful and appropriate in certain circumstances.

13. See, for example, U.S. Securities and Exchange Commission, "Form 6-K: Report of Foreign Private Issuer: Siemens Aktiengesellschaft" (2008), file number 1–15174, available at http://w1.siemens.com/investor/en/publications_events/sec_filings.htm (accessed 16 December 2008).

14. From 2005 to 2007, GE Aircraft Engines reduced the number of its consultants by 50 percent; during that same period, the number of consultants was reduced by 37 percent in Korea; 22 percent in China; and 10 percent in the Middle East.

15. Even though the exchange of gifts in business may be traditional in some societies, GE set low limits on what was "acceptable" so as to remove even the appearance of an improper payment. In none of these settings were cash payments allowed.

16. Facilitating payments—small payments for routine acts—pose a dilemma for MNCs. Such acts include: obtaining permits; processing papers such as visas, or securing services such as utilities and mail; and loading or unloading cargo or scheduling necessary inspections. These acts may be legal for U.S. MNCs under U.S. law (if "ministerial" acts, not "discretionary" acts), but acts of "petty" corruption are often nominally illegal (though widely practiced) in emerging markets. Moreover, many MNCs, such as GE, have codes of conduct that require compliance with local law, which would include compliance with non-enforced laws that prohibit various forms of petty corruption. To resolve such a dilemma, GE prohibited these payments across the globe, even if doing so caused delays, because of the company's need to comply with local law as a critical part of its performance with integrity. Payments, therefore, could only be made on an "exceptions" basis such as in cases where businesspeople sought the opinion of counsel, where there was an emergency from a business perspective, or where an individual's health and safety were threatened. Severe cases had to be raised up to more senior leaders and lawyers, who then made a decision about whether the payment was small enough and was routine enough to solve the business problem. Such decisions had to be in writing. A better approach would be to work with the local government in professionalizing and computerizing the customs service, say, to reduce the local practice of petty corruption. See General Electric, "Improper Payments," *The Spirit and the Letter* (New Haven, 2005), 18–19.

17. Such reviews can involve specific businesses or cross-business sessions in difficult countries (e.g., China) or regions (e.g., Middle East). They can involve new acquisitions that require the integration of employees and the practices of the acquiring company's culture. These reviews can involve major misses where the causes of problems, discipline, and systems change are front and center. They can be conducted by business or corporate leaders.

18. See General Electric, "Improper Payments."

19. Other examples of fostering employee awareness include: candid orientations that discuss company failures; web-based training that varies facts in the hypothetical to engage the employee; and, most important, face-to-face training where there can be real personal engagement, which addresses up-front cultural differences and explains why a global company has chosen to act differently. Beyond these steps, GE also sought bicultural and bilingual leaders and to provide leadership training shortly after a person assumed a position of importance in an emerging market so that his or her responsibilities and accountability were clearly and forcefully communicated.

20. In 2007, 4,500 matters were lodged in GE's ombuds system; 1,500 related to "concerns" about law and policy (others only sought information); 500 resulted in the finding of a violation. For improper payments, 50 "concerns" were reported in 2007 and 18 were confirmed as violations. Other methods for ensuring that an employee has a voice inside the corporation are: a strong internal audit staff, compliance reviews that start at the lowest level of the company and build up, and strong reporting relationships between the functional staff in the businesses (finance, legal, and human resources) and their senior counterparts at the corporate level.

21. For example, directors can use the following five categories to assess leadership on performance with integrity: adoption of the key principles, proper use of implementing practices, creation of an integrity culture (which can be measured by surveys and 360 degree personnel reviews), comparisons with peer companies (such as investigations or prosecutions for improper payments), and achievement of specified annual goals and objectives (such as choosing a proper local leader for China or India with the right background). The obverse, of course, is that leaders who fail in this area must suffer financial, and other, consequences. As noted in this chapter, the company must not wink at impropriety in the senior ranks or it loses all credibility with its employees.

22. At various times, GE has chosen not to do business at all in a nation, for example, in South Africa, Burma, Nigeria and, for certain kinds of "cash flow" businesses, in Russia (out of concern for money laundering).

23. Multi-national corporations' internal adherence to a robust anti-corruption policy becomes even more important for doing business, as powerful global companies emerge from the developing world. See Antoine van Agtmael, *The Emerging Markets Century: How a New Breed of World-Class Companies Is Overtaking the World* (New York, 2007).

24. The United States adopted its Foreign Corrupt Practices Act (FCPA), which bans bribes in foreign nations, in 1977 in response to Watergate revelations that U.S. companies had paid bribes to win orders in Japan, Italy, and the Netherlands. After close to twenty years of debate following the enactment of the U.S. FCPA, the OECD's Working Group on Bribery (formed in 1989) finally called for member governments to end the tax-deductibility of bribes and to make foreign bribery a crime. The convention was signed in 1997 as a result of several factors: increasing recognition that international corruption was a serious problem that should no longer be ignored and widely publicized corruption scandals in several important OECD countries.

25. The working group established it credibility by candidly criticizing those that did not enforce the convention, including influential countries such as Britain and Japan. With the exception of Britain, these nations corrected the deficiencies in the statutory law that the working group identified.

26. Seven countries are reviewed each year, and this initial review phase is not yet complete for all nations. If dissatisfied, the working group can schedule another country visit, as has been done in Japan, Britain, Ireland, and Luxembourg.

27. TI reports are based on the work of experts from its national chapters who conduct detailed inquiries in their countries. Understandably, the TI experts cannot get access to all information, but the reports are reviewed by national authorities and the OECD. These reports provide an important sense of direction, if not complete information.

28. The United States has a specialized foreign bribery enforcement office that is staffed by high quality career employees in the Justice Department's Criminal Division who have been enforcing the Foreign Corrupt Practices Act with relative diligence (regardless of the party in power) since the late 1970s. According to the 2008 TI Report, the United States has had 103 prosecutions under the act since it ratified the convention in 1999; this is almost 50 percent of all prosecutions among OECD nations, even though the United States has only 10 percent of total OECD exports. See Transparency International, *Progress Report 2008: Enforcement of the OECD Convention on Combating Bribery of Foreign Public Officials in International Business Transactions* (Berlin, 2008), 7–8.

29. TI, *Progress Report 2008,* 24.

30. In 2008, Siemens agreed to pay $800 million in fines to U.S. authorities and another $528 million to German authorities to resolve the pending bribery investigations in the respective nations.

31. United Kingdom House of Lords, Opinions of the Lords of Appeal for Judgment in the Cause: *R (on the application of Corner House Research and others (Respondents) v. Director of the Serious Fraud Office (Appellant) (Criminal Appeal from Her Majesty's High Court of Justice),* 30 July 2008, UKHL 60.

32. Heineman and Heimann, "Arrested Development," 84–85.

33. Ibid., 83, citing Susan Rose-Ackerman and Benjamin S. Billa, "Treaties and National Security," *New York University Journal of International Law and Politics,* XL (2008), 437–496. This article puts forth the proposition that national security exceptions to international treaties are not to be implied under international law; the only recognized implied exception is for "necessity" to address imminent harm and self-defense. See also Fritz Heimann and Susan Rose-Ackerman, "OECD Convention and National Security Interests," *Transparency International Policy Paper* (Berlin, 2008). Conditions of a narrow necessity exception include: a) a level of harm threshold; b) a requirement to balance conflicting interests; c) efforts to overcome national security concerns through diplomatic and other means; and d) some form of OECD Working Group review (even if in secret).

34. These countries have greatly expanded their role in international trade, and the convention's ability to achieve and maintain a corruption-free, level playing field will be undermined if these countries do not play by the same rules. Other nonmembers of the OECD have already acceded to the convention, including Brazil, Argentina, and more recently, South Africa. The OECD should also strengthen the convention, by clarifying language, to include bribes to political parties and party officials and bribes paid through foreign subsidiaries that are controlled by OECD-based parent companies.

35. Corporations have issued general anti-corruption codes of conduct through their associations; made public commitments through the World Economic Forum; announced industry-specific anti-corruption principles or activities (e.g., in financial services and extractive industries); and helped to develop anti-corruption tools through Transparency International. For example, the International Chamber of Commerce, the OECD, the World Economic Forum, and Transparency International have all promulgated statements of anti-bribery principles. The financial services industry (through the so-called Wolfsberg Group) has issued its own anti-corruption principles (focusing primarily on "know your customer" and anti-money laundering disciplines for high-risk correspondent banking relationships). A salient example of broad business group action is the World Economic Forum's Partnering Against Corruption Initiative (PACI), which claims more than 120 companies have signed up both to principles and program guidelines (but PACI has only self-reporting, not third-party verification). Another type of business initiative for companies is cooperation with developing nations. For example, the Extractive Industries Transparency Initiative (EITI) brings together leading companies in the mining and oil industries with developing-world governments to ensure that royalty payments are publicly reported. This effort addresses the widely recognized concern that countries with oil and other natural resources are among the most corrupt in the world because their leaders can secretly skim off much of the royalties paid out from these industries. EITI seeks to make such payments transparent, thereby making them harder to misappropriate. Finally, groups such as Transparency International develop practical tools so companies can move from principles to practice, for example, anti-corruption, self-assessment programs, accounting and assurance techniques, supply chain guidance, web-based training, and library resources.

36. In October 2008, the OECD Working Group on Bribery issued a blistering report on the failure of Britain to amend its anti-bribery laws, to handle the Al Yamamah investigation properly, and to implement the OECD convention fully. See *OECD Group Demands Rapid UK Action to Enact Adequate Anti-Bribery Laws* (Paris, 2008), available at www.oecd.org/document/8/0,3343,en_2649_34855_41515464_1_ 1_1_1,00.html (accessed 18 December 2008). In November 2008, the British Law Commission did recommend a revision in the UK foreign bribery laws: the creation of a new offense of bribing a foreign public official and a second new offense, applicable to corporations, of negligently failing to prevent bribery by an employee or agent. The commission stated that having adequate systems in place to prevent bribery

would be a defense to the second offense. Presumably, the British government will take some action on these recommendations in 2009. See Law Commission, "Bribery," available at www.lawcom.gov.uk/bribery.htm (accessed 18 December 2008).

37. The roles that the media and non-governmental organizations, such as Transparency International, with ninety-eight chapters worldwide, play in exposing and embarrassing companies and advocating for anti-corruption efforts are vital if these ideas are to gain currency.

38. For example, President Thabo Mbeki of South Africa accused Prime Minister Tony Blair of hypocrisy because Blair terminated the Al Yamamah investigation while Blair pressed for anti-corruption reforms in Africa. Broadly, the new UN Convention against Corruption (UNCAC) is beginning the difficult process of implementation, with follow-up monitoring yet to be established. But if the OECD fails to bring the many laggards on board—and thus erodes its own effectiveness—what is the message for UNCAC with its far more diverse 140 signatories and far more countries without a robust rule of law?

39. Heineman and Heimann, "Arrested Development," 86–87.

40. The World Bank's focus on corruption began when then President James Wolfensohn gave his "Cancer of Corruption" speech at the bank's 1996 annual meeting. For the next ten years, this anti-corruption initiative proceeded in fits and starts, with the creation of, in 1991, the Department of Institutional Integrity (INT) to investigate corruption. In March 2007, the bank issued a strategy paper on governance and anti-corruption, with an implementation plan issued in the fall of that year. During 2007, the Volcker Review Panel also examined the role of the INT in the context of the broader WB's Governance and Anti-Corruption Strategy.

41. Such efforts are aimed at establishing political stability and achieving the absence of violence; enhancing government effectiveness (e.g., quality of public services and professionalism of civil service); enacting regulations to level the economic playing field and to protect "social goods"; promoting rule of law in theory and in practice; protecting the role of the media and civil society; and controlling corruption and stopping state capture.

42. This fiduciary duty states: "The Bank shall make arrangements to ensure that the proceeds of any loan are used only for the purposes for which the loan was granted, with due attention to considerations of economy and efficiency and without regard to political or non-economic influences or considerations." See Volcker and others, "Independent Panel Review of the World Bank Group Department of Institutional Integrity," 9. As the 2007 GAC strategy paper states (p. 56), ". . . operational experience has demonstrated that protecting Bank funds can also advance local capacity."

43. See Volcker and others, "Independent Panel Review of the World Bank Group Department of Institutional Integrity," 10, 12.

44. Ibid.

45. For a development specialist's perspective see, for example, Paul Collier, *The Bottom Billion: Why the Poorest Countries are Failing and What Can Be Done About It*

(New York, 2007); for an economist's point of view, see Dani Rodrik, *One Economics, Many Recipes: Globalization, Institutions, and Economic Growth* (Princeton, 2007); for a political scientist's view see, for example, Francis Fukuyama, *State-Building: Governance and World Order in the 21st Century* (Ithaca, 2004); for the views of a business professor, see Michael Spence, *The Growth Report: Strategies for Sustained Growth and Inclusive Development* (Washington, D.C., 2008), available at http://cgd.s3.amazonaws. com/GrowthReportComplete.pdf (accessed 4 February 2009). Spence is the former dean of Stanford Business School and chair of The Commission on Growth and Development (a twenty-one-member commission that was launched in 2006 under the sponsorship of the World Bank; the governments of the Netherlands, Sweden, and Britain; and the William and Flora Hewlett Foundation). For a short summary of the debate about the meaning of "rule of law" and its relationship to economic development, see "Briefing: Economics and the Rule of Law: Order in the Jungle," *Economist* (13 March 2008), 83–85.

46. For a discussion of how global companies should address some of the toughest issues—emerging markets, acquisitions, crisis management, public policy, and reputation—with integrity see Heineman, *High Performance with High Integrity*, 100–146.

47. MNCs have limited capital, and nations with slow growth and poor institutional infrastructures will not fare well in attracting foreign direct investment (FDI). For nations where FDI is important to their economic growth, the development of institutional, as well as physical, infrastructures is critical. See Collier, *The Bottom Billion*, 154. Nations with great natural resources may attract FDI that does not include funds for institutional infrastructures, but this type of FDI leads to a set of currency, corruption, and keptocracy problems as discussed by Collier. See Collier, "The Natural Resource Trap," in his *The Bottom Billion*, 38–52. See also Joel Kurtzman and Glenn Yago, *Global Edge: Using the Opacity Index to Manage the Risks of Cross-Border Business* (Cambridge, MA, 2008). Kurtzman and Yago discuss how an index that measures corruption, legal systems, enforcement, transparency of accounting, and regulatory factors is an important measurement for businesses seeking to assess country risk.

JOHANN GRAF LAMBSDORFF

15

The Organization of Anti-Corruption: Getting Incentives Right

Corruption poses similar problems to both governments and private firms. Contracts are awarded to those paying bribes rather than delivering quality. Public policies as well as corporate strategies are distorted by side payments and resources are embezzled for private use. Due to these similarities, most of the ideas developed herein are equally applicable to public and private organizations.

Anti-corruption approaches can either relate to rules or to principles; they can be either top-down or bottom-up. This chapter reviews a variety of widely discussed approaches to anti-corruption and highlights some of the shortcomings of rules-based, top-down anti-corruption. The chapter makes the argument that many in government and the private sector can contribute to bottom-up endeavors. The chapter then emphasizes the need for bottom-up methods to complement top-down approaches. The last section seeks to reconcile top-down and bottom-up approaches and provides practical reform proposals.

Rules-Based Anti-Corruption

Many anti-corruption methods refer to rules. These rules have two dimensions. The first element is repression, which emphasizes draconian penalties and a high probability of detecting malfeasance. Since the seminal work of Becker, criminal behavior is seen as being driven by rational calculus. A fully rational, risk-neutral actor opts for criminal behavior if the expected benefit

I am indebted to Mathias Nell, Robert Rotberg, and Emily Wood for helpful comments and assistance.

exceeds the sanction multiplied by the probability of being convicted. Even if rationality is imperfect, this calculus captures many of the incentives faced by human beings. This argument is further supported by the fact that bribery, fraud, and embezzlement are less emotional, and more rational, forms of misconduct. They require sophistication, skills, and long-term planning, emphasizing the sober balancing between pros and cons. The 2003 United Nations Convention against Corruption requests that all signatory countries implement criminal codes that counter corruption. As of 2008, this approach is the most important rules-based approach to deterring criminal behavior.

Repression is an indispensable element in the fight against corruption. But judiciaries perform quite differently across countries. Data on prosecutions and court convictions related to fraud, bribery, and embezzlement reveal that such cases are common in countries such as Canada, Finland, Germany, and New Zealand, reaching annually up to 100 cases per 100,000 inhabitants.[1] But in many less developed countries these figures are drastically lower; often fewer than one single case per 100,000 inhabitants is reported. What might cause these huge discrepancies? First, law enforcement is costly and, second, such convictions require an honest judiciary. But resources for developing an honest judiciary may be in short supply, particularly in developing countries.

Apart from the costs, increasing repression also has detrimental effects. Threats of penalties and enhanced monitoring may adversely affect the intrinsic motivation of public and private employees. Thus, employees may not support the repressive actions of their superiors with their own efforts and civic engagement. To the contrary, employees are induced to fight corruption for their superiors but not for themselves. Empirical evidence exists that casts doubt on approaches that focus on formal, rules-based anti-corruption endeavors. For example, Voigt, Feld, and van Aaken investigate the impact of prosecutorial independence in containing corruption and find that *de facto* independence decreases corruption.[2] However, *de jure* independence does not exert the same impact. A similar finding related to strict campaign financing rules is reported by Stratmann.[3] Employing only formal rules may thus be insufficient for containing corruption.

Global Integrity, a Washington-based think-tank, assesses various key issues of governance and anti-corruption. These data, as presented on its website, reveal to what extent rules, in what Global Integrity calls the "legal framework," are effective in reducing corruption. It investigates issues such as elections, civil society and the media, accountability, administration, oversight, and the rule of law. Table 15-1 reveals how the "legal framework" and its "practical implementation" (another dataset assembled by Global Integrity)

Table 15-1. *Ordinary Least Squares Regressions: Perceived Corruption, Anti-corruption Rules, and Their Implementation*[a]

Dependent Variable	TI Corruption Perceptions Index		WEF Perceived Effectiveness of Anti-corruption, 2007[b]	
Independent Variable	1	2	3	4
Constant	1.8	2.34	4.72	5.27
	(2.2)	(3.2)	(4.3)	(4.7)
Anti-corruption: Legal Framework[c]	−0.042	−0.018	−0.033	−0.026
	(−3.1)	(−1.3)	(−2.0)	(−1.4)
Anti-corruption: Practical Implementation[d]	0.098	0.032	0.030	−0.001
	(5.7)	(2.4)	(2.6)	(−0.1)
GDP per capita[e]		0.12		0.056
		(6.0)		(3.6)
Observations	48	48	48	48
R^2	0.55	0.82	0.14	0.33
Jarque-Bera[f]	15.4	1.5	0.9	1.9

a. White corrected t-statistics are in parenthesis.

b. In the World Economic Forum's Executive Opinion Survey 2007, businesspeople were asked: "In your country, has the government put in place effective measures to successfully combat corruption and bribery?" The data range between 2.0 (for Argentina) and 5.9 (for Canada).

c. Data from Global Integrity 2007. The data range between 51 (for Lebanon) and 96 (for Romania).

d. Data from Global Integrity 2007. The data range between 30 (for Algeria) and 81 (for the U.S.).

e. Source of data: World Development Indicators. The data relate to 2005. It is purchasing power adjusted in current international $1,000.

f. The Jarque-Bera measures whether the residuals are normally distributed by considering its skewness and kurtosis. The assumption of a normal distribution can be clearly rejected for levels above six.

affect perceived levels of corruption in a cross-country investigation. The data on practical implementation positively correlate with Transparency International's (TI) Corruption Perceptions Index. This correlation is revealed by a coefficient of 0.098, which drops to 0.032 when controlling for GDP per capita, but it remains significant. A similar result is not found for data on the legal framework. A coefficient of −0.042 reveals that countries with a better legal framework perform worse in the Corruption Perceptions Index.

In the 2007 Global Competitiveness Survey of the World Economic Forum (WEF), businesspeople were asked about the effectiveness of anti-corruption measures. Again Global Integrity's data on practical implementation positively correlate with this WEF assessment. This correlation is revealed by a coefficient of 0.030 (this impact does not survive the inclusion of GDP per capita as a control variable). As revealed by a coefficient of –0.033, a good legal framework even decreases businesspeople's rating of successful anti-corruption. Rules-based approaches to anti-corruption are important, but such approaches neither improve a country's rating in the TI Corruption Perceptions Index nor do businesspeople perceive them to be effective. Such findings certainly do not prove that rules-based approaches are futile, but that these approaches are sometimes badly communicated to the business community or deemed insufficient by businesspeople. Certainly, these findings may also imply that more time is needed for rules-based reform to see an impact on perceived levels of corruption.[4]

The second dimension of rules-based anti-corruption relates to limits on discretion. Corruption takes place where office holders and corporate employees have leeway in carrying out their tasks. Suggestions to limit discretion relate to rotation of staff, separation of functions, standardization of rules and procedures, internal and external audits, as well as the four-eyes principle, where a second employee must verify and sign off on the decisions of his colleague.

But limits on discretion have their costs. Quite often, bureaucratic rules aimed at reducing discretion tend to produce frictional costs and run counter to the goals of a public administration. Kelman argues that anti-corruption rules imposed by legislators aim at limiting the discretion of procurement officers but instead produce unwanted outcomes.[5] Such rules aim at improving competition but divert officers from the actual goals of acquiring best-value products and services for the government. For example, procurement officers observe the performance of contractors over time. They gather experience with respect to the quality procured by contractors. But procurement guidelines often discourage the use of this experience. Such guidelines result because of fears that performance evaluations are biased or driven by bribes. This top-down distrust toward procurement officers produces unwanted outcomes because contractors might not be sufficiently sanctioned for low-quality deliveries.

Another problem arises when contracts should be awarded to the lowest-cost bidder. Procurement officers' tasks are limited to checking whether official specifications are fulfilled. A procurement official may detect that specifications were incomplete or fulfilled only at face value. Contractors, thus, look out for incomplete specifications and similar loopholes as a method for making extra profits. In an attempt to avoid this, the principal tends to add more detailed specifications. This increasing burden of specifications acts as a deterrent to bidders and suffocates competition. Anechiarico and Jacobs report evidence for such effects in New York City.[6] Rose-Ackermann criticizes Kelman's proposal for reform, fearing that risks for corruption and collusion are downplayed.[7] The dismal experience with some procurement guidelines, she argues, should serve to adjust the guidelines, but not to end anti-corruption. Alternative approaches to anti-corruption should be investigated to determine if they prove more successful. For example, a less rules-based and less top-down approach to anti-corruption may meet Kelman's approval.

Principles-Based Anti-Corruption

Some authors have argued that instead of focusing on rules, the fight against corruption should relate more to principles. This approach recognizes the many non-monetary and intrinsic motivations of officials and employees and honors their role for advancing common goals. Once these motivations are understood, it might be possible to influence behavior with prevention, controlling incentives, and fostering values within an organization.

There is a large body of economic literature that reveals how corruption may result from adverse incentives.[8] Price or quantity restrictions may produce artificial shortages, where bribery serves as a market clearing device. Import quotas, for example, produce an excess supply of export goods, and limited import licenses may be handed out in exchange for bribes.

There is consensus that anti-corruption efforts should identify such dismal distortions and tend to avoid them, where possible. But apart from such prescriptions, it appears difficult to use incentives to induce integrity. Paying someone a bonus for his or her honesty is impossible to implement. Incentives can only be given for a measurable economic surplus. But there is no yardstick that can measure honesty and the remuneration that it deserves. Second, incentive schemes imply a variation in employees' incomes, lowering the security equivalent of their pay and crowding out the risk-averse (and potentially less corrupt) from obtaining official positions. Incentive theory, at best, helps to detect the variety of organizational inconsistencies and disincentives. But incentives will hardly ever be sufficient to outbid the briber, as is sometimes suggested by formal principal-agent modeling. Realistically, incentive schemes may highlight and acknowledge individual integrity but they will fall short of producing high-powered rewards.

Rather than focus on narrow payoffs, one approach to provide the right incentives is to focus on group behavior. For example, Paine as well as Kapstein and Wempe argue that integrity comprises more than following rules.[9]

Integrity should aim at establishing a value system that provides guidance even where rules are lacking. These scholars propose training methods, aimed at coding desired behavior. These trainings can help to communicate more clearly the conflicts of interest that are unique to specific sectors and countries. Furthermore, ethical training can help to develop an atmosphere of transparency and stewardship among a firm's and a bureaucracy's employees.

Rules and principles are both needed in anti-corruption efforts. Good principles need the rules to become embedded and to serve as benchmarks for behavior. In turn, rules without principles may backfire. For example, bribing a public official is illegal, but the U.S. Foreign Corrupt Practices Act (FCPA) allows favors to be given to well-connected private businesspeople, so-called gift-partnerships, or to engage (bribe-paying) intervening purchasers in public procurement.[10] As long as businesspeople are (or claim to be) unaware of what local agents do with their consultancy fees and commissions their actions may be excused. Ironically, the clearer the rules on malfeasance are, the clearer businesspeople are on how to circumvent them. Such an adverse effect may be avoided if the underlying principles are communicated.

Ethical Investment Research Services (EIRIS) investigated the performance of almost 2,000 companies, rating whether a company had a code of conduct; whether that code prohibited bribery, gifts, facilitation payments, and political donations; whether whistle-blowing systems, ethical training, and compliance structures existed; and how well companies communicated these issues to their employees.[11] Small- and medium-sized companies scored considerably lower compared to large companies.[12] While company-specific details were not reported, this author dares to claim that multi-national firms known for their corrupt record obtained favorable scores. Laufer makes a related point with respect to Enron, a firm that was highly esteemed for its ethics management prior to its collapse.[13]

Measurements such as those performed by EIRIS relate to simple rules. Measuring a value system cannot be done in a checkbox manner. Where values are absent, companies may camouflage this deficiency with a compliance system, but one that functions superficially. Such compliance systems can be purchased from consultants and serve to eliminate responsibility if business goes awry.[14] Compliance systems help companies to conduct business free of regulatory scrutiny and corporate liability.[15]

Such compliance systems risk being substitutes for, rather than complements to, values. They camouflage problems and do not invoke change. They provide guidance on how to abide by formal rules in anti-corruption, but leave incentives unchanged. For example, although Britain has signed the OECD Convention on Combating Bribery of Foreign Public Officials, contrary to the convention's principles it stopped the Serious Fraud Office's investigation into bribes paid to Saudi Arabian officials.[16]

This shortcoming is not only a problem for anti-corruption rules. Also preventive measures sometimes do not aim at advancing a value system but camouflage an organization's true interests. Private firms, for instance, might be in a "prisoner's dilemma," paying lip service to anti-corruption, but at the same time profiting from a corrupt contract. Ethical training is given to those expected to stay clean, while the dirty work is outsourced. In the end, ethical training may simply provide firms with official excuses when their employees are caught, resulting, for instance, in exemption from corporate liability. The ethical training of bureaucrats likely faces similar limitations.

High penalties and stiff rules (for example on the taking of gifts and expenses for dining) provoke employees to seek loopholes rather than follow these new rules. Engagement with intermediaries or in joint-venture agreements allow employees to abide by the new rules while the payment of bribes continues. Although outsiders do the dirty work, those who are the target of stiffer rules can claim ignorance about bribe payments. For example, in a 2006 survey of businesspeople, Control Risks Group reported that 32 percent of U.S. companies believe that their competitors regularly circumvented anti-corruption legislation by engaging intermediaries—a higher percentage than in all other countries included in the survey (Germany, Britain, Netherlands, France, Brazil).[17] The likely reason rests with the stiffer corporate anti-corruption legislation in the United States.

This effect does not only relate to individuals but also to group behavior and collective reputation. Groups establish networks of cooperation, which give rise to more intricate ways to react to rules. Groups may react either by subordination or by collective resistance. Higher penalties, increased monitoring, or stiffer limits on discretion require acceptance by and support from these networks. Such support is desperately needed as hints by insiders close to an illegal deal are crucial for investigations. These hints require a corporate culture of anti-corruption; an atmosphere where individuals are supported by their colleagues when they cooperate with investigators.[18]

In 2007, PricewaterhouseCoopers published the Global Economic Crime Survey. This survey is based on telephone interviews with 5,428 CEOs, CFOs, and other leading managers.[19] Respondents were asked about their initial means of detecting fraud. Quite striking is the importance of internal and

Table 15-2. *Initial Hints on Detection of Fraud, Percent of Cases*

| Country | Corporate Culture | | | Corporate Control |
	Whistle-blowing system	Internal tip-off	External tip-off	Internal Audit
Russia	5	8	8	20
United Kingdom	3	14	9	19
United States		20	13	21
Denmark	7	26	7	19
Singapore	8	21	14	19
Czech Republic	16	18	7	18
South Africa	16	22	11	20
Norway	9	18	12	15
Thailand		15	19	12
Turkey	5	21	21	16
France	8	36	7	14
Germany		38	26	14
Slovenia	30	15	11	11
Switzerland	4	26	30	9

Source: PricewaterhouseCoopers (2007) and author's composition of data from country supplements.

external tip-offs.[20] These findings reveal the significance of a corporate culture; a bottom-up approach to contain corruption.

In the United States (alongside the UK and Russia) initial detection seldom comes from tip-offs (see Table 15-2).[21] A more participatory system, where employees openly contribute to anti-corruption with tip-offs, seems to operate (at least when looking at relative numbers) in Switzerland, Germany, and France. Palazzo argues that business ethics are more rules-based in the United States, while they are more "community oriented" and more relational in Europe.[22] Within such a model, managers are more trusting of their workers and informal mechanisms for social control are given higher emphasis. Such relationships contribute to a greater willingness to complain openly about the malfeasance of superiors and thus contribute to more tip-offs in Continental European businesses. In the United States the most important method for detection is internal audit, which has contributed to 21 percent of all detections. This percentage is the highest figure for all countries surveyed, suggesting a top-down, rules-based approach to corporate anti-corruption in the United States.

Limiting the Leaders

Rules and prevention require an honest leadership that successfully contains corruption among employees and bureaucrats. But fostering integrity among the leadership is difficult. Governments (as well as company boards) must limit self-seeking among their own ranks. Strong competition for leadership positions, be it general elections for public offices or tournaments for economic leadership positions, is commonly seen to be insufficient to prevent malfeasance. Rather, press freedom and a high level of transparency contribute to holding senior officers accountable.[23] This system provides a clear motivation for bottom-up approaches to anti-corruption.

Non-governmental organizations (NGOs) and citizen watchdogs have started to request more information on government operations, claiming their right to access such information. These organizations put social pressure on perpetrators, complain about malfeasance of administrators and politicians, voice their concern with respect to political priorities, and blow the whistle on criminals. Grassroots initiatives by civil society are a core contribution to anti-corruption. For many multilateral institutions this shift toward civil society has dramatically changed their daily operating procedures.[24] Building coalitions that surpass the classical boundaries of government has become essential in the fight against corruption.

The importance of bottom-up approaches is also documented at the cross-country level. Press freedom is clearly a bottom-up approach to improve accountability in the public sector and ultimately to reduce corruption. While causality is trickier to ascertain, there is substantial evidence that countries with high levels of press freedom have lower levels of perceived corruption.[25] These correlations are robust even when controlled for standard influential variables, for example income per head.

However, bottom-up approaches are not controlled as well by superiors as are top-down approaches. At times, bottom-up approaches may conflict with anti-corruption strategies that are chosen by business and political leaders. Revelations of misconduct may come at an abysmal time. Such strategies may not complement the other overall goals of an organization; these strategies may even endanger the leadership itself. But the purpose of bottom-up approaches is precisely that such approaches credibly commit a whole organization to anti-corruption efforts. Attempts fully to control anti-corruption are similar to an autocratic regime that attempts to improve its international reputation by controlling the state's media, an approach that is not widely approved.

Still, there are various problems and unanswered questions about bottom-up initiatives. Representatives from civil society are sometimes attributed the legitimacy to speak for the interests of a population at large, which is a disputable development.[26] Some scholars feel that there are few altruistic actors who may deserve such legitimacy outside elected government positions. Civil society approaches to anti-corruption are also open to abuse. The most extreme cases relate to NGOs in control of politicians who want to divert international aid into their own pockets. Thus, there are some unresolved issues relating to the proper role of NGOs and civil society in politics. However, that bottom-up anti-corruption initiatives need a critical mass of supporters in society is not disputed. Successful bottom-up initiatives must therefore embrace more than a few altruistic actors in civil society. But is it possible to recruit such actors?

Bottom-Up Anti-Corruption

There are many reasons to abstain from corruption apart from the extrinsic motivations that are commonly considered. Containing corruption is not related only to explicit top-down measures. Threats of punishment from superiors and courts may not be the most important. "Homo homini lupus" (man is a wolf to man) was Thomas Hobbes's argument for a strong state. In a top-down fashion this strong state would overcome the downside effects of individual maximizing, including corruption. Contrary to Hobbes's approach, a bottom-up philosophy asks why individuals may intrinsically avoid corruption. Morality may have only a limited role. But corrupt actors are influenced by factors such as the expected opportunism of their counterparts.[27] A briber is commonly promised future favors, but often the briber ends up paying twice or never receiving what he was promised. This unreliability of corrupt counterparts may induce honesty among potential bribers and good governance within organizations even where ethics are scarce. This effect is labeled as the "invisible foot." The unreliability of corrupt counterparts induces honesty and good governance even in the absence of good intentions.[28]

There are related reasons why individuals prefer to commit to anti-corruption. Those who are willing to take bribes are of limited value to their superiors and clients.[29] Governments have no interest in auditors who cannot abstain from falsifying their reports. Companies equally seek to guard their financial interests and would not employ auditors who are willing to take bribes rather than report corporate fraud. Investors avoid countries where governments cannot commit to protecting firms and their property rights. Such governments suffer as a consequence from limited foreign direct investments. Further, governments will not hire tax inspectors if they give in to temptations for extra income.

These effects, maybe much more than moral considerations, are responsible for the anti-corruption grassroots initiatives. Various business networks have been established with the goal of (peer-) monitoring: members helping each other commit to anti-corruption actions. Even for intermediaries, who are sometimes the facilitators of corrupt deals, a network has been established that aims at signaling honest dealings by its members.[30] In a similar spirit, Transparency International has implemented the idea of Integrity Pacts, where the procuring governmental department and all bidders agree on a monitoring system and tailor-made penalties to avoid bribery in public procurement. Such strategies must be encouraged to broaden the base for anti-corruption at the grassroots level as bottom-up methods can embrace even those who are tempted to pay and accept bribes.

Conflicts between Top-Down and Bottom-Up

Conflicts between top-down and bottom-up are standard in managerial science. These conflicts have also been well recognized in business ethics.[31] But this topic has been only slightly explored for anti-corruption. Evidence from experimental investigations for labor markets reveals that a good deal of employee behavior is based on intrinsic motivation, fairness, and reciprocity.[32] Employers may thus offer wage premiums so as to provide incentives for good performance even if this performance cannot be observed. In addition, employers may disregard applicants who are willing to work for low wages. Most interesting, employers may blindly trust that their employees are performing well. This type of trust often causes increased efforts among employees. To the contrary, increased monitoring often creates a certain level of distrust that weakens the intrinsic motivation of employees and limits their willingness to act with integrity.[33]

Experimental evidence also reveals that intrinsic motivation may limit corruption. Frank and Schulze, in their investigation of individual tendencies to engage in corruption in procurement, find that a significant number of participants did not maximize payoffs, apparently as a result of intrinsic motivations to abstain from corruption. In a later study, these scholars extended their analysis and observed that threats of penalties dilute this intrinsic motivation.[34] That is, some intrinsically motivated participants that may have abstained from taking bribes were induced by the threat of penalties to follow a maximizing strategy and take bribes.

There are other negative effects of top-down approaches. If penalties for taking bribes are imposed without mercy, bureaucrats are prevented from acting opportunistically.[35] For example, in a Bochum, Germany, court case, an employee of the road construction authority confessed to accepting bribes for contracts to mark roads. Beginning in 1987, lacking business experience, he had passed on names of competing firms in a public tender. After this incident, he received an envelope filled with DM 2,000 from the private firm who obtained the favor. In court, the employee recounted: "Suddenly I knew that I had begun to be at his [the briber's] mercy." This statement reveals how an initial small payment made the employee dependent on the briber and forced him to comply with the briber's demands afterward.[36] Quite often, a first-time small gift, taken by mistake, marks the starting point of a corrupt career. The official is confronted with the threat of a potentially large penalty for such a mistake. This threat makes him or her dependent on the complicity of the corrupt counterpart, rather than serving as a watershed against malfeasance.

We are short of a theory that reveals how to best balance top-down and bottom-up approaches. But a top-down approach can avoid some of the aforementioned repercussions by better integrating the bottom-up endeavors.

Leniency

Some anti-corruption activists employ the term "zero tolerance" to signal an uncompromising attitude toward corrupt actors. This term is morally loaded, and the attitude associated with it can backfire badly, as leniency can be an effective means to encouraging bottom-up approaches.

First, while leniency may partially reduce the deterrent effect of penalties, it is commonly assumed to lower enforcement costs and reduce future harm.[37] Second, sometimes insiders are trapped by minor malfeasance and unable to report to prosecuting authorities who have committed to zero tolerance.[38] Nell investigates the criminal codes of fifty-six countries and detects that twenty-six countries have leniency provisions for "active bribery," that is the *payment* of bribes, but only three have provisions for "passive bribery," the *taking* of bribes.[39] This situation is unfortunate as public servants need a method to turn themselves in to prosecutors with the assurance of limited personal repercussions. Public servants should thus be given incentives to blow the whistle after having obtained a bribe.

Qualifications for leniency are divergent and some approaches have been criticized. Firms are often sanctioned as a corporation if they fail to eliminate employee malfeasance. Quite often, firms are not punished if they behave properly as an organization and corruption is found to be related only to the individual misconduct of their staff. As a result, leniency is often exercised if proof is provided that compliance systems exist. Laufer argues that this type of leniency reduces the repressive pressure of the legal code, and even more worrisome, it induces firms to invest in potentially useless compliance systems rather than in eliminating actual misconduct.[40]

A related problem with leniency arises when an organization, after being suspected of malfeasance, accepts an outside monitor to impose internal reforms. This approach is currently taken by the World Bank within its voluntary disclosure program and has gained prominence in the U.S. Justice Department.[41] Such an approach is alleged to lower the deterrent effect of corporate liability, while producing verifiable compliance systems with uncertain outcomes. Proving compliance then produces an unusual game: firms have incentives to produce evidence of compliance but do not have incentives to install effective compliance systems that enhance ethical behavior.[42] This method may explain the finding by Ernst and Young who report that U.S. senior executives consider allegations of bribery or corrupt business practices to be predominantly unpleasant because they increase compliance costs.[43]

This problem arises in particular because those who engage in the compliance service industry and the associated regulatory bodies tend to overestimate the capacity of their top-down methods to actually reduce corruption. If the results displayed in Table 15-1 are also valid for corporate anti-corruption, which is not an unreasonable assumption, the capacity of top-down rules to reduce corruption is lower than commonly estimated. Leniency would in this case be linked to the wrong action. Thus, leniency should not be given to firms merely based on the idea that these organizations have good compliance systems. Such leniency is misleading as the effectiveness of compliance systems is difficult to evaluate by outsiders. Such systems can be afforded only by large companies, and they lead firms to employ ineffective anti-corruption efforts. Other forms of leniency provisions are superior in reducing corruption.

Lambsdorff and Nell modeled optimal penalties in bribery transactions and investigated the effect of leniency as an instrument for containing corruption.[44] They found that leniency in exchange for self-reporting can lower the incentives to become engaged in corruption if all of the following conditions are met: 1) self-reporting must actually increase external investigators' knowledge; 2) self-reporting must help in prosecuting others; and 3) leniency should only be given to successful corrupt actors. These conditions ensure that corrupt partners have an incentive to report each other.

While leniency in exchange for self-reporting is widely employed, the three conditions mentioned above are hardly ever matched. The third condition in particular requires some explanation. In the case of self-reporting, leniency should not be given to businesspeople who were cheated by public servants. Leniency in such a case would provide businesspeople with a credible threat to blow the whistle, which then forces the public servant to deliver on his or her promises. This threat buttresses the corrupt agreement and bottom-up anti-corruption endeavors are countered.[45] Leniency should be granted only to those businesspeople who did obtain the requested corrupt service. Like- wise, public servants who were cheated and not given a bribe should not qual- ify for leniency. In summary, one should give leniency in exchange for self- reporting, but not to those who have participated in incomplete bribe transactions.

An additional concern is whether a regulatory or prosecutorial body should have the discretion to grant leniency. Overall, discretion should be limited as judges' and prosecutors' commitments may not be credible. It is not uncom- mon that those cooperating with the authorities often receive a higher pun- ishment than negotiated with the prosecutors, so that leniency remains inef- fective and a promise of such is seen as empty. The above-mentioned recommendations may not be in line with prosecutors' ideas of fairness and deterrence. For example, if an entrepreneur self-reported after having obtained a contract, he can still be made rich by the deal and only mildly punished. While a commitment to such a penalty design is desirable for reduc- ing corruption, prosecutors and judges, who are endowed with sufficient dis- cretion, may dislike enforcing such an apparently unfair outcome. Prosecutors and judges are also susceptible to misusing their discretionary power. In the worst case, they would grant leniency in exchange for favors, increasing cor- ruption in the judicial system rather than helping to deter corruption. Thus, clear rules on leniency provision are superior to discretionary applications. Some discretion along the lines of the above-mentioned conditions, still, is unavoidable. Prosecutorial authorities must impartially determine how far self-reports have advanced prosecutors' knowledge beyond existing investi- gations, to what extent self-reports can be helpful in prosecuting others, and whether corrupt transactions were completed.

Interestingly, certain legal provisions are likely to stabilize corrupt transac- tions rather than to discourage them. Former Article 215 (2) of the Turkish

Penal Code stipulated that leniency should be granted only if the public official had not yet reciprocated on the bribe, contrary to the recommendations above.[46] Remarkably, according to this article, the bribe-giver, if self-reported, could reclaim the bribe. A culture of anti-corruption that tries to increase the risks of bribery is seriously undermined by such legislation.

Debarment

That companies, not individuals, should be punished for malfeasance so as to provide incentives for improving corporate culture is a broadly accepted concept. Where such penalties are lacking, firms may pay lip service to anti-corruption but unofficially inform their employees that getting contracts is all that counts. But *how* companies should be punished remains uncertain. Debarment and suspension of companies is an often recommended penalty and is applied in public as well as private procurement. After this system was implemented by the U.S. Department of Defense in 1983 many other countries and private companies followed this precedent.

There are many problems with this system, though. If a criminal conviction by court is required, such as in South Africa and in the EU, debarment is often imposed only after years of legal dispute. The debarment then may impact a completely altered company, now operating under a different leadership and shareholder structure. The burden of proof to convict is also high, suggesting that many cases would be decided in favor of the briber where reasonable doubts remain. The conviction process can be sped up by delegating the authority to debar to procurement officers, which is the standard in the United States. But such an allocation of authority risks losing a clear legal basis for debarment, potentially implementing the punishment without definitive evidence.

A second issue is whether procurement agencies should have the discretion to decide if bids from debarred firms should or should not be considered. If the agencies are granted such discretion, important considerations for their decisions could be recognized, such as whether a supplier is indispensable or whether the supplier has contributed to uncovering a corruption case and proactively contributed to the investigation. But a discriminatory application of debarment can easily undermine its legitimacy. For example, Karpoff and colleagues carried out a statistical analysis of the stock market valuation of U.S. defense procurement contractors who were suspended between 1983 and 1995.[47] Following the announcement of these suspensions, the stock market valuation of the respective companies dropped on average by 4.5 percent.

This effect was less pronounced for the government's most important contractors. Those ranked as important (from a list of 100 most important in all sectors) experienced only a 1.4 percent drop, whereas the remaining less important companies suffered a 14.1 percent decrease in their stock market valuation. This finding is likely related to the higher influence exerted by the former companies. The authors concluded that influential contractors benefit from these suspensions as they pay small fines but profit from the reduced competition that results from the debarment system. The authors found, further, that influential contractors did not experience a decrease in overall government contracts following a suspension. They report anecdotal evidence that contracts were postponed until the end of the contractors' suspensions, that these contractors obtained contracts as subcontractors, or that they profited from bureaucratic discretion such that contracts were awarded in spite of their being debarred.

Further, the penalty that results from debarment often does not correlate well with the magnitude of the criminal act. A small grease payment may ruin a firm that depends on government contracts, while a substantial kickback remains without consequence for a firm that does not intend to compete for future government contracts. Overall, the impact of debarment on a corporate anti-corruption culture remains uncertain. The impact may in fact become negative as bottom-up efforts are discouraged and companies that proactively report the malfeasance of their staff are still threatened with debarment. This predicament may prevent companies from reporting relevant cases to prosecutors and procurement agencies. Companies will instead threaten internal whistleblowers and try to suppress the relevant evidence. Firms should thus be given incentives to cooperate with prosecutors after their employees have finalized a corrupt deal. Such incentives are difficult to implement in systems of debarment.

Nullification

Courts commonly do not enforce agreements made by means of corrupt transactions. Instead, courts follow the principle that those who operate outside the law cannot claim the law's protection. Corrupt contracts are, thus, null and void. The nullity of the corrupt contract often entails a further legal consequence: bribes cannot be reclaimed, irrespective of whether or not the promised corrupt favor was delivered. Such a consequence presents a severe risk to bribe payers, evidenced in many cases of failed corrupt transactions.[48]

This legal judgment by the courts is important for anti-corruption as it helps to increase the risks for corrupt actors and, thus, serves to reduce corruption. To what extent courts worldwide adhere to this principle and to what extent civil laws are in line with it should be further investigated.

Some anti-corruption activists go further in their requests for nullification. Consider a contract for government construction that is induced by a bribe to a procurement official. Pope argues that governments should have the right to declare the construction contract void. Nullity would not only result for the corrupt side-agreement, but for the main contract.[49] Similar provisions are now found in various government procurement guidelines and those of private firms.

Such a practice has a dismal effect on bottom-up anti-corruption. For example, construction firms that find that their employees paid bribes are unwilling to cooperate with prosecutors and the government, fearing the nullity of their profitable contracts. Whistleblowers in these companies risk their jobs and stay silent instead. Furthermore, only companies that were successful in bribing are sanctioned by this type of penalty. Those that paid bribes but failed to get the contract can threaten self-reporting because they are not hurt by the nullity of a contract that they do not possess. Nullity, thus, stabilizes corrupt transactions rather than inducing corrupt partners to cheat each other.

Finally, if the government is uncertain about the profitability of a contract it may delegate negotiations to its most corrupt bureaucrats. If these corrupt bureaucrats take bribes, rules on nullity provide the government with the option to cancel the contract at a later stage. By threatening cancellation the government can also blackmail these companies and request better conditions. As with debarment, only the influential firms can withstand this type of extortion. As a result of this process, the government loses the incentives that prevent its bureaucracy from bribe-taking.[50]

The German company Siemens was investigated by prosecutors, the media, and internal and external investigators because of slush funds that were being amassed to bribe officials. Reacting to public pressure in 2006, a new leadership at Siemens introduced immense efforts to comply with anti-corruption standards. This openness in dealing with the problem, however, backfired. Many contracts that were obtained in the past by way of bribery were nullified and had to be renegotiated, often with less favorable conditions. Other German companies did not follow the good example set by Siemens, fearing also that their contracts would be nullified. Ultimately, these other firms are likely to fail in rebuilding their corporate culture.

Contract Penalties

In addition to debarment and nullification some procurement guidelines entail provisions for contract penalties. These penalties are implemented in the form of payments made by the contractor if bribery is detected. Such penalties have various advantages.[51] First, these penalties merely shift resources from one party to another and do not entail further social costs. Contrary to this method, debarment produces disadvantages to the public by limiting competition, while the nullification of contracts imposes costs for repeated negotiation and delays. Second, in a system with monetary penalties, civil courts (or arbitrators) provide conflict resolution, where there is a less stringent burden of proof. The risk of a wrong judgment is thus more fairly shared among the contracting parties. On the contrary, criminal courts may fail in deterring acts where reasonable doubts of misconduct remain. Third, once imposed, monetary penalties can later be revoked, without substantially disadvantaging the contractor. Debarment and nullification, on the other hand, produce social costs that cannot be recovered if a court's decision is reversed at a later stage. Penalties can be imposed quickly; a reversal of this initial decision comes at a mild cost. Contract penalties are thus an attractive option for public, as well as private, contracting.

The size of the penalty is sometimes linked to the contract value. For example, the procurement guidelines of Deutsche Bahn AG (German Railways) invoke penalties of 2 percent, 5 percent, or 7 percent of the gross contract value, depending on the seniority of the briber in the contracting firm.[52] This approach, however, is not the best. On the one hand, the gross contract value is a poor basis for determining the size of the penalty. The temptation to pay a bribe is proportional to the net profit that can be achieved with a successful bribe. In some sectors, such as retail and banking, gross revenues are large and deterrence is therefore sizable. In services such as consultancy contracts, the opposite is true, where few costs are subtracted from gross revenues, producing large incentives to pay bribes. On the other hand, bribes differ with respect to their severity. A small gift to a secretary should not entail the same legal consequences as a large kickback to a senior official or manager. Thus, a better base for penalties would be the size of the bribe (or favor).[53] Given that bribes often tend to be small, to achieve sufficient deterrence fifty times the size of a bribe may be a sufficient contract penalty.[54]

Another issue is who should be the recipient of the monetary penalty. If the penalties accrue to the procurement authority (and the principal behind it) there is an adverse incentive: the procurement authority profits from its own organizational failure. A possible adverse repercussion is that the principal will allow its employees to take bribes so as to request the monetary penalty thereafter. A better solution is to assign the penalty to a charity, perhaps after costs for the criminal investigation are subtracted. Another solution is to assign rights to restitution to the unsuccessful bidders, which can be claimed from the collected monetary penalty. Rewards to whistleblowers may also be paid from these funds.

A third question is how anti-corruption efforts should deal with companies that proactively report the bribery of their own staff. Leniency should be guaranteed in this case, perhaps reducing the penalty to ten times the bribe. This design reveals a clear advantage of contract penalties over different penalty schemes. The reduction in the penalty can be transparent and announced upfront, assigning more apparent legal rights to a firm that comes forward with evidence. On the contrary, debarment systems may also attempt to treat cooperating firms more leniently but risk a less transparent decision, favoring the influential firms.

Despite these advantages, in practice contract penalties are only seldom applied. The reasons for this failure are unclear. Such penalties may not provide advantages to influential firms, suggesting that there are political-economic reasons for these firms' disregard for such penalties. Transparency International considers contract penalties in its integrity pacts; clearly such penalties deserve more application and research.

Whistle-Blowing

Whistle-blowing systems, such as hotlines, are a first step toward bottom-up anti-corruption. But effective whistle-blowing systems must go beyond telephone hotlines where anonymous hints can be submitted. More elaborated Internet-based systems have been developed that allow prosecutors or compliance officers to interrogate the whistleblower, while the anonymity of the whistleblower is retained. Another approach is to have ombudsmen outside the company that serve as a contact to discuss issues of corruption with whistleblowers while being legally bound to keep the identity of their informants confidential. This more personal approach may be better suited for some whistleblowers, but it may also be difficult to implement for a multi-national company with employees scattered around the globe.

Stringent compliance rules are often helpful to whistleblowers. Such rules distinguish right and wrong and tend to encourage the reporting of malfeasance. But what should whistleblowers do if they observe that rules are being skillfully circumvented? And how should superiors react to such whistle-blowers? A whistleblower may report that his or her firm's payments to inter-mediaries were passed on to public officials, thus qualifying as bribery. Such a report puts a company in an uncomfortable position and may even induce a criminal liability of the company's board. Some companies hide behind their pro-forma compliance rules: their intermediaries have signed anti-cor-ruption codes and no hints exist that payments have been given to public officials. Thus, there appears to be no need to investigate further. In these cases, a whistleblower obtains little support for his actions. Anti-corruption environments should provide a forum for discussion rather than discourage employees from reporting by posting rigid rules. A true anti-corruption cul-ture requires increased due diligence and leaders that seek to clear their com-panies of all allegations.

Such an anti-corruption approach does not seem to be common practice. Instead, whistleblowers are often frustrated. In some countries, such as Ger-many, employees can be fired and face prosecution for reporting their com-pany, even in cases of severe malpractice. A culture of anti-corruption requires that whistleblowers be treated with leniency, even if they provide information to third parties. Those that make the allegations must be legally protected against harassment and be given the right to inform third parties in cases of severe malpractice.

To build such an environment, codes of conduct must be developed from the bottom up and constantly readjusted. In reality, codes of conduct are often written by external experts, imported from benchmark companies, and simply distributed to a firm's staff.[55] Ex-cathedra indoctrination on corporate ethics is likely to fail where real dilemmas arise. Even when employees are requested to confirm and approve these codes of conduct, the codes are not made part of the corporate or public culture. Kapstein's well known claim that "a code is nothing, coding is everything" deserves more recognition as a bot-tom-up method for developing a corporate culture of anti-corruption. Train-ing employees in the detection of red flags can also enhance a bottom-up cul-ture. Such training sharpens employees' awareness of gray areas where rules are still absent. To encourage the discussion of these gray areas further, helpdesks should be available for those seeking immediate advice. Such helpdesks (either by telephone or via Internet) allow employees to voice their questions, concerns, or fears without making them known to their peers, sub-ordinates, and superiors. Compliance offices must become responsive to the views contributed by employees. Without this bottom-up support, the rules invented by compliance offices will be futile or even counterproductive.

Policy Implications

By exploiting the concept of the invisible foot, anti-corruption efforts can be effectively organized.[56] This concept embraces two issues. First, economic actors want to commit to anti-corruption approaches as a means to preserve their reputations with their superiors and clients. This intrinsic motivation must be recognized and encouraged. Second, corrupt actors must be seduced to betray each other so as to destabilize corrupt transactions.

In this light, a comprehensive anti-corruption strategy must embrace both top-down and bottom-up elements. This chapter demonstrates that merciless penalties, debarment, and the nullification of contracts that are influenced by bribery fail. Such top-down approaches are in conflict with bottom-up endeavors to contain corruption. If only such top-down strategies are applied, companies will find themselves trapped in a vicious cycle, as malfeasance in the past implies penalties without pardon, lost contracts, and debarment from future contracts. Such a cycle entices companies to continue their illicit operations. In the public sector, likewise, public officials find themselves trapped after a minor error, as taking a gift qualifies one for harsh penalties. Public officials then are at the mercy of the bribers, who can force them into corrupt careers.

This chapter suggests methods for reconciling bottom-up endeavors with top-down rules. It suggests rules on leniency that serve to encourage bottom-up actions against corruption. If leniency is given to public servants who obtained bribes, self-reporting may be encouraged, helping them to end their corrupt career. Leniency should also be offered to bribers in exchange for self-reporting but only if the bribers were successful in obtaining the desired favor (for example a contract). Such a system helps to catch the higher-ups and renders bribe-taking a risky business. Contract penalties in public and private contracting can also work well, in particular when joined with rewards given to whistleblowers and with leniency for self-reporting.

Contrary to these recommendations, leniency is often given in exchange for documented anti-corruption efforts. This method is likely to fail as the success of anti-corruption efforts is extremely difficult to measure and often overestimated. Such provisions will favor the large and influential firms that can afford costly compliance programs.

Siemens has now imposed strict rules on gift-giving and dining, fixing the maximum allowances to levels below business standards. Similar rules are often defended on the premise that one must safeguard against the initial temptations of corruption. However, there are various problems with such a strategy. Due to such rigid rules some employees are captured in a circle of corrupt complicity after an initial minor error. Others simply dislike the moral rigor and feel less inclined to contribute to the development of a corporate culture of anti-corruption. Groups may (and already did in the case of Siemens) revolt against the excessively authoritarian tone of such rules. This measure may have done more harm than good.

Anti-corruption is a deserving crusade where ethical considerations are necessary to provide guidance to key actors. But morality is an insufficient guide. Instead, incentives must increase the risks of corrupt behavior and highlight the economic returns from acting with integrity.

Notes

1. See United Nations Office on Drugs and Crime, *The Tenth United Nations Survey on Crime Trends and the Operations of Criminal Justice Systems (Tenth CTS 2005–2006)* (2008), available at www.unodc.org/unodc/en/data-and-analysis/Tenth-CTS-access.html (accessed 16 January 2009).

2. Stefan Voigt, Lars P. Feld, and Anne van Aaken, "Power over Prosecutors Corrupts Politicians: Cross Country Evidence Using a New Indicator," *CESifo Working Paper* No. 2245 (Munich, 2008).

3. Thomas Stratmann, "Do Strict Electoral Campaign Finance Rules Limit Corruption?" *CESifo DICE Report* 1 (Munich, 2003), 24–27.

4. In this respect it must be pointed out that lagged variables in the regressions may have better captured the underlying logic. Unfortunately, these variables are unavailable.

5. Steven Kelman, *Procurement and Public Management: The Fear of Discretion and the Quality of Public Performance* (Washington, D.C., 1990); Steven Kelman, "Remaking Federal Procurement," *The John F. Kennedy School of Government Series Visions on Governance in the 21st century, Working Paper* No. 3 (Cambridge, MA, 2003).

6. Frank Anechiarico and James B. Jacobs, *The Pursuit of Absolute Integrity: How Corruption Control Makes Government Ineffective* (Chicago, 1996).

7. Susan Rose-Ackerman, *Corruption and Government: Causes, Consequences, and Reform* (Cambridge, MA, 1999), 60–63.

8. See Rose-Ackermann, *Corruption and Government*, 9–17; Johann Graf Lambsdorff, *The Institutional Economics of Corruption and Reform: Theory, Evidence and Policy* (Cambridge, 2007), 2–12, 59–61.

9. Lynn Sharp Paine, "Managing for Organizational Integrity," *Harvard Business Review*, LXXII (1994), 106–117; Muel Kapstein and Johan Wempe, "Twelve Gordian Knots When Developing an Organizational Code of Ethics," *Journal of Business Ethics*, XVII (1998), 859.

10. See Theodore H. Moran, "Combating Corrupt Payments in Foreign Investment Concessions: Closing the Loopholes, Extending the Tools" (Washington, D.C., 2008), available at www.cgdev.org/files/15197_file_CombatingCorruption.pdf (accessed 12 January 2009); Theodore H. Moran, "How Multinational Investors Evade Developed Country Laws," *Center for Global Development Working Paper* No. 79 (Washington, D.C., 2006); Lambsdorff, *The Institutional Economics of Corruption,* 145–147, 167.

11. See EIRIS, "Corporate Codes of Business Ethics: An International Survey of Bribery and Ethical Standards in Companies," *Research Briefing* (Boston, 2005), available at www.eiris.org/files/research%20publications/corporatecodesofbusinessethic-sep05.pdf (accessed 13 January 2009).

12. This is also noted by Erikson who argues that small- and medium-sized companies cannot afford the costs of compliance systems. But in such companies the tone at the top is key to the corporate value system. A clear commitment to anti-corruption by the leadership must be implemented. See Daniel P. Erikson, "Compliance by Small- and Medium-Size Enterprises (SMEs)," in François Vincke and Fritz Heimann (eds.), *Fighting Corruption: A Corporate Practices Manual* (Paris, 2003), 179–186.

13. See William S. Laufer, *Corporate Bodies and Guilty Minds: The Failure of Corporate Criminal Liability* (Chicago, 2006), 100.

14. See Jennifer Arlen, "The Potentially Perverse Effects of Corporate Criminal Liability," *Journal of Legal Studies,* XXIII (1994), 833–867.

15. See Laufer, *Corporate Bodies,* 101.

16. See Sope Williams, "The BAE/Saudi Al-Yamamah Contracts: Implications in Law and Public Procurement," *International and Comparative Law Quarterly,* LVII (2008), 200–209.

17. See Control Risks Group, "International Business Attitudes to Corruption—Survey 2006" (2006), available at www.crg.com/PDF/corruption_survey_2006_V3.pdf (accessed 16 January 2009).

18. Dixit and Easterly elaborate on this issue more generally. They argue that top-down and rules-based systems may destroy bottom-up informal systems. Bottom-up systems rely on trust and reputation, which are enhanced by repeated exchange and network activities. But those who milk their reputation and cheat their partners may continue with their business in a competing rules-based system, if it exists. With the emergence of such a competing system, the incentive to guard ones reputation is thus reduced. A similar argument can be made with respect to anti-corruption. Top-down rules can weaken networks that aim to contain corruption because individual members experience less of a need to establish a reputation of being committed to anti-corruption. See Avinash K. Dixit, *Lawlessness and Economics: Alternative Modes of Governance* (Princeton, 2004); William Easterly, "Institutions: Top Down or Bottom Up?" *American Economic Review: Papers & Proceedings,* XCVIII (2008), 95–99.

19. PricewaterhouseCoopers, "Economic Crime: People, Culture and Controls: The 4th Biennial Global Economic Crime Survey" (2007), available at www.pwc.com/

extweb/pwcpublications.nsf/docid/1E0890149345149E8525737000705AF1/$file/PwC _2007GECS.pdf (accessed 16 January 2009). Country supplements are available at www.pwc.com/extweb/insights.nsf/docid/6C0D9D7B1B02B1F18525736F00508A9F (accessed 16 January 2009).

20. Anecdotal evidence assigns higher importance to such tip-offs. Once tip-offs are provided, internal auditors sometimes detect evidence of further malfeasance by the same actor or misbehavior of other actors in the same department. Such detections are likely to be attributed solely to the auditor. Internal auditors often paint such a picture to boost their reputation within the company.

21. The Sarbanes-Oxley Act in the United States explicitly requires that corporate whistle-blowing systems be organized. One would have thus expected a higher relevance for whistle-blowing in the United States. This issue seems to be more than outbalanced by the other issues mentioned in this section.

22. See Bettina Palazzo, "Habits of the Heart in US-American and German Corporate Culture," in Walther Ch. Zimmerli, Markus Holzinger, and Klaus Richter (eds.), *Corporate Ethics and Corporate Governance* (Berlin, 2007), 55–63.

23. There are, however, also some problems with increased transparency. One concern is that transparency may support the monitoring of corrupt reciprocity. See Lambros Pechlivanos, "Self-Enforcing Corruption: Information Transmission and Organizational Response," in Johann Graf Lambsdorff, Markus Taube, and Mathias Schramm (eds.) *The New Institutional Economics of Corruption—Norms, Trust, and Reciprocity* (New York, 2004), 93–111. Imagine a procurement board that publishes the individual votes of its members. This increased transparency may backfire because it helps bribers monitor whether their payment to an individual member of the board was reciprocated. To the contrary, lack of transparency (in this case non-publication of individual votes) would make it easier for a board member to take bribes and cheat the briber. Likewise, non-transparent bureaucracies may at times prevent corruption, because bribers would have a hard time: 1) finding the right person to bribe and 2) observing whether the bribee reciprocates honestly. In a similar spirit, it is standard practice that public procurement requires some limits on transparency: bidders should not know their competitors' incoming bids. Some secrecy must prevail until all bids are jointly opened. Bid-rigging would be facilitated if transparency is introduced at the wrong stage. Transparency, therefore, needs to undergo a more fine-tuned interpretation. Instead of advocating unlimited disclosure of information, comprehensive information management systems that provide key data to stakeholders should be put in place. These systems' designs will remain important issues for the years to come.

24. For a recent example concerning the World Bank policy of combining top-down and bottom-up initiatives see http://info.worldbank.org/etools/BSPAN/ PresentationView.asp?PID=1685&EID=808 (accessed 16 January 2009).

25. See Lambsdorff, *The Institutional Economics of Corruption*, 46–47.

26. See Bjørn Møller, "Civil Society Romanticism: A Skeptical View. Reflections On Håkan Thörn's Solidarity Across Borders," *Copenhagen Peace Research Institute, COPRI Working Papers* No. 31 (Copenhagen, 2002).

27. Johann Graf Lambsdorff and Björn Frank, "Corrupt Reciprocity—an Experiment," *Discussion Paper of the Economics Faculty of Passau University* No. 51–07 (Passau, 2007).

28. See Lambsdorff, *The Institutional Economics of Corruption.*

29. Ibid., 58–108.

30. See the online presentation at www.traceinternational.org (accessed 16 January 2009).

31. See Muel Kapstein, *Ethics Management: Auditing and Developing the Ethical Content of Organizations* (Dordrecht, 1998).

32. See Colin Camerer, *Behavioral Game Theory: Experiments on Strategic Interaction* (Princeton, 2003), 95–100.

33. See Donald Lange, "A Multidimensional Conceptualization of Organizational Corruption Control," *Academy of Management Review,* XXXIII (2008), 710–729; Guido Palazzo, "Organizational Integrity—Understanding the Dimensions of Ethical and Unethical Behavior in Corporations," in Zimmerli, Holzinger, and Richter (eds.), *Corporate Ethics and Corporate Governance,* 124.

34. See Björn Frank and Günther G. Schulze, "Does Economics Make Citizens Corrupt?" *Journal of Governance,* IV (2003), 143–160; Günther G. Schulze and Björn Frank, "Deterrence versus Intrinsic Motivation: Experimental Evidence on the Determinants of Corruptibility," *Economics of Governance,* IV (2003), 143–160.

35. See Johann Graf Lambsdorff and Mathias Nell, "Fighting Corruption with Asymmetric Penalties and Leniency," *CeGe-Discussion Paper* No. 59 (2007); Lambsdorff and Frank, "Corrupt Reciprocity."

36. See Lambsdorff, *The Institutional Economics of Corruption,* 158.

37. See Steven Shavell, *Foundations of Economic Analysis of Law* (Cambridge, MA, 2004), 523–524.

38. This type of "entrapment" is emphasized by Shavell. See Shavell, *Foundations of Economic Analysis of Law.* A related argument is brought forward by advocates of "marginal deterrence." See Shavell, *Foundations of Economic Analysis of Law,* 518. The idea is to deter more harmful acts because their sanctions exceed that for less harmful acts. If penalties for accepting gifts are already large, bureaucrats are less deterred from providing the promised favor in return.

39. See Mathias Nell, "Strategic Aspects of Leniency Programs for Corruption Offences: Towards a Design of Good Practice," *Discussion Paper of the Economics Faculty of Passau University* No. 52–07 (Passau, 2007).

40. See Laufer, *Corporate Bodies,* 99–129.

41. See "Leniency for Big Corporations in the U.S.," *International Herald Tribune* (9 April 2008).

42. See Kimberly D. Krawiec, "Organizational Misconduct: Beyond the Principal-Agent Model," *Florida State University Law Review,* XXXII (2005), 571–615.

43. Ernst & Young, *Corruption or Compliance: Weighing the Costs,* 10th Global Fraud Survey (2008), available at www.ey.com/global/Content.nsf/International/ AABS_-_RAS_-_FIDS_-_10th_Global_Fraud_Survey (accessed 16 January 2009).

44. See Lambsdorff and Nell, "Fighting Corruption." The argument has some relation to the one provided in Arlen, "Potentially Perverse Effects." She notes that corporations that are facing liability may lose the incentive to monitor their employees: they fear that knowledge of misconduct may deem them liable. Arlen points out that these adverse effects can be overcome if information that is disclosed by a corporation cannot be used against it in criminal litigation. This is only a small incentive. Broader guarantees of lenient treatment in cases of self-reporting may provide for even stronger incentives.

45. See Paolo Buccirossi and Giancarlo Spagnolo, "Leniency Policies and Illegal Transactions," *Journal of Public Economics*, XC (2006), 1281–1297.

46. See Silvia Tellenbach, "Türkei," in Albin Eser, Michael Überhofen, and Barbara Huber (eds.), *Korruptionsbekämpfung durch Strafrecht* (Freiburg, 1997), 642.

47. See Jonathan Karpoff, D. Scott Lee, and Valaria P. Vendrzyk, "Defense Procurement Fraud, Penalties and Contractor Influence," *Journal of Political Economy,* CVII (1999), 809–842.

48. See Johann Graf Lambsdorff, "Making Corrupt Deals: Contracting in the Shadow of the Law," *Journal of Economic Behavior and Organization,* XLVIII (2002), 221–241.

49. See Jeremy Pope, "The Transparency International Source Book 2000—Confronting Corruption: The Elements of a National Integrity System" (Berlin, 2000), available at www.transparency.org/sourcebook/ (accessed 16 January 2009).

50. See Mathias Nell and Harald Schlüter, "Rechtswirksamkeit auf Schmiergeld beruhender Hauptverträge—Eine ökonomische Analyse," *Neue Juristische Wochenschrift (NJW),* XIII (2008), 895–896.

51. This type of penalty is widely recognized in the literature. See A. Mitchell Polinsky and Steven Shavell, "The Theory of Public Enforcement of Law," in Lawrence E. Blume and Steven N. Durlauf (eds.), *The New Palgrave Dictionary of Economics* (New York, 2008) (2nd edition).

52. The United States Sentencing Commission uses the value of a contract and the size of bribes as a basis for the size of penalties.

53. See A. Mitchell Polinsky and Steven Shavell, "law, public enforcement of," *The New Palgrave Dictionary of Economics Online* (New York, 2008), available at www. dictionaryofeconomics.com/search_results?q=law%2C+public+enforcement&button_ search=Search (accessed 24 April 2009). They emphasize the general principle that penalties should be equal to the social harm of an act divided by the probability of detection. This equation is motivated by the idea that individuals should carry out acts that violate criminal codes if the individual benefit exceeds the public harm. The public harm of corrupt acts is difficult to determine, however. What is the harm of a contract secured by help of a bribe if this contract would have gone to another bribe paying company anyhow? Also loss of reputation produces a harm that is difficult to measure. Relating penalties to the size of the bribe would be a feasible second-best alternative. Two further issues run in favor of this solution: First, the size of bribes is

better linked to the actual gravity of the criminal misconduct. Second, the probability of detection can be increased where public harm is particularly high, making sure that bribery does not become a dominant strategy in areas that are particularly detrimental to the public.

54. There are cases where the size of bribes or favors cannot be determined. A procurement officer, for example, may fail to report a conflict of interest and award a contract to a close relative. A "market value" for a bribe should be estimated in this case, using evidence on bribery in related cases.

55. See Kapstein and Wempe, "Twelve Gordian Knots," 857.

56. See Lambsdorff, *The Institutional Economics of Corruption,* 225.

PETER EIGEN

16

A Coalition to Combat Corruption: TI, EITI, and Civil Society

Globalization is bringing new actors to the fore: civil society organizations (CSOs) and the private sector take on an increasing role in shaping global governance together with the public sector. Governance traditionally has been associated with the institutions of the state. However, in a globalized economy, this concept is out of sync with reality. Political and economic problems such as corruption are increasingly affecting more than one state. Solutions can no longer be sought solely on the national level and only by state actors.

As traditional governing institutions are losing influence, a governance void arises. However, this chapter argues that CSOs are filling this gap and developing into a true "third sector," complementing state and commercial actors. A greater number of voluntary civic and social organizations are playing an important role where traditional actors are failing to cope effectively.

An active civil society is vital to address corruption and other challenges to global governance that exist in 2009. Civil society cannot replace the traditional governance institutions; state governments still have the democratic legitimacy to govern their countries. Private sector enterprises, particularly multi-national corporations also have become acknowledged actors in global governance. For many years, such entities have played an important role in shaping global markets. They have devised global strategies and created global assets and liabilities. The private sector has assumed a great responsibility in shaping and maintaining global governance. The role of these two traditional actors remains important and cannot be underestimated. However, both

The author thanks Tim Bittiger for his thoughtful editorial support in bringing various publications together for this chapter.

actors should be supported and complemented by CSOs, at the local, national, and global levels.

A powerful civil society can be the key element to regain the primacy of politics over the market, to rebuild the human capacity that is needed to shape the global economy into what in Germany is known as *Soziale Markt-wirtschaft*—a market that serves the people, rather than a society that has to obey the "invisible hands" of the market. The world's societies can only thrive if its people, through civic activity and its representative bodies, are involved in shaping globalization; in building better global governance.

The Plague of Corruption

The failures of governance manifest themselves in many ways, but corruption is likely one of the challenges with which the public and private sectors have the most difficulties, especially when each sector is working on its own. At the same time, corruption is a case that illustrates how a new triangular alliance of governments, companies, and CSOs can successfully join forces to address corruption's root causes.

Bribery and corruption are increasingly recognized as major scourges of society. The scale of the devastating effects that corruption inflicts on the world is immense. The World Bank Institute estimates that $1 trillion a year are paid in bribes around the world.[1] However, the damage goes beyond these figures: corruption leads to a perversion of economic decision-making. It distorts competitive markets, leads to the misallocation of resources, and ruins the investment climate. PricewaterhouseCoopers estimates that the Russian Federation alone loses $10 billion a year in potential foreign direct investments.

Corruption also diverts public expenditures away from social sectors, such as education and health, and it is one of the main reasons for the poverty that the world is facing in the twenty-first century. In this century, with the world's immense possibilities and opportunities dramatically to reduce poverty, it is unacceptable that more than 1 billion people still live under the absolute poverty line. In 2007 alone, 11 million children died before they reached the age of five of easily curable illnesses caused by poverty.

Corruption likewise violates human rights and exacerbates discrimination against those who are unable to claim their fair share of the world's resources. Former United Nations (UN) High Commissioner for Human Rights Mary Robinson proclaimed that corruption was a "crime against humanity."[2] Corruption and an unfair distribution of wealth are among the root causes of the conflicts that are ravaging large parts of the world, producing large-scale destruction and deaths; as of early 2009 such cases include the Democratic Republic of the Congo, the Sudan, Chad, and Somalia. Many of these conflicts are waged over natural resources. Oil, gas, and minerals provide sizable wealth for many countries in Africa and elsewhere, but revenues are seldom used for national development and poverty alleviation.[3]

Mobilizing for the Fight against Corruption

Poverty can be reduced by eliminating its root causes, and one such cause is corruption. Fighting corruption should therefore be a priority. The world community has attempted to solve the issue of corruption, but it is clear that societies need to do better than they have so far. Particularly during the past decades there were few organized efforts to fight international corruption. As World Bank director in East Africa, in the 1980s, I witnessed how the donor community was presented with large-scale projects, such as building hydropower stations, which provided no economic viability, were inadequate to ensure stable power supplies, and damaged communities and the environment. Although donors often had the good sense to say no to such "white elephants," these projects were nevertheless pushed through by an "unholy alliance" of suppliers, their lobbyists, and a few powerful national decision-makers. Tens of millions of dollars in bribes were paid into foreign bank accounts, to prime ministers, and to cabinet members in many countries in Africa, Latin America, Asia, and Eastern Europe. Meanwhile, projects to help children to go to school or to assist communities to improve agricultural productivity were neglected. At the time, I became increasingly aware and intolerant of this situation and consulted colleagues in the World Bank and beyond to develop a concept that would counter corruption. Unfortunately, I could not overcome the lack of understanding and the resistance at the higher echelons of the World Bank. Therefore, I decided to leave the institution and devote my time and energy to combating corruption.

In the early 1990s, I returned to Germany from Africa; while in Africa, I rallied colleagues from around the world jointly to take up the fight against corruption. My colleagues and I created Transparency International, a not-for-profit, non-governmental organization (NGO) that aims to fight the root causes of bribery and corruption. The task ahead of us seemed insurmountable. At the time, the belief was widespread among companies and governments that corruption abroad was normal and necessary to do business. Corrupt practices were simply the way business was done and were not considered damaging or immoral. The United States was the only country in the world that, in 1977, had introduced the Foreign Corrupt Practices Act, which imposed accounting transparency requirements on U.S. companies and prohibited bribery of foreign officials. In the early 1990s, foreign bribery was allowed by all other countries, and often even officially supported by their domestic governments. In Germany, for example, foreign bribery was not only a widely acknowledged business practice, it was even tax deductible and tolerated by governmental export insurance companies.[4]

Transparency International revealed that foreign corruption was not the doing of a few black sheep; it was systemic and the recognized way to do business by most members of the Organization for Economic Cooperation and Development (OECD) and beyond. The few companies that found foreign corruption to be immoral did not say so publicly, out of fear that they would be ridiculed by their peers. Exporting country governments and companies also argued that if they stopped foreign bribing, they would run the risk of losing contracts to competitors who were less scrupulous. Governments and companies felt caught in what in game theory is called the "prisoner's dilemma," where rational choice leads two players each to play to his or her own gain, even though each player's individual reward would be greater if they played cooperatively. It was this prisoner's dilemma, the lack of a level playing field, which perpetuated corruption abroad. Transparency International tried to address the issue by talking to German companies, pointing out the fact that bribery was "risky business," and illustrating that their reputation, vis-à-vis their customers, was at stake. However, these early attempts were in vain. Fear of losing their contracts was more powerful for companies than arguments for corporate responsibility and good business practice.

We then decided to take the debate to a higher level and involve political decision-makers and honest-brokers. Transparency International secured the former German Federal President Richard von Weizsäcker as chair of a series of meetings at the Aspen Institute in Berlin. At an initial meeting, company representatives were still hostile, arguing that their conduct was not bribery, that it was not wrong-doing, but common practice, and that corrupt counterparts in developing countries were to blame for setting insufficient standards. However, by 1996 some companies had run into problems over their corrupt practices, and a prominent firm had been blacklisted in Singapore, together with four companies from other countries, for bribery. The notion that bribing might be wrong entered the discussion. Company representatives in the second Aspen meeting acknowledged they were willing to change but that they were trapped in the prisoner's dilemma. At the third Aspen meeting, in early 1997, companies and Transparency International came forward with a joint plan that ensured that companies would not lose out if they stopped bribing.

Creating Islands of Integrity

Transparency International was aware that the only way to counter corruption effectively was to create a level playing field for honest companies. What started out as a necessity became the organization's major strategic strength: to provide a global network with the capacity to negotiate a common ground between three actors: state, business and civil society organizations.

Of course, this goal could not immediately be met on a global level, so Transparency International's initial approach was to identify situations where only a small number of companies were in competition. The aim of this approach was to bring those companies together and get them to pledge not to make corrupt payments to client governments. The next step was then to agree on a so-called "Integrity Pact"; a process aimed at preventing corruption in well-defined, competitive situations, such as public contracting, privatization, and licensing of mineral rights, circumscribed markets, where all competitors could be identified. The aim of this pact was for all competitors to promise each other that they would not bribe. The Integrity Pact introduced an agreement between a government and all bidders for a public contract. These actors would agree on rights and obligations to the effect that neither side would pay, offer, demand, or accept bribes; collude with competitors to obtain the contract; or engage in such abuses while carrying out the contract. The Integrity Pact also introduced a monitoring system by which CSOs provided independent oversight and accountability in the countries concerned. We called the outcome "Islands of Integrity."

The work of Transparency International gained momentum and found substantial support among companies, governments, and international organizations. A number of enterprises became corporate members of Transparency International, endorsing the initiative and publicly proclaiming their commitment to end bribery. Leaders within German companies sent an open letter to Chancellor Helmut Kohl, asking that the German government participate in an OECD convention to address the prohibition of foreign bribery. Germany took up the challenge. In 1997, together with thirty-four other OECD countries, it signed the OECD Convention on Combating Bribery of Foreign Public Officials.[5]

Transparency International's successes at the time clearly showed how the intervention by a third party—even one with no formal power—was instrumental in building bridges and in creating an escape route from the prisoner's dilemma. In the sixteen years since Transparency International was founded, a radical change in attitudes and anti-corruption legislation has taken place. The organization has been a trailblazer in convincing companies and governments, but also international organizations, to join the fight against corruption. There was still the need to monitor the implementation of the OECD convention. Other CSOs joined that effort. For instance, the International Chamber of Commerce (ICC) was active with Transparency International in convincing reluctant countries to sign and ratify the convention. For example, France had to be convinced not to insist on a "grandfather clause," which would guarantee an expiration period of ten years for all existing contract arrangements.

A decisive threshold was achieved in 1996, when World Bank President James Wolfensohn declared war on the "cancer of corruption," marking a policy shift for his organization.[6] Recognizing that corruption was, at its core, also an economic issue, the World Bank has made the fight against corruption one of its key concerns, both internally and in its member countries. A range of governments closed ranks with the World Bank and the International Monetary Fund (IMF) at the March 2002 UN Conference on Financing for Development in Monterrey, Mexico, stating that development goals were unreachable where corruption ruled.

In 2003, the UN Convention against Corruption (UNCAC) was adopted. One hundred and forty states have since signed the convention, out of which thirty-three had not yet ratified in mid 2008. Hence, the road to reaching global coverage is still long. As of early 2009, Germany has still not ratified the UNCAC, partially because it would mean that German members of parliament would no longer be legally exempt from sanctions against certain corrupt practices.

Transparency International was able to rally governments and companies for the combat against corruption because it strictly adhered to three principles. The first principle was not to work principally through confrontation but as far as possible through cooperation. Transparency International never investigated individual cases of corruption for exposure. Instead, it saw government agencies and companies as potential partners and tried jointly to find solutions with them. On the one hand, this cooperation was necessary in order to adequately respond to company predicaments—e.g., the prisoner's dilemma—and to identify win-win situations for all those involved. On the other, Transparency International pragmatically acknowledged that cooperation with traditional actors was critical, as CSOs had little power on their own to force governments and business to stop corrupt practices. Some CSO partners, especially in Africa, accused Transparency International of being too close to companies and governments—of not "attacking" corruption as did other advocacy organizations. However, as Transparency International's track record illustrates, negotiating inside board rooms or official conferences—such as the World Economic Forum in Davos—rather than protesting in the street had been the right approach to take in the fight against corruption.

The second principle that Transparency International followed was a holistic approach to fighting corruption. It recognized that criminal law, which was considered by most as the key tool against corruption, was a relatively blunt weapon that could often not be effectively used against corruption. Instead of focusing mainly on criminal sanctions, the organization developed a range of tools that would protect society in a sustainable way. The most urgent instruments needed were to address awareness building for which a range of tools were designed. The best-known of these tools is the Corruption Perceptions Index, which was first released in 1995 and has since been published each year. It ranks about 180 countries by their perceived levels of corruption. These levels are determined by opinion surveys. Similar indices, such as the Bribe Payers Index, which measures the propensity of companies headquartered in the main exporting countries, or the Corruption Barometer, which collects empirical data on corruption, complement the awareness building tool kit for advocacy and research.

Another prominent example that illustrates Transparency International's holistic approach is the so-called "Integrity System Source Book," which lays out as an annotated checklist the basic elements of its National Integrity System model, which is used to evaluate the strengths and weakness of anti-corruption architecture and its systems for a given society—a country, region, municipality or sector; it exists in more than twenty languages.

With its all-inclusive approach, Transparency International aimed to couple criminalization and punishment of corruption with preventive measures. This normally involves various elements such as building anti-corruption institutions, reviewing procurement systems, enacting freedom-of-information legislation, and raising awareness in society. The basic belief behind these efforts was that a multitude of institutions, laws, and guidelines were needed to protect society from corruption—like an immune system protects against disease. If one were missing, a gap in the system would appear and the other institutions would lose their effectiveness in the fight.

The third principle Transparency International adhered to was to decentralize its operations and structures, moving the principal responsibility to CSOs, called National Chapters, across the globe. Transparency International always believed that the combat against corruption could only be effective if it were led by society within a country, which ensures that such efforts are sustainable and have national buy-in and ownership. Therefore, it was necessary to empower CSOs in affected countries to act. The International Secretariat was established in Berlin to develop Transparency International's tools in a systematic way, to carry the international anti-corruption campaign, and to help to build in-country capacities. The secretariat now has more than 70 staff members, while Transparency International has grown to around 100 national chapters around the world, making Transparency International a truly global movement. Eighty national chapters are formally accredited members of the organization; together with close to thirty individual members, they elect the international board and contribute to its decision-making. Some country chapters are very large: Bangladesh and Argentina, for example, have several thousand members. Transparency International is a democratic movement, with the national chapters determining its overall policies, running anti-corruption programs in their own countries, and sharing their experience with and helping each other to jointly combat the root causes of corruption.

Making Natural Resource Wealth Work for Development

The tentacles of corruption reach into all sectors and areas of life, but the extractive industries are the sector in which the spoils are the greatest and where most damage is done. With increasing scarcity of natural resources, particularly energy resources, frequent booms in commodity prices, industrialized, as well as emerging, economies are scrambling for oil, gas, and minerals in Africa and elsewhere in the southern hemisphere. At the same time, we have witnessed a manifest increase in poverty and continued conflicts, with wars being fought over resources.

A phenomenon is emerging: the countries that should be the wealthiest because they have natural resources are often the poorest. Especially in Africa, most countries that are blessed with natural resources have become victims of the so-called "resource curse"; a paradox by which countries with an abundance of natural resources tend to have less sustainable development than countries without these natural resources. In the Democratic Republic of the Congo, 4 million people have died in a drawn-out civil war over the control of the country's natural resources. There are few exceptions in the developing world, but Botswana stands out as having harnessed its wealth from diamond development. The country is now among the most prosperous economies in Africa—however, this sadly remains the great exception. What are the reasons for this "paradox of plenty"? The economic phenomenon called "Dutch disease" is not the main culprit.[7] What really creates the resource curse is corruption.[8] In many countries, their powerful elites suddenly find tremendous wealth on their hands and they are faced with opportunities and challenges that are far beyond their imagination.

Again, it was CSOs that made the first attempt to tackle the resource curse that had left so many resource-rich countries poor. Nearly ten years ago, Transparency International, Global Witness, and other NGOs launched a coalition called Publish What You Pay (PWYP). This initiative aimed to help citizens of resource-rich developing countries hold their governments accountable for the management of revenues from the extractive industry sector. The PWYP coalition, as of early 2009 consisting of 300 NGOs worldwide, called for the mandatory disclosure of all payments made by oil, gas, and mining companies to host governments for the extraction of a nation's natural resources.

Many companies accepted the challenge posed by civil society, arguing that they were already publishing such information and were ready to assume their corporate social responsibility. However, several governments of resource-rich countries, most prominently Angola, did not agree with this disclosure of financial flows, insisting that companies were bound by confidentiality clauses in their investment agreements. One motivation for such criticism was certainly the enormous amount of money—including some personal benefits for the elites in power—that many governments had received without the knowledge of and accountability to the legislators and citizens of their countries. In some cases, governments threatened not to renew production rights if companies disclosed payments. This intimidation made it difficult for the private sector to fully engage in PWYP's initiative.

Faced with this obstacle, it became clear to Transparency International that the only way to advance revenue transparency was to put the onus also on host countries, convincing these countries to publish what they received from selling natural resources that belonged to their people to extractive industry companies. In 2003, Nigerian President Olusegun Obasanjo announced in a speech in Berlin that his government would not only allow companies operating in Nigeria to publish what they paid, but that he would also make such publication mandatory in Nigeria. More important, he committed his government to publish the revenues that it received from selling Nigeria's national resources to domestic and foreign companies.

With this bold and practical step, the Extractive Industries Transparency Initiative (EITI) was born; by then it had already received generous support from the UK's Department for International Development and the World Bank. The EITI emerged as a coalition of governments, companies, and CSOs that aims to achieve accountability and good governance in the extractive industries and to leverage revenues from natural resource sales for growth and development in resource-rich countries. The central concept of the EITI consists of collecting data on company payments to host governments and government revenues from companies in the extractive industries. Governments that implement the initiative are obliged to establish national multi-stakeholder EITI groups. These groups' members, coming from the government, foreign and domestic companies, and civil society, jointly ensure that data on financial flows are properly consolidated, matched, audited, and published. An implementing country that successfully follows the agreed-upon principles of EITI and its criteria will first pass to the status of "Candidate Country" and can—depending on the outcome of an independent "validation"—become a "Compliant Country."

In 2003, the EITI developed from a theoretical concept to an established initiative. The first EITI Global Conference took place in London in that the same year. At the second EITI Global Conference in 2005, an International Advisory Group (IAG) received its mandate to develop the EITI methodology. Under my chairmanship, this group of twenty experts from the three EITI stakeholder groups (governments, companies, and CSOs) and from northern as well as southern countries met more than ten times to deliberate about the future structure and operations of EITI. The IAG finally presented its recommendations to the third Global Conference in Oslo in 2006, which were detailed in the EITI IAG Recommendations. This document was approved by the more than 400 conference participants— including various ministers and the presidents of the World Bank and the African Development Bank (AfDB)—and has since been the key reference and guideline for implementing the EITI in countries.

The EITI has further elaborated its organizational structure to guide and support its implementation. At the 2006 conference, the twenty members of the IAG were appointed as the members of a newly formed EITI board, and they received a mandate to turn the EITI into a reality. The EITI International Secretariat was established in Oslo in 2007 and has since ensured that policies decided upon by the board are implemented and that the EITI principles are adhered to. While the idea of the EITI has been developing since its inception around 2000, the real day-to-day work has started with the establishment of its secretariat in 2007.

As of 2009, the EITI has had great success and it can be argued that the initiative is on its way to becoming a global standard for revenue transparency in the extractive industries. The EITI, as of early 2009, has twenty-three candidate countries combined in Africa, Asia, and Latin America.[9] A number of other countries, including Norway and Botswana, have committed to becoming EITI implementers. More recently, the deputy prime minister of Iraq has announced that his country will join the EITI. As of 2009, all of these countries have yet to reach the status of a compliant country, but in each, the initial validation efforts are underway.[10]

The EITI has many dedicated supporters and various institutions have endorsed this growing initiative. As early as 2002, British Prime Minister Tony Blair officially announced the idea of the EITI at the World Summit on Sustainable Development in Johannesburg. In the same year, George Soros created Revenue Watch, a civil society initiative that promotes transparent, accountable, and effective management of natural resource wealth to leverage revenues for poverty alleviation. A dozen or so supporting countries have since established a Multi-Donor Trust Fund, managed by the World Bank.[11] A range of agencies provide technical expertise to implementing countries, including the World Bank, the IMF, the AfDB, and bilateral donors. CSOs, such as Transparency International, Global Witness, Revenue Watch, and Oxfam play a key role in promoting the EITI. Hundreds more participate through the PWYP coalition. As of early 2009, thirty-seven oil, gas, and mining companies have endorsed the EITI, including major companies from industrialized and emerging countries, such as Exxon-Mobil, Anglo American, Chevron, BP, Shell, Pemex, and Petrobras, to name only a few.[12] Many mining companies are represented through the International Council for Mining and Metals (ICMM). The EITI has won the support of more than eighty global investment institutions that collectively managed more than $14 trillion in 2008.[13] In their final statement from the G8 summits in Heiligendamm and in Hokkaido, Tokyo, G8 leaders reiterated that they backed the EITI and encouraged emerging economies and their companies to support the initiative.[14] A resolution on revenue transparency in the extractive industries was, as of late 2008, adopted by the UN General Assembly.

The success of the EITI has not only rallied new implementers and supporters. It has also provided inspiration and incentives for wider approaches to revenue transparency. The World Bank and other agencies are discussing ways to ensure transparency across the entire value chain of the extractive industries, with the EITI at its center. Countries that produce timber are calling for an extension of the EITI into the forestry sector. Possibilities for including fisheries are also being discussed. In this context, it is important to underline that at its core, the EITI is about the consolidation and publication of financial revenue flows between the extractive companies and host governments. This narrow focus has been the key to EITI's success, providing a common denominator that is agreeable to a diverse group of stakeholders, from governments to industry and civil society. It is important that this consensus is maintained to allow the initiative to prosper. However, after an extractive sector company and an implementing country have taken this important first step toward more transparency, governments, companies, and CSOs often realize the need to increase transparency and accountability across more sectors.

Already within the existing scope of the EITI, there are a number of challenges that the EITI Board, the EITI Secretariat, and their partners have to tackle. Discussions are underway about the best way to ensure that financial flows are not only captured at the level of central governments, but also at the subnational level or in states with specific resource-rich regions—federal Nigeria with its oil-rich Niger Delta as a case in point. The capacity of all EITI stakeholders needs to be built so that they can play their role in tackling these imminent challenges. This capacity-building is relevant for CSOs, as well as for companies.

While the EITI initially was mainly associated with the oil and gas sector, its current methodology is broad enough to cover the mining sector. While significant strides have been made in the formal mining sector, such strides will be much harder to take in artisan mining. Yet, even there, work is underway to specify how revenues from small-scale mining can be covered by the EITI. In small-scale mining, both extraction and payments are generally informal and the sector is a particular challenge in this respect.

Important outreach efforts are undertaken to bring emerging economies into the EITI. Such efforts are underway in Brazil, China, India, Indonesia, and South Africa. Emerging economies are becoming important players in the extractive industries, as consumers, investors, and suppliers, all with regional and global influence. They have a crucial role to play in both ensuring and promoting transparency in the extractive industries.

The EITI is still a work in progress, and there are opportunities for further achievements, as well as challenges to such achievements. The success of the initiative lies in the magical triangle, bringing together what the *Economist* once titled the "curious coalition": companies, governments, and CSOs. By 2010, a number of existing EITI countries will be validated and fully compliant. New candidates will have joined the initiative. There is hope that the EITI will, by this time, have become the global standard for the extractive industry sector.

In February 2009, the fourth EITI Global Conference took place in Doha, Qatar. It brought together EITI implementers and supporters, political leaders, business executives, and civil society, who discussed how to increase transparency and bring the EITI forward to become a global standard for revenue transparency in the extractive sector.

Conclusion

Corruption has become a major plague on millions of people and is the main obstacle for development in a vast number of countries. The catastrophic results of corruption are known, but combating its root causes is a challenge in a world where globalization has weakened the power of traditional actors. Recognizing this, governments, companies, and CSOs are increasingly collaborating to combat corruption on the local, national, and global levels. Whether in cases of petty corruption in an African school or grand-style corruption in major industry projects, new partnerships are responding more swiftly and effectively to corruption.

Civil society organizations can make a tremendous contribution to filling the gaps that globalization has created in global governance. A free and vigilant civil society is essential if we are to tackle poverty and the challenges of globalization and to dispel the climate of despair and alienation that serves as a breeding ground for conflict, war, and terrorism. State governments often lack credibility and the global reach that is necessary to fill the gap. Businesses are torn between their commitment to corporate social responsibility and the need to turn a profit. Together with governments and companies, CSOs can develop a world with more equity and less violence and conflict, ensuring real progress for all of us and for future generations.

Notes

1. World Bank Institute, "Worldwide Governance Indicators: 1996–2006" (2007), available at www.govindicators.org (accessed November 2008).

2. "Thirteenth International Anti-Corruption Conference," *IACC Today* (2008), available at www.13iacc.org/files/NL_IACC_01_11_08_final.pdf (accessed April 2009).

3. For a standard book about this phenomenon, see Paul Collier, *The Bottom Billion: Why the Poorest Countries Are Failing and What Can Be Done About It* (London, 2008) (2nd edition).

4. See Ben W. Heineman, Jr., "The Role of the Multi-National Corporation in the Long War against Corruption," chapter 14 in this volume.

5. Fritz Heimann and Gillian Dell, *Progress Report 2007: Enforcement of the OECD Convention on Combating Bribery of Foreign Public Officials* (Berlin, 2007).

6. James D. Wolfensohn, "People and Development, Annual Meetings Address," Washington, D.C., 1 October 1996, available at http://go.worldbank.org/1NQRAFLP 50 (accessed November 2008).

7. The "Dutch disease" describes the economic situation in a country—first observed after large oil revenue inflows in the Netherlands—where one sector's growth simultaneously depletes the country's dependence on other, formerly viable sectors; hence, Africa's dependence on its extractive industry sector. It also denotes the difficulty of managing volatile inflows from natural resources exports.

8. See also Paul Collier, "The Natural Resource Trap," in his *The Bottom Billion: Why the Poorest Countries are Failing and What Can Be Done About It* (New York, 2007), 38–52.

9. Azerbaijan, Cameroon, Côte d'Ivoire, the Democratic Republic of the Congo, Equatorial Guinea, Gabon, Ghana, Guinea, Kazakhstan, Kyrgyzstan, Liberia, Madagascar, Mali, Mauritania, Mongolia, Niger, Nigeria, Peru, the Republic of the Congo, São Tomé and Príncipe, Timor-Leste, and Yemen.

10. In late 2008, Azerbaijan was the first EITI "candidate country" to have started the "validation" process.

11. The supporters of the MDTF, as of early 2009, are Australia, Canada, some of the European Commission's member states (Belgium, France, Germany, the Netherlands, Spain, and Britain), and Norway.

12. For the full list of EITI supporting companies, see www.eitransparency.org/companies.

13. Figure as of June 2008.

14. For the documents that were published from the G8 summit in Heiligendamm, see www.g8.de/Webs/G8/EN/G8Summit/SummitDocuments/summit-documents.html (accessed 18 December 2008); for the documents that were published from the G8 summit in Hokkaido, see www.mofa.go.jp/policy/economy/summit/2008/doc/doc 080709_01_en.html (accessed 18 December 2008).

CHARLES C. GRIFFIN

17

Reducing Corruption in the Health and Education Sectors

Health and education consume a significant fraction, usually half or more, of central government expenditures in low- and middle-income countries. Along with infrastructure, these two sectors dominate the activities of most national governments and, if public subsidies are effective and well targeted, are key investments to improve the capabilities and quality of life of the poor. Foreign assistance is concentrated in health and education, although it is typically not well coordinated either across donors or with domestic government spending, and many different channels and systems are used for disbursing the funds. A principal argument that donors use to defend why they do not put their assistance through government budgets in a coordinated fashion is inadequate fiduciary controls, inability to trace funds, and blatant corruption.

There is a significant literature on corruption in the health sector and a developing literature on corruption in the education sector. However, there is little systematic evidence of corruption in either sector. Nor has there been an effort to tease out characteristics of the two sectors that would help us to understand similarities and differences in interventions that might reduce opportunities and incentives for corruption. This chapter focuses on economic characteristics of the two sectors and operational opportunities for governments and donors to improve the design of their interventions so as to reduce vulnerability to corruption and its negative impact on poor parents' abilities to invest in their children.

In health, the typical diagnosis of corruption lists all of the possible areas where corruption might occur, but because so little is known empirically about it, it is nearly impossible to sort out what matters the most. Hence, recommendations for managing corruption tend to be reduced to enforcing laws, increasing community oversight, improving the pay and accountability of staff, making procurement more rule-bound and transparent, and so on. These are general types of guidance that probably would improve the situation in any sector, but they also tend to require major reforms across the board, while impact is uncertain and untested.[1] In education, more or less, the same recommendations are made, although because education also has a certification role, there are additional corruption issues and actions related to testing and accreditation.[2]

Where to Look: Expenditures in Health and Education

The possible sources of corruption lie in the elements of the delivery of services with public sector financing. Of course, there are also instances of corruption within the private sector, but the focus of this discussion is on the use of public funds. Table 17-1 is not exhaustive but provides examples of sources of corruption in health and education and attempts to distinguish between corruption and performance failures.

In terms of labor force issues, health and education services tend to be labor intensive, particularly at the primary level (in health, that would be clinic or physician services; in education, this refers to primary schools). In poorer countries, it is almost an understatement to say that these services are labor intensive, as labor costs tend to crowd out virtually all other public expenditures. Table 17-2 shows the high share of primary school budgets devoted to teacher salaries and allowances in eleven African countries.

The most important corruption issue for the labor force that has been quantified is a failure to show up for work. The most widely cited estimates come from background work for the *World Development Report 2004,* shown in Table 17-3. The numbers in the table are thought to be conservative estimates. Teachers, for example, were counted as absent only if they were full-time employees and were not present in the school during a period when they should have been teaching a class. For health workers, only those who were supposed to be present in that particular facility at the time of the visit, as reported by the facility manager, were counted if they were absent. Illness and other duties were the most commonly stated causes for absences, but these accounted for less than 3 percent of absences across the sample. In other words, excused absences could reduce the unweighted averages for all absences by only about three points.

The extent to which salary costs crowd out other expenditures is enormous. In 2006, in Latin America the average for salary costs in education was

Table 17-1. *Summary of Corruption Susceptibilities in Health and Education for Public Expenditures*

	Areas of Susceptibility in Health	Areas of Susceptibility in Education	Examples of Corruption	Failures in Performance
Labor Force	Government health workers	Government education workforce	Bribery to be appointed to a position; bribery to be placed in a specific facility; appointing unqualified family, friends, or others based on political payoffs; not showing up for work; shirking duties while on the job; demanding side payments from clients; stealing funds	Incompetence, inappropriate skills, behavioral problems, and mismangement
Supplies	Contracts for services; pharmaceuticals; consumables; food; maintenance	Contracts for textbook authors, textbooks, all aspects of publishing if the government prints books; school supplies; food; maintenance	Kickbacks; bribes; personal use of facilities and supplies; falsification of documents; awarding contracts in violation of the law; stealing government property	Failure to maintain vehicles, equipment, and buildings; allowing drugs or other consumables to expire
Capital Investment	Hospitals; clinics; laboratories; warehouses; vehicles; equipment	Schools; colleges; training facilities; publishing houses; warehouses; vehicles; equipment	Kickbacks; bribes; personal or business use of facilities and equipment; falsification of documents; awarding contracts in violation of the law	Shoddy workmanship; poor monitoring of construction; inadequate record keeping; failure to follow procurement or supervisory procedures

85 percent; in Western Europe and North America, it was 65 percent. For Latin America, that means approximately $100 per primary school pupil a year went into non-salary spending, compared to almost $2,000 for Western Europe and North America (adjusted for purchasing power parity or PPP). Because the data are only intermittently reported, it is difficult to estimate similar numbers for Africa or South Asia. But for countries in Table 17-2,

Table 17-2. *Personal Emolument in Primary Schools as a Percent of Recurrent Expenditure, 2002–2004*[a]

Country	%
Burundi	99.6
Ghana	98.2
Zimbabwe	97.6
Eritrea	97.2
South Africa	95.9
Zambia	95.3
Swaziland	93.6
Togo	85.6
Seychelles	84.9
Lesotho	75.6
Comoros	65.5

a. "Swaziland Public Expenditure Review: Strengthening Public Expenditure Policy and Management for Service Delivery and Poverty Reduction," *World Bank Report* No. 35318-SW (Washington, D.C., 2006).

Ghana, for example, spent about $300 per child, which means about $5.40 in non-salary inputs annually. For Burundi, non-salary inputs came to about half a dollar, and for Eritrea, about a dollar. All figures are in PPP.[3] There is a close relationship among low total spending, high salary costs in the total, and the tiny residual left for supplies.

Generally, spending per capita on health tends to be lower than for education, and the non-salary percentages a bit higher. An example from Karnataka State, India, is illustrative. In two districts, Chitradurga and Udupi, the Centre for Budget and Policy Studies went through accounting records at the district level to figure out what was being spent on health and education. Table 17-4 shows the results in terms of PPP, which approximately triples the raw dollar amounts. Education accounts for about 60 percent of district spending and health about 6 percent. The numbers are stated in terms of students and patients. The "All Other" category literally includes every other expenditure, including capital, supplies, electricity, vehicles, and equipment. It is not just books and drugs. The table illustrates not only the absolute differences in the costs of the two sectors but that the higher percentage of "All Other" in health translates into very little in absolute terms. In these two districts, about $25 is spent annually on non-salary inputs per pupil in primary and secondary school and between $1.45 and $2.13 per patient in health centers.

Table 17-3. *Absence Rates (Percent) of Primary School Teachers, 2002–2003*[a]

Country	Primary Schools	Primary Health Centers
Bangladesh	16	35
Ecuador	14	–
India	25	40
Indonesia	19	40
Peru	11	25
Uganda	27	37
Unweighted Average	19	35

a. Nazmul Chaudhury and others, "Missing in Action: Teacher and Health Worker Absence in Developing Countries," *Journal of Economic Perspectives*, XX (2006), 91–116.

There is even more detailed evidence in health from Karnataka State, where a public expenditure tracking study of thirty randomly selected primary care units in two districts found that pharmaceuticals accounted for just over 2 percent of the districts' health budgets. Each clinic has an allocation for drugs of 100,000 rupees, and about 6,000 patients a year, for a per-patient allocation of about 17 rupees annually, or about one dollar in PPP terms. Imagine what one dollar would buy in the United States in a pharmacy. The average stock-out of the thirty most demanded drugs in these districts was sixteen weeks, and this pattern remained consistent from 2004 to 2007. It is interesting that, with these numbers, only about 22 percent of the patients bought all or part of their drug supplies in the market. Physicians in the clinics reported that they rationed drugs by not giving the full course needed to patients so that most would get something, even if the amount given to any single patient was insufficient to solve his or her problem according to normal treatment guidelines.[4]

A third example, from Kenya, illustrates the supply problem from a national perspective. A 2009 analysis of the public sector pharmaceutical logistics system found that the public budget was able to finance only 21 percent of the annual demand for drugs. Of the top ten drugs used by the system, seven were out of stock for the year by the third month of the year.[5] The logistics system is often accused of rampant corruption, but as an element of health service delivery, the biggest problem for Kenyans is that budgets are insufficient to finance the pharmaceuticals and supplies that are necessary for it to function. However, there is a substitute for these expenditures in that Kenyans can pay for what they need on the private market, so the impact of either shortages or corruption in this part of the system can be mitigated by clients.

Table 17-4. *Spending in PPP Per Pupil and Per Patient in Two Districts in the State of Karnataka, India, 2005–2006*[a]

Sector	Chitradurga District	Udupi District
Population	1,517,896	1,112,243
Education	$245.57	$266.62
Salaries (90 percent)	$221.01	$239.95
All Other (10 percent)	$24.56	$26.66
Health	$7.61	$5.18
Salaries (72 percent)	$5.48	$3.73
All Other (28 percent)	$2.13	$1.45

a. Vyasulu Vinod and others, "Expenditure on Education and Health at the Local Level: A Study in Karnataka" (Bangalore, 2007).

Finally, we turn to capital spending. In available budgets or in projects, it is rarely completely separated from the other components of expenditure, as the following examples illustrate. In the poorest countries that qualify for concessional assistance from the World Bank, donors tend to provide almost all of the investment funds—buildings, equipment, vehicles—in health and education. Bilaterally supported projects typically follow donor procurement guidelines, or the procurements are done by the donor, tied to firms that are based in the donating country.

World Bank–financed projects tend to be far more exposed to local practices than are projects that are funded by other donors. The bank requires international competitive bidding, following its procedures, for large procurements and national competitive bidding, following approved procedures, for smaller ones. Typically the first several procurements in either category receive prior review by bank staff before the award can be made; thereafter, such a review is reserved for larger procurements. The bank "post-reviews" a sample of procurements on a regular basis as part of project supervision, so in theory any procurement at any time could be reviewed, which should act as a credible threat for those interested in side-stepping the rules.

Probably the most detailed forensic review of a donor portfolio that has ever been conducted was completed in 2008 in India by the World Bank. This review came in two parts. The first was a multi-year investigation of the $248 million Reproductive and Child Health Project (RCH) signed in 1997 and closed in 2004. The investigation found evidence of payments despite incomplete deliveries of orders, possible quality problems with drugs, possible collusion on supplies of absorbent materials, and reports of kickbacks and bribes being paid. It specifically found that two companies had colluded to win $50 million in pharmaceutical contracts.

However, it is difficult to understand even from this detailed investigation the quantitative dimensions of the fraud that might have occurred. Only one clear example is provided: in a procurement of 303,603 unit packs of Vitamin A solution, the two colluding companies won the bid at a total cost that was $506,000 more than the cost if the contract had been awarded to the lowest bidder.[6] In addition, witnesses interviewed by the bank provided accounts of kickbacks being paid to procurement officers, bribes to state officials to facilitate processing of invoices, and bribes to certify successful completion of procurements or works. As the Government of India pointed out, however, these are simply assertions reported by the bank's investigators and would not stand up in court unless the money could be followed.

In response to the bank's review, the Government of India suspended business with the two firms that were accused of colluding and brought a legal case against them. Two procurement officers were suspended, United Nations Office Project Services took over procurement responsibility for the World Bank projects, and the government took various other measures to improve management and accountability. Presumably if and when the court case is settled, there will be more information on the amount of monies lost due to the collusion, but this is the extent of the public knowledge as of early 2009.

The second investigation, prompted by the findings from the first, was a review of five more health projects in India that are supported by bank credits, totaling $569 million. All projects initially were planned to be completed in five years, but most took eight or more years to disburse fully. In Table 17-5, it is easy to see the types of problems encountered, ranging from questionable procurement practices to unfinished or deficient buildings that had been certified as complete.[7]

The six hundred pages of this two-volume report include quantitative evaluations of tenders, bid prices, and "indicators of fraud and corruption."[8] Nevertheless, it is impossible to derive from it an understanding of what might have been the value of the losses due to corruption. An exception is shown in Figure 17-1, which comes from the review of the Malaria Control Project. It suggests that possible collusion among bidders to supply insecticides for indoor residual spraying (to reduce transmission of malaria by mosquitoes) had a large effect on unit prices. The average fell from $50.82 a kilogram between 1999 and 2002 to $8.98 in the 2004 tender, approximately an 80 percent drop. Assuming the price difference was caused by collusion, the approximate amount of $30 million spent on wettable powder pyrethroids for the

Table 17-5. *Summary of Findings from the Detailed Implementation Review: India Health Sector, 2006–2007*

Project	World Bank Funding	Implementation Period	Findings
Food and Drug Capacity Building Project	$54 million	2003 to 2008	— Questionable procurement practices in tenders for 88 percent of the total value of equipment procured and a third of the works financed. — Deficiencies in delivery, use, and installation of equipment and training of staff at all fifteen food and drug laboratories.
Orissa Health Systems Development Project	$82 million	1998 to 2006	— Of 55 project hospitals, 93 percent had easily observed problems, such as incomplete construction; leaking roofs; crumbling ceilings; molding walls; or nonfunctional sewage, water, or electrical systems. Yet forty-five were certified complete. — Significant irregularities in contracting such as exclusion of the low-cost bidder in 25 percent of the contract awards.
Second National AIDS Control Project	$194 million	1999 to 2006	— Fictitious NGOs receiving contracts and government officials receiving bribes. — Lack of financial controls to track disbursements to NGOs. — Faulty blood test kits and blood bank equipment.
Malaria Control Project	$114 million	1997 to 2005	— Similar bid prices, submission of fraudulent documents, and payments to government officials in the procurement of insecticides. — Rotation of contract winners, bidders with identical phone numbers, similarity in text and layout of bids affecting 50 percent of decentralized procurement by value.
Tuberculosis Control Project	$125 million	1997 to 2006	— Central procurement seemed to have worked relatively well. — State and district procurement of pharmaceuticals and equipment showed signs of collusion, fraud, or corruption in 78 percent of contracts reviewed by value.

Figure 17-1. *Unit Prices of All Contracts Awarded for Wettable Powder*

Unit price for 10% WP or equivalent (ex-works, US$ per kg)

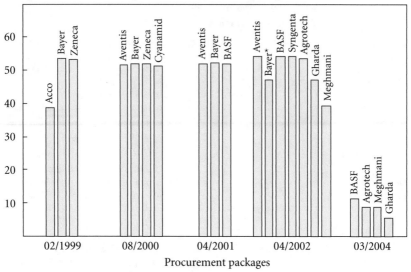

Procurement packages

Source: See note 5; graph is from p. 444.
*Bayer's price was lowered at contract award. Its original bid price was USD 55.39 per kilogram. This may suggest that there was collusion in the bids but that GOI was able to negotiate a lower price at contract signing.

pre-2004 tenders could have been reduced to approximately $6 million, suggesting an overpayment of $24 million.

In its response, the Government of India suggested that the hold of four multi-national companies over prices for wettable pyrethroids was broken by its efforts to register Indian companies so they would be eligible to participate in the procurements, which they began doing in 2001 and 2002. It argues that price competition from these newly eligible suppliers caused the reduction in 2004, which was already evident in the bids in 2002 and the procurements financed by domestic funds in 2003. Prices continued to fall in 2005 and 2006. Moreover, the government argues that the high prices prior to 2003 were assessed for reasonableness in the years that they were paid, implying that they were not out of line with international prices at the time.

In addition, the government points out that in terms of health outcomes, substantial progress was made in each of the areas addressed by these projects. [9] For example, total malaria cases declined from 1.19 million in 1997 to

0.65 million in 2004 in project states, and reported deaths due to malaria declined from 539 to 226. One can only speculate how the result might have been different had the government saved $24 million on insecticides, whatever the cause of the excess expenditure.

The Second National AIDS Control Project spent about $120 million on interventions implemented by 1,200 non-governmental organizations (NGOs) that targeted services to so-called marginal groups (such as commercial sex workers, men who have sex with men, and users of injectable drugs). Use of NGOs to provide testing, education, and counseling for these high-risk groups is common in AIDS programs because the dangerous behaviors are often illegal or frowned upon by society, so the government itself is not a logical provider of the services.

The World Bank forensic team visited the states of Karnataka, Chhattisgarh, and Maharashtra, and the municipality of Mumbai, where 103 NGOs were supported, accounting for $6.4 million of the total expenditure (about 5 percent). The World Bank examined procurement or financial documentation for 76 out of the 103 NGOs and visited 20 (the latter accounted for $126,000 of the spending). The inspection team found that financial controls for, and disbursement tracking by, the project were completely inadequate, records were either missing or incomplete, and witnesses reported that officials in the states demanded and received bribes (witnesses cited amounts ranging from 5 percent to 40 percent of the contract's value). Some contracted NGOs apparently submitted falsified claims, some were unqualified to do the work, some were fictitious, and some received payments but did not perform services. The Ministry of Health and Family Welfare conducted a review of all NGOs that provided services and terminated 25 percent of the contracts.

In addition, the bank observed serious problems with procurement and quality of HIV test kits. It found deficiencies in the decentralized procurement, quality of installation, and maintenance of blood bank equipment. It is not clear how much funding was involved in the test kits or blood bank equipment. However, if one arbitrarily assumes a 25 percent loss rate on this entire project due to corruption, incompetence, and negligence, almost $50 million would have been lost over six years, or about $8.3 million a year. The AIDS Control project was riddled with indicators of corruption, but the scale and scope of the intervention would make enforcement and prosecution costly relative to the limited value of each contract in the decentralized procurement of both NGOs and HIV test kits. Each of the twenty NGOs visited by the bank team, for example, had an average contract of just over $6,000.

Perhaps the project closest to a pure infrastructure operation was the Orissa Health Systems Development Project. Civil works composed 39 percent, and equipment, 15 percent, of total spending. The forensic team visited fifty-five hospitals, representing 35 percent of the project sites. Without belaboring the details, the team found many problems with bidding procedures, disturbingly common disqualifications of the lowest bidders, inadequate financial reporting, improper certification of works, and cost overruns. In short, the team's "indicators of corruption" meter went well into the red zone. The report is littered with photographs that document shoddy construction, poor maintenance, and unusable and dangerous equipment.

The World Bank investigation was looking for problems, and it found many. Nevertheless, despite the extensive work done by the bank on its India portfolio, it is disturbing to realize that only a small fraction of the transactions and financed activities could be observed by the team, and almost none of the money was traced with certitude to its final destination. Moreover, it is difficult, if not impossible, to identify with certainty the level of corruption that took place; how much it cost; and how to distinguish among corruption, incompetence, negligence in implementation, or poor controls that allowed sloppy work to be certified as adequate and payments to be made when they were unwarranted. It is even more difficult to single out one reason for the problems that were observed, such as rampant corruption.

It is worth noting that if these five projects plus the Reproductive Health Project were disbursed smoothly over their lifetimes, they would have accounted for roughly $100 million a year in the Indian health sector, or about $800 million over eight years. Over this same period between 1997 and 2005, public spending on health by the union and state governments in India was approximately $43 billion. The World Bank–financed projects accounted for about 1.9 percent of total public spending. Over that same period, Indians were financing out of their pockets, conservatively estimated, about $150 billion of health services.[10] Of course, the expectation is that any corruption that entered the World Bank portfolio also characterized government spending. Maybe normal government funding is characterized by a higher degree of misuse; one can only speculate.

What might this assessment mean in the Indian context? In Table 17-6, based on total estimated public expenditure on health, I have made arbitrary assumptions about its distribution across labor, supplies, and capital. The percent to labor is based on the Karnataka study, and I arbitrarily split the remainder between supplies (non-labor recurrent inputs) and capital. I then

Table 17-6. *The Possible Quantitative Dimension of Corruption in the India Health Sector (Government Health Expenditures), 2007*[a]

Category of expenditure	Assumed percentage distribution of spending (percent)	Amount (dollars)	Assumed leakage for each spending category (percent)	Amount of assumed leakage (dollars)	Percent of assumed leakage
Labor	72	8,009,423,939	35	2,803,298,379	84
Supplies	23	2,558,565,981	15	383,784,897	12
Capital	5	556,209,996	25	139,052,499	4
Total	100	11,124,199,916	75	3,326,135,775	100

a. Author's calculations based on data in *World Development Indicators 2008* and author's assumptions.

assigned an assumed leakage from each category: 35 percent for labor simply due to absenteeism (lower than the estimate presented earlier), arbitrary assumptions that an average of 15 percent for every supply contract is "skimmed" in one way or another, and that 25 percent of every investment contract is "skimmed" on average.

I make no assumptions about incompetence and negligence. The overall guessed leakage is 30 percent of public spending. Eighty-four percent of the total is due to absenteeism of staff. If we assume the leakage rate for staff is 20 percent rather than 35 percent, it still accounts for 75 percent of the guessed total. These numbers are not corrected for PPP because only the percentages matter.

Table 17-7 presents a similar estimate for the education sector. The distribution of spending is different. The published national estimate for teacher salaries in total public spending was 85 percent in 2003 and 87 percent in 2004. I chose 86 percent to apply to 2007 spending. My guesses for supplies and capital are arbitrary, as before. I also used the same leakage percentages as those used for health, except the teacher absentee rate was 25 percent for India, which I reduce arbitrarily by 5 percent, as I did for the health number (from Table 17-3). I included secondary school expenditures, so I am assuming all of these proportions apply to both primary and secondary education. The result is as we might expect—leakages are completely driven by labor costs. The guessed value of leakage is over $5 billion (about $15 billion PPP), and 87 percent of it is due to absenteeism.

Table 17-7. *The Possible Quantitative Dimension of Corruption in the India Education Sector (Public Primary and Secondary Expenditures), 2007*[a]

Category of expenditure	Assumed percentage distribution of spending (percent)	Public spending on primary and secondary education (dollars)	Assumed leakage for each spending category (percent)	Amount of assumed leakage (dollars)	Percent of assumed leakage
Labor	86	23,866,678,177	20	4,773,335,635	88
Supplies	10	2,775,195,137	15	416,279,271	8
Capital	4	1,110,078,055	25	277,519,514	5
Total	100	27,751,951,368	—	5,467,134,420	100

a. Author's calculations based on data in *World Development Indicators 2008* and author's assumptions.

Five billion, three billion, or even one billion dollars is a huge amount of money if any of these figures is remotely close to the truth—and the labor cost figures that drive the totals are likely to be conservatively estimated but not too far from the truth. The important point, though, is that probably 95 percent of the losses in this thought experiment would be petty corruption at an individual level that would be enormously difficult to monitor and stop. Improving data systems, strengthening internal auditing, simplifying and enforcing rules and procedures, making the policing of people and purchases more aggressive, and throwing the worst scofflaws in jail every year and publicizing it are important and essential steps to pursue in any governmental effort to end a culture of corruption. But all of these measures are long term, requiring a steady commitment from the top, and we should not delude ourselves that we would witness fundamental changes overnight. They require systems, plus changes in incentives and culture that are enormously difficult to develop and implement successfully. No one is under the illusion that corruption would be eradicated under any circumstance, but it could be reduced with vigilance and large investments in improving the ability to track small purchases and staff, along with a judicial system that could be relied upon to punish offenders.

A fundamental problem of the current approach to corruption is that it focuses on the areas of least importance, from an expenditure standpoint (capital spending in Tables 17-6 and 17-7, and to a lesser degree, spending on supplies), that are easiest to observe for international organizations. No element of the bank's Detailed Implementation Review (DIR) in India focused on labor inputs, only on transactions for goods, works, and services. Even so, the bank's review demonstrates how little can be known about what actually happened based on the available paper trail. It is questionable whether legal remedies could be enforced on the basis of the evidence or leads that were uncovered by the bank or that there would be much impact in preventing the same types of behavior in the future. The fundamental problem comes with labor inputs. That is a principal-agent and incentive problem of massive proportions. It is unlikely to be solved through central fiduciary or judicial means in the long or short run.

In the current methods of financing and providing education and health services in most developing countries, the government or the taxpayer takes all of the risk and assumes that the system will function successfully. If a hospital is rehabilitated but remains nearly unusable; if a piece of equipment or a vehicle is purchased but is not maintained; or if a teacher does not show up for class, the long chains of accountability mean that virtually nothing will happen to resolve the problem.[11] The next section provides a short summary of reviews of the development of financial accountability and procurement systems in Africa and Latin America, illustrating the long-term nature of changes to the accountability structure of government. Then the chapter discusses other options to improve accountability through the design of interventions.

We must of course support and encourage the longer term changes in accountability. However, in the short term, to solve problems like those illustrated in this section, it is important to design health and education programs that give citizens the self-interest and power to affect outcomes and to shift general governmental risks for performance to individual suppliers to the degree that it is possible.

Prospects for Improving Public Financial Management (PFM) and Procurement Systems

Over the past decade, the World Bank has undertaken Country Financial Accountability Assessments (CFAAs) and Country Procurement Assessment Reviews (CPARs) at least once for each of its borrowing countries. Originally, these were internal documents intended to help bank staff make decisions about fiduciary practices for bank-financed projects, especially to help determine the degree to which the bank could rely upon country systems for disbursement and procurement aspects of project implementation. Many of these documents are now in the public domain. The OECD has supported a systematic evaluation framework that is focused specifically on procurement, which has now been adopted by most CPARs.[12]

Although originally for internal purposes, these reviews also helped to document for the bank the quality of public financial management and implementation arrangements across countries. Naturally, as bank staff began to understand these issues in a more systematic way, the information began to be used for policy dialogues about improving financial management, procurement systems, and implementation arrangements in countries. In 2007 and 2008, a sample of these reviews for ten countries in Latin America and the Caribbean (LAC) and thirty countries in Africa were looked at to understand some of the lessons.

Generally the reviews looked for characteristics of sound public expenditure management systems, which include the following:

—Is there a clear legal and institutional framework for expenditure management; is the budget comprehensive; is the budget organized in terms of programs; and are revenues reconciled with spending plans?

—Is there an adequate and open system to review the budget and set priorities?

—Is the budget executed in a manner that is consistent with a high degree of accountability, transparency, and efficient management of public funds? Do these systems meet the standards of economy, efficiency, competition, and transparency?

—Is there independent scrutiny of the government's stewardship of public resources, including internal and external audits, performance monitoring, vigorous legislative oversight, and opportunities for civil society oversight?

The ten LAC countries reviewed were Brazil, Chile, Colombia, Costa Rica, Dominican Republic, Guatemala, Honduras, Jamaica, Panama, and Paraguay. These are, for the most part, middle-income countries. The review concluded that only Chile and Brazil have been making significant progress across the full set of measures, with Chile consistently seeking to improve performance over the past two decades and Brazil making noticeable progress during the past decade. Costa Rica and Panama have made some important reforms but still have many off-budget items and other peculiarities that limit their ability to plan for and meet commitments and to procure well. The remaining countries have problems across the board that they have been slow to address. Nevertheless, most have made progress at least in gaining control over the overall balance of revenue and expenditure, historically a core problem for all of them, although that gives little comfort when our interest is in the efficacy and honesty of public spending.

The procurement side of the equation is particularly troublesome. While countries may have a legal procurement framework in place, most leave procurement up to individual agencies, which develop their own unique rules and practices. Except in Chile and increasingly in Brazil, procurement is considered an administrative function that is done correctly when it follows the agency's rules to the letter rather than focusing on the desired results of economy and efficiency. Often agency-level procedural rules become so specific and costly to manage that bidding firms begin to specialize and develop ties to agencies, which erodes competitiveness and transparency. For both financial management and procurement, the focus is on *ex ante* controls and procedures, not on achieving results, except in Chile.

By far, the weakest elements in all of these countries are audit and oversight. Most important for the social sectors, which depend on decentralized implementation, whatever controls and oversight are present at the center, they quickly evaporate as distance from the capital increases.[13]

For the thirty countries reviewed in Africa, the systems are in a completely different state of development, but the results are not so different. Prior to the mid-1990s, most African countries had inadequate or nonexistent legal frameworks for PFM and procurement. Beginning in the 1990s, the World Bank and other donors embarked on a concerted effort to work with African governments to correct these problems. As in Latin America, most countries now have achieved a necessary condition for good budget management, substantial control over their fiscal balance, which is a night-versus-day improvement over the situation prevailing in most countries prior to 2000.

For procurement, most African states now have state-of-the art laws on their books that are based on the model that was developed by the United Nations Commission on International Trade Law. The problem, of course, is that there is a vast gap between law and practice. Developing the practice side of the equation is likely to take many years, as institutions and skills are developed and the practices of the past are slowly abandoned.[14]

The set of issues covered by CFAAs has been formalized in the Public Expenditure and Financial Accountability Program (PEFA), which has developed twenty-eight indicators (that are further decomposed into seventy-three detailed dimensions) to rate public financial management systems with a letter grade of A, B, C, or D, with D being the worst.[15] Norway recently scored itself, receiving a world record 17 As, 5 Bs, 4 C+s, and 2 Ds. The Ds were for lack of a comprehensive internal audit function and no systematic public reporting of resources available for municipal-based service delivery units (e.g., schools and health facilities).[16]

The PEFA scoring system has not been applied to LAC, but in Africa there has been substantial coverage. For thirty-one African countries, scores were far lower than for Norway. Although the details are quite complex, the core findings are consistent with the CPARs and CFAAs:

—Budget preparation processes are relatively stronger than execution and oversight, the same observations made for LAC in the CFAAs.

—*De jure* is rated higher than *de facto,* the "good law but poor implementation" problem.

—Processes are stronger in more homogeneous environments with few actors such as the budget department or treasury. They are much weaker where more actors or more layers are involved, such as in the decentralized operations that characterize the social sectors.[17]

In this section, I have skimmed the surface of measuring governance and accountability in public financial management and procurement to give a flavor of the feasibility of preventing or controlling the "indicators of corruption" that the World Bank's DIR of the India health portfolio uncovered. First, systematic knowledge and data on the performance of government systems are new. PEFA and the OECD's procurement frameworks have been in development for only a few years, and applications of them are even more recent. The International Budget Program's Open Budget Index, which measures many of the same phenomena, was developed in 2005 and 2006. All of the indexes show the same thing: that these accountability systems are nascent, have not reached far beyond giving governments the ability to manage overall revenues and expenditures (a tremendous achievement, but only the first stage), and are particularly weak in decentralized service delivery. We simply cannot expect this situation to change overnight and must be ready to spend decades patiently investing in better governance of expenditures. Improved technology can have an impact, but the experience in LAC suggests that new technology grafted onto dysfunctional or incomplete systems leads to possibly more efficiency and higher potential, but the systems remain dysfunctional.

Moreover, nothing discussed in this section specifically addresses the core source of leakages that is suggested by the guesswork in Tables 17-6 and 17-7: how to get human beings who are already on the job to produce. That is the critical issue in education. A class of students can be taught successfully without a classroom and without books, but it cannot be taught without a teacher. The classroom and books help. So does the principal. But they are not sufficient. A good teacher is necessary and can be sufficient to educate a child, although this is not an optimal situation.

In health, personnel are necessary but for most services are not sufficient. A nurse needs a vaccine and delivery device to complete an immunization. Both the nurse and the vaccine are necessary for success. The issue, therefore, is how to make sure the people on the supply side of the social sectors actually produce, without forgetting that other inputs are either necessary also or at least helpful.

Program Design

Given what we know about the fiduciary and accountability environment and its prospects for improvement, why would we try to organize teachers in such a way that they are accountable to overwhelmed bureaucrats in the capital rather than to parents whose children are in the school? How did we develop the idea that governments would adequately fund maintenance when it is treated as an added cost rather than a reduction in taxable income, as it would be in the private sector? Where did we get the idea that shifting all the risk of failure to taxpayers would result in a better deal for clients? How did we conclude that the government has an advantage over extermination companies in purchasing insecticide and spraying homes?

The simple lesson is that, however imperfectly, incentives need to be taken into account, particularly when control mechanisms do not operate as well as they should. In this section, I provide a number of examples of approaches.

EDUCO (Educación con Participación de la Comunidad): Community-Managed Schools in El Salvador

Slowly, but surely, across the developing world, schools are being decentralized, and school management committees or parent-teacher associations are being formed. These processes have been under way for twenty years as of 2009. However, often parental involvement is advisory to the principal or seen as a way to improve student discipline and gain community support for the school. Parents typically have no input into teacher selection, school management, or performance reviews of staff. In the EDUCO program, in contrast, the parents are in charge. It began during the civil war in El Salvador, when public services stopped functioning in the most isolated parts of the country. Parents organized their own schools as a result. Once the war ended, a decision was made to support these schools with public funding rather than to fold them into the traditional centralized school system. In 1992, public support of EDUCO started; there were 845 Community Associations for Education (ACE is the Spanish acronym; these associations operate the schools), about 1,000 classrooms, and 32,000 students. Operation was limited to pre-school up to third grade. By 2001, there were nearly 2,000 ACEs, 10,000 class-rooms, and 322,000 students, and the schools ranged up to grade 9. EDUCO schools account for about 50 percent of rural enrollments.[18] The ACEs secure classrooms, hire and fire teachers, monitor teacher performance, pay teachers, buy teaching materials for the classrooms, and closely monitor the schools. They have contracts with the Ministry of Education to provide these services.

An evaluation of the program found that EDUCO parents are poorer, less educated, and have much lower access to electricity, water, or sanitation services than are and do non-EDUCO parents (whose children are enrolled in traditional schools). Yet 75 percent of the teachers hired by EDUCO schools have a university education, compared to 37 percent in traditional schools. They have about four years of experience, compared to almost nine years for traditional school teachers. In EDUCO schools, parent associations visited the schools an average of 5.7 times in the month leading up to the evaluation, compared to 1.6 times in traditional schools. The evaluation found that EDUCO substantially expanded education opportunities for poorer rural children. While these children performed worse on standardized language and mathematics tests, when the researchers controlled for their more disadvantaged backgrounds, the differences in scores disappeared, suggesting that the EDUCO schools performed as well or better than traditional schools. Both teachers and students missed fewer days in EDUCO schools, and the close monitoring of schools by parents had a strong positive impact on learning outcomes. In short, under the most difficult conditions—poorly educated, low-income parents in remote areas of El Salvador—parental management solved many problems of access, student performance, and teacher performance.[19]

Community-Managed Schools in New Zealand

Of course, community-managed schools need not be confined to the most difficult situations. New Zealand instituted a reform in 1989 in which primary and secondary schools became autonomous, governed by boards of trustees that were composed of elected representatives (three to seven parents, one member of the staff, and one student in schools with students above ninth grade), plus unelected members (the principal of the school and other trustees that the board agrees to seat). These boards have full responsibility for the schools. They employ all staff in the school, set the school's strategic direction, ensure a safe environment, and are responsible for quality. The boards also oversee the management of personnel, curriculum, property, finance, and administration. They are required to prepare annual reports for the school that include audited accounts. The government of New Zealand transfers funds to the schools based on formulas, and teacher salaries are determined nationally so the schools do not have to negotiate compensation. Within these parameters, the boards fully manage the school, obviously with the principal being the day-to-day manager. Students have limited choice over which school they attend due to capacity constraints in popular schools. Nevertheless, this system is now twenty years old and is extremely well institutionalized.[20]

In both New Zealand and El Salvador, the Ministry of Education has transferred performance risks, and the means to manage them, to parents, who have been successful. Of course, the underlying motivation is to empower the "principals" (the parents) to monitor their "agents" (the principal and the teachers) and to have power over the agents. The Ministry of Education no longer has to run the schools, but it can provide support to the independent schools and increase their level of accountability by comparing their performances and sharing the information with parents. If Klitgaard's basic equation of corruption holds (corruption = monopoly + discretion – accountability), both the EDUCO and New Zealand approaches reduce opportunities for monopoly by opening up the schooling bureaucracy to outside scrutiny and shift control to the parents, while at the same time increasing options for students and parents.[21] Successfully increasing competition among schools would open the systems even more. Discretion is shifted to parents to a large degree, and accountability is increased. As both innovations have matured and become institutionalized, support to improve the quality and experience of all parties has increased.

The Girls' Secondary School Stipend Program in Bangladesh

There are market-based solutions to accountability problems in the education sector as well, such as providing vouchers or scholarships and letting parents and their children choose the school. The Girls' Secondary School Stipend Program in Bangladesh, which was scaled up nationally in 1994, has provided a small stipend to girls that increases each year they stay in school (grades six through ten) to cover about half of the out-of-pocket costs of attending school; a payment to the school they attend; and for the higher levels, book allowances and exam fees. In return, the girls and their parents sign a contract that the supported girl will maintain a 75 percent attendance record, achieve at least a 45 percent mark on midterm and annual exams, and remain unmarried. Each of the girls opens a bank account, where the stipend is deposited; she is often the first in her family to have a bank account. Starting at about 33 percent in 1990, by 2003 the net secondary enrollment rate of girls was

47 percent in Bangladesh, compared with 23 percent in Pakistan. A prerequisite for going to secondary school, of course, is completing primary school. The net enrollment rate of girls in primary school was 89 percent in Bangladesh, compared with 49 percent in Pakistan in 2003. By any measure, this program has been successful in getting girls enrolled.

If we look only at the World Bank financing for the stipend program from 1994 through 1999, it provided $68 million to support stipends and tuition for 1.6 million girls. That comes to about $14 a year per girl. This is an amount paid above and beyond the normal subsidies for children in schools. For this marginal payment, the school system, parents, and the girls have responded vigorously. If some of the cash losses caused today by teacher absenteeism could be redirected to programs with similar impacts, the change in productivity would go from negative to wildly positive.

The stipend program has had problems, though. Administrative costs have been about 18 percent.[22] Graduation rates for the girls have been disappointing (due to low school leaving exam results), the design of the program gave schools an incentive to enroll as many girls as possible even if there was not room for them, and there was obvious cheating by some schools and girls.

On the positive side, all of these problems came to light because of the information system that is required to make payments to girls and schools. Unlike the case of the India DIR, the money can be traced to its final destination because the whole system depends on payments against reports (e.g., enrollment, attendance, exam scores). Prices cannot be inflated to finance cash kickbacks, as the values of the stipend and tuition are fixed; only quantities can vary. The nature of the intervention creates the digital trail needed for enforcement, and it is possible to cross-check results.[23] For the same reason, conditional cash transfer programs have been successful in many environments, with low leakage rates and large impacts. The cash goes to the final beneficiary, who of course may at times be criminally zealous about getting the money. However, only a small amount is at risk with each individual or household, and data analysis can reveal problems and risks.[24]

Options in Health

In health, solving the principal-agent problem is much more problematic. Compare, for example, a primary care clinic and a primary school or a secondary school and a hospital. In education, there is a long-term relationship of eight or nine months between the principal and the agent, with a precious commodity involved (the child). Parents can acquire substantial information about performance and act on it. If they have more than one child or just talk to other parents, they can gain even more information about schools, teachers, and results. If empowered, as in EDUCO, parents have shown that they can become effective supervisors of schools. Parental capabilities to oversee are robust and can extend to secondary schools, as shown in New Zealand.

In health, contacts are more episodic, and there is a wider gulf in knowledge between the provider and the client. There are greater limitations on community oversight. The result has been the shifting of more health sector relationships into the realm of competitive markets. For example, while many countries of the former Soviet Union have had limited or easily reversed experiences with democratic reforms, most have shifted with gusto from monopolized, low-accountability, high-provider-discretion health care to systems where there is a separation between financing and provision, more consumer choice, more (but uneven) accountability, less provider discretion, and more information for everyone. These evolving health markets are far from perfect, but there has been a consistent attempt to shift from systems where public funding follows doctors and hospitals to systems where public funding follows the patient and where the suppliers compete. This change has to be accompanied by regulation and robust accreditation, neither of which develops well in government-owned and -managed health care delivery systems (in which case the regulator also delivers the service).

Increasingly, low- and middle-income countries are moving in this same direction. China, Ghana, India, Indonesia, Kenya, Mexico, Rwanda, Turkey, and Vietnam, among others, have in just the past few years started to move toward funding health services through subsidized insurance that follows the patient. As this intervention develops, ownership and control of facilities must be addressed so that hospitals and clinics are forced into more business-like behaviors. Incentives for absenteeism disappear as, with the secondary schools in Bangladesh, clients become more attractive because they are the sources of revenue. Excess delivery of services becomes the public policy problem. As facilities become independent—whether owned by the government or not—their abilities to tap private sources of investment finance increase. Overbuilding and over-equipping becomes the problem, not incomplete works and unsuitable equipment that does not function.

Conclusion

This chapter has been no more than an exploration from an operational standpoint of how to combat corruption in government health and education. Corruption can come in all three types of inputs in both sectors—labor, capital investment, and supplies. A fairly convincing story can be developed that the source of most losses in both sectors lies in shirking by civil servants. It has been measured by absenteeism surveys, although of course there are other dimensions (such as poor performance when they show up for work). There is, undoubtedly, corruption in capital investments, maintenance, logistics, and the purchase and supply of consumables, but these corrupt acts are dwarfed by shirking because labor consumes so much of public budgets, typically crowding out these other inputs. It is also difficult to tease out the losses in these other areas that are due to poor performance (rather than to corruption) of civil servants.

Corruption and poor performance can be reduced through better policing, better fiduciary systems, and better leadership. However, it is a long, slow process to change institutions that have developed certain patterns of behavior over many decades. A simple rule change does not solve the underlying problem, and the PFM performance reviews in Africa and Latin America do not instill confidence that fiduciary systems can be improved quickly.

Therefore it is important to focus on other means—paradigm shifts possibly—by which government programs are designed so that they take advantage of the self interest of the parties that are involved and put the principals in control of the agents. These changes can take place relatively quickly, even during a civil war, once the principals are given the power and information to act. They have an interest in doing so. Moreover, changing program designs are probably more reliable ways under any circumstance to improve the performance of the agents relative to what could be accomplished through central control systems. Motivation, supervision, and incentives are the issue, and they can be provided by the principals. I hope that I have demonstrated that this change can be relatively straightforward in education. Market-based solutions can also be tried in education, but much can be accomplished by reorganizing authority in the public system.

In health, it seems inescapable that greater use of markets is necessary. In that case, it is a matter of putting purchasing power in the hands of the principal—in this case, the patient—and flipping current power relationships in the public sector on their heads. As this is done, the system will quickly shift from under-delivering services to over-delivering them.

In both education and health, the post-reform shift of some power from the provider (the agent) to the consumer (the principal) reduces the need for old-style fiduciary controls on procurement. Presumably more procurement would be done at the point of service, where parents can observe closely how the money is spent, or in the market where the owner has an incentive to get value for money. As a result, much less large-scale central or state government procurement would be needed.

On the financial management side, the demands would be great to be able to follow the money and account for it by the end recipient. The recipients themselves—whether school committees, parents, or patients—will demand to get the funding or services to which they are entitled. This change gives governments the opportunity to develop systems that deliver and account for the funds. As with the Bangladesh stipend program, such systems also create a control environment in which money can be matched against receipts and performance contracts.

A new approach to reducing corruption would in the first instance focus on reducing absenteeism and shirking. It would also shift risks of non-performance nearer to the point of service delivery, where they can be observed by interested parties and acted on. It would require that parents and patients be given more authority over their agents in the classroom or the clinic. Corruption would not be eliminated, but the fiduciary systems supporting such a shift would be far more able to "follow the money," which is essential to keep a system as honest as possible.

A reasonable case may be made that the incentive-focused changes suggested here would be as long term and difficult to make as improvements in the fiduciary, or control, environment. The latter must be strengthened under any circumstance, but making a few important changes to how education and health programs operate can simplify and strengthen the impact of fiduciary reforms that are carried out, and it can allow them to be more focused. Recruiting those who have an interest in the products of the education and health systems to watch more carefully and take more responsibility for how robustly they operate is an intervention of a fundamentally different character from one aimed at changing the behavior of a procurement officer.

People worry about the time that is required to make fundamental reforms such as putting schools under control of parent-led boards. Virtually all the time cost of making that change is in the political decision-making process. Once that is done, service providers' expected behavior changes should take place quickly as the newly empowered parties start to make decisions, changing both incentives and the nature of supervision. In contrast, for fiduciary reform, not only do we face the time cost of political decision-making because of entrenched interests in the status quo, but the behavioral response is far from guaranteed. Changing the behavior of bureaucrats, service delivery personnel, and suppliers can take decades when the change is expected to come from within.

Empowering those who depend on health and education services to demand greater accountability is the key missing ingredient in efforts to reduce opportunities for corruption in the social sectors. This statement is an assertion based on the logic, suggestive guesses for India, and other evidence presented in this chapter. However, efforts to solve the problem through stricter enforcement, policing, forensic reviews, and rules have no stronger empirical or theoretical basis. Evaluation of alternative approaches is obviously in order. It is clear that poor children are getting a raw deal from their education and health systems, as are tax payers and donors. Treating corruption in education and health as a principal-agent problem broadens the set of tools that can be used to address corruption and has the potential to unleash a powerful positive output response in systems that are woefully underperforming.

Notes

1. In health, there are a number of excellent surveys with extensive bibliographies. Two good starting points are Maureen Lewis, "Governance and Corruption in Public Health Care Systems," *Working Paper* No. 78 (Washington, D.C., 2006) and Taryn Vian, "Review of Corruption in the Health Sector: Theory, Methods, and Interventions," *Health Policy and Planning*, XXIII (2008), 83–94.

2. In education, the literature is more sparse and is focused on country cases and teacher absenteeism. See Jacques Hallak and Muriel Poisson, *Corrupt Schools, Corrupt Universities: What Can be Done?* (Paris, 2007), available at http://unpan1.un.org/intradoc/groups/public/documents/unesco/unpan025403.pdf (accessed 11 March 2009); Harry Anthony Patrinos and Ruth Kagia, "Maximizing the Performance of Education Systems: The Case of Teacher Absenteeism," in J. Edgardo Campos and Sanjay Pradhan (eds.), *The Many Faces of Corruption: Tracking Vulnerabilities at the Sector Level* (Washington, D.C., 2007).

3. The calculations combine information from Table 17-1 and *Education for All Global Monitoring Report 2009* (Paris, 2008). It was published jointly by the United Nations Educational, Scientific and Cultural Organization (UNESCO).

4. Indo-Dutch Project Management Society, *Following the Public Health Delivery Trail: A Worm's Eye-View of the Health Spend* (Bangalore, 2008).

5. Sangeeta Raja and Donald A. Hicks, "Designing a Strategic Public Sector Healthcare Supply Chain for Kenya: Driving Service Improvements through Supply Chain Excellence Using Advanced Modeling Software," AIDS Campaign Team for Africa Learning Series presentation at the World Bank, Washington, D.C., 18 February 2009.

6. World Bank, Department of Institutional Integrity, *Report of Investigation into Reproductive and Child Health 1 Project Credit N0180 India* (Washington, D.C., 2005). This report is labeled "strictly confidential" but was obtained by the *Wall*

Street Journal and can be found at http://opinionjournal.com/editorial/090407 rchi.pdf.

7. World Bank, Department of Institutional Integrity, *Detailed Implementation Review India Health Sector 2006-2007 Volumes I and II* (Washington, D.C., 2007). These two volumes are available at the World Bank website at http://go.worldbank.org/ M5LSBCRY90.

8. Indicators of fraud and corruption in procurement include: "questions about meeting post qualification criteria, inconsistent findings as to whether an item meets required specifications, unsupported finding as to whether a bidder or an item meets required specifications, inconsistent requests for clarifications among bidders with same procurement, inconsistent requests for clarifications among similarly situated bidders, steering committee overrules bid evaluation committee, procurement guidelines not followed, apparent lack of thoroughness in bid package, unreasonable delay in award of contract, bid document drafted narrowly to favor specific bidder, seemingly fraudulent documents, procurement officials' inconsistent reliance on product literature." Ibid., 72.

9. The discussion of the Government of India's response is drawn from World Bank, *World Bank Response to Detailed Implementation Review India Health Sector 2006–2007* (Washington, D.C., 2008). This report is labeled "strictly confidential" but was obtained by the *Wall Street Journal* and can be found at http://online.wsj.com/ public/resources/documents/IndiaDIRBankResponse.pdf.

10. Estimates of health spending come from data in World Bank, *World Development Indicators 2008* (Washington, D.C., 2008).

11. For a complete discussion of this accountability problem, see World Bank, *The World Development Report 2004* (Washington, D.C., 2004).

12. OECD, *Methodology for Assessment of National Procurement Systems,* Version 4 (Paris, 2006), available at www.oecd.org/dataoecd/1/36/37390076.pdf (accessed 12 March 2009).

13. Omowunmi Ladipo, Alfonso Sanchez, and Jamil Sopher, "Effective and Transparent Governance of Public Expenditures in Latin America and the Caribbean: Revitalizing Reforms in Financial Management and Procurement" (Washington, D.C., 2009, forthcoming in the World Bank's *Directions in Development* book series).

14. Alfonso Sanchez, "Procurement Systems in Sub-Saharan African Countries: Hindering or Helping Improve Public Spending?" Discussion Paper (Washington, D.C., 2009).

15. See Public Expenditure and Financial Accountability Program, "Public Financial Management Performance Measurement Framework" (Washington, D.C., 2005), available at www.pefa.org/pfm_performance_frameworkmn.php (accessed 19 April 2009).

16. Håkon Mundal, *Public Financial Management Performance Report–Norway— Based on PEFA Methodology* (Oslo, 2008). The Ministry of Finance's reactions to low scores were: (a) weaknesses in procurement practices and follow-up to external audit findings would be addressed; (b) multi-year program/sector budgeting, limited extent

of internal audit, no consolidated overview of risks from autonomous agencies, and public corporations are not high priorities; (c) local health and education services are municipal responsibilities, central government will not get involved.

17. Matthew Andrews, "PFM in Africa: Where are We, How Did We Get Here, Where Should We Go?" Discussion Paper (Washington, D.C., 2009).

18. Darlyn Meza, José L. Guzmán, and Lorena De Varela, "EDUCO: A Community-Managed Education Program in Rural Areas of El Salvador," paper presented at "Reducing Poverty, Sustaining Growth—What Works, What Doesn't, and Why: A Global Exchange for Scaling Up Success, Scaling Up Poverty Reduction," Shanghai, 25–27 May 2004.

19. Emmanuel Jimenez and Yasuyuki Sawada, "Do Community-Managed Schools Work? An Evaluation of El Salvador's EDUCO Program," *The World Bank Economic Review,* XIII (1999), 415–441.

20. This paragraph was adapted from www.minedu.govt.nz/educationSectors/Schools.aspx. A brief exploration of this website will give the reader a feeling for how well this reform has become institutionalized and the resources that are available to support the boards of trustees. For a good, up-to-date narrative on some aspects of the system, see Norman LaRocque, "School Choice: Lessons from New Zealand," *Education Forum Briefing Papers* No. 12 (Washington, D.C., 2005), available at www.education forum.org.nz/documents/policy/briefing_no_12.pdf (accessed 13 March 2009).

21. Robert E. Klitgaard, *Controlling Corruption* (Berkeley, 1991).

22. Shahidur R. Khandker, Mark M. Pitt, and Nobuhiko Fuwa, *Subsidy to Promote Girls' Secondary Education: The Female Stipend Program in Bangladesh* (Washington, D.C., 2003).

23. World Bank, "Project Performance Assessment Report, Bangladesh Female Secondary School Assistance Project (Credit 2469)," Report No. 26226 (Washington, D.C., 2003); Janet Raynor and Kate Wesson, "The Girls' Stipend Program in Bangladesh," *Journal of Education for International Development,* II (2006), available at www.equip123.net/JEID/articles/3/Bangladesh.pdf (accessed 13 March 2009); Jennifer Hove, "Barriers to Girls' Secondary School Participation in Rural Bangladesh," *CPR Commentary* No. 5 (Dhaka, 2007).

24. Ariel Fiszbein and Norbert Schady, *Conditional Cash Transfers: Reducing Present and Future Poverty* (Washington, D.C., 2009).

JOMO KWAME SUNDARAM

18

Good Governance, Anti-Corruption, and Economic Development

Corruption adversely affects development in many different ways, especially by diverting resources that may be invested productively and by causing uncertainty for investors. Efficient markets are defined as those with low transaction costs, particularly the costs of negotiating and enforcing contracts. If these costs are high, markets are inefficient, and transactions, including investments, become less likely.

The economic argument for the good governance agenda can be summarized as follows. Poor economic development performance is blamed on inefficient, high-transaction-cost markets. Inefficient markets are blamed on welfare-reducing government interventions, especially those that cause insecure property rights with uncertain, potentially high-cost implications. Unstable property rights and welfare-reducing interventions are then explained by what rent seekers pay to secure economic advantage. Such payments limit the average person's ability to establish a connection between government policy and democratic accountability, allowing the abuses to persist.

Good governance indicators become necessary conditions for low transaction costs in market economies, and thus, they become preconditions for development. Consequently, good governance proponents advocate ambitious policies to break out of this trap. Unlike the traditional economic reform that focuses on economic liberalization, these approaches require many institutional reforms.

However, there is, at best, a weak and moot relationship between the requirements of the good governance agenda and improved economic performance. Other conditions needed to accelerate and sustain economic

I am greatly indebted to Mushtaq Khan, but do not implicate him in any way.

457

growth are not usually identified by the good governance approach. The key question here is whether the requirements for good governance identify the most appropriate conditions and reform priorities to accelerate and sustain economic development.

The quality of governance cannot be directly measured; so instead, proxy indicators, often based on subjective judgments and opinions, are utilized. Although many governance indicators are methodologically subjective in nature, they are widely perceived by their users as objective and utilized to draw policy conclusions and recommendations that are rarely justified.

Advanced countries score better on all governance indicators compared to both converging and diverging developing countries, suggesting that higher per capita incomes generally improve governance indicators. The data show that richer countries generally have better governance, lower corruption and so on, but the causality is unclear.[1] For corruption and other governance indicators to become developmental policy priorities, good governance should clearly enhance economic growth. This presumed relationship between governance indicators and growth rates is weak, and often disappears with the inclusion of other variables such as investment rates.[2] Even when corruption and other governance variables improve, Khan shows that overall economic performance can remain weak.

Significant differences in economic performance between converging and diverging developing countries are not explained only by good governance indicators. Data for all countries for the 1980s show a weak positive relationship between governance quality and economic growth. Governance indicators were only marginally better for converging compared with diverging developing countries, while both groups were significantly worse than the advanced countries. The large differences in growth rates between converging and diverging developing countries were not associated with significant differences in governance quality in the 1980s or 1990s. Meanwhile, the "median converging developing country" had a marginally poorer governance index compared with the "median diverging developing country."[3]

The median corruption indices for both converging and diverging developing countries were similar in the 1980s and 1990s, but both groups scored significantly worse than the advanced countries.[4] Meanwhile, although there undoubtedly are significant governance differences between converging and diverging developing countries, the differences in their governance characteristics are not identified by the good governance indicators.

Khan shows that converging and diverging developing countries do not contrast significantly in terms of their average governance characteristics, but differ significantly in terms of economic growth performance.[5] While good governance advocates claim that diverging countries will develop and thus become advanced countries by implementing good governance reforms, Khan notes that no country has ever first improved its governance characteristics and then increased its growth rate to achieve advanced country status. Once growth has accelerated, the implementation of good governance reforms may be desirable, and such reforms may even be necessary to sustain growth.

However, there is no evidence that the full good governance agenda—all the indicators that are identified as significant for development and those that are promoted by the World Bank or the Millennium Challenge Corporation—can be fully implemented in poor countries or that such reforms are preconditions for growth in poorly performing countries. Undoubtedly, poor governance may be the stumbling block to development, but in such instances, "good enough," pragmatic, or necessary developmental reforms—rather than the entire good governance agenda—have proved sufficient to remove the bottlenecks that prevent development. The governance reforms that are undertaken by developing country governments, which have been conducive to development, clearly support the case for pragmatism, rather than dogmatism, in governance reforms that are needed for development.

Such governance reforms are undoubtedly context-specific, and should therefore be conceived after careful consideration of the stumbling blocks to development, their origins or causes, as well as the factors that sustain them. Consequently, the identification and imposition of ostensibly universal best practices—irrespective of the specific governance bottlenecks to development—have probably contributed to the failure of the good governance agenda approach to reform. The universal good governance agenda is therefore problematic, not only because it demands more than is needed, and thus increases the likelihood of failure, but also, more important, because it requires inappropriate, if not anti-developmental, reforms.

Available evidence does not point to any single set of institutions that have accelerated growth in all advanced or converging countries. The World Bank recognized the critical role that the government played in East Asian development, but warned that such governance capacities were absent in other developing countries, therefore these other countries should not adopt East Asian–type strategies.[6] The bank was thus effectively asking countries with poor governance capacities to achieve new good governance capacities that no poor country had historically achieved, claiming that such governance capacities would ensure faster growth, despite the absence of evidence to that effect.[7]

The Causes of Corruption in Developing Countries

Many commentators have offered their opinions on the ostensible causes of corruption in developing countries. First, the most influential view is that corruption is principally due to the greed of public officials who abuse their discretionary powers for their own self-interest (self-seeking bureaucrats or politicians). The weakness of central government, in turn, encourages predation, a scourge in many developing countries. Anti-corruption strategies must therefore strengthen appropriate governmental enforcement capacities.

Second, weaknesses in enforcing legal rights, including property and contractual rights, produce higher costs for negotiating, enforcing, and protecting contracts. Weakly protected property rights or poorly enforced contractual rights and their associated corruption seem widespread in developing countries. However, with sustained high growth, as well as greater social and political stability, economic expectations become more stable, helping to sustain investment and growth. In other words, corruption tends to decline with sustained economic development.

Third, clientelism—or patron-client relations or "political corruption"—is often associated with efforts by politicians or others to retain or gain power. Developing countries' governments and politicians may resort to such measures to maintain political stability, often because the underlying problems (the factors that are conducive to or encourage clientelism) cannot be addressed by more conventional programs, owing to fiscal constraints. Clientelism must be regulated to limit its most damaging effects, while the ability of governments to budget and spend according to their own priorities, rather than according to those that are imposed through aid or debt conditionalties, should be enhanced to achieve social and political stability through transparent fiscal transfers to the deserving.

Fourth, corruption and rent-seeking that are associated with needed government interventions cannot be addressed simply by privatization or liberalization. The conventional critique of rent-seeking presumes that rents that are created by governmental interventions will be completely dissipated by rent-seeking behavior; thus, rent-seeking can only be wasteful. However, there is no theoretical or empirical support for this presumption, fatally undermining such a critique of rents due to government interventions. As Schumpeter acknowledged, rents constitute important incentives for innovative behavior, which are essential for economic progress. The major policy challenge then is to limit wasteful and unnecessary rent-seeking to maximize the gains from such behavior. State capacities should be strengthened to better motivate innovative and entrepreneurial behavior, while enforcing improved regulations to reduce associated rent-seeking.

While all corruption is damaging and undesirable, some types of corruption are much more damaging than others. Claiming to fight corruption in developing countries generally (by implementing a laundry list of desired governance reforms) sounds impressive and deserving of support, but such efforts ignore more feasible and targeted policies that can improve economic performance. As it is virtually impossible to address all types of corruption simultaneously, good policy should limit its focus to the types of corruption that are most damaging to development, such as corruption that results in the dissipating of investment resources. Reform priorities should respond to actual circumstances. Otherwise, anti-corruption and other governance reform efforts can adversely impact developing countries by setting unattainable targets, inadvertently causing disillusionment and reform fatigue.

Officials' Greed and Discretion

Predatory corruption occurs as a result of a central government's inability or unwillingness to prevent government officials from enriching themselves, even when such action threatens government revenue, stability, and survival.[8] Ironically, instead of strengthening state cohesion, capacity, and efficacy, some ostensible anti-corruption initiatives—such as decentralization and devolution—have instead exacerbated the problem, albeit inadvertently, by creating new opportunities for rent-seeking (for example, in the case of the Filipino and Indonesian provincial elections after Suharto).

Predation is widely considered the most important corruption challenge in developing countries; it involves government officials who use their discretionary powers to extort. Successful developing countries have been able to limit predation and extortion by limiting the ability of lower officials—or private looters in association with local officials—to abuse their discretionary powers. Where and when governments are threatened by public officials' predatory behavior, state enforcement capacities need to be strengthened and consolidated instead of having them simply eliminate developmental interventions.

The World Bank's corruption analysts and many anti-corruption advocates argue that corruption is largely due to the greed of bureaucrats or politicians who use their discretionary powers to confer personal benefits selectively or cause societal damage.[9] If the risk of detection and punishment is low, these officials are more likely to engage in this type of corruption. Although there are many varieties in such analyses of corruption contributions, Khan focuses on their similarities to describe collectively this approach as the "greed plus discretion" theory of corruption.[10]

If corruption in developing countries has been due to factors that are identified by the greed plus discretion approach, the adoption of anti-corruption measures that are associated with this approach should have significantly reduced corruption in many developing countries. However, conventional anti-corruption strategies and policies that are proposed by the greed plus discretion perspective have failed to reduce significantly corruption and sometimes, unwittingly, exacerbated the problem. Privatization should have eliminated public sector corruption; instead it created opportunities for a new type of corruption.

The main measures to address corruption that are associated with this analysis, as well as the actual outcomes from the implementation of such policies, have been summarized by Khan as follows:[11]

—reducing the discretionary powers of government officials through deregulation, privatization, and greater transparency as well as accountability. In fact, deregulation and privatization have often been accompanied by increased corruption.[12]

—improving government officials' authorized remuneration, thus raising the opportunity cost of corruption as officials risk losing these positions and incomes if found to be corrupt. Higher remuneration for state officials alone is unlikely to deter corruption unless the likelihood of punishment is also greater.

—improving the rule of law to ensure that corrupt bureaucrats and politicians will be prosecuted and punished. While the rule of law has improved in many developing countries, actual experience raises grave doubts as to whether this progress has either reduced corruption or enhanced development.

—encouraging greater transparency and civil society scrutiny of government and public affairs to enhance accountability. While setting up new institutions to enhance checks and balances, with improved transparency and accountability, attracts foreign support, these institutions have had little effect where governance is poor.[13]

—promoting democratization, devolution, and decentralization. However, there is no evidence that corruption is lower in democracies or strongly related to decentralization in developing countries.[14]

The failure of policies that have been inspired by this greed plus discretion explanation of corruption has encouraged greater attention to other types of—and explanations for—corruption in developing countries. Three other types of corruption in developing countries point to alternate causes that are not usually adequately addressed by conventional anti-corruption policies.

Government Interventions

The conventional wisdom presumes that all discretionary government interventions are undesirable, ostensibly because such interventions generate opportunities for public officials to participate in corruption. If government interventions benefit some more than others, or even benefit some at the expense of others, the inevitable rent-seeking that will occur needs to be managed to maximize these interventions' socially desirable outcomes.[15] Investment incentives are a good example of selective governmental interventions to accelerate economic development. The "losers" may need to be compensated to reduce resentment about incentives and other "privileges" that are offered to potential investors.

Governments in advanced countries play important roles in managing their economies, inevitably creating opportunities and incentives for extensive rent-seeking, much of which is not deemed illicit, as the interventions and rents are legal.[16] In advanced economies, rent-seeking is legally regulated (e.g., business lobbying within prescribed limits), whereas rent-seeking in developing countries is often unregulated, and thus, more likely to be deemed corrupt. Ironically, the blanket moralistic condemnation of rent-seeking has unwittingly served to cloud understanding of rent-seeking's nuances and how it can be appropriately regulated. Governmental interventions to help emerging big businesses in developing countries are typically not transparent; they are informal and lack wide political legitimacy.

If rent-seeking does not undermine the intended outcomes of an intervention, the resources used for rent-seeking constitute a social cost, but the net effect of the intervention can still be positive for development.[17] Developing countries can significantly reduce corruption by identifying needed governmental interventions and properly regulating such interventions, as well as related rent-seeking.[18]

For instance, industrial policy—or investment and technology policy—interventions are generally recognized as necessary for development. To minimize abuses during implementation, some governments have introduced "performance standards" to ensure that incentives are withdrawn from those who fail to meet these criteria.[19] The World Bank has acknowledged the critical contribution of "directed credit" or "financial restraint" in proactively financing industrial expansion in Northeast Asia.[20] Similarly, in Northeast

Asia, trade policy during its "catching up phase"—effective protection that was conditional on export promotion—disciplined industries, with firms enjoying trade protection, while being required to export increasing amounts of their output, and thus, more quickly becoming cost- and quality-competitive in international markets.

The possibility of corruption or abuse should not block such needed developmental government interventions, even if they are likely to involve some unavoidable rent-seeking. After all, rent-seeking remains the most significant incentive for "profit-maximizing" investor behavior (Keynes's "animal spirits"), as recognized by Schumpeter, as well as Porter's notion of "competitive advantage," which encourages firms to try to develop exclusive (monopolistic) access to rents.

Protecting Rights

In many developing countries, property claims, contractual rights, and other entitlements generally are weakly protected and often contested because of the limited governmental resources that are available for properly defining and protecting such rights. Conventional governance analysis assumes that the protection of these rights can be improved through governance reforms and reducing corruption. But establishing and maintaining property rights is expensive, and rich countries often only stabilize property rights after they achieve high levels of productivity.[21]

The protection of property rights has been estimated to account for half of all economic activity in some advanced economies. Transaction costs may vary with efficiency, but are far from negligible.[22] Developing countries are generally characterized by modest fiscal means, limiting their ability to protect property rights and reduce transaction costs. Not surprisingly, then, developing countries generally have much weaker and more contested property rights, compared to advanced countries. Consequently, non-market transfers are widespread and far more significant in developing countries compared to developed economies.[23] But again, these differences cannot only be attributed to the greed and discretion of public officials. Such non-market transfers include not only those involving bribery and corruption, but also other redistributive government interventions that are prone to abuse and corruption.

Although property rights seem to be insecure and the enforcement of contract laws leave much to be desired in many developing countries, the implications for economic performance can vary greatly. In most poorly performing developing countries, potential investors often face great uncertainty, and consequently investments tend to remain low.[24] But addressing this problem requires more than just curbing the greed and discretion of public officials. While insecure property rights and associated corruption affect most developing countries, fast-growing developing countries have often developed novel institutional capacities to provide credible commitments, ensuring reliable expectations in areas that are considered critical to potential investors. Such capacities include giving long-term supply contracts that encourage the contractor to invest so as to better supply his service.

For example, with the de-collectivization of agriculture in China from the late 1970s, the "household responsibility" system, as well as land leasing arrangements, provided flexible but nonetheless predictable expectations. These expectations induced significant investments in and effort toward farming, resulting in sustained increases in agricultural production for well over a decade. Similarly, the collective "township and village enterprise" (TVE) became the basis for significant non-agricultural growth and economic expansion, at least until the mid-1990s.

Securing Political Support and Clientelism

Limited fiscal resources constrain government capacities, especially in developing countries, with their much lower incomes and typically lower tax shares. But maintaining political stability requires sufficient fiscal resources for redistribution to secure political legitimacy and support. Most rich countries tax between a third and one half of their national income, whereas the rate in developing countries is typically less than a quarter of much smaller average incomes. In most developing countries, after civil servants are paid (in general, poorly), there is not much left for other basic services, let alone needed infrastructure. Developmental spending is often largely financed by domestic and external lending.

Political stability is difficult to maintain because the limited redistribution that is made possible through the budget cannot meet popular demands and expectations. Khan explains patron-client networks in developing countries as off-budget transfers—through such networks—in response to group demands for redistribution.[25] Often through inherently corrupt processes, political power and public resources are used to benefit particular clients to keep their political patrons in power. Thus, clientelism provides, to certain privileged client groups, what is not provided to all deserving groups. When these resources are not available through the budget, off-budget resources are likely raised through corrupt processes or through tolerating corruption by those so favored.

Khan emphasizes that while these processes are not desirable and developing countries may want to be rid of them, such corruption is not wholly due to the greed or discretion of public officials. Clearly, the chances of reducing this type of corruption are likely to remain limited until greater fiscal resources become available for redistribution. While clientelism and associated corruption are widespread in developing countries, the many varieties have different origins, often playing different roles and functions, especially in the co-optation and management of popular expectations.[26]

The tendency for reformist governments to succumb quickly to corruption suggests that transparency and accountability reforms, on their own, cannot resolve the problem. The larger issues, as well as fiscal constraints, must be addressed. Clientelist politicians win elections, even if their corruption is well-known, because they deliver, even if the delivery is biased. Appropriate governance reforms are context-specific, and unlikely to be aided by ambitious anti-corruption strategies, which are hard to implement and rarely successful.

Conclusion

No one disputes that good governance is desirable, but the issues that are raised above put forth three key concerns:

—how the desirable goals of good governance agendas have been presented as necessary preconditions for development;

—whether the good governance agenda can be successfully implemented and its goals fully achieved in a developing country, without first accelerating the country's economic development;

—whether pursuing the good governance agenda distracts from more urgent and achievable reforms that will enhance economic development prospects and will, in turn, contribute to achieving good governance.

Anti-corruption efforts—inspired by the greed and discretion analysis of corruption—can only be effective if the analysis is relevant. Hence, if a governmental intervention is only intended to create or enhance opportunities for predation for government officials, whether politicians or bureaucrats, the conventional policy agenda—economic liberalization, improved remuneration of public officials, strengthening the rule of law, and enhancing transparency—should work. Such measures are likely to be effective for checking the discretionary powers of public officials that are due to such undesirable or unnecessary government interventions. However, if corruption is principally due to other factors, such reforms are unlikely to be effective in reducing corruption, even if they can be successfully implemented.

The preceding analysis suggests that the conventional anti-corruption agenda is unlikely to be successful in developing countries, as the imposition of governance conditionalities on developing countries has no sound analytical or empirical basis. Most governance and corruption indicators that are used are subjective and somewhat arbitrary. Progress on such measures has not enhanced the developmental prospects for developing countries.

Instead, critical developmental governance capacities need to be enhanced pragmatically in developing countries to accelerate economic development. Distinguishing among different causes, sources, and types of corruption can help inform the choice of feasible reform and anti-corruption priorities. Having a long laundry list of unachievable "feel good" governance goals as immediate reform priorities distracts from the more urgent task of carrying out critical developmental reforms for developing countries.

Notes

1. See Robert I. Rotberg and Rachel M. Gisselquist, *Strengthening African Governance: Ibrahim Index of African Governance, Results and Rankings, 2008* (Cambridge, MA, 2008).

2. Mushtaq H. Khan, "Governance, Economic Growth and Development since the 1960s," in José Antonio Ocampo, Jomo K. S., and Rob Vos (eds.), *Growth Divergences: Explaining Differences in Economic Performance* (London, 2007), 285–324.

3. Mushtaq H. Khan, "Governance and Anti-Corruption Reforms in Developing Countries: Policies, Evidence, and the Way Forward," *G-24 Discussion Paper Series* No. 42 (New York, 2006), 6, available at www.unctad.org/en/docs/gdsmdpbg2420064_en.pdf (accessed 16 April 2009).

4. Ibid., 6–7.

5. Ibid., 7.

6. World Bank, *The East Asian Miracle* (Washington, D.C., 1993), 27–78.

7. Khan, "Governance and Anti-Corruption Reforms," 11–12.

8. Mushtaq H. Khan, "The Efficiency Implications of Corruption," *Journal of International Development,* VIII (1996), 683–696.

9. See, for example, World Bank, *Bureaucrats in Business: The Economies and Politics of Government Ownership* (Washington, D.C., 1996).

10. Khan, "Governance and Anti-Corruption Reforms," 12–14.

11. Ibid., 13.

12. Barbara Harriss-White and Gordon White, "Corruption, Liberalization and Democracy," *Institute of Development Studies Bulletin,* XXVII (1996), 1–5.

13. Jeff Huther and Anwar Shah, "Anti-Corruption Policies and Programs: A Framework for Evaluation," *Operations Evaluation Department Policy Research Working Paper* No. 2501 (Washington, D.C., 2000), available at www-wds.worldbank.org/external/default/WDSContentServer/IW3P/IB/2001/01/06/000094946_00121906063771/Rendered/PDF/multi_page.pdf (accessed 16 April 2009).

14. Daniel Treisman, "The Causes of Corruption: A Cross National Study," *Journal of Public Economics,* LXXVI (2000), 399–457; Tugrul Gurgur and Anwar Shah, "Localization and Corruption: Panacea or a Pandora's Box," International Monetary Fund Conference on Fiscal Decentralization, Washington, D.C., 21 November 2000. While this chapter states that there is no evidence that corruption is lower in democracies, others disagree. However, the evidence for the case in Africa is equivocal and is not corroborated in other regions such as in Asia or Latin America.

15. Mushtaq H. Khan, "Rents, Efficiency, and Growth," in Mushtaq H. Khan and Jomo K.S. (eds.), *Rents, Rent-Seeking, and Economic Development—Theory and Evidence in Asia* (New York, 2000), 21–69.

16. Khan, "Governance and Anti-Corruption Reforms," 14.

17. Khan, "Rents, Efficiency, and Growth," 21–69.

18. Khan and Jomo K.S. (eds.), *Rents, Rent-Seeking, and Economic Development.*

19. Hasan Hasli and Jomo K.S., "Rent-Seeking and Industrial Policy in Malaysia," in Jomo K.S. (ed.), *Malaysian Industrial Policy* (Honolulu, 2007), 150–171.

20. World Bank, *The East Asian Miracle,* 86–90; Chin Kok Fay and Jomo K.S. "Financial Sector Rents in Malaysia," in Khan and Jomo K.S. (eds.), *Rents, Rent-Seeking and Economic Development,* 304–326.

21. Mushtaq H. Khan, "Corruption and Governance in Early Capitalism: World Bank Strategies and their Limitations," in Jonathan Pincus and Jeffrey Winters (eds.), *Reinventing the World Bank* (Ithaca, 2002), 164–184; Mushtaq H. Khan, "State Failure in Developing Countries and Strategies of Institutional Reform," in Bertil Tungodden, Nicholas Stern, and Ivar Kolstad (eds.), *Toward Pro-Poor Policies: Aid Institutions and Globalization: Proceedings of 2003 Annual World Bank Conference on Development Economics Europe* (Washington, D.C., 2004), 165–195, available at www-wds.world bank.org/servlet/WDS_IBank_Servlet?pcont=details&eid=000160016_200405181628 41 (accessed 21 August 2008); Mushtaq H. Khan, "Determinants of Corruption in Developing Countries: The Limits of Conventional Economic Analysis," in Susan Rose-Ackerman (ed.), *International Handbook on the Economics of Corruption* (Northampton, 2006), 216–244.

22. Douglass C. North, *Institutions, Institutional Change and Economic Performance* (Cambridge, MA, 1990); Douglass C. North and John J. Wallis, "Measuring the Transaction Sector in the American Economy 1870–1970," in Stanley L. Engerman and Robert E. Gallman (eds.), *Long-Term Factors in American Economic Growth* (Chicago, 1992), 95–161.

23. Khan, "Governance and Anti-Corruption Reforms," 18.

24. Khan, "State Failure."

25. Mushtaq H. Khan, "Markets, States and Democracy: Patron-Client Networks and the Case for Democracy in Developing Countries," *Democratization,* XII (2005), 705–725; Khan, "Determinants of Corruption," 216–244.

26. Mushtaq H. Khan, "Patron-Client Networks and the Economic Effects of Corruption in Asia," *European Journal of Development Research,* X (1998), 15–39; Khan, "Rents, Efficiency, and Growth," 21–69; Khan, "Determinants of Corruption," 216–244.

Contributors

Matthew Bunn is an Associate Professor at Harvard University's John F. Kennedy School of Government. His research interests include nuclear theft and terrorism; nuclear proliferation and measures to control it; and the future of nuclear energy and its fuel cycle. Before coming to Harvard, Bunn served as an adviser to the White House Office of Science and Technology Policy, as a study director at the National Academy of Sciences, and as editor of *Arms Control Today*. He is the author or co-author of more than a dozen books or major technical reports, and over a hundred articles in publications ranging from *Science* to the *Washington Post*. He is an elected Fellow of the American Association for the Advancement of Science; a recipient of the American Physical Society's Joseph A. Burton Forum Award for "outstanding contributions in helping to formulate policies to decrease the risks of theft of nuclear weapons and nuclear materials"; and the recipient of the Hans A. Bethe Award from the Federation of American Scientists for "science in service to a more secure world."

Erica Chenoweth is Assistant Professor of Government and Director of the Program on Terrorism and Insurgency Research at Wesleyan University. She is also an associate at the Belfer Center for Science and International Affairs at Harvard University and a visiting fellow at the Institute of International Studies at the University of California at Berkeley. Chenoweth's main research interests are political violence, nonviolent and violent protest, the consequences of democratization, and repression. She is co-lead investigator (with Laura Dugan) for the National Consortium for the Study of Terrorism and Responses to Terrorism (START), a Department of Homeland Security Center of Excellence at the University of Maryland. Her project for START, entitled "Dealing with the Devil: When Bargaining with Terrorists Works," assesses the efficacy of different counterterrorism policies in the Middle East since 1980. Before coming to Wesleyan, Chenoweth taught at the University of Colorado and Harvard University.

Sarah Dix is Research Adviser to the Government of Papua New Guinea (PNG), in the Political and Legal Studies Division of the National Research Institute. She was previously Lecturer on Social Studies at Harvard University, and has worked in Latin America and Africa as a consultant and senior manager for the International Rescue Committee, the United Nations Development Programme, and the Organization of American States. She has published articles on corruption, refugee issues, and peace-building. In 2009, in PNG she is advising on the development of a national anti-corruption policy, a national survey on governance, and research on the costs of corruption.

Peter Eigen has worked on economic development for twenty-five years, mainly as a World Bank manager of programs in Africa and Latin America. From 1988 to 1991, he was the Director of the Regional Mission for Eastern Africa of the World Bank. Under Ford Foundation sponsorship, he provided legal and technical assistance to the governments of Botswana and Namibia. In 1993, Eigen founded Transparency International (TI), a non-governmental organization promoting transparency and accountability in international development. In 2005, Eigen chaired the International Advisory Group of the Extractive Industries Transparency Initiative (EITI) and became Chair of EITI in 2006. Eigen has lectured at the universities of Georgetown and Frankfurt and from 1999 to 2001 was a faculty member of Harvard's John F. Kennedy School of Government. In 2001, Eigen joined the Carnegie Endowment for International Peace as a Visiting Scholar while teaching at Johns Hopkins University's School of Advanced International Studies. He became a member of the board of the Centre for International Environmental Law (CIEL) and since 2002 has been teaching as an Honorary Professor of Political Science of the Freie Universität in Berlin. In 2004, he received the Readers Digest Award "European of the Year 2004." Since 2007 Eigen has been a member of Kofi Annan's Africa Progress Panel.

Kelly M. Greenhill is Assistant Professor of Political Science at Tufts University and Research Fellow at the Harvard Kennedy School's Program on Intrastate Conflict. She was previously Assistant Professor of Government at Wesleyan University, a pre- and post-doctoral Fellow and Visiting Assistant Professor at Stanford University's Center for Security and Cooperation, and pre-doctoral Research Fellow at Harvard University's Olin Institute for Strategic Studies. Her current projects examine nontraditional methods of coercion; counterinsurgency; international criminal networks; and the differential effects of visual versus verbal imagery on public opinion formation and change. Her first book manuscript, which focuses on the use of forced migration as a military and political weapon, is forthcoming. Her work has appeared in a variety of venues, including *International Security, Security Studies, Civil Wars,* and *International Migration.*

Charles Griffin joined the World Bank in 1992 as a Senior Economist in Human Development for Eastern Africa, where he worked for five years. From 1997 to 2001, he managed first the Social Protection group, then the Health group in the Latin America and Caribbean Region. In 2002, he became Director for Human Development in the South Asia Region. In 2004, he transferred to the same position in the Europe and Central Asia Region. Griffin took a leave of absence from the bank in 2006 to join the Brookings Institution as a Senior Fellow. Previously, Griffin was an Associate Professor of Economics at the University of Oregon, a Senior Research Associate at the Urban Institute, and Research Director for the USAID-supported Health Financing and Sustainability Project. His operational and research experience has been in public finance and service delivery related to health, education, pensions, social welfare, and water supply. In 2009, Griffin returned to the World Bank as a Senior Adviser.

Ben W. Heineman, Jr. was General Electric's Senior Vice President–General Counsel from 1987 to 2003, and Senior Vice President for Law and Public Affairs from 2004 until his retirement at the end of 2005. He is a Senior Fellow at the Belfer Center for Science and International Affairs at Harvard's Kennedy School of Government, Distinguished Senior Fellow at Harvard Law School's Program on the Legal Profession, and Senior Counsel to the law firm of Wilmer Hale. He was the editor-in-chief of the *Yale Law Journal,* and law clerk to Supreme Court Justice Potter Stewart. Heineman was Assistant Secretary for Policy at the Department of Health, Education and Welfare and practiced constitutional law prior to his service at GE. He is a Fellow of the American Academy of Arts and Sciences. His most recent book, *High Performance with High Integrity,* appeared in 2008. In 2007, he served on the Independent Review Panel on the World Bank Group's Department of Institutional Integrity (the Volcker Panel) and is a member of a World Bank Group expert advisory panel appointed by the bank to assess its governance and anti-corruption strategies.

Nathaniel Heller is Managing Director of Global Integrity. In 1999, he joined the Center for Public Integrity and began, along with Marianne Camerer and Charles Lewis, to develop the Integrity Indicators and conceptual model for what would become Global Integrity. At the center, Heller reported on public service and government accountability. His reporting on the human rights impact of post-9/11 U.S. military training abroad won awards from both Investigative Reporters and Editors and the Society for Professional Journalists. In 2002, he joined the State Department, focusing on European security and transatlantic relations. He later served as a foreign policy fellow to Senator Edward Kennedy. In 2005, Heller returned to Global Integrity.

Jomo Kwame Sundaram (Jomo K.S.) has been Assistant Secretary General for Economic Development in the United Nations Department of Economic and Social Affairs (DESA) since 2005, adviser to the president of the 63rd United Nations General Assembly, and member of the [United Nations General Assembly or Stiglitz] Commission of Experts on Reforms of the International Monetary and Financial System. He was Professor in the Applied Economics Department, University of Malaya, Kuala Lumpur, until 2004. Jomo has authored over thirty-five monographs and edited over fifty books including *Rents, Rent-Seeking and Economic Development* (with Mushtaq Khan) (2000). In 2007, he was awarded the Wassily Leontief Prize for Advancing the Frontiers of Economic Thought.

Lucy Koechlin is a Lecturer in Development Studies at the Institute of Sociology and the Centre for African Studies, University of Basel, and was, until recently, responsible for Development Policy and Research at the Basel Institute on Governance. Her major research interests include political order, civil society, poverty, and governance and corruption, with a geographical focus on sub-Saharan Africa.

Johann Graf Lambsdorff holds a chair position in economic theory at the University of Passau, Germany, and is a research consultant to Transparency International. He created the Corruption Perceptions Index, which he has been overseeing since 1995. He has published extensively on corruption and anti-corruption in leading international journals such as *Public Choice, Economics of Governance, Kyklos, Journal of Economic Behavior and Organization,* and the *Journal of International Economics.*

Robert Legvold is the Marshall Shulman Professor Emeritus of Political Science at Columbia University. He is Project Director for "Rethinking U.S. Policy toward Russia" at the American Academy of Arts and Sciences. Legvold specializes in the foreign policy of the Soviet Union and the post-Soviet states. His primary interests include the international relations of the post-Soviet region and their impact on the international politics of East Asia and Western Europe. From 1978 to 1984, he was Director of Soviet Studies at the Council on Foreign Relations and from 1984 to 1993 the Associate Director, then the Director, of the Harriman Institute. He is a Fellow of the American Academy of Arts and Sciences. His most recent books are *Russian Foreign Policy in the 21st Century and the Shadow of the Past* (2007); with Bruno Coppieters, *Statehood and Security: Georgia after the Rose Revolution* (2005); with Celeste Wallander, *Swords and Sustenance: The Economics of National Security in Belarus and Ukraine* (2004); and *Thinking Strategically: The Major Powers, Kazakhstan and the Central Asian Nexus* (2002).

Emmanuel Pok is Researcher in the Political and Legal Studies Division of the National Research Institute (NRI), Papua New Guinea. He has published articles in Papua New Guinea on electoral politics, provincial autonomy, and public policy. He has served as a domestic electoral observer.

Susan Rose-Ackerman is the Henry R. Luce Professor of Jurisprudence (Law and Political Science) and Co-director of the Yale Law School's Center for Law, Economics, and Public Policy. She was a Visiting Research Fellow at the World Bank and a Fellow at the Center for Advanced Study in the Behavioral Sciences. She has written widely on corruption, administrative law, and law and economics. Her most recent books are *Corruption and Government: Causes, Consequences and Reform* (1999), which was translated into fifteen languages; *From Elections to Democracy: Building Accountable Government in Hungary and Poland* (2005); and *Controlling Environmental Policy: The Limits of Public Law in Germany and the United States* (1995).

Robert I. Rotberg is Director, Program on Intrastate Conflict and Conflict Resolution, Belfer Center for Science and International Affairs at the Harvard Kennedy School of Government, and President, World Peace Foundation. He was Professor of Political Science and History at MIT; Academic Vice President of Tufts University; and President of Lafayette College. He is a Fellow of the American Academy of Arts and Sciences. He is the author and editor of numerous books and articles on U.S. foreign policy, Africa, Asia, and the Caribbean, most recently *China into Africa: Trade, Aid, and Influence* (2008); *Worst of the Worst: Dealing with Repressive and Rogue Nations* (2007); *Building a New Afghanistan* (2006); *A Leadership for Peace: How Edwin Ginn Tried* *to Change the World* (2006); *Battling Terrorism in the Horn of Africa* (2005); *When States Fail: Causes and Consequences* (2004); *State Failure and State Weakness in a Time of Terror* (2003); *Ending Autocracy, Enabling Democracy: The Tribulations of Southern Africa 1960–2000* (2002); and *Truth v. Justice: The Morality of Truth Commissions* (2000).

Magdalena Sepúlveda Carmona is the United Nations Independent Expert on the Question of Human Rights and Extreme Poverty. Sepulveda is a Chilean lawyer and is currently working as Research Director at the International Council on Human Rights Policy (Geneva). She lectures at several universities in Latin America and has provided technical assistance and training on human rights to NGOs, IGOs, and governments. Sepulveda has worked as a researcher at the Netherlands Institute for Human Rights, as a staff attorney at the Inter-American Court of Human Rights, and as the Co-Director of the Department of International Law and Human Rights of the United Nations–affiliated University for Peace in San Jose, Costa Rica. She also served as a consultant to the Department of International Protection of UNHCR and to the Norwegian Refugee Council in Colombia.

Daniel Jordan Smith is Associate Professor of Anthropology and Associate Director of the Population Studies and Training Center at Brown University. He has worked in Nigeria since 1989 and published on a range of topics in journals such as *Africa, American Anthropologist, American Ethnologist, American Journal of Public Health, Canadian Journal of African Studies, Cultural Anthropology, Politique Africaine, Population and Development Review,* and *World Development.* His recent book, *A Culture of Corruption: Everyday Deception and Popular Discontent in Nigeria* (2007), won the 2008 Margaret Mead Award.

Rotimi T. Suberu teaches political science and international relations at Bennington College. Earlier he taught political science at the University of Ibadan. Suberu has served as a consultant to the Nigerian government, to the EU delegation to Abuja, as well as to Washington, D.C.'s National Democratic Institute and National Endowment for Democracy. He has won fellowships and visiting positions from University of Oxford, the Woodrow Wilson International Center for Scholars, the University of Pennsylvania, Northwestern University, New Delhi's Center for the Study of Developing Societies, and from the U.S. Institute of Peace.

Jessica C. Teets is an Assistant Professor in the Political Science department at Middlebury College. Her main research interests are governance in non-democracies, the role of civil society in China and other non-democracies, and the ability of social networks to transmit information in non-transparent environments. She has published in the *China Quarterly* and the *Journal of Chinese Political Science.*

Laura Underkuffler is J. DuPratt White Professor of Law at Cornell University Law School. Previously, she was Arthur Larson Distinguished Professor at Duke Law School. She has also taught at Harvard University, the University of Pennsylvania, Georgetown University, and the University of Maine. She received the Faculty Scholarship Award at Duke in 2003 for her book *The Idea of Property: Its Meaning and Power* (2003). She has published widely in the United States and abroad in the fields of property theory, constitutional law, and the role of moral decision making in law. She has also been involved in international projects concerning property rights and regime change, and the problem of corruption and democratic governance. Underkuffler practiced litigation law for six years, and headed the appellate department of a large Minneapolis law firm. She was appointed to the Advisory Committee for the Eighth Circuit Court of Appeals on which she served for several years. She also served as special counsel in the U.S. Senate and has been a Fellow at the Woodrow Wilson International Center for Scholars.

Index

Abacha, Sani, 265, 293, 342, 355

Abdul Qadeer Khan Network: disruption of, 150, 151; financing for, 135; and nuclear proliferation, 124, 126–28, 138, 139, 142–43, 156; Pakistani protection of, 136. *See also* Khan, Abdul Qadeer

Abkhazia, criminal state of, 12

Abramoff, Jack, 38

Abubakar, Atiku, 265, 272

Academic literature on corruption, 30, 50, 167–68, 171, 207

ACB. *See* Anti-Corruption Bureau

Accountability mechanisms: antidote to corruption proliferation, 19; causing corruption, 7, 14, 312–13; in corporations, 21; effectiveness of, 343; in Guatemala, 72, 76; in Kosovo, 84; in Mozambique, 79; in Nigeria, 16; second-generation corruption estimator, 6, 52

Achebe, Chinua, 286, 292–93

Adamov, Evgeniy, 137

Adedibu, Lamidi, 272

Advanced Spectroscopic Portals, 151

Afghanistan: corrupt public officials in, 100; illicit trading by, 211; narco-terrorism in, 175; Reconstruction Trust Fund of, 88; response to corruption in, 356; and Taliban, 11, 12; weapons in, 173

Afolabi, Sunday, 265

Africa: Afrobarometer Survey for, 58; bribery in, 418; EITI candidate countries in, 426; governance assessment of, 59, 60, 317; illicit activities in, 8–9; lack of multiplier effect in, 6; management of public funds in, 444–45, 446; natural resources corruption in, 423–24; origins of corruption and bribery in, 342, 346; public reactions to corruption in, 284, 286; systemic corruption in, 13, 283, 354; transnational criminal organizations in, 111. *See also specific countries*

African Commission on Human and People's Rights, 327, 329

African Development Bank, 425, 426

African Peer Review Mechanism, 59, 60, 317

Agreement on Trade-Related Aspects of Intellectual Property Rights (TRIPS), 226–27

Air Force (Israel), 364

Air Force (U.S.), 144

Akwanga, Hussaini, 265

Alamieyeseigha, Diepreye, 267

Albania and organized crime groups, 108

Alcatel, 371

Allum, Felia, 105

Al Qaeda: financing for, 174; procurement of nuclear materials, 10, 129–30, 133, 156

Alstom, prosecution of, 371

Aluko, Jones, 269

Andreyev, Andrej, 136

Anechiarico, Frank, 393

Angola: compared to Mozambique, 79; corruption and lack of transparency in, 74–76, 86–87; Index of African Governance rating of, 74; post-conflict corruption in, 68–71; and Publish What You Pay, 424; transnational criminal organizations exploitation of, 106

Anti-Corruption Bureau (ACB, Malawi), 321, 323

Anti-corruption efforts, 416–28, 457–67; accountability systems for, 19, 314; Atlantic Council recommendations for, 219; bottom-up strategies for, 22, 326; comprehensive strategy for, 409–10; and contract penalties, 406–07, 409; and corporate debarment, 403–04, 406, 407; by corporations, 21, 22, 368–69; in developing countries, 360–61, 375, 466–67; failure of, 417–18; good governance best practices for, 458–59; for governments, 22; and human rights, 18–19, 310–11, 315, 325–31; and integrity, 393–94, 420–23; international solutions for, 188–89; legal framework for, 241–45, 390–91; measurements of, 47; mobilization of, 418–20; and natural resource wealth, 423–28; and nullification of corrupt contracts, 404–05, 406; plague of corruption upon, 417–18; of political leaders, 342, 343, 356; in post-conflict situations, 7–8; in post–Soviet Union countries, 218–25, 228–29; and poverty reduction, 418; problems with, 442–43; for proliferation-related corruption, 142–56; recommendations for, 24–25, 39–40, 63, 88–89, 141–55, 225–30, 442, 452; standards for, 312, 314; success of, 20; and sustained economic growth, 460; top-down efforts of, 354, 392, 396, 397, 399–400, 409; zero tolerance approach to, 400. *See also* Multi-national corporations; *specific countries*

Anti-corruption incentives, 389–410; bottom-up, 398–400, 405, 407–10; contract penalties of, 406–07; debarment of, 403–04; leniency for corrupt actions, 400–03, 409; limiting leaders, 397–98; nullification of, 404–05; policy implications of, 409–10; principles-based, 393–96; rules-based, 389–93; top-down strategies for, 354, 393–96, 399–400, 401, 409–10; whistle-blowing of, 407–08

Anti-Corruption Network, 221–22

Aondoakaa, Michael, 272–73

Apter, Andrew, 301–02

A.Q. Khan Research Laboratories, 127. *See also* Abdul Qadeer Khan Network

Argentina, Transparency International chapter in, 423

Aristotle, 37

Armenia: corruption in, 199; criminalized state of, 12, 229; Global Integrity Index rating of, 198; MONEYVAL member, 227

Arusha Accords, Burundian, 80

Asia: bribery in, 418; corruption in, 6, 13, 222; EITI candidate countries in, 426. *See also specific countries*
Asian Development Bank, 375
AsiaWeek on Taiwan triads, 104
Aspen Institute, 419
Atlantic Council, 200
Audit Act of 1989 (Papua New Guinea), 241, 244
Aum Shinrikyo, 129–30, 156
A User's Guide to Measuring Corruption (Global Integrity), 60
Ayoola, Emmanuel, 264–65
Azerbaijan: criminal state of, 12, 196, 229; MONEYVAL member, 227

Babangida, Ibrahim, 303
Baden, John, 28
Baker Hughes (company), 371
Balkans, organized crime in, 106–07
Balogun, Tafa, 267
Banca Nazionale de Lavoro, Italian, 135
Bangladesh: illicit trade profits of, 211; school stipend program in, 449–50; Transparency International chapter in, 423
Bank financing of corrupt activities, 135
Bashir, Omar, 355
Bayart, Jean-Francois, 287, 289
Beg, Aslam, 128
Belarus: anti-corruption efforts in, 223; as Eurasia Group member, 227–28
Benson, Bruce, 28
Betrayal as corruption, 31–32, 36, 38
Bhutto, Zulfiqar Ali, 126
Big men (Papua New Guinea), 246–48, 249, 255, 297
Bin Laden family, 174
Blair, Tony, 372, 426
Blundo, Giorgio, 291, 292
Border patrol officials, corruption of, 135–36, 211

Bosnia-Herzegovina, organized crime in, 106, 114
Botswana: anti-corruption efforts in, 345–46, 351–55; as EITI implementor, 426; strong economy of, 424
Bout, Viktor, 213
BPI. *See* Bribe Payers Index
Brasz, H. A., 31
Brazil: EITI outreach efforts in, 427; public financial management of, 444, 445
Breach of duty as corruption, 30–31, 36, 38
Brezhnev, Leonid, 204
Bribe Payers Index (BPI), 23, 109, 422
Bribery: causes of, 201–02; commonality of, 419; consequences of, 417; and contract penalties, 406–07; in corporations, 366–67; as corruption, 28, 32; as a crime, 370; facilitator for trafficking, 173; in Malawi, 318; in Nigeria, 291; and nullification, 405; preventing, 263, 375. *See also* Corruption
Britain: and Balkan organized crime, 106–07; corporate fraud detection in, 395–96; investigation of British Aerospace Systems, 372, 395; lack of corruption in, 141; literature on corruption, 37; OECD convention enforcement in, 371, 372
Brooke, James, 40
Buhari, Salisu, 266
Bulgaria, arms sales in, 214
Bunn, Matthew, 3, 4, 10–11, 124, 141, 142, 148–49, 186, 227
Burlakov, Matvei, 215
Burma, corruption in, 188, 342, 344, 356
Burundi: anti-corruption efforts of, 82; corruption and poverty in, 80–82, 87, 88; education costs in, 433; post-conflict corruption in, 68–71

Business Environment and Enterprise Performance Survey, 53, 198
Business International, 177

Cambodia: corruption in, 345; response to corruption in, 356
Canadian judiciary system, 390
Cancer of corruption theory, 47, 421
CCB. *See* Code of Conduct Bureau
CCT. *See* Code of Conduct Tribunal
Ceku, Agim, 84
Central America, illicit weapons in, 173. *See also specific countries*
Central Asia: anti-corruption efforts in, 223; failure to fulfill Program of Action controls, 226; heroin use and HIV/AIDS in, 212. *See also specific countries*
CFAAs. *See* Country Financial Accountability Assessments
Chad, corruption and conflict in, 417–18
Chàvez, Hugo, 40
Chechnya, organized crime in, 186
Chenoweth, Erica, 3, 11, 167
Chile, public financial management in, 444, 445
Chiluba, Frederick, 343–44
Chiluba, Regina, 344
China: anti-corruption laws of, 380; EITI outreach efforts in, 427; Eurasia Group member, 227–28; fulfilling Program of Action controls, 226; and General Electric, 379; health care funding in, 451; heroin use and HIV/AIDS in, 212; household responsibility system of, 465; illicit trading by, 210–11; transnational criminal organizations in, 107
Civil society organizations (CSOs): anti-corruption methods of, 252–54, 271, 397, 398; cooperation

with Transparency International, 422, 423; global governance role of, 416–17, 428; and natural resources, 424; in Nigeria, 275, 277–78; oversight and accountability role of, 420; preventing small arms proliferation, 226
Code of Conduct Bureau (CCB, Nigeria), 260, 262, 263, 268, 270, 274, 276
Code of Conduct Tribunal (CCT, Nigeria), 260, 262, 263, 274
Colombia: corruption in, 100, 167, 185–87; drug trafficking in, 11, 104–05; mafia's relationship with Russia, 108; narco-terrorism in, 175, 185–87; and organized crime, 107, 114; public financial management in, 444; relationships with Sicilian and Nigerian mafias, 108. *See also* Revolutionary Armed Forces of Columbia (FARC)
Complex interdependence, 101–02
Congo. *See* Democratic Republic of the Congo
Contact (money-transfer business), 216
Control Risks Group, 395
Convention on Physical Protection of Nuclear Material, 153, 154
Convention on the Rights of the Child, 316, 326
Corporations: anti-corruption practices of, 21–22, 368–69; bribery in, 366–67; fraud detection in, 395–96; publication of revenues, 424–25. *See also* Multi-national corporations
Correlates of War National Capabilities Index, 178
Corruption: consequences of, 6, 35, 38–39, 360, 417; defined, 27–42; definitional paradigms of, 5–8; definition of, 359; definitions of, 290,

315; and human rights, 18–19, 310–11, 325–31, 417; and leadership, 341–56; measurement of, 47–64; as moral concept, 5, 30–31, 37–41, 42; patron-clientism form of, 287–90, 296–99; in post-conflict situations, 7–8, 66–89; risk factors for, 66–68; and terrorism, 11, 167–76, 178–85, 186–89

Corruption Barometer, 422

Corruption Perceptions Index (CPI): as anti-corruption tool, 23, 57; beginning of, 422; criticism of, 52; goals of, 51; measurements of, 57, 177; most corrupt countries of, 343; rankings of, 5, 22, 109, 167, 318, 392; and terrorism, 178–79, 180; unreliability of, 5; World Map of, 324. *See also* Transparency International

Cosa Nostra, 102–03

Costa Rica, public financial management in, 444

Council of Europe: Criminal Law Convention on Corruption, 223, 224, 310; Groupe d'Etats contre la corruption (GRECO), 220, 221–22

Country Financial Accountability Assessments (CFAAs, World Bank), 443, 445, 446

Country Policy and Institutional Assessment, 198

Country Procurement Assessment Reviews (CPARs, World Bank), 443–44, 446

CPARs. *See* Country Procurement Assessment Reviews

CPI. *See* Corruption Perceptions Index

Crenshaw, Martha, 170

Criminalized states: corruption in, 207, 217–18, 224; examples of, 12–13, 196, 197; and nuclear materials, 209; in post-Soviet countries, 202; and

transnational crime organizations, 100; weakening, 218, 225, 229

CSOs. *See* Civil society organizations

Customs officials, corruption of, 135–36, 214, 267

Dariye, Joshua, 267, 268

Defense Department (U.S.), 137, 144, 150–51, 403

Democratic Republic of the Congo: corruption and conflict in, 417–18; natural resources corruption in, 423–24; transnational criminal organizations exploitation of, 106

Denmark, corruption ranking of, 345

Department for International Development (U.K.), 63, 320, 375, 425

De Sardan, Olivier, 286, 288, 291, 292

Deutsche Bahn AG, 406

Developing countries: anti-corruption efforts in, 360–61, 375–76, 378–81, 462, 466–67; causes of corruption in, 460–66; corruption in, 341, 360, 461–62; corrupt leaders of, 355; good governance indicators for, 458; judiciary systems of, 390; multinational corporations assistance for, 378–81; political instability and clientelism in, 465–66; property rights in, 464

Dhlakama, Afonso, 77

Dickens, Charles, 2

Dirty bombs, 140, 151

Dix, Sarah, 3, 14–15, 239

Doing Business 2008 (World Bank), 220

Domestic national conflicts, 66–89; corrupt opportunities of, 66–68; and post-conflict corruption, 68–85; reform proposals for, 85–89

Dominican Republic, management of public funds, 444

Drogoul, Christopher, 135

Drugs: extradition of dealers, 115; heroin use, 211–12; methamphetamine trafficking, 173; and narco-terrorism, 175, 185–87; trafficking in, 11, 104–05, 173
Dubro, Alec, 104

Ease of Doing Business Index, 109
Eastern Europe, bribery in, 418. *See also specific countries*
East Timor, response to corruption in, 356
Economic and Financial Crimes Commission (Nigeria): anti-corruption efforts of, 260, 272; charging officials with corruption, 266–67, 268, 273; policies of, 270–71; political scrutiny of, 264
Economic development, 457–67
Economic Intelligence Unit's Index on Democracy, 56
Economist: on anti-corruption coalition, 427; on Rwandan anti-corruption efforts, 354
Education, 430–54; accountability problems of, 449; in Bangladesh, 449–50; corruption reduction in, 452–54; critical issues for, 446; design and incentives for anti-corruption in, 447–51; in El Salvador, 447–48, 449; expenditures for, 430, 431–43; in New Zealand, 448–49; and public financial management improvement, 443–47; recommendations for, 430–31; solving principal-agent problem of, 450–51
Egwuba, Emmanuel, 270
Eigen, Peter, 3, 22–23, 416, 418, 425
EITI. *See* Extractive Industries Transparency Initiative
Ekeh, Peter, 284
Eliot, George, 2

El Salvador: EDUCO program of, 447–48, 449; health and education anti-corruption efforts in, 24
Enelpower, prosecution of, 371
Energy Department (U.S.), 137, 147
Enron, 394
Environmental Law Centre, 254
Enwerem, Evans, 266
Equatorial Guinea, 2
Eritrea, education costs in, 433
Ernst and Young, 401
Ethical Investment Research Services, 394
Etteh, Patricia, 266
Eurasia Group, 227–28
European Bank for Reconstruction and Development, 53, 196, 200, 375
Europe and European Union: on Balkan organized crime threats, 106–07; bribery in, 227; community-oriented business ethics in, 396; corruption in, 141–42; debarment requirements in, 403; export control systems of, 145; and Iraq supplier corruption, 130; Kosovo influence of, 83; Nigeria anti-corruption aid from, 274; peace building efforts of, 71; post-Soviet anti-corruption aid from, 225, 229; as Russian and Chinese illicit trade market, 210. *See also specific countries*
Executive Opinion Survey, 198
Export control programs, 147, 226
Extortion, 32
Extractive Industries Transparency Initiative (EITI): anti-corruption efforts of, 23; challenges of, 427–28; Global Conference of, 425; initial work of, 425–28; sector-specific measurement of corruption, 62, 76; support and endorsement for, 426
Exxon-Mobil, 359, 426

FARC. *See* Revolutionary Armed Forces of Columbia

Fatah, 167

FATF (Financial Action Task Force), 227–28, 264

Fawehinmi, Gani, 276

Fayose, Peter, 267, 268

Federal Bureau of Investigation (FBI, U.S.), 106–07

Feld, Lars P., 390

Felix Holt, The Radical (G. Eliot), 2

Financial Action Task Force (FATF), 227–28, 264

Financing of corrupt activities, 135

Finland: corruption ranking of, 345; strong judiciary of, 390

Foreign Corrupt Practices Act of 1977 (U.S.), 370, 394, 419

Foreign Intelligence Service (Russian), 214

France: corporate fraud detection in, 395–96; corrupt politicians of, 1–2; literature on corruption, 37; and OECD convention, 371, 373–74, 421

Frank, Björn, 399

Freedom House's Freedom in the World survey, 56

French Declaration of the Rights of Man and of the Citizen, 310

Fuerzas Armadas Revolucionarias de Colombia. *See* Revolutionary Armed Forces of Columbia (FARC)

Fujimori, Alberto, 103

Gaddy, Clifford, 209

Gallup International Survey, 177

Gaps in Basic Workers' Rights (International Labour Association), 56

Gates, Robert, 144

Geiges, Daniel, 126

General Electric (GE): aiding Chinese anti-corruption efforts, 379; anti-bribery policies of, 366–67, 369; anti-corruption principles of, 363–64; conditions for third parties, 365–66; corrupt dealings with Israeli Air Force, 364; integrity policies of, 364, 365; ombudsmen program of, 367; policies for gifts, entertainment, travel, and living expenses of, 366

George Mason University. *See* POLITY IV country reports

Georgia: anti-corruption efforts in, 198, 220–22, 225; corruption and criminality in, 105, 199, 205; criminal and criminalized states of, 196, 229; MONEYVAL member, 227; National Anti-Corruption Strategy of, 220; Rose Revolution in, 199, 209, 220

Germany: Balkan organized crime expansion into, 106–07; corporate fraud detection in, 395–96; failure to ratify UNCAC, 421; lack of corruption in, 141; OECD convention enforcement in, 371–72, 373–74; Siemens investigation in, 371; signing of OECD Convention principles, 420; strong judiciary of, 390; whistleblower response in, 408

Ghana: education costs in, 432–33; health care funding in, 451

Glenny, Misha, 211

Global Economic Crime Survey, 395–96

Global Integrity: anti-corruption work of, 60–61, 390–92; corruption definition, 4; corruption measurement tools, 52–53; Global Integrity Index, 52, 56, 57, 198; Integrity Indicators of, 56; ranking Malawian corruption, 321; unintentional bias or inconsistency of, 58

Global Integrity Alliance, 63

Globalization as aid for corruption, 25
Global security, threat of, 11
Global Witness, 424, 426
Godson, Roy, 101
Goh Chok Tong, 348
Golden Crown (money-transfer business), 216
Goloskokov, Igor, 134
Gonzalez, Carlos Hank, 103
Governance, 457–67; in Africa, 288; best practices for, 458–59; corruption causes, 460–66; for expenditures, 446; failures of, 417–18; indicators for, 59; and leaders, 350; measurement tools for, 47, 52, 54–55. *See also* Anti-corruption efforts
Gowon, Yakubu, 262, 344
Grange, Adenike, 266
Great Britain. *See* Britain
Green, Penny, 100
Greenhill, Kelly, 3, 8, 12, 96, 186
Griffin, Charles, 4, 23–24, 430, 440–41, 446, 452
Griffin, Peter, 125, 126, 153
Guatemala: corruption and inequality in, 72–74, 86–88; post-conflict corruption in, 68–71; public cynicism in, 101; public financial management in, 444; Truth Commission of, 73
Guinea-Bissau, transnational criminal organizations exploitation of, 106

Halliburton, 265
Hamas: motivating terrorism, 171; support and success of, 167, 171; trafficking methamphetamine, 173
Handelman, Stephen, 102
Harkat-ul-Jihadal-Islami, 211
Harris, Robert, 115
Hayakawa, Kiyohide, 130
Health care corruption, 430–54; anti-corruption efforts, 24, 451, 452, 454; critical issues for, 447; expenditures

of, 430; and principal-agent problem, 451; and public financial management improvement, 443–47; recommendations for, 430–31
Heidenheimer, Arnold, 50–51
Heimann, Fritz, 372
Heineman, Ben W., Jr., 3–4, 21–22, 227, 359, 361, 363, 366, 372, 376, 380–81
Heller, Nathaniel, 3, 6, 47, 68, 71
Heroin use: in Russia, 211–12; as threat to international welfare, 212
HEU. *See* Highly enriched uranium
Heywood, Paul, 52
Hezbollah: illicit trading by, 213; public support for, 171; and terrorism, 171; trafficking methamphetamine, 173
Highly enriched uranium (HEU): conversion to LEU, 225; and corruption, 132–33; insider theft protections for, 146; and nuclear proliferation, 129, 143; and Pakistan, 127; smuggling of, 139, 209
High Performance with High Integrity (Heineman), 361
Hobbes, Thomas, 398
Honduras, public financial management in, 444
Hong Kong: preventing corruption in, 222, 223; transnational criminal organization regional ties in, 107
House of Representatives, U.S., 251
H+H Metalform GmbH, 131
Human behavior, 341–42
Human rights, 310–31; and anti-corruption efforts, 312–15, 327–29; and corruption, 18–19, 195, 310, 325–31, 417; in Malawi, 315–24; treaties of, 316, 326; within the UN Convention against Corruption, 313, 314; of vulnerable and disadvantaged, 328–29
Human Rights Council, 316
Human Rights Watch, 16, 260, 269–70

Hun Sen, 345
Huther, Jeff, 141
Hyden, Goran, 59

IAEA. *See* International Atomic Energy
Agency
Ibori, James, 267, 268, 273
IBRD (International Bank for Recon-
struction and Development), 377,
378
Igbinedion, Lucky, 267, 268
Illegality as corruption, 28–30, 34
Illicit trade: and corruption, 195, 213;
of humans, 210; and poverty, 217;
prevention of, 188–89, 226, 228–29;
and terrorism, 168–76, 177–78,
181–84; as threat to international
welfare and security, 211–13; of
wildlife derivatives, 210–11
IMF. *See* International Monetary Fund
Immelt, Jeff, 363
Incentives. *See* Anti-corruption
incentives
INDEM (Information Science for
Democracy), 200–01
Independent Corrupt Practices and
Other Related Offences Commission (ICPC, Nigeria), 260, 263–64,
268, 270, 272, 274
Index of African Governance, 16,
55–56, 57, 74, 318, 354
India: EITI outreach efforts in, 427;
health and education spending in,
433–34, 451; health sector corruption in, 435–41; and OECD Convention, 373
Individual rights: freedom of expression, 327; information, 327–28;
political participation, 328; property, 464. *See also* Human rights
Indonesia: corruption in, 103, 344–45;
EITI outreach efforts in, 427; health
care funding in, 451

Inequality as corruption, 32–33, 36
Information Science for Democracy
(INDEM), 200–01
Insider threats to security, 146
Inspectorate of Prisons (Malawi), 320
Institute for National Affairs, 253
"Integrity System Source Book" (Trans-
parency International), 422
Intelligence agencies, 150–51
Inter-American Development Bank, 53
International Atomic Energy Agency
(IAEA), 147, 152
International Bank for Reconstruction
and Development (IBRD), 377, 378
International Budget Partnership,
52–53, 58. *See also* Open Budget
Index
International Chamber of Commerce,
377, 421
International Convention for the Sup-
pression of Acts of Nuclear Terror-
ism, 153
International Council for Mining and
Metals, 426
International Covenant on Civil and
Political Rights, 316, 326
International Covenant on Economic,
Social, and Cultural Rights, 316,
326
International Development Associa-
tion, 377, 378
International Labour Association, 56
International Monetary Fund (IMF):
aiding Mozambique's democracy,
79–80; and Angola financial man-
agement systems, 75, 76; anti-
corruption efforts of, 421; and
Eurasia Group creation, 227;
technical expertise for EITI, 426
International organized crime. *See*
Organized crime
International Secretariat, 423
Invisible foot effect, 398, 409

Iran: as market for Abdul Qadeer Khan Network, 126, 127, 128; proliferation-related corruption of, 131, 132, 141, 156

Iraq: corrupt activities with Russia, 132, 135, 214; corruption and terrorism in, 188; EITI member, 426; proliferation-related corruption of, 130–32, 141, 156; purchase of centrifuge-related equipment, 125, 153; systemic corruption in, 138

IREX Media Sustainability Index, 55

Israeli Air Force, 364

Italy: Balkan organized crime expansion into, 106–07; mafia's integral role in, 105–06, 107, 108; OECD convention enforcement in, 371; organized crime problem in, 98, 107, 115

ITERATE data set, 176–77

Jacobs, James B., 393

Jama'atul Mujahideen Bangladesh, 211

Jamaica, public financial management in, 444

Japan: aiding post-Soviet Union anti-corruption efforts, 225, 228, 229; OECD convention enforcement in, 371; organized crime problem in, 98, 103, 115; as target of Russian and Chinese illicit trades, 210

Japanese Liberal Democratic Party, 114

JE Import/Export Company, 375

Johnson, Samuel, 37

Johnston, Michael, 41, 50–51

Jomo Kwame Sundaram, 3, 24, 41, 457

Jonathan, Goodluck, 272

Justice Advisory Group, 252

Justice Department, U.S., 401

Kagame, Paul, 354–56

Kalu, Orji, 267, 268

Kanyongolo, 323

Kaplan, David E., 104

Kapstein, Muel, 393, 408

Karpoff, Jonathan, 403

Kaunda, Kenneth, 343

Kayangolu, 319

Kazakhstan: anti-corruption efforts in, 223; Eurasia Group member, 227–28; Global Integrity Index rating of, 198

Kelman, Steven, 392, 393

Kenya: bribery in, 4; health care budget and funding in, 434, 451; public opinion of corruption in, 19–20

Keohane, Robert, 101

Ketumile, Quett Masire, 352, 353–54

Khama, Seretse, 342, 346, 350, 351–54, 356

Khan, Abdul Qadeer: corrupt activities of, 126–28; penalties against, 153. *See also* Abdul Qadeer Khan Network

Khan, Mushtaq, 458–59, 461–62, 465–66

Khintsagov, Oleg, 136, 209

Kickbacks, 32

Kleiman, Mark A. R., 173, 175

Kleptocratic interdependence, 96–115; definition and origins of, 97–102; effects of, 111–15; global alliances with governments, benefits of, 107–11; growth and persistence of, 102–06, 114; political geography of, 106–11; security threat of, 8–9; weakening power of, 115. *See also* Transnational criminal organizations (TCOs)

Klitgaard, Robert, 28, 38, 50, 141, 449

KMT (Kuomintang), 104

Koechlin, Lucy, 3, 14, 17–18, 310

Kohl, Helmut, 420

Kosovar Albanian guerilla group, 211

Kosovo: anti-corruption efforts of, 76, 85; corruption and lack of accountability in, 82–84, 87, 88; Liberation Army, 84, 211; organized crime and corruption in, 114; post-conflict corruption in, 68–71; transnational criminal organizations exploitation of, 106
Kuchma, Leonid, 215
Kuomintang (KMT), 104
Kurdistan Workers' Party (PKK), 175
Kyrgyzstan: corruption in, 100, 209; criminalized state of, 12

Lambsdorff, Johann Graf, 3, 22, 105, 177, 389, 394, 401–02
Landman, Todd, 323
Latin America: bribery in, 418; civil society's anti-corruption methods in, 254; education costs in, 431–32; EITI candidate countries in, 426; and public financial management scoring system, 446; role in FARC development, 185; World Bank public expenditure reviews of, 444. *See also specific countries*
Latynina, Yuliya, 209
Laufer, William S., 394, 401
Leaders, Ethics, and Coalitions Research Program, 63
Leadership and corruption, 341–56; Lee Kuan Yew's anti-corruption efforts, 346–47; within multinational organizations, 362–65, 374–75
Lebanon, corruption in, 171
Lee Kuan Yew, 9, 342; anti-corruption leadership of, 346–50, 356; corruption suspicions about, 351
Legislative corruption, 266, 273–74
Legvold, Robert, 194
Lerch, Gotthard, 126, 128, 131, 148

LEU (low-enriched uranium), 139, 225
Levgold, Robert, 2, 3, 12, 100, 197
Lewis, Patricia, 212
Leybold-Heraeus (German company), 131
Leys, Colin, 38
Libya: aiding disruption of Abdul Qadeer Khan Network, 128; as market for Abdul Qadeer Khan Network, 126, 127; proliferation-related corruption of, 131, 141, 156
Llosa, Mario Vargas, 100
Local governmental corruption, 269–70
Los Angeles Times on North American, Mexican, and Chinese criminal collaborations, 108
Low-enriched uranium (LEU), 139, 225

Mabetex, 205
Madison, James, 100
Madrid terrorist attacks, 174
Mafia: in Colombia, 108; in Italy, 105–06, 107, 108; in Russia, 105–06; in U.S., 103, 114; in Western Europe, 108. *See also* Organized crime
Malaria Control Project, 436
Malawi: accountability systems in, 320–23, 324, 326; Anti-Corruption Bureau (ACB) of, 321, 323; anti-corruption efforts in, 315–24, 327–28; citizen empowerment in, 323, 326–27; constitutional human rights framework of, 316–17, 320; corruption in, 18–19, 318, 319, 323; culture of, 318–19, 320–22; Human Rights Commission of, 320, 321–22; human rights in, 18, 311, 316–17, 320, 325–26; Poverty and Vulnerability Assessment of 2006, 319; poverty of, 318–19

Malaysia, Scomi plant managers in, 128

Malta, corruption ranking of, 345

Markin, Boris, 133

Martins, Kenny, 269

Matrix Churchill (company), 131

Mayak Production Association (plutonium facility), 135, 137

Measurement of corruption: first measurements of, 50–53; future possibilities for, 62–64; indicators for, 54–58, 59; problems with tools for, 60–61; second-generation tools of, 52–54, 61; usefulness of, 59–60. *See also specific measurement tools*

Media: on Abramoff scandal, 38; as anti-corruption method, 25, 101, 224, 252; covering corruption, 242, 245, 293, 321; covering multinational corporations, 368; freedom of, 56, 327, 397; on Kosovo corruption, 83; reports on nuclear material payouts, 143; on Wang Baosen's corrupt activities and suicide, 38

Media Council, 253

Medvedev, Dmitri, 218, 223, 224–25

Mexico: extradition of drug dealers to United States, 115; health care funding in, 451

Mikhailov, Victor, 130, 137–38

Millennium Challenge Corporation (MCC, U.S.): anti-corruption rewards of, 47–50; good governance agenda of, 459

Millennium Development Goals, 47

Milosevic, Slobodan, 83–84, 103

MNC. *See* Multi-national corporations

Moi, Daniel arap, 355

Moldova: corruption and economic growth in, 208; criminalized state of, 12; criminal state of, 196; destroying criminalized state of, 229

MONEYVAL, 227

Monterrey process, 47

Morality: as anti-corruption tool, 398–99, 410; of corruption, 37, 40–41, 42, 141, 251; Nigerians' opinion of, 285; of political leaders, 353

Mozambique: Angola compared to, 79; corruption and market economy of, 76–80, 87, 88; post-conflict corruption in, 68–71

MPC&A Operations Monitoring project, 149

Mugabe, Robert, 342, 355

Mukasey, Michael, 96

Multi-national corporations, 359–81, 389–410; anti-bribery policies of, 366–67, 368–69; anti-corruption programs of, 359, 361–68, 393–96; compliance systems of, 394–95; contract penalties of, 406–07, 409; debarment of, 403–04, 406; in developing countries, 375–81; employee training, 367, 395, 408; enforcement of OECD Convention principles, 370, 374; leniency for, 400–01; management reviews of, 366–68; nullification of corrupt contracts of, 404–05, 406; performance and integrity of, 361–69, 379, 381, 397; role of, 360, 416–17; and third party corruption, 365–66; whistle-blowing policies of, 407–08

Musharraf, Pervez, 127, 128

Mutharika, Bingu wa', 321

Myanmar, corruption in, 188, 342, 344, 356

NACA (National Anti-Corruption Alliance), 244–45

Nagle, Luz, 186

Nagorno-Karabakh as criminal state, 12

Nahimana, Terrance, 81

Naím, Moisés, 215

Nampota, Alexious, 321

Narco-terrorism, 175, 185–87

National Anti-Corruption Alliance (Papua New Guinea), 244–45

National Council of Churches (Papua New Guinea), 254

National Identity Cards Project (Nigeria), 265

National Integrity System. *See* Transparency International

National Intelligence Council, 212

National Law and Justice Policy and Plan of Action (Papua New Guinea), 252

Natural resource endowments as corruption cause, 75

Neild, Robert, 101

Nell, Mathias, 400, 401

Nepotism, 5, 14, 32, 239, 249, 342, 351

Netherlands, OECD convention enforcement in, 371

New African Partnership for Development, 317, 323–24

Ne Win, 344, 355

New Zealand: community-managed schools in, 448–49; corruption ranking of, 345; strong judiciary of, 390

NGOs. *See* Non-governmental organizations

Nigeria, 260–82; anti-corruption crusade in, 260–78; case studies of corrupt situations, 294–95, 297–301; citizen corruption in, 293–95; Code of Conduct Bureau (CCB), 260, 262, 263, 268, 270, 274, 276; Code of Conduct Tribunal (CCT), 260, 262, 263, 274; Colombian mafia relationship with, 108; community development union of, 299–300; culture of corruption, 355–56; endemic corruption in, 264–70; executive corruption in, 265–66; forms of corruption in, 290–92; governmental corruption in, 267–69; as headquarters for transnational criminal organizations, 109, 111; and Human Rights Watch, 16, 260, 269–70; Independent Corrupt Practices and Other Related Offenses Commission of, 17; judicial corruption in, 266–67; leadership corruption in, 292–93, 342, 344, 352, 355–56; moral economy of, 305; National Committee on Corruption and other Economic Crimes of, 263; patron-clientism corruption in, 287–90, 296–99, 307; public opinion of corruption, 39, 305; social context of, 283–84, 285, 306

NIS. *See* Transparency International

Nkurunziza, Pierre, 80

Nnamani, Chimaroke, 267, 268–69

Non-governmental organizations (NGOs): anti-corruption efforts of, 377, 397, 398; and bribery, 227; Burundi influence of, 82; civil society facilitation by, 253; corrupt activities exposure by, 155–56; corrupt acts of, 439–40; and human rights, 331. *See also specific organizations*

Non-proliferation programs, 136–38, 142–48, 154–55

Noonan, John T., 27

North America: education costs in, 432; Mexican and Chinese criminal organizations in, 108. *See also specific countries*

North Korea: lack of transparency in arms sales of, 214; as market for Abdul Qadeer Khan Network, 126, 127; proliferation-related corruption of, 131, 141, 156

Norway: as EITI implementor, 426; public financial management score for, 445

Nuclear proliferation, 124–57; and
Abdul Qadeer Khan Network,
126–28; anti-corruption efforts for,
10–11, 142–44, 150–55; conspiracies
of, 148–49, 225; controls over proliferation-sensitive technologies,
144–48; and corruption, 129–38;
influenced by corruption, 10, 124;
and legislative organizations,
155–56; and media, 155–56; and
NGOs, 155–56; and organized
crime, 138–41
Nuclear Trade and Technology Analysis
unit, 152
Nwabueze, Ben, 273
Nyame, Jolly, 267, 268
Nye, Joseph, 4, 101, 170, 290

Obasanjo, Olusegun: anti-corruption
initiative of, 263, 269, 271–72, 273,
303; and civil society organizations,
275, 276; publishing corporate revenues, 424–25; removal of corrupt
officials, 264, 265
Obasanjo Farms, 266
Obeidi, Mahdi, 132
Odili, Peter, 266–67
OECD Convention on Combating
Bribery of Foreign Official: actions
for future progress, 373–75; adoption of, 370; and corporate culture,
22; mixed record of, 360, 372–73;
monitoring and enforcement of,
371, 374–75, 421; provisions of,
369–71
Office of the Auditor General (Papua
New Guinea), 242, 244
Office of the United States Trade Rep-
resentative, 210
Office on Drugs and Crime (UN), 111
Oil wealth/industry: in Africa, 418; in
Nigeria, 261, 289–90, 296, 302

Okadigbo, Chuba, 266
Olivier de Sardan, Jean-Pierre, 39
Omar, Mullah, 175
Ombudsman Commission (Papua New
Guinea), 240, 241, 242–43
Open Budget Index, 52, 56, 57, 446
Organization for Economic Cooperation and Development (OECD),
443–44, 446. *See also* OECD Con-
vention on Combating Bribery of
Foreign Official
Organized crime, 96–115; charitable
contributions by, 106; and corrup-
tion, 8, 114, 213; as economic
opportunity, 105; effects of, 114; as
global security threat, 98; in
Guatemala, 73, 74; infiltration of
police departments, 136; and
nuclear materials access, 141–54;
nuclear proliferation role of, 138–41;
in post–Cold War world, 96–97; in
post-conflict situations, 7, 67, 71
Orttung, Robert, 140
Osomo, Alice, 265–66
Osuji, Fabian, 265
Oyeyipo, Timothy, 267

Paine, Lynn Sharp, 393
Pakistan: corruption and nuclear proliferation in, 10, 125, 126–28, 132,
156; female education enrollment
rates in, 450; military and security
services corruption in, 134;
National Accountability Bureau of,
127; non-proliferation programs in,
136; Taliban success in, 12. *See also*
Abdul Qadeer Khan Network
Palazzo, Bettina, 396
Palestinian Territories, terrorist popu-
larity in, 167, 171
Panama, public financial management
in, 444

Panfilova, Elena, 224

Paoli, Letizia, 107

Papua New Guinea, 239–59; anti-corruption efforts of, 15, 240–45, 250, 251–55; corruption in, 14–15, 255; culture of, 239–40, 246–47, 253, 255; government corruption investigation in, 242, 243; legal framework of, 241–45; political leader subversion, 246–49; social accountability of, 241, 249–51; Transparency International chapter, 245

Paraguay, public financial management in, 444

Patrick, Stewart, 111

Patron-clientism, 287–90, 296–99, 460

Peace deals as anti-corruption method, 68

PEFA (Public Expenditure and Financial Accountability), 53, 445–46

People's Action Party (Singapore), 222

Perez, Carlos Andrés, 40

Peru: bribery in, 105; corruption in, 103; narco-terrorism in, 175

Petroleum Technology Development Fund, 265

Petty corruption, 4, 239, 261, 442

Phey Yew Kok, 348

Philippines, corruption in, 222, 345

Philp, Mark, 35–36

Piontkovsky, Andrei, 102

PKK. *See* Kurdistan Workers' Party

Plato, 37

Plutonium, 132, 139, 143, 146

PNG Banking Corporation, 242

Pok, Emmanuel, 3, 14–15, 239

Police departments, strengthening of, 150–51

Policies: for addressing most damaging forms of corruption, 461; for constraining individuals with access to sensitive information, 131; for post-conflict situations, 86; for protection against inside conspiracy threats, 146

Politburo (Russian), 204

Political Corruption (Johnston & Heidenheimer), 50–51

Political-criminal nexus, 101

Political liberalization, 208

POLITY IV country reports, 55, 57, 58

Pope, Jeremy, 405

Post-Cold War environment, 96–97, 115

Post-conflict situations: anti-corruption lessons of, 85–86, 88–89; common corrupt features of, 71

Post-Monterrey era of corruption, 51

Post-Soviet transition, 194–230; anti-corruption efforts for, 216–30; arms and ammunition in, 213; causes of corruption during, 201–07; consequences of corruption, 207–16; corruption in, 197, 202, 218, 228; Corruption Perceptions Index of, 12; corrupt rankings during, 198–201; economic growth in, 208; fulfilling Program of Action controls, 226; global security problems of, 12; health markets of, 451; and intrastate conflict, 215–16; moral norms of, 142–43; nuclear security in, 144–45; poorly supervised military in, 213–14; and terrorism, 216; transnational criminal organization regional ties in, 107; types of corruption during, 195–98. *See also specific countries*

Poverty: and corruption, 417–18; and human rights, 310–11

Predatory corruption, 461–62

Prevention of Corruption Act of 1960 (Singapore), 222

PricewaterhouseCoopers, 395–96, 417

Program of Action, 226
Public action in anti-corruption strate-
    gies, 253
Public Complaints Commission,
    Nigerian, 262
Public Expenditure and Financial
    Accountability (PEFA), 53, 445–46
Public interest theories of corruption,
    33–34
Public officials: alliances with transna-
    tional criminal organizations,
    102–05; anti-corruption efforts for,
    465; as corrupt actors, 8, 30–32, 68,
    199, 214, 341; and corruption by
    direct participation, 99–101; in
    Georgia, 221; in Malawi, 326; in
    Papua New Guinea, 246; predatory
    corruption of, 461–62; in Soviet
    Union, 205; whistle-blowing oppor-
    tunities for, 400
Public opinion as anti-corruption
    method, 101
Publish What You Pay initiative, 23,
    424, 426
Puerto Rico, corruption ranking of,
    345
Putin, Vladimir, 134

Radiation detectors, 149, 151
RENAMO, 77, 87
Rent-seeking: and economic develop-
    ment, 457, 460–61; in Nigeria, 289;
    resulting from government inter-
    ventions, 463, 464; in Russia, 206,
    207
Repression, as anti-corruption tool,
    389–90
Reproductive and Child Health Project
    (India), 435–36
Revenue Watch, 426
Revolutionary Armed Forces of
    Columbia (FARC): bribery used by,

185, 186; facilitation approach of,
    169, 186–87; funding of, 174, 213;
    illicit trade by, 188; narco-terrorism
    of, 175, 185–87; success of, 11–12,
    167; trafficking activities of, 11, 140
Ribadu, Nuhu, 264, 273, 275–76
Rights. *See* Human rights; Individual
    rights
Robinson, Mary, 417
Rosatom (Russia), 137
Rose-Ackerman, Susan, 3, 7–8, 14, 50,
    66, 169, 201–02, 393
Rosoboronoexport, 214
Rostekhnadzor (Russia), 138
Rotberg, Robert I., 1, 3, 20, 222, 341,
    351
El-Rufai, Nasir, 266
Russia: anti-corruption efforts of, 153,
    155, 218, 219–20, 223–25, 417;
    authoritarianism in, 207; bribery in,
    138, 200–01; collective responsibil-
    ity history in, 206; corporate fraud
    detection in, 395–96; corrupt activi-
    ties with other countries, 108, 132,
    135, 136; corruption funding in,
    216; criminalized state of, 12, 196,
    197, 206–07; economic growth of,
    194–95; Eurasia Group member,
    227–28; fair trial expectations in,
    206; Federal Security Service of,
    133; heroin use and HIV/AIDS in,
    212; illicit trading by, 210–16;
    mafia's integral role in, 105–06; mil-
    itary and security services corrup-
    tion in, 134; money laundering in,
    227; as MONEYVAL member, 227;
    moral norms of, 142–43; National
    Plan for Counteracting Corruption,
    223; non-proliferation cooperation
    with United States, 137–38, 144,
    149, 225; nuclear materials of, 134,
    209; and OECD Convention, 373;

organized crime and corruption in, 105–06, 114, 139, 186–87; Program of Action controls, 226; Transparency International ranking of, 198, 224

Russian-Georgian War, 229

Rwanda: anti-corruption efforts of, 354–55; health care funding in, 451

Saakashvili, Mikheil, 220, 222

Sagem SA (French firm), 265

Sandline International, 242

Sargsian, Aleksandr, 199

Sargsian, Serge, 199

Saudi Arabia: corrupt deals with Britain, 372, 395; proliferation-related corruption in, 133; terrorist funding from, 174

Scandinavia and Balkan organized crime, 106–07

Schaab, Karl-Heinz, 131, 153, 154

Schiavo, Giuseppe Guido Lo, 105

Schudel, Charles J. W., 323

Schulze, Günther, 399

Schumpeter, Joseph, 460, 464

Scott, James C., 4, 7, 28, 29, 33, 170, 344, 345

Security Council Resolution 1540 (UN), 10, 145, 147

Seibert, Renate, 105

Seko, Mobutu Sese, 342, 344, 355

Senate, U.S., 1

Seow, Francis T., 351

September 11 terrorist attacks, 173

Sepúlveda Carmona, Magdalena, 3, 14, 17–18, 310

Serio, Joseph D., 214

Seversk (Russian plutonium facility), 134

Sevmorput Naval Shipyard, 133

Shah, Anwar, 141

Shang Jin Wei, 177

Shata, Mohammed, 265

Shelley, Louise, 140

Sheriff (company), 215

Shining Path, 174, 175

Shlyapuzhnikov, Sergei, 134

Siberia, corrupt activities with Russia, 214–15

Sicily and Colombian mafia, 108

Siemens: anti-corruption efforts of, 409–10; bribery scandal of, 265, 363, 368, 371, 405; prosecution of, 371

Sierra Leone and transnational criminal organizations, 106

Singapore: anti-corruption efforts in, 222, 223, 345–46, 355; bribery in, 419; Corrupt Practices Investigation Bureau of, 222, 349; public officials anti-corrupt leadership, 345–50

Slebos, Henk, 126

Small Arms Trade Transparency Barometer, 214

Smirnov, Yuri, 153

Smith, Daniel Jordan: case studies of Nigerian corruption, 294–95, 303–04; experience in Nigeria, 283, 287, 293, 302; on morality of corruption, 38, 39; on Nigeria's concept of corruption, 290; on Nigeria's culture of corruption, 3, 16, 261, 283–84, 285

Social accountability as anti-corruption method, 241, 249–51

Solntsevo crime group, 214

Somalia: conflict in, 417–18; corruption in, 188

Sonangol (Nigerian company), 75, 76

Soros, George, 426

South Africa: debarment requirements in, 403; response to corruption in, 356; and transnational criminal organizations, 111

South Korea, corruption ranking of, 345

South Ossetia, criminal state of, 12

Soviet Union: criminalized state of, 204–05; non-proliferation of, 136, 142; second economy of, 203, 204; systemic corruption in, 197, 203–04. *See also* Russia

Soyinka, Wole, 264, 275–76

Special 301 report, 210

Sri Lanka: corrupt military of, 12; narco-terrorism in, 175

Stability and world peace. *See* World peace and stability

State capture, 68, 100, 102, 128, 196–97, 239

State Department (U.S.), 147

State Security Act (Nigeria), 75

State Statistics Committee (Soviet Union), 205

Statoil, 371

Stefes, Christoph H., 197, 199

Stemmler, Bruno, 131, 148, 153, 154

Stevens, Siaka, 355

Stratmann, Thomas, 390

Suberu, Rotimi, 3, 16–17, 260

Sudan: corruption and conflict in, 417–18; proliferation-related corruption in, 133

Suharto, 344–45

Sukarno, 344–45

Supreme Court of Appeals (Italian), 105

Sweden, corruption ranking of, 345

Switzerland: corporate fraud detection in, 395–96; corruption ranking of, 345; lack of corruption in, 141; organized crime in, 106–07

Syria, proliferation-related corruption of, 141

Taiwan: corruption ranking of, 345; transnational criminal organization regional ties in, 107

Tajikistan: corrupt public officials in, 100; Eurasia Group member, 227–28; Global Integrity Index rating of, 198

Taliban, 11, 175

Tan Kia Gan, 347

Taxation as cause of corruption, 106

Taylor, Charles, 355

TCOs. *See* Transnational criminal organizations

Teets, Jessica, 3, 11, 167

Teh Cheang Wan, 348

Ter-Petrosian, Telman, 199

Terrorism, 167–89; and corruption, 11, 167–76, 178–89; domestic forms of, 171; funding for, 174; and illicit trade, 168–78, 181–84; implications for, 187–89; and narco-terrorism, 175, 185–87; nuclear proliferation goals of, 129, 130; preventing access to nuclear materials, 141–54; research design for, 176–78; success of, 174–75; transnational crime compared to, 173–74. *See also specific terrorist organizations*

Terrorism Knowledge Base, 177

Thachuk, Kimberley, 185–86

Thailand, corruption in, 1, 103, 170, 345

Than Shwe, 344

Three-person rule, 146, 148–49

Tikhomorov, Dmitry, 133–34

Tilman, Robert O., 34

Timor Leste, response to corruption in, 356

Tinner, Friedrich, 126

Tinner, Urs, 128, 151

Torres, Vladimiro Montesinos, 105

Trafficking: and corruption, 8; of drugs, 11, 104–05, 173; increase of, 3; and terrorism, 11, 140, 172–73

Transdniestr: corruption in, 215; criminal state of, 12

Transition Report (EBRD), 207
Transnational criminal organizations (TCOs): and conflict situations, 106–07; and corruption, 97–99; defined, 8–9, 98–99; governmental alliances with, 107–11; growth of, 98; headquarters of, 109–11; public officials alliances with, 102–05, 107; regional ties of, 107; similarities of, 111; success of, 115; terrorist groups compared to, 173–74; threat of, 114
Transparency. *See* Accountability mechanisms
Transparency International: anti-corruption efforts of, 253–54, 313, 377, 391; on commonality of corruption, 419; on contract penalties, 407; corruption definition of, 4, 125; EITI promotion by, 426; enforcement report of, 371; founding and initial work of, 22–23, 418–23; Integrity Pacts of, 23, 399, 420; "Integrity System Source Book" of, 422; measuring corruption, 202; National Integrity System (NIS) of, 18, 52, 313–14, 315, 422; and Publish What You Pay, 424; rankings of, 194, 198, 283. *See also* Corruption Perceptions Index
Triads, 104, 107, 346
TRIPS (Agreement on Trade-Related Aspects of Intellectual Property Rights), 226–27
The Trouble with Nigeria (Achebe), 286
Turaki, Saminu, 267, 268–69
Turbiville, Graham H., 214
Turkey: collaboration with Albanian organized crime groups, 108; health care funding in, 451; leniency for corrupt acts in, 402–03; narco-terrorism in, 175; organized crime groups' relationships with European groups, 108

Turko-Kurdish groups, 107
Two-person rule, 146, 148–49

Uba brothers, 272
Uganda, corrupt military of, 12
Ukraine: anti-corruption efforts in, 218, 219, 222–23; corruption in, 194–95, 200, 215; criminalized state of, 12, 196, 229; economic growth in, 194–95; fair trial expectations in, 206; heroin use and HIV/AIDS in, 212; as MONEYVAL member, 227; Orange Revolution in, 200, 209; organized crime group trading with, 186; Program of Action controls, 226
Underkuffler, Laura, 3, 5, 27
United Nations: anti-corruption efforts of, 379; Commission on International Trade Law, 445; Conference on Financing for Development, 421; Conference on Illicit Trade in Small Arms and Light Weapons, 226; Department for Disarmament Affairs, 212; Human Development Index, 109, 318; Joint Programme on HIV/AIDS, 212; in Kosovo, 83, 84, 85; long-range missile transfer ban, 131–32; Mozambique peace negotiations of, 77, 79, 87; non-proliferation programs in, 136; Office on Drugs and Crime, 211; Protectorate, 70; Security Council Resolution 1540, 10, 145, 147
United Nations Convention against Corruption (UNCAC): anti-corruption standards of, 312–13, 375; and human rights, 315; increasing accountability, 18; as modern assault on corruption, 23; on problems posed by corruption, 310; ratification of, 223, 224, 421; rules-based approach of, 390

United Nations Development Programme, 60, 62

United States: anti-corruption efforts in, 150–52, 227; corporate anti-corruption efforts in, 395–96; corruption ranking of, 345; debarment requirements of, 403–04; export and border control programs of, 147; illicit trading and trafficking in, 104–05, 210, 216–17; improving nuclear security in, 134, 145; and Iraq supplier corruption, 130; lack of corruption in, 141; mafia in, 103, 114; non-proliferation cooperation with Russia, 137–38, 144, 149, 225; OECD convention enforcement in, 371, 373–74; organized crime problem in, 98, 106–07, 115; post-Soviet Union anti-corruption aid from, 225, 228, 229–30; and Program of Action controls, 226; "Second Line of Defense" program of, 149; two- and three-person rules of, 148

University of Maryland. *See* POLITY IV country reports

Uranium. *See* Highly enriched uranium (HEU)

Urenco (European consortium), 126

U.S. Agency for International Development (USAID), 81, 375

U.S.-Russian HEU Purchase Agreement, 137

Uvin, Peter, 324

Uzbekistan: communist party of, 204; corruption and economic growth in, 208; criminalized state of, 12; Eurasia Group member, 227–28; organized crime group trading in, 186

Van Aaken, Anne, 390

Varese, Federico, 205–06

Venal corruption, 4, 224, 286, 342–43

Vietnam, health care funding in, 451

Violence: and corruption and terrorism, 170; illicit trafficking as cause of, 173

VIP Money Transfers (money-transfer business), 216

Vladimirov, Anatolii, 106

Voigt, Stefan, 390

Volcker Review Panel, 376–78

Von Weizsäcker, Richard, 419

Wabara, Adolphus, 265

Wang Baosen, 38

Wantok, 246, 247, 248–49

War Against Indiscipline and Corruption (Nigeria), 262–63

Ward, Tony, 100

Water Integrity Network, 62

Waziri, Farida, 270

Weapons, 173, 226

Weapons of mass destruction (WMD), 9, 195

Wee Toon Boon, 347–48

Welch, Jack, 363

Wempe, Johan, 393

West Africa, illicit weapons in, 173

Western Europe: education costs in, 432; mafias in, 108. *See also specific countries*

WGIs. *See* Worldwide Governance Indicators

Whistleblowers: as anti-corruption tool, 407–08; and corporate debarment, 404; Georgian protection for, 221; and nullification, 405; rewards for, 407

Williams, Phil, 106

Wisser, Gerhard, 126

WMD. *See* Weapons of mass destruction

Wolfensohn, James, 47, 421

Working Group on Bribery, 370–71
World Bank: anti-corruption efforts of, 375–78, 379, 421; approval of EITI AIG Recommendations, 425; Bangladesh school stipend program aid from, 450; corruption definition of, 4, 99; and corruption measurement tools, 53, 63; Country Financial Accountability Assessments (CFAAs) of, 443, 445, 446; Country Procurement Assessment Reviews (CPARs) of, 443–44, 446; Doing Business surveys of, 53, 56, 61–62; and Eurasia Group creation, 227; financial management and procurement systems aid from, 445; on Georgia, 220; governance agenda of, 459; on Guatemala, 72; on India, 435–41, 442–43; industrial policy of, 463; Mozambique democracy aid from, 79–80; Multi-Donor Trust Fund of, 426; on Nigeria, 288, 298; as outside monitor, 401; on predatory corruption, 461; procedures for financed projects of, 435; and state capture, 196; technical expertise for EITI, 426; transparency efforts, 425, 426–27; on Ukraine, 200
World Bank Institute, 417
World Competitiveness Yearbook, 198
World Development Report 2004 (World Bank), 431
World Drug Report, 212
World Economic Forum, 391–92, 422

World Ethics Forum, 63
World Islamic Front for the Jihad Against the Jews and Crusaders, 211
World peace and stability, 1–25; and anti-corruption efforts, 19–25; and crime, 8–12; and human rights, 17–19; and Nigeria, 14–17; and nuclear proliferation, 8–12; and Papua New Guinea, 14–17; and Russia, 12–14; and terrorism, 8–12
World Summit on Sustainable Development, 426
World Trade Organization, 226
Worldwide Governance Indicators (WGIs): as composite indicator, 57; criticism of, 52; goals of, 51; output-input plus indicators of, 56; as policymaking aid, 57; ranking of Malawi, 318

Xinhua, 38

Yakuza, 103, 104, 109, 114
Yamamah, Al, 372
Yar'Adua, Umaru, 264, 272–73, 275, 276
Yeltsin, Boris, 223
Yugoslavia, corruption in, 103

Zaire, corruption in, 344
Zambia, corruption in, 343–44, 356
Zimbabwe, corruption in, 2, 355, 356
Zürcher, Christoph, 215–16
Zvania, Zurab, 222

The World Peace Foundation
The World Peace Foundation was created in 1910 by the imagination and fortune of Edwin Ginn, the Boston publisher, to encourage international peace and cooperation. The Foundation seeks to advance the cause of world peace through study, analysis, and the advocacy of wise action. As an operating, not a grant-giving foundation, it provides financial support only for projects that it has initiated itself. In its early years, the Foundation focused its attention on building the peacekeeping capacity of the League of Nations, and then on the development of world order through the United Nations. The Foundation established and nurtured the premier scholarly journal in its field, *International Organization*. Since 1993, the Foundation has examined the causes and cures of intrastate conflict. The peace of the world in these decades has been disturbed primarily by outbreaks of vicious ethnic, religious, linguistic, and intercommunal antagonism within divided countries. Part of the task of the Foundation is to resolve conflicts as well as to study them. The Foundation's work in Congo, Cyprus, Burma, Sri Lanka, Haiti, the Sudan, Zimbabwe, and all of Africa has resolution of conflict as its goal. The Foundation has sponsored a detailed study of negotiating the end of deadly conflict within and between states. It is also engaged in an analysis of the successes and failures of African leadership.

The Program on Intrastate Conflict, Conflict Prevention, and Conflict Resolution
On July 1, 1999, the Program on Intrastate Conflict, Conflict Prevention, and Conflict Resolution was established in the Belfer Center at the Harvard Kennedy School as a result of an association between the Center and the World Peace Foundation. The Program analyzes the causes of ethnic, religious, and other intercommunal conflict and seeks to identify practical ways to prevent and limit such conflict. It is concerned with measuring good governance, the consequences of the global proliferation of small arms, the failure and vulnerability of weak states, failed states and rogue states, UN peace building reform, with peace building and peace enforcement capabilities in Africa, conflict resolution in war-torn countries, the role of good leadership in Africa, China's influence in Africa, assessing crimes against humanity, and the role of truth commissions in conflict prevention and conflict resolution.

American Academy of Arts & Sciences
The Academy was founded during the American Revolution by John Adams, James Bowdoin, John Hancock, and other leaders who contributed prominently to the establishment of the new nation, its government, and its Constitution. The Academy's purpose was to provide a forum for a select group of scholars, members of the learned professions, and government and business leaders to work together on behalf of the democratic interests of the republic. In the words of the Academy's Charter, enacted in 1780, the "end and design of the institution is . . . to cultivate every art and science which may tend to advance the interest, honour, dignity, and happiness of a free, independent, and virtuous people." Today the Academy is both an honorary learned society and an independent policy research center that conducts multidisciplinary studies of complex and emerging problems. Current Academy research focuses on science and global security; social policy; the humanities and culture; and education. The Academy supports young scholars through its Visiting Scholars Program and Hellman Fellowships in Science and Technology Policy, providing year-long residencies at its Cambridge, Massachusetts, headquarters. The Academy's work is advanced by its 4,600 elected members, who are leaders in the academic disciplines, the arts, business, and public affairs from around the world.